herder's commentary on the psalms

edited by Edmund Kalt

translated by
BERNARD FRITZ, O.S.B.
Assumption Abbey
Richardton, North Dakota

THE NEWMAN PRESS · WESTMINSTER, MARYLAND

1961

Originally published as Volume VI, *Die Psalmen,* in *Herder's Bibelkommentar: Die Heilige Schrift für das Leben erklärt,* by Verlagsbuchhandlung Herder and Co., G.m.b.H., Freiburg im Breisgau, Germany.

Imprimi potest: Ignatius Hunkler, O.S.B.
  Coadjutor Abbot of Assumption Abbey
  March 26, 1957

Nihil obstat: Edward A. Cerny, S.S., S.T.D.
  Censor librorum

Imprimatur: Francis P. Keough, D.D.
  Archbishop of Baltimore
  June 13, 1961

preface

THE religious movement by which our age is seized has awakened among the laity, and even among our youth, a desire to learn the Catholic faith from its sources, and to live by the strength of these direct sources. This has, therefore, created a lively interest in Sacred Scripture, not only in the New Testament, but also in the Old Testament. It has set in motion the study and reading of the Catholic Bible.

As, according to the plan of Divine Providence, Pope Pius X promoted and rendered possible early and frequent Communion which awakened a greater religious life, so also the encyclical letters of recent popes have helped much to promote the study of the Scriptures and the preaching of scriptural sermons, and have urged the clergy to make the laity more acquainted with the supernatural wealth of the biblical books than heretofore. If the current biblical movement which has so fortunately begun should become greater, and if the laity should delve more deeply into biblical science, and if the sacred stream that flows from this sacred source should fructify the religious life, then, according to the instructions of the popes, the priests especially must have a correct understanding of the meaning of the sacred books and apply themselves to the diligent study of scientific commentaries. The priest must be able to obtain sufficient knowledge to appreciate this rich treasure and evaluate its religious value for Christian living.

Only insofar as the priest himself appreciates the written word of God and learns to love it, and only insofar as its strength and beauty becomes known to him, will he be able to speak to the faithful in the language of Sacred Scripture and to explain its meaning with such warmth that their hearts will be touched by it. Pope Leo XIII in his encyclical *Providentissimus Deus*, on the study of Sacred Scripture, says that it is the "peculiar and singular power of Holy Scripture, arising from the inspiration of the Holy Spirit, which gives authority to the sacred orator, fills him with apostolic liberty of speech, and communicates force and power to his eloquence."

It is a serious and sacred duty for a priest to acquire for himself biblical knowledge, not only to find in it for himself strength to strive for perfection, but also to offer to the faithful supernatural nourishment by his sermons and catechetical instruction.

The wisdom of the sacred books, however, is not evident to every man;

v

it is in many cases a treasure concealed in an acre which must be sought for and acquired. This in the first place applies to the layman who takes the Scripture in hand. The priest has acquired a certain attitude toward inquiring about the deeper meaning of biblical expressions through his theological and exegetical studies. But he, too, cannot dispense with a reliable guide. The distractions and heavy burdens of the modern care of souls do not give to the priest the time demanded and the inner peace to continue in his private work of biblical studies, to get a clearer understanding of the value of these sacred books for Christian living, and to use them for his own personal sanctity and for the edification and guidance of the souls entrusted to him.

Without an experienced guide, he runs the risk of not getting a practical appreciation of these books, of interpreting the written word of God sentimentally, and of using it in a manner which is contrary to the intended meaning of the Holy Spirit. An explanation of Sacred Scripture for pious living supposes an understanding of the literal sense and a familiarity with biblical thought. This applies particularly to the books of the Old Testament, the content and form of which are more ancient and which until now received fewer ascetic-homiletic explanations than the Gospels and Epistles of the Apostles.

We are, therefore, glad to learn that the publishing house of Herder in Freiburg has begun the publication of a biblical work which explains all biblical books with the view of aiding the formation of a practical Christian life and which takes particularly into consideration its literal sense and which emphasizes and shows the supernatural and divine in these writings and what they tell us in this generation of the twentieth century. Only a systematic and thorough work of the entire Sacred Scripture can point to beauties to which the other many ways of interpretation did not lead. This biblical work will, therefore, fill a deficiency, and meet a need especially for the clergy having the care of souls and should, therefore, be in every priest's library.

The new Bible commentary published at Freiburg will not depreciate the value of other biblical works. The directions given to the collaborators emphasize expressly that the Sacred Scripture explained for Christian living has not the task of explaining the sacred text scientifically; it supposes a scientific knowledge and builds upon it. We, therefore, do not have to fear that this new Bible treatise lessens the interest in scientific commentaries; rather, it is our hope and wish that a deeper penetration into the practical values of the sacred text, as the Freiburger commentary intends, will urge the readers to seek greater scientific explanations of God's word so that the clergy will more than heretofore apply themselves to a more extensive knowledge of Sacred Scripture. Thus both kinds of explanation will not encroach upon one another, but will be of benefit to one another, and that, along parallel ways and not along different lines, they will reach the common purpose, namely, of making known more clearly the word of God.

THEODORE CARDINAL INNITZER
Archbishop of Vienna

Vienna, March 21, 1935

introduction

I T IS AN ancient practice to use music and poetry in the service of the
worship of God. We can trace it back to the very beginning of the
history of the people of Israel. After the passage through the Red Sea,
Moses sang a song of praise to the Lord; the women took kettle-drums in
hand and sang a "Te Deum" to the powerful deliverer. So also did Debbora after the victorious battle at Thabor. When, in the time of the judges,
the religious life declined, men and youth inspired by God formed prophetic schools in order to solemnize the sacrificial services with music,
song, and religious dances.

These modest beginnings of a sort of liturgical movement the pious
King David took up after he had given a lasting dwelling place to the ark
of the covenant in the new sanctuary on Sion and after he had established
regular sacrificial service by arranging the order of the priestly and
levitical service. He established not only a choir of singers, but also
composed spiritual songs which form the groundwork of our present-day
Psalter. The Chronicler (2 Chron. 7:6; 23:18) calls David a composer of
songs. Sacred Scripture calls him the sweet singer of Israel (2 Kings
23:1). Jesus Sirach says of him: "He placed singers before the altar, and
he had them sing lovely melodies; he also gave solemnity to the feasts,
and to the end of his life he had the solemn feasts observed with splendor
in order that men might praise the holy Name of the Lord and glorify
God's sanctity in the early morning." (47:11 seq.) Even if not all seventy-
three psalms, which in the Massoretic text are superscribed by David's
name, can be traced to his authorship, it is his spirit that pervades the
entire Psalter.

The groundwork formed by David expanded in the course of centuries. To the first collection 1–41, four others were added: namely 42 to
72, 73–89, 90–106, 107–150. All the psalms are divided into five books,
each ending with a doxology; and all five books contain 150 psalms.
Toward the end of the fourth century the Psalter was already accepted in
its present form. The arrangement in the Hebrew text is different from the
arrangement in the Greek and Latin texts. Psalm 9 of the Septuagint and
Vulgate is divided into two Psalms, 9 and 10, in the Hebrew text. Psalms
114 and 115 as well as 146 and 147 of the Greek and Latin translation
form each one Psalm, 116 and 147, in the Hebrew text. In consequence of
this, the enumeration of the original text agrees with that of the Septu-

agint and the Vulgate only in Psalms 1–9 and 147 to 150. In the rest of the psalms the original is one number ahead of our text.

The psalms collected in the Psalter were not all intended by the author to be sung at the celebration of the divine service. Some songs of religious content were patterned for liturgical use by additions and small changes. That profane songs were appropriated and subsequently had their meaning changed from the original sense and were then used in the liturgy cannot be proved and has little probability. The psalms in their individual collections are not compiled according to a specific viewpoint. The only group designated by a superscription are the pilgrimage songs (Psalms 119–133). The Church has selected seven psalms as Penitential Psalms (6, 31, 37, 50, 101, 129, and 142). Since in the same psalm there are various sentiments, and certain fundamental thoughts are repeated in manifold connections, it is impossible to group them according to content and purpose. In their literary character simple prayers change into spiritual songs, hymns, and didactic poems. Only a few psalms deal exclusively with the Messianic future, and, therefore, have a prophetic character. However, in many psalms there is expressed a hope for that blessed era.

Israel is not the only nor the first nation of antiquity to have given future generations spiritual songs. Even centuries before Abraham, the Egyptians, Sumerians, Babylonians, and other nations sang hymns in honor of their gods and prayed penitential psalms to assuage their wrath. The findings and decipherings of the ancient pagan prayer literature in recent decades have enriched the knowledge of these to such an extent as to make a comparison with biblical lyrics possible. We must admit that paganism has also given us pearls of religious poetry which show a deep religious feeling. But its prayers and hymns seldom can be compared to the language of the Psalter and are far inferior to the spirit of Old Testament poetry.

There are two facts which, from a comparison of ancient pagan and Old Testament prayers, give us a knowledge of the uniqueness of the biblical poetry of the psalms. The one fact is: in the Psalter there is pulsating life; the pagan prayers are dead letters. They are today nothing more than more or less preserved mummies which no power on earth can resurrect to life; they are mummies which one admires, but will not use. But the biblical psalmody, despite its antiquity of 2500 to 3000 years, is still alive and draws millions of pious worshipers under the charm of its language and thoughts.

The temples in which the ancient nations sang hymns to their gods have fallen into ruins, and the hymns are forever silenced because no one comes to the feast. The desert sand has buried all, the temple, the gods, and their adorers, with the same shroud. Even the temple at Jerusalem has been in ruins for nearly nineteen centuries, and no stone has been left upon the other. The nation which, since the time of King David, had for a thousand years glorified God with its Psalms is dispersed throughout the world, without a sanctuary, without priest, without sacrifice. But its songs are not silenced. Even before the woe of the Lord was fulfilled by the destruction of Jerusalem, the young Christian community took the harp in hand which had fallen from the hands of the Levites, and praised the Lord-Christ of the new era with hymns of the Old Testament. The melody of their songs was sent by a great messenger into all lands throughout the centuries, and one hears today the singing of the Psalter from one end of the earth to the other, as far as the kingdom of God, the Church of the New Testament, reaches.

Surely the Psalms show traces of their great age and of their distant oriental country. Christianity has grown upon the Old Covenant, with its imperfect religious and moral views. Therefore, these songs contain matter which, from a Christian point of view, we think we cannot pray. But because, despite this, they have become the liturgical prayer book of the Church and have remained such for two thousand years, it is an evident sign that these biblical songs possess an indestructible spiritual power. They are a breath of the everlasting God whom they serve.

A second fact which gives us a knowledge of the uniqueness of the Psalter is a comparison of the ancient pagan and Old Testament piety, compelling us to establish this formula: confidence in God and the love of God are the keynote of the religious life of Israel; superstitious belief in the gods and fear of demons pervades the pagan prayers. He who knows the chaos that exists in the mythology of the gods and in superstitious practices, who has had under observation the whole life of a pagan, has the conviction that in such an atmosphere no confidence or love of the divinity can thrive.

But in rich variety the fundamental thought of God's love and confidence in him pervades all the songs of the Psalter. Sometimes we find a solemn worship of Yahwe the Creator, the Father of Israel; at other times we find a jubilant thanksgiving or a humble prayer; at other times we find a sorrowful admission of an unfaithfulness committed or a trustful cry for help in deep spiritual grief; then again a quiet meditation about the great deeds of the Lord in the history of his people or a passionate curse against the enemies of his kingdom. All of nature, from the constellations of heaven to the animals of the earth and the flowers of the field, are brought into the psalms to proclaim God's glory and love. The twinkling of the stars becomes a symphony in honor of their Ruler; the animal and plant world narrate to man the loving providence of the Creator; and the blooming meadow rejoices because the Lord has clothed it with such manifold colors. Everything points to God in order that man may admire his greatness and taste of his goodness. The meditation upon the history of Israel and of human life is found in the Psalter when it treats about confidence in God. History and life are not a mere coming and going of a changing fate; in the Psalter they become a revelation of divine wisdom in discipline and government. They make us recognize the hand which strikes to heal and which miraculously saves in order to make known to all the world His power. And finally all Messianic psalms are sung with faith, hope, and confidence.

May the prayers of the Psalter look back in quiet meditation or occupy man with the future; may they sob with the sinner laden with guilt; may they complain with the just man burdened with sorrow or lend words for all causes of anxiety, they always lead the soul above that which is earthly and transitory, above all trouble and adversity, and in faith they let man see God's fidelity and mercy. The whole variety of feelings become in themselves a prayer. Baumgartner in his *History of World Literature* judges correctly when he writes: "This fervent devotion, this longing for God, this humble submission to God, this childlike attachment to God, we find among no other people of antiquity. What the Babylonians and Egyptians have to say to their gods are frosty attentions in comparison to the inner, enthusiastic outpourings of the soul. These impetuous expressions of joy, of sorrow, of admiration, of hope, of love, which are strange to the pagan world are often manly and vigorous, and again feminine and tender, often warlike and impetuous, and often simple and intimate like the chatter of a pious child."

The inner worth of the Psalter is heightened for us by exterior dedication. It has become the breviary of the Lord. When in the stillness of the night our Savior ascended the lonely mountain heights to hold conversation with his Father, his soul poured out thoughts in the language of his divinely human heart. When he prayed in the circle of his disciples or of the people, when he attended divine service in the synagogue on the Sabbath or celebrated the great feasts at Jerusalem and ate the Paschal Lamb with his disciples, he prayed in the language of the psalms. According to St. Paul (Hebrews 10:5), the purpose of the Son of God who became man, the utterance at his coming into the world was taken from the 39th Psalm. And just as he began his work of redemption in the crib with the silent prayer of this psalm, so on the cross he closed the bloody liturgy on Golgotha by praying aloud Psalm 21.

The disciples only followed the example of their Master when they introduced the Psalter in the Christian divine service and glorified the liturgy of the New Covenant with those songs which were sung at the celebration of the bloody sacrifices of the Old Covenant. The Apostle of the Gentiles exhorts: "Sing to the Lord with thankful hearts in psalms and spiritual songs." And St. James exhorts the Christians "to praise the Lord with psalms." Since then the prayer of psalmody has ever flowed in the Catholic Church like that miraculous stream which the prophet Ezechiel saw rushing from the temple of Sion, a stream which everywhere brought new life. Since then the songs of Sion have resounded in the dark passages of the catacombs and in the large halls of the Christian basilicas. The present day liturgy of Holy Mass bears traces of an early and wide use of the Psalter at the celebration of the sacred mysteries. The priest approached the altar during the singing of the psalms by the people; during the singing of the psalms the faithful brought their gifts to the altar; and during the singing of the psalms at Holy Communion they received the Body of the Lord. The Psalter has received an important place in the ecclesiastical hours of the breviary, so that there is no hour in the year in which the prayers and the songs of the psalms do not ascend to heaven. Thus, in truth, it has become a Catholic prayer.

The greatest value of the Psalter consists in this: that its prayers and songs, as well as all parts of Scripture, were composed with the aid of the Holy Spirit, that they were inspired by him. They, therefore, contain divine thoughts expressed in human language. The Holy Spirit did not necessitate that the employed instruments affect a style corresponding to the divinely inspired ideas. He took the composers of the psalms, as they were: children of their people, of their time, and of their oriental environment; he took them with the poetic aptitudes which they naturally possessed, with their characteristics and temperament. Thus, despite inspiration, the psalms bear the character of their human composer. We, therefore, find in biblical poetry, besides the pearls of religious lyric, some songs which indicate simplicity and lack of culture. Yet, in general, the beauty of external form corresponds with the sublime content of the psalm.

The characteristic mark of biblical poetry is the elevated language. In its vividness and clearness it is scarcely surpassed by any Gentile poetry. It is inexhaustibly rich in description. The pictures are mostly taken from nature and everyday life, and sometimes from the liturgy of the Old Testament and from history. The poet knows how to give life to all creation. The stars of heaven proclaim the glory of the Lord, the massive mountains leap like calves because of joy at the great deeds of the Lord, the brooks clap their hands; heaven and earth, rain and sunshine, fields and the waves of the sea, all praise the Lord, all sing and acclaim their Creator. This vividness of poetic phantasy corresponds to the freedom of poetic form. It knows no constraint of rhyme, neither does it hold itself strictly to a determined rhythm of syllables. Here the external form does not hinder the flow of thought; the thought rather governs the external form. Only the so-called alphabetical poems make an exception. In them the beginning of the verse is bound to the alphabetical form. The rhythm of syllables is replaced by rhythm of thought, the so-called parallelism of members, which we may designate as a peculiarity of biblical poetry. The poet builds his verses in two, sometimes three, similar members which repeat the same thought either in augmented or contrasting form. This kind of poetry is especially adapted for prayer. It makes it possible for the poet to create a stronger and freer development of the thought, and for the petitioner to be more rested and to meditate more deeply upon the thought.

The poetic language, however, is only the extrinsic style of the psalm. Its true value lies in the depth of its religious content. He who seeks only aesthetic enjoyment in the biblical songs and has no understanding of the religious content will not find much pleasure in these poems. Rightly Cardinal Faulhaber tells us in the introduction to his explanation of the Vesper Psalms for Sundays and holydays: "It is necessary to let this religious keynote pervade the soul when we take the songs of Sion in hand. He who believes at the very start that he is entering into a fabulous forest of mental pictures and flowers of speech will be disappointed. We must take our shoes from our feet when we walk on this holy ground. We must bring with us a congenial religious and God-seeking soul when we open the Book of Psalms."

But even those who do not seek aesthetic enjoyment in these psalms, but rather an edified elevation of religious spirit, feel themselves disappointed. They find objection to this treasury of sacred ecclesiastical songs in the light of a hyper-Christian mentality which demands expurgation. Called into question are the so-called innocent and cursing psalms. In the former the petitioner claims a just and innocent life before the all-knowing and all-holy God; in the latter with passionate maledictions he calls God's punishment upon his and his nation's enemies.

To prevent a false judgment concerning these two groups of psalms, it is necessary to observe above all else that they, too, belong to the canonical songs of Israel and bear the divine seal. It makes no difference whether these songs, composed under the direct inspiration of the Holy Spirit, were officially entered earlier or later into the biblical canon. In both cases the very cooperation of the Holy Spirit excludes the fact that these prayers contain anything that is immoral. They may represent an imperfect morality; for they were not composed by and for men who had reached the summit of Christian perfection or at least knew of it, but were written by and for men of the Old Covenant who were to be led gradually by the Holy Spirit to the heights of perfection. Therefore this

Holy Spirit could not demand of them the standards of Christian ethics. As a mother teaching her child how to pray does not use words adapted to her own understanding but those which are suitable to the child's understanding, to its emotions, and to its moral faculties, so also the Holy Spirit in these psalms adapted himself to the understanding, emotions, and moral abilities of those men who in these prayers would speak to God and who in comparison with the mature men of Christ's era were were still babes.

The so-called "Innocence" psalms can give little offense. We must separate, above all, these songs and prayers in which the psalmist defends his innocence against calumnies and unjust suspicions. The confessions have reference only to imputed faults and crimes. These psalms should also be judged with consideration because the petitioner, impressed with the feeling that he has to bear undeserved suffering, reminds God of his righteous living. We know how easily the words are uttered by a Christian bowed down with sorrow: "O Lord, how did I deserve this?" The just man of the Old Testament suffered more than the Christian and the problem of suffering troubled him more; he had not yet seen the God-Man suffer innocently and die on Golgotha. Furthermore, the psalms were composed at a time in which the knowledge of divine retribution had not reached man so clearly as it did at the time of the Christian revelation. To the just man the observance of the moral law presented the thought of reward in this life as was strongly emphasized in the Old Testament; and it was, therefore, human to attribute grave sufferings to indifference to and disobedience of the law of God. However these prayers do not indicate that the just man was arguing about the problems of his sufferings or that they were accusations directed against God, but rather that they are confessions of faith in God's fidelity and justice usually closed with an act of confidence. Even in the very few psalms in which a confession of innocence is made, because of calumny or the pressure of suffering, it is not self-pity nor pharisaic self-justification, but a naive piety that prompts the composer. For the Israelitic petitioner a confession of innocence like that of the 25th Psalm could invite to an examination of conscience and a wholesome purpose of amendment. In this sense the Church has accepted the second part of this psalm, the Lavabo, into the liturgy of the Sacrifice of the Mass; thus should the Christian pray such a psalm of innocence.

It is more difficult to solve the problem of the cursing psalms. However, we would be too severe in saying that these psalms were inspired by a repugnant and savage lust for revenge and on that account contain cursings. Nevertheless they seem to be a discordant factor in the harmony of the Psalter. The problem, how these songs could find a place in the canon of Sacred Scripture, is not removed by questioning their inspired character or even by denying it. The opinion that cursing psalms cannot be attributed to God, that they are only then inspired when it is true that in them is shown human zeal for God and his cause and this finds expression in strong language, lacks proof. One cannot place the prayers of the canon on the same level as the citations in the historical books which, without denying the truth of inspiration, contain errors because both the divine author and the human composer of these books guarantee only the correctness of the citation but not the truth of the contents. The cursing psalms have not been accepted in the sacred treasury of the songs of Israel as cultural historical documents, but only as the language in which members of the chosen people were permitted to call down God's judgment upon their enemies and oppressors. When the apostles interpreted the two most pronounced cursing Psalms, 68 and 108, as Messianic and accepted them as prophetic, they surely did not doubt their inspired character.

We must distinguish between the contents of the psalm, the intention of the composer, and the external form. Only the content is inspired, the form is exclusively the work of the composer. That the cursings do not serve the purpose of satisfying personal revenge is self-evident. If they did, they would not have been accepted in the canon of biblical prayers; for even the Old Testament moral law considered private revenge to be opposed to the will of God (Leviticus 19:18). Revenge was considered to be an encroachment on Yahwe's rights because he has reserved the right of retribution for himself as a judicial act, and men may practice judgment only in virtue of the power which was given them by God (Deuteronomy 32:35). The cursing psalms are a call for the divine judgment when earthly justice is denied, when godlessness, defying the patient God, becomes bolder in its opposition to his law of justice. They are urgent petitions that God may humble the enemies not only of his own people but also of all the just, because they are also his enemies. Antiquity made no sharp distinction between a person and his deeds. It struck at the godlessness in the godless. The Church too prays: "We beseech thee, O Lord, crush the pride of our enemies and hurl to the ground their obstinacy with thy mighty hand."

The petition for the punishment of the enemy which is in itself justifiable, the psalmist has, indeed, clothed in rather passionate language. But the Oriental, when his passion is aroused, speaks with an excess of intense expression. And we may add to this that the poet is not satisfied with a simple petition. He depicts the judgment which should fall upon the enemy, and the enemy himself, with the vividness of his oriental phantasy. We would do him an injustice if we would strain his words and interpret them literally. They are a poetic paraphrase of the ancient principle. "An eye for an eye, and a tooth for a tooth"; wherewith one has committed crime, he should also be punished.

Frequently the form of the wish is a poetic means to express sure intervention by the punishment which has long been threatened by God. The Christian petitioner must, like the Church, overlook the unsympathetic form of the cursing psalms so displeasing to us Occidentals and pray them in the spirit of the Church. Faulhaber says: "If the Church has given these psalms a place in the official breviary, she wishes to utter an exorcism on what is bad and not on men who are bad; and to leave the demoniacal in world history to the judgment of God."

The external form of the psalms is influenced by environment and time, but the content is inspired by the Holy Spirit and is above time and the limit of national barriers. The religious songs of Israel still have much to say to the Christian. And their beauty is not superficial. Their inner wealth can be understood only by earnest study and diligent meditation. Human forms of speech and divine content are not independent of one another. We cannot exhaust the content without considering the form. He who wishes to understand what is divine in the psalms must first understand the human element involved in those psalms.

Hence it is the task of a scientific explanation of the psalms to ascertain the meaning intended by the composer, to study the characteristics of the people, the history of the native country from which they stem; to study their religion and history, their morals and customs; to take into consideration their thought and manner of speech. The psalms cannot be explained without this natural relationship. The same applies to the numerous descriptions whose profound contents can be understood only by a knowledge of Palestine and of Israelitic life. Only he who does not shun the trouble of studying all these helps will find a sure ground from which he may advance to the wealth of the supernatural world of thought. A homiletic-ascetic explanation of the psalms may never look upon a pure scientific understanding of them as superfluous, but must look upon it as a necessary help. We thus refer you here to the Catholic commentaries of Hoberg, Schulte, Knabenbauer and Thalhofer-Wutz.

The homiletic-ascetic explanation has this particular task: to emphasize the supernatural and the divine in the psalms and to make them fruitful in the Christian life. Sacred Scripture is more esteemed than any other religious book of antiquity, and we do justice to it when we value it critically, religiously, historically, and aesthetically. According to Catholic faith, God himself here speaks to us in words for which this threefold consideration is never sufficient.

The value of Sacred Scripture does not end in its cultural and historical significance. It is of value in every age and in every generation. A purely scientific explanation cannot give us a thorough understanding of the significance and purpose of the canonical scripture. This applies especially to the Psalter which has become the liturgical prayerbook of the Church and will remain such. God wishes to speak to us through the psalms and wants us to speak to him in the language of the psalms as did the chosen people of the Old Testament. On this account he has given over these sacred songs to the Church of the New Testament through Christ and the Apostles. This explanation for Christian life will lead us to delve deeply and meditatively into the meaning of God's word. Our hearts should be inflamed when Sacred Scripture is unfolded and laid before us.

contents

Contents

Contents

Contents

Herder's Commentary on the Psalms

psalm 1

Beatus vir

The happiness of the just and the evil state of the wicked

1. Blessed is the man who hath not walked in the counsel of the ungodly, nor stood in the way of sinners, nor sat in the chair of pestilence.

2. But his will is in the law of the Lord, and on his law he shall meditate day and night.

3. And he shall be like a tree which is planted near the running waters, which shall bring forth its fruit in due season.
   And his leaf shall not fall off, and all whatsoever he shall do shall prosper.

4. But not so the wicked, not so; but like the dust, which the wind driveth from the face of the earth.

5. Therefore the wicked shall not rise again in judgment nor sinners in the council of the just.

6. For the Lord knoweth the way of the just; and the way of the wicked shall perish.

I N EVERY man there is a desire for happiness, a longing and a seeking for the blessedness of heaven. There are two ways open to him: the one leads to happiness, the other leads to punishment: the way of the law and the way of sin. There is only one way that leads to the end or purpose of our existence, the way of sacrifice and self-denial, the narrow and steep path that leads to God. Our heart is restless until it rests in God. The Psalter may be called the pilgrim's book of the ascent to God. He who wishes to read and pray the Psalter with profit must follow the narrow path. The first psalm points out that path which shows the way to true happiness; it tells us what is demanded and what we will obtain by following the true path; it points out the path of error and sin which leads to the night of eternal death. Rightly, therefore, St. Jerome calls this didactic poem the Prologue of the Holy Spirit to the Psalter.

God has reserved true happiness for the just. The first part of the psalm (verses 1–3) teaches us the nature and blessedness of righteousness. True happiness and sin are irreconcilable. The requisite for

3

righteousness is hatred for sin. If this hatred for sin is not nourished, man runs the risk of falling into the unhappiness of estranging himself from God. In three clauses the psalmist shows the way of the godless. This way begins by seeking counsel from the wicked; and by no longer seeking to be guided in the path to eternal life by the light of divine truth, but by the spirit and principles of the world. Faith then loses its impelling force, sin loses its true meaning, and conscience its integrity. The protecting walls around the soul crumble. Even the just man can sin, but his sin is only a slip from the right path. But he who takes counsel from the wicked leaves the path of righteousness and enters upon the path of sinners. Then not only are his individual actions contrary to the divine law, but his whole life stands in opposition to God. This is the meaning of the word "sinner" in the fundamental biblical concept. Following this path, man finally mocks at what is holy. He feels himself at home in the circle of those who ridicule religion and virtue. He who is led astray leads others astray. He becomes a carrier of pestilence for his environment.

The second requirement for righteousness is the love of the Law. Blessed is he whose delight is in the precepts of Yahwe. The psalmist did not write these words in a spirit of pharisaism but by the inspiration of the Holy Spirit and, therefore, in the consciousness that God's gift of the Law presents a moral obligation for man. We do not only have in mind here the Mosaic Law but also every divine revelation. The knowledge of God is a requisite for the love of God. The sign of a genuine love of God is the desire of an ever deeper understanding of the Beloved, of his nature, in order to worship him, of his will in order to obey him, of his providence in order to praise him. The just man meditates on the Law day and night. His joy is the knowledge of the commandments and revelations of his God. His joy is not merely the sentimentality of religious festivities. His joy is the result of a constant zeal and love, of meditating deeply upon the things of God, and of permitting grace to enter deeply into his life.

To hunger and thirst after justice is a guarantee for eternal happiness. God does not leave the just man's desires unquenched. The psalmist compares the blessedness of righteousness to a fruit tree near ever-flowing water. For his native country this is a picture of impressive beauty. Water is indicative of life, especially for the waterless Palestine; for there it rains only in the winter covering every spot of the earth with luxuriant grass. But in the summertime nearly all brooks and ponds are dry. The hot glow of the summer sun and the burning winds from the southeast scorch grass and flowers, the leaves of the trees wither, and the parched earth permits no luscious fruit to thrive. But at the Jordan and in every dell inexhaustible springs flow into the valleys; there is everlasting spring and autumn.

4

Thus Ezechiel in a vision saw the blessing of Messianic times (47:12): "A fountain issued from the temple and became a life-giving stream; every tree at its banks retained its foliage, and its fruit continually matured." The stream is divine grace which comes from heaven and gives supernatural life to every man who accepts it. The tree is the just man, the saint united with God. He bears fruit in due time. But upon the just man there also comes the fire of suffering and trial; he also is afflicted with temptation. His supernatural strength and life, however, cannot be destroyed and as long as he remains rooted in grace, his fruitfulness cannot be destroyed. The history of the saints of all times gives testimony that in the very years of the hardest trials and in a world whose supernatural life was on the wane, the most glorious fruits of heroic virtue matured. "His foliage does not wither." For him who draws his strength from the sources of salvation, supernatural life will never die, his faith will not waver, his love will not cease, his fidelity will remain unshaken. "Whatever the just man does, prospers." For him there is no failure. Whatever is done by the grace of God is pleasing to God and will be entered in the book of life for an eternal reward. Even the babbling prayer of a little child, the insignificant work of an adult, the dire want of the poor, the patient suffering of the sick, will be entered in this book of life. For the just man death is not dying, but a transition to perfection.

But the way of the sinner ends differently. In the second part of the psalm (verses 4–6) the psalmist contrasts the lot of the just man with the fate of the godless. Earthly happiness seems to favor the child of the world more than the child of God. But he who sees deeper and reflects upon the fate of men in the light of faith will not envy the sinner's good fortune, for he will observe the emptiness of his life. Jeremias in 17:6 also contrasts the blessing of the righteous with the fate of the godless. He likens it to a plant in a waterless desert. But for the psalmist even this contrast is not sufficient. He contrasts it with chaff blown away by the wind. When the beating has been completed on the threshing floor, the farmer separates the wheat from the chaff. He first pours both into a sieve and then gathers the chaff to be burnt. He finally shovels the grain and throws it against the wind. This chaff is a picture of the life of the godless, without root, without fruit, without strength of life, without content— useless. The godless are like a sea which never comes to rest, the waves of which wash up dirt and slime. The truth of these words was once uttered by the prophet Isaias (57:20). From the rich experience of many active years in the apostolate he could express himself in this manner and every cultured nation would substantiate his claim. Any man who is not anchored in faith will be influenced by the spirit of the age; yet he is not fully satisfied with his pleasures and he finds no moral support when distress and want befall him. Worthless and useless is the life of a man who does not serve his highest purpose, does not cooperate with grace, and does not perform any work of eternal value, but only performs such works as will not stand the test of judgment.

The comparison of the godless with chaff leads the psalmist to the thought of their fate on judgment day. The cleansing of the threshing floor is a frequent figure of speech used for the judgment at the end of the world which will separate the sinners from the just for all eternity. Because of the worthlessness of their worldly life the godless cannot countenance the Judge; for who can endure his wrath, who can withstand his anger. His wrath burns like fire. Before him even the rocks melt. The just lived on earth among the godless and were oppressed, but in the eternal Sion only the just may dwell; the sinners will be expelled from the face of the Lord into eternal darkness. Their expulsion will be irrevocable. The judgment will reveal the end of their way. The Lord knows the way of the just. It is the way designed by him, the way of faith and obedience. He will redeem his promise. The path of the sinner leads away from God. The sinner loves darkness more than light; therefore his portion will be eternal night and destruction.

psalm 2

Quare fremuerunt

Christ's kingdom and his enemies

1. Why have the Gentiles raged and the people devised vain things?

2. The kings of the earth stood up, and the princes met together against the Lord and against his Christ.

3. Let us break their bonds asunder; and let us cast away their yoke from us.

4. He that dwelleth in heaven shall laugh at them: and the Lord shall deride them.

5. Then shall he speak to them in his anger and trouble them in his rage.

6. But I am appointed king by him over Sion, his holy mountain, preaching his commandment.

7. The Lord hath said to me: Thou art my son, this day have I begotten thee.

8. Ask of me, and I will give thee the Gentiles for thy inheritance and the utmost parts of the earth for thy possession.

9. Thou shalt rule them with a rod of iron and shalt break them in pieces like a potter's vessel.

10. And now, O ye kings, understand; receive instruction, you that judge the earth.

11. Serve ye the Lord with fear: and rejoice unto him with trembling.

12. Embrace discipline, lest at any time the Lord be angry and you perish from the just way.

13. When his wrath shall be kindled in a short time, blessed are all that trust in him.

EVEN the primitive Christian Church ascribed this psalm to the royal singer David (Acts 4:25). It is poetry of dramatic vividness. It has a breadth and depth of thought which can be explained only by attributing it to divine revelation. In four scenes the psalmist gives a description of Messianic times as he was permitted to see them in his prophetic vision. He describes conditions as we have experienced them in the last twenty centuries in the history of the Church. The psalmist pictures to us the revolt of the hostile powers against God and against the nascent destiny of the world-wide dominion of Christ the King.

The Anointed of Yahwe is the Messias. From Apostolic times this was the understanding of the Church. The Anointed is the Son of God, the only-begotten Son of Yahwe. The Egyptians, Babylonians, and other pagan nations believed that their rulers were begotten by gods and on this account gave them divine honors. But Israel could call its kings "Sons of God" only in a figurative sense; however in this psalm such a sonship of the Anointed of God is excluded because the emphasis is placed upon his generation from Yahwe. In biblical Hebraic language the begetting is unexceptionably a real procession. By nature the Anointed is of divine descent. Such a descent is also ascribed to the Messias by other prophets. Other kings of Israel could be called sons of God only after their ascent to the throne; their divine sonship through grace was a consequence of their kingship. But for the Anointed of this psalm the divine Sonship is the reason for his kingship and for his claim to world dominion. The divine Sonship is older than the throne. God never gave to the Davidic royal house the right to world dominion. The realm of the Davidic kingdom remained limited to Palestine even during the time of its greatest glory. No Israelite prince could think of ever ruling the then-

7

known nations. When at the ascension of a new king to the throne, an Assyrian or Babylonian poet-laureate would honor him as a ruler to whom the gods gave the power to rule all nations and the history of his country gave him a certain amount of justification. To the little king of Juda, however, who was happy if the great powers along the Euphrates and the Nile would permit him to rule his little country in peace, the words of the psalmist about the "iron rod" would be unjustifiable flattery and would be altogether inadmissible in the mouth of a poet enlightened by the Holy Spirit. The world dominion of the Messias-King, however, is a real sketch of a prophetic picture of the future.

The promise that the Messias would be a blessing to all nations was already made to Abraham. On this account the psalmist considered the Messianic future as a time of undisturbed world peace during which all nations would be glad to subject themselves to the mild sceptre of Yahwe and his Anointed. But in this psalm there is presented an altogether different picture. The psalmist sees an unwilling submission to the kingdom of God on earth, a fierce revolt against the kingdom of Christ in the entire world. The first scene (verses 1–3) leads us into the center of the revolt of the nations. New plans are continually being made and new possibilities are being weighed to supplant the throne of the eternal King. Kings, who otherwise are at war with each other, secretly plan to unite in common attack and to urge the nations to shake off the rule of Yahwe and the yoke of Christ the King. Liberty is their watchword. We do not want this God to rule over us. His blessed law is looked upon as unworthy bondage, his merciful yoke as an oppressive burden. The prophet is astonished at the blindness of the nations and of their rulers. He is angry at the world's alienation of Christ and ridicules its foolish hatred and violence; for vain and foolish is its undertaking. How can the kings of the earth, men formed from the slime of the earth, dare to revolt against the kingdom of God and his Anointed? Such a crime will not end pleasantly.

The second scene (verses 4–5) gives us a view of heaven, where God is enthroned in inaccessible majesty. It is folly to revolt against Yahwe. In a masterful way the psalmist gives with a few strokes the contrast between heaven and earth. Here is restlessness and mad passion and violent revolt of blinded men; there is the inaccessible height of their God and King who dwells in the peace of his infinite grandeur. He derides those who revolt against him and war against the kingdom of heaven. "Who dwells in heaven and laughs at them." In human language this is the answer of the Lord to the futile undertakings of his creatures. He scoffs at those who revolt against the kingdom of heaven; for it is in vain that they will try to shake off the yoke of Yahwe. He is "Adonai," the all-

8

powerful One before whom the nations are but a drop in the ocean, a speck of dust on the scales (Isaias 40:15). Revolt is insanity. God may for a long time look upon the frivolous activities of men because he is patient; but when the time of his longanimity has come to an end, the day of punishment will fall upon the disobedient in all its terror. Then the Lord will speak in his inexorable wrath. Then they will hear the judgment of rejection, the curse of God.

The picture changes again. In the third scene (verses 6–9) the Anointed appears before the rebellious nations to make his claim for world dominion and to demand submission to the sceptre. It is crime and folly to revolt against Christ the King. He is the rightful King of Sion placed there by God himself. He is the Lord of all the earth, placed by God over his kingdom in this world. The theocracy of the New Covenant, the Church, will be supra-national. It will comprise all nations; it will by its very nature be world-wide. The center of this world-wide kingdom in the prophetic picture of the future will be Mount Sion, because there the God of the world dwells in his sanctuary and there is the throne of David whose heir is to be the Messias-King. From Sion the Lord is to permit the mighty sceptre of his Anointed to rule and have dominion over his enemies (Psalm 109:2). He who rebels against the Anointed makes God his enemy.

The claim of the Messias-King to the obedience of all nations has a deeper foundation. He is the Son of God by nature not by grace. With the statement of this truth the psalm reaches its climax. Here revelation lifts the veil which in the Old Covenant otherwise hides the nature of the promised Redeemer and permits men only to surmise what the "Credo" of the Holy Mass confesses: "I believe in the Lord, Jesus Christ, the only begotten Son of God, begotten of the Father from eternity, God of God, light of light, true God of true God, begotten not created, one nature with the Father, through whom all things were made." The Anointed of Yahwe has proceeded from the nature of the Father. And the Father on the day of begetting, the day of eternity, acknowledged the Son and declared him to be his Son when he said: "Thou art My Son; this day I have begotten Thee." Not without purpose does the psalmist place this sentence in the mouth of the Father; for according to the Babylonian and Israelitic custom the father uttered it after the birth of a son begotten by him. Without doubt the psalmist wished to exclude all doubt about the true character of the divine Sonship of the Messias; for it is only on this relationship that a claim to a participation in the world dominion of his Father is based. The origin of the Messias before all creation, from the day of eternity, was not unknown to the prophets (Micheas 5:2). Now the Son reveals it to all nations because they deny his right to world-dominion. He reveals it in his Gospel and through the Church.

On the day of the eternal generation the Son of God, as the Messias, did not as yet possess world dominion. But already at that time the nations were given to him as his future dominion and the whole world as his future possession. The sons of kings inherit the throne of the father when he dies or when he resigns his kingdom. God cannot die, neither can he relinquish his dominion; but at some time he will give to the Anointed a full and equal share of world dominion and will have him participate in his unlimited power. He shall be the lord of the whole world and shall dispose of the nations as his possessions just as the Father is lord and possessor. He shall be possessor as soon as he completes his task of the redemption of mankind and makes his claim of ownership. This pledge in the psalm is more than a king's word; it is God's word which will be infallibly kept without any reservation. The prophet already sees it fulfilled; for the revolt of the nations is directed against the claim of the Messias to world dominion. We see that this claim was realized when Christ rose from the dead, and ascended into heaven, and sitteth at the right hand of God (Psalm 109:1). But on the day of the eternal generation God has assured his Son not only unlimited possession and the right to rule the nations, but he also has provided him with infinite power in order that he might be able to maintain his right. He who does not willingly submit to his rule will feel the power of his justice. As the potter breaks to pieces a useless vessel, so God will destroy every nation that revolts against his rule. History gives testimony that this has been fulfilled.

The undeniable right of Christ the King's claim to world dominion demands from the nations and princes the duty of submission. Therefore in the fourth picture the psalmist turns to the kings with the admonition to subject themselves to the rule of Yahwe and his Anointed. Their own common sense and the welfare of the people demand it; for in view of the irresistible power of God and his Son, it is folly to seek peace and happiness by revolting against him. There is only one way of obtaining the true welfare of the nations; namely, by unreserved submission to the law of God. "Serve ye the Lord in fear." Obedience should be given not with a slavish fear of the iron rod, but with reverence that is rooted in the belief in God and in his Anointed. His right to rule is everlasting. Therefore with a joyful enthusiasm and with holy reverence they should worship the Anointed of the Lord as their King because of his infinite greatness and majesty. In the ancient Orient it was the custom for the vassal to signify his submission to the kingly lord by kissing his feet. Therefore the psalmist closes with the admonition: "Kiss the Son." In the Greek and Latin text, however, the psalm repeats the warning against revolt. Accept discipline before it is too late, for the day of judgment is not far off. He who has entered upon the wrong path will be struck by the curse of God on that day; but he who lives in Christ will obtain eternal peace and blessing.

psalm 3

Domine, quid multiplicati

The prophet's danger and delivery from his son Absalom: mystically, the passion and resurrection of Christ

1. The psalm of David when he fled from the face of his son Absalom. (2 Kings 15).

2. Why, O Lord, are they multiplied that afflict me? Many are they who rise against me.

3. Many say to my soul: There is no salvation for him in his God.

4. But thou, O Lord, art my protector, my glory, and the lifter up of my head.

5. I have cried to the Lord with my voice; and he has heard me from his holy hill.

6. I have slept and have taken my rest: and I have risen up, because the Lord hath protected me.

7. I will not fear thousands of the people surrounding me; Arise, O Lord, save me, O my God.

8. For thou hast struck all them who are my adversaries without cause: thou hast broken the teeth of sinners.

9. Salvation is of the Lord, and thy blessing is upon thy people.

IN HEBRON, Absalom had given the sign of rebellion against his own father and a large number of inhabitants had seceded from David. Weeping, barefooted, with veiled head, accompanied by six-hundred faithful followers, the king fled past Mount Olivet into the desert of Jericho. But even there he was not safe; for he had to fear that Absalom with his twelve-thousand men would pursue and surround him in the darkness of the night. David could not rely on human help. What could an army of six-hundred warriors do against an army twenty times its size? His adversaries were triumphant and suggested that their victory was a sign that God had rejected his anointed. However the king was not despondent. When in the desert the first night came upon the pursued king, he went to sleep with a confidence in God's protection and the Lord permitted him to awake to a new morning which gave him the opportunity to cross the Jordan. According to the superscription the psalm was composed on this occasion. It is David's morning prayer after the first night during his flight. Having been accepted in Israel's collection of hymns, the psalm has become a prayer for all who have experienced great affliction from without as well as great spiritual suffering. It is a pattern that should pervade our prayer in similar situations.

The psalm begins with a complaint to God (verses 2–3). Man has need of unburdening his heart to others when afflicted with sorrow. The very thought of finding consolation and sympathy will lessen his sorrow. No one has a greater understanding of human sorrow than the infinitely good God; and no one knows better how to console than the God of consolation. Therefore David does not complain to his faithful followers. He does not accuse his son nor his people, but lays bare his distress before God. He tells God how bitterly he is disappointed by his subjects and what sorrow his experience has caused him. He knew that he had enemies, but that there were so many he did not surmise. What was still more bitter for him was that many saw in his fate a punishment from God, a sign of divine rejection. It is true that during his life he had sinned gravely against God, but he had also done penance and received pardon from God. Thus he cannot admit that there is no salvation for him, that he will no longer obtain any favors from God.

David makes his complaint before God, but his prayer is not an accusation against him. It is made because of his faith in divine providence (verses 4–5) and because of his confidence in God's merciful love. How easily man forgets all the gifts and benefactions which the heavenly Father has showered upon him when he is tried and disciplined. Doubts arise in his mind about God's justice and kindness and from his lips we hear reproaches: "How did I deserve this?" The creature enumerates before his Creator all the good things he has done, all the debts which the Lord owes him, his servant. Not so the royal petitioner. In his anguish he seeks and finds peace of soul by considering how fatherly God has guided him through the vicissitudes of life for so many years. How often had he seen his life threatened by Saul and his followers? But he was always protected by God as the large shield protects the warrior. Did he not frequently have reason to thank and praise God and extol his fatherly providence? When anxiety and spiritual affliction humbled him, it was God who encouraged him and brought happiness to him again. David now reflects upon all the requests he had made to the Lord by his constant petitioning. He knows no prayer that did not find a hearing. He remembers no cry which God did not answer with rich blessings from the sanctuary on Sion. It is the psalmist's consolation that the good God still loves.

From the past the petitioner turns to the present in which there is so much suffering. It gives him reason for a triumphant hope (verses 6–7). Was it not a miracle of divine love which in that first night kept David from all dangers and hindered a surprise attack by Absalom upon his father? God was near his anointed. Now it is certain that his affair is well taken care of by the Lord. This consciousness leaves him triumphant in his affliction. When God is with him, he has nothing to fear even from a large army. Thus has it always been proved in the life time of the psalmist that God does not permit a trial to befall a faithful follower which is above his strength to resist. David could count himself among the faithful followers of God; for to feel in suffering the loving and protecting hand of God is a sign of genuine love of God.

His prayer is a petition replete with confidence (verses 8–9). The psalmist is certain that he will be heard. How often as a shepherd David had defended his flock from wild animals and had crushed the predators' heads with his club that he might keep them from their prey. God is his shepherd. He will not permit a just man to be destroyed by the godless. He destroys them and takes away from them their booty, even though they already seem to triumph. God is the Good Shepherd. For men there is no salvation in any other, nor for whole nations. There is no other name by which they may find salvation. Faith in the Good Shepherd gives us strength to overcome all discouragement.

psalm 4

Cum invocarem

The prophet teaches us to flee to God in tribulation

1. Unto the end, in verses, a psalm for David.

2. When I called upon him, the God of my justice heard me; in my distress, thou hast enlarged me. Have mercy on me and hear my prayer.

3. O ye sons of men, how long will you be dull of heart? Why do you love vanity and seek after lying?

4. Know ye also that the Lord hath made his holy one wonderful; the Lord will hear me when I shall cry unto him.

5. Be ye angry and sin not; the things you say in your hearts be sorry for them upon your beds.

6. Offer up the sacrifice of justice, and trust in the Lord; many say: Who showeth us good things?

7. The light of thy countenance, O Lord, is signed upon us; thou hast given gladness in my heart.

8. By the fruit of their corn, their wine, and oil, they are multiplied.

9. In peace in the self same I will sleep and I will rest.

10. For thou, O Lord, singularly hast settled me in hope.

THE day on which David fled from his son Absalom, and which he began with the morning prayer of the third psalm, came to an end; and night again fell upon the persecuted king. But with prayer and the consciousness that God's providence watches over him, the agony of his soul quickly subsides. The Lord had even taken care of the temporal needs of the refugee, and had sent him help in the desert. Full of faith and confidence the king was filled with a holy joy because of God's goodness, and a profound peace came to his soul. No discouragement, no emotion of hatred, no spirit of revenge, disturbed his rest. In his happiness of being united with God, he thought of those men who were deprived of this peace; he thought of his foolish enemies, and of his faithful and discouraged friends. There is a strain of Christian piety and evening devotion in this psalm. Therefore, the Church has accepted it as an evening prayer for Compline on Sundays and feast days.

The Christian evening prayer is that of thanksgiving; for every day in which the soul is united with God in Christ is a precious day filled with gifts of the divine love and goodness. Such a soul now elevates itself in thankfulness to God during his night prayer and meditates on God's fatherly kindness. With such uplifting of his soul to God, David, too, closes his day even though the wealth of Christ's graces have not been at his disposal. Even though he is still a refugee, he does not think of his present adversity, nor dwell upon the present afflictions of his life. He

14

meditates upon the manifestations of divine favor which helped him to overcome all trials. He views the bright side of his day's activities. He recalls how the Lord, as the true defender of a just cause, assisted him whenever he asked for help; how he was always near him, as a deliverer, whenever there was no other escape from danger. The experiences gave the prayerful David the assurance that his prayers would not go unheard, that God would not deny his protection on this night and on all future occasions and that his enemies would not succeed. So also the Christian in his life should not be discouraged, but in thankfulness, confidence, and love should place himself under the protection of divine providence.

In the evening the Christian's attitude should be that of reconciliation with the offender, and with all who persecute the Christians and the priests, the anointed of the Lord. And Christ teaches us this at the end of his earthly life: "Father, forgive them; for they know not what they do." David also thought of his enemies and prayed for them in verses 3–6. He himself could not speak to them. He, therefore, confided his petition to the Lord that he might guide them by his mysterious grace. It was David's wish that as men of judgment and culture, they might recognize their blindness. These men believed that they could justify their calumnies and persecutions of the chosen before God and conscience. The psalmist prayed that they might see their self-deception concerning the success of an affair that was contrary to the will of God and, therefore, a sham and a lie. The Lord could not be untrue to himself. He could not permit his work to be destroyed by human arrogance. He had called David from his shepherd life. He had disciplined him in the strict school of suffering; he had given him victory and power over his enemies; he had given him, who was a man after his own heart, wisdom, that he might rule the people of God in the name of that same invisible, eternal God. How could God now permit him to become a victim of a ruthless rebellion? The enemies of the anointed should know that he who is just is the stronger even when to all appearances he seems defenseless and can only defend himself by the weapon of prayer. Unbridled passion and inordinate pride cause blindness of intellect; quiet and humble reflection opens the eyes of the mind and permits man to see the error of his conduct. Therefore the prayerful petitioner does not ask God to pass a judgment of condemnation upon his enemies, but to give them light and grace. We may criticize the mistakes of an anointed one, but rebellion against God-willed authority and order is not justifiable. David's enemies rejoiced over their momentary success and celebrated magnificent victory services on Sion. But God took no pleasure in the thanksgiving services of brutal men whose successes he permitted for a short time for reasons known only to his inscruta-

15

ble wisdom. He found no pleasure in them because they carried out their own plans, contrary to the wishes of God, instead of submitting unreservedly to the norms of his law.

There is no special merit in trusting in God when all of one's wishes are fulfilled. Yet, it can become difficult to keep a Christian optimism when all hope for the future seems lost. As long as David was victorious, his faithful followers had no doubt about the Lord being with him. But when the people deserted him and he had to flee into the desert from the army of Absalom, his followers became depressed and quickly gave up hope in the king's cause. Who will grant us success? David would have far more reason to give way to pessimism because in one day he lost the throne, the people, his child, and his home. But his faith in God's fidelity and love proved to be stronger than the temptation to discouragement and despondency. Should God turn his countenance from him and deprive him of his bounteous grace because a foolish son rebelled against his father? Not one moment would rob him of the assurance of God's mercy and love. At this evening hour in the desert he had only one petition; namely, that God would remove the bandage from the eyes of his discouraged friends, so that they might see the brightness of the divine countenance shedding light upon them like a victorious banner announcing temporal deliverance and joy of soul. It is only from a belief in God's fidelity to his promises and a confidence in his help that they could acquire courage and remain with the king in the desert in the darkest hours of his life. David himself knows nothing of discouragement. Like St. Paul, his heart is full of confidence and joy despite adversity. Although impoverished and dependent upon the sympathy of others, he would not have the pure joy which the consciousness of divine favor gives to the soul taken from him and would not exchange it for the joy which would be given him by the possession of earthly goods. The joy that comes from union with God is the fruit of the spirit and gives peace of heart; and peace with God gives security. He who lives under the protection of God can rest securely even when he is surrounded by a thousand dangers. His protection gives greater security than many legions of soldiers. Thus this beautiful evening song is recited with sentiments of peaceful assurance of God's love.

psalm 5

Verba mea auribus

A prayer against the iniquities of men

1. Unto the end, for her that obtaineth the inheritance. A psalm for David.

2. Give ear, O Lord, to my words, understand my cry.

3. Hearken to the voice of my prayer, O my king and my God.

4. For to thee will I pray; O Lord, in the morning thou shalt hear my voice.

5. In the morning I will stand before thee and will see, because thou art not a God that willest iniquity.

6. Neither shall the wicked dwell near thee; nor shall the unjust abide before thy eyes.

7. Thou hatest all the workers of iniquity; thou wilt destroy all that speak a lie. The bloody and the deceitful man the Lord will abhor.

8. But as for me in the multitude of thy mercy, I will come into thy house; I will worship towards thy holy temple, in thy fear.

9. Conduct me, O Lord, in thy justice; because of my enemies, direct my way in thy sight.

10. For there is no truth in their mouth; their heart is vain.

11. Their throat is an open sepulchre; they dealt deceitfully with their tongues; judge them, O Lord. Let them fall from their devices; according to the multitude of their wickedness cast them out; for they have provoked thee, O Lord.

12. But let all them be glad that hope in thee; they shall rejoice forever, and thou shalt dwell in them. And all they that love thy name shall glory in thee.

13. For thou wilt bless the just. O Lord, thou hast crowned us, as with a shield of thy good will.

A NEW day has dawned. In the court of the holy tabernacle the priests arrive to make preparations for the morning offering. They face Mount Olivet in order to lay the offerings on the flames of the altar as

17

soon as the first rays of the sun appear over the eastern heights. In his castle King David prepares himself for his walk to the sanctuary, in order that by his participation in the sacrifice he might obtain protection and blessing for the new day. The thoughts which occupy his mind on the way are expressed by this psalm. The psalm can serve every Israelite in his preparation for the bloody morning sacrifice; it can also serve the Christians as an "Introit" to the unbloody morning sacrifice of the New Covenant.

Who goes to the sanctuary goes to the king, seeking relief and asking for help (verses 2–4). Grave responsibilities rest upon David's shoulders and still heavier do the secret plots of his enemies oppress him. At the beginning of the day he is confronted with many cares. These he places before the Lord at the morning sacrifice. He speaks to the Lord about the many dangers which deceitful and treacherous men put in his way. Against these he can seek effective protection only with his God and King. To him, the earthly king, admission is granted, as it is to all, who seek justice and protection from God (2 Kings 15:2). The duty of the king is to defend the cause of the oppressed and persecuted. But God is the just king of his people to whom all may come with their petitions; he is also David's God and king. Therefore he hastens to seek help in the temple sanctuary that he may place his affairs in the early dawn before the throne of the Most High. Prayer in the early morning hours may be considered the first fruits of the new day and this concept gives assurance that it will be heard. Thus the psalmist prepares himself by the spiritual offering of prayer; he gathers his thoughts, preparing them on the altar of his heart, that they may ascend to heaven like the smoke from the altar of holocausts. The psalmist looks confidently to heaven that the sun of divine mercy may shine upon him upon this new day.

He who wishes to go to the sanctuary must examine his conscience before he approaches the holy God (verses 5–7). "For no one is holy but the Lord" (1 Kings 2:2). He cannot be pleased with sin; for sin by its very nature is opposed to God. Therefore the blasphemer is cut off from union with God. He has not the right of a guest in the tabernacle of Yahwe; he may not participate in the precious banquet of grace which the Lord prepares for his guests. The holy God is not only displeased with sin, he hates it as much as he loves virtue. He can meet the refusal of submission to his will only with an ardent hatred and punitive justice. But what creature can endure the wrath of an almighty God? How could a godless man face a pitiless and strict Judge who with the wrath of his lips can destroy the blasphemer? He who dwells and rules in the sanctuary is the searcher of hearts. He is infinite truth. No lie or hypocrisy can deceive him. All untruth and treachery is an abomination to him. He not only hates those who tell lies and are guilty of calumny and detraction; he destroys them; he casts them into eternal darkness; he moves them far from him into the night of damnation.

But the just man may in all confidence enter the house of the Lord, the dwelling place of the merciful God (verses 8–10). The psalmist, too, is a just man, not because of his own merit, but thanks to the abounding love of God. Meditations upon this love occupy the royal petitioner on his way to the holy tabernacle. It was God's grace that permitted him to be born a member of the chosen people, of that people which could boast of having God so near. No Gentile nation could make this boast about their gods (Deuteronomy 4:7). Joyful about this divine grace David at another time exclaimed: "Blessed is he whom thou hast chosen and taken to thee: he shall dwell in thy courts" (Psalm 64:5).

It was divine love that urged him to acquire an ever more profound knowledge of the majesty of Yahwe and through it a greater reverence for the sanctuary. Therefore, humbly and thankfully the psalmist confesses: "I will come into thy house: I will worship towards thy holy temple in thy fear." The way to the temple reminds him of the spiritual way to God, the way of virtue. For dangers lurk around us, dangers that threaten because of our own spiritual weakness, dangers from satanical, evil men who seek every possibility of bringing about the fall of the just man. If a man wishes to walk the way of the commandments, God himself must lead him and remove all dangerous obstacles that lie in his way. The help of the Lord is so much the more necessary when there are very dangerous opponents. Just as Satan clothes himself in the form of light in order to deceive men about his purposes, so the godless conceal their true purpose by flattering speech. Their mouth speaks peace, but their soul plans destruction. Their throat is a grave which never closes, but receives new victims with insatiable greed.

At the close of the psalm the prayer is changed into a sacrificial prayer for all (verses 11–13). The enemies of the anointed are also the enemies of God. The liturgical divine service is not for the individual only. The psalmist is conscious of the fact that he is a member of a large society whose sufferings and joys he must share. As a member of this society David prays that God may destroy the enemies of his kingdom and shatter their ruthless plans. He prays that the Lord may protect his faithful followers against the enemies and against all dangers; he prays that God may be to them a refuge in all adversity. Then they will rejoice because of his power and fidelity, and they will realize that God loves those who love him. The psalmist is sure that his prayer will be heard. The rich experiences of his own life give testimony that the Lord blesses the righteous and protects them as a large shield protects the body.

19

psalm 6

Domine, ne in furore

A prayer of a penitent sinner, under the scourge of God.
The first penitential psalm

1. Unto the end, in verses, a psalm for David, for the octave.

2. O Lord, rebuke me not in thy indignation, nor chastise me in thy wrath.

3. Have mercy on me, O Lord, for I am weak; heal me, O Lord, for my bones are troubled.

4. And my soul is troubled exceedingly: but thou, O Lord, how long?

5. Turn to me, O Lord, and deliver my soul; O save me for thy mercy's sake.

6. For there is no one in death, that is mindful of thee; and who shall confess to thee in hell?

7. I have labored in my groanings, every night I will wash my bed; I will water my couch with my tears.

8. My eye is troubled through indignation; I have grown old amongst all my enemies.

9. Depart from me, all ye workers of iniquity; for the Lord has heard the voice of my weeping.

10. The Lord hath heard my supplication; the Lord hath received my prayer.

11. Let all my enemies be ashamed and be very much troubled; let them be turned back, and be ashamed very speedily.

THE Church has rightly classified this poem as one of the seven penitential psalms. This impressive song was not occasioned by any personal sin of David, but rather by a persecution wrought by his enemies. It may even be the persecution by Saul and his followers. But it is a pattern for penitential sinners who sincerely seek reconciliation with God. The most profound affliction of the soul is separation from God (verses 2–4). For months David, conscious of his innocence and believing in God's providence, bore his sufferings with submission. But this source of strength, like the patience of Job, began to waver. The night of abandonment by God seemed to overpower him and the thought troubled his soul that God had withdrawn his love and grace, that God was displaying His wrath because of his sins, that his sufferings were the bitter fruit of his sins against God and God's resultant curse. How helpless a man feels himself when he is in an open field without protection, exposed to the fury of the elements, fearing that the next flash of lightning will strike him. This is only a weak picture when compared to the condition of a sinner who has deserved God's anger and who, because of his sins, may be punished with eternal death. The thought of having come under the curse of God troubled David so much the more because with his whole soul he had desired that Yahwe should be the God of his heart and his portion eternally. He humbly begged not for a mitigation of his punishment; he was willing to bear any sufferings and atone for his guilt. He asked only for a sign showing that God was not angry with him; he asked only for a ray of mercy and grace. Discipline out of love effects healing, but the punishments of divine wrath must finally exhaust the strength of any man. A cross which the love of God imposes, does not destroy, but strengthens peace of soul. But the curse of God troubles the soul in its deepest recesses. From the depth of his soul the psalmist cried to God: Lord, how long? How long wilt thou refuse to listen to the pleading of my soul which is in such great affliction? How long must I call upon thee until thou hearest me?

The psalmist looks in vain for a sign from heaven. The Lord still seems to show his anger toward him. And thus a second appeal is made to heaven for God's mercy, a cry to spare his life, a cry for temporal and eternal life. With contrite heart a sacred vow dedicates his life to the Lord; for only a living man can praise the Lord (verses 5–8). It is for his own glory that the Creator has given spiritual life to man: that he may praise his holy name, relate his wonderful deeds, and speak of the greatness of his works (Sirach 17:7). The dead do not praise God. In the underworld, in the limbo of the just, the praise of the Lord does not resound, because those who silently await redemption do not behold the wonderful works of God. In hell the praises of God come to an end for all eternity. Only he who lives can praise God (Isaias 38:19). If God grants the psalmist a longer life, he will serve him more faithfully. He will play the harp all the days of his life in Yahwe's honor. But now the harp has fallen from the hands of one who is sick unto death. No songs of jubilation come from his mouth. Instead only sobs are heard. Tears fill his eyes and the still of the night is painful to him. The joy of life no longer shines in his countenance. Worry and tears have dimmed his sight and the attacks of his enemies have exhausted his strength. God, who does not want death, but life, must be moved by this misery.

21

The penitential cry of the sinner remains unheeded if it is not accompanied with the hope of reconciliation with God (verses 9–11). It is only a trust in his mercy that gives strength. The cry of the psalmist was accompanied by an unconquerable faith in God "whose mercy is great" (Isaias 55:7). We may be surprised at the sudden change of sentiment in this song. It is the genuine fruit of a strong faith and of prayer for the light of God's love. Thus the petitioner has raised himself from the abyss of despondency to the assurance of reconciliation with God, and he now triumphantly demands that his enemies depart. "Away ye tempters of mistrust and despondency! Away with you who rejoice at my suffering and expect my defeat!" They have triumphed until now, but God has heard the cry of his anointed and he will answer his prayer. For they who cry unto the Lord will not be disappointed. But his enemies will be disappointed and put to shame. God may permit their wickedness for a while in order to try the just and purify them and even lead sinners back to the right path but he will not permit them to conquer. They who thought victory already in their hands see their plans frustrated. They will be put to shame and take flight when they approach the divine Judge who will utter the terrible "Depart."

psalm 7

Domine, Deus meus

David, trusting in the justice of his cause, prayeth for God's help against his enemies

1. The psalm of David which he sang to the Lord, for the words of Chusi the son of Jemini (2 Kings 16).

2. O Lord my God, in thee have I put my trust: save me from all them that persecute me, and deliver me.

3. Lest at any time he seize upon my soul like a lion, while there is no one to redeem me, nor to save.

4. O Lord, my God, if I have done this thing, if there be iniquity in my hands:

5. If I have rendered to them that repaid me evils, let me deservedly fall empty before my enemies.

6. Let the enemy pursue my soul, and take it, and tread down my life on the earth, and bring down my glory to the dust.

7. Rise up, O Lord, in thy anger; and be thou exalted in the borders of my enemies.
And arise, O Lord my God, in the precept which thou hast commanded:

8. and a congregation of people shall surround thee.
And for their sakes return thou on high.

9. The Lord judgeth the people.
Judge me, O Lord, according to my justice, and according to my innocence in me.

10. The wickedness of sinners shall be brought to nought: and thou shalt direct the just; the searcher of hearts and reins is God.

11. Just is my help from the Lord, who saveth the upright of heart.

12. God is a just judge, strong and patient: is he angry every day?

13. Unless you will be converted, he will brandish his sword; he hath bent his bow, and made it ready.

14. And in it he hath prepared the instruments of death, he hath made ready his arrows for them, that burn.

15. Behold he hath been in labour with injustice; he hath conceived sorrow and brought forth iniquity.

16. He hath opened a pit and dug it; and he has fallen into the hole he made.

17. His sorrow shall be turned on his own head; and his iniquity shall come down upon his crown.

18. I will give glory to the Lord according to his justice; and will sing to the name of the Lord the most high.

S AUL goaded by envy and driven by a mania for persecution suspected his faithful armor-bearer of high treason (1 Kings 22:8). The slanderous accusations of his courtiers strengthened his suspicions and provoked him to take measures to rid himself of the defenseless David by force (1 Kings 26:19). Thus David had to flee unable to justify or defend himself. The Law knew no other judge above the king excepting God alone. The psalmist turned to him and beseeched him to pass judgment upon his calumniators. The psalm became a community hymn and a prayer for those who were innocent and yet calumniated. It became a prayer for the Church against her calumniators and persecutors. Ancient tradition has called the Benjaminite Saul a Kushite or Ethiopian because of his heartlessness toward David. The Ethiopian people were stereotyped as archsavages.

When unscrupulous men attack a defenseless man with the treacherous weapons of lies and slander using their influence to deny the victim the right to defend himself, no power on earth can hinder the injured person from having recourse to God and from confidently appealing to the supreme divine Judge. David was defenseless but strong in his confidence in God (verses 2–3). Not many persuasive words are needed before the all-knowing and all-just God. Simply, and yet persuasively the psalmist utters his petition for protection and gives his reason for it. The slanderers are compared to blood thirsty animals who attack their victim from the rear and tear him to pieces. When all human help against persecutors is at an end, God himself must intervene in behalf of the defenseless; for as author and supreme guardian of the moral order he may not rest until justice prevails.

A requisite for petitioning the divine Judge is innocence (verses 4–6). David may confidently approach God who searches the heart and reins. He knows that he is not guilty of the injustice with which his enemies intentionally malign his reputation. He has not only served his king and his country in the battles against Goliath and the Philistines, the archenemies of the kingdom, but he has also magnanimously preserved the life of Saul when he could have revenged himself upon him for the wrongs he had suffered (1 Kings 24:4 seq. and 26:6 seq.). He has not repaid anyone with evil who without reason betrayed him to his enemies. David knows himself to be free from any criminal attacks against the life and rule of the rightful king, the crime of which he was accused. And thus he can even challenge the divine Judge. He wants to be an outlaw whose life is proscribed and whose honor is dragged through the mire if he can be proven guilty. The language of the psalmist is also the language of the Church. The Church can in all tranquility challenge her slanderers by appealing to the judgment of history.

The psalmist has protested his innocence before the all-knowing God and now expresses the wish that God may make his just cause known to all the world (verses 7–11). God's longanimity, which is here especially described as the sleep of God, allowed the enemies of David to continue their plotting against him so that their insolence went beyond all limits. Their malice must challenge the wrath of God and his just punishments. He who has established the judiciary office for the protection of the unjustly persecuted and for the preservation of right order cannot permit this order to be disregarded for any length of time without inflicting punishment. The divine judge is the Lord of the universe before whose judgment seat all nations must appear. Thus the view of the psalmist is enlarged: the individual judgment becomes a world judgment. David's affair becomes an affair of all the just, indeed, an affair of God himself. Saul and his followers become representatives of the enemies of the kingdom of God. The nations are assessors and witnesses of the judicial act; they should know that the Lord defends the rights of his anointed. The court has assembled, God ascends his sublime tribunal, and the judgment of the nations begins. The contents of the strophe and the solemn tone of speech point to the fact that the climax of the psalm is to be sought in this judgment. Now David full of confidence in the justice of his cause and with a good conscience approaches the steps of the throne and begs for the judicial intervention of God. He does not speak for himself only, but for all just men. His words are similar to the expectations of Israel; namely, that in the Messianic judgment all sins and sinners will forever be excluded from the kingdom of God and that the just alone will rule upon a new earth. The psalmist does not have to fear the judgment. The judge is a searcher of hearts and of incorruptible integrity. The judgment will be in his favor and favorable to all the just; for God is the protection of his anointed and of all who with sincerity intend to walk the way of his commandments.

The court proceedings have ended. An explicit publication of the court's decision is not needed. It can only be a condemnation of all that is contrary to God's law; for he who touches the anointed touches the apple of God's eye (Zacharias 2:8). However a last opportunity to receive God's grace is given to the slanderers. On this account the psalmist gives admonition to be converted before the execution of the judgment (verses 12–14). The conversion admits no delay; for the divine punitive judgment may fall upon them any day. God is already prepared like a warrior ready for battle. Weapons are frequently the symbols of the divine wrath and punishments: the sword is sharpened, the bow is bent, the arrows are made ready. Glowing and burning arrows were used to set fire to a besieged city. The burning arrows of the divine wrath ignite the eternal fire which will never be extinguished.

The history of the world is a record of judgments passed upon the world. The fates of blaspheming men and nations are types of the eternal retribution (verses 15–18). Those who attack the anointed of the Lord and his church eventually come to a sad end. An example is the fate of Saul. Out of jealousy he strove to pierce David with a lance and in his despair he threw himself upon his sword. The wicked with all their planning and restless striving are likened to a woman who suffers a miscarriage as the fruit of her anxieties. They see themselves not only bitterly deceived, but also hindered in their progress. The misery which they

25

intended for others has become their own disaster. Two proverbs from the life of a hunter depict the fact which they experienced. The hunter falls into the pit which he has dug. The stone hurled from the sling strikes the head of the marksman. But the just man sees these punishments and praises God's justice and his infinite Majesty.

psalm 8

Domine, Dominus noster

God is wonderful in his works, especially in mankind, singularly exalted by the Incarnation of Christ

1. Unto the end for the presses: a psalm for David.

2. O Lord our Lord, how admirable is thy name in the whole world. For thy magnificence is elevated above the heavens.

3. Out of the mouth of infants and sucklings thou hast perfected praise, because of thy enemies, that thou mayest destroy the enemy and the avenger.

4. For I will behold thy heavens, the works of thy fingers; the moon and the stars which thou hast founded.

5. What is man, that thou art mindful of him? or the son of man that thou visitest him.

6. Thou hast made him a little less than the angels, thou hast crowned him with glory and honour.

7. Thou hast set him over the works of thy hands.

8. Thou hast subjected all things under his feet, all sheep and oxen: moreover the beasts also of the fields.

9. The birds of the air, and the fishes of the sea, that pass through the paths of the sea.

10. O Lord our Lord, how admirable is thy name in all the earth.

THE Eighth Psalm is a song that will never grow old. Its truths will be more understood the more natural science delves into the unfathomable mysteries of the universe and sees in them the infinity of the Creator, and the more profoundly Christian thought understands the excellency of the supernatural image of God in man so much favored by God.

The littleness of man before God, of man who is only an atom in the visible creation, is the first truth that this psalm presents (verses 2–5). The royal singer is occupied in meditation of the starry heaven. The brilliance of innumerable stars moving quietly through the wide firmament is a uniquely splendid scene which we can admire almost every night. But there are hours in which the believing soul is especially receptive to the revelations of this supernal world and in which the greatness of God in his creation becomes an impressive experience to him. The soul then has a presentiment of the sublimity of the divine Name, that is of the divine nature, which is written on the firmament. There we find a reflection of his glory. The revelation of the starry heaven concerning the infinite greatness of the Creator is so clear and convincing that even a child understands it. When a mother points to the twinkling stars and tells her child that God has made them, the baby folds its little hands to praise and worship him with babbling sincerity. This childish prattle must put to shame the unbelievers who refuse to recognize the divine Creator in the greatness and beauty of his works. The child as an advocate of God passes judgment upon all of God's adversaries. Those who think themselves wise are condemned as fools by the childlike faith of simple people.

Even men of antiquity with little knowledge of the vast universe of constellations were aware of their own littleness and nothingness when from mountain heights wrapped in night stillness, they looked into the starry heavens. They were aware of their meagerness before the Creator of this world "who spoke and they were made; who commanded and they appeared" (Psalm 32:9). How little, how like a speck of dust in an unending universe must not modern man appear to himself, the contemporary who numbers the stars by the millions and measures their sizes and distances! And how conscious he must be of his littleness before God who created this world with his fingers! Should man be astonished if the infinite God would forget and overlook his own nothingness? But he does not ignore him; he guards him and heaps upon him proofs of his tender love. If God would limit himself to this, it would be for this very condescension and goodness that man should owe him eternal thanks and would be obligated to praise him. But God has done far more.

The dignity of man through the grace of God is the second sublime truth which this psalm presents to our consideration (verses 6–10). According to the testimony of Sacred Scripture, the solemn words with which the Creator of the world initiates the creation of man must convince us that man far surpasses all created things, excepting the angels:

27

"Let us make man to our image and likeness" (Genesis 1:26). He made man according to his own image; for he gave him a free will, intellect, speech, vision, hearing, rationality; he gave him understanding, wisdom, and knowledge; he permitted man to participate in his divine nature and to partake in his dominion over other creatures. Man was to rule over the fishes of the sea, and the birds of the air, and the cattle and beasts of the field, and the serpents that crawl upon the ground (Genesis 1:26). It is true the contrast between God and man despite all this is infinitely great. Yet, clothed in the reflection of God's glory and given a glorious participation in divine dominion, the psalmist considers man to be a little below the angels. In a picturesque manner he enumerates the creatures subjected to the king of creatures; in procession they pass according to their different kinds as if they were worshiping him: the domestic animals, small and large; the wild beasts of the prairies; the birds of the air; the fishes of the seas and rivers. He could have also mentioned other kingdoms of this extensive creation but he is satisfied with those that are mentioned in the list of creation.

At the end of the song the psalmist returns to the thought of the prologue. "Lord our God, how admirable is thy name upon all the earth." In the beginning of the psalm these words are a cry of astonishment concerning the glory of the Creator who is revealed in the starry heaven; but the closing words are a jubilant thanksgiving for the merciful elevation of man above all creatures, excepting the angels. The Christian has a special reason to recite this "Te Deum," because more than the royal singer can surmise, God has condescended to clothe him with honor and glory; for by giving man sanctifying grace God has made him a participant in the divine nature.

psalm 9

Confitebor tibi, Domine

The Church praises God for his protection against her enemies

1. Unto the end, for the hidden things of the Son. A psalm for David.

2. I will give praise to thee, O Lord, with my whole heart: I will relate all thy wonders.

3. I will be glad and rejoice in thee: I will sing to thy name, O thou most high.

4. When my enemy shall be turned back: they shall be weakened and perish before thy face.

5. For thou hast maintained my judgment and my cause: thou hast sat on the throne, who judgest justice.

6. Thou hast rebuked the Gentiles, and the wicked one hath perished: thou hast blotted out their name forever and ever.

7. The swords of the enemy have failed unto the end: and their cities thou hast destroyed, their memory hath perished with a noise.

8. But the Lord remaineth forever. He hath prepared his throne in judgment.

9. And he shall judge the world in equity, he shall judge the people in justice.

10. And the Lord is become a refuge for the poor: a helper in due time in tribulation.

11. And let them trust in thee who know thy name: for thou hast not forsaken them that seek thee, O Lord.

12. Sing ye to the Lord, who dwelleth in Sion: declare his ways among the Gentiles.

13. For requiring their blood he hath remembered them: he hath not forgotten the cry of the poor.

14. Have mercy on me, O Lord: see my humiliation which I suffer from my enemies.

15. Thou that liftest me up from the gates of death, that I may declare all thy praises in the gates of the daughter of Sion.

16. I will rejoice in thy salvation: the Gentiles have stuck fast in the destruction which they prepared.
Their foot hath been taken in the very snare which they hid.

17. The Lord shall be known when he executeth judgments: the sinner hath been caught in the works of his own hands.

18. The wicked shall be turned into hell, all the nations that forget God.

19. For the poor man shall not be forgotten to the end: the patience of the poor shall not perish forever.

20. Arise, O Lord, let not man be strengthened: let the Gentiles be judged in thy sight.

21. Appoint, O Lord, a lawgiver over them: that the Gentiles may know themselves to be but men.

Psalm 10 according to the Hebrews

1. Why, O Lord, hast thou retired afar off? Why dost thou slight us in our wants, in the time of trouble?

2. Whilst the wicked man is proud, the poor is set on fire: they are caught in the counsels which they devise.

3. For the sinner is praised in the desires of his soul and the unjust man is blessed.

4. The sinner hath provoked the Lord, according to the multitude of his wrath he will not seek him.

5. God is not before his eyes: his ways are filthy at all times.
   Thy judgments are removed from his sight: and he shall rule over all his enemies.

6. For he hath said in his heart: I shall not be moved from generation to generation, and shall be without evil.

7. His mouth is full of cursing, and of bitterness, and of deceit: under his tongue are labor and sorrow.

8. He sitteth in ambush with the rich in private places that he may kill the innocent.

9. His eyes are upon the poor man: he lieth in wait in secret like a lion in his den.
   He lieth in ambush that he may catch the poor man: to catch the poor, whilst he draweth him to him.

10. In his net he will bring him down, he will crouch and fall, when he will have power over the poor.

11. For he hath said in his heart: God hath forgotten, he hath turned away his face not to see to the end.

12. Arise, O Lord, let thy hand be exalted: forget not the poor.

13. Wherefore hath the wicked provoked God? for he hath said in his heart: He will not require it.

14. Thou seest it, for thou considerest labor and sorrow that thou mayest deliver them into thy hands.
    To thee is the poor man left: thou wilt be a helper to the orphan.

15. Break thou the arm of the sinner and of the malignant: his sin shall be sought and shall not be found.

16. The Lord shall reign to eternity, yea, forever and ever: ye Gentiles shall perish from his land.

17. The Lord hath heard the desire of the poor: thy ear hath heard the preparation of their heart.

18. To judge for the fatherless and for the humble, that man may no more presume to magnify himself upon earth.

THE Hebrew text in its present form divides the ninth psalm of the Septuagint and Vulgate into two psalms, but unrightly so. Not taking into consideration the alphabetical arrangement which is found in both parts (although the arrangement is no longer complete), both sections suggest an original unity, because in both parts we find the same expectation of a Messianic judgment and only one outlook for the end of time, at which, according to the prophetic prognostications the Gentile nations will be destroyed and all oppressions of the members of the earthly kingdom of God will cease. David believed that the fulfillment of the first promise had already begun in the victories over the neighboring Gentile nations, but the fulfillment of the second promise; namely, the cessation of the injustices of godless men seemed to him in the distant future. Therefore, in the first part (verses 2–20) he thanks God for the victories over the pagan nations and in the second part he begs God to destroy the evil men so that the time of persecution may end. The Christian considers the victories of the Church over the pagan world and over all her enemies and persecutors.

In an uninterrupted march of conquests David had vanquished the hostile neighboring countries and had forced them to pay tribute: the Philistines, the Moabites, the Amalekites, the Edomites, the Syrians and the Ammonites (2 Samuel 8). Having returned home from his campaigns he relinquished the sword, took the harp in hand and sang with sincere heart a song of thanksgiving for the victories of Yahwe over the pagan world (2–11). In a spirit of humility he did not think of attributing the great successes to his own power and efficiency. In his eyes they were wonderful deeds of God, the invisible Ruler of Israel, whose instrument he was permitted to be. Again the king did not so much rejoice about the defeat of the enemies, but was jubilant in the fact that the true God, whom he loved and revered had revealed his power and majesty to the Gentile world and had so clearly proved the powerlessness of its gods. He also rejoiced in his God for the reason that the wonderful successes were another proof that God, in truth, dwelt among his people and that all the powers on earth could not destroy his kingdom. When David after the close of the campaign reviewed the past, it became evident to him that although the enemies had been so sure of victory when they went to war, they were impelled by an invisible power to seek safety in flight. Like clouds driven by the wind, like chaff blown away by the storm, they were dispersed and fell before the terrible majesty of Yahwe.

David's thoughts, however, did not dwell long on these victories; his views were now directed to the future; the singer became a prophet. He looked upon the defeats of the pagan world around him in the light of the Messianic judgment. His words about the complete collapse of the enemy are not poetic exaggerations of his victories. They merely point to the end which now began to be realized. Two facts seemed clear to the mind of the psalmist. The enemies of the kingdom of God disappeared without any trace in history (verses 5–7), and God alone and his kingdom will continue forever (verses 8–11). The places upon which the battles for the kingdom of God were fought were places of the divine judgment. This was true in the Old Covenant. God himself often intervened miraculously in these battles and they were decisively in favor of his people. But at the end of time he will establish his tribunal for all nations. Then he will speak to the Gentiles in his wrath. He will defeat and destroy them with his almighty word so that the very remembrance of their name will be erased for all eternity. The cameo of the future that David beheld has become a reality. All nations that had at one time or another subjugated the people of the Lord have disappeared from the earth. Not only the little tribes of Palestine, but also the great world emperors on the Euphrates and on the Nile, the mighty empire of the Persians, and the world-wide empire of Rome have disappeared; their cities like Nineveh and Babylon, Memphis and Thebes, Susa and ancient Rome were destroyed, and only their eternal ruins are records of their ancient greatness. Such is the end of all enemies of the kingdom of God; so it is also for the enemies of the New Covenant God and the persecutors of the Church of Christ.

Yahwe rules upon the ruins of world kingdoms and over their great cities forever and ever; for he alone and his kingdom will last forever (verses 8–11). No power can overthrow his throne and no rebellion can deprive him of his rights as supreme Judge; for he is not lord and judge by the will of men. He himself has established his tribunal for judgment. His power has its basis in his own divine nature. And thus he rules the world in justice. As Judge he has no respect of persons and of nations. Even the mighty nations are before him as a drop in the sea, as a speck upon a scale. They cannot hide themselves from his judgment. They may for some time oppress and persecute the members of the kingdom of God, but the kingdom will continue and its members will triumph. The Judge of the world proves himself to be a strong defender of the oppressed. He is their protector in the time of need. He makes peace follow upon war and liberty upon oppression. These facts give to all believers, who acknowledge God as the all-faithful, a joyful confidence. He who does not place his entire confidence in men, but seeks refuge with the Lord, will not be disappointed. This is a truth which David saw verified in his own life, and which in his prophetic vision he saw fulfilled at the Messianic judgment of the nations.

For the psalmist, however, it was not sufficient to give thanks and sing songs of praise as king alone in the name of his people (verses 12–19). The entire congregation of God, the Church, should unite with him in his joyful song of thanksgiving. For it is in the midst of Sion that the victorious God dwells. When the rulers of the Gentile world-empires returned home from their victorious conquests, the royal city echoed with the jubilations of its citizens. The victorious king was met with hymns and garlands and the fame of his gods was proclaimed in the subjugated countries. Could Sion in view of the glorious deeds of its God and King remain silent? And would it be satisfied by merely singing its hymns within the walls of Jerusalem? The members of the Church must bring the renown of their God to the nations that they too may acknowledge and praise him. In the destruction of the enemies of Israel the Lord has again proved himself to be the avenger of his people. According to Mosaic Law every murderer was in danger of blood-revenge, and the nearest relative of the murdered person had to inflict the punishment. The protection of the people of the Covenant God has taken upon himself. Every injury inflicted upon the enemies was a new proof that Yahwe exercised just punishment and that he was attentive to the cry of the oppressed.

The song of Sion begins with a cry for help not only because the commonwealth is again suffering what it has suffered in the past, but because it is again encompassed by enemies and will remain so until the final judgment. Thus every liberation gives to the praying Church more confidence that the gates of hell shall not prevail against it. Often she appeared as if she were at the door of Death's domain, but God always gave her new life. Often the enemy rejoiced at her collapse, but the Church always revived. He cannot permit the Church to perish, because he has entrusted to her the glad tidings of salvation and his miraculous power. At the gates of Sion, that is, in the congregation of God, the praise of the Lord shall be proclaimed and the thanksgivings of the redeemed shall ascend to heaven. This is her divine mission. (The meetings of the people took place at the gates of the city.)

Sion views the hearing of prayers in the light of Messianic times. Sin is its own avenger. What history has already verified will be proclaimed to the world on judgment day. The powers that were intent upon destroying God's kingdom tumbled into the pit into which they intended to topple Sion. They were caught in the same traps which they laid for the Church. They did not want to be reminded of God and will now be eternally forgotten by him. They brought about their own destruction and are now burned in the abyss of hell. On the day of the world judgment it will be made known that God has remembered his followers in their adversity, and that they are not to be disappointed in their hopes. The psalm closes with the petition that the time of fulfillment may not be far off, that the growing malice and presumption so hostile to God may find a master in the Lord, that the world may learn that even the mightiest on earth are mere men formed from the dust of the earth, mere chaff before an infinite God.

The view of the psalmist and of the praying congregation turns again from the end of time to the present. The Messianic judgment had its beginning, indeed, in the victories of Yahwe over the Gentiles, but the members of the kingdom of God still suffer under the weight of persecutions by unscrupulous men. And the cry to heaven for help has not yet been answered by God. It appears as if God had abandoned them in their affliction. And thus as a supplement to the prayer of thanksgiving a petition is added that Yahwe may intervene by punishing the persecutors.

Second Part of Psalm 9 according to the Hebrew Text

In order to prove the necessity of divine intervention the psalmist describes the activities of the godless (verses 3–11). In passage after passage he gives a description that is applicable to the persecutions of the faithful of all times. In his long-suffering, God permits the deeds of wicked men to go unpunished in order to try the faithful. But because of his patience the audacity of the wicked grows so that they shamelessly boast of their malice, and with ridicule and blasphemy challenge the justice of God. They deny the greatness of God with which they must reckon. They do not believe in his judgment; for them there is no God. They have no conscience. They carry out their infamous plans because they fear neither divine nor human punishment and haughtily despise their opponents. Such men feel themselves entirely secure. In their unbounded self-conceit they are sure that they will not fail, that nothing can hinder their endeavors. They give their tongue full liberty. Every means by which they may destroy their opponents is lawful to them: lying, calumny, oppression, and violence. They are not afraid of murder and assassination. Like brigands they conceal themselves in the courts to attack their victims. They lie in wait for their victim as the lion in the thicket lies in wait for his prey, as the hunter watches the wild beast to catch it in his snare. With ruthless violence they overpower the weak. They do evil because they do not fear God and do not believe in retribution.

In order that a stop may be put to these activities the psalmist turns to God with the petition that he may intervene with his punitive justice (verses 12–17). God should no longer endure this wickedness; for he is Yahwe, the Lord and King of Israel. He is also the God and judge of the oppressors and blasphemers. On this account he should no longer countenance their blasphemies and denials of his majesty and providence. As King of Israel, God is the father of the poor and persecuted. He knows their needs and has promised to take vengeance upon the enemy. Trusting in his fidelity the unfortunate and abandoned make known their affliction to him. He should, therefore, appear in judgment and forever stanch the violence of the godless.

The psalmist is sure that his prayer will be heard. For the Lord will not permit himself to be dethroned by the godless. The day will come on which not only the physical pagan world, but also the totality of pagan culture, whatever is of a worldly nature within the kingdom of God on earth will be eradicated and destroyed. On that day the petition of the faithful will be heard. They will then become strong and will triumph over the godless. God will love them. The oppressed will obtain justice and never more will man who crawled from the dust of the earth challenge the Lord.

psalm 10

In Domino confido

The just man's confidence in God in the midst of persecutions

1. Unto the end, a psalm for David.

2. In the Lord I put my trust: how then do you say to my soul: Get thee away from hence to the mountain like a sparrow?

3. For, lo, the wicked have bent their bow: they have prepared their arrows in the quiver: to shoot in the dark the upright of heart.

4. For they have destroyed the things which thou hast made: but what has the just man done?

5. The Lord is in his holy temple, the Lord's throne is in heaven: His eyes look on the poor man: his eyelids examine the sons of men.

6. The Lord trieth the just and the wicked: but he that loveth iniquity hateth his own soul.

7. He shall rain snares upon sinners: fire and brimstone and storms of winds shall be the portion of their cup.

8. For the Lord is just, and hath loved justice: his countenance hath beheld righteousness.

DAVID saw himself persecuted at the court by envious and treacherous enemies. They looked with disfavor upon the young son of Jesse because of the confidence which his royal master had in him. They used all possible means to have him removed from his place and from the royal court to which God's providence had called him. Their activities were so much the more dangerous, because their attacks upon him were not open but insidious. They sought to undermine his favor by casting suspicions upon him with their slander.

Wisdom advised flight (2–3). David's friends viewed the situation from a human viewpoint. They saw the young, defenseless man in the hands of influential, crafty, and unscrupulous opponents. Just as a bird escapes the hunter by flight into mountain caverns, so David, they advised, should flee from his difficulties. To give emphasis to their advice they picture the greatness of the threatening danger and the futility of David's precarious position. As the hunter in his hiding place waits for the favorable moment to strike at his unsuspecting victim, so also David's enemies wait for a favorable opportunity to ruin him. Of what use is piety, conscientiousness, and fidelity, when the pillars upon which the social order rests have no honesty, sincerity, or fear of the Lord? From malicious and treacherous attacks flight from danger is the only remedy. This advice is the voice of human wisdom; a voice of temptation escaping danger; a voice relinquishing a position which God has bestowed; a voice evading the attacks of the enemy, evading the cross and sacrifice.

Confidence in God gives courage to persevere (verses 4–7). The psalmist compares his confidence in God with the advice of human wisdom. This is no presumption. From the natural viewpoint he is defenseless and powerless and must become a victim of his enemies. But the Lord in whom he trusts and whom he serves is Almighty God. He is king, infinite and supreme; his palace is heaven; there is his throne. Worldly statutes can be annulled by men, but not God's laws. David's enemies are indeed dangerous, because they do not attack openly and work their guile secretly. But the Lord in whom he trusts is the all-knowing God who sees all things, to whom no secret plots are unknown, whom no hypocrisy deceives. He knows the difficult situation of the persecuted man. He tests the just man. To him virtue is not unknown. He also tries the godless and sees their sins and hates them with the infinity of his holy Being. And what God must hate is subjected to his inexorable judgment. Like a violent storm it falls suddenly upon the sinner. Like fiery darts the punishment strikes him. There is no escape. Like the fire and brimstone which once fell upon Sodom is the fiery breath of the divine wrath falling upon the sinner. This is the wrathful portion of the beaker which God gives the sinner and which he must drink to the dregs. Just as God hates sin, so he also loves justice, and virtue, and all who practice goodness. The Lord will reward him who suffers patiently, believing and hoping in God's protection. The Lord will reward him who does not abandon the position assigned him. If a just man resolutely looks to heaven at a time when heaven seems closed to him, God will reward his fidelity with the blessing of special union with him; his portion of the chalice is the knowledge of God. The psalmist does not think as yet of the vision of God in the next world, but of a special union with him in the Messianic era when all the godless will be excluded from the society of the just.

psalm 11

Salvum me fac

The prophet calls for God's help against the wicked

1. Unto the end; for the octave, a psalm for David.

2. Save me, O Lord, for there is now no saint: truths are decayed from among the children of men.

3. They have spoken vain things everyone to his neighbor: with deceitful lips and with a double heart they have spoken.

4. May the Lord destroy all deceitful lips, and the tongue that speaketh proud things.

5. Who have said: We will magnify our tongue: our lips are our own. Who is Lord over us?

6. By reason of the misery of the needy, and the groans of the poor, now will I arise, saith the Lord.

7. I will set him in safety, I will deal confidently in his regard.

8. The words of the Lord are pure words: as silver tried by the fire, purged from the earth, refined seven times.

9. Thou, O Lord, wilt preserve us: and keep us from this generation forever.

10. The wicked walk round about: according to thy highness, thou hast multiplied the children of men.

WHEN among men godlessness and moral corruption grows, when fidelity and sincerity disappear from public life and religious life is on the wane, discouragement takes hold of the just man so that he will speak as the Prophet Elias: "The children of Israel have abandoned the covenant, and have destroyed thy altars, only I alone remained faithful" (3 Kings 19:10). His view is veiled; everywhere he sees only wickedness and does not observe that there is still profound and manly fidelity in the land. A similar temptation may have confronted David at the time of Saul's persecution. His enemies were socially friendly and flattered him because of his heroic deeds, but privily they prepared his downfall by calumny and inferred suspicions. What he had to experience in his proximate surroundings, he had to endure in the entire nation; insofar as there, too he had the same sad experience. All lies and hypocrisy, all falseness is an abomination to the Eternal Truth. Therefore the faint-hearted David waits daily for the judgment of the Lord who will put an end to all hypocrisy; his waiting and his cry become more and more impatient as the godless, relying on their own power, become more and more presumptuous. The less responsible the small and great dictators believe they are before God, the more they revel in their false sense of security. They boast of their own heroism. With the written and spoken word they seek to control the masses. With the terrible weapons of lies, calumnies, and distortions of truth they eliminate truth. They feel themselves to be lords and will not acknowledge anyone as their superior.

Faith conquers the fainthearted spirit of David. He meditates upon the divine promises and finds in them God's answer to his anxious cries. The answer is found in many pages of Scripture. When God's patience with the wicked has been exhausted, he will rise in judgment, putting an end to the sorrows of the oppressed and persecuted, giving to them the long promised redemption. There will then no longer be any suffering,

injustice, and corruption. God has withheld the day and hour of intervention and punishment, but his promises will certainly be fulfilled; for
God's word is truth. It is like silver cleansed seven times from all dross,
free from all human imperfection and uncertainty. Therefore the just man
never has reason to be discouraged or despondent. A godless generation
may seek to oppress and ruin him, but it cannot do him more harm than
God will permit. God is the protector and defender of his followers. He
is a safe and powerful protector. May the wicked boast about their power
and pretend to be lords, they will at long last be humbled; the greater
their pride and the greater their haughty bearing, the greater will be
their humiliation and their downfall.

psalm 12

Usquequo, Domine

A prayer in tribulation

1. Unto the end, a psalm for David.
   How long, O Lord, will thou forget me unto the end? How long dost thou
   turn away thy face from me?

2. How long shall I take counsel in my soul, sorrow in my heart all the day?

3. How long shall my enemy be exalted over me?

4. Consider and hear me, O Lord, my God. Enlighten my eyes, that I never
   sleep in death.

5. Lest at any time my enemy say: I have prevailed against him. They that
   trouble me will rejoice when I am moved.

6. But I have trusted in thy mercy. My heart shall rejoice in thy salvation. I
   will sing to the Lord, who giveth me good things: Yea I will sing to the
   name of the Lord, the most high.

"BECAUSE thou wast acceptable to God, it was necessary that temptations should prove thee" (Tobias 12:13). These words which
Raphael speaks to old Tobias express a truth which we find verified in the
lives of all the saints and in the souls of all who fear God. Sufferings are

the school of the cross which leads to progress in virtue whether through bodily sufferings, spiritual anguish, the hostilities of evil men, or temptations by Satan. It is true that God does not permit man to be tempted beyond his strength (I Corinthians 10:13). But the brooding may be heavy and enduring and the strength of man may be close to exhaustion. David, too, had to experience such spiritual sufferings and this psalm has its basis in affliction. The conduct of the psalmist is a pattern for all who are subjected to grave temptations.

David complains before God, but he does not express any self-pity (vv. 2–3). For months, perhaps for years he felt that he was persecuted by Saul and that his life was threatened by him. As an outcast he had to seek refuge in the desert. All his prayers seemed to be in vain. When a cloud of loneliness and abandonment enveloped him, he felt himself abandoned even by God. Of this spiritual abandonment the Twenty-first Psalm gives a touching expression: "My God, my God, why has thou forsaken me; for from my salvation are the works of my sins. O my God I shall cry by day, and thou wilt not hear; and by night and it shall not be reputed as folly in me." Every day brings new dangers and with them new thoughts to overcome these dangers. The longer divine help is delayed, the bolder will the enemy be, and the more unscrupulous will be his persecutions.

David prays to God (verses 4–5). The impetuous agitation of his soul was quieted by the complaint and now ends in a suppliant prayer; for in the conversation with God the petitioner has again and again found strength to keep on carrying the cross. He prays for a merciful sympathetic love; for his strength seems to be exhausted. The hero is weak and must succumb at the next onset. God must help for His honor's sake. If the enemy would be permitted to boast of his fall who always had placed his confidence in the Lord, how great would be the evil laughter! How hell would rejoice in the victory!

David trusts in God (verse 6). He trusts that the enemy will not triumph; for in his battles he does not confide in his own strength, but in the help of God alone. He feels himself strong with this aid although he appears to be extremely weak. His trust in God's help is so great that he already rejoices at the coming hour of victory. When it has come, he will sing to the Lord a hymn of thanksgiving.

psalm 13

Dixit insipiens

The general corruption of man before our redemption by Christ

1. Unto the end, a psalm for David.
   The fool saith in his heart: There is no God.
   They are corrupt, and are become abominable in their ways: there is none
   that doth good, no not one.

2. The Lord hath looked down from heaven upon the children of men, to see if
   there be any that understand and seek God.

3. They are all gone aside, they are become unprofitable together: there is none
   that doth good, no not one.
   Their throat is an open sepulchre: with their tongue they acted deceitfully:
   the poison of asps is under their lips.
   Their mouth is full of cursing and bitterness: their feet are swift to shed
   blood.
   Destruction and unhappiness are in their ways: and the way of peace they
   have not known: there is no fear of God before their eyes.

4. Shall not all they know that work iniquity, who devour my people as they
   eat bread?

5. They have not called upon the Lord: there have they trembled for fear,
   where there was no fear.

6. For the Lord is in the just generation: you have confounded the counsel of
   the poor man, but the Lord is his hope.

7. Who shall give out of Sion the salvation of Israel? When the Lord shall have
   turned away the captivity of his people, Jacob shall rejoice and Israel shall
   be glad.

G ODLESSNESS in its last analysis is a denial of God; for he who believes
in a personal God, in a remunerator and punisher cannot remain
godless. From the sinful conduct of so many members of his people the
psalmist concludes that there is a practical and a theoretical denial of
God. For instruction he gives an illustration of its nature and its consequences.

The nature of the denial of God is known by its causes and effects (verses 1–3). It is a folly, a culpable lack of knowledge, an unwillingness to know. "All men are fools who lack the knowledge of God, and who from the visible perfection of nature cannot perceive their Maker, who by meditating upon his works cannot find their Author" (Book of Wisdom 13:1 seq.). The denial of God is the source of depravity. He who is indifferent about God has neither the will nor the strength to obey his holy Law. What statistics teach with their numbers the psalmist saw in his immediate surroundings; he saw it in the entirely demoralized paganism —corruption everywhere. The conduct of the godless is an abomination before God. Only what is normally good and of value before God is in conformity to his holy will. The godless cannot conduct themselves according to the demands of the divine Law. The psalmist sees this fact confirmed by the infallible judgment of God. Anthropomorphically he permits God to look down from heaven upon the children of men to find if anywhere the denial of God and a moral life can be compatible; he questions whether or not a man can be a fool denying God while at the same time wise in the practice of virtue, a man who perhaps unknowingly would be concerned about the divine Law and seek God by fulfilling his Law. But the all-wise and all-seeing God comes to another conclusion: all have departed from the way of the Law; all have degenerated; all are spiritually indifferent, morally corrupt; there is no exception.

In this confirmation by God there is already a judgment upon those who deny God. This judgment is passed because they cruelly and ruthlessly oppress the people of God. They devour the people as they devour bread. The Prophet Micheas describes the conduct of the godless in a more gruesome manner. "Who have eaten the flesh of my people, and who have flayed their skin from them: and have broken and chopped their bones as for the kettle, and as flesh in the midst of the pot" (Micheas 3:3). They act thus because they do not believe in Yahwe, because they do not call upon him and do not fear him. But the day will come on which they will fear, on which they will tremble before God. It will be the day of judgment on which they will acknowledge that the Lord whom they have denied, actually exists and even now stands on the side of the just. The just man trusts in God in all persecutions. God does not permit his plans to be obstructed by the godless. On the day of judgment he will proceed from Sion and salvation will come to Israel who will greet it with jubilation.

psalm 14

Domine, quis habitabit

What kind of men shall dwell in the heavenly Sion

1. A psalm of David
Lord who shall dwell in thy tabernacle? Or who shall rest in thy holy hill?

2. He that walketh without blemish, and worketh justice.

3. He that speaketh truth in his heart, who hath not used deceit in his tongue. Nor hath done evil to his neighbor: nor taken up a reproach against his neighbors.

4. In his sight the malignant is brought to nothing: but he glorifieth them that fear the Lord. He that sweareth to his neighbor, and deceiveth not:

5. He that has not put out his money to usury, nor taken bribes against the innocent.
He that doth these things shall not be moved forever.

THIS little psalm probably belongs to the pilgrim songs. They were sung when the travelers were going up to Sion, to the temple, in order to awaken a righteous sentiment among the pilgrims. It contains thoughts that might occupy the minds of Christians when they go to church. There are men who in their visits to the divine service fulfill their duties only outwardly and in whom spiritual union with God is lacking. The psalmist does not have these in mind. He has in mind those men who in their ascent to the sanctuary admit that the external expression of worship must be accompanied with proper internal dispositions, who recognize the obligation of being in union with God even outside the divine service. This is expressed by a portrayal of hospitality. In the Orient, hospitality meant more than treating a passing stranger well. Hospitality meant a union between the master of the house and the stranger. Being a guest and tarrying with God in the holy tabernacle, or upon the mountain of Sion in the spiritual sense, means union with God. There is a question here: who shall be admitted to union with God?

The psalmist gives the answer by enumerating three moral requisites. The first condition for union with God is irreproachable conduct, a conduct in conformity to the mind of God, not according to the spirit of the world; for only what is holy can be united to the infinite Holiness. On this account the Lord gives the command through Moses: "Be ye holy, because I am holy" (Leviticus 11:45). "Sanctify yourselves and be holy, for I am Yahwe, your God" (Leviticus 20:7). The second requisite, a corollary of the first, is a life of righteousness; that is, a life according to the norm of the divine Law, a life which God gives and owns, a life which means the fulfillment of all laws. Such was the complete obedience God demanded from his chosen people in the Old Covenant. Therefore Moses said to Israel: "We shall be a righteous people if we insist on obeying the entire Law before the Lord our God" (Deuteronomy 6:25).

The third requisite for union with God is a conformity of our inner attitude with our external conduct. God is not deceived by external sham or pretense. Isaias calls this make-believe, a mere external presence at the solemn divine service in the temple, a trampling in the fore-courts, because the body comes to the house of God, but the soul is occupied with worldly things.

The love of God and the love of man cannot be separated from one another. The love of God without the completion of our social duties is unthinkable. The psalmist places the honor and good name of the neighbor first. Lying and calumny are an abomination to the Lord. How could he be pleased if men praised him and at the same time calumniated and cursed their neighbor who is made to the image and likeness of God? Union with God excludes all uncharitableness to the neighbor whether it be in word or in deed. Another social duty which union with God demands is assistance to those who fear God, furtherance of their interests, and promotion of their welfare. These have the first claim to our honor and respect, not so the godless who are rich and powerful in their abandonment of God. A third duty is honesty and fidelity. He who by oath makes a promise to his neighbor, must keep it; for God is unchangeable fidelity. Taking advantage of one's neighbor is an abomination before God. The last social duty is to assist one's neighbor in his need. The Mosaic Law forbade taking interest on a loan given to a poor man of one's own religion and race (Exodus 22:25). No one should take advantage of the personal need of another. The same consideration demands that no bribes be accepted in the courts and thus even the poorest shall obtain justice. He who fulfils all these duties is worthy of union with God and will find in it strength and security.

psalm 15

Conserva me, Domine

Christ's future victory and triumph over the world and death

1. The inscription of a title to David himself.

2. Preserve me, O Lord; for I have put my trust in thee.

3. I have said to the Lord, thou art my God, for thou has no need of my goods.

4. To the saints, who are in his land, he hath made wonderful all my desires in them.

5. Their infirmities were multiplied: afterwards they made haste.

6. I will not gather together their meetings for blood-offerings, nor will I be mindful of their names by my lips.

7. The Lord is the portion of my inheritance and of my cup: It is thou who wilt restore my inheritance to me.

8. The lines are fallen to me in goodly places: for my inheritance is good to me.

9. I will bless the Lord who hath given me understanding: moreover my reins also have corrected me even till night.

10. I set the Lord always in my sight; for he is at my right hand, that I be not moved.

11. Therefore my heart hath been glad and my tongue hath rejoiced: moreover my flesh also shall rest in hope.

12. Because thou wilt not leave my soul in hell: nor wilt thou give thy holy one to see corruption.

13. Thou hast made known to me the ways of life, thou shalt fill me with joy with thy countenance: at thy right hand are delights even to the end.

ACCORDING to the superscription and according to the testimony of the Apostles Peter and Paul, the psalm was composed by David. The Apostles interpreted it as directly Messianic and as pointing to the resurrection of Christ. Thus Peter said in his first Pentecostal sermon: "David spoke with a look into the future about the resurrection of Christ; for neither shall he be left in hell, nor will his flesh see corruption" (Acts 2:31). The Apostle gave his own interpretation and not that of the Jews of his time who seem to have applied the meaning to David himself. The divine Master himself had interpreted the psalm in the same manner as Peter did. Shortly before his ascension into heaven Christ had to reproach the Apostles because they did not understand the Scriptures. He proved to them that he had to die and rise from the dead. When, therefore, Peter in his first sermon, ten days after the Ascension of our Lord, proved from the 15th Psalm that the Messias had to rise from the dead, without doubt he must have received this knowledge from the teaching of Jesus. According to the decision of the Biblical Commission of the 1st of July, 1933, the action of Peter is a biblical testimony for the direct Messianic character of this psalm. Before the Jews at Antioch in Pisidia Paul also affirmed that the psalm points to the Resurrection of Christ because David had died and had seen corruption (Acts 13:34). If the psalm is Messianic, and it is, Bellarmine has rightly called it the psalm prayer of Gethsemane, the prayer of Christ to the Father. It surely has a profound meaning, if we consider it in this respect. As the angel on Mount Olivet pointed out to the praying Saviour the glorious fruit of suffering, so here, too, the praying Messias placed before our view the fruits of his suffering.

The beginning of the psalm is an ejaculatory prayer which comes from the heart of the Saviour struggling with the fear of death. "Preserve me, O Lord, for I have put my trust in thee." And now picture after picture clearly passes before the spiritual vision of the Messias. The fruits of his suffering are the redeemed (verses 2–4). The redemption of fallen mankind is the great work of the Father and of the Son. God himself does not need this work; for he is infinitely rich and happy. His perfection and happiness cannot be increased by anything, not even by the sacrificial death of the Son. He does not need the redemptive act of the Son. It is not for his own sake that he has given him to us, but that all may believe and become blessed. For the sake of man he has accepted the grace of Redemption. It was for humanity that God satisfied the ardent desire of the Messias begging the forgiveness and salvation of men. The saints that are in his kingdom, the Messianic kingdom on earth and in heaven, are the first glorious fruits of his redemptive death. They are legion from all countries, speaking all languages; they are nations no man can count. But it does not include all men, not even all of the chosen people. The more the prophecy progresses, the clearer is the prophetic vision that a great part of Israel will be excluded from the Messianic salvation and will be rejected, because it has broken the covenant of Yahwe and has turned to the practice of idolatry. These will not participate in the joys of the redeemed, but their lot will be suffering and bitterness. Because they have rejected Yahwe, the Messias will also exclude them from his kingdom. This exclusion is expressed in a picture of that time. The Messias does not take part in their bloody sacrifices. They are an abomination to him. They are forever disregarded.

Even if through the guilt of men the fruit of the redemption will not be a hundredfold, the personal fruit of his sufferings will remain undiminished; it is the eternal union of the Messias with God (verses 5–8). The Lord is the portion of his inheritance and of his cup. When Israel had conquered the promised land under the leadership of Josue, the land was divided among the various tribes and to every family was allotted a portion of the land as a lasting inheritance. The second picture is taken from a banquet at which the host filled a beaker for every guest. The portion of the beaker for the Messias is God Himself whose infinite happiness is the precious drink that is offered to him. The Messias is not yet in possession of this heavenly inheritance. He still lives on earth and must first taste the bitterness of suffering and death. But God is not only the inheritance. It is he who has assured this possession by his divine word. Thus the heavenly inheritance is not a mere hope. It is already an assured possession, even if it has not yet been entered upon. It shall be a reward for his obedient suffering and death. In view of the future glory the Messias rejoices. A desirable possession has come to him; indeed, glorious is his inheritance. When no eyes have seen nor ear heard, and when it has not entered into the mind of any man what God has prepared for those that love him, how can we measure the length and the breadth, the height and the depth of glories that will come to the Messias, the much-beloved Son of the eternal Father. In view of this unspeakable glory he recognizes how good God has been to him when he made known to him his will in the decree of suffering, when he did not take from him the chalice of suffering, but made him drink it. Day and night, even in the night of suffering he must praise God for it. What should he fear? Even when he must walk through the valley of the shadow of death, he has nothing to fear. The Lord is near. He stands at his right, a true defender and a powerful helper.

The third precious fruit of the sufferings is the Resurrection and the Ascension (verses 9–11). Beyond the night of death the Messias sees the glorious day of the Resurrection; therefore his soul may rejoice. He must indeed die and commit his body to the grave, but he has the assurance that his rest in the grave will be followed by a resurrection before his body decomposes. The soul descends into Limbo, but only for a short period. God will not leave him in the kingdom of the dead. The Lord will not permit the Holy One, the Messias, to see corruption. That the psalmist

47

here had in mind "corruption," and not the grave, is verified by all ancient translations as well as by Peter and Paul. From the fact that the body of David saw corruption proves that the petitioner was not David, nor any other ordinary man; for the law of corruption applies to all. The body of the Messias was to rise before it might decompose. Here it is also indicated that the Resurrection will take place two or three days after death. The Resurrection will be followed by the Ascension. God will lead the Resurrected from death and the grave to the glorified life of heaven which will be given to him without limitation of time. With the Father he will participate in his plenitude of happiness; for the right hand of the Lord will grant him the unending joy of the Godhead.

The psalm is also a Gethsemane prayer for every Christian soul in sorrow. The call to the kingdom of God, the hope of entering the heavenly kingdom, and of entering upon the eternal inheritance with all the saints, the assurance of a future resurrection and ascension are here on earth a powerful source from which the Christian may draw strength and joy in suffering, so that his soul may overflow with joy in all tribulation.

psalm 16

Exaudi, Domine, justitiam

A just man's prayer in tribulation against the malice of his enemy

1. The prayer of David.
   Hear, O Lord, my justice: attend to my supplication.
   Give ear unto my prayer, which proceedeth not from deceitful lips.

2. Let my judgment come forth from thy countenance: let thy eyes behold the things that are equitable.

3. Thou hast proved my heart, and visited it by night, thou hast tried me by fire: and iniquity hath not been found in me.

4. That my mouth may not speak the works of men: for the sake of the words of thy lips, I have kept hard ways.

5. Perfect thou my goings in thy paths: that my footsteps be not moved.

6. I have cried to thee, for thou, O God, has heard me: O incline thy ear unto me, and hear my words.

7. Show forth thy wonderful mercies, thou who savest them that trust in thee.

8. From them that resist thy right hand keep me, as the apple of thy eye. Protect me under the shadow of thy wings.

9. From the face of the wicked who have afflicted me. My enemies have surrounded my soul.

10. They have shut up their heart: their mouth hath spoken proudly.

11. They have cast me forth and now they have surrounded me: they have set their eyes bowing down to the earth.

12. They have taken me, as a lion prepared for the prey: and as a young lion dwelling in secret places.

13. Arise, O Lord, disappoint him and supplant him: deliver my soul from the wicked one with thy sword.

14. from the enemies of thy hand: O Lord divide them from the few of the earth in their life: their belly is filled from thy hidden stores.
They are full of children: and they have left to their little ones the rest of their substance.

15. But as for me, I will appear before thy sight in justice: I shall be satisfied when thy glory shall appear.

IN THE Fifteenth Psalm the Messias has praised God because he had revealed to him the decree of suffering and had ordered him to drink the chalice of suffering; for having done so, a glorious inheritance has come to him, the eternal plenitude of joy before the countenance of the Lord. The Sixteenth Psalm also speaks of a hope in the blessed vision of the Lord. The petitioner has learned something of the happiness in suffering through his life of suffering and persecution. Blessed are they who suffer persecution for justice's sake; for theirs is the kingdom of heaven. According to the superscription David is the composer of this psalm.

The psalm begins with a confession of innocence (verses 1–5). This is the reason for the address to the divine Judge. Only he who suffers for a just cause and who can offer his prayer to God with guileless lips can expect that the Lord will pledge himself for his cause; for ultimately it is God's affair when one of his faithful servants is persecuted by godless men. Despite his many faults and sins David could count himself among the faithful servants of God, and therefore could appear before the divine judgment seat with a good conscience to receive the verdict of guilt or innocence. Before the all-seeing God everything lies open. Much explanation is not needed. The Lord knows the intentions of the persecutors and all their injustices. He knows the sufferings of the persecuted and their intentions. God cannot be deceived and he cannot deceive himself. He permits adversity to overshadow his servants to test their fidelity and love. He searches their hearts not only in the light of day, but also in the hours of the night, in fortune and misfortune, in order to bring to light the secret plans and intentions of the soul. He tested David in the fire of tribulation as silver and gold in the smelter are tested for their purity, but found no dross, no admixture of anything dishonorable. As long as godlessness and injustice prevailed and triumphed, and virtue was disregarded and ridiculed, never had the psalmist approved the conduct of wicked men, never in his life had he made any compromises. The ways in which God's Law, his calling and his education had led him were harsh and tortuous. They demanded self-abnegation, unselfishness, strength of will, living faith, and confidence in God. David persevered in these ways because the Lord willed it and how he willed it! No threats on the part of heartless men, no enticements by friends who were weak in faith, no temptation to seek flight from persecution and to leave his post, could keep him from continuing on the way designated by the divine Will. He continued to walk firmly on the path of duty.

Conscious of being a just man and as such a sufferer for a just cause, he now places before God the petition for deliverance (verses 6–12). The psalmist has often during his life experienced that one does not beg help from God in vain. His cries for help have never remained unanswered. This encourages him not only to pray for a willing ear but also for a miracle of divine mercy. The enemies are powerful and numerous. The danger is great and he needs extraordinary assistance to give liberty and peace to the oppressed. The psalmist believes that such help will be given him. He believes that with God everything is possible, that God will exceed his requests, that God will reward his servant seeking protection against his adversaries. David places himself under this divine protection in order to be guided by his divine love, to be protected as a man protects the pupil of his eye. David would prefer to be secure against every attack and protected by Divine Providence, defended like a fledging under its mother's wing. The Lord indeed has promised to protect his people as the apple of his eye, and to carry them like the winging eagle if they will but remain faithful to him (Deuteronomy 32:10). David begs most fervently for God's protection because the enemies are oppressing him severely and are surrounding him to destroy him. No one has any consideration for his rights, nor do they care about his troubles. They all have lost the proper attitudes toward right and justice. They know no sympathy for the needs of their opponents. They have no knowledge of nobility. Their speech is haughty and insolent because they do not fear God and do not believe in his judgment. David had to flee to save his life. But it was not enough for his enemies to make it impossible for him to remain at the court of Saul, they even pursued him into the desert. They wanted to surround him and put an end to him. Like a lion which goes out in the evening to seek prey, like a young lion in the thicket awaiting its kill, they also spy upon David to catch and destroy him.

No man challenges God's judgment in vain. Therefore the psalmist concludes with certainty that retribution will come (verses 13–14). He begs and prays that God may intervene, oppose, and crush the enemy of his faithful servant. God's word, the sword of his judgment, shall save him from wicked men; God's powerful hand shall save him from his enemies. What the psalmist expresses as a wish, he is sure will be fulfilled. He expects not only a temporal punishment, but he also sees a punishment of eternal separation in Messianic times. His enemies are men of the world. They cater to the spirit of the wicked world and their portion is only of this world. Even temporally they are excluded from the Messianic kingdom. They have already received their reward in this life. The Lord has permitted them to live in material luxury. This, however, was permitted them for lawful enjoyment only. He gave them numerous descendants to whom they could bequeath their riches. But in view of eternal rewards the psalmist would not care to exchange with the enemies. Wealth and earthly happiness are transitory. They end with death. The true happiness of the just descends only when they have closed their eyes to the sorrows of the present. The godless are thrust out into exterior darkness. But those who love God in this life come to the vision of God and will be filled with happiness emanating from God. Here the psalmist does not speak of the knowledge of God obtained through faith. Every visit to the sanctuary of Jerusalem was called a vision of God because of the effects of grace. He speaks here of the eternal vision of God after the awakening from the sleep of death. The conclusion of the psalm is a presage of that which Paul in the light of Christian revelation acknowledges to show the ultimate worth of suffering and persecution. He wrote (2 Corinthians 4:17–18): "That which at present is momentary, a light affliction, prepares for us above measure an eternal weight of glory; while we look not at the things which are seen, but at the things which are not seen. For the things which are seen are temporal, but the things which are not seen are eternal."

psalm 17

Diligam te, Domine

David's thanks to God for his delivery from all his enemies

1. Unto the end for David, the servant of the Lord, who spoke to the Lord the words of this canticle in the day that the Lord delivered him from the hands of all his enemies and from the hands of Saul.

2. I will love thee, O Lord, my strength.

3. The Lord is my firmament, my refuge and my deliverer. My God is my helper, and in him will I put my trust. My Protector, and the horn of my salvation, and my support.

4. Praising I will call upon the Lord: and I shall be saved from my enemies.

5. The sorrow of death surrounded me: and the torrents of iniquity troubled me.

6. The sorrows of hell encompassed me: and the snares of death prevented me.

7. In my affliction I called upon the Lord, and I cried to my God.
And he heard my voice from his holy temple: and my cry before him came unto his ears.

8. The earth shook and trembled: the foundations of the mountains were troubled and were moved, because he was angry with them.

9. There went up a smoke in his wrath: and a fire flamed from his face: coals were kindled by it.

10. He bowed the heavens, and came down: and darkness was under his feet.

11. And he ascended upon the cherubim and he flew: he flew upon the wings of the winds.

12. And he made darkness his covert, his pavilion round about him: dark waters in the clouds of the air.

13. At the brightness that was before him the clouds passed, hail and coals of fire.

14. And the Lord thundered from heaven, and the highest gave his voice: hail and coals of fire.

15. And he sent forth his arrows, and he scattered them: he multiplied lightnings, and troubled them.

16. Then the fountains of waters appeared, and the foundations of the world were discovered. At thy rebuke, O Lord, at the blast of the spirit of thy wrath.

17. He sent from on high and took me: and received me out of many waters.

18. He delivered me from my strongest enemies, and from them that hated me: for they were too strong for me.

19. They prevented me in the day of my affliction and the Lord became my protector.

20. And he brought me forth into a large place: he saved me, because he was well pleased with me.

21. And the Lord will reward me according to my justice: and will repay me according to the cleanness of my hands.

22. Because I have kept the ways of the Lord, and have not done wickedly against my God.

23. For all his judgments are in my sight: and his justices I have not put away from me.

24. And I shall be spotless with him: and shall keep myself from my iniquity.

25. And the Lord will reward me according to my justice; and according to the cleanness of my hands before his eyes.

26. With the holy, thou wilt be holy; and with the innocent man thou wilt be innocent:

27. And with the elect thou wilt be elect: and with the perverse thou wilt be perverted.

28. For thou wilt save the humble people; but wilt bring down the eyes of the proud:

29. For thou lightest my lamp, O Lord: O my God, enlighten my darkness.

30. For by thee I shall be delivered from temptation; and through my God I shall go over a wall.

31. As for my God, his way is undefiled: the words of the Lord are fire-tried: he is the protector of all that trust in him.

32. For who is God but the Lord? or who is God but our God?

33. God who hath girt me with strength; and made my way blameless.

34. Who hath made my feet like the feet of harts: and who setteth me upon high places.

35. Who teacheth my hands to war: and thou hast made my arms like a brazen bow.

36. And thou hast given me the protection of thy salvation: and thy right hand hath held me up:
And thy discipline hath corrected me unto the end: and thy discipline, the same shall teach me.

37. Thou hast enlarged my steps under me; and my feet are not weakened.

38. I will pursue after my enemies, and overtake them: and I will not turn again till they are consumed.

39. I will break them, and they shall not be able to stand: they shall fall under my feet.

40. And thou hast girded me with strength unto battle; and hast subdued under me them that rose up against me.

41. And thou hast made my enemies turn their back upon me, and hast destroyed them that hated me.

42. They cried, but there was none to save them, to the Lord: but he heard them not.

43. And I shall beat them as small as the dust before the wind; I shall bring them to nought, like the dirt in the streets.

44. Thou wilt deliver me from the contradictions of the people: thou wilt make me head of the Gentiles.

45. A people, which I knew not, hath served me: at the hearing of the ear they have obeyed me.

46. The children that are strangers have lied to me, strange children have faded away, and have halted from their paths.

47. The Lord liveth, and blessed be my God, and let the God of my salvation be exalted.

48. O God, who avengest me, and subduest the peoples under me, my deliverer from my enemies.

49. And thou wilt lift me up above them that rise up against me: from the unjust man thou wilt deliver me.

50. Therefore will I give glory to thee, O Lord, among the nations, and I will sing a psalm to thy name.

51. Giving great deliverance to his king, and showing mercy to David his anointed: and to his seed forever.

D AVID had reached old age when he composed this psalm of deep piety and of poetic beauty and strength. God had cleansed him in the onerous school of suffering and had confirmed him in humility and the love of God. He reviewed the many successes of his past life in order to give glory and honor to the eternal and invisible King of Glory. In thankful love he dedicated this glorious song to him. He also had the people sing it on public occasions; for David's career was a reflection of the history of his kingdom, of the Old Testament kingdom of God. And this kingdom, in turn, was in itself and in its vicissitudes a type of the Church of the New Testament. Thus this beautiful song will always be of value as a thanksgiving psalm.

The psalm begins with a thankful confession of thankful love (verses 2–4). The prologue is the keynote to the entire psalm. "I will love thee, O Lord, my strength." God's claims to the love and thanks of his anointed and of his people are well founded. The poet enumerates the many manifestations of love God has shown; they rightly demand a return of love. "The Lord is my strength." He is an inexhaustible source of power for his servants. He is the rock upon which they stand securely, even when the enemy's assaults are like seething waves. He is the rock that supports and holds fast the house of Israel. He is the firm and impregnable fortress. He is refuge when dangers threaten. He is the protector with whom every one is secure. His divine providence is like a large shield covering the warrior from which the arrows of the enemy must recoil. He is the lion of salvation, the strength which gives safety and liberation. This great and mighty God is all goodness and fidelity to those who honor him. He who in his need and affliction calls upon him, upon the most holy God, will be delivered from his enemy. This was the experience of King David. It was experienced a hundredfold in his life. In this psalm he summarizes all the adversities of his life and all the liberations by God in one single need and in one single liberation.

The first part of the psalm (verses 5–20) depicts the divine work of deliverance. The affliction was great (verses 5–7). How often was not David confronted with death and destruction? During the flights from Saul and Absalom, he was like one suffering shipwreck and clinging to a plank, a toy of the raging storm and tossing waves. The afflictions came upon him like onrushing floods that drew him defenseless into the abyss. The monster of death was approaching like a huntsman who tangles his victim in a net. These are impressive pictures of the greatest human needs. In the depth of such afflictions David cried to God: Will he who dwells in his holy temple above the stars hear the weak voice of man in the uproar of the elements? God did hear his voice; for all the turmoil on earth is not strong enough to stifle the cry wrenched from a just man.

God did hear the cry. The Saviour comes (verses 8–16). When the eternal Judge will descend from heaven to hold judgment on earth, a dreadful fear of his majesty will weigh heavily upon all nature like the gathering of heavy storm clouds. On this account the biblical pictorial language preferentially has the Lord appear in stormy weather when he reveals himself as Judge and Lawgiver. Then the earth will tremble and quake because of the wrath of Almighty God; the mountains will totter and will be shaken to their foundations. Then as the Prophet Nahum says: "Who can stand before the face of his indignation? And who shall resist in the fierceness of his anger? His indignation is poured out like fire and the rocks are melted by him" (Nahum 1:6). When the infinite God is angry, his whole inner being is one glow of fire. In his wrath there streams from his nose a hot breath like smoke from a fire. A consuming fire issues from his mouth. Thus the poet depicts in an anthropomorphic manner the terribleness of God's punishment challenged by sin. Threatening clouds appear on the horizon. It is getting dark in the sky; clouds are lowering and it appears as if the entire heaven were resting on the mountains. It is as portentous as the pillar of cloud veiling the divine glory. A windstorm arises and drives the clouds before it. He whose throne is above the cherubim is carried upon their wings. Over the Ark of the Covenant in the Holy of Holies the cherubim were indicators of God's presence. When the Lord appears at judgment, they will accompany his majesty revealed in the storm. But again and again the clouds separate; a brilliant light like glow of shattered coals breaks through the clouds. Then the clouds again come together and a hailstorm falls upon the earth. The thunder rumbles and in it the Lord's powerful voice resounds so that the mountains quake and man and beast tremble. Here and there the lightning flashes in the heavens like burning arrows of the divine wrath. In the tumult of the elements and in the raging storm the waves mount and furrow so that the floor of the sea becomes visible and the foundations of the earth are laid bare.

During the storm God descends from heaven and comes to save his anointed (verses 17–20). The poet again takes up the picture of a shipwrecked person fighting against the waves, tossed to and fro by the storm. The Lord sees the futile struggle with death. He reaches out his strong arm and draws him from the waves to safe ground. The mighty waters are the powerful enemies who have fallen upon the weak opponent. David is probably thinking of the years of Saul's persecution when he with a few faithful followers opposed a well-equipped army; or of those sad days when his own son encompassed him with an army twenty times superior to his. Those were difficult times, but the Lord did not permit his anointed to be defeated. In those days he proved himself to be a mighty support like the horn of salvation. When there was no way of escape, he rescued David from the encirclement of his enemies and frustrated their ruthless plans. And when David asked himself: Why did the Lord do this? He knew only one answer: because he loved me. God does not need men, kings, or nations; he is not obligated to any of his creatures. Thus every help that man receives from the Lord is a revelation of God's infinite goodness.

This thought leads us to the second part of the psalm (verses 21–31). This part gives us the motives for the divine love. God the all-holy loves that which is holy; therefore, he loves all those who walk in innocence, who obey his commandments and occupy themselves with his word. David too believes in the extraordinary divine guidance in his life, in divine providence, and especially in the frequent miraculous deliverances from adversities. He sees in these affairs God's love for him, an approval by God of his own fidelity to the Lord, and heaven's blessing for his justice. It is not contrary to the spirit of humility when a man gives testimony that he has never knowingly and maliciously trespassed against the divine commandments. Humility is truth. David could speak of his fidelity to God, because he had never allowed himself to be seduced to unfaithfulness through the godlessness of his enemies and his long period of suffering. He had never disregarded the statutes of the Lord. Even in misfortune they remained his joy and the object of his meditations. Even in his sorrows he had never refused fidelity and obedience to his God. On the contrary, because the Law, the word of God, was always an active impetus, he lived the Law, and carefully tried to avoid disregarding it. How well David willed at all times to conform his will to the will of God, his own noble words testify when Semei cursed the king who was fleeing from Absalom: "If he curses, he does it because the Lord has told him: Curse David. Who dare say! Why do you do that?" (2 Kings 16:10). According to the law of retribution which the just God practices most reliably, David could recognize in the deeds of the Lord his love toward him and also the rewards of his own fidelity and love.

God's dealing with man is a reflection of man's conduct toward God. He who is kind and merciful will receive kindness and mercy from God. He who is faithful to God will receive from God manifestations of his fidelity. A man who is innocent, without guile, who gives himself up to God unreservedly, God will consider as his friend and will bestow upon him his entire love. But with a sinful man God will deal according to his sinfulness. The history of the people of Israel, scrawled on many pages, confirms this kind of divine action. The Book of Judges is especially filled with proofs that the fundamental reason for oppression or for peace, for victory or for defeat, is to be found in the relation that existed between the people and Yahwe. When the people were faithful to the statutes of the Lord and served him without guile, the Lord was merciful to them and liberated them from every affliction. But if in their pride they rebelled, he permitted pestilence, hunger, and war to come upon them and humble them. The life of David also testifies to the norm of the divine conduct. Because he had faithfully served, God permitted his light to fall upon him. Light is the symbol of fortune and happiness. The light burning in a house is a symbol of posterity. This reference in 3 Kings 11:36 is to express the posterity of David which was to culminate in the Messias. Here perhaps the king silently meditated upon the shining light because when in thankful love and piety he resolved to build a house to the Lord, the Lord promised that he would build a house, the cornerstone of which would be the Messias. How often it entered into David's life—the Lord probing the darkness with the light of his grace. With God his weakness became irresistible strength. There was no obstacle that he could not surmount. What do all the armies mean when the Lord of hosts fights on the side of his anointed? What do all fortifications mean if God will make all surrender to his faithful servant? God alone is a greater power and security than legions of well-equipped warriors and well-fortified cities. He to whom the Lord has promised protection may be sure of that protection. God's ways are not crooked; his ways are straight and without blemish and do not lead into error. His word is reliable, precious gold cleansed by fire. He is a protecting shield for all who in danger take refuge with him.

In thankful love David reviews all the afflictions of his past life and all the liberations granted through God's love. Now in the third part of this psalm (verses 32–46) he takes a broader view. During his life God gave even greater proofs of his love than deliverance from evil. His thankfulness impels him to tell this also; namely, that he has accomplished all great things only by God's grace. Indeed, there is no source of strength other than Yahwe because there is no god other than him. There is, therefore, no other secure protection than God alone. From this inexhaustible source David has drawn his strength. It is a gift of God. As a cincture holds together a garment so the Lord has surrounded and endowed David with strength. Still more! The Lord has not only given him great strength that he might surmount all obstacles; but he himself has removed many difficulties that his anointed might attain his purposes without hindrances. With strength there was united another gift of God; namely, the speed of a hart. In a surprise attack he would vanquish his enemy. Thus by God's grace David rose to the apex of his power and renown. God also helped him in the use of weapons and disciplined his army for war. Only extraordinary human strength could stretch the brazen bow. Along with great strength the Lord granted him extraordinary protection. He gave him the shield of salvation and protected him from all dangers with his help. His right arm supported him. His grace gave him remarkable strength. Enormous difficulties came into David's life. For many years was he persecuted by Saul. Having become king, not all tribes gave him their allegiance. Then followed the wars against the Gentile neighboring nations, and lastly great difficulties arose because of the rebellion of Absalom. But God delivered him from all adversities and strengthened him in his sufferings so that he never wavered.

Equipped with God's strength, his weapons, and protection David could begin wars with his enemies and finish them victoriously. Standing at the horizon of his life's activities he now saw himself ruler of a country that extended from the river of Egypt to Syria. All the nations of these territories were subjected to him and had to pay tribute. His country enjoyed security and peace; for the conquered would not dare to rebel again. The psalmist again thankfully emphasizes that these victories were not due to his own merit, but that they were victories of God. For it was he who guided his king with strength, who subjugated his opponents for him. He had defeated his enemies and had put them to flight. It was only because of this that the king could crush those who out of hatred persecuted him and his people. The Gentiles in their affliction called upon their gods, but their gods frozen in stony impassivity did not hear them. The godless enemies of David within the nation of Israel cried to Yahwe because they feared the king's sword; yet the Lord paid no heed to their cry and thus their defeat was inevitable. With God's help David dispersed his enemies like dust driven before the wind, like the dirt of the street trampled upon by men. When David ascended the throne, all the neighboring kingdoms were restless. They tried to hinder the growing power of Israel.

Now all warfare is ended and David is the ruler of his enemies. Many a king not waiting until David's warriors crossed the borders of his country subjected himself before he met the conqueror and not daring to resist paid homage to the king of Israel. The people voluntarily opened the gates of their fortified cities in order to submit to the irresistible power of David.

The psalmist closes his song of thanksgiving with a litany resembling a song of praise (verses 47–51). Yahwe the invisible Lord and King of Israel be praised. He had been a mighty protector of his anointed. Praised be God who liberated him. Praised be God who permitted him to take vengeance upon his enemy, who subjected all the Gentile nations to him. Praised be the Liberator from the many and cruel enemies. Praised be

59

the Giver of victory, to the faithful and mighty Protector. This song of praise should not be limited to the small territory of the kingdom of David and of the people of Israel. The Gentile kings brought the fame of their gods into the countries they conquered. David's victories should not bring renown to himself. They should bring about an acknowledgment of the one true God among the nations and should prepare the ways of salvation for them. Therefore David wishes to proclaim the sublime name of the Lord among the Gentiles also. King David feels himself especially called for this duty because of his relation to the Messias. God has given to him the great grace of having the Saviour of the world as his descendant. To him was given the great favor that his royal race should last for all time, crowned by him whose kingdom and throne was to continue forever. Thus the song of thanksgiving ends in the worship of Christ the king through whom all live and have their being.

psalm 18

Coeli enarrant

The works of God show forth his glory: his law has greatly to be esteemed and loved

1. Unto the end, a psalm for David.

2. The heavens show forth the glory of God, and the firmament declareth the work of his hands.

3. Day to day uttereth speech, and night to night showeth knowledge.

4. There are no speeches nor languages where their voices are not heard.

5. Their sound has gone forth into all the earth: and their words unto the ends of the world.

6. He hath set his tabernacle in the sun, and he, as a bridegroom coming out of his bridechamber, hath rejoiced as a giant to run the way:

7. His going out is from the end of heaven, and his circuit even to the end thereof: and there is no one that can hide himself from his heat.

8. The law of the Lord is unspotted, converting souls: the testimony of the Lord is faithful, giving wisdom to little ones.

9. The justices of the Lord are right, rejoicing hearts: the Commandment of the Lord is lightsome, enlightening the eyes.

10. The fear of the Lord is holy, enduring forever and ever: the judgments of the Lord are true, justified in themselves.

11. More to be desired than gold and many precious stones, and sweeter than honey and the honeycomb.

12. For thy servant keepeth them, and in keeping them there is a great reward.

13. Who can understand sins? From my secret ones cleanse me, O Lord:

14. And from those of others spare thy servant.
If they shall have no dominion over me, then shall I be without spot: and I shall be cleansed from the greatest sin.

15. And the words of my mouth shall be such as may please: and the meditation of my heart always in thy sight.
O Lord, my helper and my redeemer.

THE eternal God has created two suns as proclaimers of his wisdom, love and power: the great star of the day to give to the earth warmth and light, and the spiritual light of the Law and supernatural revelation in order to give light to man on his journey through life. Holy Scripture has called the Old Testament Law, the light of God, the light of the Lord, the unchangeable light. The New Testament has called the Gospel the true light, the miraculous light, the glad tidings of the glory of Christ. In this psalm the psalmist has praised the glory of both suns which will never grow old. The more scientific investigation had made known the wonders of the starry heaven, and the deeper men have delved into the mysteries of the supernatural revelation, the more the biblical song of the sun gains in spiritual truth and glad approval.

The first part of the psalm (verses 2–7) speaks of the glory of the material sun, the sun in the kingdom of nature. Among all the works of visible creation none other has made so deep an impression on the mind of the pious Israelite; none has spoken with such impressive language about the greatness of God as the immensity of the firmament and the remarkable beauty of the constellations. In holy joy Isaias cries out: "Lift up your eyes and see who hath created these things, who bringeth out their host by number and calleth all by their names: by the greatness of his might and strength and power not one of them is missing." In the almost cloudless heaven of the Orient, day after day proclaims the praise of its master and each night the stars sing the praises of their Creator. At its setting, the sun bears witness to the divine majesty and at its rising gives testimony of him before the morning dawn. The stars do not give a sound which the ears can hear, but yet their testimony is so manifest that even a child can understand and their language is so distinct that everyone can comprehend. Only those of stubborn will refuse to understand. As far as the firmament extends over the earth, the stars shine brilliantly and proclaim the glory of the Creator. Their testimony is given in all lands, over all seas, in all desert places, unto the ends of the earth.

The king of all the works of God is the sun whose kingdom extends over the entire system. In roaring fire has the Lord placed the testament of his tabernacle, a testament which daily must run its course. Morning after morning it appears in the east glistening like a burnished hero eager to complete his task. It climbs the eastern sky warming the whole earth and in the evening sinks, red with the flush of toil.

Progressing in thought the psalmist passes to the second part (verses 8–15), to the thought of the spiritual sun, the law of revelation. It is only with the second sun that the divine work of creation is completed. What the material sun is for nature, that the Law and revelation is for the human soul; namely, light and life. What the psalmist has to say of the Old Testament Law applies in its complete meaning to the Law of the New Covenant, the Christian revelation. As the power of the natural sunlight is recognized by its effects so also the power of the divine light. The psalmist shows the advantages of the heavenly light by the sacred number of seven. The first advantage of the Law and revelation, above all human laws and doctrines, is perfection. Divine revelation is a sun without spots, a reflection of the eternal light, an outpouring of the glory of God. He who occupies himself with it, who studies it, and meditates upon it, finds consolation for his soul. He finds strength and confidence. The written Law is a complement of the testimonies of God. The Old Testament pictured the "Tables of the Law," written by the fingers of God, as "the precious archives of his holy will." All books of Holy Scripture are testimonies. They are reliable because they have been sealed with the seal of the Holy Spirit. They give the child and the ordinary man a wisdom and knowledge of the most profound questions of life which put to shame the wisdom of the world. The precepts of the Lord are good because they are an expression of his own goodness, of his holy will. They give joy to the human soul; for the profoundest and clearest source of human joy is God and only loving conformity to his will gives true happiness. Because the Law comes from God, the Law is not only good, but also clear; his utterances are explicit and understandable. He who submits to their truths will himself be pure. The Law supposes the fear of the

Lord. Reverence for God is the motive for fulfillment, and the fear of the Lord should be the purpose of man's education. The fear of the Lord is pure. Its source is the sanctity of God which eternally remains immaculate. It will remain so eternally because the demands of the divine sanctity will never grow old, will never cease; heaven and earth may pass away, but God's word is above all changes of time. The Statutes of the Lord are true because they rest upon an absolute moral foundation; they are just despite their unchangeableness; they take into account man's abilities and thus he can arrange his life according to them. On this account there is nothing more precious than the Law. He who has once learned the Law will find it more desirable than the most refined gold. There is nothing more sweet and pleasant than the Law, even the most excellent honey. Therefore the Book of Proverbs says of the wisdom given to man through the Law: "It is well for man that he has attained wisdom and insight; for to have attained wisdom is more valuable than gold. It is more precious than pearls and everything that one desires. It is a tree of life for those who seize it and for those who hold it. It brings happiness" (Proverbs 3:13).

The psalmist speaks from personal experience. He has meditated deeply and has obtained instruction from it. He has not only read the Law and reflected upon it, he has also tried to conform his life to it. Without man's assumption of the divine commandments the word of God is like a seed which is not put in the ground. A life according to the Law has its reward; for the observance of the Law gives peace of soul now and assurance of eternity. But who can say that he fulfills the Law in all things? Even the best men will break some law of God unknowingly and unwillingly. Such transgressions God will look upon with mercy and will forgive because of his infinite love. But man is not even secure from grave faults. He is always exposed to the influence of the spirit opposed to God. This spirit may deprive him of reverence for divine Law and of fear of divine judgment; for to resist the spirit of the world, the help of divine grace is necessary for weak human nature. Therefore, no one who wants to walk the way of the Law should rely upon himself alone, but should pray perseveringly that God may preserve him from the wicked spirit and may not permit this spirit to prevail over him. God will be pleased with him who takes pleasure in the Law of the Lord and meditates upon it with untiring zeal. His prayer and praise of God will be mercifully received and his petitions will find a willing ear. All his endeavors and cares will give him joy and consolation on the paths laid out for him by God. The Lord will be a protector to the just man in all dangers of life. To the just man the Lord will be a deliverer from all evils of body and soul.

psalm 19

Exaudiat te Dominus

A prayer for the King

1. Unto the end, a psalm for David.

2. May the Lord hear thee in the day of tribulation: may the name of the God of Jacob protect thee.

3. May he send thee help from the sanctuary: and defend thee out of Sion.

4. May he be mindful of all thy sacrifices: and may thy whole burnt offering be made fat.

5. May he give thee according to thy own heart: and confirm all thy counsels.

6. We will rejoice in thy salvation: and in the name of our God we shall be exalted.

7. The Lord fulfill all thy petitions: now have I known that the Lord hath saved his anointed.

8. Some trust in chariots, and some in horses: but we will call on the name of the Lord our God.

9. They are bound, and have fallen: but we are risen, and are set upright.
O Lord, save the king: and hear us in the day that we shall call upon thee.

Before the kings of Israel went to battle against a Gentile nation they had sacrifices and gifts offered in the sanctuary to obtain victory from the most high God, the invisible King of Israel, the Guide in all battles. The priests and people, the king and his warriors surrounded the altar upon which the high priest offered the sacrifice. It was an army of petitioners. All were filled with the consciousness that not the number of warriors, nor the strength of weapons, but the will of God would decide the outcome of the war. This army of petitioners around the altar of holocausts is a type of the militant Church on earth which is assembled around the altar begging for victory in the battle for God's kingdom.

Whilst the flames devour the sacrifice on the altar, the sacrificial prayer of the people ascends to heaven (verses 2–6). Times of war are times of affliction; for it is only in times of peace that a nation can prosper, and only in times of peace can the militant church of God unfold its blessings effectually. In times of war the man of faith feels his dependence upon God more deeply than in times of peace; for it is in his hands that war and peace, victory and defeat rest. Therefore the people of faith gather around the altar to offer up prayer for the warrior of God's cause that he may strengthen and protect them in dangers as he protected the patriarch Jacob journeying to and from a strange country. God is indeed everywhere and hears all prayers. But he himself has made the sanctuary on Sion a place of grace that he may dwell there, that his eyes may be continually watchful and his ears always attentive to the prayers that are offered in this place. From the altar his blessings will flow. The sacrifice of the king must be pleasing to the Lord because thousands of his people pray with him that God may accept the gifts and sacrifices which his servant offers, that he be mindful of all the gifts which he has given to the sanctuary. A remarkable sympathetic feeling is manifested between the people and their leader when they show confidence in his plans. By raising up their hands in prayer they may contribute to the fact that the Lord will grant the king his wish and thus all his plans will prosper. The victory is certain. The people who had interested themselves in the war will also have the right to participate in the joys of the victory and to boast in the power of Yahwe their God. With the petition that God may fulfill the prayer of the king the sacrificial prayer of the people ends. God cannot resist such prayers. With the closing words of the priest, the divine service ends. When an entire nation prays with its king in this manner, when at his departure for war he is accompanied by the prayers of his people, there can be no doubt that the Lord will assist his anointed, that he will hear him from his throne in heaven and will give him his powerful assistance in victory. The enemies of David relied on their own superior strength and on their chariots (which Israel at that time did not yet use). They trusted in superior equipment with which the little Israel could not equip itself. But Israel relied on its God. In many battles God had granted the weak minority the victory and the hostile majority he had destroyed. It is impossible for the Gentile world to defeat the kingdom of God. The Gentile nations will collapse and pass away, but the people of God will stand fast and his kingdom will continue forever. This is not presumption, but rather confidence that victory will be realized even if the times are difficult. The closing words again take up the petition of the people that God may grant victory to the king, that he may hear the people as often as they pray to him.

psalm 20

Domine, in virtute

Praise to God for Christ's exaltations after his passion

1. Unto the end, a psalm for David.

2. In thy strength, O Lord, the king shall joy: and in thy salvation he shall rejoice exceedingly.

3. Thou hast given him his heart's desire: and hast not withholden from him the will of his lips.

4. For thou hast prevented him with blessings of sweetness: Thou hast set on his head a crown of precious stones.

5. He asked life of thee: and thou hast given him length of days forever and ever.

6. His glory is great in thy salvation: glory and great beauty shalt thou lay upon him.

7. For thou shalt give him to be a blessing forever and ever: Thou shalt make him joyful in gladness with thy countenance.

8. For the king hopeth in the Lord: and through the mercy of the most high he shall not be moved.

9. Let thy hand be found by all thy enemies: let thy right hand find out all that hate thee.

10. Thou shalt make them as an oven of fire, in the time of thy anger: the Lord shall trouble them in his wrath, and fire shall devour them.

11. Their fruit shalt thou destroy from the earth: and their seed from among the children of men.

12. For they have intended evils against thee: they have devised counsels which they have not been able to establish.

13. For thou shalt make them turn their back: in thy remnants thou shalt prepare their face.

14. Be thou exalted, O Lord, in thy own strength: we will sing and praise thy power.

K ING DAVID returned to Jerusalem from a victorious battle and went up to Mount Sion to thank the Lord for his success. Just as the people had accompanied him at the departure of the army with their prayers, so now they assembled in the courts of the sanctuary for a solemn "Te Deum." The faithful crowd rejoiced and was well disposed because they saw in the glorious victory of the king over the neighboring Gentile nations a renewed confirmation of the promise made to David and a confirmation of the final Messianic victory over the entire Gentile world. David's victories are types of the victories of Christ the King over the enemies of his reign. The psalm becomes a song of thanksgiving for the militant Church and an expression of confident expectation of her future triumph.

The first part of the psalm (verses 2–7) celebrates the victory of the king as a great deed of the Lord. David went to war in order to fight against a Gentile nation for the Lord and to secure peace for God's kingdom. The Lord was with him and his army. Now King David, joyful in his victory, stands in the midst of his people with hands uplifted toward the sanctuary and thanks God who had given him success and who had revealed himself as the mighty Ruler of his people. He himself intones the hymn of praise to the King of glory. The people join enthusiastically in David's jubilation and thanksgiving because the victory with the help of Yahwe was a new sign from heaven that their king was protected by God and stood in his grace; for the Lord has fulfilled David's wishes, has heard his prayer and has permitted all the plans he had made for war to succeed. He granted him victory over his enemies, removed the threatening danger from his people, and allowed him to return home with rich booty from the field of battle.

God gave him more than he deserved or dared to request. Even before the king stretched out his hands in prayer to beg for the blessing of God, the blessing was granted him. The Lord had placed upon his head a golden crown. His rule was recognized by all the world. He gave him renown and dominion over his enemies. David prayed for protection and for the preservation of his life; the Lord promised him not only a long life, but also a continued existence of his house and kingdom. All other kingdoms may pass away; all other houses may perish; all other thrones may collapse, but his kingdom, his royal house and throne will continue forever. The Messianic King will be the heir to his throne. The glorious victories with God's help, the Messianic promise of the eternal existence of his throne, the distinction of being the progenitor of the Messias enhanced the glory and renown of his kingdom; for no king could boast of having a descendant called by God to be a mediator of God's blessings for the entire world and a source of blessings for all times.

67

David accepted this unique distinction with indescribable joy before the countenance of the Lord. Thus God made many enemies of Christ the King the footstool of his feet. He placed upon his head the glorious crown of a world kingdom. He gave him eternal life, eternal glory and supremacy, and made him a blessing for all times.

The victories which David attained through God's help brought about the glorious end of his endeavors; namely, the attainment of peace for his country. They also gave him a sure guarantee for the future of his kingdom (verses 8–14); simply, that no power on earth could subdue it. The people viewed the future with confidence in God. They were certain that God's kindness would never forsake them, and on that they would never waver in their confidence. Despite the many victories obtained, new enemies will appear to war against the kingdom. New wars will ensue, but the victorious king will vanquish these enemies and all who oppose his throne and kingdom will feel the strength of his right arm. When the king faces his enemies, they will feel the glow of the threatening punishment. The glow of his wrath will burn them as the glow of coal in the fire oven. The appearance of the king means their destruction; for the Lord will destroy them in his anger and the fire of his anger will devour them. Their race will be exterminated and their name will disappear and be forgotten for all times. This will be the fate of all who have raised their weapons against the kingdom of God. They may now make ruthless plans for the destruction of his kingdom. They may intend to overthrow his throne, a throne destined to continue forever, but armed even with treachery and force they will find it impossible. The king will put them to flight and disperse them. His punishment will strike them in the face like a deadly arrow. That will be the future of the kingdom and of its enemies. The time has not yet come. The people still suffer under a threatening danger, but with longing they look for the day of deliverance, for the day on which the Lord will reveal his power to the enemy. Then Israel will sing the great "Te Deum" and will praise the Lord with harp and song. Still more are the conquests of the Church guarantees of its promised triumph. Christ's powerful will withstands all enemies who revolt against his kingdom. His judgment will crush them as it has already crushed and erased the memory of many. We have only to pray that he may not delay and to praise him for his power.

psalm 21

Deus, Deus meus

Christ's passion and the conversion of the Gentiles

1. Unto the end, for the morning protection, a psalm for David.

2. O God, my God, look upon me: Why hast thou forsaken me? Far from my salvation are the words of my sins.

3. O my God, I shall cry by day, and thou wilt not hear: and by night, and it shall not be reputed as folly in me.

4. But thou dwellest in the holy place, the praise of Israel.

5. In thee have our fathers hoped: they have hoped, and thou hast delivered them.

6. They cried to thee, and they were saved: they trusted in thee, and were not confounded.

7. But I am a worm, and no man: the reproach of men, and the outcast of the people.

8. All they that saw me laughed me to scorn: they have spoken with the lips, and wagged the head.

9. He hoped in the Lord, let him deliver him: let him save him, seeing he delighteth in him.

10. For thou art he who hast drawn me out of the womb: my hope from the breasts of my mother.

11. I was cast upon thee from the womb. From my mother's womb thou art my God.

12. Depart not from me. For tribulation is very near: for there is none to help me.

13. Many calves have surrounded me, fat bulls have besieged me.

14. They have opened their mouths against me as a lion ravening and roaring.

15. I am poured out like water: and all my bones are scattered. My heart is become like wax melting in the midst of my bowels.

16. My strength is dried up like a potsherd, and my tongue hath cleaved to my jaws: and thou hast brought me down into the dust of death.

17. For many dogs have encompassed me: the council of the malignant hath besieged me.
They have dug my hands and feet.

18. They have numbered all my bones, and they have looked and stared upon me.

19. They parted my garments amongst them: and upon my vesture they cast lots.

20. But thou, O Lord, remove not thy help to a distance from me; look toward my defense.

21. Deliver, O God, my soul, from the sword: my only one from the hand of the dog.

22. Save me from the lion's mouth; and my lowness from the horns of the unicorns.

23. I will declare thy name to my brethren: in the midst of the church will I praise thee.

24. Ye that fear the Lord, praise him: all ye the seed of Jacob, glorify him.

25. Let all the seed of Israel fear him: because he hath not slighted nor despised the supplication of the poor man.
Neither hath he turned away his face from me: and when I cried to him he heard me.

26. With thee is my praise in a great church: I will pay my vows in the sight of them that fear him.

27. The poor shall eat and shall be filled and they shall praise the Lord that seek him: their hearts shall live forever and ever.

28. All the ends of the earth shall remember and shall be converted to the Lord. And all the kindreds of the Gentiles shall adore in his sight.

29. For the kingdom is the Lord's; and he shall have dominion over the nations.

30. All the fat ones of the earth have eaten and have adored: all they that go down to the earth shall fall before him.

31. And to him my soul shall live: and my seed shall serve him.

32. There shall be declared to the Lord a generation to come: and the heavens shall show forth his justice to a people that shall be born, which the Lord hath made.

THE psalm is a lamentation. The superscription and tradition ascribe it to David. But neither David nor any other just man of the Old Covenant, be he king or prophet, can really be the petitioner. We know of no historical person who had experienced things similar to those of the petitioner. And still less do we know a person whose redemption from death could have had such an effect on the Gentile world both as to extent and as to time. Only one has suffered so much, Jesus Christ. Only his redemption from death through the resurrection had such effects both in extent and in time. The Church, therefore, has from the beginning, interpreted this psalm as Messianic. Even the Apostles have seen in the sufferings of Christ the fulfillment of this psalm. Yet David was not a mere instrument of the Holy Spirit used to prophesy the Passion of our Lord Jesus Christ. The prayer also flowed from his own soul filled with sorrow. But his own suffering is submerged vicariously in the sea of suffering of his great descendant. The Good Friday vision which he was vouchsafed to see was the divine answer to the "eli, eli, lama Sabachtani." Thus it is that the suffering of Christ which he describes is no longer his suffering, but the suffering of Christ. The description of suffering is the description of the Passion of the Lord. The fruits of the suffering are exclusively the Messianic blessings of the Redemption. David is only an interpreter of the man of suffering whom he saw on the cross in his vision; he is the herald of another's sufferings.

In the first strophe (verses 2–12) the lament of the suffering Christ corresponds to the complaint of the psalmist. Perhaps it is an expression of David's sentiments when he received information concerning the revolt of Absalom and the secession of the entire people, when barefooted and weeping, he fled to Mount Olivet and then took refuge in the desert. The happiness of his union with God left him and the Lord seemed to have abandoned him. As the winter rains raise the rivers to such heights that they finally break through the dams, so the ever-growing, fomenting sorrow filled his soul: "My God, my God, why hast thou forsaken me? Why dost thou not hear the cry of a tortured soul?" Day and night he cries to heaven, but no angel of consolation appears. Heaven remains closed. Has not the Lord promised answer to persevering prayer? Did not Judith give expression to the old common belief of Israel when she said to the despondent inhabitants of Bethulia: "Know that the Lord will hear your prayer if you continue perseveringly with fasting and prayer before him" (Judith 4:12). But he does not acquire the spiritual peace in prayer. The eyes of the petitioner turn to the sanctuary on Sion. There God dwells in the midst of his people; there his ears are always open to the prayers of those who pray to him, and his heart is always ready to bestow mercy upon the afflicted. And, indeed, how many bowed down with sorrow make pilgrimages to this place of grace and return home encouraged and redeemed! How often do the courts of the sanctuary echo with the congregation's songs of praise and thanksgiving? There is no

71

people whose God is so near as Israel's God is to those who call upon him. Why does the anointed of the Lord in his deep sorrow cry in vain in the sanctuary of divine love? None of the patriarchs who had recourse to the Lord was disappointed in his confidence. Joseph prayed in the Egyptian prison and was liberated and elevated; Moses and Aaron interceded for the people and mercy was granted them; Josue prayed for success in his war against the Amorrhites and God gave him victory; Gedeon and Samuel asked for miraculous signs and the favors were granted them. As often and in whatever circumstances the fathers called upon God, their petitions were granted. The sacred books which were preserved with the ark of the covenant, the books that narrated these wonderful deeds are, so to say, votive tablets which a thankful people placed in the sanctuary as a testimony to the prayers that were answered.

Why does God deny to the anointed what he so liberally granted to the fathers? Was their suffering greater than David's? Did their suffering challenge the sympathy of an all-merciful God? It is unthinkable that the anointed in his misery compares himself to a worm creeping along the way and trodden under foot. One has sympathy with any man who suffers much affliction. Yet, the petitioner found not only no mercy, but received mockery and derision in his sufferings; for those who saw his affliction mockingly shook their heads in malicious joy and made grimaces. No one showed any sympathy to him in his pitiful condition. When God has withdrawn, the soul seeks consolation from men. But it is doubly hard to be obliged to forego this also. And it is triply hard in such hours of abandonment by God to be despised on his account and see oneself branded as one rejected by God. Superficial men looked upon every suffering as a punishment from God and estimated the enormity of the sin by the greatness of the suffering. Therefore it was a cruel mockery when they said: "He has always trusted in God that he would save him. He surely should help his most beloved. Does he now show that he is God's most beloved?" The psalmist asks himself if the consciousness that he was in God's grace could have been a terrible self-deception? The entire past contradicts such an idea. Was it not God's love that gave him life? Could he not, because of Divine Providence, rest at the breasts of his mother? Did not Divine Providence guide him lovingly in the days of his youth? Was he not directed to the all merciful God by his pious mother? Was not the Lord his God from the first moment of his earthly existence? If God should abandon him now in this great affliction when everyone else has forsaken him, who should help him? Thus the lamentation closes with the outcry: Depart not from me; for tribulation is very near; for there is none to help me. The Messias has uttered his complaint before God through the mouth of the psalmist. But to give greater emphasis to his cry for mercy, he unrolls in the second part of the psalm (verses 13–23) before the eyes of the Lord three pictures of the passion. These reveal three gruesome afflictions.

The first passion picture: He is taken captive by cruel enemies. A rabble, a mob of unsympathetic and violent men, has thrown itself upon him, has taken hold of him to put him to death. He can only compare its savagery and cruelty with that of wild and untamed beasts, with that of the steers of Basan, a country east of the Sea of Genesareth. On account of their great strength these steers are often mentioned in Sacred Scripture. He compares the inordinate desire for revenge to the thirst of blood-hungry, savage animals which cannot be stilled. No kind words of sympathy reach his ears, but instead a wild tumult, the "crucifige" of a hateful and mad rabble, a roaring like that of a ravenous lion that throws itself upon its victim.

The second passion picture: Mistreatment persists until the victim is completely exhausted. From the comparisons we may surmise what the Messias had to suffer from these savage men. Because of blows and mal-treatment the blood flows to the ground and with the blood the strength of life vanishes like water that one pours on hot ground. From violent pulling the members of the body are out of joint. All these sufferings the soul experiences with undiminished vehemence along with the feeling of abandonment by God. Like soft wax which receives every impression, so also mockery and mistreatment leave indelible and deep traces on the tender heart and sensitive mind. In the unchecked fire of suffering all energies of the soul are exhausted. They dissolve like wax in the fire. A burning fever consumes the last powers of the body. The tongue cleaves to the palate because of a burning thirst. And no one makes a move to refresh him with a cooling drink, not even the Lord; for God himself has given the enemies power over his servant. He has humbled him and brought him to the brink of death, so that he appears more like a corpse than a living being.

The third passion picture: He is nailed to the cross and robbed of his garments. Just as scavenger dogs in the Orient go about seeking their prey and fall upon it to lacerate it, so the rabble of malicious men sur-round the Messias. They rush upon him and nail him to the cross. That the psalmist has thought of a real nailing to the cross is shown by the mean-ing of the employed Hebrew word which means to hollow out. The oldest translation and the entire Christian antiquity also give this interpretation. The prophecy is all the more remarkable because the Israelites of those days did not know anything about punishment by crucifixion and it can-not be proven that the neighboring nations used this punishment at that time. By nailing the victim to the cross the limbs of the crucified were violently stretched. Through the skin and through the lacerated flesh the bones could be counted. He is a picture of unspeakable suffering. But those who stand around the cross have no sympathy. They stare at him as if he were on display and take delight in his pangs of death. Joking rudely the executioners divide his garments among themselves; they have taken his last possession from him. It was customary in Israel to strip off the clothes of those condemned to death and to execute them in their nakedness. That the garments were usually divided among the executioners is not reported by a single witness. But the prophecy is so much the more remarkable insofar as at the crucifixion of Christ incidental circumstances were literally fulfilled so that the Evangelist John thought that he ought to refer to this sketch of the prophetic description of suffering (verses 19:24).

The vitality of the crucified is about to be exhausted. The Passion is about to end. The hour of departure from this life has arrived. The Messias begins the last agony to which all human assistance is denied, the battle in which life and death contend with each other. In this contest only God's power can strengthen him. Thus the dying Messias cries out for the last time that the Lord may be near him and not delay with his help. Already death has stretched out its hand for his precious life; the sword is drawn which cuts asunder body and soul. Like a hungry scavenger it has thrown itself upon its prey in order to rob him of his life. The Messias, too, has only one soul. It cannot always be the booty of death and of the grave. Like a man attacked by a lion and dragged away in its jaws for devouring, like a man impaled on the horns of a wild buffalo is hurled to the ground and is trodden upon by its heavy hoofs, as such a man cries for help, so the Crucified cries for help in his last and greatest suffering. And with the Messias's cry for help his vow also ascends to heaven. If God hears him and gives him life again, he will thank him every day of his new life and will proclaim his name and glory to his brethren, to God's family of the redeemed. He will glorify him in the congregation, the Church of the New Covenant.

Heaven has heard the cry of the dying Messias. He is still hanging on the cross struggling with death, but he is certain of deliverance and exaltation. The dawn of Easter Sunday sends into the regions of time its beams of light and in this light he sees the fruit of his sufferings, the great blessings of his work of the Redemption (verses 24–32). He already sees himself in the circle of those who fear God, of the members of his people longing for salvation. He sees himself proclaiming to them, according to his vow, the name of God, his power and goodness which reveal themselves in the Resurrection and Transfiguration of the Crucified and in the act of love of the Redemption. Making known the glad message of the

Resurrection is the first fruit of the Passion. All who awaited Redemption should rejoice. They should praise and glorify the Lord. All generations of Jacob should worship him with reverence; the tribes of Israel, the redeemed Israel of the New Covenant should adore him. The Messias is still poor, deprived of everything, despised, derided, and blasphemed; but God has not despised him. He remained near him in his night of abandonment and heard his prayers. Such knowledge must strengthen all in the confidence that God will also command the morning of deliverance to follow upon the night of suffering.

The second fruit of the Passion is the unique sacrifice of Messianic times, the Eucharistic Sacrifice. The resurrected Christ, the Messias, will render thanks by a votive offering which will be celebrated in the great Messianic congregation, the Church, forever, so that the true adorers may participate in it at all times. The Old Testament votive offering was a thanksgiving sacrifice for restored peace with God, for regained union with God. With this sacrifice there was connected a sacrificial banquet at the place of the sanctuary. It was an expression of this union with God. The prophet Malachias says of this sacrifice that it will be offered in all places from the rising to the setting of the sun and that the name of God will be glorified among all nations (Malachias 1:11). According to the Law (Deuteronomy 6:11) the poor, the widows, the orphans, and the strangers were invited to partake of these votive offerings at the sacrificial banquet. In the Eucharistic Sacrifice of the Messias there is also a sacrificial banquet of which the poor may partake, and also the sufferers and the needy who expect help from God, and all poor who hunger and thirst for justice and to whom peace has been promised. The effects of this Eucharistic Banquet will be supernatural. As many as partake of this Eucharistic Meal will be sated, and being sated their souls will be filled with joy. They will consider themselves blessed because they have sought the Lord. They have ardently longed for him and will themselves praise the Lord who has showered so many graces upon them. By the strength of the Eucharistic Banquet their souls will live forever. The Sacrificial Banquet is a food, the partaking of which has eternal spiritual consequences. The Protestant interpreter Delitsch remarks: "Does this not suggest the thought about the sacramental Eucharist in which the second David ascends the throne through suffering and death and makes us partake of the fruits of his offering?"

The third fruit of the Passion is the conversion of the Gentiles, the spread of the Church over the entire earth, and the catholicity of Redemption. The sermon of the resurrected Christ will penetrate into the pagan world and its people will remember the Lord for whom they gave up their gods. The pagan world will be mindful of its Creator and his

75

revelations and will return to the house of God which like the prodigal son they had so ungratefully abandoned. Those who have bent their knees to a lifeless idol will now prostrate themselves before Yahwe and worship him. And thus the prophetic word will be fulfilled that every knee shall bend before the Lord (Isaias 45:23) and that the temple shall be a house of prayer for all nations (Isaias 56:7). To the Lord belongs the ruling power over all nations because he is their creator. To spread into the world the knowledge of the divine claims to this rule and to dispose the Gentiles to acknowledge the world dominion of Yahwe will be the supreme task of the Messias, in order that the one God may be worshiped; that there be one God, one faith, and one Church. Then among all Gentile nations the Messianic Sacrifice will be celebrated. Gentiles, too, will partake of the Eucharistic Banquet. The rich and the mighty of the world will give up worldly pleasures and will desire to partake of the Banquet of the Lord. All men on earth will feast on this Banquet. They will live eternally by the strength of this Food. The Messias himself will dedicate his transfigured life to the glorification of God, and the human race which he has purchased with his precious blood will serve the Lord. The witnesses of the redeeming death of the Messias and of his resurrection will narrate to the coming generation the incomprehensible deeds of God's love and of his Anointed and the coming generations will in turn proclaim the glad tidings from century to century until the end of time. And all generations that come and go will look up to heaven with sincere thankfulness to God who loved the world so much as to sacrifice his own Son for our redemption. They will say: He has done it. Then they will look up to the Messias and his cross and will likewise say: He has done it. Our deliverance and our redemption, our salvation and blessedness is God's work, our Redeemer's greatest deed.

psalm 22

Dominus regit me

God's spiritual benefits to faithful souls

1. A psalm for David.
   The Lord ruleth me: and I shall want nothing.

2. He hath set me in a place of pasture. He hath brought me up on the water of refreshment.

3. He hath converted my soul. He hath led me on the paths of justice, for his own name's sake.

4. For though I should walk in the midst of the shadow of death, I will fear no evils, for thou art with me.
Thy rod and thy staff, they have comforted me.

5. Thou hast prepared a table before me, against them that afflict me.
Thou hast anointed my head with oil, and my chalice, which inebriated me, how goodly is it!

6. And thy mercy will follow me all the days of my life.
And that I may dwell in the house of the Lord unto length of days.

THERE is a sentiment of joyful tranquility and spiritual peace pervading this psalm which can only be found in a soul that has learned to know how good the Lord is to those who love him and place their confidence in him. In this psalm we have a slight presentiment of the happiness of heaven about which St. John speaks in the Book of Revelation. He seems to have borrowed his thought from this psalm: "They shall no more hunger nor thirst, neither shall the sun fall on them, nor any heat. For the Lamb which is in the midst of the throne shall rule them and shall lead them to the fountains of the waters of life, and God shall wipe away all tears from their eyes" (Revelation 7:16-17). The psalmist giving us a picture of the Good Shepherd and of the Host is thinking about Yahwe, but he also has in mind the Messias who in the Gospel calls himself the Good Shepherd. There is also a reference to the Eucharistic Banquet which the psalmist describes in the foregoing psalm in which Christ is taken. In this Sacrament the remembrance of his suffering is celebrated, the heart is filled with grace, and a pledge is given of future glory.

God is my shepherd (verses 1-4). I shall not want anything. This is the keynote of the song: total satisfaction through Divine Providence. The word *shepherd* meant more for the Israelites than it does for us today. Many times the shepherd was the possessor of the herd which he himself tended or entrusted to the care of his sons or daughters. Out of love for his flock he cared for its needs and bravely encountered the dangers that were inherent in his calling. For his herd he sought green pastures, leading them to drinking places, and protecting them against robbers and wild animals. Without fear a herd could be entrusted to such a shepherd. Isaias has given us a description of the Good Shepherd in the following words: "He shall gather together the lambs with his arm, and shall take them up in his bosom, and he himself shall carry them that are not young" (Isaias 40:11). He who belongs to the herd of the Divine Shepherd shall want nothing. For whatever a true shepherd does for his herd, that the Lord with infinite care does for man and above all else for the human soul.

He has set me in a place of pasture. In Palestine when the winter rains are over, the sun burns upon the steppes. The green pastures become fewer and then the shepherd must frequently go far from home with his herd to find suitable grazing land. The world is like a sun-parched steppe because upon it the rain and dew have ceased to fall. Therefore God leads his sheep into another world, into the kingdom of God, into the glorious pastures of supernatural Truth, into the eternal meadows where the soul finds nourishment in abundance, nourishment that satisfies, gives health and strength of life. God leads men to the waters of refreshment, to the fountains where graces flow abundantly, graces that can still the thirst for peace, joy, and happiness. He who drinks natural water will thirst again, but he who will drink of the water which I shall give shall not thirst forever. The water which I shall give will be to him a fountain of eternal life (John 4:13). If this was true about the revelations of the Old Covenant and of the Old Covenant sanctuary, it is more true about the revelations of Jesus Christ and about the treasures of grace stored up in his Church.

Only truth and grace can refresh the soul of man because it is from God, and the soul has an unquenchable thirst for God and the things of God. And on this account it is only God who can give refreshment. God alone can lead the soul on the right path to truth and grace. Christ is the way, the truth, and the life. God leads the soul to Christ for his name's sake. Reception into the fold of God is an unmerited grace. It is not our merit. It is God's gift (Ephesians 2:8). The Lord has made himself the shepherd of his people out of pure love. He has taken upon himself the duties of a shepherd out of pure love; he has also made us the sheep of his herd. But even in the life of a man united with God the way leads him through the shadow of death, through the days of corporal and spiritual suffering and persecutions. But even if all this should happen, even if the way should finally lead through the shadow of death, through the fears and anxieties of the last hours of life, the man of God has nothing to fear. Who shall be disheartened and afraid of his salvation as long as God dwells within his soul? God's staff, the Shepherd's staff, which points the way to the last end, the Good Shepherd's rod which defends against the attacks of the enemy and wards off all dangers is a secure guarantee that the soul will overcome all difficulties and will come to a good end. The word of the psalmist has found a strong echo in the heart of the Apostle of the nations: "Who shall separate me from the love of Christ? Shall tribulation or distress, or famine, or nakedness, or danger, or persecution, or the sword? But in all things we overcome because of him that has loved us. For I am sure that neither death, nor life, nor angels, nor principalities, nor powers, nor things present, nor things to come, nor might, nor height, nor any other creature, shall be able to separate us from the love of God, which is in Christ Jesus, our Lord" (Romans 8:35 seq.).

God is my host (verses 5–6). The psalmist changes the picture. In place of the Good Shepherd the hospitable host enters the picture; in place of the sheep, the wanderer in a strange land; instead of the green pastures, the banquet; the water of refreshment becomes the overflowing beaker; the shadow of death becomes the way upon which the enemies lie in wait. The second comparison is also taken from daily life in the ancient Orient. These people esteemed very highly the practice of hospitality. The psalmist uses this comparison in order to show with what prodigal love God protects man who as a stranger seeks strength and protection in his holy tabernacle. Like a noble host God receives man as a highly esteemed friend and feeds him bounteously and honorably. He himself sets the table, anoints his head, and hands him the beaker. Without worrying about his enemies who are lying in wait for him, the stranger can enjoy the hospitality; for not one will dare to enter the tabernacle. What was only a similitude for the psalmist in order to show the happiness of those who dwell in the house of God has become in the New Covenant a wonderful reality. In truth God sets the table for all who as members of his Church seek rest and protection in the house of God during their pilgrimage through life. He gives them the Bread of Heaven and the full beaker of God's love and the richness of his grace, the beaker of his Precious Blood, and anoints him with the sevenfold gift of the Holy Spirit. No enemy, no power in the world nor in hell can disturb the happiness of this hospitality; for nothing can separate us from the love of God which is in Christ Jesus. Thus the happiness of union with God, the precious enjoyment of God's mercy and grace remains in the soul of such a man throughout his life. Happiness and grace are constant companions on the way to everlasting happiness. For he whom the Lord has called to his kingdom, he for whom the Lord has made room, as guest may dwell in his house. Even death cannot destroy this union with God: "For thee my flesh and my heart hath fainted away: thou art the God of my heart, and the Lord that is my portion forever" (Psalm 71:26).

psalm 23

Domini est terra

Who are they that shall ascend to heaven? Christ's
triumphant ascension thither

1. On the first day of the week, a psalm for David.

2. The earth is the Lord's and the fullness thereof: the world and all that dwell therein.

3. For he hath founded it upon the seas, and hath prepared it upon the rivers.

4. Who shall ascend to the mountain of the Lord? And who shall stand in his holy place?

5. The innocent in hands, and the clean of heart, who hath not taken his soul in vain, nor sworn deceitfully to his neighbor.

6. He shall receive a blessing from the Lord, and mercy from God his Saviour.

7. This is the generation of them that seek him, of them that seek the face of the God of Jacob.

8. Lift up your gates, O ye princes, and be ye lifted up, O eternal gates: and the king of glory shall enter in.

9. Who is the king of glory? The Lord who is strong and mighty, the Lord mighty in battle.

10. Lift up your gates, O ye princes, and be ye lifted up, O eternal gates: And the king of glory shall enter in.

11. Who is this king of glory? The Lord of hosts, he is the king of glory.

For twenty years the Ark stood far from its sanctuary in the house of Aminadab. When David took Jerusalem and the freedom of the country was secured, he erected a new tabernacle to the Lord on Mount Sion and had the Ark carried in solemn procession to Jerusalem. This psalm most likely belongs to the songs that were chanted on this occasion. It is a profession of faith by the people accompanying the Ark. It is a profession of faith in him who broods invisibly over the Ark of the

Covenant. "I believe in Yahwe, the almighty Creator of the universe. I believe in the Holy One of Israel, in the King of glory." The thoughts of this psalm are very suitable for meditation before receiving the Eucharist.

The first article of the Creed: the Creator of the universe enters (verses 1–2). The Lord who broods over the Ark of the Covenant and who wishes to reside in the tabernacle on Sion is the Lord of all creation, of all things, and of all beings that are in heaven and on earth. The heavens with its myriads of stars are his. He called them and they said: "We are here." "How they shine and give joy to him, who created them" (Baruch 3:35). His is the earth and its plants with their wonderful multiplicity. His are all the animals, large and small. His are all men in all times and places. Everything is his unlimited possession, because with his all-mighty power he called all things into being. From the testimonies of the Divine Power at creation the psalmist selects an example that makes a particularly great impression. God made the gigantic earth with its majestic mountains on a vibrating foundation; he built it on seas and waters, yet it stands so firm as if it were grounded on a rock. The idea that the earth stands on subterranean waters was commonly believed among the ancient peoples. This belief was engendered by the fact that when digging they found subterranean water. For the psalmist this world picture is a testimony to God's power in creation.

The second article of the Creed: the Holy One of Israel enters (verses 3–6). He who broods on the Ark of the Covenant and wishes to dwell in the tabernacle has in his Law given the command to his people: "Be ye holy because I, Yahwe, your God am holy" (Leviticus 19:2). In order to remind the Israelites of this command, the choir of singers asks the question of the festive pilgrims: Who may ascend to the mountain of the Lord? Who may stand in his holy place? The question is important. Did not many of the inhabitants of Bethsames die a sudden death because with irreverential curiosity they looked upon the Ark of the Covenant when the Philistines brought it back to them? (1 Kings 6:19). Was not Oza struck dead when he touched the sacred Ark with unconsecrated hands? (2 Kings 6:6).

God does not demand of those who wish to approach him to have their hands filled with rich gifts; he does not exact offerings and sacrifices, but he does demand a pure heart and clean hands. God does not need sacrifices and gifts; for everything belongs to him. What God wants is the sacrifice of the will and faithful obedience to his Law. Thus Moses instructs his people: "And now Israel what doth the Lord thy God require of thee, but that thou fear the Lord thy God, and walk in his ways, and love him, and serve the Lord thy God with thy whole heart and with thy whole soul" (Deuteronomy 10:12). The Lord is not satisfied with a merely

81

external observance of the Law so that only the hands appear clean. He looks upon the soul, upon the pure intention. He who wishes to serve God with his whole soul must not set his mind on vain things, upon what is worldly. The Lord does not wish the soul to be divided in its service. The purity of intention must correspond to the purity of speech. The love of God cannot be reconciled with the abuse of his holy Name. He who in the Name of God promises something to his neighbor must keep his promise in God's Name, for his Name is holy as God himself is holy.

Only an intention that is pleasing to God is blessed by him. In the sanctuary the fruits of the grace of redemption are opened to him alone who has a good intention; for only such a man is justified and enriched with graces. What the psalmist has said in a few words is a small catechism on morality placed in the hands of all who seek God and wish to appear before the face of the God of Jacob; that is, those who wish to come to the place of grace, who wish to enter his holy tabernacle. Only the true seekers of God will find the Lord, will receive his grace.

The third article of the faith: the King of glory enters (verses 7–11). The procession which accompanies the Ark of the Covenant has arrived at the gates of the temple and the God brooding above the cherubim wishes to enter the sanctuary. So also Christ the King stands before the human soul and with his grace asks for admission. The gates are too small, too narrow, and too low to admit the most powerful and majestic King. The choir, therefore, demands that they be made larger. This demand is at the same time an admonition to the people to open their hearts to the King of glory, to remove from their hearts everything that is too narrow and too small for the love of God, to show willingness to make sacrifice, and to receive the great King with lofty aspirations. For everything that is narrow and little in the love of God, in faith, confidence, obedience, and self-sacrifice is unworthy in the sight of the sublime Ruler.

The gatekeepers within the walls inquire concerning the King of glory. The question prompts the choir to intone a hymn praising the glory of the King. The King clothed with God's glory is Yahwe, the strong Hero, powerful in war. He who enters is the conqueror in many battles, who has vanquished the enemies of his kingdom and humbled them. The psalmist may have thought of the many battles that had been won through God's intervention in favor of his people; he may have recalled the victories which he had obtained through God's help.

They cannot close the gates to such a mighty and victorious King. Therefore there is given a second request to raise the gates so that the King of glory may enter. Who should be so foolish and presumptuous as to refuse the request? But again the watchers at the gate ask the question: Who is this King of glory? The answer of the choir is another description of the great King. The King of glory is the Lord of Hosts. He is the king not only of Israel but of all nations. He is also ruler of the heavenly spirits. The innumerable legions of those wise and powerful spirits are under his command and at all times fulfill his will gladly. Now they open the gates and the King of glory enters that he might plant his throne upon Sion.

psalm 24

Ad te, Domine, levavi

A prayer for grace, mercy, and protection against our enemies

1. Unto the end, a psalm for David.
   To thee, O Lord, have I lifted up my soul.

2. In thee, O my God, I put my trust; let me not be ashamed.

3. Neither let my enemies laugh at me: for none of them, that wait on thee, shall be confounded.

4. Let them be confounded that act unjust things without cause.
   Show, O Lord, thy ways to me, and teach me thy paths.

5. Direct me in thy truth, and teach me: for thou art God my Saviour; and on thee have I waited all the day long.

6. Remember, O Lord, thy bowels of compassion: and thy mercies that are from the beginning of the world.

7. The sins of my youth and my ignorances do not remember.
   According to thy mercy remember thou me: for thy goodness sake, O Lord.

8. The Lord is sweet and righteous: therefore will he give a law to sinners in the way.

9. He will guide the mild in judgment: he will teach the meek his ways.

10. All the ways of the Lord are mercy and truth, to them that seek after his covenant and his testimonies.

11. For thy name's sake, O Lord, thou wilt pardon my sin: for it is great.

12. Who is the man that feareth the Lord? He hath appointed him a law in the way he hath chosen.

13. His soul shall dwell in good things: and his seed shall inherit the land.

14. The Lord is a firmament to them that fear him: and his covenant shall be made manifest to them.

15. My eyes are ever towards the Lord: for he shall pluck my feet out of the snare.

16. Look thou upon me, and have mercy on me; for I am alone and poor.

17. The troubles of my heart are multiplied: deliver me from my necessities.

18. See my abjection and my labor; and forgive me all my sins.

19. Consider my enemies for they are multiplied, and have hated me with an unjust hatred.

20. Keep thou my soul and deliver me: I shall not be ashamed; for I have hoped in thee.

21. The innocent and the upright have adhered to me: because I have waited on thee.

22. Deliver Israel, O God, from all his tribulations.

For men upon earth the only real concern is to attain their last and supreme end, to attain salvation through our Lord Jesus Christ (1 Thessalonians 5:9). The people of the Old Covenant were already directed to this end. Tobias says: "We are children of the saints and expect the blessed life which God will grant to those who will not waver in their fidelity to him" (Tobias 2:18). As the end cannot be viewed except by faith, so also the way to that end cannot be known except by revelation, and cannot be walked except by the assistance of divine grace. God must show the way and lead us on it. This was done in the Old Covenant through the wisdom of the Law. "God found out all the way of knowledge and gave it to Jacob his servant and to Israel his beloved. Afterwards he was seen upon earth, and conversed with men" (Baruch 3:37-38). In the New Covenant Christ came as the way, the truth, and the life. The psalmist, thoroughly convinced of the necessity of divine teaching and guidance in this acrostic psalm, beseeches the Lord to show him the way which he must walk to attain the happiness of revering him and to protect him against all dangers that threaten him, the pilgrim, on his way to his final end.

The psalmist is anxious about his salvation (verses 1-3). Afflictions, opposition from without, and hateful suspicions had oppressed his soul. Godlessness seemed to triumph over the fear of the Lord; faithlessness to the Law over fidelity to the Covenant. He who in such a situation does not anchor his thoughts and life on faith, will err on the way, succumb to temptation, and give up all confidence in God. For such and for all who are tempted to despair the psalmist wrote this psalm. Despite all adversities and afflictions he himself raised his mind to God in order to receive through prayer and meditation light and strength from above. With the confidence a child has in its father and mother he places all his anxieties in the hands of God; for the Lord cannot abandon those who love and serve him. He cannot abandon those who because of their reverence and piety toward God are subjected to animosity. How the enemies of God would rejoice if they brought about the downfall of a just man, because he in whom he had placed his confidence defected. How hell rejoices when a friend of the Lord is guilty of a breach of fidelity! The psalmist does not believe in such a triumph; on the contrary he is certain that virtue will triumph, that the godless will be punished and be put to shame. He says with the prophet Jeremias: "But the Lord is with me as a strong warrior; therefore, they that persecute me shall fall, and shall be weak. They shall be greatly confounded because they have not understood the everlasting reproach which shall never be effaced." The godless will be ashamed and undeceived when on the day of judgment they will see the just in their transfiguration. "Therefore we have erred from the way of truth and the light of justice hath not shined unto us and the sun of understanding hath not risen upon us. We wearied ourselves in the way of iniquity and destruction, and have walked through hard ways, but the way of God we have not known" (Wisdom 5:6–7).

Many try to show men the way of happiness, but true happiness is found in God alone, and the Lord alone knows the way. God must show the way of salvation to us (verses 4–7). God has, indeed, revealed his will in the Law and in the Gospel. Everyone can read it there. But the right interpretation and correct knowledge God himself must give. Therefore the composer of Psalm 118 prays: Give me insight that I may observe the Law and keep it with my whole heart (Psalm 118:34). The Lord has made known his truth; there is no other truth that leads us to our last end. Only with the light of grace is the truth known. God alone can instruct in the truth; only his spirit can help us delve more deeply into this truth and only by his light can we get a clear knowledge of divine Truth. He alone can comprehend his own eternal decree of salvation, the conferring of blessings upon men. He alone is the God of salvation. He alone can give it and refuse it. The longer a man walks along the path of the Law, the deeper he delves into the revealed truths. The stronger supernatural life pulsates in him, the greater will be his confidence in God's gracious guidance; for when a man who is called to salvation wills to err on the way, the Lord will no longer accompany him. Then God's abounding love and grace would be without fruit. But how could God forget to manifest his love to weak man? His weakness reaches back to the fall of the first man in Paradise. God's love extends into eternity. As little as God can cease to exist, so little can his infinite love come to an end. It is so abounding and great that it can forgive and erase all the sins of men. If God would remember all sins, all the sins of youth, all the sins of indifference and unfaithfulness, all transgressions of his commandments because of lack of knowledge, and would deign to withdraw his hand and his grace from men, who could attain salvation? Therefore the psalmist prays that God may not be mindful of his transgressions, but that he may be mindful of his own infinite mercy and kindness.

The cry of a sinful but humble man relying on God's grace alone will not remain unheard. God's grace shows him the entire way (verses 8–11). The prayer now becomes a meditation upon the divine Goodness. The Lord abounds in merciful love toward the sinner. He does not wish the death of the sinner, but that he may be converted and live. Throughout the entire Sacred Scripture we find praises of God's goodness and fidelity: "O Lord, the Lord God, merciful and gracious, patient and of much compassion, and true" (Exodus 34:6). He manifests his goodness toward a sinner that is penitent. "But to the penitent sinners he hath given the way of justice, and he hath strengthened them that were fainting in patience and hath appointed them the lot of truth" (Sirach 17:20). Also to the humble who do not rely on their own knowledge and ability alone, but who rely also on God the Lord shows the way of the Law. "God resists the proud, but to the humble he gives grace" (James 4:6). Only to those who submit to his will and permit themselves to be led does the Lord teach his way. He leads them on the way of virtue to the heights of perfection. The path by which God leads men according to his will and eternal decrees are grace and truth, but only those will see the glorious effects of the divine love and fidelity who are faithful to his covenant and cherish his Law in their heart. He, therefore, who wishes to experience God's love and fidelity must not only meditate upon and understand the Law, but must have in mind the greatest grace and the fulfillment of the greatest promise; namely, salvation. God by his nature is goodness and fidelity, but the glorious effects of the divine love and fidelity only those will experience who remain true to his Covenant and cherish his Law in their hearts. He, therefore, who wishes to experience God's goodness and fidelity may not merely meditate upon, but must also live the Law. God must demand fidelity in return for his fidelity; he must demand love for love. Because of his goodness every sin deliberately committed is rank ingratitude and because of God's unwavering fidelity every act of human unfaithfulness is a grave fault. But every thought of God, of his divine nature, of his promise of forgiveness and mercy to the penitent sinner gives the confidence that God will no longer be tolerant of his sins.

Great are the blessings that await man at the end of God's way. He who is led by God is happy (verses 12–15). In a few words the psalmist depicts the happiness of the just who permit themselves to be guided by God. To him who fears God, the Lord shows the way. This way he must walk in order to attain his eternal destiny. God assists him in all affairs pertaining to eternity and in all cares of life and gives him security. He gives him clearness of understanding and correct judgment which no worldly wisdom can give. Already here on earth he who permits himself to be guided by the hand of God is happy and contented; for nothing can happen to him which the wisdom and love of God does not permit. He knows no fear because he knows that to those who love God and trust in him all things turn out well. He lives happily because with confidence he may expect participation in eternal happiness; for according to the divine promise the generations of the just will possess the land. They will be members of the Messianic kingdom in its blessed completion. From this the sinner is excluded forever. The just will inhabit the land and the innocent will dwell there, but the godless will be eradicated from the land and the faithless will be uprooted (Proverbs 2:21). Even now the just are deigned worthy of the friendship of God. The Lord makes a covenant with them and thus he will no longer call them his servants but his friends and confidants.

"A friend of the king" was one of the highest titles of honor which in ancient times a ruler could bestow on a faithful officer and trustworthy counselor. In the book of the Old Testament only Abraham is called the friend of God. But every man who fears God is given the honorable title of friend when he permits himself to be guided by God and God then permits him to partake of all good things that are proper to a friend. Because of such divine goodness man must always look up to God, follow his counsel in all things and have full confidence in his protection. He who directs his thoughts to God does not find it necessary to be anxious about the way. He does not need to fear that snares will be laid for him; for God unbinds his feet if perchance he has fallen into a snare. God will not let him fall who has sought his protecting hand. With this description the psalmist wishes to say that God leads the just man through all difficult situations of life and dangerous occasions to the end of his earthly wanderings.

At the end of the psalm the meditation on the goodness of God and on the happiness of the man who is led by God, changes into a petition to keep him on the right path (verses 16–22). There are three dangers on the way to our last end. The first is the loneliness into which the God-fearing man may fall. The world does not understand him; it despises and ridicules him. He has no one to whom he can utter his complaints and from whom he may seek consolation. When God withdraws consolation for a time, man may in his abandonment become despondent. The second danger is sin and anxiety about sin, not only about those that have been committed, but also those that may be committed again and again because of human frailty. His soul is anxious because everywhere there are hindrances that make him fear; everywhere there are needs that disturb his joy in God and the quiet enjoyment of peace. At every step the just man must rely on the mercy and grace of God. He must rely upon his goodness, upon his willingness to forgive sin, and upon his protection in all adversities. If the Lord would not continually watch in such needs, who could ever attain his end? The third and greatest danger comes from the great number of enemies that threaten his salvation. There are men who are determined to corrupt the just man and entice him to commit sin. There is also the enemy within man, the evil concupiscences. There is Satan who goes about like a roaring lion seeking whom he may devour; his hatred is insatiable. In the face of such enemies man is powerless. Only with God's power can he vanquish them. Therefore, man must pray daily to the Lord with the psalmist that he may save his soul from the dangers that surround him, that he may save him from falling. He must place himself under the protection of God's power and love and have firm confidence that God will not disappoint him. Innocence and righteousness, true piety and a sincere willingness to be obedient to the Law of God should be the defense given to him by God. And as protectors on the way, they should be of help to the pilgrim that he may not fall into the danger of entering on to wrong paths. The Lord who wills the end and has shown the way will not deny us these companions. As for individual men, so also for an entire nation has God set a sublime purpose and shown it the way to salvation. A nation too is beset with dangers and on that account may fail in its task. Therefore the psalmist himself or a compiler of later times has added the petition that the Lord may deliver the people from all adversities.

psalm 25

Judica me, Domine

David's prayer to God in his distress, to be delivered, that he may come to worship him in his tabernacle

1. Unto the end, a psalm for David.
   Judge me, O Lord, for I have walked in my innocence: and I have put my trust in the Lord, and shall not be weakened.

2. Prove me, O Lord, and try me; burn my reins and my heart.

3. For thy mercy is before my eyes; and I am well pleased with thy truth.

4. I have not sat with the council of vanity: neither will I go in with the doers of unjust things.

5. I have hated the assembly of the malignant: and with the wicked I will not sit.

6. I will wash my hands among the innocent; and will compass thy altar, O Lord.

7. That I may hear the voice of thy praise: and tell of all thy wondrous works.

8. I have loved, O Lord, the beauty of thy house: and the place where thy glory dwelleth.

9. Take not away my soul, O God with the wicked: nor my life with bloody men.

10. In whose hands are iniquities: their right hand is filled with gifts.

11. But as for me, I have walked in my innocence: redeem me, and have mercy on me.

12. My foot has stood in the direct way: in the churches I will bless thee, O Lord.

THE psalm may have been written in the times of David's great trials, in the time of the persecution by Saul. The mention of the sanctuary does not militate against this. The friendly relationship which David had at his ascension to the throne with the high-priest Nobe permits us to conclude that he was not an infrequent guest at the place of the holy tabernacle. A passionate hatred haunted him, but he knew that he was innocent of any misconduct against the king. He never had any connections with the opponents of Saul, but faithfully fulfilled his duty as a subject, and even when he was ostracized he would not harm the life of the king. Therefore he could call upon God with a good conscience and peacefully await his just decision. He could have the confidence that God would not inflict upon an innocent man the punishment that was due to the godless. As a community song the psalm became a prayer that the Lord might protect the just man and intervene against the enemy of his salvation and support him in his determination to remain faithful and not permit him to die the death of a blasphemer.

The psalm begins the petition for assistance in the conflict with the enemy of his salvation (verses 1–2). Paul speaks of a conflict which a Christian must wage not only against flesh and blood; that is, against man's own concupiscences but also against principalities and powers, against the rulers of darkness, against the spirits of wickedness in high places (Ephesians 6:12). It is a conflict for God, for the greatest good of man, for his own salvation. The natural powers of man are not sufficient to resist hostile powers greater than his own. God must intervene for him in order that he may not succumb. The God-fearing man who conscientiously tries with the grace of God to walk the way of innocence, of obedience to the Law, may with confidence rely on God's assistance; for the Lord allows no one to be tempted beyond his strength and he does not deny his help to him who does not confide in his own strength alone, but places his trust in the help of the Most High. The confession of innocence is no self-praise, no self-deception, but the testimony of a good conscience. God, the all-seeing and all-wise, who searches the heart and the reins knows the good will of his servant and must strengthen it. He knows that his piety and fidelity to the Law is not external sham, but that it is profoundly and spiritually true.

There are certain characteristics of the psalmist's union with God which confirm the self-confession of conscience about his state of grace. A sign of union with God may be seen in the joy one takes in the Law and in revealed truth. Jesus Sirach calls such a one blessed: "Blessed is the man that shall continue in wisdom, and that shall meditate on his justice, and in his mind shall think of the all-seeing eye of God. He that considereth her ways in his heart and hath understanding in her secrets, who goeth after her as one that traceth, and stayeth in her ways. He who looketh in at her windows and hearkeneth at her doors. He that lodgeth near her house, and fastening a pin in her walls sets up his tent nigh unto here where good things shall rest in his lodging forever" (Ecclesiasticus 14:22 seq.).

A second characteristic of union with God is hatred for sin. He who seeks friends where lying and hypocrisy prevail; he who habitually seeks companionship with infidels and immoral men can have no friendship with God; for the enemies of God cannot be friends of his servant and confidant. This in the first place means Satan and the spirit of the world, the archenemies of the Lord. This means not only to have personal intercourse, but to give one's consent to their godless principles.

A third characteristic of union with God is love for the house of God and interest in the liturgical worship of God. A servant of sin takes no pleasure in the service of the heavenly Lord. But the just man goes to the sanctuary because he knows that he is free from grave sins. The priest had to wash his hands before he approached the altar of sacrifice in order to be reminded of the sanctity demanded by God. What with him was a symbolization was also a symbol of a good conscience. In view of the active participation of the just man at the divine service this symbol was of importance. To a religious man the mere external presence at a sacrifice is not sufficient; he attentively follows what is going on at the altar and unites himself with those who are offering the sacrifice. He takes part in the sacred songs with which the priest and the people glorify the Lord. In the language of the psalms he proclaims God's wonderful deeds to the people, the deeds of his love, and the fulfillment of his eternal decree of salvation. He who truly loves God manifests this love and reverence in the house of God where he dwells in his glory. It was the unique privilege of the holy tabernacle that God himself dwelt in the Holy of Holies. Splendid temples, however, were erected for false gods. On this account the faithful Israelites had a great desire to return to the house of God at Jerusalem. Yet both the tabernacle and the temple were only a shadow of the Catholic House of God showing forth God's glory.

Where these three characteristics of the supernatural union with God are found, there is no presumption or self-deception on the part of the psalmist when he concludes that God is pleased with this union. But it would be presumptuous if the believer would think that this precious possession belonged to him and could not be lost. Therefore the psalmist closes his prayer with the petition that he may be preserved from the fate of the godless (verses 9–12). When the Lord withdraws his grace, then even the just man will be lost; for without God's help one cannot attain salvation. Therefore the just man must pray in all humility: "Take not my soul away with the wicked." Take not away from me eternal life as those who because of their crimes on the life and property of their neighbor are excluded from the kingdom of heaven. He must pray daily that God will deliver him from all evil, that he may walk in innocence of life. God's grace and mercy alone can grant him this. To this petition the just man must add a holy vow of thanksgiving. When the Lord helps him to walk righteously, when by his grace he removes all obstacles to salvation, then it is his duty to thank the Lord for it and to praise him not only privately but publicly and to serve God with zeal and to promote his honor.

psalm 26

Dominus illuminatio

David's faith and hope in God

1. The psalm of David before he was anointed.
   The Lord is my light and my salvation, whom shall I fear?
   The Lord is the protector of my life: of whom shall I be afraid?

2. Whilst the wicked draw near against me to eat my flesh
   My enemies that trouble me, have themselves been weakened, and have fallen.

3. If armies in camp should stand together against me, my heart shall not fear.
   If a battle should rise up against me, in this will I be confident.

4. One thing have I asked of the Lord, this will I seek after; that I may dwell in the house of the Lord all the days of my life.
   That I may see the delight of the Lord, and may visit his temple.

5. For he hath hidden me in his tabernacle; in the day of evils, he hath protected me in the secret place of his tabernacle.

6. He hath exalted me upon a rock: and now he hath lifted up my head above my enemies.
   I have gone round, and have offered up in his tabernacle a sacrifice of jubilation: I will sing, and recite a psalm to the Lord.

7. Hear, O Lord, my voice, with which I have cried to thee: have mercy on me and hear me.

8. My heart hath said to thee: My face hath sought thee: Thy face, O Lord, will I still seek.

9. Turn not away thy face from me: decline not in thy wrath from thy servant. Be thou my helper, forsake me not; do not despise me, O God my Saviour.

10. For my father and my mother have left me: but the Lord hath taken me up.

11. Set me, O Lord, a law in thy way, and guide me in the right path, because of my enemies.

12. Deliver me not over to the will of them that trouble me: for unjust witnesses have risen up against me: and iniquity has lied to itself.

13. I believe to see the good things of the Lord in the land of the living.

14. Expect the Lord, do manfully, and let thy heart take courage, and wait thou for the Lord.

IF SANCTITY fundamentally means nothing more than conversion and an elevation of a worldly life to a life with God, in and for God, a constant conduct according to the will of God, and a constant communication with God, even though this is as yet imperfect and bound by earthly ties, nevertheless there is a true and real participation in God's glory and happiness, an inflow and overflow of it in the heart and life of man. The composer of this beautiful psalm is one of those great souls for whom union with God is a source of supernatural joy which no adversity can quell. To the psalmist union with God is like the brilliant sun that even changes suffering. Union with God is a necessity of life. How poor, helpless, and abandoned man would be in this world without God. As fruits of true union with God the psalmist has experienced a twofold blessing even during this life. Above all else it brings about a joyful confidence in all tribulations. The psalmist gives us a remarkable description of these blessings in verses 1–6. The Lord is the light and salvation of every one who fears him and who is united with him by grace. Just as night follows day, so in man's life there are moments of light, joy, and happiness followed by dismal moments of affliction and need. After times of spiritual peace follow times of conflict and temptation. When the brilliant star of faith has become extinguished or has never risen, man can find no escape from the darkness that surrounds him. A pessimism and despondency takes hold of him. But when faith and love for God rule his life, the Lord permits to shine upon him the light which dispels all darkness and awakens in man a realization of the eternal values of all tribulations. Faith teaches us that God is salvation, the saviour of his servants, the physician who cures all weaknesses and gives to the soul supernatural strength and life. Faith and experience tell the just man that God is his protector. Everyone must ask protection from him. Why then should he be discouraged? Since God is with him, who will successfully carry on war against his enemy? Godless men may have the intention of devouring his flesh; that is, according to biblical language: they may have the intention of destroying him morally by calumny and false suspicions. They may oppress him severely, but they can only do as much as God will permit and may only persecute him as long as God will allow. But as soon as God's hand touches them their power vanishes and they fall. Even when an entire army marches against the just man and encompasses him so that no escape seems possible, he who is united with God has nothing to fear from even armies; for he who is under the protection of God has a helper who is more powerful than all the armies of the world. With one word he can crush them to dust and deprive them of their weapons. And when the battle has begun in which the just man is confronted with a power a hundredfold greater than his, indeed, even if the power of hell stands opposed to him, no one can rob him of his peace and confidence because he has sought refuge with God, a citadel that cannot be taken.

Since union with God offers such consolation and gives such confidence, the just man can only wish that this union may never be broken during his life. The psalmist accompanies his plea with the petition that he may dwell all his life in the house of God and that he may be permitted to meditate in his temple about the loveliness of the Lord. Tarrying in the temple, the house of God, is an expression and a sign of spiritual union with God and of trustful intercourse with the Lord; for only he who loves the house of God and who values the divine intimacy so much that he wishes to remain in his sanctuary all the days of his life, who finds in God the object of his entire love and sees in him the object of his desire, only such a one will wish to see the loveliness of the revelations of his glory and to penetrate more deeply into the richness of his divine Love which lies concealed from men in the tabernacle. Such a one knows the sanctuary as a place of refuge. According to the Mosaic Law the sanctuary gave the right of asylum. He who took refuge there and touched the horns of the altar of holocaust was secure against his persecutors because neither hatred nor revenge should penetrate the sanctuary. The dwelling of the Lord in the spiritual sense also is a place of refuge in times of adversity and persecution from the enemies of salvation. There he who is united with God finds protection. The evil enemy may not dare to come near the most high God. God gives to the just man the security afforded by an invincible mountain fortress. With consciousness of such security the man united with God can boldly raise his head before all his enemies and face all dangers. He is certain of victory and of the defeat of his opponents. Therefore he offers sacrifice to the Lord in jubilant thanksgiving and praises him with song and harp.

Union with God gives confidence in prayer (verses 7–10). It does not make prayer unnecessary. Even the man who lives in the grace of God, who enjoys the love of God must pray and beseech God. To him the Book of Sirach has given the admonition: "Stand firm in the lot set before thee, and in prayer to the most high God. . . . Let nothing hinder thee from praying always" (Ecclesiasticus 17:24 and 18:22). The psalmist too is mindful of the divine admonition to seek the countenance of the Lord. For it is a general law which God has given to man that in all his solicitude he should pray to him in his sanctuary; for here particularly will he pay attention to the needs of him who comes to him and will open his heart and will manifest his merciful love. The divine plan of salvation warns that the union with God can be lost, that the just man can maintain this union only with constant prayer for God's help. When the Lord turns his countenance away from man, when he withdraws the assistance of his grace, it means for him futility and collapse. Therefore the man who fears God must always pray that the Lord may not withdraw his grace, that because of the faithlessness of his servant he may not be wrathful and turn away from him, that he may be merciful and help, that he will again guide him and not cast him away. There is no other God that can save him. There is no other that can give man happiness. He who has been abandoned by God has also lost eternal salvation. But God will not forsake him, who being united with him, prays for perseverance in good. If a father and mother would abandon their baby or if the parents would be deprived of their children, yet God would take the just man lovingly into his house and profusely manifest his love toward him, a love which the world has refused him.

Just as union with God gives the assurance that prayer for divine grace will not remain unheard, so it also gives assurance of divine guidance (verses 11–14). The just man united with God cannot dispense with divine guidance without which he would soon miss the right path and take the wrong way. He needs direction because of the enemies who lie in wait to destroy him, to tear him from time and eternity. Because of human weakness no just man can omit the petition: "Lead us not into temptation." If God would withdraw his hand, even a very holy man would be powerless and would succumb to the attacks of the enemies who seek his eternal destruction. Even union with God does not make prayer unnecessary. Do not subject me to the wrath of my enemies; for deceitful tongues oppose me and seek my destruction. Union with God gives the glad certainty that the Lord will not abandon his servant, but will lend him a sure hand that will lead him to his last end. The just man gladly confesses with the psalmist: "I am sure that I will see God in the land of the living." He will be permitted to see God's goodness and will enjoy it in the kingdom of the true supernatural and transfigured life. Again the psalmist reflected upon the Messianic kingdom in which God's love will be revealed in its fullness to the redeemed. And the hope for the kingdom of the eternal vision of God, of the eternal happiness of eternal life springs alive like a bubbling fountain. With this assurance the soul can express the hope: "Hope in the Lord and be consoled; take courage and wait for the Lord."

psalm 27

Ad te, Domine, clamabo

David's prayer that his enemies may not prevail over him

1. A psalm for David himself.
   Unto thee will I cry, O Lord: O my God, be not thou silent to me lest if thou be silent to me, I become like them that go down into the pit.

2. Hear, O Lord, the voice of my supplication, when I pray to thee; when I lift up my hands to thy holy temple.

3. Draw me not away together with the wicked; and with the workers of iniquity destroy me not.
   Who speak peace with their neighbor, but evils are in their hearts.

4. Give them according to their works, and according to the wickedness of their inventions.
   According to the works of their hands give thou to them: render to them their reward.

5. Because they have not understood the works of the Lord, and the operations of his hands: thou shalt destroy them, and shalt not build them up.

6. Blessed be the Lord, for he hath heard the voice of my supplication.

7. The Lord is my helper and my protector: in him hath my heart confided, and I have been helped.

And my flesh hath flourished again, and with my will I will give praise to him.

8. The Lord is the strength of his people, and the protector of the salvation of his anointed.

9. Save, O Lord, thy people, and bless thy inheritance: and rule them and exalt them forever.

K ING DAVID seems to be bowed down in sorrow before the Old Testament tabernacle. He appears before the Holy of Holies. There God's glory broods over the Ark of the Covenant in his mysterious presence of grace. It is always a sign of vivid faith, tender love, and spiritual union with God when man bears sorrow and does not complain to other men, but makes it known to the Lord alone in order to receive consolation, strength, and help from him. Nobody can protect against the treacherous and dangerous activities of hypocritical and conscienceless men as does the all-knowing God; for he knows the secret plotting and secret thoughts of the godless. Because he is almighty and all-just he has also the power and the will to punish these evil men according to the measure of their malice.

The psalmist casts himself before the throne of the most high God. He stretches out his hands towards him and begs for protection against his enemies (verses 1–5). For a long time, altogether too long, they have carried on their nefarious activities against the innocent. Heretofore God remained silent. He did not intervene to protect the honor and rights of his anointed and to make the godless feel his justice. But they have become more bold and insolent in their plotting because they thought that, since God was silent, he favored them. It is time that God speaks to the evil-doers the language of punishment, in order that their eyes may be opened. David is not concerned with transitory loss but rather with what should be and should not be when his opponents are enemies to his eternal salvation. If God would permit them to do as they pleased and would deny the just man his assistance, then even saintly men would be in danger of losing their souls and of being cast into hell with the godless. In this great affliction the persecuted makes a pilgrimage to the sanctuary, appears before the throne of the Most High, raises his hand in prayer, and asks for help; he prays sincerely and appeals to the divine Heart that he may hear him and answer his prayer.

God cannot refuse his protection to the just; for if the just man would succumb to the persecutions of his enemies, his fate would not be different from what his enemies must expect according to the divine threat even though he is not spiritually like them. They are wicked and deceitful men who speak to the innocent with honeyed words but who at heart are mongers of destruction. They cannot please God; for their lies and hypocrisy are an abomination to him. That the just may not be vanquished by them, God must forestall their destructive plans with his punitive justice. He should punish them as they deserve lest the just be defeated by their attacks. It was not a spirit of revenge that prompted the psalmist to speak these words. It was rather zeal for the honor of God. The triumph of godless men does harm to the cause of religion. The enemies of the servants of God are God's enemies. They are blind to the just and merciful providence of God. They have no mind for the decrees of salvation; they have no understanding of the nature of sin and of the value of redemption; they have no understanding of God's deeds of love, of the miracles he wrought for the benefit of men. Since they are bent on the destruction of God's kingdom in the souls of men and upon establishing a kingdom of godlessness, they themselves deserve to be destroyed and never again to be established.

The psalmist has made his complaint. God has now ceased to be silent and has heard his prayer. The petition, therefore, is changed into a prayer of thanksgiving for God's protection (verses 6–9). Praised be the Lord for having heard my cry. God is much pleased when a man, tried by suffering, comes to him and tells him the desires of his soul in order that through his mercy he may obtain consolation. But God does not always grant the request. To many he speaks as he did once to Paul when he besought the Lord that the messenger of Satan might depart from him: "My grace is sufficient for thee; for power is made perfect in infirmity" (2 Corinthians 12:9). Then too he does not permit the destruction of the enemy to follow immediately upon the petition, but prefers to strengthen David in his perseverance and patient waiting. He strengthens him in his confidence that he might rejoice in the consolation which flows so richly from the tabernacle into his soul. For this he gives praise and thanksgiving in his song. What the royal singer himself has experienced he narrates to his people in his song. Not only is one powerless against the enemies of God if God does not give his help, but the entire people is helpless. When God is excluded, the enemy of good order has easy play; but when the fear of God is the foundation of civic life, the nation draws from supernatural sources. Then God becomes for the people a strong fortress. Therefore David closes this psalm with a prayer for the entire nation: Give salvation to thy people and bless thy inheritance, guide and bring it to eternal happiness.

psalm 28

Afferte Domino

An invitation to glorify God, with a commemoration of his mighty works

1. A psalm for David, at the finishing of the tabernacle.
   Bring to the Lord, O ye children of God: bring to the Lord the offspring of rams.

2. Bring to the Lord glory and honor: bring to the Lord glory to his name: adore ye the Lord in his holy court.

3. The voice of the Lord is upon the waters; the God of majesty hath thundered. The Lord is upon many waters.

4. The voice of the Lord is in power: the voice of the Lord in magnificence.

5. The voice of the Lord breaketh the cedars: yea, the Lord shall break the cedars of Libanus.

6. And shall reduce them to pieces, as a calf of Libanus, and as the beloved son of unicorns.

7. The voice of the Lord divideth the flame of fire.

8. The voice of the Lord shaketh the desert: and the Lord shall shake the desert of Cades.

9. The voice of the Lord prepareth the stags: and he will discover the thick woods: and in his temple all shall speak his glory.

10. The Lord maketh the flood to dwell: and the Lord shall sit king forever. The Lord will give strength to his people: the Lord will bless his people with peace.

THUNDERSTORMS are not frequent in Palestine and the people feel the greatness and violence of these storms with a depth of emotion. Perhaps the song was composed under the impression made by one of these storms passing over the land. In deep sounding, heavy rumbling it begins at the sea in the west, passes over the Lebanon range of mountains and then further to the southeast, to the Syrio-Arabian desert.

During the storm the Lord manifests his power. The psalm considers the storm as a means of divine revelation. By it Israel should surmise the glory of Yahwe who is its king and the God of salvation. The tongues of men cannot worthily praise almighty God before whose thundering voice all nature trembles. Therefore the call to praise the Lord ascends to the angels, who, because of their proximity to the most high God, are called sons of God (verses 1–2). They should glorify his name and praise his power and majesty. As heavenly spirits they know all things better than men know them. They see God's majesty in its sublime clarity. From the powers of nature they comprehend better than the human mind God's eternal glory in its height and depth. In the name of the chosen people the angels should worship the Lord. They should worship him in their holy beauty, in the garment which God has given them which makes them more worthy to adore the Lord of creation than sinful men created from the created dust of the earth. By describing a thunderstorm in its effect the psalmist attempts to visualize the majesty of God as shown in his creatures (verses 3–9). The storm appears over the sea in the northwestern horizon. The thunder accompanied with blinding flashes of lightning rumbles and drowns the noise of the stormy sea and the howling of the mad wind. In all this turmoil the Lord approaches visibly. A thunderstorm upon the sea is a majestic scene of nature. In the midst of the turmoil of the elements the roaring of the thunder is terrifying. If God's voice is so powerful in nature, how terrifying will it be when in his holy wrath he will speak directly to man from his judgment seat, when in his holy wrath he will address the godless: "Depart from me ye cursed!" The storm passes from the sea eastward to the Lebanon mountains. The storm falls with violence upon the beautiful cedar forests. It breaks to pieces trees centuries old, trees thick and high with long branches. They lie splintered on the ground; their beauty is gone. Terrified by the rolling thunder and the lightning flashes which echo in all the caves and gulleys, the massive mountain chain begins to quake because of the violence of the storm and the crashing of the falling cedars. The bending of the trees when the storm takes hold of them, when seen from a distance, looks to the poet like leaping calves. Even the Sarion, a Phoenician name for the Great Hermon, which reaches a height of 3000 meters, seems to leap like a young buffalo. It too is restless when the lightning flashes continuously, breaking the darkness and shattering the forests which cry in the storm. If inanimate nature trembles when the Lord passes in the storm, how will weak man be able to stand when the Lord will come upon him with grim wrath? The storm passes on further to the southeast, to the Syro-Arabian desert, and unloads itself upon the desert of Cades, south of

Palestine. Even this silent desert becomes restless because of the terrible rolling of the thunder.

Lightning and thunder terrify the timid herd in the thicket, so that they give birth before the time. So terrible is the storm that the trees are rooted up and hurled down.

Even the congregation gathered in the sanctuary is frightened by the terrible majesty of Yahwe and cries out at the flashes of lightning: "What glory!"

When the storms rage, the heavens open their sluices and the rain falls from the clouds in a great downpour. The parched soil is being prepared for the winter seeding. The eternal Lord rules over these water-floods like a king. With the powers of nature he rules to punish and to save. The psalmist prays that God may judge the enemies of his people and destroy them and that he may give the strength and the blessing of the Messianic peace to Israel.

psalm 29

Exaltabo te, Domine

David praises God for his deliverance and his merciful dealings with him

1. A psalm of a canticle, at the dedication of David's house.

2. I will extol thee, O Lord, for thou hast upheld me: and hast not made my enemies to rejoice over me.

3. O Lord, my God, I have cried to thee, and thou hast healed me.

4. Thou hast brought forth, O Lord, my soul from hell: thou hast saved me from them that go down into the pit.

5. Sing to the Lord, O ye saints: and give praise to the memory of his holiness.

6. For wrath is in his indignation: and life in his good will.
In the evening weeping shall have place, and in the morning gladness.

7. And in my abundance I said: I shall never be moved.

8. O Lord, in thy favor, thou gavest strength to my beauty.
Thou turnedst away thy face from me, and I became troubled.

9. To thee, O Lord, will I cry: and I will make supplication to my God.

10. What profit is there in my blood, whilst I go down to corruption?
Shall dust confess to thee, or declare thy truth.

11. The Lord hath heard, and hath had mercy on me: the Lord became my helper.

12. Thou hast turned for me my mourning into joy: thou hast cut my sack-cloth: and hast compassed me with gladness.

13. To the end that my glory may sing to thee, and I may not regret: O Lord my God, I will give praise to thee forever.

A CCORDING to the superscription this psalm was composed by David for the dedication of the house of God and is frequently said to have been used at the time of the plague which God had inflicted as a punishment upon Israel because of the pride of the king which prompted him to take up the census of the people (2 Kings 24). In this instance the psalm must have been composed for the dedication of the altar which David had erected at the place of the future temple structure. The expression *house of God* does not militate against this because every consecrated place can be designated by this appellation. In this psalm the royal singer also gives thanks for his and his people's deliverance from the plague. He voluntarily confesses his arrogance and his presumption security for which the Lord has punished him. The psalm should be an admonition for all not to be proud and self-confident, but to be humble and to rely on God's grace.

The introduction of the psalm (verses 2–4) gives the reason for the song of thanksgiving. It does not indicate a specific time in the life of David. But there is nothing to prevent us from connecting the poem with the celebration of the dedication of the altar on Mount Moriah. David's enemies in foreign parts as well as within the country were already jubilant because soon the hour of retribution would come. They were glad and watched the spread of the plague and hoped that the king himself would die from it. But God did not permit this. When David and the elders appeared in penitent garbs and cast themselves before the Lord and begged him to desist from his punishment, the Lord put a stop to the plague. If the plague had continued, David too would have finally succumbed to it. But God in his mercy preserved him from certain death because of his contrition and prayers. Many thousands had died from the plague though it had lasted less than a day. Even David had to fear death. But God saved him; he had to draw his soul, as it were, from the underworld; he had again given to him the life which was believed to be lost.

The punishment had fallen on the entire people and in its termination they all rejoiced. The psalmist, therefore, calls on the entire chosen people to celebrate a service of thanksgiving to the Lord and to praise his holy Name with songs and the playing of the harp; for he has again proven himself not only as an all-holy and infinitely just God but also as a merciful deliverer. In its effects the punishment bore fruit even though the plague lasted only a few hours. The punishment testified that God's wrath is brief for him who does penance and is converted to the Lord. Literally the word of the Lord has been fulfilled for Israel: "In the evening weeping shall take place and in the morning gladness." The sufferings which God sends are only of one night after which a new morning follows. But for him who remains faithful to the Lord there is no night that follows the bright day of divine grace.

Happiness, wealth, prosperity, and success are frequently the cause of self-elation and of a sense of false security. David too after all his victories and successes nourished a false sense of security. This he himself confesses in this psalm (verses 7–11). He believed that his prosperity was such a sure thing that he no longer had to fear. He thought that he would continue in this great prosperity. In his proud self-satisfaction he ordered a census to be taken. He no longer considered that it was God who had given him victory over his enemies and who had given to Mount Sion, the center of fortifications, such strength that no enemy would dare to attack him. It was on this account that the Lord let the disastrous plague fall upon him which made him amend his proud sense of security. God, whose favor he reckoned to be a matter of fact, veiled his countenance before him, withdrew his protection, and thus David was very much disappointed. But now David acknowledged that he had taken a false path and had been turned away. In all humility he now acknowledged his helplessness and stretched out his hand to the Lord in prayer, beseeching him to cease in his wrath and not to destroy him. He vowed to the Lord that he would dedicate his life to the praise of his holy Name. Of what profit would it be to the Lord if his servant became victim of a plague which would hurl him into the kingdom of the dead. The dead cannot praise his love and fidelity because sadness reigns in their place. Only the living experience God's kindness and fidelity, only the living can honor God. May the Lord permit grace to prevail and may he prove himself to be a great helper because of the holy and solemn vow

103

which the king, prostrate before the Lord in the dust of the sanctuary, makes for the sake of his people.

God has accepted the vow and commanded the plague to cease immediately. The lamentation is changed into jubilation; now the penitential garb is exchanged for a festive garment and songs of thanksgiving and joyous dances are celebrated because of God's mercy and grace. David's soul rejoiced. This joy shall never again be taken from him in this life. Never again shall this song be silenced in his soul. He will always praise the Lord and thank him.

psalm 30

In te, Domine, speravi

Prayer of a just man under affliction

1. Unto the end, a psalm for David, in an ecstasy.

2. In thee, O Lord have I hoped: let me never be confounded: deliver me in thy justice.

3. Bow down thy ear to me: make haste to deliver me.
   Be thou unto me a God, a protector, and a house of refuge, to save me.

4. For thou art my strength and my refuge: and for thy name's sake thou wilt lead me, and nourish me.

5. Thou wilt bring me out of this snare, which they have hidden for me: for thou art my protector.

6. Into thy hands I commend my spirit: thou has redeemed me, O Lord, the God of truth.

7. Thou hast hated them that regard vanities to no purpose.
   But I have hoped in the Lord.

8. I will be glad and rejoice in thy mercy for thou hast regarded my humility, thou hast saved my soul out of distresses.

9. And thou hast not shut me up in the hands of the enemy: thou has set my feet in a spacious place.

10. Have mercy on me, O Lord, for I am afflicted: my eye is troubled with wrath, my soul, and my belly.

11. For my life is wasted with grief: and my years in sighs.
    My strength is weakened through poverty and my bones are disturbed.

12. I am become a reproach among all my enemies, and very much to my neighbors; and a fear to my acquaintance. They that saw me without fled from me.

13. I am forgotten as one dead from the heart. I am become as a vessel that is destroyed.

14. For I have heard the blame of many that dwell round about. While they assembled together against me, they consulted to take away my life.

15. But I have put my trust in thee, O Lord: I said: thou art my God.

16. My lots are in thy hands. Deliver me out of the hands of my enemies; and from them that persecute me.

17. Make thy face to shine upon thy servant; save me in thy mercy.

18. Let me not be confounded, O Lord, for I have called upon thee.
    Let the wicked be ashamed, and be brought down to hell.

19. Let deceitful lips be made dumb. Which speak iniquity against the just, with pride and abuse.

20. O how great is the multitude of thy sweetness, O Lord, which thou hast hidden for them that fear thee!
    Which thou hast wrought for them that hope in thee; in the sight of the sons of men.

21. Thou shalt hide them in the secret of thy face, from the disturbance of men. Thou shalt protect them in thy tabernacle from the contradiction of tongues.

22. Blessed be the Lord for he hath shown his wonderful mercy to me in a fortified city.

23. But I said in the excess of my mind: I am cast away from before thy eyes. Therefore thou hast heard the voice of my prayer when I cried to thee.

24. O Love the Lord, all ye his saints; for the Lord will require truth, and will repay them abundantly that act proudly.

25. Do ye manfully, and let your heart be strengthened, all ye that hope in the Lord.

I⊤ is difficult to get an idea of the greatness of the physical and mental suffering to which young David was subjected in the time of Saul's persecution. The picture of suffering which he draws in this psalm lets us surmise the sufferings he had to endure which became more severe as time went on. But it is also difficult for a Christian to get a clear understanding of his piety which withstood all storms and of his confidence in God, so firm that in the midst of all tribulation his heart was jubilant. If despite the example of Christ and the greater graces and clearer understanding of the eternal value of suffering we do not attain the heroic confidence of an Old Testament saint, then in shame we should lay aside these sacred songs and kneel down in the next room, and unseen, weep because of our shameful cowardice at the least tribulation (Schegg). The psalm gives us an insight into the great soul of David. His song is a pattern of a genuine prayer of petition in grave need. David appears before the Lord and in spirit casts himself before the tabernacle to make his complaint. But he does not begin with the complaint but with a confession of his confidence. After he has lifted his mind from earthly things into the supernatural realm and his view has become clear through faith, he pictures briefly and succinctly his suffering. After this portrayal follows the pathetic and humble, childlike and trustful petition.

The prayer breaks the bonds that have troubled his heart. The thought of God's goodness fills his soul with consolation and joy; for he is sure that the Lord will hear him. The great sufferer has cast himself in all humility before the tabernacle of his God to seek protection from him; for the Lord alone is the rock for all times. He begins his prayer with a confession of his confidence (verses 2–9). Confidence in God's justice, love, and fidelity are absolute conditions for every prayer of petition if the petitioner expects to be heard. Hope that the prayer will be heard is so much the more justifiable when it is consistent with the divine Justice to give help in the affair and if the need for help is great. He who because of his faith, of his fear of the Lord, and of his position in the kingdom of God is mocked and persecuted, can rely on God's assistance. These reasons justified David in great measure in making his petition because he was hated, calumniated, and persecuted; for the Lord had chosen him to be king and had him anointed king in Saul's place. There is only one thing that he begs from God; namely, that he may no longer delay in extricating him from the encirclement of his enemies, that he may be to him a fortress in which he may conceal himself, a strong fortified house which gives him security. Christ also teaches us to pray for this: "Lead us not into temptation and deliver us from all evil." Deliver us from all enemies and from all dangers to our eternal salvation that surround us in this world.

That God alone can be a protector of the just man is also a reason for confidence in his help. Hounded by Saul and spied upon everywhere there was no security for the life of David, no rock upon which he could save himself, no fortress in which he could take refuge; but there was confidence that the Lord in his mercy would show him the way for his Name's sake. God cannot permit that one whom he has chosen and anointed be always calumniated and persecuted. For the sake of his own honor and for the sake of justice he must defend his servant. The Lord frees him from the snares that had been laid for him. He gives him protection and defense. But the Lord is far more merciful. He is the only security both for the life of the soul and body; For without his grace we can do nothing. This inability, willed by God, constitutes a reason why we should trust in his power and help. God's power and grace is made evident by the weakness of man.

When man in his need surrenders himself to God without reserve and acknowledges no other deliverer but him alone, we find in this submission another motive for confidence. Thus David commended his spirit, his soul, his whole life into the hands of the Lord. God has created and formed him; he is God's work. David again places this work into the hands of his Creator. There it is securely tended; for God loves what he has made and he saves him who puts his trust in him. God is a faithful God who will not disappoint the servant who trusts in the Lord. God hates only those who exchange his glory for worthless idols, who place their hope in superstitious practices, and who do not repay his justice, love, and fidelity with confidence.

David's confidence has its foundation in the numerous gifts and graces he has received in the past. How often was he not in danger when he fled from Saul? But again and again the Lord looked upon his misfortune and freed him. He saw his need and saved him. Now he casts himself down before the face of the Lord mindful of his past help; indeed, his soul rejoices in the memory despite the present affliction which prompted him to approach the tabernacle. He is joyful because of the mercy of the Lord which was so often showed his servant. The thought of the many deliverances from threatening danger, of the deliverances from the encirclement of the enemies is now a consolation. In days of affliction many easily forget the beneficent deeds which God has done previously for them. And regrettably so, for nothing attracts the divine Mercy more than tears of present suffering mingled with thankful joy for past demonstrations of love.

The consideration of the motives that moved the heart of God to grant his merciful help rejuvenated the soul of David and strengthened his confidence in the Lord. With such sentiments the following description of his suffering is given (verses 10–14). It is a cry for divine mercy. Long years of physical and mental sufferings diminish life's vigor. Despite his youth David feels that he has aged. His eyes are weakened because of his many tears. Throughout the years he had to bear much sorrow. Without any assurance that soon there will be an end to his tribulation even the strongest man will finally succumb.

No human consolation being given such troubles finally become unbearable, especially when they are accompanied by a feeling of total abandonment. What the psalmist says of his loneliness is not to be taken altogether literally. It is only a partial picture of his abandonment. The fact that the enemy mocked at him and laughed at his helplessness can be easily understood. Nothing else was to be expected. When men who were his acquaintances, neighbors, friends, and even relatives had no sympathy with him in his sorrow, when they despised him as if he were cursed by God because they did not believe in his innocence, his cross became doubly hard to bear. David had to suffer their defection from him because they were afraid of being suspected by Saul. They made common cause with his enemy because they feared that they might be put to death. The situation was such that it appeared as if all his friends and acquaintances had died. It was a hard trial to be chosen by God, to be king, and yet to be despised as a useless sandal which one throws away in order to be rid of it. If the shepherd had remained in the house of his father, he would, indeed, have remained unknown, but he would have lived happily and in peace. But now his enemies had conspired against him and hated him because of his calling, and continually formed new plots to destroy him. No matter which way he turned, everywhere he met terror and mischief; whatever he heard was mockery, calumny, and threatening words.

Many words are not necessary when a man makes known his sorrow before God; for he knows all about it. Man multiplies words for the sake of his own soul because the vivid description of his needs gives fervor to his prayer. In this fervor David laid bare his sufferings and ended his prayer with a humble and confident petition (verses 15–19). For all his tribulations he did not waver in his confidence in God. "I trust in thee; thou art my God, so I speak." Faith in Yahwe, his God, the all-merciful, almighty, and faithful God, is his indestructible rock, the foundation of his hope, his strong support in all his suffering. The man who believes in God knows that he will not be left to fate, but that his life rests well in God's hands. He knows that nothing will happen to him that the infinite love of God does not want or permit, and that he cannot wish or permit anything which is contrary to his wisdom, justice, and fidelity. The Lord has called David to his kingdom. Therefore he could confidently expect that he would deliver him from all enemies and persecutors and that he would guide him to his destined end. Upon him who is a servant of the Lord, who has been called to his service, God will shine the smile of his countenance. From him who is his faithful and wise servant he will not withdraw his mercy. God will not refuse his aid when asked for grace and help. In his prayer David manifested faith and confidence: "O Lord do not disappoint me when I cry to thee." He who trusts in the Lord will never be disappointed, but the enemies will be disappointed in their hope because God will not grant success to their plans now nor in eternity when they will hear the irrevocable judgment upon their life. When their deceit is made known and their hypocrisy is revealed, they will be silenced. Then they who laughed at the just and persecuted them will be rejected and humbled. They who in their pride mocked others will be subjected to derision eternally.

David did not hope and pray in vain. It is true he was not freed immediately from the persecutions of the enemy, but coming from the tabernacle of the Lord he was consoled and assured that his prayer would be heard. Therefore he ends his prayer with a thanksgiving for the expected answer to his prayer (verses 20–25). He who goes to God for consolation and help experiences how great God's goodness is. There in his tabernacle he has stored up the plenitude of his goodness for those who revere him. The Lord opens the treasures of his infinite love to him who comes to the tabernacle and prays in all confidence that his prayer will be heard. God will show him mercy. He will grant favors to him with such liberality that all men will acknowledge God's goodness and praise him. With his countenance he will protect those who come to him. He will place them under the protection of his gracious presence in the Holy of Holies. The tabernacle becomes a place of refuge where David is protected from the crude rabble of wicked men and against the persecutions of lying tongues. For such love God should be praised at all times. Never should his praise die on the lips of the children of his house; for God proves himself to be a fortress for the just man who takes his every refuge in the Lord. In this city of God mercy and grace will be given to him. Afflictions may beset even the most God-fearing man, making him feel abandoned and rejected by God. David also had to experience such terrible moments which caused him to utter: "My God, my God, why hast thou forsaken me." This only, however, when discouragement and despondency had beset his soul. But reflecting he realized that such moments were only passing trials and that God never refused to grant his petitions.

From this experience all God-fearing people, all members of the kingdom of God, should learn that they must love God at all times with their whole soul, believe in him, and place their trust in him unreservedly. God will not abandon him who remains faithful to him even in his most dire need. But God will make the proud man who relies only on his own powers feel his hand. As exalted as he thought himself to be, so low will he be humbled. From these truths and experiences all should learn to trust in God, should draw new strength from him and give up discouragement; for those who hope in God raise themselves like an eagle toward the sun and do not tire; they walk and do not weaken (Isaias 40:30).

psalm 31

Beati quorum

The second penitential psalm

1. To David himself, understanding.
   Blessed are they whose iniquities are forgiven, and whose sins are covered.

2. Blessed is the man to whom the Lord hath not imputed sin, and in whose spirit there is no guile.

3. Because I was silent my bones grew old; whilst I cried out all the day long.

4. For day and night thy hand was heavy upon me: I am turned in my anguish, whilst the thorn is fastened.

5. I have acknowledged my sin, and my injustices I have not concealed.
   I said I will confess against myself my injustice to the Lord: and thou hast forgiven the wickedness of my sin.

6. For this shall every one that is holy pray to thee in a seasonable time.
   And yet in a flood of many waters, they shall not come nigh unto him.

7. Thou art my refuge from the trouble which hath encompassed me; my joy, deliver me from them that surround me.

8. I will give thee understanding, and I will instruct thee in this way, in which thou shalt go: I will fix my eyes upon thee.

9. Do not become like the horse and the mule, who have no understanding.
   With bit and bridle bind fast their jaws, who come not near unto thee.

10. Many are the scourges of the sinner, but mercy shall encompass him that hopeth in the Lord.

11. Be glad in the Lord, and rejoice, ye just, and glory, all ye right of heart.

AFTER his sin of adultery with Bethsabee and the murder of her husband Urias, King David for a long time tried to conceal his crime from the public eye and even would not admit nor confess it before God and his prophet. Though he tried to quiet pangs of conscience, it was in vain that he strove to obtain peace of mind. Before this, even in the direst hardship he had had peace. He would have finally succumbed both in body and soul in this spiritual conflict if God in his goodness had not showed his mercy and had not released him from this situation through the candid words of the prophet Nathan, if God had not given him the grace and moral courage to sincerely and contritely confess his guilt. In the happiness of regained peace and in thankfulness for the undeserved divine pardon, David composed this psalm. Because of his own experience he wished to teach other sinners how foolish it is to delay a confession of one's guilt until the punishment of God drives one to it. He wished to show what happiness there is in the consciousness of being reconciled with the Lord. The psalm is the second in the series of ecclesiastical Penitential Psalms.

Great is the happiness of regained peace of soul (verses 1–2). Happy is the man who is freed from the bonds of sin. St. Augustine describes this happiness in his confessions: "Thou didst take sin from me and didst enter in its place; thou sweeter than all pleasure, even though not for flesh and blood; thou more brilliant than all light, but spiritually as the most profound mystery, thou more exalted than all honor, but not for those who consider themselves exalted." Such joy and happiness entered the heart of the royal penitent when the prophet Nathan absolved him in the name of the Lord. The introductory words of the psalm sound like an echo of that joy of a soul redeemed from the heavy burden of sin and from the divine wrath: "Happy he whose guilt has been forgiven, whose sins have been remitted." Indeed, happy is the man who has become reconciled to God and now knows that the Lord has dropped his sins into the depths of the sea, that his name has been erased from God's book of guilty souls, and that his misdeeds are no longer subjected to divine punishment. David was permitted to enjoy the happiness of a regenerated life in full measure because no guile remained in his soul. Not only was his confession sincere (otherwise the all-knowing God would not have granted him pardon), he also freed himself from all attachment to the sin he had committed and from the desire of satisfying his wicked propensities. Now he was really free, free from those tangles with which sins bind men, free through the love of God and his grace.

David experienced the happiness of the forgiveness of his sins so much the more because he had for a long time kept his sin a secret and had to taste how evil it was to have offended God, the Lord, grievously. The

111

psalmist gives a warning and admonition to all sinners by his clear instruction about the sting of a bad conscience which had troubled him (verses 3–7). The more his pride deterred him from admitting his twofold crime and the longer he remained silent the more severely his conscience reproached him. He had to experience the truth of the words: "He who conceals his sins will not obtain any blessing" (Proverbs 28:13). It was vain to silence the admonishing voice of God. Weeks and months he resisted better knowledge, until the constant discord in his soul weakened even his bodily powers. All the joy which had so often manifested itself in song and in the playing of his harp had left him. His soul, troubled by his guilt, could only weep and lament. Since the day of his sin the hand of the Lord lay heavily upon him. The thought that the all-just God was angry at him, that the anger of the most high God rested upon him, humbled him. This thought did not give him any rest day and night. It was in vain that he tried to forget his sins. No matter what he would do, the pangs of an evil conscience kept on troubling him. After a long and wearisome battle the resistance to grace was finally broken; his pride was vanquished. When the prophet Nathan approached David in the name of the Lord and chided him for his conduct, the victory was won. Now nothing kept David from making an open confession of his guilt before God and his prophet. As if God in his love were waiting with great longing for the hour of conversion, the king, having begun his confiteor: "I will confess my transgression . . ." heard the consoling words from the mouth of the prophet, "The Lord has forgiven your guilt, thou shalt not die" (2 Kings 12:13).

In view of such experience it is folly for a sinner to refrain from confessing his guilt and to close his lips to a sincere confession. No devout man, no member of the chosen people of God, should attempt to quiet the pangs of conscience, but should pray for the grace of conversion, as long as God is willing to give him this grace, and confess his sins contritely before Yahwe who alone has the power to forgive and to pardon. The admonition of the royal singer is of great value to the devout man of the New Testament, to every member of the Church of Christ because the Lord has entrusted to it the sacrament of reconciliation. May adversities, temptations, and sufferings come upon him, he who is reconciled with God stands upon firm ground. Tempests will not harm him. The waves of destruction cannot hurl him into the abyss. God is his protection. He sustains him even in the greatest need. No matter which way he turns, everywhere the divine Mercy meets him; everywhere the loving divine Providence extends his hands and leads him happily out of all adversity. As long as David lived in the state of sin he was subjected to the wrath of God, but in the state of grace and in union with God, God's love and mercy protect him that he might praise him and be happy.

From the twofold experience which David had under the burden of an unconfessed sin and during the time of happiness of restored peace of soul, in verses 8–11 the psalmist makes the practical application: "Do not delay penance." He addresses his words to the sinner to show him the right way to peace and reconciliation with an outraged God. His eyes are directed to him because he wishes to give him well-meant advice. He who has willfully sinned against God must willingly and unhesitatingly be converted to him and his guilt shall be forgiven. In his sinful condition man should not act like an irrational animal, like a horse or a stubborn mule who stubbornly refuse to be governed. Man may not delay his conversion until God forces him by his punitive justice to mend his ways. Grave punishments await the impenitent sinners; indeed, the gravest of grave punishments when death overtakes them in their impenitence. But he who trusts in the infinite mercy of God and sorrowfully but confidently approaches the all-merciful Lord will obtain pardon for his guilt. God will encompass him with his love and mercy as if he had never sinned. How thankful every devout Israelite must have been who had been called to be a member of a people whose God possessed the power and love to forgive a penitent sinner his guilt! How he must have rejoiced at the fact that God would restore the sinner. But far more blessed are they who are called to the Church of Jesus Christ; for in it flow the healing waters of the holy sacraments that wash away all guilt. Therefore these latter have far more reason to rejoice in the Lord and to be glad because of the grace of elevation as children of God than did the members of the Old Covenant.

psalm 32

Exultate, justi

1. A psalm for David.
   Rejoice in the Lord, O ye just: praise becometh the upright.

2. Give praise to the Lord on the harp; sing to him with the psaltery, the instrument of ten strings.

3. Sing to him a new canticle: sing well unto him, with a loud noise.

4. For the word of the Lord is right: and all works are done with faithfulness.

5. He loveth mercy and judgment: the earth is full of the mercy of the Lord.

6. By the word of the Lord the heavens were established; and all the power of them by the spirit of his mouth.

7. Gathering together the waters of the sea, as in a vessel: laying up the depths in storehouses.

8. Let all the earth fear the Lord and let all the inhabitants of the world be in awe of him.

9. For he spoke and they were made: he commanded and they were created.

10. The Lord bringeth to nought the counsels of the nation: and he rejecteth the devices of people and casteth away the counsels of princes.

11. But the counsel of the Lord standeth forever: the thoughts of his heart to all generations.

12. Blessed is the nation whose God is the Lord: the people whom he hath chosen for his inheritance.

13. The Lord hath looked from heaven: he hath beheld all the sons of men.

14. From his habitation which he hath prepared, he hath looked upon all that dwell upon the earth.

15. He who hath made the hearts of every one of them: who understandeth all their works.

16. The king is not saved by a great army: nor shall the giant be saved by his own great strength.

17. Vain is the horse for safety: neither shall he be saved by the abundance of his strength.

18. Behold the eyes of the Lord are on them that fear him: and on them that hope in his mercy.

19. To deliver their souls from death, and feed them in famine.

20. Our soul waiteth for the Lord: for he is our help and protector.

21. For in him shall our heart rejoice: and in his holy name we have trusted.

22. Let thy mercy, O Lord, be upon us, as we have hoped in thee.

I N THEIR history the chosen people, the kingdom of God of the Old Testament, had won many victories over the Gentile nations which were much more powerful than the kingdom of Israel. They won their battles with the assistance of the Lord and often by his immediate intervention during the battles. We need only to be reminded of the events in the times of Josue, Debbora, Gedeon, Samuel, and David. The thirty-second psalm may have had its origin in a similar victory won by the assistance of God. When in later times they sang this song in the court of the temple, it was done in thankful remembrance of the great past deeds of Yahwe and to keep alive in the people the faith and confidence that in the future also the gates of hell should not prevail against the kingdom of God. Because this promise in its highest sense is meant to refer to the Church of Jesus Christ the psalm should be sung by Christians again and again as an object of meditation. It builds up a faith in the truth of God's word and gives us the confidence that his word will be fulfilled.

The psalmist requests the just and righteous to praise God (verses 1–5). They are by grace the living members of his kingdom. They should make the interests of his covenant their own. They should have an understanding of the sublime acts of God. What he has kept from the worldly-wise, that he has made known to the humble and poor in spirit. Therefore they are capable, worthy, and obligated to sing praises to the invisible king. Their song of thanksgiving should be accompanied by the music of the harp and by the psaltery, the ten-stringed instrument. They should sing a new song to the Lord. Inspired to thank God they should again and again sing praises to God who has done such great deeds for his people; for every deed of deliverance which the Lord has done is important enough to deserve praise by songs accompanied by the sounding of instruments. Every one of God's deeds of deliverance is another testimony and a guarantee that his word is true and that his promise of the eternal existence of his kingdom is reliable. Thus the prophet Isaias said: "Look upon Sion the city of our solemnity: thy eyes shall see Jerusalem, a rich habitation, a tabernacle that cannot be removed: neither shall the nails thereof be taken away forever, neither shall any of the cords thereof be broken. Because only there our Lord is magnificent: a place of rivers very broad, and spacious streams: no ship with oars shall pass by it, neither shall the great galley pass through it. For the Lord is our judge, the Lord is our law-giver, the Lord is our king, he will save us" (Isaias 33:20–22). God loves justice and righteousness; he hates all injustice and brings it before his judgment seat. Everything that is contrary to God's Law cannot continue for any length of time. However God is also mercy and love; the whole earth is filled with his goodness. He is good to all who know him and serve him. The Lord is not only true and faithful in his promises, just and kind, he has also the power to fulfill his promises. He can inflict justice upon his enemies and give loving help to his people. In order to emphasize what he says, the psalmist provides truths for meditation.

The first truth: God is so powerful that with one word he created the world (verses 6–9). The gods of the pagans, according to their legends, have only after severe battles taken from the Titans the rule of the world.

But God with one word has created the world, has called into existence the constellations with the breath of his mouth. Modern astronomy realizes the tremendous meaning of this verse. God with one act of his divine will has brought into existence the constellations consisting of uncountable heavenly bodies in a space the extent of which the human mind cannot measure. God has also given them their law of movement. The second miracle of the divine power of creation is the immense body of water which comprises 70 percent of the earth's surface. In a manner of course and with the ease with which an oriental water-seller fills his bottle made from hide of a goat skin, with water drawn from a well, indeed, without any effort whatever, the Creator has gathered these immense water masses, filled up the deep places, kept the waters, so to say, in storage to give moisture to the land. Should man not fear the almighty power of the Creator; should he not revere his infinite majesty? The Lord speaks through the mouth of the prophet Jeremias: "Will you not fear me; will you not repent at my presence? I have set the sand a bound for the sea, an everlasting ordinance, which it shall not pass over: and the waves thereof shall toss themselves, and shall not prevail: they shall swell and shall not pass over it" (Jeremias 5:22). When God created the world he only said: Let light be made; let the firmament be made; let the stars in the heavens be made; and they appeared and began to fulfill their task. He commanded the earth to bring forth plants in abundance; he commanded and the sea was filled with fishes and animals inhabited the earth. At his command they appeared in great variety. How then could man successfully resist the will of the Almighty?

The second truth: no revolt against the will of God is so great that he cannot put it to naught (verses 10–12). From the beginning of the kingdom of God how many plans were made by the godless to destroy it? How many wars were carried on against Israel after it had gone out of Egypt and since God had chosen it as his people on Mount Sinai? It was in the midst of his people that the Saviour was to appear. The world powers on the Euphrates and the Nile had overrun this little country with their great armies. They could bring great afflictions upon Israel because the Lord wanted it so, but they could not destroy it. God frustrated their plans. The plans of the Lord, however, no human power can frustrate. The divine decree that through Israel the Messianic salvation was to be given to the world remained firm. Even the faithlessness of his chosen people could not upset his plan. Heaven and earth may pass away but his word shall never remain unfulfilled. How happy Israel must have been because the mighty and faithful God had chosen it as his special possession. It did not need to fear for its future existence; it did not need to fear that the glorious promises would not be fulfilled. God does not permit himself to be led into error through his plans of world government. "Happy is the nation whose God is the Lord." This saying may be applied in a greater measure to the Church of the New Covenant; for to it was given the promise by Christ that the gates of hell should not prevail against it.

The third truth: no human activity, however secret, is so hidden that the Lord does not see it (verses 13–15). The Lord is all-knowing. From the great height of heaven he looks down upon the earth and not a single one of the many children of men escape his notice; none could live if he did not supply their wants. His looking down upon the inhabitants of the earth means that he also provides for them, that he guides and leads them by his divine providence. God does not only see men, he also knows their secret thoughts and desires. He himself has created the heart which according to the understanding of the ancient people was the seat of all spiritual activities. Should he not know in all of them their secret thoughts and desires? Nothing can remain concealed from him; no plots against his people and against his kingdom can be concocted which he does not know. He knows all activities and permits them to be carried out only insofar as they are consistent with his eternal decrees.

The fourth truth: God's protection outweighs all human power and strength (verses 16–19). Israel compared to its enemies had only a small army. At the time of David it knew nothing about cavalry or chariots. The kingdom of the New Covenant, the Church of Christ, also possesses no means of defense. Yet of what profit were the 185,000 men to the Assyrian king Sennacherib when he besieged Jerusalem? Of what use was gigantic strength to Goliath? When the general fought against Debora, he had many horses and chariots while the tribes of Israel fought only with swords and bows. But neither chariots nor horses helped him win the victory because the Lord of heaven fought against him. The history of the kingdom of God of the New Testament is also rich in examples of God taking from the hands of earthly powers the weapons which they used against his kingdom. God is never on the side of those who rely on their own powers only; he always defends those who love and worship him, who place all their hopes in his assistance, and in patience wait for his good favor, even when death threatens their life and when famine lies heavy upon the land. Confidence in God never disappoints.

He who in faith has meditated upon these four truths of the psalm will realize that peace is to be found in the confidence he has in the all-powerful, faithful, and merciful God. May times of affliction come upon his kingdom and upon its members, God always remains the helper and the strong shield. He who abides with him shall never be disappointed. He who meditates profoundly upon the greatness, power, fidelity, and love of

God, who reads about them in the book of nature and history will know that the Lord is to him an unfathomable source of true joy. The psalmist saw him do great things and still greater things does he expect from him for his Name's sake. For Yahwe's Name, his majestic nature, is for the people a sufficient reason for its strong faith and hope. The psalm closes with the petition that God may show his mercy to his faithful servant according to the measure of his confidence.

psalm 33

Benedicam Dominum

An exhortation to the praise and service of God

1. For David when he changed his countenance before Achimelech, who dismissed him, and he went his way. (1 Kings 21)

2. I will bless the Lord at all times: his praise shall be always in my mouth.

3. In the Lord shall my soul be praised: let the meek hear and rejoice.

4. O magnify the Lord with me: and let us extol his name together.

5. I sought the Lord, and he heard me: and he delivered me from all my troubles.

6. Come ye to him and be enlightened: and your faces shall not be confounded.

7. This poor man cried, and the Lord heard him: and saved him out of all his troubles.

8. The angel of the Lord shall encamp round about them that fear him: and shall deliver them.

9. O taste and see that the Lord is sweet: blessed is the man that hopeth in him.

10. Fear the Lord, all ye his saints: for there is no want to them that fear him.

11. The rich have wanted, and have suffered hunger: but they that seek the Lord shall not be deprived of any good.

12. Come, children, hearken to me: I will teach you the fear of the Lord.

13. Who is the man that desireth life: who loveth to see good days?

14. Keep thy tongue from evil, and thy lips from speaking guile.

15. Turn away from evil and do good: seek after peace and pursue it.

16. The eyes of the Lord are upon the just: and his ears unto their prayers.

17. But the countenance of the Lord is against them that do evil things: to cut off the remembrance of them from the earth.

18. The just cried, and the Lord heard them: and delivered them out of all their troubles.

19. The Lord is nigh unto them that are of a contrite heart: and he will save the humble of spirit.

20. Many are the afflictions of the just: but out of them all will the Lord deliver them.

21. The Lord keepeth all their bones, not one of them shall be broken.

22. The death of the wicked is very evil: and they that hate the just shall be guilty.

23. The Lord will redeem the souls of his servants: and none of them that trust in him shall offend.

WHEN David was informed by his friend Jonathan of the irreconcilable hatred of Saul, he fled to the Philistine territory in the hope that he would remain unknown and that he could live there in security. He was recognized, however, and brought before Achis, the king of Gath. Achimelech was the common title given to the Philistian kings, just as Pharaoh was the title of the Egyptian kings. To save his life David pretended to be insane. He succeeded in deceiving the king and the latter commanded him to leave his territory immediately. The superscription of this psalm is in agreement with the passage in 1 Kings 21:11–16 where the event is narrated. The passage attributes David's fortunate deliverance to his fear of God. The psalm belongs to the alphabetical psalms and is especially of a didactic character. It urges the practice of the fear of the Lord and indicates the nature and the blessings of this virtue.

Because of the great difference between the creature and God, every single benefaction of God to his creature is an act of infinite condescension and incomprehensible love and as such it is of great importance that the thankful sentiment in the heart of man should never be extinguished. Therefore the psalmist will not cease to thank and praise God for his deliverance. But his thankfulness will not remain concealed in his heart! He shall proclaim that with which his heart is filled in order that others

119

may learn God's goodness, and that they also with him may glorify God. The greatest proofs of the Lord's love are found in the prerogatives of man's soul. Can there be a greater elevation for man than that the infinite God condescends to manifest in man his love and mercy? Therefore the psalmist wishes to proclaim loudly God's mercy and grace. Others also who are visited with sorrow and adversity should hear how good the Lord has been to him in order that they too may call upon him with confidence, and because of this confidence in God, the helper, rejoice and join in the praises of the Lord's mercy. He calls upon all cross-bearers to glorify God with him and to praise his great Name.

He who wants to taste the sweetness of the Lord must put his trust in him. But trust in God can only thrive in a soul which fears the Lord. Hence the psalmist begins his psalm of thanksgiving with a recommendation to fear the Lord (verses 5–11). He himself has experienced its value. In great affliction he sought the Lord in constant trustful prayer and it was not in vain. The Lord delivered him from bad situations and freed him from all fear and anxiety. Everyone who with the same confidence turns to God and seeks him with a lively faith will experience his merciful love. Never will shame and disappointment redden the countenance of one who in joyous hope looks to God for help. His countenance will rather show joy and happiness for having received and experienced so richly God's goodness. From the numberless examples that give testimony to this the psalmist chooses only one. Perhaps he himself is the poor man deprived of all necessities and abandoned by all. When he now looks back to the most difficult years of his life, he can only rejoice and thankfully acknowledge that the Lord has always heard his prayers and has been a helper and guardian in all his great needs. God sends his angels as protectors of his servants. The protection is compared to a strong and equipped army, a fortress upon which every enemy attack fails. Everyone who fears God has an angel as a powerful protector; for the Lord has commanded his angels to carry the just on their hands, as it were, so that not even their feet should stumble upon a stone that lies on the way.

Only the man who fears God has this protection; only he can taste how good the Lord is. The satisfaction which the palate enjoys feasting at a delicious banquet is only a weak likeness to the spiritual satisfaction of the soul when it partakes of the divine Love. The hymn *"Jesu dulcis memoria"* sings of the preciousness of this love when it speaks of the God-Man. "How consoling to the penitent, how mild to those that seek thee, how good to those who present their complaints to thee, but what about those who carry thee in their heart. No tongue can express, no letter can write, only faith alone can help comprehend how great the love of Christ is." Hence the psalmist calls upon all the saints (they are all the members of the chosen people of God) to fear the Lord and to revere him with a thankful love. God will not permit him who fears the Lord to suffer excessive need. The prophet calls the fear of the Lord the greatest treasure (Isaias 33:6). It is possible that a rich man who has acquired wealth cannot enjoy it, that despite his possessions he may famish and suffer from hunger. But it is impossible that a man who fears God, who longs for the knowledge and love of the Lord, who seeks union with him, will lack true good. If he has God and his grace, he has all. Suffering and deprivation mean nothing to him; for the possession of the greatest good and the hope of eternal life outweighs all perishable goods. Hence there is nothing more conducive to this greater wealth than the fear of the Lord.

The psalmist adds a short instruction about the nature of the fear of the Lord (verses 12–15). Those who are longing for salvation he addresses as children. It is the tender address which the Master used in his instructions to the disciples. The fear of the Lord is the beginning of salvation. He who during this earthly life does not want to miss the blessings of God and wishes to enjoy spiritual happiness, who strives for eternal life and a never-ending union with God must walk the way of the fear of the Lord. There is no other way to true and lasting happiness. Many sins are committed by the tongue. It is therefore an established fact that the command to keep one's tongue in check should have the first place. The Apostle James says: "When anyone thinks that he is pious, but does not discipline his tongue, he deceives himself and his piety is mere sham" (James 1:26). "But he who guards his tongue and mouth, keeps his life from tribulation" (Proverbs 21:23). The second demand of the fear of the Lord is the avoidance of evil and the practice of good works. Avoid evil and do good is the summary of all commands and prohibitions, the meaning of obedience to the Law. Only in this way can man find peace. For the godless there is no peace. This peace with God and with oneself is a precious goal which one must seek as a priceless pearl, which one must pursue as a hunter stalks a wild animal.

For the sake of this peace man must fear God and keep his commandments. In order to urge his listeners still more, the psalmist indicates the blessings of the fear of the Lord (verses 16–23). The man who fears God is especially a child of Divine Providence. The pious Jew, Jesus Sirach, speaks strikingly of him: "The spirit of those that fear God is sought after and by his regard shall be blessed; for their hope is in him. He that feareth the Lord shall tremble at nothing, and shall not be afraid; for he is his hope. The soul of him that fears the Lord is blessed. The eyes of the Lord look upon them that fear him. He is a mighty protector" (Sirach 34:14). But the Lord looks wrathfully upon the godless and the anger of offended sanctity and justice means collapse and destruction. "The mourning of men is about their body, but the name of the ungodly shall be blotted out" (Sirach 41:14). It is indeed true that the godless frequently enjoy earthly

121

prosperity while those who fear God are visited with sorrow and adversity. But the Lord lightens the burden that he lays upon them. When they call upon him he hears them and delivers them from their need. When the just man is sick at heart, when spiritual strength is needed, it is then the Lord consoles his servant, helping him and raising his dejected spirit. "According to the multitude of my sorrows in my heart, thy comforts have given joy to my soul" (93:19). The love of God for the just man does not exclude the fact that he will be confronted with sufferings. It is God's very love that sends him trials. "Whom God loves he disciplines as a father does his child which he loves!" (Proverbs 3:12). But the Lord will not permit him to be lost; he will not permit things to come to extremes, but will remove all tribulations before the godless will triumph over him. Even in the midst of the greatest sufferings God looks down condescendingly upon his servant. God guards all his servants so that not one shall perish. This is the precious certainty of a man who fears God. This certainty lifts him above all affliction and gives him strength to bear patiently and to wait until God wills to put an end to his suffering. For the just man, suffering will never be the cause of eternal death, but sin and malice will kill the blasphemer. He who hates the man that fears God must be punished for his hatred; for he who hates him, hates God and he who strikes him strikes the apple of God's eye. But just as death is the punishment of the godless, so also eternal reward will be the lot of those who fear God. God redeems the souls of his servants from all suffering, from all passing sorrows, from all deceptions. For those who fear the Lord death is a deliverance in the true sense of the word. He who trusts in God at all times, who seeks help and consolation from him, who trustingly believes in his power will not rue it for eternity.

psalm 34

Judica, Domine, nocentes me

David in the person of Christ, prayeth against his persecutors: prophetically foreshowing the punishments that shall fall upon them

1. For David himself.
   Judge thou, O Lord, them that wrong me: overthrow them that fight against me.

2. Take hold of arms and shield: and rise up to help me.

3. Bring out the sword, and shut up the way against them that persecute me: say to my soul: I am thy salvation.

4. Let them be confounded and ashamed that seek after my soul.
Let them be turned back and be confounded that devise evil against me.

5. Let them become as dust before the wind: and let the angel of the Lord straiten them.

6. Let their way become dark and slippery; and let the angel of the Lord pursue them.

7. For without cause they have hidden their net for me unto destruction: without cause they have upraided my soul.

8. Let the snare which he knoweth not come upon him; and let the net which he hath hidden catch him: and into that very snare let them fall.

9. But my soul shall rejoice in the Lord; and shall be delighted in his salvation.

10. All my bones shall say: Lord, who is like to thee?
Who deliverest the poor from the hand of them that are stronger than he: the needy and the poor from them that strip him.

11. Unjust witnesses rising up have asked me things I know not.

12. They repaid me evil for good: to the depriving me of my soul.

13. But as for me, when they were troublesome to me, I was clothed with hair-cloth.
I humble my soul with fasting; and my prayer shall be turned into my bosom.

14. As a neighbor and as an own brother, so did I please: as one mourning and sorrowful so was I humbled.

15. But they rejoiced against me, and came together: scourges were gathered together upon me, and I knew not.

16. They were separated, and repented not: they tempted me, they scoffed at me with scorn: they gnashed upon me with their teeth.

17. Lord, when wilt thou look upon me? rescue thou my soul from their malice: my only one from the lions.

18. I will give thanks to thee in a great church: I will praise thee in a strong people.

19. Let not them that are my enemies wrongfully rejoice over me: who have hated me without cause, and wink with the eyes.

20. For they spoke indeed peaceably to me; and speaking in the anger of the earth they devised guile.

21. And they opened their mouth wide against me; they said: Well done, well done, our eyes have seen it.

22. Thou hast seen, O Lord, be not thou silent: O Lord, depart not from me.

23. Arise, and be attentive to my judgment: to my cause, my God, and my Lord.

24. Judge me, O Lord my God according to thy justice, and let them not rejoice over me.

25. Let them not say in their hearts: It is well, it is well, to our mind: neither let them say: We have swallowed him up.

26. Let them blush, and be ashamed together, who rejoice at my evils.
Let them be clothed with confusion and shame, who speak great things against me.

27. Let them rejoice and be glad, who are well pleased with my justice, and let them say always: The Lord be magnified who delights in the peace of his servant.

28. And my tongue shall meditate thy justice, thy praise all the day long.

K ING DAVID prays for divine punishment upon his enemies. However he does not pray as a private person, but as a chosen and anointed king over God's chosen people, as a visible representative of the invisible King. The attacks of his enemies are directed against his position as king. On this account God considers the enemies of his anointed and of his people his own enemies. He has sworn to himself that he would mete out punishment upon them because of their maliciousness. "If I should whet my sword as the lightning and my hand take hold on judgment, I will render vengeance to my enemies and repay them that hate me" (Deuteronomy 32:41). Because the malice of the blasphemers had now gone beyond all bounds, the psalmist wishes to remind the Lord of this oath that he may fulfill it. Many writers have placed the words of this psalm in the mouth of the Messias and the liturgy of the psalm, for the Monday of Holy Week, seems to be dominated by the thoughts of this psalm. The use of this psalm is justifiable insofar as David in his person and in his life is a type of Christ.

The psalmist begins his prayer with the petition that God may appear in judgment against the enemy and prove that he is the God of salvation for his anointed. The comparison of the divine judgment with a battle of God against his and his people's enemies is very common in the Old Testament. Already in the Book of Deuteronomy the Lord speaks through

Moses: "I will make my arrows drunk with blood and my swords shall devour flesh, of the blood of the slain and of the captivity, of the bare head of the enemy" (32:42). In the Book of Wisdom (5:19 seq.) the armor of God is mentioned and stands for his judgment. The armor is his justice; the helmet is his unmistakable judgment; the shield his sanctity; and the sword is his grim wrath. Therefore David clothes his petition with the demand that God may begin his conflict with the enemy. He should take hold of the large and small shield. God is frequently called the Shield of the just, a shield for all who seek his protection (Proverbs 30:5). The petition means: Take thy shield and arms; show thyself a shield to me; grant me thy protection and help. Moreover the Lord should defend him against his enemy with his spear so that he may not dare to do his utmost against his anointed; his grim wrath should strike the enemy that in the future he may not harm him. God should say: I am thy salvation. God's word is infallibly effective. When God has assured man of his salvation, of his help, and of his deliverance from all adversity, then the adversity has already ended.

The petition for punishment is given in detail in the first part of the psalm (verses 4–10). The enemies of the anointed have decided on the last and decisive plot. They now seek his life. But they shall not carry out their intention; they shall find an insurmountable obstacle in God's power and in shame and disgrace they shall depart. Even before they will begin to carry out their nefarious plans, they will take flight before the grim wrath of God like chaff that is blown away by the wind. The angel of the Lord, the protector of the kingdom of God and the executor of his judgment will pursue them so that every trace of them will disappear. Even a hasty flight will not save them from destruction. Their way will be dark. God will strike them with blindness so that they will not see the abyss to which they are hastening. Their way will be slippery; they will trip and fall. The avenging angel of the Lord will not give them a chance for rest.

The enemies have deserved the punishment so much the more because they did not meet David in open warfare; they did not use honest weapons against David, but were treacherous in their recourse to detraction and calumny, by secretly casting suspicion upon him and attacking his honor, by undermining his reputation and causing the people to lose confidence in him that they might bring about his downfall. But their false suspicions and accusations were groundless and could not endure the light of veracity. According to the divine Law of retaliation, by their treachery they will bring destruction upon themselves. They will be caught in the very snares they have laid for the anointed; they will fall into the very pit they have dug for him. This punishment will especially fall upon the leader, the soul of the resistance against David. The judgment will come.

With God's help the persecuted will triumph over the persecutors. Then he will rejoice in the Lord because the malicious enemy did not win the victory despite his strength; for God the all-powerful had vanquished him. Then his entire self, body and soul, will be the herald of the great deeds of God. Where among the gods is there one who will save the weak and helpless from the power of the strong ones on earth? What god will protect the weak from unscrupulous exploitation? Yahwe alone has the power. And it is upon this that the psalmist builds his confidence and unwavering hope.

David reckoned that God's punishment would soon take place because the malice of the enemy had grown beyond bounds (verses 11–18). He sees himself brought before the judgment seat by the enemies to give an account of himself. Detractors stand up against him and question him of things which he knows not. They accuse him of many crimes which he has never committed and which are altogether contrary to his nature. He never did anything wrong to his accusers; he did but good to them; in fact, he was a blessing to them. But now they expel him. He is without a home, lonely, abandoned. He had given shelter to many and had been a friend and helper in every need. David can point to the fact that he had taken a sincere interest in all the cares and sufferings of those who are now heartlessly expelling him.

He sympathized with those who were struck with sickness. He performed acts of penance and by humble incessant prayer he sought to obtain from God the restoration of their health. A friend and a brother could not sympathize more with them in their affliction. He could not do more for them than he had done. His sympathy for them was as true and sincere as that of a mother at the sickbed of her beloved child. But all this tender love did not make an impression on his enemies. When affliction befell him, they had no sympathy; they rather greeted his downfall and were glad of it. Even more they planned to increase his misfortune and plotted to bring about his ruin. They heaped on him injustice after injustice, on him to whom they should have been grateful; they undermined his good reputation and deceived the unsuspecting with hypocritical friendliness. They concealed their real intentions. They placed snares in order to find reasons for accusing him. For all the misfortune which befell him they had bitter ridicule; they gnashed their teeth in hateful glee. For a long time the Lord had looked silently upon the activities of these men and the psalmist now anxiously asks: How long will his patience endure the devilish malice against his servant and how long will he be silent about the triumph of godlessness? The enemies are encircling the anointed and throw themselves upon him like bloodthirsty lions. They want to rob him of his life, his only life. The description of the enemy's malice closes with

126

a vow by David that he will thank the Lord when he has freed him from the power of his opponents. He will thank God not only privately but before the great congregation; he will praise him before all the people; he will praise the name of this Lord before all the world, this Lord who has redeemed him.

In the third part of the psalm (vv. 19–28) we again have a petition for a punishment. If before he has described the malice of the enemy, he now begs God that the malicious may not be triumphant. The opponents of David had begun their animosity in trivial pretense; their hatred against the king had no justifiable reason. He had done great things for his people. He had united them politically and religiously; he had given them peace from within and security from attacks of the neighboring nations; he had subjected the neighboring Gentile nations; he had taken care that the Law was observed and that the religious life was enhanced. The Lord had blessed his work. His successes, however, awakened the envy and jealousy of some of the leaders of his people while others were dissatisfied because under his rule they did not receive any preferences. God cannot permit that such men should triumph over the anointed of the Lord. Their attacks were not only upon the king, but they also stirred up strife and dissatisfaction among the people. Among a satisfied people their plans could not succeed; they had to incite the people and create unrest. Therefore the restlessness of war was carried infectiously to the peaceful who refused to join them in the sickness of their plotting against the king and who wished to live in peace and in the fear of the Lord. These too they persecuted maliciously and unjustly because they would not be of service to them in their criminal intentions. The description of the enemies' malice closes with a vow of David that he will thank the Lord after he has freed him from the power of his enemies. He will praise him before all the people. Before all the world he will praise the God who delivered him.

All this God has seen. Being all wise nothing lies concealed from him. This gives the psalmist the assurance that God will help in due time. He therefore begs God to be silent no longer; he begs that he may no longer delay his help so that crime will no longer triumph. When God in his patience and long-suffering allows the godless to continue and does not punish evil, the poet imaginatively calls the delay "the sleep of God." In Psalm 120 the psalmist says: "He who guards thee does not sleep." The petition therefore that the Lord may awake is an expression meaning that he may no longer close his eyes to the need of his servant but must defend his rights. If God does not judge in favor of his servant, does not defend him and pass punitive judgment upon his enemies and free the persecuted, the godless will rejoice and say: ha! this is altogether according to our wish. We have devoured him. But God cannot permit such triumph of malice. The justice and fidelity of God demand that shame and disgrace fall upon them who rejoice at the misfortune of the anointed, who boast that they can overthrow the king without being punished. But when punishment has been inflicted upon the enemy, the faithful followers of David who defend him in his right will rejoice. They will recognize God's justice and fidelity to his promise when he punishes the criminals and gives victory to the king, when he seeks the welfare of his anointed and not his destruction.

psalm 35

Dixit injustus

The malice of sinners and the goodness of God

1. Unto the end, for the servant of God, David himself.

2. The unjust hath said within himself, that he would sin: there is no fear of God before his eyes.

3. For in his sight he hath done deceitfully, that his iniquity may be found unto hatred.

4. The words of his mouth are iniquity and guile: he would not understand that he might do well.

5. He hath devised iniquity on his bed, he hath set himself on every way that is not good: but evil he hath not hated.

6. O Lord, thy mercy is in heaven, and thy truth reacheth even to the clouds.

7. Thy justice is as the mountains of God, thy judgments are a great deep. Men and beasts thou wilt preserve, O Lord.

8. O how hast thou multiplied thy mercy, O God: But the children of men shall put their trust under the covert of thy wings.

9. They shall be inebriated with the plenty of thy house: and thou shalt make them drink of the torrent of thy pleasure.

10. For with thee is the fountain of life: and in thy light we shall see light.

11. Extend thy mercy to them that know thee, and thy justice to them that are right of heart.

12. Let not the foot of pride come to me: and let not the hand of the sinner move me.

13. There the workers of iniquity are fallen; they are cast out and could not stand.

THERE are two great mysteries on earth that stand in opposition to one another. The one has its source in hell, the other comes from heaven. They are the mysteries of sin and grace. The psalmist speaks of both, not in general terms, but in their effects upon men.

He first describes the mystery of sin (verses 2–5). He does this that the glories of divine grace may shine forth more brilliantly upon the dark background of human wickedness. He describes sin in its deepest source, in its seductive nature, and in its corruptive effects. As the just man is influenced in his thoughts, words, and actions by his love for God so the godless men are influenced by the Satanic power of sin. Sin has taken possession of them; it dominates their thoughts and desires and their whole life. How does sin come to such regency? For the soul the fear of God is the protecting wall against this uncanny enemy. The Book of Proverbs says: "Through the fear of the Lord one avoids evil" (Proverbs 16:6). Again: "By the fear of the Lord one hates sin" (Proverbs 8:13). And Jesus Sirach writes: "The fear of the Lord dispels sin; he who is without the fear of the Lord will never be a just man" (Ecclesiasticus 1:27). When this protecting wall has fallen, Satan takes possession of the soul. Sin is the more dangerous because of its enticing and seductive nature; it deceives man in regard to its destructiveness. It convinces the sinner that God is not concerned about the doings of men and to the godless it speaks in the words of Malachias: "He laboreth in vain that serveth God. And what profit is it that we have his ordinances and that we have walked sorrowfully before the Lord of hosts. Wherefore now we call the proud people happy; for they that work wickedness are built up and they that tempted God are preserved" (Malachias 3:14–15). What the godless speak is wicked and false and what they do is evil. They do not know how to act wisely and well. Isaias describes their activity as follows: "There is none that calleth upon justice, neither is there anyone that judgeth truly: but they trust in a mere nothing, and speak vanities: they have conceived labor and brought forth iniquity: their works are unprofitable works, and the work of iniquity is in their hands: their feet run to evil, and make haste to shed innocent blood: their thoughts are unprofitable thoughts: wasting and destruction are in their ways. They have not known the way of peace and there is no judgment in their steps: their paths are become crooked to them; everyone that treadeth in them, knoweth no peace" (Isaias 59:4ff.). By night the evil man plans destruction

129

against his neighbor and during the day he seeks to carry out his plans. Finally there is no crime from which the sinful man is not deterred.

With the mystery of sin the psalmist contrasts the mystery of grace (verses 6–10) and describes its glory in a spiritual hymn. Grace in its effect is a consequence of God's love. He who wishes to appreciate its value must appreciate the infinity of God's fidelity. For this there is no earthly measure. Can a man measure the distance between earth and heaven or the heights of the clouds over land and sea? God's love from which grace emanates is greater than heaven, is immeasurably high above the earth, and his fidelity is more sublime than the lofty clouds themselves. If anyone would want to appreciate fully the value of grace, he would have to understand God's justice and the infinite wisdom of his decrees. The justice which justifies man and gives him grace is anchored in God's nature as the eternal mountains are anchored to the depths of the ocean. And his decrees which from eternity have determined the ways of grace are the fruit of a wisdom and knowledge that are broader and deeper than the world's ocean. Adding to this, God's goodness is so inexhaustible that it distributes eternally its gifts to all creatures, to men and animals alike.

In this divine love, the breadth, length, height, and depth of which only God can fathom, men may seek protection as a young bird seeks shelter in the shadow of the wings of its mother. How precious is grace! It makes man the special object of Divine Providence and heavenly protection. It gives him a portion of all the goods and joys of the house of God. It nourishes him with the best and gives him to drink of the infinite stream of God's heavenly joy. If already the just man of the Old Covenant acknowledged and praised grace as a nourishment from God and as a replenishment of heavenly joy even though he could not understand so profoundly the spiritual wealth and beauty of grace as the just man of the New Covenant, how much greater should not the Christian appreciate the value of grace. In a much greater measure is grace the source of spiritual life in the New Covenant, a life in which we see God's light. The just man of the Old Covenant knew not only a spiritual life which consisted in obedience to the commandments, but also a higher life which consisted in the participation of the divine Life. The spiritual life he could lead, but the higher life he could only obtain when God gave him the grace. Grace raised him far above the natural life. But he had no idea of the greatest of graces; namely, the grace that was the source of supernatural life, of a life that raises the recipient to the family of God, that makes him God-like. The just man of the Old Covenant saw in the aura of grace the divine light. Revelation permitted him to know something of the providence and nature of God who is the light and in whom there is no darkness. But to us the light shines much brighter because of the revelations made by Jesus Christ and in this light we can see more clearly him who dwells in inaccessible light.

Grace is not a possession that cannot be lost; therefore, the psalmist concludes his hymn with the petition that God may continue to love them who love and praise him, that he may manifest his justice to all, that he may give grace and salvation to all who with a sincere heart seek him and long for him. The man of grace is confronted with grave dangers from a proud world and from wicked men. Should God subject the just man to the malice of sin and through it bring about his fall? This will never happen. With a lively faith in God's love and with a glad hope the psalmist sees the downfall of his enemies, of the enemies of his salvation. Those who have sought the ruin of the just man have themselves fallen. Those who have sought to deprive him of his union with God have themselves been rejected eternally. They will never rise from the abyss.

psalm 36

Noli aemulari

An exhortation to despise this world, and the short prosperity of the wicked, and to trust in Providence

1. A psalm for David himself.
   Be not emulous of evildoers: nor envy them that work iniquity.

2. For they shall shortly wither away as grass, and as the green herbs shall quickly fall.

3. Trust in the Lord, and do good, and dwell in the land, and thou shalt be fed with its riches.

4. Delight in the Lord, and he will give thee the requests of thy heart.

5. Commit thy way to the Lord, and trust in him, and he will do it.

6. And he will bring forth thy justice as the light, and thy judgment as the noonday.

7. Be subject to the Lord and pray to him. Envy not the man who prospereth in his way; the man who doth unjust things.

8. Cease from anger, and leave rage; have no emulation to do evil.

9. For evildoers shall be cut off; but they that wait upon the Lord, they shall inherit the land.

10. For yet a little while, and the wicked shall not be: and thou shalt seek his place, and shalt not find it.

11. But the meek shall inherit the land, and shall delight in abundance of peace.

12. The sinner shall watch the just man: and shall gnash upon him with his teeth.

13. But the Lord shall laugh at him: for he foreseeth that his day shall come.

14. The wicked have drawn out the sword: they have bent their bow, to cast down the poor and needy, to kill the upright of heart.

15. Let their sword enter into their own hearts, and let their bow be broken.

16. Better is a little to the just, than the great riches of the wicked.

17. For the arms of the wicked shall be broken in pieces; but the Lord strengtheneth the just.

18. The Lord knoweth the days of the undefiled; and their inheritance shall be forever.

19. They shall not be confounded in the evil time; and in the days of famine they shall be filled:

20. Because the wicked shall perish. And the enemies of the Lord, presently after they shall be honored and exalted, shall come to nothing and vanish like smoke.

21. The sinner shall borrow, and not pay again: but the just showeth mercy and shall give.

22. For such as bless him shall inherit the land: but such as curse him shall perish.

23. With the Lord shall the steps of a man be directed, and he shall like well his way.

24. When he shall fall he shall not be bruised, for the Lord putteth his hand under him.

25. I have been young, and now am old; and I have not seen the just forsaken, nor his seed seeking bread.

26. He showeth mercy, and lendeth all the day long, and his seed shall be in blessing.

27. Decline from evil and do good, and dwell forever and ever.

28. For the Lord loveth judgment, and will not forsake his saints: they shall be preserved forever.
The unjust shall be punished, and the seed of the wicked shall perish.

29. But the just shall inherit the land, and shall dwell therein forevermore.

30. The mouth of the just shall meditate wisdom: and his tongue shall speak judgment.

31. The law of his God is in his heart, and his steps shall not be supplanted.

32. The wicked watcheth the just man, and seeketh to put him to death.

33. But the Lord will not leave him in his hands: nor condemn him when he shall be judged.

34. Expect the Lord and keep his way: and he will exalt thee to inherit the land: when the sinner shall perish thou shalt see.

35. I have seen the wicked highly exalted, and lifted up like the cedars of Libanus.

36. And I passed by, and lo, he was not: and I sought him and his place was not found.

37. Keep innocence, and behold justice: for there are remnants for the peaceable man.

38. But the unjust shall be destroyed together: the remnants of the wicked shall perish.

39. But the salvation of the just is from the Lord, and he is their protection in the time of trouble.

40. And the Lord will help them and deliver them: and he will rescue them from the wicked, and save them, because they have hoped in him.

DISPARITY between the prosperous life of the godless and the life of poverty of the just frequently exists. For the faithful members of the chosen people it was a severe test of their faith in God's justice and of their confidence in his promises; for the Lord had solemnly promised his blessings, both spiritual and corporal, for the family, home, and field, to those who would remain obedient to his Laws, but upon those who would be faithless he uttered a curse (Deuteronomy 5:28). With the increasing clearness of the future the Messianic picture, the expectation of an equalization in the fullness of time, became more vivid and solved the problem of the sufferings of the just. But there still remained bad feeling among the lower classes. The composer of the Book of Job has taken up the question and pointed out the disciplinary value of suffering. In this alphabetical song the psalmist has also taken a stand in this regard. He wishes to show that the disparity is only apparent and limited in time and that jealousy of the good fortune of the godless is foolish and without foundation.

It is foolish for anyone to excite himself about the fact that wicked men prosper, that they acquire wealth and influential positions, and that all their undertakings prosper because the good fortune of the sinner is only for a time (verses 1–6). All earthly possessions are not lasting. These possessions can be lost quickly through death or other happenings. They can be lost as quickly as they have been acquired. Their insecurity might be compared to the perishability of grass and of the herb in the field. Under the influence of the winter rain they sprout and grow up and in a short time cover the fields with luxuriant green. But as soon as the south-east wind with its withering heat blows over it or the summer drouth comes, they wither and lie dried up on the ground. On the contrary it is wise to put one's trust in God and to keep the commandments even when God's blessing is delayed. It is wise to remain in the land and to progress in faithfulness to the Lord and the Covenant. The psalmist does not give to the word "land" a strictly geographical meaning, but a spiritual and religious signification. He means the place of union with God, the Messianic kingdom, the temple of the Old Covenant. He who does not strive inordinately for perishable goods, but has his joy in God alone will be truly joyful and satisfied; for only God can satisfy the human heart. All earthly pleasures leave the soul dissatisfied. When man has freed himself from all inordinate attachment to the things of this world and finds pleasure in God alone, he always sees his wishes fulfilled; for he desires nothing that is contrary to the Divine Will, nothing that the Lord would have to deny him. Of what use is it to fret and worry about the cross which the Lord lays upon the shoulders of the just man? Is it not better to leave everything in the hands of Divine Providence? Is it not better to leave the way, the life with its thoughts and endeavors, its work and suffering in God's hands? The Lord guides him in wisdom and love who confidently gives himself up to his guidance. The Lord will always lead us to what is best for us. When the man who fears God is accused of injustices, when suspicions are cast upon him or when he is calumniated, God will see to it that justice is done to him, that his innocence will come to light; and then his innocence will be held in honor by men so much the more. If his rights have been taken from him or curtailed, it will come to light as the light of the noonday sun.

It is foolish to become excited about the good fortune of the godless. For the true value of life is to be judged according to its purpose (verses

7–15). It is God himself who brings happiness and sorrow according to his own good will. If he allows tribulation and adversity to come upon his servant, he should carry his burden quietly and willingly; he should bear the sufferings laid upon him by the Lord and wait patiently until it pleases God to deliver him from them. He should not become excited when good fortune comes to cheaters, schemers, and other evil men. It is God's business to distribute his goods and not the affair of man. Of what use is it to become angry at inequality and hold a grudge against the rich and against those who live in luxury? Such dissatisfaction and anger only leads to sin. It is wrong to murmur because God is good to such who according to human reckoning are undeserving of his goodness. God is free to do as he wills. And yet he is not unjust; for at some time or other things will be equalized. When the final judgment will come, the godless will be separated. For them there will be no room in the congregation of the saints. Those however who are submissive and in their troubles trust in the Lord will be heirs of the land, of the Messianic promise, and of heavenly happiness. It will be only a short time until all the wealth of the godless, all their prosperity, all their renown will come to an end. The rich, the prosperous, and those of repute will disappear from this world and will soon be completely forgotten. Even the place where they lived will be completely obliterated. But the just man who suffers and quietly submits to the will of God, who magnanimously endures his suffering and conforms his will to the will of God will inherit the land, will enjoy the blessings of the Messianic kingdom, will be refreshed with the plenitude of beatific salvation. Therefore the just man has no reason to be jealous of the perishable fortune of the godless.

It is true that the just man must suffer from the unscrupulousness and heartlessness of evil men. Because his faithfulness to the Law and his God-fearing life are a continual reproach to their fruitless endeavors they gnash their teeth at him in their grim hatred. But even this is no reason for murmuring and complaining; for they who persecute the just man will not escape punishment. God sometimes permits the persecution of his servants, but not because he is unable to hinder the enemies' activities. Evil men may boast about their power, but God in heaven laughs at their presumption. He permits them to do as they please for some time, but the day of their punishment is already determined; he sees the hour of punishment approaching. The enemies of the just are men who fear no act of violence. They draw the sword and bend the bow; they attack him openly to bring about his downfall or they persecute him secretly like the hunter who kills the wild animal from the rear with his bow. They have only one purpose in mind; namely, to cause the downfall of every man who walks the just way of the Law. But their violent deed finally redounds upon themselves. God frequently punishes the sinner by the very sins which he commits. The sword that he has drawn against others pierces his own heart; his crime will be to him a punishment and ruination. His bow will be broken before the arrow can be on its way to pierce the victim. God frustrates the attempt to injure the just.

Moreover it is foolish for a just man in his poverty to envy the godless because of their wealth. Small possessions and virtue are more precious than wealth and sin (verses 16–26). The psalmist contrasts the modest possession and position of the God-fearing man with the luxury and reputation of the godless. Faith and experience have taught him that virtue surpasses all wealth and reputation in value and compensates for the want of earthly possessions. In view of death the worthlessness of all perishable things and the value of what is eternal is easily seen. How quickly the arm of the sinner breaks! How easily everything collapses that gave him power and support in life! Wealth, position, reputation, and health! In one day all these things can perish. Even when one has enjoyed all these things to the end of his life, death takes everything away; nothing of all these things follow him into the grave. But the arm of the just man never breaks; for God himself is his arm: the Lord is his support which never breaks down. "Be not afraid, when a man shall be made rich, and when the glory of his house shall be increased. For when he shall die he shall take nothing away: nor shall his glory descend upon him" (Psalm 48:17–18). God knows the days of his just ones, he knows all the changes in their lives, he knows every moment in their existence. Because he knows them, he blesses them and enters them in the book of life for eternal rewards. No anxiety, no suffering, no worries are forgotten. Even if evil days shall fall upon the just, their confidence in God's providence will not disappoint them. When famine befalls a country or scarcity occurs so that even the rich must go hungry, the Lord will feed his just ones as he fed the prophet Elias in a miraculous manner in the home of the widow of Sarepta.

How different is the fate of the godless! Isaias has strikingly given the contrast: "Behold my servants shall eat and you shall grow hungry; behold my servants shall rejoice and you shall be confounded; behold my servants shall praise for joyfulness of heart and you shall cry for sorrow of heart and shall howl for grief of spirit" (Isaias 65:13–14). How beautiful is a valley, the valley of Sharon, in the springtime of the year when all is in blossom; but when the south wind blows, all beauty vanishes. This is a description of the fate of the wicked. Today blooming life; tomorrow they are struck by the glowing breath of the divine wrath; all glory has faded. As a cloud of smoke is taken up by a slight wind and is dispersed and disappears, so the eternal Lord puts an end to the prosperity of the wicked. Their possession falls from their hands. One single misfortune can make them beggars so that they do not have even enough to pay back a loan or escape slavery because of debt. There is no blessing upon wealth that has been dishonestly obtained. But the just man can well distribute his modest income and even then will not be poor. The more he gives, the more abundantly God bestows his blessings. But they who are blessed by the Lord will inherit the land of promise. They will be accepted into the Messianic kingdom and will enter into the possession of the heavenly inheritance. But the Lord curses the godless; they will have no portion of the promised inheritance, they will be cast out and will be abhorred by all the world. They will inherit the wind.

God carefully guides the steps of all that are pleasing to him. He guides them to the glorious end of the Messianic and heavenly inheritance. He takes them, as it were, by the hand so that they will not miss their glorious purpose. If despite all this anyone will stumble on the way or if he will have the misfortune of assenting to sin, God will not permit his fall. His hand will support him that he may again take courage and walk along the path of virtue with a firm step. The psalmist from his own experience knows and can prove that God will not abandon a just man, that the Lord will even permit his children and his children's children to partake in the fruits of his piety. For a time he may suffer need, for God permits this as a trial. However it has never been heard that a just and God-fearing man was completely impoverished and that his children had to beg for bread. Even if he is not rich, he still has so much that he can give to others and can mitigate other's sufferings. This spirit of kindness we find in his descendants so that they are a blessing for their time and surroundings.

The sinner is not to be envied because he is rich and can satisfy all his desires, but the just man should be envied; for only virtue makes one truly happy (verses 27–36). We find true spiritual and lasting happiness only in the land of the Lord in union with God. "The learned in word shall find good things: and he that trusteth in the Lord is blessed" (Proverbs 16:20). Only the just man can live in a blessed union with God. He who does not want to be rejected from this earthly paradise must avoid sin and practice virtue. For God loves justice and, therefore, also loves men who constantly practice justice, virtue, and obedience to the Law. For this reason he does not abandon the pious. The godless shall be destroyed; they must depart to a distance from God eternally, but the God-fearing will continue their existence forever with God; for "the just shall live forevermore and their reward is with the Lord and the care of them with the Most High" (Wisdom 15:16). The patient sufferers will possess the land which is now dominated by godlessness. They are called to rule in the Messianic kingdom and they will be citizens of this kingdom and will enjoy its blessings for all eternity.

Even now the just man is abundantly blessed and his life has a greater spiritual value than all the joys of the sinner. He can give answer to the greatest and most profound questions that trouble the life of a man and for which a child of the world knows no answer. His mouth speaks wisdom. He knows the answers to the questions about God, his nature, and his works. He knows about the origin of the world and its highest purpose; he can answer questions about the origin of man and about the purpose of his existence; he knows the meaning of his earthly existence. He does not only sense the problem of evil, he also knows the source of evil and the consequences of it. The tongue of the just man also speaks what is right. He knows what is right and in his speech he is independent of time, place, and the opinion of men; he knows that right binds all the inhabitants of the earth, that there is an absolute norm of morality upon which the order of society is based. This sublime knowledge, free from all error and hypocrisy, he obtains from the Law of God. This Law is not mere superficial material for knowledge; it is written in his heart; it is the norm for his union with God. His own will and endeavors do not make the Law. Therefore he does not falter in his steps whilst the godless meander through life without a purpose. The clearness of the knowledge of his purpose in life and of the way he has to walk gives him a peace and security in his progress which must make the man of the world envious.

The godless spy upon the just man and seek to take his life; they drag him before the courts in order to accuse him of guilt. They may pronounce him guilty and pass punitive judgment upon him, but before God this judgment has no value; for him it does not exist. Therefore he does not leave the accused in the power of his enemies. To these truths the psalmist adds the admonition that in all conditions and difficulties they should confide in the Lord and never abandon the way of the commandments and of fidelity to the covenant. Him, who perseveres, the Lord will exalt over his enemies. He will give him undisturbed possession of the land of which the evil man claimed to be the absolute possessor. The prosperity of the enemies of God is of short duration. The psalmist can prove this by his own experience. He knows of an unbelieving man, rich and powerful, and well-established like a mighty cedar of Lebanon. But soon this proud cedar was overthrown. Wealth, power, and reputation were all lost. There was not a splintered trace of his former greatness.

The psalmist closes with a practical application (verses 37–40). He who wishes to obtain lasting happiness should not walk the way of sin. It will not lead him to salvation. Man should keep his conscience free of

138

all guilt and beware of every injustice against God and man. Then at the end of his life when he reviews his past he may peacefully look ahead to the future. The just man may enjoy his life in spiritual peace. His salvation is secured; for it is given by the Lord, the true and faithful God. He cannot find a better guarantor for the future. God is also not only a guarantor for the future, he is also a refuge and saviour in every present need. When afflictions come from which God does not spare his people and cannot spare them, he stands at their side supporting and consoling them; he delivers them from the power of the enemy; he saves them. When the danger is greatest, he delivers them. When the enemy believes himself sure of success, then does the Lord all these things for those who trust in him without reserve.

psalm 37

Domine, ne in furore

A prayer of a penitent for the remission of his sins. The third penitential psalm

1. A psalm for David, for a remembrance of the Sabbath.

2. Rebuke me not, O Lord, in thy indignation: nor chastise me in thy wrath.

3. For thy arrows are fastened in me: and thy hand hath been strong upon me.

4. There is no health in my flesh, because of thy wrath: there is no peace for my bones, because of my sins.

5. For my iniquities have gone over my head: and as a heavy burden are become heavy upon me.

6. My sores are putrified and corrupted, because of my foolishness.

7. I am become miserable, and am bowed down even to the end: I walked sorrowful all the day long.

8. For my loins are filled with illusions: and there is no health in my flesh.

9. I am afflicted and humbled exceedingly: I roared with the groaning of my heart.

10. Lord, all my desire is before thee: and my groaning is not hidden from thee.

11. My heart is troubled, my strength hath left me: and the light of my eyes itself is not with me.

12. My friends and my neighbors have drawn near, and stood against me: And they that were near me stood afar off.

13. And they that sought my soul used violence.
And they that sought evils to me spoke vain things, and studied deceits all the day long.

14. But I as a deaf man, heard not: and as a dumb man not opening his mouth.

15. And I became as a man that heareth not: and that hath no reproofs in his mouth.

16. For in thee, O Lord, have I hoped: thou wilt hear me, O Lord my God.

17. For I said: Lest at any time my enemies rejoice over me, and whilst my feet are moved, they speak great things against me.

18. For I am ready for scourges: and my sorrow is continually before me.

19. For I will declare my iniquity: and I will think for my sin.

20. But my enemies live, and are stronger than I: and they that hate me wrongfully are multiplied.

21. They that render evil for good, have detracted me, because I followed goodness.

22. Forsake me not, O Lord my God: do not thou depart from me.

23. Attend unto my help, O Lord, the God of my salvation.

THE third ecclesiastical Penitential Psalm most likely bears upon the twofold crime which David committed against Bethsabee and Urias. Since the time of this twofold crime, misfortune upon misfortune has fallen upon the royal penitent. The child of his sin had to die. His son Amnon raped his own sister and was therefore murdered by his brother Absalom and the latter rebelled against his father in order to take from him his kingdom. The king had to flee into the desert in order to save his life. Nearly the entire nation had broken with him and refused loyalty to him. Then David realized how great a crime he had committed and that God was angry at him. And this troubled him more than the loss of his children. He then turned to God in prayer and besought him from the depth of his soul to free him from the curse of his wrath and receive him again in his favor. What the psalmist experienced in body and soul is a type of the misery which mankind had suffered since the days of original sin and the psalm becomes a prayer for all children of Adam for redemption and reconciliation.

The prayer begins like the first Penitential Psalm with the suppliant petition that God may not punish his sin in his wrath but in fatherly love. The contrite petitioner does not ask that the deserved punishment be remitted and not even mitigated; for he must acknowledge that God is just in his judgments (Tobias 3:2). He only wishes that God will not punish him in his wrath and that by his penitential suffering God will heal him and be reconciled to him in merciful love.

The petition in the first part of this psalm (verses 3–9) has for its object the misery of sin which is compared to a grave sickness. For David himself the portrayal was not a clear picture and it is also not for any sinner; for sin brings misery to soul and body. Like arrows which deeply pierce the flesh the divine visitations struck the heart of David. God's punishing hand struck and lay heavily upon him. All the manifold evils that have come into the world as a result of sin are likened to painful arrows. Since the original sin in paradise the hand of the Lord lies heavily upon the human race. The consciousness of not being guided by Divine Providence, but of being pursued by the divine wrath man cannot long endure, neither spiritually nor physically. At some time or other all strength and energy must break down. And thus it appeared to David that a grave sickness afflicted his body. "There is no health in my flesh because of thy wrath; there is no peace for my bones, because of my sins." Mankind suffering from the consequences of original sin is compared to a sick body bleeding from a thousand wounds. What Isaias says of his own people may be said of mankind in general: "The whole head is sick, and the whole heart is sad. From the sole of the foot unto the top of the head there is no soundness: wounds and bruises, and swelling sores: they are not bound up, nor dressed, nor fomented with oil" (Isaias 1:5–6). Who will be astonished about this condition when David had to acknowledge that his iniquities had gone over his head and lay upon him as an unbearable burden. The world still unredeemed, as St. Paul portrays it in his Epistle to the Romans, has sunk so deeply that sin and crime cover it like the muddy waters of a swamp. And as they preferred not to have God in their knowledge, God delivered them up to a reprobate sense. The world sighs under the weight of a guilt which it can never erase.

As long as David had not fully gotten rid of the folly of his sin and had not realized the greatness of his guilt, as long as God was still angry, so long he could not close the wounds inflicted by sin. And without the proper care they will fester. In a world which does not want to admit the real need of humanity, follies and blindness are added to the burden of

141

guilt. Thus the wounds inflicted by sin remain open and the growing moral corruption festers and becomes more and more difficult to heal. Guilt, however, does not only bring about spiritual sickness, it is also a soporific of joy. David had to admit that since he had fallen into sin and guilt bothered his conscience, he no longer had a day of joy. Sad and with bowed head he walked along like a broken man. Lack of genuine cheerfulness is also the sign of the unredeemed and of a generation estranged from God. Sin brings misery upon nations. Man needs the happiness of a good conscience for spiritual health and for union with God. He cannot deprive himself of this union with God for any length of time without grave injury to his soul. Just as a continued fever robs the body of strength and vigor of life and affects the members and organs, so also sin and the glow of the divine wrath affect the soul. Sin with its uncanny power acts like a cancer which gradually affects the entire man. All willingness to higher and nobler endeavor is put to naught. But the spirit of man is not contented with this. The heart is restless and longs for spiritual health, peace, and reconciliation; and from the troubled soul there comes a cry for redemption. The many sacrifices of the pagans, the killing of their own children to reconcile their gods, the eternal unrest of a godless world give testimony that the heart desires peace and redemption.

Health of soul and reconciliation with God are always possible as long as there is still a desire for true redemption. To prove this is the purpose of the second strophe of the psalm (verses 10–15). David's soul was filled with the desire for redemption. God knew his desire for peace and heard his sighs for reconciliation. But as St. Paul says in his Epistle to the Romans: "There is a longing and a sighing for redemption throughout all creation subjected to the slavery of destruction, a seeking for peace and a weeping because of the lost happiness of life" (Romans 8:22). The more the intellect comes to the understanding that God alone can redeem and that all endeavors of self-redemption are fruitless, so much the more will the heart seek peace with God.

Sin's work of destruction is very great. Under the burden of his guilt David felt himself old and broken, his strength weakened. In vain does the world attempt to seek redemption by its own power; all endeavors are futile. Its spiritual outlook has disappeared so that it can scarcely see a glimmer of hope.

Who can eliminate the misery of sin? All men, even the best acquaintances and friends cannot remove the stain of sin; no human power can free us from the misery of sin. David too had to experience this. He did not wish to say that all his friends had abandoned him because six hundred men remained faithful to him and followed him into the desert and were sympathetically concerned about him. But they could do nothing about his spiritual need and his guilt. His friends could not help him and his enemies mocked and calumniated him; they laid snares for him in order to bring about his fall and they did not shun lying and detraction to complete his fall. And to all this David had to remain silent because he had become guilty in the sight of his supreme Lord. He felt himself a deaf and dumb man who could not defend himself. Without being able to contradict he had to endure all suffering. So also the world cannot complain about the suffering which the powers of hell have inflicted upon it, but must be mindful of its guilt.

If David had to remain silent to men because of his guilt, he could, nevertheless, cry to God for help and expect that his prayer would be heard; for God will redeem (verses 16–23). With this confidence he awaited God's favor. God's grace is also the light which shines into the darkness of unredeemed paganism. The psalmist bases his confidence on four reasons. God cannot help the enemies of the anointed; for to him he had given the glorious promise of the future in order to promote his own glory. God cannot permit his downfall lest the enemies may triumph. God cannot permit the power of hell to frustrate his plan of salvation. God will redeem because without his merciful help man will succumb to the power of hell. If God withdraws his protecting arm, the sinner can fall deeply at any moment and it will be impossible for him to rise from the fall without God's help. If God does not help, then the pang of guilt remains eternally. But he who confesses his sins and is sorry for them will by God's mercy be freed from their bonds; for a contrite and humbled heart God will not despise. Confession and contrition are indispensable conditions for pardoning. Our Lord will have mercy upon a contrite soul. The more powerful the enemies become, the greater will be their hatred, the greater will be the desire to bring about his fall, the greater will be the injustice which they commit, and the stronger will be their aversion to him who is hated. Despite these four reasons for hope in redemption, this psalm closes not as the first and second penitential psalms did with an expression of joyful confidence, but with a suppliant petition that God may not abandon the petitioner, that he may remain near him and hasten to help and save him. The psalm closes with the fundamental thought of the entire psalm that without God there is no redemption.

psalm 38

Dixi custodiam

*A just man's peace and patience in his sufferings: considering
the vanity of the world, and the providence of God*

1. Unto the end, for Idithun himself, a canticle of David.

2. I said: I will take heed to my ways: that I sin not with my tongue.
I have set a guard to my mouth, when the sinner stood against me.

3. I was dumb, and was humbled, and kept silence from good things: and my
sorrow was renewed.

4. My heart grew hot within me: and in my meditation a fire shall flame out.

5. I spoke with my tongue: O Lord, make me know my end.
And what is the number of my days: that I may know what is wanting to
me.

6. Behold thou hast made my days measurable: and my substance is as
nothing before thee.
And indeed all things are vanity: every man living.

7. Surely man passeth as an image: yea, and he is disquieted in vain.
He storeth up: and he knoweth not for whom he shall gather these things.

8. And now what is my hope? Is it not the Lord? And my substance is with
thee.

9. Deliver thou me from all my iniquities: thou hast made me a reproach to
the fool.

10. I was dumb, and I opened not my mouth, because thou hast done it.

11. Remove thy scourges from me. The strength of thy hand has made me
faint in rebukes.

12. Thou hast corrected man for iniquity. And thou hast made his soul to
waste away like a spider: surely in vain is any man disquieted.

13. Hear my prayer, O Lord, and my supplication: give ear to my tears.
Be not silent: for I am a stranger with thee, and a sojourner as all my
fathers were.

14. O forgive me, that I may be refreshed, before I go hence, and be no more.

SUFFERING and adversity can come upon a man who fears God with such vehemence that there may arise a spiritual conflict as to whether in view of the good fortune of the godless one should murmur against Divine Providence or bow down submissively to the will of God. The psalmist too was in such a situation. He fought with the temptation of doubting God's justice and love and was close to submitting to this doubt. In this psalm he has written down for the benefit of all the just who are afflicted with sorrow what has prevented him from committing this grave sin and from being defeated and how he has obtained the victory.

In a few verses the poet describes the spiritual combat (verses 2–4). In view of the carefree life and activity of the godless which he saw before him every day, he has decided to be wary. No word of complaint against God about his fate should escape his lips. It was his firm purpose not to sin with the tongue. It was a purpose inspired by the fear of the Lord. It was his purpose to keep his tongue in check as long as the wicked, whose destruction he had expected for a long time, were still prosperous. He kept his resolution; he submitted to his sufferings and remained silent. But in order not to encounter the danger of breaking his resolution, he strove to drive from his mind the troublesome thoughts of contrasting the life of sinners and their prosperity with his own fidelity to the Law and his grievous affliction. But it was impossible not to think of it; for the disparity troubled him more and more day by day because of the weight of his cross. The more he strove to get the thought from his mind, the more his sorrow which he tried to overcome grew. The more he tried to silence himself, the more he thought about the reasons of the disparity; and the more he meditated, the more mysterious the ways of God appeared to him. Like fire the unsolved question burned in his bosom and demanded an answer. The psalmist loosed the bond of his tongue not to complain, however, but to inquire from God. May God permit him to know the transitoriness of human prosperity that he may not value it too highly; may he also, because of the shortness of human life, grant him the peace of a sorrowless future.

The solution of the apparent disparity between the conduct and fate of men lies in the transitoriness of human happiness (verses 5–7). A pleasure that has a sad ending, a good that can be lost suddenly loses its value to every thoughtful man and loses much of the temptation to purchase it at any price. For God who reckons with infinity, all perishable things are too insignificant to give to his servant as a divine reward. The better the perishableness of all earthly goods is known, the easier the just man consoles himself when he must deprive himself of them and the less he will envy the godless because of their possessions. Therefore the psalmist begs the Lord for a deeper knowledge. Let me know my end and the number of my days. He does not ask to be permitted to die in order to escape this spiritual conflict, but that by the divine light he may clearly realize the perishableness of this life and remove the troublesome conflict from him. The Lord granted him his petition. But now it is clear to his mind that the days of a man's life when compared to eternity are only a hand's breadth long. Indeed, in the eyes of God the entire length of a man's life is less than a second; it is like nothing. As the breath from the mouth quickly vanishes in the air, so life passes and never comes again. Even the strong man is nothing but a passing shadow, a phantom. And yet men make so much ado and take so much care about nothing. They plague themselves to heap up treasures and do not know for whom they gather them. Ecclesiasticus says: "It happens that man laboreth in wisdom, and knowledge, and carefulness, and he leaveth what he hath gotten to an idle man: so this also is vanity and a great evil" (Ecclesiastes 2:21).

A further consolation is hope in God (verses 8–12). Men who hope in God observe the pleasures and goods which the children of the world enjoy and compare the transitoriness of everything that is earthly with the unchangeableness of things eternal. The fate of all men rests in God's hands; he distributes all things according to the norm of his justice and love, both sufferings and joys. He who has acquired the supernatural virtue of hope and has not lost it will not be defeated in his spiritual combats. The psalmist can claim that he at all times waited for the Lord and placed all his hope in him alone. The hope in God's goodness puts the confident petition on his lips that because of the shortness of time the Lord may soon grant him blessings and justice. In affliction man often forgets his guilt before God. But the psalmist admits that he has sinned and that he has deserved punishment from God. According to Old Testament belief there existed a necessary relation between sin and a divine visitation. The pardoning of sin, therefore, was a necessary condition for the restoration of the privilege of receiving temporal blessings from God. The psalmist prays that the Lord may pardon his sins so that because of his sad condition he may not become an object of mockery to his enemies. In the consciousness of his guilt he bore his sufferings with resignation. The thought that God's hand rested upon him, the hands of him who is all just and good, has given him strength to bear his sorrow patiently. But this does not hinder him from begging God to restore him to grace. Man's weakness must finally submit to the strong punishing hand of God; for when God punishes man on account of his sin, his strength of life will gradually diminish. Man in comparison to his Creator is only a breath.

At the close the psalmist again begs for a mitigation of his suffering. He begs that God may pay heed to his tears because man is so prone to

146

sickness. Man is like a guest who tarries in a country only for a short time and then travels further; he is like a citizen who has no possessions in the land, but is one who is borne up with, who is under the protection of a stranger. But the just man is a guest of God and a denizen in the land of the Lord as all the forefathers were. May the Lord be friendly to his guest, may he not deny protection to a member of his kingdom, and may his wrathful countenance be turned away from him. For soon death will come which will bring him into the underworld where the sun of the divine grace will no longer shine.

psalm 39

Expectans expectavi

Christ's coming and redeeming mankind

1. Unto the end, a psalm for David himself.

2. With expectation I have waited for the Lord, and he was attentive to me.

3. And he heard my prayers, and brought me out of the pit of misery and the mire of dregs.
   And he set my feet upon a rock, and directed my steps.

4. And he put a new canticle into my mouth, a song to our God.
   Many shall see, and shall fear: and they shall hope in the Lord.

5. Blessed is the man whose trust is in the name of the Lord; and who hath not had regard to vanities, and lying follies.

6. Thou hast multiplied thy wonderful works, O Lord my God: and in thy thoughts there is no one like to thee.
   I have declared and I have spoken: they are multiplied above number.

7. Sacrifice and oblation thou didst not desire: but thou has pierced ears for me.
   Burnt offering and sin offering thou didst not require:

8. then said I, Behold I come. In the head of the book it is written of me

9. that I should do thy will: O my God, I have desired it, and thy law in the midst of my heart.

147

10. I have declared thy justice in a great church. Lo, I will not restrain my lips. O Lord thou knowest it.

11. I have not hid thy justice within my heart: I have declared thy truth and thy salvation.
    I have not concealed thy mercy and thy truth from a great council.

12. Withhold not, O Lord, thy tender mercies from me: thy mercy and thy truth have always upheld me.

13. For evils without number have surrounded me; my iniquities have overtaken me, and I was not able to see.
    They are multiplied above the hairs of my head: and my heart has forsaken me.

14. Be pleased, O Lord, to deliver me; look down, O Lord, to help me.

15. Let them be confounded and ashamed together, that seek after my soul to take it away.
    Let them be turned backward and be ashamed, that desire evils for me.

16. Let them immediately bear their confusion, that say to me: 'Tis well, 'tis well.

17. Let all that seek thee rejoice and be glad in thee: and let such as love thy salvation say always: The Lord be magnified.

18. But I am a beggar and poor: the Lord is careful for me.
    Thou art my helper and my protector: O my God, be not slack.

THE royal singer was in great need. Perhaps this song was composed during the time when David had to flee into the desert from his son Absalom. But despite the bad situation he carried no grudge against his enemies, and against God he allowed no mistrust to enter his soul. He reviewed the more difficult times when he was persecuted by Saul during which he so often experienced the liberating power of the Lord and his condescending love. The consciousness of having thanked the Lord for his great and kind deeds in his behalf, not only privately, but also publicly in his songs, and by proclaiming his power, wisdom, and fidelity, gave him despite his guilt of sin a glad hope that God both now and in all future times would save him and put to naught the plans of his adversaries. In his thankfulness toward God he saw the way to the divine heart and it moved him to new proofs of his love. David in his conduct is a type of the Christian who in his thankfulness for the graces of redemption received since his baptism prepares himself for the reception of new graces. He is also a type of Christ. Therefore St. Paul puts the verses 7–9 into the mouth of the Lord on his entry into the world (Hebrews 10:5).

The psalmist calls to memory the graces received (verses 2–4). In the days of persecution by Saul, David had never lost confidence in God's justice and fidelity. Many of the psalms composed at that time give testimony of this. He believed and hoped in the Lord and with great confidence relied on his help. God always lovingly condescended to hear his prayers. At that time he often felt like a man thrown into a dark dungeon and abandoned to starvation or like a man sinking in a swamp. But God always came to his help and placed him upon firm soil so that he could walk without faltering. This is also a picture of mankind's condition since Adam's sin.

Without the divine Redemption all would have continued into moral degradation and would have perished because of their estrangement from God. Christ had to redeem men and save them from the abyss of sin through baptism and penance and place them on the firm foundation of faith and grace so that they could walk safely and securely to their eternal destiny. The divine proofs of love which the royal singer experienced inspired him to sing a new song, a song of praise for his deliverer. In this song the wonderful deeds of God's love are continuously commemorated. We also experience them continuously and, therefore, filled with a holy reverence and strengthened in our confidence we are inspired with similar sentiments of praise and thanksgiving. David believed and felt that the Lord did not manifest his fidelity, power, and goodness to him in order to keep the knowledge of them to himself, but that he should proclaim them so that others may know them and praise the Father who is in heaven.

The psalmist thanks God for the gifts received (verses 5–11). The miraculous deliverance from many dangers has shown how wise a man acts who places his confidence in the Lord, who is not discouraged in adversities, who does not become faithless to his God, who does not associate himself with godless men, who does not seek counsel and help in the idolatrous service of false gods and in superstitious practices. For the chosen people, God is the only power and love who can and will help. What he has done for David was only one example in the endless chain of miraculous deeds of liberation which had begun with the call of Abraham. In this chain, deed upon deed is added until Christ performs the supreme act; namely, that of the resurrection and glorification of all the just. God's decrees of salvation are so profound and his miracles are so astounding that nothing can be compared with his deeds of salvation. If we would attempt to enumerate all of them and proclaim them, we would never come to an end so great is their number.

At that time when through God's intervention all of the godless plans of Saul failed, David asked himself the question: "What shall I render to

149

God for all that he had done for me?" Should he give God a thanksgiving offering of many sacrificial animals? If God had desired this from him, he would have led the refugee to the sanctuary. The Lord wanted no sacrifice, neither holocausts, nor gifts; that is, neither bloody nor unbloody sacrifices, neither holocausts for adoration nor sacrifices of atonement for sins committed. God wants man, his obedient will, not animals; for all bloody and unbloody offerings mean nothing to God when the sacrifice of obedience is denied him. Therefore Samuel once spoke to Saul: "Is God pleased with holocausts and thanksgiving offerings as much as he is with obedience to his commands? Obedience is better than sacrifice; to hear is better than the fat of the ram" (1 Kings 15:22). God has given men ears that they may hear his words and cherish them in their heart. Because God wished obedience as a sign of grateful love, David uttered his: "Here I am." By these words he obligated himself to obey the Book of the Law, the archive of God's will. In this book we find especially written the laws for kings, which he had to learn; namely, to fear the Lord his God and to respect all the words of his doctrine and of his Law (Deuteronomy 17:19).

It was David's pleasure to obey God; he had his joy in the Law; he meditated upon it day and night (Psalm 1:2). The content of the Law was for him an affair of conscience. The Law was inscribed deeply in his heart. Just as the Old Testament sacrifices were empty ceremonies if not accompanied with the sacrifice of glad obedience, so are also the prayers of thanksgiving, all songs of praise, and all gifts of a Christian, worthless and unattended by God, if not accompanied by proper dispositions, by a willingness to obey, and by a love of the holy will of God. But David in his thankfulness was not satisfied with the sacrifice of obedience: he proclaimed the message of God's redeeming love to all the people. What filled his heart he proclaimed with his lips. The all-knowing God gave testimony of this and would abide by this testimony in the future. In his songs he always praised the just providence of God. He proclaimed to men God's decree of salvation, his fidelity, mercy, and truth. The knowledge which he had acquired he did not allow to remain a dead letter, unfruitful knowledge stored in his own mind; he published it to the Old Testament assembly of God in order that it might grow in the knowledge and fear of the Lord. This is the most noble gratitude for all the proofs of God's love and favors that he had received and for all the enlightenment; namely, to make use of his heavenly talents and to bring others who were still estranged from God nearer to him by his words, example, and love.

God by his justice, love, and fidelity had frequently saved the psalmist in the past. He, therefore, thanked the Lord for all by his fidelity to the Law and by singing his songs before all the people. The consciousness of having done this gives him courage and confidence in his present need. Because he had received so many gifts before, he petitions again (verses 12–18); for God does not change. Troubles surrounded him like an army. Absalom revolted. The nation became unfaithful to its ruler. The sufferings indeed were not undeserved. David confessed openly and admitted it. The punishment for his sins came upon him. The guilt of his sins was so great that he could not deny his transgressions; they became more numerous than the hair of his head. If they had not been so great, God would not have laid such heavy penance upon him. He almost lacked courage to beg the Lord for pardon. But his faith in God's everlasting mercy and the consciousness that he had always been thankful to God for his help impelled him to pray with confidence that God might graciously help him and that he might not delay with his help.

The enemies are seeking his destruction. By God's intervention and protection their plans will prove unsuccessful. Ashamed they must surrender or retreat before the divine Power and clear the field. Consternation will come upon all who rejoiced at the misfortune of the king and showed satisfaction at his affliction. But all who seek God's salvation shall see the destruction of the enemies of the anointed and his own miraculous deliverance. They shall rejoice and praise the greatness of Yahwe. How glorious the promised deliverance must be by which all godlessness will be eradicated since God even now reveals his power so miraculously. Despite his misery and abandonment the psalmist does not doubt that God will not forget him, that he will care for him; for he is always his helper and deliverer. In his entire petition and especially at the close we observe the glad assurance that the Lord will not delay his help. To him who always thankfully acknowledges God's help and favors, who faithfully seeks to return love for love, the Lord will always show mercy when affliction befalls him, when the number and burden of his sins make him restless. God will redeem him from his distress; the plots of the enemies will not succeed, even those of his hellish enemies. The psalmist will experience the greatness of God's love.

psalm 40

Beatus qui intelligit

The happiness of him that shall believe in Christ, notwith-
standing the humility and poverty in which he shall
come: the malice of his enemies, especially
of the traitor Judas

1. Unto the end, a psalm for David himself.

2. Blessed is he that understandeth concerning the needy and the poor: the Lord will deliver him in the evil day.

3. The Lord preserve him and give him life, and make him blessed upon earth: and deliver him not up to the will of his enemies.

4. The Lord help him on his bed of sorrows: thou hast turned all his couch in his sickness.

5. I said: O Lord be thou merciful to me. Heal my soul, for I have sinned against thee.

6. My enemies have spoken evil against me: when shall he die and his name perish?

7. And if he came in to see me, he spoke vain things: his heart gathered together iniquity to itself.
He went out and spoke to the same purpose.

8. All my enemies whispered together against me: they devised evils to me.

9. They determined against me an unjust word: shall he that sleepeth arise again no more?

10. For even the man of my peace, in whom I trusted, who ate my bread, hath greatly supplanted me.

11. But thou, O Lord, have mercy on me, and raise me up again: and I will requite them.

12. By this I know, that thou hast a good will for me: because my enemy shall not rejoice over me.

13. But thou hast upheld me by reason of my innocence: and hast established me in thy sight forever.

14. Blessed be the Lord, the God of Israel, from eternity to eternity. So be it. So be it.

THE words: "Blessed are the merciful, for they shall obtain mercy . . ." were uttered by Jesus, but the truth contained in them was not unknown in the Old Testament. Because of the strong emphasis placed on the law of retaliation, a doubt could easily arise about the truth of this promise, especially when an Israelite practiced great charity and showed merciful love towards his neighbor but received little sympathy and mercy when he himself was afflicted with grievous sickness or had to suffer need. To assuage and console such disappointed persons David tells them in this psalm what experiences he himself had when he was sick and how he himself never doubted the truth of this promise, but saw in his bitter experience only a passing divine visitation which changed nothing in the decree of the divine Love.

The psalmist places the beatitude of mercy at the beginning of his instruction (verses 2–4). Blessed is he who shows sympathy to the weak. In evil days the Lord will save him. The prophet Isaias has announced the divine promise in spirited words: "Deal thy bread to the hungry, and bring the needy and harborless into thy house: when thou shalt see one naked, cover him, and despise not thy own flesh. Then shall the light break forth as the morning, and thy health shall speedily arise, and thy justice shall go before thy face, and the glory of the Lord shall gather thee up. Then shalt thou call and the Lord shall hear: thou shalt cry, and he shall say: here I am" (Isaias 58:7–9). The Lord protects the life of the merciful man and keeps him from falling; he makes him happy and guards him against his enemies that their hatred and madness may not harm him. If sickness befalls a man who is generous and kind to his neighbor, the Lord will refresh him on his sick bed and will restore him to perfect health so that no trace of his sufferings remains.

Despite the glorious divine promise the psalmist now compares the unmerciful treatment with his own great mercy (verses 5–10). In his grievous sickness he found out that the generous and sympathetic love which he showed to his neighbors even when practiced in an heroic degree for the mitigation of their sufferings was only repaid by being unmercifully treated by his fellow man in his own afflictions. It was during his sickness that his enemies carried on their whispering campaign against him, the rightful ruler, and urged the people to rebel against him. He therefore begged the Lord to restore his health so that he could put an end to the ruthless activities of his enemies. But while he was beseeching God for the restoration of health, his adversaries awaited his death. They had no word of sympathy for him in his sufferings, but rather rejoiced when bad news came from the palace about his condition. They spoke with gleeful satisfaction about his coming death and hoped that with his life the memory of him would also be extinguished. In their heartlessness some of them even appeared at the sick bed of the king pretending sympathy with him in his sufferings, but really intending to find means that would be to his disadvantage and to convince themselves that the end would soon take place. Outside of the palace the associates stood and waited for a favorable report. There they spoke to each other in whispers and carried on hateful conversations against him, plotting and wishing him evil. In their joy they believed that it was a fact that his sickness would end in death, that the king was incurably sick, that he would never again leave his bed. For the psalmist the anguish about such ruthlessness and heartless duplicity was heightened because one of his best friends was found among them, a man to whom he had given his fullest confidence, a man whom he had permitted to sit at the royal table with him, and whom he had made an associate. This man had joined his archenemies and rebelled against his kingdom. Such was the experience of David despite his practice of mercy even toward enemies such as Semei. Yet he did not doubt for one moment about the truth of the divine promise.

The psalmist closes his song with the repetition that God may give him the beatitude of mercy (verses 11–13). He beseeches the Lord that God might again restore his health so that he might punish the enemies of the throne for their ruthless and heartless conduct. This petition should not be considered as serving the purpose of satisfying the passion of revenge but of defending justice and God's honor because David's enemies were also God's enemies who established the kingdom. Therefore his restoration to health and the punishment of the rebels was to be a sign that the Lord had not withdrawn his love from the anointed and that he was still being protected by the mercy and goodness of God. David knew that he was not guilty of the things his enemies accused him. Therefore he was certain that God would not permit him to be vanquished as long as he lived, that his kingdom would enjoy the promise of continued peace until the appearance of the Messias. The psalm ends with the confidence that divine mercy will not be denied to a merciful man. Verse 14 does not belong to this psalm, but forms the conclusion of the first book with a doxology.

psalm 41

Quemadmodum desiderat

The fervent desire of the just after God: hope in afflictions

1. Unto the end, understanding for the sons of Core.

2. As the hart panteth after the fountains of water; so my soul panteth after thee, O Lord.

3. My soul hath thirsted after the strong living God. When shall I come and appear before the face of God?

4. My tears have been my bread day and night, whilst it is said to me daily: Where is thy God?

5. These things I remembered, and poured out my soul in me: for I shall go over into the place of the wonderful tabernacle, even to the house of God. With the voice of joy and praise; the noise of one feasting.

6. Why art thou sad, O my soul? And why dost thou trouble me?
Hope in God, for I will still give praise to him: the salvation of my countenance,

7. and my God. My soul is troubled within myself: Therefore will I remember thee from the land of Jordan and Hermoniim, from the little hill.

8. Deep calleth on deep, at the noise of thy flood-gates.
All thy heights and thy billows have passed over me.

9. In the daytime the Lord hath commanded his mercy: and a canticle to him in the night. With me is prayer to the God of my life.

10. I will say to God: Thou art my support. Why hast thou forgotten me? And why go I mourning, whilst my enemy afflicteth me?

11. Whilst my bones are broken, my enemies who trouble me have reproached me;
Whilst they say to me day by day: Where is thy God?

12. Why art thou cast down, O my soul? And why dost thou disquiet me?
Hope thou in God, for I will still give praise to him: the salvation of my countenance, and my God.

PSALM 41 · *Quemadmodum desiderat*

How biased is the observation that the religious life of Israel was based upon the fear of God's strict justice and of his tyrannical rule is seen from this touching song of the soul's ardent longing for its God and for the sanctuary of Sion. This psalm is one of the most precious pearls of biblical lyric. Here we find an intense longing side by side with sorrowful remembrances, a glad hope with apprehensive doubt, passionate complaint with fervent petition. The unknown singer from the tribe of Levi of the Korahites has composed this song at the headwaters of the Jordan. He was expelled from his country. He gave expression of the conflict in his soul between human discouragement and confidence in God. In a threefold refrain, faith in God's fidelity and love gradually banishes the temptation to despondency. Thus the song which starts with sentiments of fervent longing ends with a joyous hope of a speedy return home. The psalm may well be used by a man who feels himself abandoned by God, by a soul that feels itself forsaken here on earth and longs for eternal union with God in the heavenly sanctuary after the manner of the Apostle of the Gentiles who longed to be dissolved in Christ and to be with him.

The psalmist begins his song with the sad remembrance of the many hours of grace in the sanctuary (verses 2–6). His homesickness for Sion and his longing for the edifying religious festivities in Jerusalem is great and his soul yearns for the nearness of God like a hart which in the heat of the summer sun yearns for refreshing waters. When in the summertime the brooks of Palestine and even the wells are dried up, (here the poet intentionally selected the feminine, the weaker animal) the hart, languishing for thirst, stands among the rocks over which the waters had flowed and seeks ardently for water to still her burning thirst. So also every believing soul, banished from the sanctuary, thirsts and yearns for God, the only source of living water, the water of grace which flows unto eternal life. If God alone is the source of supernatural and eternal life, then the house of God is the well-house where the water of supernatural and eternal life is found and from which the water can be drawn. Therefore the banished psalmist begs the Lord day by day in prayer: When may I return to Sion? When may I appear before thy countenance; that is, before thy throne of grace in the sanctuary? Certainly God is everywhere, even in the place of banishment. He is the God in near places and in foreign parts (Jeremias 23:23). But in the Old Testament where he especially bestowed his blessings was Sion, as in the New Testament it is the Catholic Church.

The psalmist asks: why did the Lord permit my expulsion from the Holy City? Is the voice of the people, which believes him to be banished by God, also God's voice? These remarks of contempt which accompanied his banishment continuously sound in his ears. They mocked him because he relied on his God and looked for his help. And now the otherwise-strong man evidently weeps. His sorrow has taken away his appetite to eat. Excluded from every divine service, from all festivities, he in his great sorrow remembers those days when as a member of the chosen people he was permitted to join in with God's assembly and to worship the Lord. He remembers how he would make pilgrimages to the sanctuary in the company of noble men on the great feast days of the year; he recalls how he could joyfully join in the festive songs that were intoned by the crowds of glad pilgrims in the courts of the sanctuary while the high priest in his beautiful pontifical vestments surrounded by many priests and levites would make the sacrificial offering. Will he ever again participate in this edifying festivity? Humanly speaking he might answer "no" to the question, but believing in God's fidelity and merciful love he will answer "yes." Indeed, faith will not admit any despondency in the soul. On this account the psalmist in the first refrain requests his listeners not to allow the comparison between the sad present and the glorious past to make them crepe-hangers and not to give up hope, but to have confidence in the Lord for whom it is an easy thing to remove all obstacles for their return home. Their confidence will not remain unrewarded. He will again be permitted to praise God in his sanctuary as his Lord and Saviour. Faith also gives consolation to a Christian soul which has a notion of the glory of the heavenly liturgy in the joy of the saints. This faith strengthens him in the joyous hope of the return home to the eternal Sion.

The encouragement given to the psalmist's soul has not entirely pacified him. He still feels an urge to have a conversation with God hoping to obtain mercy (verses 7–12). He wishes to pray to him who has said: "Cast thy care upon the Lord, and he shall sustain thee: he shall not suffer the just to waver forever" (Psalm 54:23). From the place of his banishment at the source of the Jordan near the slope of the Great Hermon and the mountain of Misar the psalmist turns his thoughts to the distant sanctuary. Misar is probably the mountain that is separated from the Hermon by the Wadi Ghasab. Here the Jordan rushes over the rocks in many waterfalls down into Lake Huleh. But this beautiful natural scene does not amuse the banished king; in it he only sees his misfortune mirrored. Just as wave upon wave foams and rushes over the rocks, so sorrow rushed upon him and unmercifully afflicted his soul. Yet this soul in the midst of so much sorrow felt the merciful hand of God and heard his consoling voice. Like a friendly messenger the Lord offered his mercy and love; by day and at night the Lord let him feel the nearness of his mercy. Thus the psalmist in his abandonment did not remain silent in his songs of thanksgiving and his hands were uplifted in trustful prayer to God, his rock, the source of true life.

It is not indignation nor a defiant protest against Divine Providence which makes him utter the words: "Why hast thou forgotten me?" It is a humble petition of his sorrowful soul for the solution of a mystery of Divine Providence. It is a mystery. There is only one God, only one rock upon which the just man can build. But where can he find a hold if this God forgets him, if his only support forsakes him? Why does the Lord permit the enemy to harass his faithful servant? Why does he permit the godless to rejoice while the just man spends his days in sadness? The ridicule of the godless is worse than scourges. They ridicule his reverence for God and mock at his confidence in him day after day. They say: where is now his God? We are indifferent about his commandments; we ask no question about what he wants; and yet we are rich and without cares. We are powerful and perform acts of violence without any fear of Yahwe's judgments. Thus they laugh at him who walks the way of the Lord and places his hope in him. Because of this mystery of Divine Providence the psalmist is in deep sorrow and wonders why the Lord allows the godless to prevail over his faithful servant. In the second refrain faith is again the victor. Why is my soul perturbed, why dost thou trouble me? Can God who even in my banishment manifested his love to me, abandon me and permit me to become a victim of the enemy? Their momentary triumph is only a trial, a test of my confidence. Therefore, my soul, await in confidence the day of your return home where you will be able to visit with your God in his sanctuary and praise him. To the Christian soul in banishment, God also manifests his great love, a greater love than he showed to the Old Testament just. In all adversities and persecutions the Christian should remain confident that God does not reject his own, but tests his confidence and prepares him for the return to the heavenly sanctuary.

psalm 42

Judica me, Deus

The prophet aspireth after the temple and altar of God

1. A psalm for David.
   Judge me, O God, and distinguish my cause from the nation that is not holy: deliver me from the unjust and deceitful man.

2. For thou art the God of my strength: Why has thou cast me off? And why do I go sorrowful whilst the enemy afflicteth me?

3. Send forth thy light and thy truth: they have conducted me, and brought me unto thy holy hill, and into thy tabernacles.

4. And I will go in to the altar of God: to God who giveth joy to my youth.

5. To thee, O God my God, I will give praise upon the harp: Why art thou sad, O my soul? And why dost thou disquiet me?

6. Hope in God, for I will still give praise to him: the salvation of my countenance, and my God.

THE sufferings of the present time have awakened the remembrance of the past and this remembrance has answered his humble question and complaint. Now the complaint becomes a petition for a return home (Psalm 42:1–5). The psalmist was unjustly forced to leave his native land. His banishment was the deed of foolish men incited by an unprincipled leader. Lying, deceit, and criminal intrigue had triumphed over justice. There was no earthly court that would open the way for his return to his native country. The psalmist, therefore, turns to God, the Supreme Judge, that he may carry on the trial for him and help him to obtain his right. God is the defender and protector of justice. He is the fortress and refuge of the just. But since he is this why has he deprived his servant of the protection of his sanctuary? Since God is the fortress of the oppressed why does he permit his enemies to triumph while he is bowed down with sadness? In the darkness of this mystery may the Lord send forth a ray of light, may he reveal his divine will and fulfill his promise of fidelity. God in his love and fidelity should again lead the banished back to his home to Yahwe's holy mount of Sion, to his dwelling place in the sanctuary of Jerusalem. Then he will approach the altar of the Lord with his sacrificial gifts; for it was God who had given pleasure and joy to his youth. Then he will sing joyfully for having regained union with God. He will take his harp in hand and sing a song of praise to the Lord.

God's promise of fidelity will never disappoint and his love will never cease. Has therefore his soul reason to be depressed? Must not the belief in God's fidelity and love allay the storm within his soul? For the last time faith speaks to the soul. I will trust in God and again praise him. A joyous hope, a glad assurance make him utter these words. In spirit the psalmist sees himself on his way to his native land, on the way to the sanctuary in order to give a thank-offering to the God of the joy of his youth, to sing a song to him and accompany it by the playing of his harp. Without the assistance of God, the Christian too cannot withstand the

159

enticements of an unholy people, the attacks of external and internal enemies. Without God's light and love; that is, without his truth and grace he cannot walk the way to the heavenly Sion. Faith demands of the Christian that he confidently prays and hopes in God.

psalm 43

Deus auribus nostris

The Church commemorates former favors and present afflictions under which she prays for succor

1. Unto the end, for the sons of Core, to give understanding.

2. We have heard, O God, with our ears: our fathers have declared to us,
   The work thou hast wrought in their days, and in the days of old.

3. Thy hand destroyed the Gentiles, and thou plantedst them: thou didst afflict the people and cast them out.

4. For they got not the possession of the land by their own sword: neither did their own arm save them.
   But thy right hand, and thy arm, and the light of thy countenance: because thou wast pleased with them.

5. Thou art thyself my king and my God, who commandest the saving of Jacob.

6. Through thee we will push down our enemies with the horn: and through thy name we will despise them that rise up against us.

7. For I will not trust in my bow: neither shall my sword save me.

8. But thou hast saved us from them that afflict us: and hast put them to shame that hate us.

9. In God shall we glory all the day long: and in thy name we will give praise forever.

10. But now thou hast cast us off, and put us to shame: and thou, O God, wilt not go out with our armies.

11. Thou hast made us turn our back to our enemies: and they that hated us plundered for themselves.

12. Thou hast given us up like sheep to be eaten: thou hast scattered us among the nations.

13. Thou hast sold thy people for no price: and there was no reckoning in the exchange of them.

14. Thou hast made us a reproach to our neighbors, a scoff and derision to them that are round about us.

15. Thou hast made us a byword among the Gentiles: a shaking of the head among the people.

16. All the day long my shame is before me: and the confusion of my face hath covered me.

17. At the voice of him that reproacheth and detracteth me: at the face of the enemy and persecutor.

18. All these things have come upon us, yet we have not forgotten thee: and we have not done wickedly in thy covenant.

19. And our heart hath not turned back: neither hast thou turned aside our steps from thy way.

20. For thou hast humbled us in the place of affliction: and the shadow of death hath covered us.

21. If we have forgotten the name of our God, and if we have spread forth our hands to a strange God:

22. Shall not God search out these things: for he knoweth the secrets of the heart.
    Because for thy sake we are killed all the day long: we are counted as sheep for the slaughter.

23. Arise, why sleepest thou, O Lord? Arise, and cast us not off to the end.

24. Why turnest thou thy face away and forgettest our want and our trouble?

25. For our soul is humbled down to the dust: our belly cleaveth to the earth.

26. Arise, O Lord: Help us and redeem us for thy name's sake.

IN THE history of the church we find Thabor and Mount Olivet, times of peace and liberty, times of struggle and persecution, times of victory and times of defeat, times in which the enemy triumphs. When oppression falls upon a part of the Church, the kingdom of God considered as a whole remains faithful to Christ. We are then confronted with the mystery of divine wisdom. This mystery is the more incomprehensible when persecution for the sake of our faith is more severe, lasts longer, and losses to the Church are greater. The chosen people were confronted with

161

such a mystery in the era of its history when this psalm was composed. The army of Israel had marched against the Gentile nations, against men who blasphemed Yahwe, who wanted to destroy his kingdom and place the banners of their gods upon the pinnacles of the temple at Jerusalem. It was a struggle for the very existence of the faith and of the Covenant of the Old Testament. And yet the Lord permitted the warrior of his cause to experience a disastrous defeat and the hatred of the Satanic Gentiles to terrorize the land of Yahwe. Since the sources of Israelitic history are few, it is not possible to determine the time of the defeat here mentioned with any exactness. The conjectures of the interpreters are centuries apart.

The psalm looks in retrospect to the glorious time when Israel under the leadership of Josue took possession of the Promised Land (verses 2–4). Every page of its history testifies that all victories of the past were the work of God. What he has done in the far distant past after the redemption of his people from Egyptian captivity has been narrated from generation to generation in order that the descendants might always be mindful of the miraculous deeds of the Lord. It was the Lord that rooted out all the pagan tribes that lived in Canaan. He did as the gardener who cleanses his garden of its weeds. He planted his people in the land that it might take roots, grow, and become strong. He destroyed the Canaanites, the Amorrhites, the Hittites, and other tribes so that they disappeared from the pages of history altogether. But Israel became more numerous and more powerful. By its own strength it could never have become the possessors of that land whose inhabitants were stronger in number and weapons and could depend upon unconquerable fortifications. Josue and his warriors could not ascribe the conquest of Canaan to the power of his sword. Neither their armor nor their skill in warfare could bring about victory, but only the arm of God could do this. God gave them victory by his irresistible power and his shining countenance; that is, by his grace and love which he manifested to the people of his choice not because they deserved it, but because he loved them. The annals of the Church also record remarkable events in which paganism accepted the good tidings and gave place to the Christian kingdom of God in which his power and grace revealed themselves so wonderfully.

The conviction of the fathers that all success was due to the Lord, and the belief in his power which destroyed all the enemies brought about the conviction that even now no victory is possible without God (verses 5–9). This belief dominated also the living generation at the time of the psalmist. It was Israel's king and God who had promised the descendants of the patriarch help in their quest of salvation. Only with the power of the Lord could Israel defend itself and vanquish the enemies that surrounded it. Only in the name of God would they have the power to crush their enemies, not for their own renown and advantage, but for the honor of God and for the preservation and growth of his kingdom. The people relied on this power at that time. They did not put their trust in natural means of defense. They did not put their trust in weapons. They knew from experience that with natural means alone the wars of the Lord could not be fought victoriously. God does not use such men as his instruments who think that they do not need his help and grace in the battles for the preservation and spread of his kingdom, who rely on their own strength and who would like to claim the renown for themselves alone. Therefore Israel in times of threatening danger expected that the Lord would keep the oppressors of his people within their own boundaries and put them to shame because they hated Israel on account of its God. God cannot permit his own work to be destroyed by Gentiles, the enemies of his kingdom. Thus Israel may at all times boast of its God, dedicate its songs of victory to him, and praise his glorious name in its prayers and songs. The members of the Church also must be mindful of the fact that the kingdom of God of the New Covenant cannot continue to exist and grow by mere natural means alone. It is only with God that it can conquer; it is entirely dependent on his help.

Even at this time the warriors of Israel thought that they went out with God to carry on war; they went to war with the confidence that the Lord would again lend his strong arm to the nation. But they were disappointed. The army met a serious defeat (verses 10–17). Thus the Lord did not accompany them when they left the sacrifice and sanctuary to meet the enemy. He abandoned his people, rejected them, and deeply put them to shame before the enemy. Courageously the warriors had marched out against the enemy with the war cry: "The sword of the Lord . . ." but they could not withstand the onrush of the enemy. Their lines were broken; they fell back and had to leave their native land without protection and to surrender it to the Gentiles to be plundered. Like sheep that are selected for the slaughter and which the owner sells here and there to be eaten, so God has delivered his people to the enemies that they may destroy it and disperse its members throughout the world. God has made the victory very easy for the enemies and has demanded no reward from them. But what advantage did God get from the defeat of his own people? The Gentiles did not thank him; but praised their gods, and worshiped them as victors over Yahwe, the God of Israel. Israel, God's possession, and his chosen people which should have been at the head of nations, became the object of mockery and derision to its Gentile neighbors. The fate of Israel became a raillery among the Gentiles, a proverb with which they wished their enemy misfortune:

"May it happen to him as it happened to Israel." All shook their heads in astonishment at the greatness of the defeat and in malicious joy at the misfortune of Yahwe's people. And thus even the lost battle did not put an end to their shame. Every day brought new shame and reproach. Therefore longingly the people waited for the intervention of the Lord, but each day brought new disappointment. They could no longer show themselves among the nations, for shame covered their countenance when they had to bear the derision and mockery of the enemies and they were not able to defend themselves.

It is understandable that God's silence was an insoluble riddle, an impenetrable mystery, and so much the more so because Israel had to suffer grievous defeat, ridicule, and calumny notwithstanding its fidelity to God (verses 18–23). There were times in which the Lord rightly abandoned his people because they had become unfaithful to him. But in this instance it had been mindful of the Covenant and faithfully kept the commandments. The great commandment ("The Lord is our God, the Lord alone! Thou shalt love the Lord thy God with thy whole heart, with thy whole soul, and with all thy strength.") they had conscientiously observed (Deuteronomy 6:4 seq.). The law was written in their heart and had become the norm and rule of their conduct of life. And Israel had kept the Law until it came to the field of jackals, in that dreadful wilderness and uninhabited district where the armies confronted each other and the army of Israel was defeated and dispersed, and where the dreadful disaster had come upon the battlefield like the shadow of death. Did God not know about innocence of his people? If Israel had become unfaithful to the covenant made with Yahwe, if it had not revered his holy Name and had forgotten it, if it had worshiped the gods of the Gentiles, and if it had stretched out its hands to them in prayer, he would have known about their faithlessness and would have punished them long before; for to him who knows the deepest and innermost recesses of the heart, the activities of an entire people cannot remain concealed. It is impossible that the enemies of God's kingdom would be the instruments of God's punitive justice; for Israel was hated and persecuted by the Gentiles because it remained faithful and true to the covenant of Yahwe, because it gave honor to Yahwe alone and denied it to the Gentile gods. If the Gentiles were not instruments of Yahwe's punishment, then God permitted his people to be defeated in the defense of their holy faith; he permitted thousands to fall for the sake of the covenant, to be made prisoner of war, and to go into captivity. And for Yahwe's sake new dangers and greater tribulations are threatening Israel. They are like sheep led to the slaughter whom the sword may strike any day.

St. Paul has appropriated the words of the psalmist for the Christians suffering persecution: "For thy sake we are always in danger of death; we are esteemed as sheep led to the slaughter" (Rom. 8:36). But being sure of victory he adds: "But in all we remain victorious through him who has loved us." Such peaceful and triumphant faith, such assurance of divine love in its affliction Israel had not yet attained. The cry to God (verses 24–27) with which the psalm concludes reveals something more about the restlessness of the heart which would determine for the Lord the time of help. The people imagine that the Lord is asleep, that he does not bother about the affairs of the people, or that he rejected them forever. Because of their unrest they ask the impetuous question: "Why dost thou conceal thy countenance? Why art thou unmindful of the misery and need of thy people?" God is like a man who would turn his countenance away from the thousandfold woe. He is not a man without sympathy. He is not like the rich man living in luxury who is unmindful of the needs of his fellowman, or tries to forget him. The condition of the people must move the Lord. Because of the hard oppression by the enemy, because of the burden of a curse and affliction Israel is bowed to the ground, humiliated in the dust, incapable of rising. The psalm closes with the ejaculation: Arise, O Lord, to help us, save us for thy Name's sake. God's honor among the Gentiles depends much on the fate of his people.

psalm 44

Eructavit cor meum

The excellence of Christ's kingdom and the endowment of his Church

1. Unto the end, for them that shall be changed, for the sons of Core, for understanding, a Canticle for the beloved.

2. My heart hath uttered a good word: I speak my works to the king. My tongue is the pen of a scrivener that writeth swiftly.

3. Thou art beautiful above the sons of men: grace is poured abroad in thy lips; therefore hath God blessed me forever.

4. Gird thy sword upon thy thigh, O thou most mighty.

PSALM 44 · *Eructavit cor meum*

5. With thy comeliness and thy beauty set out: proceed prosperously, and reign.
Because of truth and meekness and justice: and thy right hand shall conduct thee wonderfully.

6. Thy arrows are sharp: under thee shall people fall, into the hearts of the king's enemies.

7. Thy throne, O God, is forever and ever: the sceptre of thy kingdom is a sceptre of uprightness.

8. Thou hast loved justice and hated iniquity: therefore God, thy God, hath anointed thee with the oil of gladness above thy fellows.

9. Myrrh and stacte and cassia perfume thy garments, from the ivory houses: out of which the daughters of the kings have delighted thee in thy glory.

10. The queen stood on thy right hand, in gilded clothing; surrounded with variety.

11. Hearken, O daughter, and see, and incline thy ear; and forget thy people and thy father's house.

12. And the king shall greatly desire thy beauty; for he is the Lord thy God, and him they shall adore.

13. And the daughters of Tyre with gifts, yea, all the rich among the people, shall entreat thy countenance.

14. All the glory of the king's daughter is within in golden borders,

15. clothed round about with varieties. After her shall virgins be brought to the king: her neighbors shall be brought to thee.

16. They shall be brought with gladness and rejoicing: they shall be brought into the temple of the king.

17. Instead of thy fathers, sons are born to thee: thou shalt make them princes over all the earth.

18. They shall remember thy name throughout all generations.
Therefore shall people praise thee forever; yea, forever and ever.

ACCORDING to the general ecclesiastical interpretations this psalm is not a worldly marriage song composed for the marriage of Solomon or for any other king of Juda. Such a song would not have been accepted in the Canon. It is an allegory which portrays the union of Israel as a type of the Messianic Church with the Messias. It describes the marriage of a king with a king's daughter. The spouse is explicitly called God. What the Canticle of Canticles gives us in six songs is here epitomized in a few

166

verses. The Israelites were well acquainted with the allegory. It was already known in the Books of Moses where opposition against the Sinai covenant was branded as adultery. We find allegories in the prophecies of Osee, Isaias, and Jeremias. The entire chapter 16 of Ezechiel is an allegory. In this allegory we find an intimation to the mystery of the Church, which St. Paul uses when he calls the Church the body of Christ.

The poet, prophetically enlightened, saw in the sublime figure of Christ an incomparable beauty and an heroic strength, a glorious being of royalty and divinity. His soul was enraptured by the vision and his heart was filled with joy and holy enthusiasm. What he saw in his meditation he wished all the citizens of his nation to enjoy in order that their longing for salvation might bear fruit and permeate their religious life. Thus he used his poetic gift in the service of the most majestic King and composed this prophetic song about Christ the King of Messianic times.

The first part of the psalm (verses 3–10) depicts the majesty of Christ the King. The psalmist saw in spirit a being of incomparable beauty; for the divinity in him shone through the veil of humanity and the unsurpassable nobility of soul gave to the figure a precious charm. From his lips flowed goodness and affability. Every word that came from his mouth bespoke kindness (*see* Luke 4:22). Such beauty was not of this world; it was a radiation of the inner richness of grace and of heavenly blessings. From this we can surmise with what plenitude of the Holy Spirit he has been endowed by God.

In the Messias his supernatural beauty is paired with his great plenitude of power, he is already described as a ruler who can break nations as if they were mere pottery. Longing to enjoy the blessed rule of Christ the King, the psalmist begs him to gird himself with his sword and to establish the kingdom of God on earth. The Messianic kingdom is described by the prophetic poet as an earthly national kingdom, but in truth it is a spiritual kingdom. The sword symbolizes the judiciary powers with which the Messias on the day of the Lord will strike and destroy the enemies of God. Therefore the psalmist calls the sword the splendor and majesty of the King. When the Messias will appear he will defend truth, meekness, and justice; he will manifest his strength in these three means of salvation. He will stand for truth and fidelity. He will remove all hindrances that human malice may put in the way. He will fulfill the divine promises of salvation, and will establish his kingdom, the Church, as an eternal means of salvation. He will be meek and merciful; for he will give relief to the oppressed. The bent reed he will straighten and the glimmering wick he will light. He will take up the cause of justice. He will come to plant God's justice upon earth, to reconcile men, and to sanctify them. Being mindful of these facts the psalmist wishes success

167

to the king. May he not delay longer to ascend his war chariot and enter upon his holy war. The ancient Oriental kings were accustomed to participate in battle upon war chariots. A hero like the Messianic king will perform wonderful deeds with his right hand with which he wields his weapon. Pictures of ancient times show us how in battle they fought from their chariots with bow and arrow. The arrows of the Messias are not without a point; they are not blunt. They will not strike without effect. His judgments are not weak and ineffectual. Like sharp arrows they pierce the heart, destroy whole nations and their kings. No power on earth can resist them. He who associates himself with the enemies of the Messias has sealed his own defeat.

The Messias is a divine King; his throne will continue forever; his dominion will never end. The Septuagint has already used the Hebraic name *"Elohim,"* that is *God,* in the vocative. The psalmist has also used it in addressing the Messias; and in the following verse has placed it side by side with Yahwe, the ordinary name of God and his Anointed. The Septuagint used the two names in the same sense. From this passage St. Paul in his Epistle to the Hebrews (1:8) has proven the superiority of Christ over the angels. Already the second psalm proves the claim of the Messias to world dominion. It also proves that his power to break down all resistance is due to his divinity. No power on earth can overthrow his throne. His kingdom, the Church, carries within itself no germ of decline as all earthly kingdoms do, neither will it be destroyed by enemies from without. "The sceptre of this kingdom." The fundamental characteristic of its ruler is integrity and justice. Beside catholicity in time and place, integrity is a characteristic of the kingdom of Christ. It is the outstanding mark of the prophets of this kingdom.

Justice has its foundation in the very nature of the Messias. He is the holy one who hates iniquity. He is not only just himself but he considers it his supreme task to propagate justice as a requisite for peace. Therefore God has distinguished him and has anointed him with the oil of gladness above all his associates. The anointing with the oil of gladness is an anointing which causes joy. This may refer to the anointing of a king and to the giving of royal powers and graces to carry out his responsibilities. The Messias-King, because of the plenitude of power and grace given to him, will surpass all kings on David's throne and all kings in the world. The psalmist may also have had in mind the marriage banquet at which the host anointed the guests with oil. Individual guests may have been especially distinguished by the amount of oil used and by the quality of the nard. In this sense the psalmist wishes to say that the Messias more than all the other guests, who as associates participate in the joys of the

royal wedding banquet, is distinguished by God. God has exalted him
and given him a name which is above all other names (Philippians 2:9).

When God clothes himself with human nature, as with a garment,
there comes from that garment the odor of heavenly glory. In the royal
palace there was a custom of burning aloe and cassia, dried blossoms and
rinds of cinnamon, and the dried juice of myrrh to create a smoke that
would permeate the garments of all persons that were in the rooms of the
palace. This smoke gave a pleasing scent. So also the garment of the
Messias emits the scent of the glories of heaven. Beside this glory the
music of the harp resounds from the palace and from the rooms plated
with shiny white ivory. There are virgins, daughters of kings, waiting for
the marriage with the king. They stand there in beautiful garments, the
gifts of their royal spouse.

Only such are allowed to enter into union with him who wear the
wedding garment which has been presented by the king, the garment of
sanctifying grace. They are Gentiles called to the Messianic kingdom
who now await the hour of spiritual espousal. The place of honor is to
the right of the spouse. It belongs to the main bride, to the chosen people
of the Old Covenant, to the Church in its Old Testament preparation. Her
dress surpasses in beauty that of the other royal daughters; the best gold
from the land of Ophir is her jewelry. To Israel belongs the childhood of
God, the glory of the Covenant, the giving of the Law, the divine service
and promises. To her belong the patriarchs and prophets and from them
Christ is descended according to the flesh.

The psalmist has sung about the beauty and majesty of the groom.
The hour of the marriage has come. In the second part of the psalm
(verses 11–18) the bride of the king is of the greatest interest. The poet,
the friend of the groom, who leads the bride to him, addresses and asks
her to give herself up to the Messias-King unreservedly. The New
Covenant with Christ admits no obstinate adherence to the obsolete
forms of the Old Covenant, no proud boasting of descent from Abraham.
In the New Covenant there is no distinction between Jew and Gentile,
between circumcision and uncircumcision, but there is a new creation.
Israel must cease as a nation, must forget its father's house and the Old
Covenant in which it has grown up in order that it may be God's people
in the New Covenant. By his grace the Lord has endowed Israel with a
supernatural beauty that it might be worthy of being the spouse of the
Messias.

Now the king asks for this beautiful bride. He demands that Israel,
the bride, be obedient to his will; for he is Adonai, the Lord. When
Esther because of her beauty was brought into the palace of Assuerus,

she had to give herself up to a pagan. This was indeed difficult. He whom the supreme King calls to spiritual union dare not resist his call. He must give himself up to him with an undivided love; for he that loves father and mother more than him is not worthy of him. The giving up of nation and home is outweighed by the honor and respect that is given to the bride for the sake of the king. The poet already sees the nations approach. They give expressions of homage to the queen on the day of her espousal and petition her for gracious favors. The speakers for the nations are the daughters of Tyre, the city proud of its liberty and wealth. The independent city reverently approaches the royal bride. In a long procession the representatives of the richest nations of the earth follow with gifts in their hands.

He who observes the procession of the worshiping people with their wealth and sees their precious gifts will conclude from the glory and renown of the queen how great is her dignity for which all admiration is due. The external beauty in the large courts of the palace is only a weak semblance of the beauty within the rooms of the royal palace. The true beauty of the Church is concealed to those who stand outside. The true beauty is found in its inner life. The poet sees the bride in her garment; it is a reflection of her divine beauty and glory; it is a participation of the divine riches. Only in this precious apparel is she led to eternal union with Christ. Now the moment has come for which the bride in the Canticle of Canticles has longed. "The king leads me into his chamber. We will rejoice and be glad; we will praise thy comeliness: more than wine" (Canticles 1:3). The moment of Messianic time has come when the Church enters in the heavenly Sion and when for all eternity she may have the most intimate communication with him. In her brilliant garment, in her wealth of grace and merits, and accompanied by all the virgins, the converted pagan nations, who as friends follow the bride, she enters the palace of the heavenly King to enjoy his beauty and love, the source of all true joy. The one that has been chosen and the many who have been chosen by her and her friends will walk with joy and jubilation through all his rooms. There is an endless procession of nations to the sanctuary of the New Covenant. In his great enthusiasm over the procession of nations, the psalmist addresses the king himself. They lead her to thee. With this remark he indicates his joy because they all come to him who is so highly esteemed by the poet.

From the spiritual espousal a glorious progeny shall issue. In the place of the fathers, the patriarchs, and the great men of the Old Testament, the sons, the children of the Church, the saints will appear in endless numbers. There will be princes from the entire world. Like princes they will be respected in all times and places. They will make his name known and bring the glad tidings of his kingdom into all the world until the end of time. The message will spread more and more, new nations will hear it and join the procession that goes up to Sion in order to learn the Law of the Lord. All nations will be accepted in his sanctuary until the praise of Christ the King will echo in the entire world and will never cease to be sung in all eternity.

psalm 45

Deus noster refugium

The Church in persecution trusteth in the protection of God

1. Unto the end, for the sons of Core, for the hidden.

2. Our God is our refuge and strength: a helper in troubles, which have found us exceedingly.

3. Therefore we will not fear, when the earth shall be troubled; and the mountains shall be removed into the heart of the sea.

4. Their waters roared and were troubled: the mountains were troubled with his strength.

5. The stream of the river maketh the city of God joyful: the Most High hath sanctified his own tabernacle.

6. God is in the midst thereof, it shall not be moved: God will help it in the early morning.

7. Nations were troubled, and kingdoms were bowed down: he uttered his voice, the earth trembled.

8. The Lord of armies is with us: the God of Jacob is our protector.

9. Come and behold ye the works of the Lord: what wonders he hath done upon earth:

10. making wars to cease even to the end of the earth.
He shall destroy the bow, and break the weapons: and the shield he shall burn in the fire.

11. Be still and see that I am God. I will be exalted among the nations, and I will be exalted in the earth.

12. The Lord of armies is with us: the God of Jacob is our protector.

IN THE year 701 the general of the Assyrian King Sennacherib appeared before the gates of Jerusalem with an army of 185,000 men and demanded the city to surrender. But at that time the Lord let King Ezechias know through the Prophet Isaias: "Wherefore thus saith the Lord concerning the king of the Assyrians: He shall not come into the city, nor shoot an arrow into it, nor come before it with shield, nor cast a trench about it. By the way that he came, he shall return, and into this city he shall not come, saith the Lord. And I will protect this city, and will save it for my own sake, and for the sake of David my servant" (Isaias 37:33–35). The prophet records further that the angel of the Lord went out and slew the entire army of the Assyrians and Sennacherib had to return to Nineveh. This miraculous deliverance of Jerusalem may have been the occasion for this psalm. It became a joyful profession of confidence that no power on earth nor of hell could prevail against the kingdom of God, a confession which the poet put into every strophe.

The believing Israelite trusted in the Lord without reservation because he had at all times proved himself to be a helper in all needs (verses 2–4). The history of the chosen people is rich in testimonies which mention God as a refuge and a power. Thus the psalmist begins his song with a joyful and jubilant "Credo" in God, a great helper of his people and of his Church. His confidence is anchored so strongly in his faith that even the greatest revolutions and dangers could not shake it. When mighty kingdoms are threatened by revolts and wars, when revolutions threaten its very existence, Israel will not give up hope because of such turmoil. When storms break in upon the nation, Israel will not despair; for the Lord of the heavenly hosts, whom many legions of spirits obey, is with his people. The God of the patriarchs is also the protector of their sons. If a single angel of the Lord slew 185,000 Assyrians in one night, what power an entire host of God would be! The first strophe is therefore a confession of confidence in the helper in all needs.

The Holy City cannot be destroyed for God lives on Sion (verses 5–8). The city enjoys a stream. Isaias in 8:6 speaks of the still-flowing water of Sion as a symbol of the peaceful Divine Providence and of his abounding grace among his people. In 66:12 he speaks of a stream of peace which the Lord will permit to flow to Jerusalem. On such a stream of divine grace and love the psalmist is also meditating here. As in a stream, wave follows upon wave, so God's grace flows continually to the city of the Lord. This grace is like a broad river that surrounds Sion and protects it. Its encirclement is the cause of joy because it is a sign that the Lord dwells within its walls and has chosen it as his sanctuary. God is in truth in the midst of his people; therefore the city of God can never cease to exist. When danger threatens, God shows his protecting hand before the inhabitants become aware of it. Even before morning dawned he had destroyed the proud army of the Assyrians in front of the walls of Jerusalem. The time of affliction is often as short as the duration of one night. Divine Providence gives his people a peaceful confidence. When the Assyrians went out with their armies, the nations against which the preparations for war were made, trembled.

Kingdoms trembled at the marches of the enemy's legions. But this terrifying power of the Assyrian king vanished before the almighty God of Israel; for at one thundering word of the almighty God, not only people and nations tremble, but also the whole earth. With joyful pride, therefore, Israel acknowledges in the second refrain: "This almighty God at whose word all inhabitants of the earth and all kingdoms must tremble; the Lord of heavenly hosts, he is the protector and refuge of his people Israel."

The great deeds which the Lord has done for his people and his holy city are known to all the world. With them he has proved himself to be the mighty protector of his kingdom (verses 9–12). Outside the walls of Jerusalem the fields were covered with the corpses of the Assyrians which the angel of the Lord had slain. The psalmist, therefore, invites the inhabitants of the city and of the entire country to behold the miracle of the Lord and to convince themselves of his power and greatness. The destruction of the Assyrian power before the gates of Sion is only a prelude to the divine judgment on the day of the Lord. God will then break all resistance against his kingdom and rule. He will put an end forever to all wars. He will break every bow that is aimed at his people; the spears will be bent and all shields will be burned. Then will the time come about which Isaias speaks: "The swords will be turned into ploughshares and the spears into pruning knives; no nation will war against his neighbor, and no one will prepare for war" (Isaias 2:4). Since Yahwe is so powerful, it is folly to wage war upon his kingdom.

From the history of this kingdom and from the fate that befell those who fought against it, all should know that Yahwe alone is God, ruler of all nations, the Lord of the entire world. Israel may well boast that the majestic God is with his people, that the God of Jacob is the refuge of Israel.

What the psalmist says here about Jerusalem is a weak counterpart of the indestructibility of the Church of Christ. May storms rage more destructive than earthquakes and typhoons the rock of Peter will remain firm; for upon it the Lord dwells. Majestic is the stream of grace that flows from the tabernacle. It is a protection which no power on earth can make ineffectual. The Church saw world kingdoms destroyed; it saw many nations revolt but the almighty word of God destroyed them. The Church itself does not waver. Its history is rich with the wonderful deeds of God. He always came to its assistance. He who reads the pages of its history must be astounded. That the Church has outlasted all attacks is a sign of its indestructibility. God breaks all weapons that are used against it. Therefore every war that is waged against the Church is a foolish undertaking. On this account we, too, with the psalmist may cry out to the enemies of the kingdom of God that they should desist from attacking the Church and acknowledge God's greatness in the Church.

psalm 46

Omnes gentes, plaudite

The Gentiles are invited to praise God for the establishment of the kingdom of Christ

1. Unto the end, for the sons of Core.

2. O clap your hands, all ye nations: shout unto God with the voice of joy.

3. For the Lord is high, terrible: a great king over all the earth.

4. He hath subdued the people under us: and the nations under our feet.

5. He hath chosen for us his inheritance, the beauty of Jacob which he hath loved.

6. God is ascended with jubilee: and the Lord with the sound of trumpet.

7. Sing praises to our God, sing ye: sing praises to our king, sing ye.

8. For God is the king of all the earth: sing ye wisely.

9. God shall reign over the nations: God sitteth on his holy throne.

10. The princes of the people are gathered together, with the God of Abraham: for the strong gods of the earth are exceedingly exalted.

THIS psalm was composed at a time when Israel had subjected all neighboring Gentile nations and made them pay tribute. God had condescended to come to his people and with his help to humble its enemies. Now after the victorious wars, he returned to heaven while Israel was offering a sacrifice of praise and thanksgiving in the sanctuary. The psalmist saw in these victories an omen of the promised Messianic time during which all nations will subject themselves to Yahwe and will join the chosen people.

Israel returned to Sion from the victorious battles and with the sound of trumpet marched to the sanctuary to thank God for his help; for his power had subdued the nations (verses 2–5). The Gentiles too should join the procession and accompany them in their applause and victory dances in honor of Yahwe. They should sing along in the jubilant songs that ascend to heaven; for Israel is the nation of Messianic salvation from which blessing goes out into the world. The destruction of the kingdom would, therefore, be an irreparable loss to all nations. Hence all the world should now rejoice because of the successes of the kingdom of God, of the Church of Jesus Christ; for through it the blessing of the Redemption is given to all nations. Yahwe is the lord of the world, the most high God; there is no other God beside him. The victories of his people which are his work have shown how terrible is his power and how mighty is his sceptre which as king of the world he wields over all nations. First the Lord has shown his power in as much as he has forced the Gentile neighboring nations to subject themselves to Israel's rule. He has subdued the nation under his feet and thus has placed his feet upon their necks. The Lord in an especial manner is the invisible king of Israel; he has chosen this people as his possession and has given to Israel Canaan as its inheritance. The enemies were powerful and so determined to possess the land that the inheritance seemed to be lost. But by miraculous deeds the Lord gave the land to his people a second time and confirmed it to be their possession. And thus Canaan became the pride of the descendants of Jacob in a greater measure than it had been for the patriarchs themselves; for God had given the land to Israel for an inheritance as a sign of his mercy and love.

God had come down from heaven to assist his people in its wars; now he again returns to heaven, accompanied by the jubilant victory songs of the returning troops and the sounding of trumpets because he has revealed himself as King of the world (verses 6–10). The joyful songs and the jubilant voices ascend to his heavenly throne while the king with his faithful followers go up to Sion. But the jubilant songs must not cease with the celebration of the victory; for Yahwe is king not only of yesterday and today but of all times. Therefore his praise must be proclaimed forever. The psalmist requests all to thank and worship God the King. The object of veneration should be the world dominion of Yahwe; for he is king of all the world. The gods of the Gentiles receive honor only in the small territory of their devotees, but the kingdom of Yahwe knows no boundaries. The praise of so mighty a King must be wise and worthy of his majesty. It is true the world kingdom is not as yet acknowledged by the Gentile nations. But the psalmist sees the promised era approaching when the Lord will sit upon his heavenly throne and the nations from all parts of the world will approach to acknowledge him as the one true God and to serve him. Then there will be one God and one Lord over all nations, one kingdom that comprises the entire world. The leaders of the nations will join the people of the God of Abraham, the chosen people of Messianic times, the Church. Then the mighty ones of this earth will also be incorporated into the congregation of God. When all the nations and princes have bent their knees before the most high God, then he will have proved himself to be the sublime God, almighty before the world.

psalm 47

Magnus Dominus

God is greatly to be praised for the establishment of his Church

1. A psalm of a canticle. For the sons of Core, on the second day of the week.

2. Great is the Lord, and exceedingly to be praised in the city of our God, in his holy mountain.

3. With the joy of the whole earth is mount Sion founded, on the sides of the north, the city of the great king.

4. In her houses shall God be known, when he shall protect her.

5. For behold the kings of earth assembled themselves: they gathered together.

6. So they saw: and they wondered, they were troubled, they were moved.

7. Trembling took hold of them. There were pains as of a woman in labor.

8. With a vehement wind thou shalt break in pieces the ships of Tharsis.

9. As we have heard, so have we seen, in the city of the Lord of hosts, in the city of our God: God hath founded it forever.

10. We have received thy mercy, O God, in the midst of thy temple.

11. According to thy name, O God, so also is thy praise unto the ends of the earth: thy right hand is full of justice.

12. Let mount Sion rejoice and the daughters of Juda be glad, because of thy judgments, O Lord.

13. Surround Sion and encompass her: tell ye in her towers.

14. Set your hearts on her strength; and distribute her houses, that ye may relate it in another generation.

15. For this is God, our God unto eternity, and forever and ever. He shall rule us for evermore.

During the reign of King Josaphat, 872–849, the Gentile Amorrhites, Moabites, and Edomites had united against the kingdom of Juda and were preparing themselves for war at Engaddi and in the desert of Tekoa, only a few hours distant from Jerusalem. Then Josaphat with his entire people prayed to the Lord, and God removed the threatening danger without the Israelitic troops having used their swords. He created discord among the confederate troops and thus they fought each other and disbanded. When the king with his warriors looked down from the heights on the extensive flats below, he saw the desert covered with corpses. The king then returned to Jerusalem to thank the Lord in the sanctuary for the miraculous deliverance from the great danger. Terror fell upon all the nations and tribes roundabout when they received the news of the intervention by Yahwe in favor of his people (2 Chronicles 20). This event may have been the occasion of this psalm. The composer gave to this prayer of thanksgiving the form of a song about Jerusalem, the city sanctified and protected by God. The contents of the psalm may be applicable in a far greater measure to the Church, the Sion of the New Covenant. The Church is in a much more exalted sense the city of the great king, and its history, too, records many miraculous deeds of deliverance.

The psalm (verses 2–4) begins by praising the Lord and Jerusalem, the city of God. Great is Yahwe the God of Israel; his name is worthy of the highest praise. What Jesus Sirach says about the greatness of God manifested in creation may also be said about his greatness as revealed in the history of his people and kingdom. How can we glorify him? The Almighty is above all his works. The Lord is majestic and exceedingly great and his power is admirable. Glorify the Lord as much as you can and he will excel all the glory that is given him; his magnificence is wonderful. Bless the Lord; exalt him as much as you can, for he is above all praise. When you glorify him do it with all your energy and be not weary; for you can never glorify him enough (Ecclesiasticus 43:30–34). This great God dwells in Jerusalem, on the holy Mount Sion, the type of the Church of Christ. Sion does not tower above the mountains round about. It is much lower than the snow-capped summit of the Great Hermon. Nevertheless it has a pleasant height and deserves to be called the delight of the whole world. On this mountain God has placed his throne of grace; from here the Messianic blessing was to flow into the world. Mount Sion in the northern part of Jerusalem has the unique privilege of being the city of the great king, of being the city on the mountain whose light shines into the darkness of paganism. The Church of Christ in its external splendor and means of power cannot be compared to the wealth and power of the world. But it deserves much more than Jerusalem to be called the joy of the world; for God dwells in its tabernacles, God who alone is the truth and without whom there is no grace. The miraculous deliverance of Sion from great danger and its preservation from the attacks of the confederate heathen kings has again shown to the world that Almighty God, the Lord of the world, dwells in his castle and is a sure protector of his kingdom. So also the Church sees in every divine punishment of the enemy a new guarantee of the promise that the gates of hell shall not prevail against it. The Church sees a new confirmation that the Lord is, in truth, with it.

Now the psalmist describes the miraculous deliverance of the city (verses 5–9). The kings of the Ammonites, the Moabites, and Edomites had formed a confederacy and had marched against the city of Jerusalem. They were tribes related among themselves and with Israel but on that account their hatred was more intense than that of the other Gentile nations and their attacks were more dangerous. They were already encamped at the borders of the kingdom of Juda and already could see from the distance the gold-covered pinnacles of the temple. But seeing the temple there came upon them a spirit of blindness and hatred which caused discord among them. Those whom hatred against the kingdom of God had brought together now fought each other. In the confusion of the many who had fought this fratricidal war the Jews recognized the strong hand of God. They trembled for fear like a woman in labor. It was impossible to take a firm stand against the approaching army of Israel. Whoever escaped the sword in war sought safety in flight, leaving the corpses and booty to the enemy. As a violent storm from the east blows over the Great Sea and shatters the great ships of Tharsis, so God's wrath scattered the proud army of the confederates. As a matter of note: all large ocean ships that were built according to the pattern of ships going to Tharsis, a Phoenician colony in Spain, were called *Tharsis ships*. What remained after such storms was only a few planks which were carried along by the waves into the open sea. In the pages of Sacred History one reads of the divine promises of protection and of the great and wonderful deeds of their fulfillment. Now they themselves experienced the truth of God's word that Sion would not be destroyed; for it is the city of God. In the history of the Church we have also experienced century after century the wonderful deeds of the Lord. The enemies unite that together they may vanquish the hated Church, but God brings discord among them and destroys them before they can fulfill their purpose.

After the easy victory King Josaphat went up to the sanctuary to thank the Lord. The psalmist now requests a thanksgiving to God (verses 10–12). In the temple the people should be mindful of God's great favor and thank him for the love he has shown to his city. But the thanksgiving and praise should not be limited to the courts of the temple. Yahwe is God of the whole people. His name, his nature, his revelations are of great significance to the whole world. It is befitting that his renown should be made known to the Gentile world, indeed, to the ends of the earth that all may know that Yahwe is a just God who will not permit anyone to attack his people without being punished, and who grants his servants blessing and deliverance. The justice of the Lord was the cause of Israel's redemption. Therefore Sion should be jubilant and its daughter-cities should rejoice; for their existence stands and falls with Jerusalem's existence and fall. They should rejoice and glorify God because he inflicts punishments upon the Gentiles. Every member of Christ's Church when he reflects upon the wonderful deeds of God must feel himself obligated to give thanks to God in like manner. He should proclaim the name of the Lord in the whole world in order all may acknowledge God's justice and praise his judgments.

To doubters the news of the miraculous deliverance of Sion may have seemed unbelievable; therefore the psalmist challenges the world to convince itself that the city was destroyed (verses 13–15). When they march around the walls they will see that none of the towers that had been erected for defense had crumbled, that not even a stone had been broken. The ramparts stand undamaged because the enemy could not scale them; no burning arrow was hurled into the citadel or into the palaces. They should observe this and narrate to succeeding generations God's wonderful act of deliverance. All should feel the majesty of the Lord and acknowledge it. Thus Yahwe is the true God; he is our God forever and ever. This acknowledgment should be accompanied by a petition that God may guide his people throughout all times. The Church too remains untouched in its faith and in its sources of grace from the attacks of the enemy. He who meditates on the holy city of God must be astonished at its indestructibility throughout the centuries. Every child of the Church may joyfully acknowledge and say: This is our God; he is our God forever. And all should pray that the Lord may guide their Church and protect it.

psalm 48

Audite haec, omnes gentes

The folly of the worldlings, who live in sin,
without thinking of death or hell

1. Unto the end, a psalm for the sons of Core.

2. Hear these things, all ye nations: give ear all ye inhabitants of the world.

3. All you that are earthborn, and you sons of men: both rich and poor together.

4. My mouth shall speak wisdom: and the meditation of my heart understanding.

5. I will incline my ear to a parable: I will open my proposition on the psaltery.

6. Why shall I fear in the evil day? The iniquity of my heel shall encompass me.

7. They that trust in their own strength, and glory in the multitude of their riches,

8. no brother can redeem, nor shall man redeem: he shall not give to God his ransom.

9. Nor the price of the redemption of his soul: and shall labor forever,

10. and shall still live to the end.

11. He shall not see destruction, when he shall see the wise dying: the senseless and the fool shall perish together. And they shall leave their riches to strangers:

12. and their sepulchres shall be their houses forever: their dwelling places to all generations: they have called their lands by their names.

13. And man when he was in honor did not understand: he is compared to senseless beasts and is become like to them.

14. This way of theirs is a stumbling block to them: and afterwards they shall delight in their mouth.

15. They are laid in hell like sheep: death shall feed upon them.
And the just shall have dominion over them in the morning; and their help shall decay in hell from their glory.

16. But God will redeem my soul from the hand of hell, when he shall receive me.

17. Be not thou afraid when a man shall be made rich, and when the glory of his house shall be increased.

18. For when he shall die he shall take nothing away; nor shall his glory descend with him.

19. For in his lifetime his soul will be blessed: and he will praise thee when thou shalt do well to him.

20. He shall go in to the generations of his fathers: and he shall never see light.

21. Man when he was in honor did not understand: he hath been compared to senseless beasts, and made like to him.

For thousands of years the complaint has been made in the world that earthly possessions, wealth, honor, luxury and health are unequally distributed, that there are rich and poor, aristocrats and plebeians. The complaint became more and more vociferous in times when social differences made themselves felt more bitterly. This inequality can become a grave test to the faith when wealth falls into the hands of the godless and is denied to those who fear God. The spiritual combat of the pious and patient Job gives testimony of the gravity a just man may suffer in spiritual difficulties.

Therefore it is of the greatest importance to give to earthly possessions their real value and a proper appreciation of the happiness of evil men. Death, and rewards, and punishments after death give us a correct idea and appreciation. The psalmist wishes to indicate these sources of knowledge. Both parts of his instruction end with a refrain.

To give to earthly possessions their proper value and to use them properly is for all men an important decision. That the goods of this life are so unequally distributed troubles men at all times and in all places. Therefore the psalmist asks all the people to pay heed to his instructions.

All the inhabitants of the earth should give him full attention. The question is not only directed to the plebeian masses who are not blessed with earthly possessions, but also to the upper classes who can satisfy their heart's desires. The rich and the poor alike have reason to occupy themselves earnestly with this question. The poor must do so because they have a wrong idea of the value of possessions and honor and on that account become dissatisfied and murmur against God; the rich must do so that in view of death and the hereafter they may not become too attached to their earthly possessions and misuse them. Worldly wisdom cannot solve the problem but will try to remove the inequalities by force and violence. Only faith can solve the problem. It is therefore heavenly acumen and not human wisdom which the psalmist proposes. It is his only concern to clothe his proposal with the right words. Prophets sometimes took harp in hands when they awaited a divine illumination and information in order to collect their thoughts and remove all distractions from the outside world. Thus the composer of this psalm takes the harp in order to concentrate on the divine instruction and with God's wisdom to solve the great problem during his song.

In the first part of his instruction (verses 6–13) the psalmist points to the end of man's earthly life. He tells us that death equalizes everything. In times when capitalism uses the power of money without any consideration for others and exploits the socially weak and causes anxiety and worries to the oppressed, there is also danger to the faith. Such a condition is fertile ground for revolutions. But the just man should not allow himself to be led astray under such difficult circumstances. He should not permit himself to be led into error by false judgments and wrong actions. It is just under such circumstances that he must try to acquire a knowledge of the true value of earthly possessions in the light of death and eternity. The rich man trusts in his power as if he could never lose it; he boasts about the greatness of his possessions because with them he can satisfy all his needs; haughtily he looks down upon the masses of the people, upon the poor and the humble. But his possessions, even if he counts them by the hundreds, do not save him from death. He may do anything he wishes with his money and indulge in luxury; he may make men submissive to his will, but he cannot make death submissive. With all his possessions he cannot bribe God to make an exception of him. Even if he would make an offering of millions, God would not take ransom money. There is no bribe able to cancel the law of death. Even if ransom were a possibility, the richest man could not accumulate enough because the price demanded by the Lord for life and death is infinite. Even if during all his years he would restlessly try to acquire money, if he would gather the possessions of a lifetime, they would not reach. Freedom from death, the immortality of the body lost in paradise cannot be bought by any earthly means. Even the richest man on earth must die and descend into the dark grave.

The godless rich are reminded almost every day that death makes no exception and shows no preferences; they see wise and just men die who because of their faith found true wisdom and union with God. They also see fools and evil-minded men die who cannot take along with them into the grave any of their possessions. They hear roundabout of laughing heirs who have inherited luxuries without any trouble of their own, luxuries which another has gathered by much wearisome work for many years. The rich man has accompanied many friends to the grave and has there seen with his own eyes that nothing has remained for them of all of their possessions. The preciously decorated and ventilated rooms of their palaces they had to exchange for the narrow dark and damp grave in which they must always remain. For those who possessed great estates not even enough room is given for their corpse to be stretched out. In this respect the rich man has nothing more than what the ordinary man has. But while enjoying more than what the ordinary man has, while enjoying his luxuriant life, he does not want to know anything about death, he does not want to be reminded of death and the grave although both are surely his lot at the end of his life. Therefore he is likened to the irrational animal which likewise does not think of death, which without care about its end lives only for the day.

Death which equalizes everything is in itself not a satisfactory solution of the problem. If there were no other life than our earthly life, the inequality of our lot would be an unbearable burden. How could we then have faith in God's justice and love? Our faith demands that there will be an equalization in the next world. Thus the meditation of the psalmist turns to the second part (verses 14–21) to the life after death. The psalmist teaches us that the next life will bring about a just equalization between the godless rich and the just poor. Godlessness blinds those who are blessed with earthly goods. The rich man trusts in his good luck. He acts as if he were going to live forever. He does not think of death and judgment which will take the bandage from his eyes. The godless rich who go into eternity may be likened to a herd of sheep which are enclosed within a fence and are watched by a shepherd. The fenced place is hell. To this place the shepherd, Death, drives the sheep and watches the entrance so that for all eternity none of the sheep will escape. They are closed up in hell forever. Never will they see the light. Hell will never be a place of joy and comfort. The eternal night has begun. But after the night of bodily death there follows for the just the morning dawn of a new, blessed life with God. Those who have been oppressed and trodden down by the godless will rule over them. They are now victors over enemies to whom they had patiently submitted. It is true their souls also must enter the underworld, but there they await the glad day when the Lord will awaken the body from the grave and will unite it with the soul for a new and blessed union. On the morning of the Resurrection of the Messianic time God will take them with him. As the just before their death lived in union with God and were permitted to be his guests in the place of the sanctuary, so for eternity they will be members of the transfigured kingdom, fellow-citizens of the saints, and members of the household of God when the promised Messianic time has come.

From this instruction about death and about reward and punishment in the next world the psalmist makes an application for the just (verses 17–21). He who reflects upon this earthly life with all its crosses and sufferings and contrasts it with the heavenly transfiguration and compares the present privations with the eternal inheritance prepared for him, cannot be envious of the rich man, even if the glory of his house increases. The rich man cannot take along with him the least of his possessions when he dies and is carried to the grave. His possessions remain here and will come into strange hands. He may say with the godless rich man in the Gospel and consider himself blessed: "My soul, thou hast laid aside rich possessions for many years; now take a rest, eat and drink, and be merry" (Luke 12:19). He may boast before others that with his wealth he may live in luxury, but this passes quickly. In his zeal the psalmist here speaks to the rich in direct address. The word of the Lord is applicable to him: "Thou fool, in this night thy soul shall be demanded of thee. What thou has garnered, whose shall it be?" (Luke 12:20). He must die like all his forefathers have died and will be burned with them. He will nevermore see the light of the sun because for the godless there will be no resurrection to a new life. He is destined to eternal death, to the eternal night of death. But even this serious truth makes no impression upon such blind men; they do not take it to heart. In the enjoyment of life they don't want to hear or know anything about death or the hereafter; they ignore it so that they do not have to think about it; they are like animals that have no understanding; they live thoughtlessly because there is no eternity for a beast.

psalm 49

Deus deorum

*The coming of Christ who prefers virtue and inward
purity before blood victims*

1. A psalm for Asaph.
   The God of gods, the Lord hath spoken: and he hath called the earth.
   From the rising of the sun to the going down thereof:

2. out of Sion the loveliness of his beauty.

3. God shall come manifestly: our God shall come, and shall not keep silence.
   A fire shall burn before him: and a mighty tempest shall be round about
   him.

4. He shall call heaven from above, and the earth, to judge his people.

5. Gather ye together his saints to him: who set his covenant before sacrifices.

6. And the heavens shall declare his justice: for God is judge.

7. Hear, O my people, and I will speak: O Israel, and I will testify to thee: I
   am God, thy God.

8. I will not reprove thee for thy sacrifices: and thy burnt offerings are always
   in my sight.

9. I will not take calves out of thy house: nor he goats out of thy flocks.

10. For all the beasts of the woods are mine: the cattle on the hills, and the
    oxen.

11. I know all the fowls of the air: and with me is the beauty of the field.

12. If I should be hungry, I would not tell thee: for the world is mine, and the
    fullness thereof.

13. Shall I eat the flesh of bullocks? Or shall I drink the blood of goats?

14. Offer to God the sacrifice of praise: and pay thy vows to the Most High.

15. And call upon me in the day of trouble: I will deliver thee, and thou shalt
    glorify me.

16. But to the sinner God hath said: Why dost thou declare my justices, and
    take my covenant in thy mouth?

17. Seeing thou hast hated discipline: and hast cast my words behind thee.

18. If thou didst see a thief thou didst run with him: and with adulterers thou hast been a partaker.

19. Thy mouth hath abounded with evil, and thy tongue framed deceits.

20. Sitting thou didst speak against thy brother, and didst lay a scandal against thy mother's son.

21. These things hast thou done, and I was silent. Thou thoughtest unjustly that I should be like to thee: but I will reprove thee, and set before thy face.

22. Understand these things, you that forget God: lest he snatch you away and there be none to deliver you.

23. The sacrifice of praise shall glorify me: and there is the way by which I will show him the salvation of God.

T HE Old Testament worship of God had its climax in the daily sacrifice for it was the main act of worship. The Law had for this service detailed regulations. According to the intention of the divine Lawgiver they were to serve as a proper external expression of the inner reverence for the majesty of God. But because of the external form of the sacrifice the inner sentiment and disposition might be neglected and thus might lose its meaning and value. The Mosaic Law already indicated the necessity of a proper disposition at the sacrifice when it taught the commandment of the love of God with one's whole soul and heart as the greatest commandment. It looked upon this commandment as a compendium of the entire Law. The prophets, especially Amos, Isaias, and Jeremias, fought against the growing externalism of worship with all their strength and eloquence. They did not oppose sacrifices as such. This was far from them. They only stressed the worthlessness of sacrifices when they were not offered in the spirit of a living faith. They emphasized the necessity of a proper inner disposition. The composer of this psalm gives the same advice as these prophets. There is no proof needed that he did not intend to criticize the sacrificial worship itself; for it is unthinkable that a psalm which had rejected the sacrificial service as displeasing to God would have been sung during the sacrificial service or that it would have been accepted in the collections of songs sung at the divine services. What the psalmist says of the externalism of the Old Testament sacrifices may also be applied to the sacrifice of the New Covenant. It is true that the Holy Mass is a sacrifice which in itself is of infinite value, but the participation at the Mass may be a mere external soulless act. The demand of a live faith and proper dispositions is applicable to all.

The truth about which the psalmist wishes to speak is a serious truth and he meditates profoundly upon the relations that should exist between man and God; therefore his language too is grave and solemn. In the introduction he permits God himself to speak (verses 1–6). God himself rejects a soulless cult. This condemnation comes from the mouth of the most high God and is not the personal opinion of the psalmist. The Lord comes from Sion, from the place of grace in Israel. He seems to pass judgment upon his people. He calls all the earth, all the inhabitants of the earth from east to west to be attentive to his words. Whatever he has to say about the true worship of God concerns not only Israel, but men of all times and places; it is meant for us. At the very place of the sanctuary God is witness of the externalism of worship. Before his very tabernacle men of his kingdom who are called to worship him believe that they do not have to give him their whole heart and soul. Therefore the holy place which deserves to be called the dwelling place of the Most High, the crown of beauty, the perfection of beauty, becomes a place of divine judgment. The psalmist sees the Lord appear. A brilliant light is seen; for God is light and his garment is light. He shines a beam of his divine glory upon men that they may recognize his majesty and worship him. Because he appears as judge fire and storm are his heralds: fire which devours sinners and the storm which blows them away like chaff. Heaven and earth are called upon to be witnesses to the act of judgment. Thus Moses once called upon heaven and earth to be witnesses that God has given his people the choice of life and death for the observance or non-observance of the Law, the choice of curse or blessing in order that they may not excuse themselves and say that they have a lack of knowledge of their duties towards God and of the consequences of their disobedience to them (Deuteronomy 30:19). So also Isaias called upon heaven and earth to be witnesses to the thanklessness and faithlessness of Israel and to the justice of the divine punitive judgment (1:2). So also now they should be witnesses to the divine admonition and warning which the Lord gives to his people about its soulless worship. The witnesses are invited. The angels as servants of the divine justice are commanded to assemble the accused, the saints, and the members of the chosen people and to bring them before the judge. With them the Lord has made a covenant which was sealed with a sacrifice. This sacrifice was the outward expression of obedience, fidelity, and worship. They had made this sacrificial covenant an empty affair. Now the Judge appears and the heavens announce that the judgment begins. Sacrificial service and the fulfillment of the Law are the objects of the transaction.

The judgment begins with the accusation of externalism at the sacrificial service (verses 7–15). The Judge takes up the word: "Hear my

187

people; let me speak; Israel, I want to admonish you." Right is on his side; for he is God, the Creator of the world, the Infinite, the Most High whom all creatures must serve and whom they cannot satisfy with a few external practices. He is the God of Israel who in virtue of the covenant can make special claims upon his people. He has chosen them and from all nations of the earth has made them his special possession and has called them to worship and glorify him. There are likewise many reasons for the Christians to worship him in spirit and in truth. It is true that Israel had not neglected the sacrificial service. It had offered the sacrifices prescribed by the Law for every day and for the feast days; it had offered many voluntary sacrifices. The Lord knows that daily a holocaust was burnt upon the altar and that blood was poured at the foot of the altar. He does not accuse his people on the point of external offerings because he does not need them.

What could the external bloody offering give him? Even if Israel sacrifices a thousand steers and many thousands of sheep and goats, as Solomon did at the occasion of the dedication of the temple, what do these gifts mean to an infinite God? He cannot receive what he already possesses. All the wild animals of the forest, all beasts roaming in the mountains are his possession. All the birds that nest among the rocks the Lord knows because they owe him their existence and are daily depending on his divine Providence. Whatever moves in the fields, large and small, belongs to God. Man has only the use of the divine possessions. He cannot give anything which God cannot claim as his possession. All of the sacrificial gifts cannot enrich God. Neither can they serve the purpose of filling the divine need for food. He to whom the universe belongs with all its plants, fruits, and animals has no need to beg man for nourishment even if it were possible that he be hungry. In this respect the sacrifices are no offerings to God, because as a pure spirit he needs no food. How could he eat the flesh of steers and drink the blood of goats? From all this Israel should know that the external sacrifice gives nothing to God for which he would have to be thankful. For him such gifts are worthless and obtain their worth only through the internal disposition and prayer. The Lord does not want the flesh and blood of animals, but he does want the faith, love, worship, and obedience of man. Only when sacrifice is the external expression of the internal disposition is it pleasing to God. The sacrifice of the New Covenant has indeed an infinite value and cannot lose it by the externalism of those who participate in it, but it loses its value as a sacrifice of adoration and thanksgiving for the individual Christian when he participates in it only externally with neither true devotion nor spiritual union between himself and his God.

In the Old Covenant God wanted man, not his animals, in the sacrificial service; he wanted praise and thanksgiving from a believing soul and not merely the folding of hands and many words. Man should not omit the sacrifices, but he should remember that his soul is demanded in sacrifices of praise and thanksgiving and that a sacrifice made in connection with the making of a vow has value only when the soul is really filled with a grateful love for God. In times of tribulation it is not the bloody sacrifice that makes the Lord decide to send help, but the humble prayer and faith of the petitioner in the God who will liberate his people so that they may praise his name and give him glory. God's honor is the supreme purpose of all divine worship and the highest purpose of man's existence. It is only through the surrender of the will, a lively faith, a thankful love, and true obedience that this purpose can be fulfilled and not by the giving of things which are worthless in God's sight.

Externalism at the sacrificial service is a disregard of the first table of the Decalogue. The divine Judge has also reason to complain about the disregard of the second table, about the externalism in the observance of these laws (verses 16–23). In the Epistle to the Romans Paul has pointed to such men who speak much about the Law of God, but disregard it in important things with the following words: "Thou that teachest another, teachest not thyself: thou that preachest that men should not steal, stealest; thou that sayest men should not commit adultery, committest adultery; thou that abhorrest idols, committest sacrilege; thou that makest a boast of the law, by transgression of the law, dishonorest God" (Romans 2:21–23). Such hypocrites speak much about the wisdom and necessity of the Law to keep the people disciplined, but they themselves refuse to submit. They hate to be educated in the Law and to be instructed in moral integrity. They do not themselves keep God's laws, but throw them, as it were, behind their backs as worthless things. The hypocrite very well knows the Commandments: "Thou shalt not steal and thou shalt not commit adultery." Nevertheless, he makes common cause with thieves and adulterers. He knows well that the eighth commandment forbids giving false testimony, lying, and detraction. But his mouth knows only wicked, uncharitable and detractive speech, deceit, and falsehood. Even the nearest relative, a brother, is not safe against slander and detraction. In man the contrast between knowing and doing is an abomination and will not go unpunished. The hypocrite must be detected otherwise he might think that God does not consider his life to be sinful because he does not punish him. The present judgment which he may not spurn should be a warning to him. The punishment will come. God in his wrath and in his abhorrence for such hypocrisy will put an end to such men who serve him only outwardly, who honor him only with their lips but whose hearts are far from him.

Then too there will no longer be salvation for them; for it is terrible to fall into the hands of the living God. At the close, the psalmist summarizes both demands for a true sacrificial service and for the fulfillment of the Law. Only he who brings to God a sacrifice of praise, only he who praises God with a lively faith and a thankful love honors the Lord; and only he who walks on the right path of the Law and does not only talk about it shall receive salvation from God. He shall see and enjoy salvation.

psalm 50

Miserere

The repentance and confession of David after his sin.
The fourth penitential psalm

1. Unto the end, a psalm of David.

2. When Nathan the prophet came to him, after he had sinned with Bethsabee (2 Kings 12).

3. Have mercy on me, O God, according to thy great mercy.
   And according to the multitude of thy tender mercies, blot out my iniquity.

4. Wash me yet more from my iniquity, and cleanse me from my sin.

5. For I know my iniquity, and my sin is always before me.

6. To thee only have I sinned and have done evil before thee: that thou mayst be justified in thy words, and mayst overcome when thou art judged.

7. For behold I was conceived in iniquities: and in sins did my mother conceive me.

8. For behold thou hast loved truth: the uncertain and hidden things of thy wisdom thou hast made manifest to me.

9. Thou shalt sprinkle me with hyssop, and I shall be cleansed: thou shalt wash me, and I shall be made whiter than snow.

10. To my hearing thou shalt give joy and gladness: and the bones that have been humbled shall rejoice.

11. Turn away thy face from my sins: and blot out all my iniquities.

12. Create a clean heart in me, O God: and renew a right spirit within my bowels.

13. Cast me not away from thy face: and take not thy holy Spirit from me.

14. Restore unto me the joy of thy salvation: and strengthen me with a perfect spirit.

15. I will teach the unjust thy ways: and the wicked shall be converted to thee.

16. Deliver me from blood, O God, thou God of my salvation: and my tongue shall extol thy justice.

17. O Lord, thou wilt open my lips: and my mouth shall declare thy praise.

18. For if thou hadst desired sacrifice, I would indeed have given it: with burnt offerings thou wilt not be delighted.

19. A sacrifice to God is an afflicted spirit: a contrite and humbled heart, O God, thou wilt not despise.

20. Deal favorably, O Lord, in thy good will with Sion: that the walls of Jerusalem may be built up.

21. Then shalt thou accept the sacrifice of justice, oblations and whole-burnt offerings: then they shall lay calves upon thy altar.

THE Fourth Penitential Psalm, the "Miserere" has become an ecclesiastical penitential psalm because of the Christian interpretation of sin as an offense against God and the co-interpretation of grace as the only source of reconciliation and perseverance. Since it is now used as a prayer of contrition, it needs no other explanation. This psalm composed by the penitent David, the Church uses on all occasions that require and call for an attitude and spirit of penance. When David had become guilty of adultery with Bethsabee the wife of his murdered officer Urias and had concealed his twofold crime from the people, when he had refused to admit his sin, God sent to him the prophet Nathan that he might awaken the conscience of the king and remind him of the gravity of his guilt. The grace of God sought entrance into his soul and David did not refuse admission. He listened to the voice of the Lord and was willing to do penance. When the prophet spoke to him, it was at once clear that before he had refused to see that he had not only done an injustice to two of his subjects, but that he had also offended God, his supreme Lord. Thus he confessed his guilt before God and his prophet (2 Kings 12:1 seq.). But he was not satisfied with this confession. The people who were necessarily scandalized at the sins of the king should also know of his conversion. Thus he composed for the accompaniment of his harp this

thoughtful penitential psalm in order that all who might have imitated
the king in his sins may now follow him on his way of penance.

The psalm begins with a petition for divine pardon (verses 3–8). King
David had sinned grievously against the love and grace of God. It was
unmerited love which called him away from his herd of sheep to the
kingship. During the years of persecution by Saul, God's love had guided
him in a wonderful manner to the throne and had helped him to vanquish
all the enemies of his kingdom while giving him the Messianic promise
for the eternal existence of his house. But despite the many manifestations
of love the king stretched out his hands to acts of injustice and repaid
favors with disobedience. Where should he now go to obtain pardon for
his sins against the Lord? He could not appeal to God's justice; for the
divine judgment passed upon him was just. He, therefore, appealed to
God's offended love, to the heart of God which is great in pardoning
(Isaias 55:7). Therefore this penitential psalm begins with the petition:
"Have mercy on me, O Lord, according to thy love; erase my misdeeds
according to thy great goodness." If before his unconfessed sins weighed
heavily upon his conscience and robbed him of so much joy, so now the
acknowledgment of the real nature of his sins, especially of the grievous
sins which oppressed him, not only awakened in him a sincere longing to
be freed from his double guilt, but also to be cleansed from every sin.
"Wash away my entire guilt and cleanse me from my sins." That is a sign
of genuine sorrow when it has its source in the true love of God, when
man is not only sorry for the grave sins he himself has committed, but
when he detests every sin from the depths of his soul because it is an
offense against God and a stain that is hateful in the sight of God.

He who is sorry for his sins in a manner pleasing to God and wishes to
obtain pardon for them sees them in their true nature; namely, as offenses
against God. This is required before we can ask pardon from God. For a
long time David may have tried to convince himself that he had only
done an injustice to two persons and that he had not infringed upon the
rights of God. He may have believed that Bethsabee could bear the loss
of her husband if he himself took her to wife. That every sin is a breach
of the commandments of the first table and primarily an offense against
God he, as many before and after him, would not admit. But when grace
entered his soul, he acknowledged his guilt. Now his sin was before him
day and night in its true nature and it did not leave him until he heard
the redeeming words of pardon. As long as man does not consider his
offense against his neighbor a sin against God, he will also deny God the
right to punish and will look upon every divine punishment as an injustice. But he who has recognized that every sin against one's neighbor
is a rebellion against God's will and then has recourse first to God and

then to his neighbor will cry out with David: "Against thee have I sinned and have done what is evil in thine eyes." By his confession the sinner acknowledges the right of the Lord to punish and says his "amen" to his judgment. Thus David's open confession was a justification of the judgment which the Lord had passed upon him through the Prophet Nathan. But this justification of God by the penitent sinner should also be the reason for God's mercy and reconciliation.

The psalmist sees another reason for divine forgiveness in the face of original sin. All men are born with guilt upon their souls and in sin are they conceived by their mothers. The psalmist in referring to the taint of human nature through original sin does not wish to excuse his own sinful act or to give extenuating circumstances before his divine Judge. This is far from him. He wishes to indicate the root of all his sins before his heavenly Physician and to indicate the first cause of his sin to him from whom he expects and begs a complete healing. A sickness of soul that is deeply rooted no human physician can heal. Only almighty God can heal it. But a healing which removes only the outward appearance of sin, which only covers the sin without curing the root of the evil is inconsistent with divine truth and sincerity. God wants man to purify himself from the guilt of sin, to free himself from all attachment to sin and from every inclination to unfaithfulness to the will of God. What Paul demands from Christians was already the highest ideal for the psalmist: "Let not sin, therefore, reign in your mortal body, so as to obey the lusts thereof. Neither yield ye your members as instruments of iniquity unto sin: but present yourselves to God as those that are alive from the dead: and your members as instruments of justice unto God: for sin shall not have dominion over you: for you are not under the law, but under grace. What then? Shall we sin because we are not under the law but under grace? God forbid" (Romans 6:12–15). Such a cleansing which excludes every future deliberate sin can only be effected by grace. Therefore David begs God to give his soul wisdom, that true wisdom which consists in the love of God and in reverence for God (Sirach 1:14). God must permeate the soul and its most secret recesses with his grace.

Such a cleansing of the entire inner man from sin is the first act of divine Love after the sinner in sincere repentance has approached his God and has longingly desired a complete healing. The second deed of divine Love is the renewal of the life of grace, union with God. Therefore David adds to his prayer for pardon the petition for a renewal of life (verses 9–15). David begins with an urgent request that God may remove all sin from his soul in order that he may again be admitted to union with him. He clothes his petition with a description of Hebrew cult life. Every Israelite by the touch of a dead person became levitically unclean and

was excluded from the sanctuary for seven days. He had to have his uncleanness removed by a priest. The cleansing from sin was effected by
purification water sprinkled with a twig of hyssop (Numbers 19:11).
Levitical uncleanness was considered a prototype of sin and its effects.
Hence it was not removed by a simple washing like other levitical defile-
ments which lasted only until evening. But it needed the mediation of a
priest, the representative of God. Every sinner must go to God to be
cleansed from his sin. God will restore him to his friendship and to
sanctifying grace. But the psalmist wants his purification to be so perfect
that no trace of sin will remain, that his soul will be made cleaner and
whiter than snow.

When, therefore, the sinner has heard from God or from his representative the consoling words, "Be of good heart, thy sins are forgiven
thee . . ." the soul is rejuvenated and true joy returns to it. This true
joy can be found only in union with God. The new life of the soul is
also imparted to the body which with the soul has suffered under the
weight of guilt and under the sting of a bad conscience. The whole man
rejoices, is seized by the happiness of being at peace with God; all dejection is at an end. David was conscious of the great multitude of sins
which he had committed since the time of his youth. In the 39th Psalm
he confessed that they were more numerous than the hair of his head. But
because of God's love neither the number nor the grievousness of his sins
was an obstacle to God's mercy. When God turns his countenance away
from sins, they are no longer there; they are erased for all times so that
they can no longer testify against the sinner.

When through the Lord's mercy all transgressions are cleansed from
the soul, the Lord may recreate a sinful heart, may create a new heart
which is not only free from guilt, but which is also strong for a new life
in and for God. Justification, the spiritual change in the sinner to a child
of grace, is so great a miracle of divine power and love that the psalmist
calls it a work of creation, as St. Paul did in his deeper knowledge of the
nature of justification (2 Cor. 5:17 and Galatians 6:15). According to
Ezechiel 36:26 the new heart is a heart filled with the spirit of God who
brings it about that the soul of man walks the way of the divine commandments and precepts. The renewal of the inner man depends on the
cooperation of man, not only to be receptive of the new life from God,
but also to persevere and perfect it. Remaining in the state of grace is
dependent on another gift of God, the grace of perseverance. For this the
psalmist also prays: "Create a clean heart in me, O God, and renew a
right spirit within my bowels." The grace of perseverance on the way of
virtue is as necessary as it is unmerited. Even the most saintly man must
be anxious about his salvation and eternal happiness; for God may

deprive him of this grace. Of this the psalmist is convinced. Therefore he constantly prays to the Lord that he may not turn his countenance away from him, that the Holy Spirit may not withdraw his sanctifying strength, his grace from him. The psalmist closes his petition for a renewal: may God give him joy in his restoration to grace, make him strong, and give him a willing spirit so that he may persevere in the state of justification; may he strengthen his will and desire for eternal salvation; may he keep his zeal alive to continue praying for salvation and to strive for it. When the Lord mercifully accepts a penitent sinner and absolves him from his guilt, when he creates in him a new heart, then such a testimony of divine mercy can become an incentive for other sinners to walk the same way and be converted to God. David would contribute to this. When the Lord grants his request, he will give testimony to the richness of his grace and love; for God will give it to those who ask for pardon.

As soon as the grace of God has completed its work of purification and renewal, the soul reconciled with God and united with him must feel the impulse not only to thank the Lord but also to praise him before all men because of the miracles of his goodness. David especially felt this tendency because the Lord had given him the talent of glorifying his name in songs. Yet even in his songs the Lord had to give his assistance. Therefore the psalmist closes this penitential psalm with a petition for the grace of worthily thanking him (verses 16–21). The absolution from the guilt of the bloody deed which David had committed in the murder of Urias will be an occasion for praising God's justice; that is, his grace that justifies and sanctifies. Only a soul which knows that it no longer has to fear the wrath of God, that it is permitted to enjoy the richness of his grace and love can sing jubilantly. Guilt closes the mouth of man; he cannot sing joyfully the praises of him whom he has gravely offended and whose wrath he has challenged. Absolution opens his mouth. But even in another sense God must open the mouth of the psalmist. He must give him the thoughts and language that he may worthily praise him. He must give to the song the spiritual power to inspire other men with the love of God. The royal singer needs this grace; for the Lord demands no other thanks from him than a song in which he may use his talent to give glory to God. The king would have been willing to offer sacrifices in great numbers. But God did not make the remission of sins in Israel depend upon the offering of bloody sacrifices. The sacrifices of atonement did not of themselves have the power "ex opere operato" to erase sins. The sacrifice pleasing to God which in the Old Testament could bring about reconciliation with God was a contrite spirit, a contrite and humbled heart. Only sentiments of humility and contrition can move God to forgive sin, but even these cannot merit forgiveness. David does not say

195

that he will not give a thanks-offering to the Lord. This without doubt he did not want to say. He only wishes to say that God places greater importance on the inner sentiment of thankful love than on the external gift because the latter only receives its value before God by the inner disposition.

The epilogue of the psalm (verses 20–21) is often considered a liturgical addition from the time of the exile. But it may have belonged originally to the Davidic song if interpreted in the light of the Messianic future. The original text does not speak about the reconstruction of the walls of Jerusalem, but about the building of an extension. The fall of David and his reconciliation with God was a type of the destiny of his people. Israel too expected a time of great grace and of continued union with God; it hoped for a greater Jerusalem which was to be the residence city of the Messias and a spiritual center of the world. It is this glorious time of Sion that David is desiring; for in those days when the reconstruction of Sion shall be accomplished, sacrifices shall be offered by his people which shall be pleasing to God. Not an often sinful and faithless people will offer sacrifice to him, but a redeemed and holy people will burn holocausts before the Lord. The prophet here speaks in the language of the Old Testament and of the Law in order to give emphasis to the value of worship of Messianic times. Young steers were the most valuable material for sacrifice which could be offered according to the Law of the Lord. In the kingdom of the New Covenant the faithful shall offer what is most valuable for sacrifice and all will worship and adore the Lord with what is most precious.

psalm 51

Quid gloriaris

David condemns the wickedness of Doeg, and foretells his destruction

1. Unto the end, understanding for David.

2. When Doeg the Edomite came and told Saul: David went to the house of Achimelech (1 Kings 22:9).

3. Why dost thou glory in malice, thou that art mighty in iniquity?

4. All the day long thy tongue hath devised injustice: as a sharp razor, thou hast wrought deceit.

5. Thou hast loved malice more than goodness: and iniquity rather than to speaking righteousness.

6. Thou hast loved all the words of ruin, O deceitful tongue.

7. Therefore will God destroy thee forever. He will pluck thee out, and remove thee from thy dwelling place: and thy root out of the land of the living.

8. The just shall see and fear, and shall laugh at him and say.

9. Behold the man that made not God his helper: but trusted in the abundance of his riches, and prevailed in his vanity.

10. But I, as a fruitful olive tree in the house of God have hoped in the mercy of God forever, yea, forever and ever.

11. I will praise thee forever, because thou hast done it: and I will wait on thy name, for it is good in the sight of thy saints.

I N VAIN did Jonathan, the son of Saul, attempt to reconcile his father with David; for the king remained firm in his determination to kill David. When the latter was informed about this by his friend, he took to flight without providing himself with food and weapons. He arrived at Nobe where at that time the sacred tabernacle was located and begged the high priest Achimelech for bread and a sword. The old man gave him some of the shewbread and the sword of Goliath which was kept in the sanctuary. The Edomite Doeg, a caretaker of the royal herds, was witness to this occurrence. He informed Saul of it and accused the high priest of treasonable intentions. Hereupon Saul ordered all priests of Nobe to come to him and then gave the order to kill them. When none of the bystanders dared to stain their hands with the murder of the priests, Doeg stabbed them himself with a dagger (1 Kings 21 seq.). The superscription of this psalm refers to this event. History tells us nothing about what happened later to the murderer. The psalmist predicts for him the lot of all murderers and godless. Doeg has become a type of all enemies of priests.

David gives us first of all a description of the malice of the persecutor, of the cruel brutal man (verses 3–6). In order to obtain the good graces of the king, he murdered the innocent and defenseless priest. Only a profligate and unscrupulous man could offer himself to take the place of an executioner to satisfy the passionate hatred of Saul against David. But it was the sign of deepest degradation to boast about such a shameful deed before other men. This dreadful deed was directed against David himself; for it was an attempt to frighten everyone and to deter them from giving any assistance to the refugee. But as the hatred of the enemy grew from day to day and sought his destruction, so also God's love watched over him daily in order to protect him and keep him from the hands of his opponents. All the thoughts and endeavors of Doeg, the creature of Saul, were malicious, cunning, and deceptive. He cared little about the injustice of his acts as long as they were of advantage to him. Therefore he was not ashamed to carry on espionage at the place of the sanctuary and to accuse the high priest who innocently wished to perform an act of charity for David. He had the effrontery to accuse the high priest before the king of being guilty of treason. There is no excuse for such wickedness. Such crime can only be the work of a man who is no longer capable of a good deed, who can no longer pass a just judgment, and for whom lying and calumny have become a necessity. Such criminal actions can only come from a man who finds it a pleasurable necessity to cast suspicions upon his neighbor and to bring misery upon him by calumny and deceit when his position and life challenge his godless mind.

God tolerates such malice for a time, but at last he will pass judgment upon the malicious. The psalmist sees the punishment fall upon the persecutor, Doeg (verses 7–9). This unprincipled man has ruined not a few and has taken the life of many priests. There will come a time when the Lord will destroy him forever. He will deprive him of his position and wealth. Then he will be like an uprooted tree which having come to its end withers and is burnt by fire. He will be excluded from the life of the Messianic kingdom forever. The persecuted just man can often be the witness of divine retribution; he can experience the Lord's punishment for such who attack his priests. He will be witness of God's punishment at the end of days. Then he will laugh at his persecutors. This laugh by no means portrays malicious joy or satisfaction at seeing vengeance enacted. The Book of Proverbs forbids us to rejoice over the downfall of an enemy and to jubilate in his overthrow (24:17). The laughing of the just man is like the laughing of God about his enemies (Psalm 2:4). It is a vivid expression for the triumph of the persecuted on the day of retribution and for the satisfaction over the victory of justice over injustice. It is a happy surprise concerning the miraculous providence of God. The law of retribution will fall upon the enemy of the priest. He trusts in his wealth or in his secure position and boasts that he does not need God, faith, grace, or mercy. But the supports on which he depends collapse now and forever.

David now contrasts the fate of the persecutors with that of the persecuted (verses 10–11). The priests of Nobe became victims for David because God protected his royal servant from death. The traitor will become an uprooted tree, but the persecuted stands firm and may be compared to a thriving olive tree in the house of God. Just as a healthy olive tree always draws new strength of life from the soil, so also the just man receives new strength of life in the house of God; that is, in his union with God. For in the house of God, in his union with God, supernatural strength and life come to him. This gives him strength to do what is good so that he is always sure of the divine mercy and may look confidently into the future. The Lord with whom he is united punishes the persecutor and rewards the persecuted. To both, divine fidelity and justice will reveal themselves. David, too, longs for this revelation in his great time of need and confidently hopes to praise the Lord on this account. The day of retribution has not yet come; the godless still control the just, the servants of God. But the name of the Lord, his divine goodness to his servants, will make itself known in its true light before all the pious in the circle of the chosen people of God. As a shining example the psalmist will patiently and confidently await the day.

psalm 52

Dixit insipiens

The general corruption of man before the coming of Christ

1. Unto the end, for Maeleth, understanding to David.
   The fool says in his heart: There is no God.

2. They are corrupted, and become abominable in iniquities: There is none that doth good.

3. God looked down from heaven on the children of men: to see if there were any that did understand, or did seek God.

4. All have gone aside, they are become unprofitable together: there is none that doth good, no not one.

5. Shall not all workers of iniquity know, who eat up my people as they eat bread?

6. They have not called upon God: there have they trembled for fear, where there was no fear.

199

For God has scattered the bones of them that please men: they have been confounded, because God hath despised them.

7. Who will give out of Sion the salvation of Israel? When God shall bring back the captivity of his people, Jacob shall rejoice, and Israel shall be glad.

THIS psalm agrees almost word for word with Psalm 13. Here the name *Elohim* is used for the name of God while in Psalm 13 the name *Yahwe* is used. The wording of the sixth verse of Psalm 52 is different and seems to refer to an historical event, probably to the siege of Jerusalem in the year 701. Perhaps in this instance the fools were many inhabitants of Jerusalem who no longer believed in God, no longer placed their confidence in him. They no longer feared the Lord and his wrath, but trembled at the threats of the Assyrian King Sennacherib and his generals encamped before Jerusalem with 185,000 men. There was no reason for fear; for God had given through Isaias the solemn assurance that the enemy would not shoot one single arrow into the city and would not set foot into the fortifications. What the Lord had foretold was soon fulfilled. During the night the angel of the Lord slew all Assyrians who were in the camp and put to shame Sennacherib who was so confident of his victory. This event surely should have opened the eyes of the godless in Jerusalem to the greatness of God and his fidelity. The miraculous deliverance of Jerusalem brings to the mind of the psalmist the promise of deliverance and salvation for Sion at the end of time. Therefore he ends his psalm with the wish that the Messianic salvation for Israel will soon take place. When the great change in the fate of the people of God has come, then too, the time of the eternal heavenly peace will have arrived in which Israel and Jacob, the people of the God of the New Testament, will rejoice. Eternal praise will sound in the streets of Jerusalem.

psalm 53

Deus, in nomine tuo

A prayer for help in distress

1. Unto the end, in verses, understanding for David.

2. When the men of Ziph had come and said to Saul: is not David hidden with us? (1 Kings 23:19).

3. Save me, O God, by thy name: and judge me in thy strength.

4. O God, hear my prayer: give ear to the words of my mouth.

5. For strangers have risen up against me, and the mighty have sought after my soul: and they have not set God before their eyes.

6. For behold God is my helper: and the Lord is the protector of my soul.

7. Turn back the evils upon my enemies; and cut them off in thy truth.

8. I will freely sacrifice to thee, and will give praise, O God, to thy name: because it is good.

9. For thou hast delivered me out of all trouble: and my eye hath looked down upon my enemies.

ALTHOUGH David had to protect his own life against the attacks of Saul, yet his love for his native country urged him to come to the assistance of the city of Keilah besieged by the Philistines. His service however was badly repaid despite the success of the city's inhabitants. When Saul appeared upon the scene, they wanted to deliver their saviour to his archenemy. But David was warned and fled from Keilah into the desert of Ziph, southeast of Hebron. Then the Ziphites made known to Saul the place of David's concealment and declared themselves willing to lead him to the haunt in the desert. But Saul had to cancel his pursuit because the Philistines were invading his land. The psalm leads us back to the time when David saw his enemy approaching and again suddenly departing (*See* 1 Kings 23). The first part asks for help against the approaching enemy, the second thanks God for the miraculous deliverance.

David beseeches God for help (verses 3–5). He sees himself surrounded everywhere by traitors who watch his every step and report them to his enemy Saul; he sees himself surrounded by an army which is led by a king who is afflicted with a mania for persecution. Yet with his increasing need, his faith in God's power and his confidence in God's love also increases. God's name, his being, which here means his power, wisdom, and justice will help him and God's power will bring about justice for him. As long as the Lord still hears him and as long as he can present his complaint to him, so long will he not be discouraged and give up his cause as lost. He relies so much the more on God's help because his enemies are godless, proud, and insolent men who care little about the Law of the Lord and do not think themselves responsible to God and his judgment, who are guided by their pride and are led to deeds of violence. God-fearing men would have never allowed themselves to be misled by Saul to persecute the anointed of the Lord and to seek his life.

Unexpectedly and quickly God heard the psalmist's petition. The

201

psalmist thanks God for his unexpected miraculous deliverance (verses 6–9). David's companions did not have the same strong faith in victory as their leader. But now since Saul's troops departed so quickly, he could say to them: "Behold God is my helper, the Lord is my soul's support." The experience of such a sudden deliverance from the greatest need must have also strengthened their confidence that the Lord was with them. But for Saul and his followers it must have been a sign that a more powerful being; namely, God, who guides nations and men, had vanquished them. At the very moment when they hoped to obtain their purpose they had to relinquish their success. They had so completely surrounded David that according to human reckoning there was no chance of escape. It was then that the Lord sent the Philistines to the rear of Saul's army so that Saul and his forces could not obtain their end without endangering themselves and their country. The devices which they intended for David now became a threat for themselves and finally became a catastrophe for Saul and sealed his defeat. This is a scene which often repeats itself in the history of the Church. The enemies believe that they have attained their purpose, but in the end must admit that by their blind hatred they have sealed their own destruction. David promises the Lord a sacrifice of thanksgiving when he is delivered from the hands of his enemies. Then he will praise his name in his songs because he has proved himself the all-good God. When he can offer such sacrifice to the Lord, then he has experienced that God has freed him from all adversity, then he has seen the destruction of his enemies, then what the Lord has promised has been fulfilled; namely, that the Lord will not permit anyone to strike his anointed without punishing him.

psalm 54

Exaudi, Deus

*A prayer of a just man under persecution from the wicked;
it corresponds to Christ persecuted by the Jews
and betrayed by Judas*

1. Unto the end in verses, understanding for David.

2. Hear, O Lord, my prayer, and despise not my supplication:

3. be attentive to me and hear me. I am grieved in my exercise, and am troubled,

4. at the voice of the enemy, and at the tribulation of the sinner.
For they have cast iniquities upon me: and in wrath they were troublesome to me.

5. My heart is troubled within me: and the fear of death is fallen upon me.

6. Fear and trembling are come upon me: and darkness hath covered me.

7. And I said: Who will give me wings like a dove; and I will fly and be at rest?

8. Lo, I have gone far off flying away; and I abode in the wilderness.

9. I waited for him that hath saved me from pusillanimity of spirit and a storm.

10. Cast down, O Lord, and divide their tongues: for I have seen iniquity and contradiction in the city.

11. Day and night shall iniquity surround it upon its walls: and in the midst thereof are labor,

12. and injustice, and usury and deceit have not departed from its streets.

13. For if my enemy had reviled me, I would verily have borne with it.
And if he that hated me had spoken great things against me, I would have perhaps have hidden myself from him.

14. But thou a man of one mind, my guide, and my familiar.

15. Who didst take sweetmeats together with me: in the house of God we walked with consent.

16. Let death come upon them: and let them go down alive into hell.
For there is wickedness in their dwellings: in the midst of them.

17. But I have cried to God: and the Lord will save me.

18. Evening and morning, and at noon I will speak and declare: and he shall hear my voice.

19. He shall redeem my soul in peace from them that draw near to me: from among many they were with me.

20. God shall hear, and the Eternal shall humble them. For there is no change with them, and they have not feared God:

21. He hath stretched forth his hand to repay.
They have defiled his covenant,

22. they are divided by the wrath of his countenance: and his heart hath drawn near. His words are smoother than oil, and the same are darts.

23. Cast thy care upon the Lord, and he shall sustain thee: he shall not suffer the just to waver forever.

24. But thou O God, shall bring them down into the pit of destruction.
Bloody and deceitful men shall not live out half their days; but I will trust in thee, O Lord.

WHEN Absalom gave the sign of rebellion at Hebron, a messenger came to Jerusalem and informed David of it. All Israel joined Absalom. The king immediately decided to leave the city in order to avoid the shedding of blood and to save his own life. Accompanied by 600 faithful followers he took the way to the Judean desert. When he came to Mount Olivet, the news was brought to him that his confidential friend had joined the conspirators. At the summit of the mountain where one can obtain a glorious view of the city of Jerusalem, David again faced the city and the sanctuary and prayed. The psalm makes us think of the prayer of our Lord in the garden of Gethsemane. It is not only the same locality that gives us this thought, but also the similarity of the situation of both petitioners. Persecuted by their enemies, by their own people who do not want them as their king, driven out, betrayed by a friend whom they trusted, both David and Christ await the attack that is to be made upon them.

Driven out of the city by his own son, betrayed by his friend and abandoned by his people, there was no other refuge left for David but God alone. Before he crossed Mount Olivet in order to descend into the desert, he again turned his face to the sanctuary on Sion and raised his hands in prayer. It began with a Gethsemane prayer (verses 2–9). "O God, pay heed to my prayer, and despise not my petition." To lose within a few hours his son, his friend, his home, and his people was painful to endure. All this and the anxiety of a father about the wrongdoing of his son and the worry of a king about the welfare of a deceived people have caused him great sorrow and confusion. To this could be added the uncertainty of his own fate. Only God's love consoles; only God's grace can pacify and strengthen. The Lord will not refuse to pay heed to the prayers of an afflicted heart.

While David raised his hands in prayer, he heard from the distance the noise and turmoil of the enemy who was about to march against Jerusalem. His heart trembled. Why should it? All those who approached sought to bring disaster upon him who was the rightful king, who was called to this dignity by God himself. With passionate hatred they rebelled against their ruler who had always showed them a devoted love. When Jesus reflected upon the sufferings which were about to befall him, he was sad and afraid. He was sorrowful unto death and the fear of death took hold of him even though his humanity stood in unique relationship to God through the union of his human nature with his divine nature in one divine Person. Because of this union he could draw immediately on the infinite divine strength. From this it is easy to understand that a just man, indeed, even a saint may be filled with anxiety and fear when he feels that death is approaching. One can easily understand that an ordinary man like David would tremble, that fear would take hold of him lest in the near future greater affliction would come upon him, that under the first impression caused by the evil reports brought to him, a dread took hold of him and the vista of the future looked black before him.

In his distress David wished to be far away from man in the deepest solitude in order to find rest and peace there. Thus Elias too fled to the desert of Sinai to escape persecution and to be able to forget his bitter experiences (3 Kings 19:1 seq.). And in a later period the Prophet Jeremias longed for a traveler's inn way out in the steppes so that he would no longer have to look upon the degradation of his people. David had similar sentiments; he too wished to fly away like a dove which seeks to escape the hunter in hasty flight. His desire was to flee far away where the hateful enemies could not pursue him, to escape into the solitude of the desert. There in quiet peace and undisturbed stillness of nature the noise and tumult of his enemies would not reach him; his soul might be at rest. There he would wait until the frightful turmoil would come to an end, until the people would come to their senses and the Lord would lead him back to the city and place him on his throne. For him there was no other liberator who would free him from this great distress. The Lord was his only hope.

In this Gethsemane prayer for a safe flight into the solitude of the desert for awaiting there the end of his tribulation, the psalmist utters a curse upon his enemies (verses 10–16). Being concerned about the city, the psalmist expresses the wish that the rebels will come to a disagreement and that thus their malicious undertaking will collapse. When the descendants of Sem in their foolish stubbornness attempted to build a tower at Babylon, the summit of which was to reach heaven, the Lord caused a confusion of languages. Quarrels arose in their ranks so that they had to desist in their plans. David wishes a similar shame upon the rebels; for a divine intervention is necessary lest the city fall into ruins. The rebels had made great promises to a people gullible enough to accept Absalom as their king. But instead of the peace which prevailed in Jerusalem under the sceptre which was wielded by David's strong hand, rebellion with all its bad consequences now prevailed. Heretofore justice and right were the guardians of the city day and night so that no injustice could enter. But now injustice took over the guardianship. Brawls and violence encompassed Sion at its walls. On account of them misery and affliction entered the city and prevailed in it. Joy, peace, and happiness left it and with them the fear of God. Law and order no longer ruled, but violence and destruction reigned supreme. Even in the market place, the place for court proceedings and commerce, justice and honesty have disappeared. Cheating and oppression, self-seeking and spoliation of the poor have taken their place. How could the people expect justice, sincerity, and honesty from those who with lying and calumny incited rebellion against the rightful king and who by force and treachery had taken authority into their own hands. Juda and Jerusalem have not received what they expected.

The fate of Jerusalem was of much concern to David because in a few days much of what he had built up in years of hard labor had been destroyed; yet what caused him more sorrow was the treachery of his friend Achitophel. When his enemies mocked at him, cast suspicions upon him, and afflicted him, the king could endure it silently. One does not expect anything else from one's enemy. One can get out of his way and avoid meeting him. One can prepare himself for his attacks. But one cannot easily protect himself against a man who hypocritically pretends to be a friend and who becomes a traitor to him who had the greatest confidence in him.

David had given Achitophel high marks of distinction; he had even permitted him to sit at table with him. He never allowed him to feel his superiority and dignity as king. He rather treated him as an equal. The friendship which he had made with him was sincere and the confidence which he had showed him was unlimited. The composer of the Second Book of Kings remarks that the king valued the advice of Achitophel as much as advice given to him by the high priest (16:23). Even in all public places David made known his love for Achitophel. He was allowed to accompany the king when he went to the tabernacle to participate in the public divine service on the Sabbath and feast days.

The conduct of Achitophel towards David and his shameful deed of treason are types of the relationship of the Apostle Judas to the God-Man Jesus Christ and the most shameful, wicked deed of treason ever perpetrated by a servant against his master. Christ said of Judas that it would have been better if he had not been born. David too pronounced prophetically a judgment in the form of a curse upon the rebels and upon the betrayer. He saw the picture of another rebel, of the Levite Core and his followers who rebelled against Moses and Aaron. Moses at that time came before the people and said: "If these men die the common death of men, and if they be visited with a plague wherewith others also are wont to be visited, the Lord did not send me. Then immediately the earth broke asunder under their feet, and opening her mouth, devoured them with their tents and all their substance. And they went down alive into hell, the ground closing upon them" (Numbers 16:29 seq.). Just as Core and his associates had rebelled against a people's leader appointed by God, so also the revolt of Absalom and his party and the betrayal of Achitophel was directed against a ruler called by God. Therefore they deserved a like punishment. Eternal death comes upon them; hell opens its mouth to swallow them alive. This fate must befall them because evil has become natural to them and a conversion can no longer be expected.

The thought of judgment upon the godless rebels strengthens the confidence of David that God will save him and bring him back to his throne and thus the song of the psalmist ends with sentiments of hope (verses 17–24). With greater confidence, he expects his prayers to be heard and he continues to cry to the Lord until he pays heed to his prayers. In his suffering he will bring his complaints to the Lord morning, noon, and night. The custom of praying three times a day; namely at the time of the morning sacrifice, at noon, and at the time of the evening sacrifice seems to have been an ancient one. Daniel was accustomed to pray three times a day (Daniel 6:11–14). The Acts of the Apostles testifies to a prayer at the sixth and the ninth hour; that is, at nine and twelve o'clock (Acts 10:3). With the three times of prayer the psalmist probably wishes to say that he will pray perseveringly and increasingly.

In the Old Testament there was a conviction that God would not refuse to pay heed to persevering prayer (*See* Judith 4:12). Hence David is also certain: "He will hear my prayer." God will give him peace. Against all expectations of his enemies God will free him from the present adversity and will so decisively defeat the rebels that no one will again dare to approach him with evil intentions. The psalmist considers this confidence to be based first of all on the great number of the godless and faithless: "A great many are against me." The more helpless the servant of the Lord is against the powers of darkness the more he is admonished to depend on the help of the Lord and the more he may hope that his help will be given to him; for God reveals his power in the weakness of men.

A second reason for David's confident hope is found in the godlessness and obduracy of his opponents. Their rebellion is not only directed against the authority of a king, but also against the authority of God. They no longer believe in God's power and judgment. Hence they do not fear him; they do not think of changing their attitude and of being converted. Such disregard of his own Being God cannot continue to tolerate. He who has been enthroned as King and Judge from all eternity cannot permit himself to be dethroned by men but will guard his right. Achitophel the traitor will especially feel the divine wrath because he has not committed an ordinary crime against his king. His crime was also a breach of the bonds of friendship; it was a double breach of fidelity. Punishment will fall upon him more surely because God has uttered a curse upon all hypocrites and liars. Jesus Sirach says of the hypocrite that the Lord hates him (27:27). The hypocrite appears to be friendly, but his arms are not for peace but for war. His words flow smoothly, but in reality they are swords ready for war and murder.

An inner voice answers the psalmist's confident prayer: "Bring your troubles to the Lord; he will protect you; he will not always let the just man stagger." God carries man's troubles in as much as he gives him strength to bear them and lightens the burdens by his grace, consolation, and enlightenment about the eternal value of suffering. Man brings his troubles before the Lord because he expects strength for endurance or a mitigation of suffering. The Lord will not disappoint him who does this. The God-fearing man does not waver, but the godless the Lord will hurl into the abyss of hell. He who stains his hands with murder and deceit will not live half of a lifetime; he will meet a violent death. This prophetic word has been fulfilled on the worst enemies of David. Saul fell upon his own sword; Achitophel hanged himself; Absalom was stabbed when in his flight his hair became entangled in the low branches of an oak and he remained hanging there. Such punishments of God upon persecutors strengthens the sufferers' confidence in God. Bowed down with suffering which came upon him so suddenly the psalmist, nevertheless, was full of confidence and descended from Mount Olivet into the Judean desert. In a short time his hope was fulfilled. His enemies were defeated and he could again return to the city and his throne.

psalm 55

Miserere mei, Deus

A prayer of David in danger and distress

1. Unto the end, for a people that is removed at a distance from the sanctuary; for David, for an inscription of a title (or pillar) when the Philistines held him in Geth.

2. Have mercy on me, O God, for man hath trodden me under foot. All the day long he hath afflicted me fighting against me.

3. My enemies have trodden on me all the day long: for they are many that war against me.

4. From the height of the day I shall fear: but I will trust in thee.

5. In God I will praise my words, in God I have put my trust: I will not fear what flesh can do against me.

6. All the day long they detested my words: all their thoughts were against me unto evil.

7. They will dwell and hide themselves: they will watch my heel. As they have waited for my soul,

8. for nothing shalt thou save them: in thy anger thou shalt break the people in pieces O God,

9. I have declared to thee my life: thou hast set my tears in thy sight, as also in thy promise.

10. Then shall my enemies be turned back. In whatsoever day I shall call upon thee, behold I know that thou art my God.

11. In God will I praise the word, in the Lord will I praise his speech. In God have I hoped: I will not fear what man can do to me.

12. In me, O God, are vows to thee with which I will pay, praises to thee.

13. Because thou hast delivered my soul from death, my feet from falling: that I may please in the sight of God, in the light of the living.

ACCORDING to the superscription the same cause existed for this psalm as for Psalm 33. David had fled into the territory of the Philistines in order to escape the persecutions of Saul. Here he believed himself secure. But he was soon recognized as victor over Goliath, taken prisoner, and led before King Achis. Being of an acute mind he pretended before the king that he was insane and thus escaped death (1 Kings 21). In this psalm which brings to memory those terrible hours of imprisonment, David described his distress and how his faith at that time gave him a confident hope of deliverance. This psalm gives us an Old Testament enlightenment of the words of St. Paul in the Epistle to the Hebrews: "Our nature is not fearfulness which leads to destruction, but faith which leads to life" (11:39). The refrain (verses 5 and 12) emphasizes this thought.

David would have succumbed to the double burden of persecution and flight had not faith kept his confidence alive; for confidence in God takes away fear (verses 2-5). His experiences give testimony of this.

When in his flight he reached the borders of Palestine, he felt himself secure. But the Lord did not wish that his anointed should depend on human security. While in his native country with death lurking everywhere, he could avoid all snares that were laid for him but he was soon arrested in a foreign land where he expected no danger. He had to realize that he had enemies in all places, enemies who in their hatred sought revenge and were determined to kill him. Wherever he went, he saw himself confronted by his enemies and his life endangered. Their number was large and their hatred and boldness great against a helpless man. There was no other refuge left for him but to trust in God; only in God's hands was his life secure.

Many others in similar situations would have been discouraged and would have given up all hope for a better future. But David's faith and confidence in God were anchored deeply in his soul and had given him such spiritual strength that he could not waver despite all the adversities from without. When fear came upon him (as he himself confesses in this psalm), then he reminded himself of the eternal truths, of the divine promises of God's truthfulness and fidelity, of his power and goodness. What he said to himself in such hours when dejection, fear, and despondency tried to possess his soul we find in the ejaculatory refrain verse: "In God will I praise my words, in God have I put my trust: I will not fear what flesh can do against me." He who lives in intimate union with God is positive that the divine promises will be fulfilled in him. He may boast that divine manifestations of mercy are meant for him. David could say this about the promises which were announced to him through the Prophet Nathan concerning his own person. Confidence rests upon the assurance of the fulfillment of God's word. And confidence in God, fructified by the love of God, knows no fear. "What can flesh do to him?" In comparison to God all human power is nothing but sand. All men are transitory and frail creatures which one breath of God can destroy.

The thought that God knows all things was for David a great consolation and gave him peace of mind; for God's knowledge of man's needs gives confidence. In a few words the psalmist describes the distress which the godless activities of his enemies have caused. It is a type of the spiritual need of every man who knows that he is encompassed by the enemies of his salvation seeking his destruction. David's enemies belittled his activities. They passed a destructive criticism on all his words and actions; they interpreted everything falsely; they accused him of evil intentions because their hatred made them incapable of passing just judgments. Secretly they spied upon him; everywhere he saw himself surrounded by spies and traitors who watched his every step. They sought accusations against him; they looked for reasons to put an end to his life.

The Lord cannot permit such evil actions to go unpunished. Those who were not receptive to admonition, who had a seared conscience, and who would no longer believe in divine punishments because of their obduracy could not be saved, for upon the day of judgment an irrevocable judgment will be spoken upon men and upon whole nations.

But the persecuted just man need not fear judgment. Redemption and the blessing of salvation will be his lot. God knows his sufferings; he has written them down in the book of life. All the tears which he has shed in his distresses are, so to say, gathered by God in a goat-skin bottle like the container in which the Israelite kept wine or water. Indeed, God booked every tear for the day of eternal retribution. When the godless will appear before the Judge, the tears which they caused others to shed will give testimony against them and will demand their condemnation; for the persecuted, however, they will be the cause of their blessedness. The enemies of David still rage; the Lord has given them power over the anointed, but David is already certain that God has heard his prayer and what he has asked will be granted. When the time has come, all that is necessary on his part is to call upon God and the enemy will take flight; for God is with him. This faith and happy assurance impels the psalmist to take up again the thought of the first refrain in a larger form in the second refrain: "In God I will praise the word, in the Lord will I praise his speech." His union with God based on faith gives him the glad certainty that the Lord will fulfill his promise which he has given to the just man. Therefore the psalmist puts his trust in God and his confidence takes away all fear and anxiety about his future. Since every sorrow and fear is marked down for eternal reward, there is no reason for discouragement in suffering or for abandonment of faith, love, and fidelity to the Lord.

The psalmist now passes over his present adversity and looks into the future when his prayer will be heard and rewarded. He sings a song of thanksgiving for his rewarded confidence (verses 13–14). God cannot disappoint him in the confidence which he has placed in him; he cannot be unfaithful to his word. Therefore in the midst of his suffering from which according to human judgment there is no escape, David thinks of the fulfillment of his vow and of the thanksgiving sacrifices which he will offer to the Lord in the sanctuary; for in the happiness granted to him he will not forget his Liberator and great Benefactor. That the Lord had given him quick-wittedness at Gath and kept him from certain death, that he did not let him fall but placed his feet on firm ground, David realized. But he also realized that all this was not merely a gift of divine goodness but also implied a task. He says: God has saved me from the fall in order that I may walk before him in the light of the living. The psalmist does not think here merely of the light of the sun which shines upon the living, but most likely and especially of the light that gives supernatural life which stands in contrast to the night of sin, the light of grace. In this light which shines upon those living in union with God the psalmist will walk before God. He will walk the way of obedience and love enlivened by faith. He to whom God grants his help should by the light of grace become a light to others that they, too, may walk the way that leads to God and to his grace.

psalm 56

Miserere mei, Deus

The prophet prays in his affliction and praises God for his delivery

1. Unto the end. Destroy not. For David, for an inscription of a title when he fled from Saul into the cave (1 Kings 24).
   And in the shadow of thy wings will I hope, until iniquity pass away.

2. Have mercy on me, O God, have mercy on me: for my soul trusteth in thee.

3. I will cry to God the most high: to God who hath done good to me.

4. He hath sent from heaven and delivered me: he hath made them a reproach that trod upon me. God hath sent his mercy and his truth:

5. and he hath delivered my soul from the midst of the young lions. I slept troubled.
   The sons of men whose teeth are weapons and arrows, and their tongue a sharp sword.

6. Be thou exalted, O God, above the heavens, and thy glory above all the earth.

7. They prepared a snare for my feet: and they bowed down my soul.
   They dug a pit before my face: and they are fallen into it.

8. My heart is ready, O God, my heart is ready: I will sing and rehearse a psalm.

9. Arise, O my glory. arise psaltery and harp: I will arise early.

10. I will give praise to thee, O Lord, among the people: I will sing a psalm to thee among the nations.

11. For thy mercy is magnified even to the heavens: and thy truth unto the clouds.

12. Be thou exalted, O God above the heavens: and thy glory above all the earth.

R EPEATEDLY David was forced to seek refuge in a cave in order to escape the persecutions of Saul. The psalm was most likely composed at the time when he concealed himself in the caverns of Engaddi west of the Dead Sea and was pursued and surrounded by Saul with three thousand men (1 Kings 24:1 seq.). However, David in the midst of threatening danger was sure that his cry for help would be heard and thus he prepared his soul to give thanks to the Lord. He was already planning to express in words his joy about the deliverance and to make them harmonize in a song accompanied by the harp. The psalm is a song full of childlike confidence in God, a canticle of faith in God's mercy and fidelity which no distress will cause him to doubt. It is also a festive song in honor of God's goodness and tells us of David's typical faith. Each strophe ends with a refrain which requests God to reveal the glory of his mercy and fidelity to the world.

It is a severe test of the faith to know that one is called by God to a responsible position, such as, to be ruler of the kingdom of God, of the people of Israel, and to see oneself exposed to the worst persecutions for months and even years because of this call. To keep alive one's confidence in God's mercy and fidelity under such circumstances and not to waver and give up is the characteristic of a hero. This psalm reveals the hero. David relies on God's mercy and fidelity (verses 2–6). He knows that the ravines and caverns cannot offer him a lasting protection because he is everywhere spied upon by traitors. Yet he does not give up; for what deserts and mountains cannot do, that God's mercy and grace will do for him. Persecuted and pursued like a deer he knows that he is well taken care of by God. While in his flight he passes over the mountains in all haste, his heart calls upon the Lord and he places himself under the protection of his merciful Divine Providence which covers him as a mother bird covers its young ones with its wings until the danger is passed.

Two facts strengthen his confidence: God's power and his fidelity. The Lord is the Highest. We may put obstacles in the way for men, but not for almighty God. The almighty Lord has chosen David for his kingdom; he will in due time complete his work and place the one whom he has

213

called upon his throne. "For he who has called you is faithful and will do this" (1 Thessalonians 5:24). As long as man does not become unfaithful to his calling he may rely on God's mercy and fidelity. May thousands of his enemies encompass him so that there is no way of escape, God in heaven can free him from the hands of his persecutors and put all their plans to naught. David is convinced of this. God whose mercy is unbounded and whose fidelity is unchangeable will also reveal his mercy and fidelity to him. Like heavenly lights they will shine into the darkness of his distress. The danger which hovers over David is great; his enemies are like bloodthirsty lions. The spears and arrows with which they have armed themselves are, as it were, the teeth of beasts in human form and the sharpened sword is the lion's tongue thirsting for human blood. The confession of confidence in the first refrain is a petition that God may rise from his throne in heaven, that he may reveal his heavenly majesty by saving the anointed from his great trials and reveal to all the world the splendor of his majesty and the glory of his mercy and fidelity.

David is certain of being heard and saved so that he is even now ready with his thanksgiving song (verses 7–12). The experiences in his life which he thankfully reviews justify him in doing this. How often did his enemies lay snares and traps in order to catch him! How often was he betrayed by those to whom he showed himself a benefactor and whom he thought he could trust. Through such treachery he suffered much; but God never forsook him. Those who dug a pit for him, who planned his destruction became victims of their own treachery. Twice Saul himself fell into the hands of him whom he persecuted and twice he should have thanked the magnanimity of the persecuted become captor. And now God will again liberate David and put an end to his trials. David already contemplates how he can clothe his sentiments of thanks with suitable words; he prepares himself to praise the mercy of the Lord in a song and accompany it with his harp. For a long time zither and harp which he so highly appreciated were silenced. Now he awakens them from their slumber for a thanksgiving song to the Lord; now he will try to obtain from them notes of jubilation. He does not want to wait until the Lord permits the glorious day of liberty to come. He is already certain of being heard. Full of thankful joy he wishes to sing before the morning dawn of a better time. This song should not cease in the forecourts of the sanctuary but the praise of the divine mercy and fidelity should be sung in the whole world and God's glory should be proclaimed among the nations.

What David has intended with this psalm has been literally fulfilled; for in the whole world and in all languages God's mercy and fidelity are proclaimed by this song. And truly! To him who reads the sacred books and searches in the pages of world, ecclesiastical, and human history

God's mercy and fidelity become an absolute certainty and he must admit that they deserve to be proclaimed in all the world and at all times. They are so sublime that man's utterances about them are not sufficient to proclaim their greatness. As high as the heaven is above the earth, so sublime is God's mercy. As high as the clouds hover above the earth, so much does God's fidelity surpass everything that is upon the earth. After the second refrain the entire psalm ends with the petition: As the Lord reveals his glory in the heavenly constellations and as in the splendor which he has spread over the entire heaven he makes known his glory over the whole earth, so may he manifest his mercy and fidelity in their effects upon humanity.

psalm 57

Si vere utique

David reproveth the wicked, and foretelleth their punishment

1. Unto the end. Destroy not. For David, for an inscription of a title.

2. If in every deed you speak justice: judge right things, ye sons of men.

3. For in your heart you work iniquity: your hands forge injustice in the earth.

4. The wicked are alienated from the womb, they have gone astray from the womb: they have spoken false things.

5. Their madness is according to the likeness of a serpent: like the deaf asp that stopped her ears.

6. Which will not hear the voice of charmers; nor of the wizard that charmeth wisely.

7. God shall break in pieces the teeth in their mouth: the Lord shall break the grinders of the lions.

8. They shall come to nothing, like water running down: he hath bent his bow till they be weakened.

9. Like wax that melteth they shall be taken away: fire hath fallen on them, and they shall not see the sun.

10. Before your thorns could know the brier; he swalloweth them up, as alive, in his wrath.

11. The just shall rejoice when he shall see the revenge: he shall wash his hands in the blood of the sinner.

12. And man shall say: If indeed there shall be fruit to the just: there is indeed a God that judgeth them on earth.

THIS psalm most likely belongs to the same period as the two preceding psalms. David addresses the tyrants of the country, especially Saul and his followers who do not want to recognize his claim to the kingship given him immediately by God and who on that account persecute him. They are doing an injustice to all who are partisans of David. Because they are hardened in their malice punishment for their obstinacy will fall upon them. The enemies of David are a type of the enemies of the Church and its members. God's punishment of the rebels will be a warning for the enemies of the Church. The psalm is a memorial of God's justice which does not permit his servants to be oppressed without punishment.

In the first place the psalmist mentions the godless conduct of the tyrants (verses 2–6). Saul and his partisans at the royal court appealed their right of persecuting David because they considered him an enemy of the state even though they did not grant him a hearing and gave him no chance of defending himself. This they had in common with all tyrants; namely, that they ruthlessly made use of their power and pretended to be guardians of justice and of the civil order and falsely claimed that the injustice was on the side of their opponents. David rightfully reproaches them: "He who wishes to be guardian of the civil order must practice integrity and justice towards all and judge impartially without respect of person; he may not lay burdens upon others which he himself refuses to carry." The opponents of David are far from possessing a sense of justice and conscientiousness. They frequently mention the word *justice* but they do not show that they are guardians of justice; they rather prove that they are unjust. Their heart is full of malice; they do evil with full deliberation and they are no longer capable of a quiet consideration of the consequences of their acts. Into their scale of justice they throw violence and injustice.

David does not find the conduct of these men to be strange. They were godless and unprincipled before they came to power. They grew up and became leaders in those principles according to which they are now conducting themselves. Now that they have power their malice can freely develop. Indeed, from their earliest youth, from their mother's breast

216

they have imbibed their godless principles. Therefore they cannot be receptive to any good influence. Requests, admonitions, and warnings make no impression upon them. The poison of unbelief and injustice which they carry within themselves is dangerous and as deadly as the poison of snakes. He who has once imbibed their poisonous principles must succumb to them. He who has once imitated their unjust practices will be ruined by them. As little as a dove can be enticed from its hiding place by the allurement of an asp, so little can the obdurate tyrants in their godlessness be converted to a different way of life. Just as there are snakes that cannot be charmed by the art of the snake-charmer, so there are men who are so hardened in malice that every attempt to change their attitude and to awaken their conscience is futile.

Thus futile were all of David's attempts to convince Saul and his partisans of the injustice of their actions. He thought that, perhaps, at least the thought of God's judgment might in some way influence their obduracy. Therefore in the second part of the psalm he points to the end of godless tyrants. Already in the Old Testament hardness of heart, obduracy, was looked upon as a sign of divine rejection. So said an unknown prophet to the godless king Amasias of Juda: "I know that God is minded to kill thee because thou hast done this evil, and moreover hast not hearkened to my counsel" (2 Chronicles 25:16). The psalmist's petition that the Lord may hold judgment upon the tyrants is a conviction clothed in many pictures. The Lord will destroy them because they are unreceptive to all good advice. The first picture is taken from the life of a shepherd. The shepherd carried a club with him as a weapon to defend himself against wild animals and to save his sheep by breaking the teeth of the animal. So also God will take away from the tyrant every possibility of continuing in his injustices. The Lord makes him disappear leaving no traces behind. When in Palestine the winter rains have ceased, the water runs into the brooks but these soon dry out. So also the Lord takes away from these tyrants their power under the glow of the divine wrath. Their power wanes until it finally disappears altogether. They may still attempt to create mischief, but their calumnies and fictitious suspicions no longer have any effect; they are like arrows from which the points have been removed. Their influence and power is gradually taken from them as the snail, about which the psalmist speaks in poetic hyperbole, that through mucous discharge propels and disintegrates itself. The tyrants will be as if they had never been; they will be as a stillborn child who never saw the light of day, who never received a name, who was taken from the womb of the mother and put into the grave. The Lord snatches the blasphemers away suddenly when they have life and strength. Before they can successfully carry out their godless plans the punishment overtakes them. The psalmist uses a comparison from daily life which should illustrate the evildoers' shortness of life. In Palestine the thorn was used for burning material in the kitchen because its glow heats the pot quickly and the heat continues for a long time. But the evil feel the wrath of God quicker than the pot begins to feel the heat of the burning thorn.

The Lord permits the just man to be witness of the punishment which he inflicts upon his persecutors. He had to observe for how long a time injustice prevailed unhindered, as if eternal love and justice paid no attention. Therefore he should also witness the punishment. The joy of the just is not the joy of a satisfied feeling of revenge about the retribution; for revenge and the fear of God cannot be reconciled. It is a joy about the victory of justice and about the revelation of God's power and fidelity. The judgment upon the obdurate tyrants will be a terrible one. It will be according to the measure of their malice and obstinacy. The psalmist compares it to a destructive defeat in a bloody battle. From it men will acknowledge that God does not permit those to go unpunished who persecute and oppress his servants, that he blesses a virtuous life here on earth, and that he rewards them by punishing the oppressors. They will realize that God does not allow himself to be mocked, that there is still a God who judges here on earth.

psalm 58

Eripe me

A prayer to be delivered from the wicked, with confidence in God's help and protection; it corresponds to Christ and his enemies, the Jews

1. Unto the end, destroy not, for David, for an inscription of a title, when Saul sent and watched his house to kill him (1 Kings 19).

2. Deliver me from my enemies, O my God: and defend me from them that rise up against me.

3. Deliver me from them that work iniquity: and save me from bloody men.

4. For behold they have caught my soul: the mighty have rushed in upon me.

5. Neither is it my iniquity, nor my sin, O Lord: without iniquity have I run, and directed my steps.

6. Rise up thou to meet me, and behold: even thou, O Lord, the God of hosts, the God of Israel.
   Attend to visit all the nations: have no mercy on all them that work iniquity.

7. They shall return at evening, and shall suffer hunger like dogs: and shall go round about the city.

8. Behold they shall speak with their mouth, and a sword is in their lips: for who, say they, hath heard us.

9. But thou, O Lord, shalt laugh at them: thou shalt bring the nations to nothing.

10. I will keep my strength to thee: for thou art my protector.

11. My God his mercy shall prevent me.

12. God shall let me see over my enemies: slay them not, lest at any time my people forget.
    Scatter them by thy power: and bring them down, O Lord, my protector.

13. For the sin of their mouth, and the word of their lips: and let them be taken in their pride.
    And for their cursing and their lying they shall be talked of

14. when they are consumed by thy wrath: and they shall be no more.
    And they shall know that God will ruin Jacob, and all the ends of the earth.

15. They shall return at evening, and shall suffer hunger like dogs: and shall go round about the city.

16. They shall be scattered abroad to eat: and shall murmur if they be not filled.

17. But I will sing thy strength: and will extol thy mercy in the morning.
    For thou art become my support, and my refuge, in the day of my trouble.

18. Unto thee, O my helper, will I sing, for thou art God my defense: my God my mercy.

AGAIN the spirit of jealousy had overcome Saul, and again he hurled the spear at David after the latter had returned home from the victorious war against the Philistines. David escaped to his own home, but the king had it surrounded by mercenary troops during the night that the hated one might not escape and that he might be killed in the morning. But his wife Michol warned him and helped him escape through an unguarded window of the house. He then went to the Prophet Samuel. Saul also sent his henchmen to this place. But the spirit of God took hold of them and hindered the imprisonment of David. Saul was also possessed by the same spirit when he himself went to Samuel to get the hated weapon bearer in his power. Under the impression that God intervened to protect David, Saul realized his injustice and again reconciled himself for a short time with David (1 Kings 19:9 seq.). From this situation the song may be understood according to the superscription. The refrain at the close of each strophe (verses 10 and 18) seems to say that the miraculous deliverance made an impression on David himself. God is the fortress with whom all unjustly persecuted may take refuge in confidence.

Sometimes God permits that a just man is deprived of all human protection and assistance and must carry his cross alone in order that with greater determination he may seek strength and protection in God. David too had to go through such a school. When Saul in his hatred began to persecute him, David stood all alone. Even his friend Jonathan was not in a position to protect him against the murderous plans of his father Saul, especially since at court there were many men who would allow themselves to murder David. At that time there was only one protection. God's power and fidelity were his only hope. To call upon the justice of God was his only means of being saved (verses 2–6). Thus in this psalm David raises up his hands to the Lord in prayer that he may save and protect him against the murderous plans of his adversaries. He is his God who created him, who called him to the kingship and had him anointed, who served him with his power and love. Help is needed for the danger is great. The murderers hired by Saul follow him at every step to apprehend him and to kill him. He cannot expect mercy from godless men who make no ado about thrusting the sword into the breast of an innocent man in order to obtain favor with a king who is possessed by mad jealousy. Only God can protect him from falling into their hands.

No matter where he flees, everywhere they pursue him and spy upon him; they hunt him as they would a savage animal. They band together and they are not ashamed of entering into the home of the prophet in order to take the hated man by force. All this David must permit to be done to him, although until now he has faithfully served his king and his country and merited only their gratitude. They chase him as if he were a criminal and they prepare themselves for a decisive blow against him who shortly before had obtained a decisive victory against the archenemy of the kingdom, the Philistines. Until now, God in his patience has quietly looked down upon the activities of Saul and his partisans, as if he slept and did not know anything of the difficulties of his anointed. Therefore David cries out loudly, "Wake up!" that God may come to his assistance with his power because he is fighting alone against a power much greater than his own. He prays that the Lord may look down upon him in his mercy. God should awaken; he has shown patience long enough towards his enemies and persecutors; now let him speak the language of his justice in his judgment. In their heathen audacity they no longer understand any other language. As faithless traitors they do not deserve forbearance. The relation of Yahwe to his people and to his anointed demands punishment; for he is the invisible King, the Lord of hosts who has made David his visible representative and has called him to be the visible ruler of his people. He is Israel's God who cannot bear this heathen conduct.

David has called upon the Lord to pass judgment and in spirit he sees that the judgment is executed (verses 7–10). The rabble which Saul had hired to satisfy his hatred may be compared to a pack of savage scavengers which during the day lie in hiding and at night roam through the oriental streets. Every evening they come howling for hunger and greedily seek their prey. Thus Saul's henchmen go out at night with a passionate desire to shed David's blood and put him to death. The venom is on their lips: abusive language, blasphemy, and calumny. Their words are like sharpened swords that are intended for the destruction of the hated one. They ask no question about God; they think so little about responsibility and about punishment that in their insolent godlessness they say: "God does not hear it! He does not trouble himself about men and what they do." But they deceive themselves about God's patience and forbearance. The Lord laughs at their speech and mocks at their dastardly boldness. Of what importance is it to the eternal Judge whether the godless want to believe in his judgment or not? Even if they want to close their eyes to this truth, the ears will some day hear the judgment of rejection. The Lord laughs at their folly and in his infinite supremacy mocks at their activities. In the sure expectation of the punishment upon his persecutors the psalmist can even now play the harp to accompany his song which will praise God as his salvation and glorify him as his strong fortress.

Faith in God's justice and fidelity, and confidence that the Lord will not permit him to be defeated, him whom he has selected to rule his kingdom, gives David an assurance that God's love will help in his present difficulties and that he himself will be witness of the divine punishment of his enemies. This will be proof of his own innocence and of God's selection; and in him God's justice and fidelity will prove itself victorious. The psalmist hopes that God's punishment will be a lasting remembrance of the divine justice (verses 11–18). May God not remove the evildoers from the face of the earth; for then the lessons of his judgments may soon be forgotten. The Lord should select such a punishment which will serve at all times as a warning to his people so that others may be deterred from the way of godlessness and that no one will dare to raise his hand against the anointed of the Lord. The enemy should be driven by God's power and should wander about restlessly, finding a refuge nowhere, finding no place of rest and peace. They should be trodden upon to show that the Lord is the protector of his anointed and defends him in all attacks because they have practiced treachery and deceit. Their pride and arrogance shall become snares into which they themselves shall fall. The cursings which they have uttered against the victims of their hatred shall fall upon their own heads. May God not eradicate them altogether from the land, but in his wrath may he morally destroy them. May he humiliate them that all men may know from the punishment that has come upon them that Yahwe still rules over his people, the descendants of Jacob, and that it is not his will to have his rule diminished by the godless.

David is certain that the Lord will not permit him to be defeated by his persecutors. Perhaps they will be like scavengers which every day at nightfall prowl around the streets for nourishment and howl because of their unstilled greed for prey. When such dogs find no food, they growl because their hunger annoys them. The prey for which Saul's accomplices in crime seek every day in order to satisfy their desire for revenge is David himself. They pursued him everywhere to apprehend him. But God did not permit that they should satisfy their desire to kill him and thus their passion became a torture to themselves. While his persecutors sought in vain to apprehend him, he could intone a song of praise to the Lord in honor of his power which protected him and did not permit the enemy to have their way. In the morning he will sing about God's mercy because the Lord has proved himself a strong fortress, a secure refuge in the time of need. His song is for the Lord who protected him in all dangers, who gave him protection as if he were in an invincible castle. He will praise the Lord as his God and as the object of his love.

psalm 59

Deus, repulisti nos

After many afflictions the Church of Christ shall prevail

1. Unto the end, for them that shall be changed, for the inscription of a title, to David himself, for doctrine,

2. When he set fire to Mesopotamia for Syria and Sobal; and Joab returned and slew off Edom, in the vale of the saltpits, twelve thousand men [2 Kings 8].

3. O God, thou hast cast off and hast destroyed us: thou hast been angry, and hast had mercy on us.

4. Thou hast moved the earth, and hast troubled it: heal thou the breaches thereof, for it has been moved.

5. Thou hast shown thy people hard things: thou hast made us drink the wine of sorrow.

6. Thou hast given a warning to them that fear thee: that they may flee from before thy bow, that thy beloved may be delivered.

7. Save me with thy right hand and hear me.

8. God hath spoken in his holy place: I will rejoice and I will divide Sichem; and I will mete out the vale of tabernacles.

9. Galaad is mine, and Manasses is mine: and Ephraim is the strength of my head. Juda is my king:

10. Moab is the pot of my hope. Into Edom I will stretch out my shoe: to me the foreigners are made subject.

11. Who will bring me into the strong city? Who will lead me into Edom?

12. Wilt not thou, O God, who hast cast us off? And wilt not thou, O God, go out with our armies?

13. Give us help from trouble: for vain is the salvation of man.

14. Through God we shall do mightily: and he shall bring to nothing them that afflict us.

K ING DAVID had vanquished the Philistines to the west and the Moabites to the east and had made them tributaries. Then the Syrians of Mesopotamia in the north and the Syrians of Seba, who lived north of Damascus as far as the Orontes, became restless. When David with his army marched against this enemy which threatened the northern boundary of his kingdom, the Edomites from the south entered the kingdom devastating and burning the territory that had no armies to defend it. The inhabitants sought to save their lives by flight. These alarming reports strongly affected the victorious king. From David's mood in these hours this psalm had its origin. Soon after, David sent troops to Edom under the command of his General Joab who vanquished the Edomites in the salt-valley, the modern Wadi-el-Melach in the vicinity of Petra south of the Dead Sea (*See* 2 Kings 8 and 1 Chronicles 18.). The song was intended to

223

be a memorial of God's help and at the same time to teach the correct attitude toward material reversals. But it was also intended to be an instruction for individual souls who in their progress are visited with humiliating degradations.

The first part (verses 3–7) gives us the impression which the invasion of the Edomites made upon David. A grave setback after glorious conquests is not an accidental misfortune. The pious king saw therein an act of Divine Providence, an act of the divine wrath. According to the first impression the Lord has rejected his people, he has dispersed it in every direction by the invading enemy. In his first disappointment he did not think that such misfortune could also be a visitation of divine love, of love which tries to keep man humble when there is danger of self-complacency. Humility brings back to man's mind the sense of human weakness when the temptation arises to ascribe victory to one's own power. Oppressed by the bad news, David presents the need of his people in his complaint to the Lord. The whole land is terrified and restless; the feeling of security has disappeared. The predatory invasion had inflicted as much harm as if the land had been visited by a severe earthquake. Only God can heal the wounds and close them again. The blow struck harder because it was so sudden and unexpected. In the midst of the transports of joy over the acquired victories of the king, God gave his people the beaker of his wrath, the bitter chalice of suffering. As intoxicating liquor deprives man of his reasoning so also the wrath of the Lord and misfortune has taken from the people their strength and deliberation. At other times God had been a strong shield behind whom the people were secure against a world of enemies. Because God alone can save, David cries for help that his all-powerful right hand may intervene and deliver his people from affliction.

The king has complained about his need before God; he has sincerely manifested his sorrow to him. He does not despair, but draws strength from faith in God's word (verses 8–10). Just as the Lord has given to the Church of the New Testament the promise of eternal existence and the members of the Church gain strength in times of war and persecution from faith in his word, so David also is mindful of the divine promises given to the patriarchs and to Moses. The God throning upon the Ark of the Covenant in the sanctuary had assured them the possession of the land of Chanaan, the selection of Israel as the chosen nation, the subjection of the Gentile nations, and membership in the kingdom of God. The psalmist is mindful of each of God's promises. God promised to give Sichem and the Succoth valley to Israel. Sichem is situated in the land west of the Jordan at the foot of Mount Garizim and the Succoth valley is situated south of the Jabbok river in the country east of the Jordan. They are places sanctified through Jacob and here represent all of Palestine. God had given to the tribes of Israel the land as a lasting inheritance. Galaad, that is, the tribes of Ruben and Gad, as well as the tribe of Manasses had settled in the land east of the Jordan; the rest of the tribes, Ephraim and Juda, being mentioned as representatives because they were the leading tribes settled west of the Jordan. Ephraim, the most powerful of the twelve tribes, was to be the helmet on the head of the Lord; to him was entrusted the external protection of the kingdom. But Juda was to be the sceptre in the hand of the Lord; through Juda God wanted to rule his kingdom. According to God's word the Gentile world will also serve the Lord. Moab shall serve the Lord as a wash basin for his feet and Edom as a footstool. By this description the psalmist wishes to say that the Gentiles will be completely subjugated. In the ancient Orient the victors were accustomed to place their foot on the neck of the vanquished kings, and thus, so to say, use them as a footstool (Psalm 109:1). The Philistines will at some time adore the true God.

The remembrance of the divine promises has strengthened David's confidence and has again given him peace; he has been humbled by the defeat, but not discouraged (verses 11–14). The experience that he could do nothing by his own power, that only God gives victory, impels him now to have confidence in the help of the Lord and to march against the Edomites in order to punish them for their cowardly act and to destroy their fortifications and their city. David is certain that the Lord will again lead the humbled people to victory, that he again will be with his army as he has been before in many battles; for the defeat could not have been a sign of rejection, but only a trial. From it David with his people had learned to depend entirely on God. Therefore in his war against the Edomites he does not think of seeking alliances; for all human help is folly if God does not bless his work; all human help is superfluous when God is not the helper. God gives the victory, not the weapons or the strength of the army. But he does not give victory to those who have no courage and at every setback hang their hands and wait until God intervenes; he gives victory to those only who again take up the battle with unwavering courage. Not to the cowardly and idle, but only to heroic fighters does God give strength to defeat and make harmless the enemy who has become powerful.

psalm 60

Exaudi, Deus

*A prayer for the coming of the kingdom of Christ,
which shall have no end*

1. Unto the end, in hymns for David.

2. Hear, O Lord, my supplication: be attentive to my prayer.

3. To thee have I cried from the ends of the earth: when my heart was in anguish, thou hast exalted me on a rock. Thou hast conducted me;

4. For thou hast been my hope: a tower of strength against the face of the enemy.

5. In thy tabernacle I shall dwell forever; I shall be protected under the covert of thy wings.

6. For thou, my God, hast heard my prayer: thou hast given an inheritance to them that fear thy name:

7. Thou wilt add days to the days of the king: his years even to generation and generation.

8. He abideth forever in the sight of God: his mercy and truth who shall search?

9. So will I sing a psalm to thy name forever and ever: that I may pay my vows from day to day.

PERHAPS this psalm stems from the time when David had to flee from Jerusalem before Absalom and tarried at Mahanaim on the other side of the Jordan. The rebellion of his son compelled him to deny himself the proximity of the sanctuary and to leave his residence city. And yet the king remained confident. When an enemy stormed the outer walls of a fortification, the inhabitants with the soldiers withdrew to the castle which was situated in the highest part of the city and which had many turrets and was especially fortified; it served the besieged as a last refuge. David may be likened to a fortification whose outer works is taken by the enemy. He withdrew to the strong citadel, to the strong tower of the castle. The strong tower is God, intimate union with him. Here David sought protection against those who had deprived him of the external union with God and had striven to claim the throne given to him by God. From David's conduct all were to learn that in every adversity protection is to be sought with God, the strong tower, and in him is to be sought the filiation of God and his eternal inheritance.

Banished from the sanctuary on Sion David directs his view from Mahanaim to the mountains of Juda where the heights of Jerusalem greet his eyes. Toward the place of God in the Holy of Holies, to the tabernacle of the Old Covenant he extends his hands in suppliant prayer. Where should he seek protection against the enemy who is marching towards him? God's love is the tower which protects against all danger (verses 2–5). So also the Christian must raise his hands toward his God concealed in the tabernacle; for the word in the Book of Proverbs is also meant for him: "The name of the Lord is a strong tower: the just man runneth to it, and shall be exalted" (18:10). The emergency compelled David to leave his sanctuary and he feels as badly as if he were banished to the ends of the earth. Cut off from the source of divine grace and mercy he believes that he must languish like a wanderer in a waterless desert. Many learn to appreciate the house of God and its source of grace when they must do without for a long time. But the psalmist longed for the sanctuary since the first day of his flight from Jerusalem because through faith and experience he has learned to appreciate its great value. And yet as a house of God and as a place of grace it was only a shadow of the Catholic House of God and of the fullness of its grace. David is afraid that far from the holy tabernacle his strength will fail him in the storms which he will encounter. Therefore he humbly beseeches God that he may strengthen him from Sion, that he may free him from all dangers stationed on a high rock which the waves cannot reach and the enemies cannot ascend. May God lead him to the place where his feet will again be on solid ground.

To expect such help from God was neither bold nor presumptuous. He could at all times rely on the Lord; for God had proved himself a firm tower in every need! Here David may have thought of the difficult times during Saul's persecutions. If at that time David had not relied upon the Lord, he would have collapsed both physically and spiritually. If God had not shown himself to be a strong protection he would have succumbed under the persecutions of the enemy. God becomes a high rock that withstands all storms and a tower which no earthly power can reduce through grace and union with man who gives external expression of devotion by visiting him in the sanctuary. To dwell eternally in the tabernacle of God means, therefore, to remain united with the Lord in faith and grace. It means to be able at all times to place oneself under his protection as the chickling hides itself under the wings of the hen; for when God is with us who can be against us? It is significant that David did not first

227

ask for the return to the throne, that he was not concerned about his restoration to his royal power, but that he begged for the return to the house of God that nothing should separate him from the love of God.

With great confidence the psalmist hopes that his prayer and his vow will be heard because the Lord has promised him the throne and the kingdom as a lasting inheritance. And God's word is a tower which assures the promised inheritance (verses 6–9). The Lord has given to all who fear him and obey his Law an inheritance for all times. Even though the material possession in Palestine may here be the first thought, yet this inheritance may be considered a type of the Messianic blessing. A part of this blessing was God's promise about the eternal existence of his throne and kingdom which David had received through the Prophet Nathan. Relying on this promise he does not for one moment doubt that he will return to Jerusalem. Therefore his thoughts are no longer occupied with the sad present affairs but rather about the future of his house. It is a wish and at the same time a confession of faith in God's promise that he will add to the days of the king many more days, that he will continue to reign in his descendants through all generations until the Messias himself will ascend the throne of his progenitor. Protected by God's countenance, by his love and fidelity, may the kingship of his house endure throughout all times into eternity. Already the Targum, the Aramaic translation of the Psalms, has referred these words to the Messias. It stands at the end of the series of Davidic Psalms; in it David's kingdom continues to all eternity because he sits at the right of the Most High. Mercy and fidelity are his nature. They are the guardians of his throne and the supports of his kingdom. As long as his rule lasts, so long is the inheritance secure to them who are united with him; for in him, I say, in whom, we also have been called by a special choice, having been predestined in the purpose of him who works all things according to the counsel of his will (Ephesians 1:11). Since the Lord gives him this grace, the psalmist wishes to remember thankfully all the days of his life this fact and always to praise his name. In his songs he will fulfill the vow of eternal gratitude which he has made in the hours of need.

psalm 61

Nonne Deo

The prophet encourageth himself and all others to
trust in God and serve him

1. Unto the end, for Idithun, a psalm of David.

2. Shall not my soul be subject to God? For from him is my salvation.

3. For he is my God and my Saviour. He is my protector, I shall be moved no more.

4. How long do you rush in upon a man? you all kill, as if you were thrusting down a leaning wall, and a tottering fence.

5. But they have thought to cast away my price; I ran in thirst: they blessed with their mouth, but cursed with their heart.

6. But be thou, O my soul, subject to God; for from him is my patience.

7. For he is my God and my Saviour: he is my helper, I shall not be moved.

8. In God is my salvation and my glory: he is the God of my help, and my hope is in God.

9. Trust in him, all ye congregation of people: pour out your hearts before him. God is our helper forever.

10. But vain are the sons of men; the sons of men are liars in the balances: that by vanity they may together deceive.

11. Trust not in iniquity, and cover not robberies: if riches abound, set not your heart upon them.

12. God has spoken once, these two things have I heard, that power belongeth to God,

13. and mercy to thee, O Lord; for thou wilt render to every man according to his works.

S T. AUGUSTINE has said that the heart of man was created for God and that it remains restless if it does not seek its rest in him. Man in serene happiness and prosperity may feel no need for God as long as he is deceived about true value. But when suffering and adversity beset him it becomes evident that he can keep an inner calm only when in childlike confidence he submits himself to God and bears his suffering in quiet surrender; for only in God is the soul at rest. From him comes salvation. The truth of this saying the psalmist has experienced in his own life so full of adversity. On this account he is impelled to tell his troubles to others in order that in their own needs they may not depend on men but seek salvation and peace with God alone. He begins every strophe with this thought that it may be deeply impressed on his memory and that it may be inscribed in his soul indelibly.

In the first strophe (verses 2–5) the psalmist permits his own life experience to speak: only with confidence in God can the soul be at peace. David endured a school of suffering even before God permitted him to ascend the throne to which he had been called. Even during his reign he was not spared from severe visitations. In all adversities he depended on God's assistance and the Lord never denied him help whenever he called upon him. Whenever his soul was troubled he went to the Lord and he was pacified with the first coursing pulsation of divine love. God always proved himself to be the only rock and protection. To the heights of security in God the wild seething waves could not reach; there every attack of the enemy collapsed. His refuge was at all times a place of peace; although his enemies rage from without, they dare not touch him. The Lord was to him an invincible fortress which thousands of Saul's warriors could not take. From this experience is explained David's indomitable strength and confidence which for years withstood persecution and met all attacks. According to human reckoning, the affair of the psalmist was lost; for in great numbers the enemy attacked a single man who was deprived of all human help and surrounded by spies and traitors. He was compared to a crumbling wall which one further blow might topple, a wall sutured and breached waiting for the final assault. The attacks of the opponents caused great anxiety to David because it was their intention to cast him from the height to which God had led him by his call to the throne. They were so much the more dangerous because they fought him with the venomous weapons of lies and calumny. They were men who concealed their true nature, who pretended to be his friends and associates, but at heart hated and cursed him. In all these severe visitations David always found peace with God; there his heart found rest when he wept and made his complaint.

In this rich divine communication it should be realized that the soul finds peace with God, no matter how violently the storms rage within and without. Hence the psalmist directs his words to the people. The first admonition is: Have confidence in God and the soul will be pacified (verses 6–9); for, in truth, all help comes from God. He alone is the rock and protection; he alone is the strong citadel against the enemy; he alone guards and gives support to his children that they may not stagger. David has really found with God what others seek among creatures: salvation and honor, strength and protection. He has not sought salvation, the saving of his life or honor on the way of self-reliance, but he has placed himself in the hands of God and he was not disappointed. God proved himself, indeed, a rock, a strong protector, and a secure refuge. Therefore all should seek peace of soul with God along the same path. The path is unreserved confidence in God's justice, love, and fidelity. Confidence makes one communicative and leads to infinite Goodness. It makes one pour out the desires of the heart afflicted with sorrow. Jesus Sirach warns against opening one's heart to every ingratiating person, because he might return the confidence with ingratitude. With God deception is excluded. He who opens his heart to him will find consolation. God will take him under his powerful protection. The very consciousness of God's love and power protects, and to be safe under his guardianship gives to the soul inner peace.

Again the psalmist gives the predominant thought in his mind; namely, that his soul finds peace in God alone because every real help comes from him alone. He alone is the rock and protection and strong citadel. He who builds upon this rock will not waver; he who takes refuge in his citadel is secure from enemies. From this he draws a conclusion which causes him to give the second admonition: "If you do not put your trust in transitory things, your soul will remain peaceful" (verses 10–13). It is folly to put one's trust in men, may they be ever so powerful and influential. The Prophet Jeremias (17:6) curses him who places his confidence in men and turns his thoughts and desires away from God. Such a one he compares to a plant which lives in the dried and unfruitful soil of the steppes. Even the sons of men, the great and the mighty of the land, are liars. They deceive and are found wanting on the scales. When we place them on a scale and the need which they should have relieved on the other scale, their scale will rise high, for they weigh like a breath. If it is folly to rely on such, then it is also foolish presumption to put one's hope in unjust gain or upon growing wealth. He who depends on wealth whether it was justly or unjustly acquired will not obtain peace. He will have the experience about which the Book of Ecclesiastes speaks: "For what profit shall a man have of all his labors, and vexation of spirit, with which he hath been tormented under the sun? All his days are full of sorrows and miseries, even in the night he doth not rest in mind: and is not this vanity" (Ecclesiastes 2:22–23).

The twofold admonition not to depend on men and not to put one's trust in injustice and wealth, the psalmist bases on two great truths. The one should fill the oppressed with a confidence in the Lord; it is the truth that to God belongs all power and love. He alone is almighty. He alone can in every adversity, no matter how great, help effectively. For him there are no impossibilities, no obstacles which he, as Lord of all things, cannot overcome. God is also love and mercy. He has understanding and sympathy for the sufferings of mankind and a heart to console and heal. The second truth should deter man from every injustice and should encourage him to endure patiently all persecutions. It is the truth that God is just and rewards everybody according to his works. The day will come when all the works of men will be tried in the fire of judgment, and only that which proves to be gold and silver will be given eternal reward. This faith in eternal retribution can really bring peace to the heart of man; it does not only give peace to the soul, but it can even give joy in suffering.

psalm 62

Deus, Deus meus, ad te

The prophet aspireth after God

1. A psalm of David when he was in the desert of Edom.

2. O God, my God, to thee do I watch at break of day.
   For thee my soul hath thirsted; for thee my flesh, O how many ways!

3. In a desert land, and where there is no way and no water: so in the sanctuary have I come before thee, to see thy power and thy glory.

4. For thy mercy is better than lives: thee my lips shall praise.

5. Thus will I bless thee all my life long: and in thy name I will lift up my hands.

6. Let my soul be filled with marrow and fatness: and my mouth shall praise thee with joyful lips.

7. If I have remembered thee upon my bed, I will meditate upon thee in the morning:

8. because thou hast been my helper. And I will rejoice under the covert of thy wings:

9. my soul hath struck close to thee: thy right hand hath received me.

10. But they have sought my soul in vain, they shall go in the lower parts of the earth.

11. They shall be delivered into the hands of the sword, they shall be the portions of foxes.

12. But the king shall rejoice in God, all they shall be praised that swear by him: because the mouth is stopped of them that speak wicked things.

I T IS the possession of God above all else that gives to man's life its true value. The loss of God creates a spiritual vacuum; for there is nothing which can replace the highest Good and man's last End. In the Old Testament merely spiritual union with him in the sanctuary was the greatest happiness. When King David had to flee into the desert from Absalom, he lamented nothing so much as the separation from the gracious presence of God in the holy tabernacle on Sion. Such great longing took possession of him that he believed he would have to die in a strange land. It is just such a sentiment that he expressed in this psalm. It finds an echo in every soul which sincerely seeks spiritual union with God. Thus this psalm becomes a Communion prayer.

The first strophe (verses 2–4) gives expression to the longing of a soul thirsting for God; it is, as it were, a prayer of preparation for spiritual or real communion with the Lord. The soul also needs nourishment for spiritual and supernatural life. When the body has no pleasure in eating and drinking, it is sick; so also the soul is sick when it has no hunger nor thirst for justice and for God. Therefore it is a sign of spiritual health when man longs for grace which can be found only in union with God, just as a wanderer in a dry and waterless desert longs for cool water. The fountain from which grace flows, the sanctuary where the soul in union with God always finds new strength of life is the Holy of Holies, that Old Testament tabernacle of God among men where the Lord broods over the cherubim of the Ark of the Covenant. To the bodily eye he is a hidden God, seen only by the eyes of faith. Faith sees him; it sees his power and glory and would like to see him more clearly and more profoundly; it would like to obtain more knowledge of him, would like to feel more strongly the rays of his love. The spiritual life which the soul shares in union with God and the love which it receives from the God dwelling in the sanctuary is far more precious than natural life. It is a wealth which outweighs a natural life full of pleasures. He who once tastes how sweet the Lord is will forever praise the Lord with his lips.

The longing of the psalmist is stilled; his soul has at last celebrated a spiritual union with God. In the second strophe (verses 5–9) he speaks of

the happiness of a soul united with God. This happiness of union with
God is so great, that on the lips of him who experienced it, the praise of
God will never die out. Every day which the Lord gives David he will
praise him because of his goodness and raise his hands in his name. He
will call upon him daily and glorify him. One single communion with God
is a gift so precious that the long life of man is not sufficient to thank him
worthily. As the body is sated with marrow and meat, that is, satisfies
fully its pleasure in food with choice delicacies, so the soul finds true and
full satisfaction in the spiritual banquet which God offers in its union
with him. It is a food which is unto eternal life. The word of the Lord
may be applied here: "He who will come to me will no longer hunger;
who believes in me will no longer thirst" (John 6:35). Hence, songs of
jubilation flow from the psalmist's lips; his mouth will not tire in praising
the Lord for the wonderful appeasement of hunger. But his thankfulness
shall not be a momentary sentiment, not a single emotion of the soul in
the first joy of the partaking. A long time after he has left the sanctuary
and the immediate sweetness of his happiness comes to a close, his mind
will always be occupied with thoughts about the good God who has
enriched him with so many graces. Indeed, his happiness does not leave
him sleep; even during the night his thoughts are occupied with it and
from one night watch to the other he thinks about God's glorious gift of
grace. And his soul has good reason to be happy and contented. God who
has united himself with him is his powerful helper. When God is with a
son of man who will be against him? Who will separate him from his great
Love? Men who are united with God are joyful; for they know that they
are protected by loving Divine Providence as a chickling is protected by
the wings of the mother hen. Thus David could feel himself protected by
God in his flight from Absalom and his heart was full of joy despite all
tribulation.

The knowledge that a man united with God is under an almighty
Protector is the second great effect of union with the Lord; hence the
psalmist speaks in the third strophe (verses 9–12) about the security of
the soul protected by God. Every new association with God binds the
bond between the Creator and his creature tighter and stronger. Love
grows; the joy in association with God becomes greater; the anxiety that
he may again lose this union gives place to a feeling of assurance. Man
becomes controlled by a joyful confidence that the hand of the Lord holds
and supports him in order that he may not stumble and fall. Here lies the
source from which David drew his own strength which in the difficult
times of his son Absalom's rebellion sustained him. He was certain that
God's justice upheld him and that those who sought his life would quickly
receive God's punishment. Those who not only revolted against their king,

but even revolted against the Lord, will be excluded from union with God; they will be cast out eternally into the abyss of hell. This punishment will take place; the prayer of the psalmist may hasten it. Those who persecuted him with the sword and who have pursued him into the desert will fall by the sword of God; they will be cast from Sion and their corpses will rot in the desert and become a prey of jackals. Then the banished king will again enter Jerusalem and will rejoice in the Lord who has not abandoned his anointed. He who swears by the Lord, who honors him, and calls upon him will glory in his God on that day. The mouth of him who tells lies will be forever silenced. That will be the final fate of all who persecute a soul united with God and who strive to break this union with God. But the souls of the just after all the sufferings of this life will enter into the heavenly Sion. In this sense the Apostle Paul writes: "Indeed it is just on the part of God to repay with affliction those who afflict you and to give you, who are afflicted, rest with us at the revelation of the Lord Jesus who will come from heaven with the angels of his power. These will be punished with eternal ruin away from the face of the Lord and the glory of his power when on that day he shall come to be glorified in his saints and to be marveled at by all those who have believed" (2 Thessalonians 1:6–10).

psalm 63

Exaudi, Deus, orationem

A prayer in affliction, with confidence in God, that he will bring to nought the machinations of persecutors

1. Unto the end, a psalm for David.

2. Hear, O Lord, my prayer, when I make supplication to thee: deliver my soul from the fear of the enemy.

3. Thou hast protected me from the assembly of the malignant; from the multitude of the workers of iniquity.

4. For they have whetted their tongues like a sword: they have bent their bow, a bitter thing,

5. to shoot in secret the undefiled .

6. They will shoot at him on a sudden, and will not fear: they are resolute in wickedness.

   They have talked of hiding snares: they have said: Who shall see them?

7. They have searched after iniquities: they have failed in their search. Man shall come to a deep heart:

8. and God shall be exalted. The arrows of children are their wounds:

9. and their tongues against them are made weak. All that saw them were troubled;

10. And every man was afraid. And they declared the works of God and understood his doings.

11. The just shall rejoice in the Lord, and shall hope in him: and all the upright in heart shall be praised.

WITH enemies who fight with honest intentions and in a knightly manner, one can come to an agreement and a sincere peace even when they have a superior force. The dangerous enemies are those who use poisoned weapons, who avoid open attacks, and who treacherously shoot their arrows from ambush. They are such whose means of fighting are lies and calumny, who pretend that they mean well, but at heart plan mischief. Against such enemies even the strongest are helpless. With such weapons the enemies fought David in order to make life impossible for him both at the court of Saul and later as king. Because of this he typified Christ and the fate of the Church of Jesus Christ. In this psalm he throws light on the conduct of calumniators and announces to them God's punishment.

Against lies and calumny, against malicious attacks in secret neither bodily strength nor human wisdom are of any help; only God's assistance can be of avail. For this reason David turns to God with his complaint and petition. He begins his song with the petition for divine protection against the calumniators (verses 2–3). May God hear his complaint and save his soul and his life from the terror of his enemies; may he secure him against the attacks and plots of his enemies. As for any other refuge that might give him security, there is none; no other punishment but the divine can put an end to the machinations of the mighty and influential opponents. He will therefore place himself under the protection of God against the rabble of evil men who calumniate and persecute him and against the raving madness of evildoers.

In order to give emphasis to this petition before God the psalmist describes the activities of his detractors (verses 4–7). They are like robbers, who lie in hiding in order to surprise the unsuspecting wayfarer.

They possess sword and arrow. The sharp sword is their tongue; hence the Book of Proverbs says: "They have swords in their mouth instead of teeth." Their injurious talks are like sharp arrows which inflict painful wounds. Calumniators direct litanies of venomous words against innocent and God-fearing men. If David had been as godless as his opponents, they would not have hated him; but his piety and faith in the Law provoked their opposition. Because they were godless and the Law of the Lord was of no concern to them they ignored all of his just claims without fear and sought his downfall by treacherous means. David could have been on his guard against one calumniator; but it was impossible for him to defend himself against the many who attacked him according to a common plan and who mutually strengthened each other in their ruthlessness, men who in craftiness tried to surpass each other in laying snares for him. The heart of man which has once given itself up to its passions is unfathomable in its malice. "The heart is perverse above all things, and unsearchable. Who can know it?" (Jeremias 17:9). Always new injustices are plotted and planned in secrecy.

The heart of man may be deep in malice, but not as profound as the knowledge of God who searches the heart of man. He knows the activities of the godless and has decided the fate of the calumniators (verses 8–11). The Lord does not permit the innocent to be defeated. Suddenly when evil men believe that they can deliver a decisive blow and destroy their victim, God intervenes with his judgment. The poisoned arrows of their calumnies become the arrows of the divine Wrath; and the sword which they carried becomes the sword of divine Punishment which inflicts incurable wounds. Their lies and calumnies will be their own ruin. The judgment reveals their shameful activities and brings about their downfall so that all who experience it are terrified at the frightfulness of the divine punishment. They must recognize in it the hand of God. God's judgment does not only give retribution, but has in mind higher purposes. It should awaken in others a fear of God's justice and should deter them from lying and calumny. The fall of the godless should serve the glory of God and urge others to meditate upon the works of the Lord. The just should realize how powerful and faithful is their divine Lord and King. Therefore they shall rejoice and be glad and be loyal to him in all sincerity. The judgment should strengthen them in their confidence in his justice and love in order that trusting in him they may take refuge with him in every adversity.

psalm 64

Te decet

God is to be praised in his church to which all
nations shall be called

1. To the end, a psalm for David. The canticle of Jeremias and Ezechiel to the people of the captivity when they began to go out.

2. A hymn, O God becometh thee in Sion: and a vow shall be paid to thee in Jerusalem.

3. O hear my prayer: all flesh shall come to thee.

4. The words of the wicked have prevailed over us: and thou wilt pardon our transgressions.

5. Blessed is he whom thou hast chosen and taken to thee: he shall dwell in thy courts.
We shall be filled with good things of thy house, holy is thy temple;

6. Wonderful in justice,
Hear us, O God our Saviour, who art the hope of all the ends of the earth, and in the sea afar off.

7. Thou who preparest the mountains by thy strength, being girded with power:

8. Who troublest the depth of the sea, the noise of its waves.
The Gentiles shall be troubled,

9. And they that dwell in the uttermost borders shall be afraid at thy signs: thou shalt make the outgoings of the morning and of the evening to be joyful.

10. Thou hast visited the earth, and hast plentifully watered it; thou hast many ways enriched it.
The river of God is filled with water, thou hast prepared their food: for so is its preparation.

11. Fill up plentifully the streams thereof, multiply its fruits. It shall spring up and rejoice in its showers.

12. Thou shalt bless the crown of the year of thy goodness: and thy fields shall be filled with plenty.

13. The beautiful places of the wilderness shall grow fat: and the hills shall be girded about with joy.

14. The rams of the flock are clothed, and the vales shall abound with corn: they shall shout, yea, they shall sing a hymn.

PERHAPS this psalm was composed for the time of the Easter festivities. After the winter rain, nature is clothed in a festive garment. The mountains and hills are covered with lush green; in the fields the grain is beginning to ripen and all the meadows are alive with milling herds. The people too have put on their festive garments. In large crowds the faithful are making their pilgrimage to Jerusalem in order to thank the Lord again for the grace of redemption from captivity and for having chosen them as his people, for protection against their numerous enemies, and for all other earthly favors. The wide courts of the sanctuary have been filled with a joyful and enthusiastic crowd which jubilantly joins in singing hymns which the choir of singers chant to the accompaniment of harps. The thanksgiving of the people is given for a threefold blessing from God: the blessing of favors received, the blessing of preservation, and the blessing of nourishment. To thank the Lord for the prospect of a good crop seems to have been the primary reason for the singing of this psalm. It dedicates five verses to the thanksgiving for a good harvest while for the other two gifts of God only two and four verses are given respectively. But the psalm is especially a psalm of thanksgiving for a good crop, because a rich harvest is the result of God's favor and of peace with God. The giving of grace, preservation, and sustenance are also the threefold blessing which God bestows upon the members of the Church of Jesus Christ. With these he blesses them from heaven.

Praise should be given to God who dwells on Sion, the type of the New Testament sanctuary. With this thought in mind, all the pilgrims go up to Jerusalem; with this thought the choir of the Levites greet them. In the hymn which they sing, they wish to make all conscious of how great are the claims of the Lord to the praise of his people. Many did not need this special proof; they went up to Sion to redeem their vows and to offer God a thanksgiving sacrifice because he had heard their prayer. But faith in the promise which God had made to Solomon from his throne upon the Ark of the Covenant led to Jerusalem even those who with some anxiety made the pilgrimage: "My eyes shall be open and my ears attentive to the prayer of him that shall pray in this place. For I have chosen and have sanctified this place, that my name may be there forever, and my eyes and my heart may remain there perpetually" (2 Chronicles 7:15–16). Therefore all flesh, the entire people of Israel with all its requests comes to this place of grace from which all God's blessings flow.

239

The first and most precious of God's blessings which Israel has received from the Lord, the psalmist places at the beginning; namely, the blessing of God's special favor (verses 4-5). This blessing meant for Israel reconciliation with God, election, and enrichment with goods of a higher and supernatural life. The people who appear in the sanctuary know well that they are not worthy of the blessings of the Most High; for from the first day of their history they have rebelled against the Lord. Indeed, they have even exchanged the glory of God for the figure of a worthless idol. Nevertheless God has forgiven them and is even now quick to forgive. Israel may consider itself blessed because almighty God, the Lord of the universe, has chosen it from among all nations and has selected it as his special possession. He has placed his dwelling in their midst to be among them that they might approach him in the courts of his temple. Here the people receive the plenitude of the supernatural graces of his house; here they receive truth and grace which alone can truly satisfy the desires of the human heart. They rejoice in the sanctity of their temple which alone deserves to be called the house of God and the gate of heaven. The first blessing, that of reconciliation, is only a weak image of the rich blessings with which the Christian is endowed by being called to the Church, with which he is filled in the House of God of the New Covenant. Therefore it is befitting to praise God in the tabernacle.

The second of God's blessings for which the people should be thankful is the blessing of preservation (verses 6-9). When the people of Israel read in the pages of their history, they found many extraordinary punishments recorded which had been inflicted upon the enemies of the kingdom of God. This was particularly so in the times of Josue, Debbora, Gedeon, David, and others. There they could read how terrible the justice of the Lord revealed itself against all oppressors of his people and how wonderfully God revealed himself as the Saviour of his people, as the God of salvation. This just providence of Yahwe continues to manifest itself throughout all ages; again and again he answers the petitions of his people with great new deeds of his power. Many Gentile nations, hearing in distant countries word of the providence of God for his people, placed their own hope and confidence in God's mercy that he might aid their needs.

Israel itself is not astonished at such manifestations of the Lord's power for the preservation of his people; for it knows him as the Creator and Preserver of the universe. He alone by his almighty power has placed the gigantic mountains so that they stand eternally. Infinite power is the girdle of his garment. He rules the sea with his power; for he is the Lord of the storm and by his command the tossing waves are stilled. Even the pagan nations are astonished about a power which in vain they seek among their gods and are stricken with terror when they witness the power of Yahwe over nature and its powers. They are full of reverence for the greatness and majesty of the God of Israel when they see his miraculous signs. Even the most distant lands receive the message of his greatness. The out-going of the morning and of the evening, the uttermost east and west, the Orient and the Occident praise his majestic Being and rejoice in him. However at the time of the psalmist the pagan world had not yet come to such knowledge and acknowledgment of Yahwe. David looks into the Messianic future in which, according to the words of the prophet, all nations until the end of the earth will bend their knees to the Lord. The second blessing of God has also come more richly to the Church of Christ. For this its remarkable preservation and spread give testimony; the Orient and Occident now praise the true God. Therefore it behooves the members of this kingdom to give praise to the invisible King.

The third of God's blessings for which Israel wishes to thank God is the blessing of sustenance (verses 10–14). The people in Palestine especially were conscious of their dependence upon God in this matter. Who would give them sunshine and rain at the right time? If the rain does not come at the right time or is not sufficient, crop failure and famine are the result. The harvest yield depends on the winter rains. Therefore an advantageous rain for seeding and growth was for Israel as great a blessing from God as a good harvest for which they had to thank the Lord as we learn in this psalm. The people are joyful; for the Lord has drenched the soil with rain and has blessed them richly. God's water courses were filled with water. The rain fell in streams from the clouds to the earth and the Lord prepared the soil for the growth of the grain. With the early rain he drenched the soil so that the ground which had been dried by the summer sun softened and the seed could be sown in its furrows. With God's blessing the green sprouted from the ground saturated with moisture. If the year has begun with such rich blessings in nature so that a glorious harvest can be expected, then God will continue his work and crown the year by rewarding all their work with a rich harvest. Where the Lord walks showering his blessings over the meadows, there everything grows in abundance. Even the steppe, the pasture land, is covered with green velvet. The hills are festively wreathed with a wealth and variety of flowers and the soil in the valleys is covered with grain. Everywhere there is joy and gladness; mountains and valleys, fields and meadows rejoice and sing to the Lord.

241

psalm 65

Jubilate Deo

An invitation to praise God

1. Unto the end, a canticle of a psalm of the resurrection.
   Shout with joy to God, all the earth.

2. Sing ye a psalm to his name: give glory to his praise.

3. Say unto God: How terrible are thy works, O Lord! in the multitude of thy strength thy enemies shall lie to thee.

4. Let all the earth adore thee, and sing to thee: let it sing a psalm to thy name.

5. Come and see the works of God: who is terrible in his counsels over the sons of men.

6. Who turneth the sea into dry land, in the river they shall pass on foot: there shall we rejoice in him.

7. Who by his power ruleth forever: his eyes behold the nations; let not them that provoke him be exalted in themselves.

8. O bless our God, ye Gentiles: and make the voice of his praise to be heard.

9. Who hath set my soul to live: and hath not suffered my feet to be moved.

10. For thou, O God, hast proved us: thou hast tried us by fire, as silver is tried.

11. Thou hast brought us into a net, thou hast laid afflictions on our back.

12. Thou hast set men over our heads.
    We have passed through fire and water, and thou hast brought us out into a refreshment.

13. I will go into thy house with burnt offerings: I will pay thee my vows.

14. Which my lips have uttered.
    And my mouth hath spoken, when I was in trouble.

15. I will offer up to thee holocausts full of marrow, with burnt offerings of rams: I will offer to thee bullocks with goats.

16. Come and hear all ye that fear God, and I will tell you what great things he hath done for my soul.

17. I cried to him with my mouth: and I extolled him with my tongue.

18. If I have looked at iniquity in my heart, the Lord will not hear me.

19. Therefore, hath God heard me, and hath attended to the voice of my supplication.

20. Blessed be God, who hath not turned away my prayer, nor his mercy from me.

IN THE history of the chosen people there was added to the manifestations of God's power of the past a new great deed of God when the angel of the Lord slew the proud army of the Assyrian King Sennacherib before the walls of Jerusalem in one night, so that the king had to leave the country in flight and never again dared to set his foot on Palestinian soil. It was the work of Yahwe which astonished even the pagan world. This psalm no doubt directs our attention to this miraculous deliverance of Sion. It may be ascribed to the pious King Ezechias. The change of the singular to the plural of the composer of the psalm will find an easy explanation in that the king speaks in his own name and in the name of his people. The deliverance of Jerusalem from the threatening danger of Sennacherib was already looked upon in Old Testament writings as a type and guarantee of the invincibility of the kingdom of God. Hence the psalm is also a song of thanksgiving for the miraculous preservation of the Church despite the severe storms which have come upon it and its members.

The collapse of the proud emperor of Assyria caused without any human intervention was an event which made even the Gentiles look up and listen and be astonished at the power of the God of Israel. Thus the psalmist begins with a challenge to all nations to praise Yahwe (verses 1–12). Ezechias in his great need begged the Lord: "And now, O Lord our God, save us out of this hand: and let all the kings of the earth know, that only thou art the Lord" (Isaias 37:20). Now he observes that his prayer is heard and in spirit he sees the entire world bowed down in worship before Yahwe. Acclaim God all ye nations, sing praises to the glory of his name, let your praises echo! Even the enemies of God must be astonished at the grandeur of his works; they cannot refuse to acknowledge his power. How inept the power of their gods, of whom they had been so proud, must appear. When a single heavenly servant of almighty God can destroy a whole army, how great must be the power of almighty God himself. The more this knowledge penetrates the Gentile world, the more does the glory of his name become evident. Then the time will come about which God speaks through the Prophet Isaias that every knee shall bend before the Lord and every tongue shall swear by him (45:23).

The God who so miraculously delivered Jerusalem from the danger of the enemy is the same who from the beginning guided Israel and who will eternally rule the nations. The psalmist exhorts the Gentiles to meditate upon the works of the Lord in the history of his people and learn about his magnificent guidance of the children of men. He once upon a time delivered Israel from the Egyptian captivity; he separated the waters of the Red Sea so that his people could pass through it dry-shod; at the end of the journey through the desert he stopped the flow of the Jordan until all Israel could pass over to the promised land. Israel has every reason to rejoice about its all-powerful God. This God still lives as the miraculous Assyrian defeat testifies and he remains King for all eternity. He guides not only the history of his people which he has chosen for himself, but also the history of the whole world. His eyes look down upon all nations; none can withdraw from his rule; a rebellion against his throne and against his kingdom will never lead to victory.

The deliverance of Jerusalem from an encirclement of 185,000 Assyrians is a sign that the Lord also looks upon the Gentile nations; that they, too, must subject themselves to his power and feel his almighty hand. They should acknowledge this and join in the song of praise which Israel sings to its God. Where can we find a divinity who could save his devotees from such great affliction, a god as great as Yahwe who saved the people of Israel. It had already considered itself lost. How could Sion defend itself since the entire country was already in the power of the enemy and famine threatened because the land could not be cultivated? How could Ezechias hold the city since it was deprived of all help and exposed to attacks by an enemy many times greater than his own army? How could his army sally forth since the inhabitants lost courage, and surrender was the only hope? The deliverance was a miracle like a resurrection from the dead, a true return to life; it alone had saved Israel from collapse. God had permitted the war in order to try his people in the smelter of suffering and cleanse it as one cleanses silver. The time of peace and prosperity had estranged many from God; religious life had degenerated to externals; even pagan superstition and idolatry were introduced among the people of God. The time of tribulation was a smelter in which the dross was separated and the silver was cleansed.

Everything that is unholy, worldly, and pagan should be removed from the people of the Lord and from the kingdom of God that Israel may seek God alone and put all its trust in him. That is also the purpose of the afflictions which God permits to come upon his Church.

The Lord permitted snares to be laid for his people by the enticing promises which King Sennacherib made to the population of Jerusalem if they would willingly surrender the city. God permitted this in order to test whether they would place greater faith in the promises of a man than in the promises of God. In order to try their confidence in God, he placed upon them the heavy burden of war and the siege of the city. For two years the enemy had devastated the land; the people were oppressed by the heavy burdens which the enemy laid upon them in their plundering of the poor. They had to pass, as it were, through fire and water. But again and again the Lord restored their strength and fulfilled the word which he had uttered through the mouth of the prophet Isaias: "Fear not: when thou shalt pass through waters, I will be with thee, and the rivers shall not cover thee; when thou shalt walk in the fire, thou shalt not be burnt, and the flames shall not burn in thee; for I am the Lord thy God, the holy One of Israel, the Saviour" (Isaias 43:2–3).

In the first part of the psalm Ezechias invited all nations to behold the works of the Lord for his people and with him to praise God. Now he goes to the sanctuary to keep his vow which he had made in the time of distress. The second part of the psalm (verses 13–20) gives us the thanksgiving of the king. When he saw the many corpses of the enemy lying before the walls of the city he was urged to thank the Lord in the sanctuary and to have the sacrifices offered which he had vowed. When he knew that there was no escape from disaster, he turned to the Lord in prayer and vowed a thanksgiving offering. What he had promised with his mouth should be given to the Lord without delay. He ordered the best of his flock to be brought to the temple to be burnt upon the altar. When God manifests his almighty power and the infinity of his love to help man, it would be unnatural for him to haggle with God about the measure of his thanksgiving. It is true that God looks less upon the external gift than upon the internal disposition; but the disposition impels the will to dedicate only the best to the Lord.

The king is not satisfied with merely offering a dead gift for a sacrifice which goes up in smoke upon the altar; with his mouth he wants to proclaim to all who fear God how great a favor the Lord performed when he granted his petition. Now he narrates to the people how he cast himself before the Lord in the sanctuary when their only thought was to surrender the city to the enemy. He knew that only a miracle could save them, but he had the confidence that the Lord would not despise the request of a miracle. And he was not deceived. Scarcely had he entered the sanctuary when the Lord informed him through the Prophet Isaias: "I will protect this city and will save it for my sake and for my servant David's sake" (Isaias 37:35). Thus the king, his anxiety abated, could leave the house of God with a "Te Deum" on his lips. Again it has been proved that God does not refuse a request which comes from a soul brimming with absolute faith and confidence, from a soul pleasing to

245

God. He who has not such confidence, but prays and doubts at the same time need not expect any mercy. The Lord has paid heed to the petition of his servant. The king tells this with jubilant heart that all may hear and know. Not by his own strength did he redeem the city. It was the power of prayer that broke the might of the Assyrian king. Thus the thanksgiving celebration was ended with a hymn about the divine Love who hears the prayers of men and does not refuse mercy to his servant.

psalm 66

Deus misereatur

A prayer for the propagation of the Church

1. Unto the end, in hymns, a psalm of a canticle for David.

2. May God have mercy on us and bless us: may he cause the light of his countenance to shine upon us, and may he have mercy on us.

3. That we may know thy way upon earth: thy salvation in all nations.

4. Let people confess to thee, O God: let all people give praise to thee.

5. Let the nations be glad and rejoice: for thou judgest the people with justice, and directest the nations upon earth.

6. Let the people, O God, confess to thee: let all the people give praise to thee:

7. The earth hath yielded her fruit.
   May God, our God, bless us.

8. May God bless us: and all the ends of the earth fear him.

As every important victory of Israel over the Gentile neighboring nations was interpreted by the prophets as a prelude to the Messianic judgment of nations, so they also saw in an unusual rich harvest a symbol of the spiritual blessings of the coming time of salvation in which all the world would partake. This psalm seems to have been originally a song of thanksgiving after a good harvest, but has also become a mission prayer; namely, that the Lord may also fulfill the hopes of the Messianic blessing. The poet has added this prayer to the petition of the priestly blessing; for God must first let his mercy and grace shine upon Israel that according to the eternal decree it can be a light and a mediator to the Gentiles. Then on earth one may see the way to salvation (verses 2–3). The nations will find that the Lord has led them in all mercy (verses 4–5). They will rejoice because of the blessings that have come to them (verses 6–7). The closing verse returns to the thought of the introductory verse.

Daily at the close of the morning and evening sacrifice, a priest uttered a blessing upon the people as Aaron did upon Israel: "The Lord bless thee, and keep thee. The Lord show his face to thee, and have mercy on thee. The Lord turn his countenance to thee, and give thee peace" (Numbers 6:24–26). The psalmist prays that this blessing may come upon Israel that the Gentile world may know the way of God to salvation. The light of Sion would have a greater attraction for the Gentiles if the effects of the gifts for salvation would shine more gloriously in the very people of God; for when the Gentiles see the life of those who expect redemption and then seek it, they also will have a longing for redemption and say: "Come let us go up to the mountain of the Lord, and to the house of the God of Jacob; and he will teach us his ways, and we will walk in his paths: for the law shall come forth from Sion, and the word of the Lord from Jerusalem" (Isaias 2:3). Therefore it was in the interests of the mission to the Gentiles that the Lord pour forth the fullness of his grace. In this sense the psalmist prays for the fulfillment of the priestly blessing; in this sense we too must pray the psalm that the life of the Christians may reveal to the nations the happiness of redemption and show them the way to salvation.

When the Messianic salvation has become a reality among the Gentiles and the light of knowledge has shone upon them, then will all nations adore the one true God and in union with Israel they will praise him; then Yahwe's name will be glorified from one end of the earth to the other. Then the vision of the Prophet Isaias will be fulfilled (Isaias 24:14 seq.) who heard the nations in the West and in the East and on the coasts of the seas jubilate and acclaim the glory of the Lord which revealed itself to them; and who heard from the ends of the earth songs of praise to the one true God. The sorrow that afflicted the Gentile world will soon be changed into joy; for the Gentiles have themselves experienced that the Lord judges the nations in justice, that is, that he guides and directs them. They will realize that the Lord does not limit his mercy to Israel and that he does not exclude the Gentiles from his love, that their ways too will finally lead to the kingdom of his grace.

When the Gentiles have walked the way of salvation and have become co-citizens with the saints and children of God, and when the decree of redemption comes to its completion, the Gentiles will be astonished about the miracles of salvation and will praise God because of his wisdom and love. They will see the curse of original sin taken from the earth; and God's blessing, which was taken from Adam by God's punitive judgment, will fructify in an astounding manner. The paradisaic fruitfulness is a type of the fullness of grace which God pours out on the redeemed from the new heaven and earth where justice reigns (2 Peter 3:13). The glimpse into the Messianic future has awakened in the psalmist a longing for the fulfillment of what he has seen. Therefore he renews his petition with which he has started that God may give grace to his people abundantly, that the Gentiles may know the Lord from the light going out from Sion and that they may fear him.

psalm 67

Exurgat Deus

The glorious establishment of the Church of the New Testament prefigured by the benefits bestowed on the people of Israel

1. Unto the end, a psalm of a canticle for David himself.

2. Let God arise, and let his enemies be scattered: and let them that hate him flee from before his face.

3. As smoke vanishes, so let them vanish away: as wax melteth before the fire, so let the wicked perish at the presence of God.

4. And let the just feast, and rejoice before God: and be delighted with gladness.

5. Sing ye to God, sing a psalm to his name, make a way for him, who ascendeth upon the west: the Lord is his name.
   Rejoice ye before him: but the wicked shall be troubled at his presence,

6. Who is the father of the orphans, and the judge of widows.
   God in his holy place:

7. God who maketh men of one manner to dwell in a house.
   Who bringeth out them that were bound in strength; in like manner them that provoke, that dwell in sepulchres.

8. O God, when thou didst go forth in the sight of thy people, when thou didst pass through the desert:

9. The earth was moved, and the heavens dropped at the presence of the God of Sinai, at the presence of the God of Israel.

10. Thou shalt set aside for thy inheritance a free rain, O God: and it was weakened, but thou hast made it perfect.

11. In it shall thy animals dwell: in thy sweetness, O God, thou hast provided for the poor.

12. The Lord shall give the word to them that preach good tidings with great power.

13. The king of powers is of the beloved, of the beloved; and the beauty of the house shall divide spoils.

14. If you sleep among the midst of lots, you shall be as the wings of a dove covered with silver, and the hinder parts of her back with the paleness of gold.

15. When he that is in heaven appointeth kings over her, they shall be whited with snow in Selmon.

16. The mountain of God is a fat mountain: a curdled mountain, a fat mountain.

17. Why suspect, ye curdled mountains? A mountain in which God is well pleased to dwell: for there the Lord shall dwell unto the end.

18. The chariot of God is attended by ten thousands; thousands of them that rejoice; the Lord is among them in Sinai, in the holy place.

19. Thou hast ascended on high, thou hast led captivity captive; thou hast received gifts in men.
Yea for those also that do not believe, the dwelling of the Lord God.

20. Blessed be the Lord day by day: the God of our salvation will make our journey prosperous to us.

21. Our God is the God of salvation: and of the Lord, of the Lord are the issues from death.

22. But God shall break the heads of his enemies: the hairy crown of them that walk on in their sins.

23. The Lord said: I will turn them from Basan, I will burn them into the depth of the sea:

24. That thy foot may be dipped into the blood of thy enemies; the tongue of thy dogs be red with the same.

25. They have seen thy goings, O God, the goings of my God: of my king who is in his sanctuary.

26. Princes went before joined with singers, in the midst of young damsels playing on timbrels.

27. In the churches bless ye God the Lord, from the fountains of Israel.

28. There is Benjamin a youth, in ecstasy of mind.
    The princes of Juda are their leaders, the princes of Zabulon, the princes of Nephthali.

29. Command thy strength, O God; confirm, O God, what thou hast wrought in us.

30. From thy temple in Jerusalem, kings shall offer presents to thee.

31. Rebuke the wild beasts of the reeds, the congregation of bulls with the kine of the people; who seek to exclude them who are tried with silver.
    Scatter thou the nations that delight in wars:

32. Ambassadors shall come out of Egypt: Ethiopia shall soon stretch out her hands to God.

33. Sing to God, ye kingdoms of the earth: sing you to the Lord, sing ye to God.

34. Who mounteth above the heaven of heavens, to the east.
    Behold he will give to his voice the voice of power:

35. Give ye glory to God for Israel, his magnificence, and his power is in the clouds.

36. God is wonderful in his saints: the God of Israel is he who will give power and strength to his people. Blessed be God.

AFTER King David had conquered Jerusalem and had taken his dwelling in the castle, his first care was to erect a sanctuary for the Lord on Sion and to bring the Ark of the Covenant which for many years had been at Cariathiarim, 12 kilometers northwest of Jerusalem, in the house of Abinadab, to the new tabernacle erected for that purpose. This psalm was composed for that event. Considered in the light of prophecy it was more than an act of reverence for the Ark of the Lord. For with the entry into Sion, Yahwe had visibly taken possession of that city which was to be the starting place of his kingdom. The transferring of the Ark therefore became an important event in the history of the Messianic salvation. In this sense it was also understood by the psalmist. Therefore in this psalm he reviews the acts of divine Providence occupying the throne on the Ark from the time the covenant was made upon Sinai until the entry into Sion and he also views prophetically the Messianic future. His meditations accompany the procession from Cariathiarim until the arrival in Jerusalem. We may call the psalm the "Lauda Sion" of the Old Covenant.

"Praise, O Sion, thy leader, thy shepherd and ruler, with prayer and songs of praise." For there are many similarities between the triumphant processions in honor of Yahwe of Sion and the Eucharistic processions of the Church. The Eucharistic processions of the Church celebrate the fulfillment of that which was foreshadowed in the Old Testament. The Ark of the Covenant as the throne of the invisible glory of God seen by the eyes of faith is a type of the monstrance; its solemn transfer is a type of the triumph of the Eucharist. The meditations are partly typical, and partly a direct prophetic preview of the blessings that were to come from God in the history of the Church and from God dwelling in the tabernacle and of the blessings that will continue to come from him. Paul sees in the entry of the Lord to Mount Sion a type of the Ascension of Christ to heaven and the possession of his eternal throne (Ephesians 4:8). By doing so he has interpreted the psalm in its most profound prophetic sense.

In the beginning of the procession (verses 2–7) the psalmist brings back to memory the departure from Sinai, and the power and love of God throning above the Ark of the Covenant. He who wishes to accompany the Lord in this triumphal procession must be permeated with right dispositions and a vivid consciousness of his majesty. When God on Sinai gave the signal for departure by the appearance of the pillar of the cloud, Moses prayed: "Arise, O Lord, and let thy enemies be scattered, and let them that hate thee flee from thy face" (Numbers 10:35). What Moses asked from the Lord during his journey through the desert the poet sees fulfilled in the history of his people. For whenever Yahwe arose for the protection of his people, the enemies and haters of his people had to take to flight. His wrath no human greatness and power can resist. A breath of wind is sufficient to disperse an ascending cloud of smoke, and a little fire is sufficient to melt wax. This is a description of the weakness of sinners and blasphemers. They vanish when the breath of God strikes them and their strength is gone when the glow of the divine Wrath falls upon them. And they perish before his countenance when he appears in judgment. As terrifying as the Lord is to those who hate him and wage war upon his kingdom, so good is he to all who love and worship him. "The Lord preserveth the souls of his saints; he will deliver them out of the hand of sinners. Light is risen to the just, and joy to the right of heart" (Psalm 96:10–11). Union with God is an inexhaustible source of pure and holy joy. Those who give themselves with their entire soul to God will learn to understand God's word. "And they shall fear and be troubled for all the good things and for all the peace that I will make for them" (Jeremias 33:9). They will be glad before God's countenance and jubilate for joy.

In view of the majesty of God seated upon the Ark of the Covenant

251

the psalmist requests all who participate in the procession to sing songs of jubilation. "Sing as well as thou canst: to sing his praise worthily can hardly be done." The Lord, whom they accompany, is Yahwe, the eternal Being; that is his name and his infinite nature. He is the one and only true God, eternal and infinite in his being, almighty in his works and all merciful in his love. But to sing songs of jubilation is not sufficient to give God befitting honor. Those who sing must also be preparers of the way and heralds of his glory that others, too, may believe in his glory and worship him. Those who already enjoy union with God have every reason to rejoice; for the eternal King is not an inaccessible ruler who treats his subjects as slaves. He is the father and defender of his people. He is the father of orphans abandoned by an earthly father; he is the advocate of the widows who are deprived of the protection of a man. The way to the throne of the sanctuary is open to all, and there is an invitation to all. "Come to me all ye who are troubled and heavily laden, and I will refresh you" (Matthew 11:28). As a father and advocate he has received his people from the beginning. He has given to those who were without a country, who lived in slavery in Egypt, a home in Canaan, as he had promised to the patriarchs. He has led all who suffered slavery and persecution in Egypt to freedom and prosperity. Only those who were unreceptive to his admonitions, who had rebelled against him could not enter the peace of the promised land, but had to die in the desert. The liberation of the Israelites from the Egyptian captivity and the leading of the homeless into the promised land was looked upon by the prophets as a type of spiritual redemption from the slavery of sin and of the call of the pilgrims on earth to the kingdom of God, the Church, and to heavenly happiness. Those whom the Lord had called should not be satisfied to be mere participants in the triumphant Eucharistic procession; they are bound more than the Israelites to be heralds and preparers of the way to his glory.

On the way to Jerusalem (verses 8–15) the psalmist calls to mind the forty years journey in the desert and reminds Israel how God at that time was the leader and provider of his people (verses 8–11). It needed only a few reminders; for to all of the participants in the procession the miracles of the divine Love were well known. But for us it is not easy and not without some difficulty to determine the meaning of such reminders throughout the entire psalm. God himself undertook to lead his people in the pillar of a cloud that they might securely reach the promised land. On this journey God revealed his majesty by miracles and signs. He appeared in his power at the making of the covenant on Sinai so that all Israel feared and trembled. The earth quaked; from Mount Sinai thick smoke arose as from a furnace, and the Lord descended in fire (Exodus 19:18).

Thunder roared over the mountains; the lightning flashed continually in the dark clouds (Exodus 20:18) and rain poured from the skies. This God revealing himself in his terrifying majesty on Mount Sinai is the same God who reigns above the Ark of the Covenant. This mighty God proved himself to be a father during the journey in the desert. He lovingly cared for his children. He gave gifts to his people and refreshed his inheritance, his own possession, his chosen people when they were famishing. At their petition he sent them quail and nourished them with bread from heaven; he opened the rocks and water issued from them; he let streams flow through the dry land (Psalm 104:40). The Lord crowned his works of deliverance by leading Israel into the land of Canaan, into the land where milk and honey flows. He had prepared this land for his people that they might carry out undisturbed his mission. In its seclusiveness it formed a natural barrier against attacks from without and its fertility supported its population without much care.

Israel by its own strength could not have conquered Palestine, could not have taken the strong fortifications. Therefore the psalmist reminds his people that God was the giver of the promised land (verses 12–15). It was he who helped Josue in conquest after conquest; it was he who helped Debbora vanquish the Canaanites at Jabin, who had delivered the Madianites into the hands of Gedeon. Successes followed one another so rapidly in the history of Israel that virgins were accustomed to celebrate the victories with music and dance and to proclaim in great numbers as messengers of God the great deeds of the Lord. The Lord of hosts was with Israel because he had chosen it as his much beloved people. He gave rich booty to it which it could use for the decoration of his tabernacle and temple. The beauty of the house can be interpreted as referring to Israel itself, the occupant of the land of Canaan. The poet, who in this part of the psalm relied much on the canticle of Debbora (Judges 5) could also have thought of Debbora, who as "mother of Israel" was the pride of her people and who distributed much booty after the battle of Thabor. After all these victories the country presented a picture of peace and quiet. The psalmist compares it to a dove, the symbol of peace. The comparison is appropriate because in biblical poetry the dove is also used as a symbol of Israel. At that time when the Almighty with his strong arm vanquished the Canaanite kings and brought peace to his people, snow fell on Selmon. The psalmist reminisces about this event which supposedly took place on Selmon near Sichem. The biblical sources narrate nothing about it; it is therefore impossible to interpret the meaning of these words. God throning upon the cherubim in the sanctuary was the leader, provider, and protector of his people, but the Eucharistic King in a much greater measure is the leader, protector, and provider of his Church; for he himself is the way, the truth, and the life; he is the bread of heaven; he is the rock that accompanies us and gives victory to the Church.

Upon entry into Jerusalem (verses 16–24) the procession ascends Mount Sion. This gives the psalmist the occasion to show his appreciation of selecting Sion as the place of the sanctuary (verses 16–19). The pagans considered the highest mountains of the land as the dwelling places of their gods. In the eyes of God, however, the Law holds that the little and insignificant is to be preferred, because God is not dependent upon externals for his glorification. Therefore he did not select the highest peak in Palestine as a place for his throne upon earth. He did not select the great Hermon which with its three summits extends along the west border of the land of Basan. He rejected Hermon which has a height of nearly three thousand meters, Hermon whose snow-caps are everywhere the sign of the approach to the land of Canaan. This huge mountain may look with envy and jealousy upon the lowly Sion which overlooks no more than the other hills in the proximity of Jerusalem. God did not select the king of the Palestinian mountains for his dwelling place; he preferred the insignificant Sion. Here he celebrates his entry with myriads of angels who had surrounded him on Mount Sinai (Deuteronomy 33:2) and with which he is also surrounded in his invisible throne in the holy tabernacle. Since the Lord celebrates his solemn entry into his city, the psalmist cannot help thinking of the innumerable host of his chariot fighters, of his blessed spirits. Because God with his court which on Sinai was witness to the making of the covenant, now enters Sion, Mount Sinai is compared to Sion. Sion is more than Sinai because here the Lord establishes his throne forever and all who ascend this mountain are admitted to the throne of grace. Nevertheless Sion is only a shadow of the eminence and glory of the smallest Catholic chapel in which God takes up his dwelling place in truth and reality. As victor the Lord also takes with him the captives; for the completion of the description this also is appropriate. First of all, the psalmist thought of the captives of war which David used as slaves in the most humble services of the sanctuary, and then of the captive Jebusites who formerly lived on Sion and who, after the taking of the fortifications, had to make room for David and his God.

The priests have placed the Ark of the Covenant on Mount Sion and the choir of singers invites all to greet God their King (verses 20–24). Praise ye the Lord! Day by day, God, our help, sustains us. What the Psalmist comprises in a short confession, that in a later period the Lord assures to his people through the Prophet Isaias in the following memorable words: "Hearken to me, O house of Jacob, all the remnant of the house of Israel who are carried by my bowels are borne by my womb. Even to your old age I am the same, and to your grey hairs I will carry you: I have made you, and I will bear: I will carry and I will save"

(46:3–4). Yahwe alone, in truth, is a Saviour, a God that can help. He can save where every other help seems impossible; he can even deliver from the grave and from the underworld.

Death, to which all men must submit, must obey the power of God. He alone can release from spiritual death. Therefore he also has the power to protect his people and his kingdom from all dangers that threaten from numerous enemies on all sides. Even if they were savage and brutal men who would not be deterred from any evil deed, against God they could do nothing. God shall break the heads of his enemies; he shall break their proud stubbornness. No one can escape his judgment. May these blasphemers hide themselves in the caverns of Basan, in the mountains of Hauran, the all-present and all-knowing God will find them; for he knows their hiding places. If it were possible for them to hide themselves in the depth of the sea, God's almighty power would drag them from the deepest abyss. The punishment will be absolute. The judgment upon the adversaries of the kingdom of God is frequently described as a horrible defeat at which the blood of the enemy flows in streams and the corpses of the fallen lie unburied and serve as food for the scavengers and jackals. With this description the psalmist wishes to say that all who hate God and wage war upon his kingdom prepare themselves for their own shameful destruction.

The solemn transfer of the Ark of the Covenant to Sion ends with the worship of God as the King of Israel (verses 25–32). The psalmist first speaks of the worship given by Israel (verses 25–28). In the same order in which the people accompany the Ark of the Lord from Cariathiarim to Sion, they pass by the throne of the most high God. It is a solemn procession in honor of Yahwe, the King, who has taken possession of his sanctuary. At the head of the procession are the choirs of singers chanting hymns and psalms; the harp players who accompany the songs with instruments follow the singers. Among them is David clothed in a linen ephod. On both sides the virgins dance and beat the kettle drums. Behind them in an immense procession walks the multitude of people that had taken part in the triumphant entry. To those who are the descendants of Israel, the offspring of the patriarchs, the request is made to praise the Lord; for he is the God of Abraham, of Isaac, and of Jacob. He is the God who made promises to the fathers, the fulfillment of which the present generation has partly seen and which it partly expects in the Messianic future. Among the tribes of Israel two southern tribes are especially mentioned. One is Benjamin which is indeed small in numbers, but especially distinguished by God since Sion is situated in its tribal territory. Therefore it worships the Lord with great enthusiasm. The princes of Juda follow. Their tribe gives the kings to Palestine and from this tribe the Messias-King will be born. As representatives of the northern tribes, Zabulon and Nephthali are mentioned. In the journey through the desert they with Juda formed a vanguard. They came from the northern part of the kingdom to show that they were united with Sion and its sanctuary.

The kingdom of Yahwe should not be limited to Israel; it should comprise all nations. Therefore the worship of Israel alone is not sufficient worship for the honor that is due to God. The worship of all nations shall complete this worship (verses 29–32). The jubilant, faithful people assembled on Sion are conscious of this and thus the psalm turns into a prayer that the Lord may complete the work which he has begun by taking possession of Sion. Jerusalem shall be the starting point of the Messianic world. May God manifest his power from the sanctuary and strengthen the work in the interest of Sion. When he diffuses the light of his Messianic glory over Jerusalem, the princes of the Gentile nations will come and worship the eternal King of Sion with their gifts; and the people will follow the example of the princes from all countries of the earth. Isaias, enraptured by the glory of the Messianic descriptions of the future, pictures in spirited language the procession of the nations to Sion: "Arise, be enlightened, O Jerusalem, for thy light is come and the glory of the Lord is risen upon thee. And the Gentiles shall walk in thy light and kings in the brightness of thy rising. Then shalt thou see and abound and thy heart shall wonder and be enlarged; when the multitude of the sea shall be converted to thee, the strength of the Gentiles shall come to thee" (Isaias 60:1 seq.). However this glory is a picture of the future. The Gentile nations are not inclined at this time to worship the God of Israel, they are even now filled with hatred and are planning war for Israel's destruction. They would like to destroy completely God's people who have been tried by so many adversities. Among these nations the psalmist mentions Egypt, the beast among the reeds. The crocodile is often considered a symbol of Egypt in the Old Testament. The great powers of the earth have united with Egypt. They are the cattle and all their calves; that is, the satellite nations dependent upon them are the calves. Against these the Lord must direct his powerful word in order that they may acknowledge his supremacy. Then the nobility of Egypt will come to Sion and be converted; Ethiopia also will hasten to worship and raise its hands to the Lord seeking help in his sanctuary. All kings of the earth will follow them, and the kingdom of Yahwe will comprise the entire world.

The psalmist even now requests all nations and kingdoms of the earth to praise God (verses 33–36). "You kingdoms of the earth, praise the Lord." The song of praise should be sung to the supreme King who reveals his majesty in the heavens. Who would dare to resist the all-powerful God? Therefore give honor to God. Give honor to the God of

Israel. By his majesty he governs the people whom he has chosen and in his people he reveals his power which reaches to the clouds and comprises heaven and earth. Indeed, God who dwells in the sanctuary, who performs wonderful deeds in his tabernacle, demands reverence. There abides the source of strength and power for his people. In a much higher sense is the tabernacle of the New Testament a source of strength for the Church and all its members. Therefore, we too should praise and thank the Lord.

psalm 68

Salvum me fac, Deus

Christ in his passion declares the greatness of his sufferings and the malice of his persecutors, the Jews, and foretells their reprobation

1. Unto the end, for them that shall be changed, for David.

2. Save me, O God: for the waters are come in even unto my soul.

3. I stick fast in the mire of the deep: and there is no sure standing.
   I am come into the depth of the sea: and a tempest hath overwhelmed me.

4. I have laboured with crying; my jaws are become hoarse: my eyes have failed, whilst I hope in my God.

5. They are multiplied above the hairs of my head, who hate me without cause.
   My enemies are grown strong who have wrongfully persecuted me: then did I pay that which I took not away.

6. O God, thou knowest my foolishness: and my offences are not hidden from thee.

7. Let not them be ashamed for me, who look for thee, O Lord, the Lord of hosts.
   Let them not be confounded on my account, who seek thee, O God of Israel.

8. Because for thy sake I have borne reproach; shame hath covered my face.

9. I am become a stranger to my brethren, and an alien to the sons of my mother.

10. For the zeal of thy house hath eaten me up: and the reproaches of them that reproached thee are fallen upon me.

11. And I covered my soul in fasting: and it was made a reproach to me.

12. And I made a haircloth garment: and I became a byword to them.

13. They that sat in the gate spoke against me: and they that drank wine made me their song.

14. But as for me, my prayer is to thee, O Lord; for the time of thy good pleasure, O God.
In the multitude of thy mercy hear me, in the truth of thy salvation.

15. Draw me out of the mire, that I may not stick fast: deliver me from them that hate me, and out of the deep waters.

16. Let not the tempest of water drown me, nor the deep swallow me up: and let not the pit shut her mouth upon me.

17. Hear me, O Lord, for thy mercy is kind; look upon me according to the multitude of thy tender mercies.

18. And turn not away thy face from thy servant: for I am in trouble, hear me speedily.

19. Attend to my soul, and deliver it; save me because of my enemies.

20. Thou knowest my reproach, and my confusion, and my shame.

21. In thy sight are all they that afflict me: my heart hath expected reproach and misery.
And I looked for one that would grieve together with me, but there was none: and for one that would comfort me, and I found none.

22. And they gave me gall for my food, and in my thirst they gave me vinegar to drink.

23. Let their table become as a snare before them, and a recompense, and a stumbling block.

24. Let their eyes be darkened that they see not; and their back bend thou down always.

25. Pour out thy indignation upon them: and let thy wrathful anger take hold of them.

26. Let their habitation be made desolate, and let there be none to dwell in their tabernacles.

27. Because they have persecuted him whom thou hast smitten: and they have added to the grief of my wounds.

28. Add thou iniquity upon their iniquity: and let them not come into thy justice.

29. Let them be blotted out in the book of the living; and with the just let them not be written.

30. But I am poor and sorrowful: thy salvation, O God, hath set me up.

31. I will praise the name of God with a canticle and I will magnify him with praise.

32. And I shall please God better than a young calf that bringeth forth horns and hoofs;

33. Let the poor see and rejoice: seek ye God and your soul shall live.

34. For the Lord hath heard the poor: and hath not despised his prisoners.

35. Let the heavens and the earth praise him; the sea, and everything that creepeth therein.

36. For God will save Sion, and the cities of Juda shall be built up.
    And they shall dwell there, and acquire it by inheritance.

37. And the seed of his servants shall possess it; and they that love his name shall dwell therein.

A N OLD tradition (*See* Romans 11:9) designates David as the composer of this touching prayer; it contains nothing that would contradict this. The psalm must stem from a time in which the royal sufferer despite his zeal for the sanctuary of the Lord was misrepresented, attacked, and hated by many. The conduct of his own wife Michol (2 Kings 6:20) gives testimony that he, because of his zeal, had to suffer much mockery and derision. The description of his spiritual distress seems to be far above the reality, and verses 23–29 are hard to understand as coming from the mouth of David refusing to revenge himself on Semei who had cursed him apparently with the permission of God (2 Kings 16:9 seq.). It is also hard to understand that these verses should come from the mouth of a man who speaks under the inspiration of the Holy Spirit. The psalm finds a satisfactory explanation only when we accept the interpretation of the fathers and ancient commentators that the royal singer speaks in the name of his great descendant, the Messias, and that his complaint and prayer may find its application in the complaint and prayer of Christ on the cross. Even the Apostles understood that this psalm applied to Christ (John 2:17 and 15:25) and to the fate of the Jewish people (Romans 11:9 seq.). John saw in the giving of vinegar to our Lord, when he was thirsty, a fulfillment of the twenty-second verse. The Apostle Peter (Acts 1:20) based the necessity of an election of another apostle to take the place of the traitor Judas on this psalm. He saw here a typical fore-shadowing of the rejection of Israel and of the call of the Gentile world. The cursing psalm is therefore a prophecy, a prophetic announcement of the redemption and of the divine judgment upon the Jewish people. David saw and experienced a vision similar to that of Psalm 21, the holy hour of Christ on Golgotha.

The introduction of the psalm (verses 2–4) reminds one clearly of Psalm 21. It is a cry for help in the greatest need. Weeping under the burden of the heavy cross, David looks up to heaven with tearful eyes. There appears to him in a veiled mist the figure of the Messias, suffering excruciating pain and approaching death, surrounded by enemies; like an echo of his own cry to God he hears the Messias's cry for help. The Anointed sees inescapable death before his eyes as a man floundering in a deep morass, thrashes and cannot find solid ground for his feet. He faces certain death, like one drowning, helplessly struggling against the waves. Strength leaves him and his members no longer give him any service and the waves go over his head and mercilessly engulf him. These are pictures of the death-struggle of the Messias who feels himself abandoned by all, even by God. In vain has he cried for help; nobody pays heed to his cries and now his voice fails him. He looks around to all sides to see if help is near, but no matter how imploringly his weakened eyes beg for help, no one steps forward to assist him. Even heaven does not open to deliver him from death's anguish.

But the Lord must and will have mercy upon his Anointed so that hell's malice will not conquer. What the Messias gives as a reason for his cry for help should be given in the language of a prayer and should be a guarantee for Israel that the decisive battle with the Satanic powers may not bury all hope for salvation but will bring about the promised Redemption. There are also as many guarantees that the stream of blessings flowing from the grace of the Redemption will never be exhausted in the Church. The first guarantee is: The Messias suffers innocently for the guilty (verses 5–7). The number of his enemies is great. They persecute him with an ardent hate. They are powerful. They have sufficient power at their disposal to put him to death. But number and power do not judge guilt and innocence. Their hatred is unjustifiable; their pretexts are foolish and their accusations are so many lies. Who, when reading this psalm, will not be reminded of the rabble that noisily demanded the death of Christ, and of the false accusations of the Sanhedrin which in the pretended interests of religion and of the welfare of the people obtained the sentence of death from Pilate. Christ should make restitution for what he has not stolen; he should suffer death for the wrong he has not done. In the mouth of the Messias these words contain a deep prophetic truth: his suffering and death should again restore the honor to God which was denied him by the sin of man. God knows the true reason of the sufferings and death of his Anointed. He knows that he dies for the guilt and sins of others. He is lacerated because of the crimes of men; he is scourged because of their misdeeds; he is punished for their welfare; stripes should be their salvation (Isaias 53:5). His innocence cannot be doubted even for the sake of the just who in their material and spiritual needs place their trust in the Lord; for he is the Lord of all before whom even the godless must bend their knees. He is the Lord of hosts whom numberless legions of angels obey. He is the God of Israel who in the solemn making of a covenant promised salvation to his people. If the Lord would permit his Anointed and his work of redemption to be defeated, how bitterly would all those who seek God be disappointed. The death of the most just Man would mean the end of all their hope.

A second guarantee: the Messias suffers for God's honor (verses 8–13). If the Messias had come to fulfill the worldly national desires of his people they would have greeted him with acclaim. But he appeared to defend God's honor and to prove to the world that its works are evil (John 7:7). Therefore they hated and despised him and heaped suffering and shame upon him; he was despised and detested (Isaias 49:7). He came to Israel as the promised Messias, but Israel knew him not; he came to his own and his own received him not (John 1:11). They estranged themselves even more from him; some of his relatives did not believe in him. With great zeal he worked for his Father's house, for his kingdom, for the spiritual temple which he intended to build. But in vain. The servant of God complains through the Prophet Isaias: "I have labored in vain, I have spent my strength without cause and in vain" (49:4). Through his zeal for God's honor he drew the hatred of the godless upon himself (*See* Romans 15:3). How many Israelites have despised the prophets, and at last John the Baptist, because of the strict lives they led? (*See* Matthew 11:8 and Luke 7:33). Thus they also ridiculed Christ. Godless men who have lost the consciousness of sin and penance ridicule him who does penance for others' sins; such ridicule was heaped upon the Lord. He did not lead a strict ascetical life as did his predecessors; he did not wear penitential garb; the prophets did not make penance a requisite for the Messias. Fasting and penitential garb are only symbols of the mission of his life; namely, to atone for the guilt of men. The godless have no understanding whatever for such a mission even to the present day. The Prophet Isaias (28:7 seq.) had to experience how drunkards in frivolous mockery made his sermons the object of their jokes. With derision and mockery the enemies of Jesus accompanied the Crucified to his death. Mockery and derision are still his portion in the world.

Near death the Messias cries to heaven. Now the moment has come when he is to make satisfaction to the justice of God. Now the time has come for kindness and love and mercy; the hour for the glorification of the Messias has come (verses 14–22). It is the time about which Christ said: "Father, the hour has come; glorify thy Son, that thy Son may glorify thee" (John 17:1). Thus the Anointed turns to the inexhaustible love and to the unchangeable fidelity of the Father who leads the servant of God from the deepest distress to the promised glory. The need is still at hand. Hence he cries again to heaven. He again presents the need of his petition with the same emphasis as at the beginning of the psalm. The danger which would make him sink into the bottomless mire and which would draw him into the depth of a flood of suffering still threatens. The hour of decision has come for God. If the flood will overwhelm his Servant and engulf him in its depth, if the abyss would close in upon him, Satan and hell will have conquered. But the Lord will help. The cry for help will certainly be heard. The reason for this certainty is based on God's infinite love. This love is so sympathetic and kind it cannot look upon the affliction of the Anointed without the greatest sympathy. It is so inexhaustibly deep and so great that it will never disappoint confidence. The second reason for this certainty lies in the greatness of the danger and in the necessity of speedy help. It is sufficient for God to know that his Servant is in need in order to send him speedy aid. He will not and cannot hide his countenance from his affliction. He must help even for the enemy's sake, otherwise the enemy will claim the victory and rejoice. Therefore the Messias prays incessantly: Come, rescue my soul from this danger of death in order that they may know that thou art with me and that they will be put to shame.

God knows about the disgrace they had brought upon his Anointed; for he was witness of his suffering. He witnessed the opprobrium with which they afflicted him. He saw how his enemies scourged, derided, mocked, blasphemed, and spat upon him (Isaias 50:6). Before the all-knowing God nothing remains concealed; all the enemies of his servant are known to him. He also knows their heartlessness and knows how severely his servant suffers under the shame which they inflicted upon him. This disgrace afflicts him so much the more because he finds no sympathy anywhere. All his friends and acquaintances have forsaken him; he is surrounded by his enemies, who have no words of consolation for him, no sympathy for him. On the contrary they increase his suffering and pour into his beaker of suffering the bitter gall of ridicule and the sour vinegar of blasphemy. In this descriptive sense the words are well used; they have found a literal fulfillment in the death of Christ.

The divine punishment will fall upon these heartless and obdurate enemies (verses 23–29). The judgment of rejection for the chosen people and for the enemies of Christ, as God has foretold through the prophets, will be passed upon them. The prayer of the Messias is not a prayer that is prompted by a spirit of revenge, but is a prophetic utterance that punishment will come upon them for the sake of the Anointed and that it will come soon after his death. The prophecy found its literal fulfillment in the fate of the Jewish nation, especially in the destruction of the temple.

"Their table has become a snare to them." Paul (Romans 11:9) applies these words to the obstinate Jews and their rejection. What should have contributed to their strength and blessing turned out to be disastrous for them. In the Messianic promises God had spread out for Israel a precious banquet; it was their feast to which they could make claim before all others. But they rejected it. According to Isaias 8:14, God who was to become a sanctuary for Israel became a snare and a net for the inhabitants of Jerusalem. Thus what should be salvation for them is their destruction. In their unbelief they looked upon the dying Servant of God with malicious joy and their eyes feasted upon his misery and their spiritual vision was taken from them. A veil was placed before their eyes so that they did not recognize the truth. They abused their power in order to maltreat the Messias; because of this their loins are sick and trembling. Breathlessly they drag themselves along under the weight of their misery. In their hatred and passion they raged against their innocent Victim in order to destroy him; now the Lord will pour out his grim wrath and in his wrath will pass his terrible punitive judgment upon them. This judgment is pictured in a few strokes. The enemies have excluded the Messias from the community of his people; they have expelled him like a criminal from human society and now wish to cast him out of the land of the living; they want to kill him. On this account God will devastate and lay waste their native country. They will be cast out and wander homeless in the world. This punishment will fall upon them not only because they had shown no sympathy to the fate that befell the Messias, but also because they helped to increase his sufferings. They would not realize that God permitted him to suffer for the guilt of all. But the greatest punishment will be their own obstinacy and their exclusion from the Messianic salvation. When God withdraws his grace from them, their guilt will increase from day to day; for only one great grace, a miracle of the merciful love of God, can heal their blindness. They will not be included in the list of the citizens of the Messianic Sion. As sons of Abraham they were called to supernatural life, but now they have forfeited this call. On the day of judgment they will be excluded from the community of the just; they will suffer the fate which the First Psalm already announced to the godless.

The Messias is sure of being heard; therefore he closes his prayer with a vow to thank and praise God (verses 30–37). He is still in anguish and full of sorrow. Enemies full of hatred still surround him; he again directs his petition to God that he may grant him help and lead him from the depths of his misery to a happy new life. Then he will proclaim to the brethren the name of the Lord. Then will he sing of his power and love which revealed itself in the redemption of the Anointed and he will glorify his mercy with a song of praise. Such a sacrifice of praise and thanksgiving will please God more than the sacrifice of steers and bulls even though these according to the Mosaic Law were considered the most excellent material for sacrifice. Even with the most valuable gift, sufficient honor cannot be given to God. It cannot be compared to the gift which the Messias gives to him by his praise and thanksgiving. The deliverance of the Anointed is for all God-fearing men a source of rich consolation and a guarantee of redemption from all of their adversities; for that which was given to him by God in his suffering, the Lord will also give to them. With his grace and mercy God will give to their soul a new life. God hears the cry of the poor begging for help and he does not close his ear to their petitions. He consoles them for the sake of the Messias and makes them rich through his grace. And him, who is one of his children, he does not despise, even when his hands are shackled by misery and sin; for he has the power and love to free him for Christ's sake. With the work of the Messias, the new era foretold by the prophet begins. In this era all creation is redeemed from the curse and rejoices because of the blessing of the Redemption. Heaven and earth and the sea and all creatures that live rejoice and praise the Lord who also redeemed them. When that time has come, the time of redemption for Sion shall also have arrived. Then the devastated and desolate cities of Juda will again be built up; then the banished children of Israel and those dispersed all over the world will return and settle again in their native country. The new Sion will again take possession of the land of promise. As once upon a time, after the redemption from the Egyptian captivity the land of Canaan was distributed among the tribes for a lasting inheritance, so the servants of God, the sons of the Messianic kingdom, will receive a portion of the new kingdom and all who love the Lord will be citizens of this kingdom; for only the just shall dwell therein.

psalm 69

Deus in adjutorium

A *prayer in persecution*

1. Unto the end, a psalm for David, to bring to mind that the Lord saved him.

2. O God, come to my assistance: O Lord, make haste to help me.

3. Let them be confounded and ashamed that seek my soul.

4. Let them be turned backward, and blush for shame that desire evils to me. Let them be presently turned away, blushing for shame that say to me: Tis well, tis well.

5. Let all that seek thee rejoice and be glad in thee; and let such that love thy salvation say always: The Lord be magnified.

6. But I am needy and poor; O God, help me.

7. Thou art my helper and my deliverer: O Lord, make no delay.

WITH a few changes we find this psalm to be a repetition of Psalm 40. The name Yahwe is here exchanged with Elohim. The prayer here ends with a petition which is based on the poverty and misery of the petitioner while in the former psalm, it ends with a confession of confidence. With this change our psalm has become a cry for help in need and is therefore a prayer that can be used by one who is in grave danger of bodily and spiritual suffering. The Lord should not favor the plans of those who endanger the life of the petitioner, lest they succeed and in their malicious joy be glad at the fall of a just man. May God make them feel his power in order that they will depart in shame. When all who seek God and long for salvation see the salvation of the just, they will praise the Lord as their Redeemer. The petitioner cannot help himself; he is poor and miserable and his collapse is near. Thus may God not be slow with his help and may he prove himself as a God of salvation.

psalm 70

In te, Domine

A prayer for perseverance

1. A psalm for David. Of the sons of Jonadab, and the former captives.
In thee, O Lord, I have hoped, let me never be put to confusion.

2. Deliver me in thy justice, and rescue me. Incline thy ear unto me, and save
me.

3. Be thou unto me a God, a protector, and a place of strength that thou
mayest make me safe, for thou art my firmament and my refuge.

4. Deliver me, O my God, out of the hand of the sinner, and out of the hand
of the transgressor of the law and of the unjust.

5. For thou art my patience, O Lord: my hope, O Lord, from my youth.

6. By thee have I been confirmed from the womb, from my mother's womb
thou art my protector. Of thee shall I continually sing.

7. I am become unto many as a wonder, but thou art a strong helper.

8. Let my mouth be filled with praise, that I may sing thy glory; thy greatness
all the day long.

9. Cast me not off in the time of old age: when my strength shall fail, do not
thou forsake me.

10. For my enemies have spoken against me, and they that watched my soul
have consulted together.

11. Saying: God has forsaken him: pursue and take him, for there is none to
deliver him.

12. O God, be not thou far from me: O God, make haste to my help.

13. Let them be confounded and come to nothing that detract my soul: let
them be covered with confusion and shame that seek my hurt.

14. But I will always hope; and will add to all thy praise.

15. My mouth shall show forth thy justice, thy salvation all the day long.
Because I have not known learning.

16. I will enter into the power of the Lord: O Lord, I will be mindful of thy
justice alone.

17. Thou hast taught me, O God, from my youth: and till now I will declare thy wonderful works.

18. And unto old age and grey hairs: O God, forsake me not.
Until I show forth thy arm to all the generation that is to come: thy power,

19. And thy justice, O God, even to the highest great things thou hast done: O God, who is like to thee?

20. What great troubles hast thou shown me, many and grievous: and turning thou hast brought me to life, and hast brought me back again from the depths of the earth.

21. Thou hast multiplied thy magnificence: and turning to me thou hast comforted me.

22. For I will also confess to thee thy truth with the instruments of psaltery: O Lord, I will sing to thee with the harp, thou holy one of Israel.

23. My lips shall greatly rejoice, when I shall sing to thee, and my soul which thou hast redeemed.

24. Yea, and my tongue shall meditate on thy justice all the day, when they shall be confounded and put to shame that think evils to me.

THIS psalm shows manifold relations to the older Davidic songs. The introduction (verses 1–3) agrees almost word for word with the beginning of the Thirtieth Psalm. The Hebrew text mentions no composer. The Greek and Latin translations ascribe the prayer to David. The poet describes himself as an old man. From the context it does not seem impossible that David composed the psalm in his old age which did not remain free from grave troubles. Upon the rebellion of Absalom another rebellion followed under the leadership of the Benjaminite Seba whom almost all Israel, with the exception of Juda, joined (2 Kings 20). Furthermore history relates that at this time Palestine suffered a failure of crops and for three years in succession there was a shortage of food. David was taken prisoner by his own people and would also have been captured during an invasion by the Philistines if Abisai had not rescued him. In his old age he did not have the strength to defend himself against the enemy (2 Kings 21). It is certain that the writer of this psalm was a man who had experienced hard times in his long life and that he had been saved from dangers only through miracles. But in his old age he had to suffer bitter sorrow and his enemies looked upon this as a sign of divine rejection. But he is a man whose old age is honored for his unwavering confidence in God's help, confidence which nothing can shatter. His song therefore has a charming attractiveness which also influences a Christian in his adversities. Its purpose is to teach that he to whom the Lord has been a source of hope and confidence in early youth may also trust in him in old age.

The psalmist belongs to that class of happy men who can confess that God has been a source of hope from the days of his youth (verses 1–6) and who may also find in him consolation and confidence in old age. Therefore he can approach God and say: "Let me not come to shame, for I have always trusted in thee." The eternal truth has been given to all who rely on it, the divine assertion that they will not be disappointed. The petitioner can with greater certainty rely upon this affirmation when he suffers innocently, when he is persecuted for justice's sake, and when he himself has not abandoned the path of justice; for divine justice cannot permit innocence to be defeated. On this account the Apostle John wrote: "Beloved, if our heart does not condemn us, we have confidence toward God and whatever we ask, we shall receive from him" (1 John 3:21–22). The confidence of the psalmist is based upon the experiences of a long life of suffering during which the Lord has always proved himself a castle on a rock, a refuge strong as a firmly built house, a protection in all storms. To the old God will not deny what he has so freely granted to the youth.

He cannot do this; for the enemies of his servant are sinners who do not concern themselves with the Law. They are godless men who are not afraid of committing injustices and violence. To such the Lord will not relinquish a weak old man who never placed his confidence in anyone but in him alone. To whom else should he have gone in his affliction than to him? Just as the eyes of a slave are directed to the hand of his master (Psalm 122:2), so he turned his eyes to the Lord of all, hoping and confiding in him; for Yahwe was his only hope in the days of his youth. Now in his old age looking back on his past life, the psalmist may say without any exaggeration: "I relied upon thee from the day of my birth. Thou wast my protection from the days of my youth; therefore, I praise thee forever."

A man who has placed himself from the very beginning under the protection of God and who in an extraordinary manner has experienced this protection on numerous occasions may confidently hope that God will also be his protection in old age (verses 7–13). The poet had to face grave dangers. The help granted to him by God was often beyond human expectations and surpassed in such great measure all human capabilities that many considered it miraculous. He himself had to consider his deliverance as a miracle; in his astonishment he had to admire the power and fidelity of the Lord and his love towards his servant. Therefore his mouth was full of thanksgiving and praise and he praised the Most High day and night. What God has so liberally granted to the youth he cannot deny to the old man; he cannot refuse to an old man, who is deprived of natural strength, the means to defend himself against the violent deeds of his enemy and against every injustice. Because of his old age he is so much the more dependent upon God's help. Unscrupulous men take advantage of the weakness of age. They speak evil about an old man; they slander and calumniate him. They are not even satisfied with this; they rob an old man of his honor and consult with each other how they can be rid of the old man. Because the Lord has not intervened in their activities they are inclined to conclude that God has abandoned and rejected their opponent. They consider God's long-suffering a consent to their wrongdoing. Therefore the psalmist begs that the Lord who through all the years of his life was near him will not depart from him in his help-less old age and will not delay in giving him assistance. Not he who prays to God and confides in his help should submit to the blows of his persecutors and come to shame, but the evildoers who perform injustices that cry to heaven should receive punishment. They should perish and depart in shame.

When the poet looks back upon his long life, his soul is filled with gratitude and he renews his courage to accept new afflictions that might come to him. He has always hoped in the Lord and his praise of the faithful divine Helper was never silenced. He will hope for the rest of his days because old age too should praise the Lord (verses 14–19). When his physical strength has diminished, he will so much the more proclaim God's praise and add new songs to the old ones. He will speak about the grace of the Lord. He will speak about his rich experiences of life; he will speak about God's love that youth may know and trust in him. God's manifestations of mercy are innumerable. Even if on every day which the Lord gives him he praises divine grace, he will never be able to grasp its greatness and beauty and will never be able to celebrate it suitably. Every day he will meditate upon the great deeds of the Lord and thus will he occupy himself in his old age. If David is really the composer of this song, then the Seventeenth Psalm testifies how the old king reviewed his long life and everywhere found traces of divine love and grace impressed upon the memory of his past life. This sublime occupation of old age is the harmonious echo of a life that has been dedicated to the praise of God. The psalmist can say for himself that for him it was a pleasant occupation. God himself has instructed him, insofar as he let him experience the miracles of divine goodness and gave him the talent to praise him in songs. Since God's mercy accompanied him all the days of his life to his old age, his praise of him should never cease. If the Lord continues to manifest his love even in old age, then he can narrate the miracles of God to his children and grandchildren; he can proclaim God's power, majesty, and love. There is no being that is like to God in manifestations of love.

The psalmist has become old, but his spirit remains young, because it has always drawn from God new strength of life. He has met many difficulties in his path of life. He has seen many evil days; but whenever under the burden of adversities he was on the verge of collapse, the Lord would refresh him and give him new life. When he was near death, God drew him out of the depth of his misery. Therefore he will dedicate the last days of his life to the praise of God (verses 20–24). God indeed had humbled him and permitted his enemies to mock him. But that the Lord humbles in order to exalt has been verified in him. Every new humiliation raised his honor and God's consolations outweighed the many sufferings he endured patiently. Thus as an old man and in all thankfulness he will take the harp in his trembling hands and sing God's eternal and inviolable fidelity which so evidently has proved itself in his life. With zither in hand he will praise the Holy One of Israel who has defended persecuted innocence and has been zealous about the honor of his servant. With the accompaniment of zither and harp his lips shall acclaim; for his soul is filled with joy and jubilation because the Lord has redeemed him and saved him from destruction. Great were the dangers, but God's merciful love was still greater. Every day his tongue will glorify God, will proclaim God's mercy and grace to all. With jubilant gratitude he will narrate how in shame his enemies had to cease persecuting him because the Lord protected him and how they were disgraced and put to shame who sought his destruction.

psalm 71

Deus, judicium tuum

A prophecy of the coming of Christ and of his kingdom prefigured by Solomon and his happy reign

1. A psalm on Solomon.

2. Give to the king thy judgment, O God: and to the king's son thy justice. To judge thy people with justice, and thy poor with judgment.

3. Let the mountains receive peace for the people: and the hills justice.

4. He shall judge the poor of the people, and he shall save the children of the poor: and he shall humble the oppressor.

5. And he shall continue with the sun, and before the moon throughout all generations.

6. He shall come down like rain upon the fleece: and as showers falling gently upon the earth.

7. In his days shall justice spring up, and abundance of peace, till the moon be taken away.

8. And he shall rule from sea to sea, and from the river unto the ends of the earth.

9. Before him the Ethiopians shall fall down: and his enemies shall lick the ground.

10. The kings of Tharsis and the islands shall offer presents: the kings of the Arabians and of Saba shall bring gifts.

11. And all the kings of the earth shall adore him, all nations shall serve him.

12. For he shall deliver the poor from the mighty: and the needy that had no helper.

13. He shall spare the poor and needy: and he shall save the souls of the poor.

14. He shall redeem their souls from usuries and iniquity: and their names shall be honorable in his sight.

15. And he shall live and to him shall be given of the gold of Arabia; for him they shall always adore: they shall bless him all the day.

16. And there shall be a firmament on the earth on the tops of the mountains, above the Libanus shall the fruit thereof be exalted: and they of the city shall flourish like the grass of the earth.

17. Let his name be blessed forevermore: his name continueth before the sun. In him shall all the tribes of the earth be blessed: all nations shall magnify him.

18. Blessed be the Lord, the God of Israel, who alone does wonderful things.

19. And blessed be the name of his majesty forever: and the whole earth shall be filled with his majesty. So be it, so be it.

20. The praises of David, the son of Jesse are ended.

IN THE earliest ages of the Church this psalm was interpreted as Messianic; the oldest Jewish tradition also considered it to be Messianic. The Targum, an Aramaic translation of the Hebrew text, has translated the first verse of this psalm: "God gave the decision of thy judgment to the King-Messias and thy justice to the son of King David." The Peshitto, the oldest Assyrian translation of the Old Testament, in the superscription calls it a prophecy of the advent of the Messias and of the call of the Gentiles. The thoughts of this psalm have throughout a Messianic character. There are hopes and expectations which according to the prophecies will be fulfilled in the fullness of time. The Hebrew text tells us that it is a psalm of Solomon, while the Septuagint tells us that it is dedicated to Solomon but composed by David. In 2 Kings 23:1 there seems to be a similarity between the last words of David and this psalm. This passage speaks of future kin, of the glory of his kingdom and contains a petition for a quick advent.

The singer directs his view into the Messianic future and to the eternal King of the Messianic kingdom. About him Isaias says: "His empire shall be multiplied, and there shall be no end of peace: he shall sit upon the throne of David, and upon his kingdom: to establish and to strengthen it with judgment and with justice: from henceforth and forever: the zeal of the Lord of hosts will perform this" (9:6). Filled with a longing to live during this glorious era he stretches out his hands towards heaven and prays that this kingdom may come. He begs first of all for the blessing of salvation for Israel (verses 2–7). David in the revelation of the Second Psalm has heard the word of the Lord to the Anointed: "Ask of me, I will give thee the Gentiles for thy inheritance and the uttermost parts of the earth for thy possession." Now he considers that the time has come that God should paternally transmit to the Messianic King judgment, the right to rule, the divine power of king, the sceptre of the kingdom. Then the desired time will come when all injustice will disappear from the earth and the poorest will obtain justice. Isaias says: "The fruits of justice will be eternal peace and security; then his people will settle down in the fullness of peace; they will dwell in their homes in all security and in quiet places" (32:17). Just as after winter rains the grass grows in abundance on mountains and hills, so the rule of the Messias will bring upon the entire land of Israel a wonderful spring. Everywhere there will be peace and justice, a blessing for the people of the Lord. The Messias will judge the poor with justice and will decide impartially for the oppressed of the land. He will slay brutal men with the staff of his mouth and will kill evil men with the breath of his lips; for justice is the girdle of his loins and fidelity the guard of his lips. Then all complaints about injustices and spoliation of the poor will be silenced. Then the poor will be treated like the rich and the humble like the proud.

According to the prophet this condition of justice will never end because the rule of the Messias will last eternally. That this may come to pass is the earnest desire of the psalmist who speaks in the name of all the poor and oppressed. As long as the order of nature lasts, may the expected King live and rule. The laws of nature which the sun and moon obeyed for so many thousands of years with such regularity are a type of the eternal and unchangeable decrees of the Lord. Here they are also a type of the eternal continuance of the Messianic kingdom. The coming of the Messias may be likened to the coming of the winter rain. When during the summer months the sun burns the meadows clipped by the flocks to a short, dry brown, the soul thirsts for the blessing of a fructifying rain. When finally the clouds pour forth rain, all nature breathes; the withered plants begin to flourish and new life awakens in the meadows. The ground is ready to receive the new seed. In Messianic times a fructifying rain of grace will fall from heaven, a new life will be awakened. Under this Messianic rain of grace a glorious harvest will ripen; justice will flourish and peace will reign until the moon will no longer give her light. Isaias says: "At that time swords will be changed into ploughshares and spears into pruning knives: no nation will make war upon its neighbors; there will no longer be any preparation for war" (Isaias 2:4).

The blessings of Messianic times will not be confined to Israel. The blessings of the Redemption will also be for the Gentile world (verses 8–15). The dominion of the Messianic King will comprise the entire world. All nations will be subjected to him. His dominion will extend from sea to sea, from the Euphrates to the ends of the earth. This drawing of the boundary lines in the literal sense has in mind the ideal limitations of the kingdom of Israel under Solomon; that is, the extent of his influence. But the psalmist also wishes to give us a picture of the world-wide dominion of the Messias in the Messianic sense. The acknowledgement of the Messianic kingdom does not only mean a confirmation that the Messias is the rightful king of Sion, but it also means a real and complete subjugation of the Gentile world under his sceptre. It will hail him as King. Those who were his enemies and had to feel the power of his arm will bend their knees before his majesty and will throw themselves before him into the dust that he may use them as his footstool (Psalm 109:1). From the ends of the earth the Gentile kings will come to worship him and present their gifts. As representatives of the kingdoms and nations of the West appear the kings of Tharsis, of the Phoenician colony in Spain, and the kings of the islands; that is, of the islands and coastlands of the Mediterranean Sea. The East is represented by the kings of Saba (Hebrew Sheba) and of Seba. The Sebaeans were descendants of the tribe of Cham who lived on the west coast of the Red Sea; the Sabaeans to which in the history of Solomon, the queen of Saba belonged, were a north-Arabic commercial people who traded in incense, balsam, gold, and precious stones. All the rulers of the earth and their subjects will join them. They will hasten to Sion to pay their respects and reverence to the King of kings and to the Lord of lords and to subject themselves to his sceptre. In the future they will no longer serve their gods, but will worship the Anointed of the Lord and Yahwe. Him alone will they adore.

The Gentiles hasten to the Messias because they long for the blessing of redemption and salvation. Stronger even than in Israel were the social contrasts among the Gentile nations. There were the great differences between the few rich and mighty and the great multitude of the poor, despondent, oppressed, and enslaved. They all sighed for deliverance, for a deliverance that would give them justice and peace. More than Israel did the Gentiles suffer under Satanic slavery from which no earthly power could redeem them. Like a brilliant light the message of redemption through Christ shone in the darkness. Among the Gentile people the ardent desire prevailed for a Being that would understand their need, that would sympathize with them in their physical and moral misery, that would and could be a support to them so that the life of the poorest and weakest would not perish. The psalmist sees all these make their pilgrimages to Sion, to him who said to them: "Come to me all ye who labor and are burdened and I will refresh you." They do not come in vain; for the Messias will free them from all oppressions with which they are burdened. No act of atrocity will humiliate them in the future; for their blood and their life is precious in the sight of the Messias. He despises no one; no matter what nation, what color, what race he represents; no matter what his position in life may be. He offers the Redemption and his blessing to all in the same measure. The happy condition of the poor will never end because the Messianic King will never die. He lives and rules forevermore. He remains the same yesterday, today, and forever. Therefore he also receives at all times the worship of his subjects. They bring him Saba's gold, the most precious that the earth yields. They pray not because he himself, the eternal King, needs the prayers of his subjects that he may remain an ideal ruler; but rather they pray for him because prayer is a cooperation in the propagation of his kingdom and at the same time a promulgation of the honor of his name. The mission prayer is the most precious gold, a gift of thankful worship for the blessing of redemption and salvation.

In the Epistle to the Romans the Apostle Paul speaks about a sighing of all nature for redemption from the heavy burden of original sin and for enlightenment. To the future Messianic picture of the prophet belongs also the redemptive blessing of nature (verses 16–17). Therefore the description of the kingdom and of the rule of the Messianic King which is drawn for us in this psalm would not be complete if it did not describe the fruit of the Messianic blessing. In those days there will be no crop failures, no desert places, no bare mountain summits. Everywhere in the country there will be golden crops of grain, even on the highest mountain peaks that reach into the regions of the eternal snow the grain will rustle like the leaves of the trees of Lebanon. Men will also beget children. The descendants in the Holy City will be as numerous as the grass of the earth. Even according to the promise which God gave to the patriarchs, the members of the Messianic kingdom will be more numerous than the sands on the seashore and the stars of heaven. Never will the generations die. Throughout all the centuries the name of the Messias will be glorified by them. As the plant sprouts and grows and develops its fruit and matures, so also the glory of Christ will issue forth and grow. It will grow from century to century to an ever more glorious exaltation until at the end of the world his glory shall be complete when all who have been called to eternal happiness will reach their full number and give their celestial worship to the immortal King of eternity. Then all the tribes of the earth shall be blessed in him and will praise the Lord for having been made worthy of his eternal blessing.

The following verses do not belong to the psalm. They form the doxology for the closing of the Second Book of Psalms. This is an extraordinary solemn form of closing; it is an echo of the sublime thoughts of the last psalm of this book, an echo of the last words of the Messianic royal song. Praise the Lord, the God of Israel, who alone does wonderful deeds. Praised be his holy Name eternally and may his glory fill the earth.

psalm 72

Quam bonus Israel Deus

The temptation of the weak upon seeing the prosperity of the wicked is overcome by the consideration of the justice of God who will quickly render to everyone according to his works

1. A psalm for Asaph.
   How good is God to Israel, to them that are of a right heart.

2. But my feet were almost moved; my steps had well-nigh slipped.

3. Because I had a zeal on occasion of the wicked, seeing the prosperity of sinners.

4. For there is no regard to their death, nor is there strength to their stripes.

5. They are not in the labor of men: neither shall they be scourged like other men.

6. Therefore pride hath held them fast: they are covered with their iniquity and their wickedness.

7. Their iniquity hath come forth, as it were from fatness: they have passed into the affection of the heart.

8. They have thought and spoken wickedness: they have spoken iniquity on high.

9. They have set their mouth against heaven: and their tongue hath passed through the earth.

10. Therefore will my people return here: and full days shall be found in them.

11. And they said: How doth God know? And is there knowledge in the Most High.

12. Behold these are sinners, and yet abounding in the world they have obtained riches.

13. And I said: Then have I in vain justified my heart, and washed my hands among the innocent.

14. And I have been scourged all the day: and my chastisement hath been in the mornings.

15. If I said: I will speak thus; behold I should condemn the generation of thy children.

16. I studied that I might know this thing; it is a labour in my sight.

17. Until I go into the sanctuary of God, and understand concerning their last ends.

18. But indeed for deceits thou hast put it to them: when they were lifted up thou hast cast them down.

19. How are they brought to desolation? they have suddenly ceased to be: they have perished by reason of their iniquity.

20. As the dream of them that awake, O Lord; so in the city thou shalt bring their image to nothing.

21. For my heart hath been inflamed, and my reins have been changed:

22. And I am brought to nothing, and I knew not.

23. I am become as a beast before thee: and I am always with thee.

24. Thou hast held me by my right hand: and by thy will thou hast conducted me: and with thy glory thou hast received me.

25. For what have I in heaven? And beside thee what do I desire upon earth?

26. For thee my flesh and my heart hath fainted away; thou art the God of my heart, and the God that is my portion forever.

27. For behold they that go far from thee shall perish: thou hast destroyed all them that are disloyal to thee.

28. But it is good for me to adhere to my God, to put my hope in the Lord God:
That I may declare all thy praises, in the gates of the daughter of Sion.

THE greater the contrasts in the social order are at a particular time, the greater the contrast between the opulence of the few and the need of the great mass of the people, the greater the disregard of the godless towards religious men, the more decidedly does the question demand an answer: how can this be reconciled with the justice of God? Why are happiness and godlessness, need and piety found side by side? The Prophet Jeremias asks this question from God: "Why doth the way of the wicked prosper? Why is it well with all of them that transgress and do wickedly? Thou hast planted them and they have taken root; they prosper and bring forth fruit" (12:1–2). This question comes up again and again and can daily become a serious temptation to doubt the just, wise, and kind providence of the Lord. Therefore it is also to be expected that in the Psalter this question is repeated and asked by different composers in order to find a way out of the difficulty. The composer of this psalm also fought this temptation and first found peace and enlightenment in the sanctuary. Here again he became conscious of the blessing of union with God with which all transitory happiness of the sinner cannot be compared. With this he shows the only correct way. The more a man meditates upon his existence in the light of the supernatural and values it accordingly, the less will he be tempted to appreciate earthly goods above their real value.

The psalmist begins his instruction with a clear, but personal question (verses 1–3). He puts the article of faith that God is love at the very beginning. God is kind to his chosen people and to every member of the chosen people insofar as they are submissive to his holy will. The poet speaks to men who have faith; therefore he builds his doctrine upon this foundation. Faith must always be the starting point in interpreting correctly the mystery of Divine Providence. The knowledge that God is love, however, does not exclude the temptation to doubt this truth. Even the psalmist despite his fidelity to his faith was close to succumbing to this temptation. He was a daily witness of the way godless men who were not concerned about God and his will led a carefree life, indeed, who in their happiness boldly and blasphemously boasted about their wickedness. Envy and jealousy arose in his soul and the incongruity between their happiness and sinful conduct became a mystery to him which he could not solve.

In order that the reader of the psalm may be able to enter deeply into the inner difficulties which cause him trouble in solving the mystery, the composer describes picturesquely the inconsistency of happiness and wickedness in the life of the godless (verses 4–9). In the world there is much physical suffering, but often only the wicked enjoy exuberant health; their bodies are strong and well-nourished and thus they reach old age. Thus they do not worry about death. The thought of it does not come to their mind; neither does the thought of reward and punishment in the other world disturb them. They live a life of pleasure and they do not want to be hindered in the enjoyment of it. While thousands of others plague themselves to prolong their lives and with hard work eke out an existence, they live luxuriantly. They know nothing about the care and worry of supporting themselves. Therefore they have no understanding about the situation of those who must struggle for the needs of a living; they have neither sympathy nor mercy. Haughtily they look down upon the mass of people. Pride is their pleasure, their jewelry; it rests upon them like a precious necklace upon the neck. Everywhere they try to force their will upon others in order to satisfy themselves even when others are ruined thereby. Violence clothes them like a mantle. Because they do not fear the Lord and ask no questions about his laws and deny the hereafter and eternal punishment they set no limits to their pleasures. Thus sin thrives among them as bounteously as the herb in fertile soil. Others may criticize their unscrupulous conduct, that does not bother them. When just men remind them of their responsibility before God, of the last judgment, and of eternity, they have only mockery and derision for an answer. At the height of their happiness and power they feel themselves above religious considerations. To them the authority of God amounts to nothing. "They have set their mouth against heaven." In their bold utterances they even mock the Most High and challenge his wrath. Everywhere in the world, wherever they go, they have the word and rule and tyrannize all with their tongue.

For many men the happiness of the godless is a grave temptation (verses 10–14). When among a people faith has disappeared and the thought of the next world no longer rules their conduct of life, the danger is near that the great mass of them will strive to make life as comfortable as possible and will walk along the path of sin since they see no other path. Those who have no judgment believe that they may conclude from the prosperity of many religiously indifferent men that the Lord does not trouble himself about the affairs of men, that he in his own happiness in the infinite heights of heaven pays no attention to the ways of men upon earth whether they follow the path of his commandments or avoid it. They say to themselves: if God were concerned about the affairs and activities of men who ask no questions about him, indeed, who knowingly commit sin and blaspheme him, it would be impossible for them to have peace and become richer and richer. That among believers who are poor such ideas might become prevalent will not cause astonishment since the tempter even approached the just man Job and whispered to him: "What did your fear of God and your piety profit you? Where is the Lord's reward for your love and for the sacrifice of obedience? Since despite your virtue you are visited by many sufferings and grave cares while the blasphemers of God are rich and happy, was it not useless that you carefully avoided every sin? Every day has brought you new plagues and troublesome work, and every morning when the sun rose again from the east and brought a new day, another divine punishment came upon you, as if your burden was not yet heavy enough for the Lord." Thus the tempter speaks to many and many allow his enticements to influence them and they abandon the way of justice and virtue.

So also the tempter approached the psalmist and whispered to him in a similar manner, but he did not listen; he sought the solution of the problem in the light of faith (verses 15–20). He who wishes to explain the contrast between the life and prosperity of the godless with that of the just by the denial of the divine sanctity, justice, and love shows that his thoughts, which should be based on faith err and that he has lost his faith; for God is and remains by his very nature holy, just, and good. The psalmist could not follow the wrong path. But he too had to experience that his natural knowledge was not sufficient to interpret the mystery of the Divine Providence. He did not doubt that God does not deny his justice and love when he gives happiness to the godless and sufferings to the just. But what remained a puzzle to him was the matter of reconciliation. The more he thought about it, the more difficult the solution became to him. Then it became clear that the answer must come from heaven. Therefore he took the only right path. In his troubled spirit he went to the temple to pray to God for supernatural light. His petition was heard; the Lord first of all pointed out to him the final fate of all the godless which can be known by faith alone.

Viewing things in relation to the last end of man, the happiness of the godless may be compared to walking on an icy path from which one can easily slip and fall. Joy and wealth are no blessings for the godless, but stones on which they may stumble and fall; they are constant dangers and occasions of sin which increase the wrath of God. When death comes to the godless, they will realize this; when once this sham of glory collapses, then of all their happiness only desolate ruins will remain. Their life looked to them like a paradise; now suddenly in the light of eternity it looks like a desert. They felt themselves deeply rooted in happiness and gave no thought to the purpose of their existence; now they are swept away by the wrath of the divine justice; they must perish for fright when they hear the irrevocable judgment of condemnation. Now their life is an empty dream which on awakening is nothing but a play of fancy. The Lord considers and despises the entire life of the godless when after long and patient waiting, he finally calls them to the general and final judgment.

From the knowledge that the happiness of the godless is only sham the psalmist draws the conclusion. It is foolish to abandon God for the sake of false happiness (verses 21–28). What profit would it have been to him if he had given in to the temptation, if he had allowed himself to become embittered against God and man, and if he had become jealous because God had blessed the godless? He would have gained nothing; he would have only been further removed from the solution to the problem. It would have been nonsense to rebel against God; for if he would overcome the temptation by divine enlightenment, he could acquire some knowledge of the mysterious providence of God. In the light of faith and grace streaming from the sanctuary he realized that it is good for man to remain faithful to the Lord even when he punishes, that it is good to allow oneself to be led by his good hand even when human reason does not see the correctness of the way. God leads man according to the norm of his eternal wisdom and he guides him to an eternal happy end. When the life of the just man is a path of thorns and he goes through the shadow of the valley of death, the light of faith and hope shines into the darkness so that the humble sufferer may at the end of his path see endless glory with God. He who abandons God for the sake of tinsel happiness has given up everything; for in heaven and upon earth there is nothing outside of God that can satisfy the human soul. Even heaven without God would be no place of happiness. Wherever God is, there is happiness. This God is the eternal inheritance of the just man. Even when the physical man wastes away, when bodily strength is consumed through suffering, and the heart suffers from anguish, God even then remains the protector, the firm support in a tattering existence. When the just man loses everything else, when death takes life from him, God remains with him; he cannot be taken from the just man by any human power of the world or of hell; even death does not separate from God; for he is the eternal possession of the just man.

At the conclusion of the instruction the psalmist again stresses clearly how the divine Judge equalizes the apparent disparity. He who hates God may prosper in this life, but he will be excluded from participation in the Messianic happiness; his life ends in eternal misery. But for the just man, poverty and need are only passing occurrences, only a deprivation of external possessions. Despite all this he enjoys a happiness in his union with God which outweighs the possession of all earthly goods and which he does not lose even through death. At the end of his life man sees the eternal loss of all temporal goods, but the just man sees his gain and the beginning of an eternal happiness if he has placed his entire hope in the Lord. At the gate of the Messianic Sion; that is, in the assembly of the saints and blessed, he will praise God's wonderful deeds.

psalm 73

Ut quid, Deus

A prayer of the Church under grievous persecutions

1. Understanding for Asaph.
   O God, why hast thou cast us off unto the end: why is thy wrath enkindled against the sheep of thy pasture?

2. Remember thy congregation, which thou hast possessed from the beginning. The sceptre of thy inheritance which thou hast redeemed: Mount Sion in which thou hast dwelt.

3. Lift up thy hands against their pride unto the end: see what things the enemy hath done wickedly in the sanctuary.

4. And they that hate thee have made their boasts, in the midst of thy solemnity. They have set up their ensigns for signs.

5. And they knew not both in the going out and on the highest top. As with axes in a wood of trees.

6. They have cut down at once the gates thereof, with axe and hatchet they have brought it down.

7. They have set fire to thy sanctuary: they have defiled the dwelling place of thy name on the earth.

8. They said in their heart, the whole kindred of them together: Let us abolish all festival days of God from the land.

9. Our signs we have not seen, there is now no prophet: and he will know us no more.

10. How long, O God, shall the enemy reproach: is the adversary to provoke thy name forever?

11. Why dost thou turn away thy hand: and thy right hand out of the midst of thy bosom forever?

12. But God is our king before ages: he hath wrought salvation in the midst of the earth.

13. Thou by thy strength didst make the sea firm: thou didst crush the heads of the dragons in the waters.

14. Thou hast broken the heads of the dragon: thou hast given him to be meat for the people of the Ethiopians.

15. Thou hast broken up the fountains and the torrents: thou hast dried up the Ethan rivers.

16. Thine is the day, and thine is the night: thou hast made the morning light and the sun.

17. Thou hast made all the borders of the earth: the summer and the spring were formed by thee.

18. Remember this, the enemy hath reproached the Lord: and a foolish people hath provoked thy name.

19. Deliver not up to beasts, the souls that confess to thee; and forget not to the end the souls of thy poor.

20. Have regard to thy covenant: for they that are the obscure of the earth have been filled with dwellings of iniquity.

21. Let not the humble be turned away with confusion: the poor and needy shall praise thy name.

22. Arise, O God, judge thy own cause: remember thy reproaches with which the foolish man hath reproached thee all the day.

23. Forget not the voices of thy enemies: the pride of them that hate thee ascendeth continually.

THE destruction of so many churches through the malice and power of Communism deeply move the heart of every Christian. Sadness and sorrow takes hold of us when we picture to ourselves the smoking ruins of a sanctuary in which through generations, perhaps through centuries, the praises of the Most High resounded and which now ruthless hands have desecrated and destroyed. It is not the works of art whose loss we lament so much as the sacrilege which cries to heaven for vengeance. How great must be the sorrow of those who have seen their own house of God, which they loved so much, lie in ruins. Such considerations may in some measure put us in the mood of this lamentation about the destruction of the Jerusalem temple by the Babylonians in the year 587. It was a sanctuary unique in its kind; for only here the Lord dwelt among his people and ruled in his glory over the Ark of the Covenant in the Holy of Holies. On this account the believing Israelite loved his house of God; it was his pride and his greatest joy. Therefore the news about its destruction inflicted an incurable wound.

How could almighty God permit the desecration and destruction of his own sanctuary, the place of his dwelling upon earth, through the hands of ruthless Gentiles? A terrible mystery, terrible because the first question implies another anxious thought. The Lord could have preserved the temple. Why did he not? Is the loss of the house of God a sign of the rejection of the people (verses 1–3)? The question was important to Israel because the temple was the only sanctuary and with its destruction the special presence of God among his people ceased. The psalmist cannot at all understand that God should have rejected his people forever; that his wrath over the unfaithfulness of the flock which he pastured for centuries with the great love of a good shepherd could be satisfied only by a lasting rejection. It is impossible that the Lord will relinquish his choice of Israel and will no longer be mindful of his congregation. He cannot give up his work and withdraw his decree. In vain then would he have redeemed his people from the Egyptian slavery and have taken it as his special possession; the redemption and preservation of Israel and the miracles he had wrought would all have been futile. In vain would have been the greatest grace; namely, his dwelling on Sion in the midst of his people if after the destruction of the temple he would abandon Israel. It is impossible that the destruction of the temple implied the rejection of the people; for then the enemy would triumph over Yahwe. They could then ruthlessly rule unpunished in his dwelling place upon earth and become an abomination of desolation in the holy place. When God will again direct his steps to the ruins, when he will direct his attention to their hopeless condition, the sanctuary will again rise from its ruins.

As if it were necessary to draw God's attention to the abominations in the temple, the psalmist describes the outrages of the enemy in the sanctuary. Where for centuries the praises of the most high God were sung and where harps and zithers were played for the praise of Yahwe, where prayers and thanksgivings of a believing people ascended to heaven, rude pagan soldiers now rioted and blasphemed. On the pinnacles of the temple they placed their standards as testimonies of the victories of their gods over the God of Israel. In their blind rage they destroyed everything which the zeal, art, and industry of Solomon and four hundred years of other kings had done to beautify the sanctuary. They tore down the gates as if they had to clear the way in the thicket of a forest. With hatchet and axe they ruined the precious carved work on the door-wings and on the wainscoting of the inner compartment of the sanctuary. Nothing was spared from the rude violence of the barbarians. After they had plundered or destroyed all, they threw firebrands into the temple and razed the proud structure of Solomon to the ground. On the place where Yahwe throned over the cherubim of the Ark of the Covenant only ruins, blackened by fire and smoke, remained. In their hatred against Israel the Babylonians wished to fully eradicate the worship of Yahwe and, therefore, not only to destroy the temple but also to erase every remembrance of the Lord and every place of prayer from the land. Even if the erection of separate synagogues became universal only after the exile, it is not only possible but also probable that in earlier times buildings were locally erected in which people assembled for prayer and the reading of the Scripture. The fact that pious Israelites were accustomed in pre-exilic times to gather around a prophet on the Sabbath day testifies to the need of celebrating religious functions in common on the Sabbath days far from Jerusalem.

The psalmist believes that he may give a negative answer to the question as to whether the destruction of the temple also meant the rejection of the people. With this, however, the question was not yet answered as to why the Lord permitted such abominations in his holy tabernacle and why it now lies in ruins. Thus the poet asks a further question: why does not God take things in hand in favor of the temple (verses 9–17)? The Lord does not make a move; he works no miracles to protect the sanctuary and to revenge himself because of its destruction. Why does he delay? The psalmist complains because there is no prophet living in Israel who can explain how long this sad condition of the house of God will continue. And yet it should be the concern of every pious Israelite. How long will the godless Gentiles blaspheme the most high God and remain unpunished? How long may they mock him? How long may they deride the Israelites because of the supposed impotency of the God of Israel? The equanimity with which God bears this is a mystery to him and becomes a grievous temptation. Surely God's power has not diminished! His right hand has not suffered a diminution of strength! He could intervene at any moment as in ancient times and defeat and destroy the enemy. Why does he hold back? Why does he conceal his power in his bosom or in the sash of his garment? Should one not expect that in his holy wrath he would strike in order to silence the blasphemers and to revenge the sacrileges committed in the sanctuary? This condition cannot last forever; for the Lord is the king of Israel. He is not since yesterday, not since the time of Sinai, but from eternity. When in eternity the decree of creation and redemption for Israel was made, he became king of the chosen people. Since the eternal election he has revealed his power over creatures in his great deeds.

He has divided the Red Sea so that its waves stood like walls and he led Israel through it. In the sea he broke the heads of the dragons. By the dragons the psalmist means the Egyptian army which perished in the floods of the sea. The dragon, that is, the crocodile, is a symbol of the Egyptian kingdom. The leviathan is also a poetic expression for the crocodile. To the biblical account concerning the destruction of the Egyptian army the poet adds the description that the corpses were thrown on shore by the waves and became the food of vultures, scavengers, and hyenas. The transition through the Red Sea was only the first link in the great chain of miracles. In the waterless district of the journey through the desert the Lord let water spring from the rock and brooks flowed in order to give Israel drink. On the other hand by his word he stopped the Jordan from flowing in order to give to his people a dry way to the promised land. Such unheard-of wonders Yahwe could work because he was the lord of all creation and of every order of nature. His is the day and his is the night; for he has created the changes and he has given them the name of light and darkness. He has formed the lights in the sky which according to immutable laws bring about the change of day and night. He has made a law for the sea and has limited it by the mainland and these limits are never to be passed. A divine command which nature obeys is the change of seasons. Thus all creation with all its order and appearances must obey the mighty will of God and none of these creatures revolt against the order of nature.

Such a powerful and mighty King may not permit godless men to blaspheme him and deride him; he may not permit the Gentile people to mock at him and blaspheme his holy Name. Therefore the psalmist in conclusion directs his petition to God for the salvation of his people (verses 18–23). Israel cannot save itself by its own strength. It is as defenseless as a dove which cannot defend itself. Israel is itself the defenseless dove of God. In the Canticles of Canticles the people are likened to a dove. It is impossible that the good God, the Father of the poor, will forget his poor people and will forever give them over to the power of the Gentiles; for he has made a covenant with this people. They have become his chosen people whose interests he will look after and protect. When the army of the Babylonians invaded the kingdom of Juda, many inhabitants fled to the mountains and into the desert and concealed themselves in caves in order to escape the cruelty which they would have to suffer from the hands of savage warriors. The Lord cannot disappoint those who in their great affliction hasten to him and in all confidence cry to him for help; he cannot abandon them without paying heed to their cries. He must have mercy upon them; for who should honor and give praise to his holy Name when his adorers have been put to death? God's honor is therefore at stake; it is God's own concern to save his people; for the Gentiles have no word of praise for him, but only blasphemy and ridicule everyday. There are ignorant men who laugh at what they do not know; hence Yahwe must show his power in order that they may know and learn to fear him. Until now the Lord has not intervened. The enemies of God still rage against his people; their blasphemies against God still ascend to heaven. Therefore the psalmist again calls to the Lord: "Do not forget it."

psalm 74

Confitebimur tibi

There is a just judgment to come: therefore let the wicked take care

1. Unto the end, corrupt not, a psalm of a canticle for Asaph.

2. We will praise thee, O God: we will praise, and we will call upon thy name.

3. We will relate thy wondrous works: when I shall take a time, I will judge justices.

4. The earth is melted, and all that dwell therein: I have established the pillars thereof.

5. I said to the wicked: Do not act wickedly: and to the sinners: Lift not up the horn.

6. Lift not up your horn on high: speak not iniquity against God.

7. For neither from the east, nor from the west, nor from the desert hills:

8. For God is the judge.
   One he putteth down, and another he lifteth up.

9. For in the hand of the Lord there is a cup of strong wine full of mixture.
   And he hath poured it out from this to that: but the dregs thereof are not emptied: all the sinners of the earth shall drink.

10. But I will declare forever: I will sing to the God of Jacob.

11. And I will break all the horns of sinners: but the horns of the just shall be exalted.

THE Israelitic people were severely harassed by the armies of the enemy who endangered the existence of the kingdom. But they relied on the divine promises that the Lord would protect them against destruction. Perhaps this psalm belongs to the time of King Ezechias and presupposes the invasion of the Assyrian army into the kingdom of Juda and the prophecy of the Prophet Isaias about the deliverance of the country from the Assyrian danger. Because of these prophecies, despite the great danger that threatened the country, a spirit of optimism pervades the psalm, an echo of that confidence with which Isaias foretells the futility of all attacks against his native country, the future home of the Messias. "Gather yourselves together, O ye people, and be overcome and give ear, all ye lands afar off: strengthen yourselves and be overcome, gird yourselves and be overcome. Take counsel together; and it shall be defeated: speak a word and it shall not be done: because God is with us" (8:9–10). In the destruction of the Assyrians before the walls of Jerusalem, 701 B.C., the prophet himself saw a guarantee of the eternal existence of the Messianic kingdom to which the promise was given that the gates of hell should not prevail against it. Thus in the background of this psalm there is also the expectation of a Messianic judgment. Therefore the meaning of this psalm is not misinterpreted if the Christian applies it to the fate of the enemies and persecutors of the Church.

The enemy has gravely afflicted the land of Juda so that it bleeds from a thousand wounds, and yet the psalmist foretells with the optimism of a strong faith the victory of God's people (verses 2–6). He trusts with such certainty in the divine promise that he intones a solemn "Te Deum" with the accompaniment of the harp, even at a time when the enemy was still in the country. Great God, we praise thee; Lord, we praise thy power; we honor thy name worthy of reverence and proclaim with song thy wonderful deeds. Who could doubt God's fidelity and be despondent even when the punishment upon the enemy is delayed. To determine the right time

287

of intervention is God's affair and his inviolable right. To determine for
God the time of help and to reproach him because he allows his people
and his Church to be persecuted (Judith 8:12) is a language which does
not impel him to mercy, but inflames his wrath. Every member of the
kingdom of God should be satisfied if the Lord intervenes at his own good
time and passes his punitive judgment upon the enemy. Even if the
enemy becomes furious and rages so that the whole world trembles and
is threatened with destruction, God is mightier than he. He holds the
pillars of the earth firm; he does not permit the foundation of the moral
order to be undermined by godless men, but strengthens them again by
the judgment of destruction which he passes upon the enemy. Therefore
the psalmist warns the assailing enemy that it should not depend on the
strength of its armies and that it should not boast about its power. Isaias
permits the king of the Assyrians to speak in an overbearing manner: "By
the strength of my own hand I have done it and by my own wisdom I
have understood: and I have removed the bounds of the people, and have
taken the spoils of the princes, and as a mighty man pulled down them
that sat on high. And my hand hath found the strength of the people as a
nest; and as eggs are gathered, that are left, so have I gathered all the
earth, and there was none that moved the wing, or opened the mouth, or
made the least noise" (10:13–14). He who revolts against God and directs
his strength against the Almighty upon whom Israel builds its future, he
who derides him, commits sin not only against the Lord, but against himself also because beneath the Rock he will be crushed.

When the Assyrian King Sennacherib demanded the surrender of
Jerusalem he informed the inhabitants that it was useless to expect help
from Egypt, the broken reed. The psalmist answers this demand by
saying that Israel relies only on the help of God (verses 7–9). It does not
expect any help from any part of the world; it relies only on assistance
from God. He is the judge over all kingdoms and nations; in his hand lies
the fate of all men and kingdoms; it is he who gives victory and defeat;
for victory in war does not depend on the greatness of the army, but on
the help that comes from heaven (1 Machabees 3:19).

The enemies of the kingdom of God should also learn history. They
should learn that no one may attack the work and possessions of the Lord
without being punished; for now and then there is a nation, a human
power, upon which a divine judgment is passed. The psalmist expresses
his thoughts with a description. God always carries the beaker in his hand
which is filled with his wrath which is, as it were, a strong, intoxicating
wine mixed with spices. Now this or that person must drink from the
beaker and empty it to the dregs; he must accept the punishment of the
Lord in its full strength.

And thus also the present enemy must empty the beaker of God's wrath; he too will not be spared from it. Therefore the psalmist rejoices and will always be glad and will sing songs to the faithful God of Israel; for he has given his divine word and will keep it. He will break all power of the sinners and will give greater strength to the just. Even if godlessness now triumphs to a great extent and justice is persecuted and despised, at the end of time when the Messias comes to judge the nations, the promise about the victory of the just will be fulfilled.

psalm 75

Notus in Judaea

God is known in his Church: and exerts his power in protecting it. It alludes to the slaughter of the Assyrians, in the days of King Ezechias

1. Unto the end, in praises, a psalm for Asaph: a canticle to the Assyrians.

2. In Judea God is known: his name is great in Israel.

3. And his place is in peace: and his abode in Sion.

4. There hath he broken the powers of bows, the shield, the sword and the battle.

5. Thou enlightenest wonderfully from the everlasting hills.

6. All the foolish of heart were troubled.
They have slept their sleep; and all the men of riches have found nothing in their hands.

7. At thy rebuke, O God of Jacob, they have all slumbered that mounted on horseback.

8. Thou art terrible, and who shall resist thee? From that time thy wrath.

9. Thou hast caused judgment to be heard from heaven: the earth trembled and was still.

10. When God arose in judgment, to save all the meek of the earth.

11. For the thought of man shall give praise to thee: and the remainders of the thought shall keep holiday to thee.

12. Vow ye, and pay to the Lord your God: all you that are round about him
bring presents.
To him that is terrible.

13. Even to him who taketh away the spirit of princes, to the terrible with the
kings of the earth.

ACCORDING to the superscription of the Septuagint and Vulgate this
psalm refers to the defeat of the Assyrians by which Jerusalem was
relieved from the greatest danger. It can only refer to the defeat of the
year 701 in which 185,000 of the besieging army were slain by the angel
of the Lord (4 Kings 19:35) as so frequently commemorated in the
psalms. The thoughts of the psalm, indeed, may naturally be interpreted
as referring to this miraculous event. The psalmist wishes to show how
the attacks of the enemy against the people and kingdom of God must
contribute to the glory of God; for its wrath shatters against the rock of
his almighty power. God had permitted the invasion of the Assyrians into
the kingdom of Judea and for Judea had willed all the severe attendant
sufferings that his power might be made known so much the more gloriously to the Gentiles. This too is the profound divine meaning of all the
attacks which the Lord permits against his Church. Its preservation and
constant spread despite the everlasting attacks of its enemies are a continuous miracle of the divine power and the seal of the divinity of his
kingdom.

Great is the God of Sion (verses 2–4). This was the first thought of the
psalmist when he received news about the miraculous deliverance of
Jerusalem. Again, as so often before in the many centuries of the history
of the chosen people, the Lord has revealed his wonderful power, has
revealed the greatness and majesty of his kingship. Israel knows the
sublimity of his name and the incomprehensibility of his divine nature.
Every new great deed impresses the picture of his greatness ever deeper
and more indelibly upon the minds of the faithful people. With a justifiable pride Jerusalem may boast about this great God putting up his lasting
dwelling place within the walls of the city, about his holy tabernacle
standing on Mount Sion. Since the Lord dwells on Sion a divine guarantee
is given for the continued existence of his holy city and for an undisturbed peace. No enemy climbs over its walls; no Gentile nation enters
its gates. In truth, before its very gates God breaks the arrows of the
Assyrians. Through the Prophet Isaias God had given King Ezechias the
assurance that the enemy would not shoot a single arrow into the city.
This promise was literally fulfilled. Because before the 185,000 men could
begin their attack on Sion, God through his angel mowed them to the
ground.

290

The psalmist now describes in a poetic manner the coming of God in judgment upon the Assyrians (verses 5–7). When the Lord comes to judgment, he permits the light of his glory to shine: "His brightness shall be as the light: horns are in his hands" (Habacuc 3:4). In the glow of divine light the angel of the Lord appeared from heaven upon the ancient mountains of Palestine to descend into the camp of the Assyrians. The weapons fell from the most courageous; these were felled by the breath of the avenging angel and they slept the eternal death. The hands which they threateningly raised against the Lord and his holy city lost their strength and refused their service. Horse and rider not able to defend themselves against the approaching evil died of fright. One hundred and eighty-five thousand men fell, killed by the power of one angel. By the word of Yahwe whole armies fall in one night.

The poet gives expression of his astonishment at God's deed (verses 8–11). Nothing brings man so overwhelmingly to the consciousness of the infinite majesty and terrible power of God as when he himself is witness of an astounding miraculous punishment. He feels his own weakness, and terror takes hold of him at the almighty power of the Judge. How may a child of man rise against God and resist him when he uses only one of his angels to destroy a large army of the enemy in so short a time? Even all creation is astonished at such power. When the Lord of heaven arose in judgment in order to redeem his persecuted people, he brought deliverance to them; and when he inflicted punishment upon the enemy, the whole world trembled with fear because of this judgment. The world was hushed; it was suddenly attentive when the noise of weapons ceased and the battle cries from the walls of Jerusalem were suddenly silenced. Thus the punishment that fell upon the army of the Assyrians meant peace for the people of Israel and for the sufferers upon earth it meant a guarantee that the Lord has the power and love to save all who adore him.

Everybody must give honor to the Most High; even the wrath of the enemy glorified God (verses 11–13). This is a law of divine Order that everyone who rebels against the Lord and his kingdom must contribute to the honor and glory of God. Israel may have asked itself: why does God permit the ruthlessness of the Assyrians against his chosen people. It now sees God's intentions. God wished to reveal to all the world that the power of the enemy which no city could withstand had to break down before the walls of Jerusalem, the city of God. However with the defeat of the Assyrians their power is not completely destroyed. There is still a remnant left; that is, there is still a remnant of people enraged against Israel. But even their plots must contribute to the glory of God. Hence this remnant will be, as it were, the garment with which the Lord will gird himself; he will attire himself with its destruction. Israel will at all times praise God and offer him thanksgiving gifts because it has been favored and is permitted to dwell in the invincible city of peace. All should worship the awe-inspiring God with their gifts. What he has done before the walls of Jerusalem can happen again at any time. He will break the pride of his enemy and will have all earthly kings feel his mighty power until they acknowledge him and bend their knees before him.

psalm 76

Voce mea

The faithful have recourse to God in trouble of mind with confidence in his mercy and power

1. Unto the end, for Idithun, a psalm of Asaph.

2. I cried to the Lord with my voice; to God with my voice, and he gave ear to me.

3. In the day of my trouble I sought God, with my hands lifted up to him in the night, and I was not deceived.
   My soul refused to be comforted:

4. I remembered God, and was delighted, and was exercised, and my spirit swooned away.

5. My eyes prevented the watches: I was troubled and I spoke not.

6. I thought upon the days of old, and I had in my mind the eternal years.

7. And I meditated in the night with my own heart: and I was exercised and I swept my spirit.

8. Will God then cast off forever, or will he never be more favorable again?

9. Or will he cut off his mercy forever: from generation to generation?

10. Or will God forget to show mercy? Or will he in his anger shut up his mercies?

11. And I said, Now have I begun: this is the change of the right hand of the Most High.

12. I remembered the works of the Lord: for I will be mindful of thy wonders from the beginning.

13. And I will meditate on all thy works: and I will be employed in thy inventions.

14. Thy way, O Lord, is in the holy place: who is the great God like our God?

15. Thou art the God that dost wonders. Thou hast made thy power known among the nations.

16. With thy arm thou hast redeemed thy people, the children of Jacob and Joseph.

17. The waters saw thee, O God, the waters saw thee: and they were afraid, and the depths were troubled.

18. Great was the noise of the waters: the clouds sent out a sound. For thy arrows pass:

19. The voice of thy thunder is in a wheel. Thy lightnings enlightened the world: the earth shook and trembled.

20. Thy way is in the sea, and thy paths in many waters: and thy footsteps shall not be known.

21. Thou hast conducted thy people like sheep, by the hand of Moses and Aaron.

At the time of the composition of this psalm the people of Israel were suffering great affliction. What kind of affliction it was cannot be clearly seen from this psalm. Yet from the meditation on the deliverance of the people out of Egypt we may infer that it was invaded by inimical neighbors or by one of the world powers. This affliction must have lasted a long time; for the need of the people was of such concern to the psalmist that nothing could console him. Then he took Israel's book in hand and read and meditated upon the wonderful deeds which the Lord had done for the redemption of his people. From this meditation he drew the consolation and confidence that the Mighty is not willing to permit Israel to go to ruin at the present time.

The psalmist first seeks consolation in prayer (verses 2–5). He cries to the Lord that he may hear him; he does not cease calling upon him until he pays heed to the needs of his people. He feels that the needs of his native country are his own; they have become his needs and anxieties. This is a sign of the inner attachment to his native country, also of a spiritual attachment to his home, the Church. Its sorrow is the sorrow of all its members and all pray together to the Almighty for the prevention of affliction. The singer of this psalm sought strength and consolation from God, and again and again raised his hands towards the sanctuary although his soul did not find consolation in anything else. It may not have been easy to persevere in prayer when his soul did not find peace, but to God such a soul is pleasing whose prayers increase in strength. There are severe and long-lasting visitations by which the Lord guides his people and his Church, and his silence to suppliant prayer becomes, even to a God-fearing man, a mystery. Every thought about the "why" causes only new anxiety so that under the weight of uncertainty man laments and suffers. This occurred to the psalmist. Whole nights his eyes would not close because of the greatness of sorrow; his soul languished; his spirit was stupified; and the hands outstretched in prayer dropped exhausted. Then in spirit he turned away from the sad present and thought only about the past.

In the Book he read the history of Israel, about God's wonderful deeds of earlier times, about the great love and mercy of God toward his people. The more he read the more vehemently he felt the present desperation of his native country. Even the remembrance of the great past did not give him peace of soul; on the contrary there arose in him a spiritual combat (verses 6–11). Whole nights he meditated and thought about why the Lord had changed his attitude toward the people he had chosen. He thought and worried about the past and present in order to understand the obscure ways of the Lord and from understanding them to find consolation. Unceasingly thoughts troubled him. Is it possible that God will reject his people forever? Can the Lord take back his promises? Can these promises which threw so much light on the history of the Old Testament come to naught; can they which shine like stars in the night lose their lustre? Is it possible that the mercy of God becomes exhausted, that his sympathy for the needs of his people is at an end? Can the Lord forget his loved ones? Has he already forgotten them? These are questions which a soul oppressed with sorrow will ask itself because it finds no escape from its affliction. The more the psalmist worried, the greater became the unrest in his soul. How should he explain the attitude of God? From his troubled soul he constantly hears the answer that God's right hand must have weakened. Formerly the Lord held his almighty right hand protectingly over his people and his city; formerly he distributed with his right hand an abundance of his blessings and slew the enemies of his name. Now he withdraws his arm and closes his hand. But what should become of Israel if the Lord has really abandoned it? Certain collapse is inevitable. This is the great anxiety of the psalmist.

Yet such a despondent thought is no balm for a soul with high aspirations. The mind of the poet revolts against such thoughts. He again takes the Book of History in hand and meditates deeply upon the great deeds of the Lord, upon the miracles he had wrought in the past (verses 12–21). They are recorded on many pages of those writers who themselves were witnesses of the great deeds of Yahwe. The reading captivates him so much that in meditating upon the glorious deeds which the Lord had done for Israel in former times he forgets the sorrowful present. He stands enraptured at the sanctity and the infinite greatness of God confronting him in the description of his deeds. God alone is holy in his commands. The ethical sanctity of God was not unknown in the Old Testament, yet here probably the poet is thinking about sanctity in the sense of the super-worldliness and absolute sublimity of God; perhaps he is thinking about the words of Moses (Exodus 15:11): "Who is like to thee among the gods, O Lord? Who is like to thee glorious in holiness, terrible and praiseworthy, doing wonders?" Only he can work miracles and has through great deeds manifested his powers to the nations. They are so much interwoven with the history of Israel that its history would be an insoluble mystery if one would try to eliminate from it the great deeds of the Lord. The preservation of the people in the midst of a pagan and inimical surrounding was alone a continual miracle of God, just as the preservation of the Church is. But even the very beginning of the history of the chosen people, the exodus from Egypt, cannot be explained without the extraordinary intervention of God. It was God's arm which at that time redeemed the descendants of Jacob and Joseph from captivity.

The psalmist became absorbed in the history of these miracles and thereby obtained peace of heart. Only in this manner can it be explained why at the close of this psalm, he does not mention a word about the need of his people and about the sorrow of his own soul but ends rather with a meditation upon the miracles during the exodus from Egypt (verses 17–21). In a vivid manner he brings back to memory the great day when the Lord in a miraculous manner led the people through the Red Sea. The waters of the Red Sea became witnesses of the power of Yahwe. They trembled when they heard his almighty word; they fell back and stood like iron walls. The sea trembled in its depths when the waters retreated and the mysteries of the abyss lay open to men's view and a hot wind touched its bottom; for the first time since the creation it was dried. The Lord appeared in a terrible storm and the powers of nature obeyed his command. From the clouds came a torrential downpour of rain; the thunder roared above the waters, and lightning crackled through the sky and illuminated the night. The whole earth seemed to be illuminated; it trembled and quaked because of the powerful, thunderous voice of the Lord; it trembled at the infinite majesty of Yahwe and in fearful expectation of his work. In the midst of this turmoil of the elements and through the high waves of the sea, God's power paved a way for his people. All this happened without God becoming visible; there was no trace of him to be seen; only from the miracle was his presence evident. Through the prepared way the Lord permitted the people to be led by Moses and Aaron. Like a shepherd that passes over the steppe, peacefully pasturing his herd, God led his people along the bottom of the sea from slavery to liberty. The psalmist said this miracle was sufficient.

At that time at the Red Sea the situation of the people was a desperate one. Without the miraculous intervention of God deliverance was impossible. The Lord worked the miracle. Thus he can also open a way of escape in the present difficult situation. The psalmist does not expressly speak here of this hope and trust, but there is an unspoken sentiment in his soul with which the psalm ends.

psalm 77

Attendite

God's great benefits to the people of Israel, notwithstanding their ingratitude

1. Understanding for Asaph.
   Attend, O my people, to my law: incline your ears to the words of my mouth.

2. I will open my mouth in parables: I will utter propositions from the beginning.

3. How great things have we heard and known, and our fathers have told us.

4. They have not been hidden from their children, in another generation.
   Declaring the praises of the Lord, and his powers, and his wonders which he hath done.

5. And he set up a testimony in Jacob: and made a law in Israel.
   How great things he commanded our fathers, that they should make the same known to their children.

6. That another generation might know them. The children that should be born and should rise up, and declare them to their children.

7. That they may put their hope in God and may not forget the works of God: and may seek his commandments.

8. That they may not become like their fathers, a perverse and exasperating generation. A generation that set not their heart aright: and whose spirit was not faithful to God.

9. The sons of Ephraim who bend and shoot with the bow: they have turned back in the day of battle.

10. They kept not the covenant of God: and in his law they would not walk.

11. And they forgot his benefits, and his wonders that he had shown them.

12. Wonderful things did he do in the sight of their fathers, in the land of Egypt, in the field of Tanis.

13. He divided the sea and brought them through: and he made the waters to stand as in a vessel.

14. And he conducted them with a cloud by day: and all the night with a light of fire.

15. He struck the rock in the wilderness: and gave them to drink as out of the great deep.

16. He brought forth water out of the rock: and made streams run down as rivers.

17. And they added yet more sin against him; and they provoked the Most High to wrath in the place without water.

18. And they tempted God in their hearts, by asking for their desires.

19. And they spoke ill of God; they said: Can God furnish a table in the wilderness?

20. Because he struck the rock, and the waters gushed out, and the streams overflowed.
Can he also give bread, or provide a table for his people?

21. Therefore the Lord heard, and was angry: and a fire was kindled against Jacob, and wrath came up against Israel.

22. Because they believed not in God: and trusted not in his salvation.

23. And he had commanded the clouds from above: and had opened the doors of heaven.

24. And had rained down manna upon them to eat, and had given them the bread of heaven.

25. Man ate the bread of angels: he sent them provisions in abundance.

26. He removed the south wind from heaven: and by his power brought in the southwest wind.

27. And he rained upon them flesh as dust, and feathered fowls like the sand of the sea.

28. And they fell in the midst of their camp, round about their pavilions.

29. So they did eat, and were filled exceedingly, and he gave them their desire.

30. They were not defrauded of that which they craved. As yet their meat was in their mouth:

31. And the wrath of God came upon them. And he slew the fat ones among them, and brought down the chosen men of Israel.

32. In all these things they sinned still: and they believed not for his wondrous works.

33. And their days were consumed in vanity, and their years in haste.

34. When he slew them, then they sought him: and they returned, and came to him early in the morning.

35. And they remembered that God was their helper: and the most high God their redeemer.

36. And they loved him with their mouth, and with their tongue they lied unto him.

37. But their heart was not right with him; nor were they counted faithful in his covenant.

38. But he is merciful, and will forgive their sins: and will not destroy them. And many a time did he turn away his anger: and did not kindle all his wrath.

39. And he remembered that they are flesh: a wind that goeth and returneth not.

40. How often did they provoke him in the desert: and move him to wrath in the place without water?

41. And they turned back and tempted God: and grieved the holy one of Israel.

42. They remembered not his hand, in the day that he redeemed them from the hand of him that afflicted them.

43. How he wrought his signs in Egypt, and his wonders in the field of Tanis.

44. And he turned their rivers into blood, and their showers that they might not drink.

45. He sent amongst them divers sorts of flies, which devoured them: and frogs which destroyed them.

46. And he gave up their fruits to the blast, and their labors to the locust.

47. And he destroyed their vineyards with hail, and their mulberry trees with hoarfrost.

48. And he gave up their cattle to the hail, and their stock to the fire.

49. And he sent upon them the wrath of his indignation: indignation and wrath and trouble, which he sent by evil angels.

50. He made a way for a path to his anger: he spared not their souls from death, and their cattle he shut up in death.

51. And he killed all the first-born in the land of Egypt: the first fruits of all their labor in the tabernacles of Cham.

52. And he took away his own people as sheep: and guided them in the wilderness like a flock.

53. And he brought them out in hope, and they feared not: and the sea overwhelmed their enemies.

54. And he brought them into the mountain of his sanctuary: the mountain which his right hand had purchased.
And he cast out the Gentiles before them: and by lot divided to them their land by a line of distribution.

55. And he made the tribes of Israel to dwell in their tabernacles.

56. Yet they tempted, and provoked the most high God: and they kept not his testimonies.

57. And they turned away, and kept not the covenant: even like their fathers they were turned aside as a crooked bow.

58. They provoked him to anger on their hills: and moved him to jealousy with their graven things.

59. God heard and despised them, and he reduced Israel exceedingly as it were to nothing.

60. And he put away the tabernacle of Silo, his tabernacle where he dwelt among men.

61. And he delivered their strength into captivity: and their beauty into the hands of the enemy.

62. And he shut up his people under the sword: and he despised his inheritance.

63. Fire consumed their young men: and their maidens were not lamented.

64. Their priests fell by the sword: and their widows did not mourn.

65. And the Lord was awakened as one out of sleep, and like a mighty man that hath been surfeited with wine.

66. And he smote his enemies on the hinder parts: he put them to an everlasting reproach.

67. And he rejected the tabernacle of Joseph: and chose not the tribe of Ephraim.

68. But he chose the tribe of Juda, Mount Sion which he loved.

69. And he built his sanctuary as of unicorns, in the land which he founded forever.

70. And he chose his servant David and took him from the flocks of sheep: he brought him from following the ewes great with young.

71. To feed Jacob his servant, and Israel his inheritance.

72. And he fed them in the innocence of his heart: and conducted them by the skillfulness of his hands.

THE history of the people of Israel is principally a history of redemption; it tends to the fulfillment of the Messianic promises in Christ. It shows the way upon which the Lord led his people to this goal and also the obstacles which Israel put in the way of divine guidance. This goal the writers of biblical history always had in mind; we may, therefore, call it a prophetic history. On this account the presentation of events gives us important material for meditation and serious thought. For this reason the psalmist gives us a section of its history for reflection. He starts with the fact that God himself has chosen the city of Jerusalem with its Sion as his dwelling and the house of David as the bearer of royal power. According to the predictions of the prophets, Jerusalem was to be the starting place of Messianic rule and the house of David the center of the worldwide kingdom. From history the psalmist proves that the claims of Ephraim were not justifiable and the rejection of its leadership warrantable. He wishes to show that this tribe throughout the centuries when it could have played a leading role and when the sanctuary was entrusted to its protection, made itself unworthy of this responsible position and was therefore rejected by God. This reflection upon the history of the past becomes a warning to the chosen people and to every member of this people an admonition to walk worthy of their calling at all times.

In the introduction to this psalm the psalmist speaks about the duty and purpose of meditating on historical facts. Teaching about the past of God's chosen people deserves full attention. The history of the chosen people cannot be compared with the history of any Gentile nation. The psalmist therefore demands attention to his words. He speaks in proverbs; he wishes to proclaim the riddles of the days of yore. His song explains the ways of God. He explains what deep wisdom pervades the divine actions and what deep meaning there is in his deeds. Indeed these actions of God seem to me to be mysteries. Men think them to be incomprehensible and unjust. On this account they stubbornly resist and do not want to submit. Because the history of Israel is so intimately connected with the development of the doctrine of salvation and is guided by eternal wisdom, all is of such great importance that nothing may be overlooked. Therefore it is God's will that their knowledge of the patriarchs will be passed on to their children. Their children should again pass it on to their children and to their children's children that the remarkable deeds of the Lord and the proofs of this power may not be forgotten.

There is no choice between remembering and forgetting the past; for the Lord has placed a duty upon the fathers to instruct their children about the history of God's people. In the Pentateuch the admonition is again and again repeated to be mindful of God's deeds. Thus the Lord speaks in the giving of the Law on Sinai: "Keep thyself, therefore, and thy soul carefully. Forget not the words that thy eyes have seen and let them not go out of thy heart all the days of thy life. Thou shalt teach them to thy sons and to thy grandsons" (Deuteronomy 4:9). The remembrance of the great deeds of the Lord should strengthen faith in his power and fidelity so that in view of his great deeds all may place their hope in God alone and that they may never forget what the Lord has done to the fathers, which was a blessing also for their descendants, and what God has demanded from his people for the keeping of the covenant. They should know from the chastisement that fell upon the unfaithful ancestors that God does not leave unpunished the disobedience and unfaithfulness of men. They should know that he rejected them even though he had chosen them and delivered them from the servitude of Egypt. Neither will he have mercy on the present generation if it is like its forefathers.

After this introductory explanation that the history of the past must be a lesson for the present, the psalmist passes over to the next lesson of his instruction: the rejection of the tribe of Ephraim. From the long period of Israel's history in which the political leadership had been given to this tribe he gives the reason for its rejection. He begins with the attitude of the fathers during the desert journey (verses 9–39). Ephraim was, if not in numbers, the most important tribe of Israel because of its influence. This tribe was a descendant of Joseph. It was to Joseph that this tribe and his brothers owed much gratitude.

And because the patriarch Jacob gave to this tribe the blessing of primogeniture, they thought themselves to have the right of the leadership of God's people. They were well-armed and counted many men of military efficiency. Besides it happened that Moses had selected as leader of the Israelitic army a man from this tribe; for Josue belonged to the tribe of Ephraim. But this tribe at the very beginning showed itself unworthy of leading the people of the Lord. Although experts in the use of bow and arrow, the sons of Ephraim retreated on the day of battle. This to be understood literally probably points to the time of the high priest Heli and to the war against the Philistines during which the Israelites fled and surrendered the Ark of the Covenant and the sanctuary at Silo to the enemy. The battlefield was situated in the territory of Ephraim in which Silo also was situated. One would therefore expect that the Ephraimites would have protected the sanctuary and would have defended it to the last man and that they would have fought with all their might to regain the Ark of the Covenant. But they fled and surrendered Silo and the tabernacle to the Philistines without battle.

The psalmist blames this conduct on the religious indifference of the tribe, to the breaking of the covenant made with God. That Ephraim permitted the godless conduct of the sons of Heli in the sanctuary at Silo, that Ephraim at Solomon's death induced the northern tribes to revolt against the temple and to worship a golden steer at Bethel is proof that at least the majority of the tribe no longer lived according to the commandments of God. They were no longer mindful of the great miracles by which the Lord helped their forefathers in the exodus from Egypt. In order to make the present generation realize the greatness of their ingratitude the psalmist reminds them of the great deed of the Lord. He reminds them of the miracles which the Lord wrought at Tanis in Egypt (the resident city of the Pharaohs at that time) in order to force Pharaoh to allow the Israelites to depart. He also mentions the passage through the Red Sea and the Lord's division of the waters so that they were dammed up and stood like walls on both sides and the entire people walked through unharmed. He also reminds them that Yahwe himself took over the leadership of Israel and guided the people by a pillar of cloud during the day and a brilliant pillar of light during the night. He finally reminds them of the miraculous gift of water. God split the rocks in the desert and let water flow from them in such abundance that both men and animals could drink to satiety. Like brooks and streams the water flowed from the rocks. When the Lord gives, he gives with divine liberality.

Despite these astounding miraculous events which had forced the mighty Pharaoh to submit to the great Yahwe, the fathers continued to sin in the desert obstinately resisting the most high God and challenging his

experienced. A heavy hail killed men and beasts, destroyed trees and vineyards and all the fruit that was beginning to ripen. The hail was accompanied by great storms which seldom occur in Egypt. Many head of cattle were killed by lightning. God afflicted the country with destructive pestilences, terrible messengers of God that destroyed both men and beasts. Finally the avenging angel slew all the first-born of the Egyptians, the descendants of Cham; all that opened the womb of the mother had to die in one night.

The generation living in Canaan had not only forgotten the miracles which the Lord had worked for the deliverance of his people in Egypt, but it also forgot the benefit it had received by giving to it the land of Canaan (52–58). Like the shepherd who in the morning leads his herd from the small fold into wide pastures, so God has led his people from slavery through the desert. The Egyptians pursued Israel in order to bring it back into Egypt by force, but the Lord led his people through the Red Sea and submerged the army of the enemy in its waters. And thus he brought Israel to the holy city which his powerful right hand had taken when he sent David to conquer the fortifications of the Jebusites. The Lord expelled the Gentiles who lived in Canaan. He granted victory to the army of Israel; he permitted Josue to divide the land among the twelve tribes of Israel in order that they might settle there. And yet even when they were in full possession of their new country, the people continued to murmur against Yahwe; even in the new land they disobeyed the divine command and provoked God's wrath. Just as their fathers in the desert had done, so they too departed from the way of the Lord; they became unfaithful to God and worshiped pagan gods. They who had been called and chosen for Yahwe's service failed in that service like a crooked bow. They especially provoked God by permitting the Canaanites to seduce them into worshiping in high places and making images which were forbidden by God. Everywhere in the country they erected sun pillars and sacred posts, symbols of Baal and Astarte.

Their continual unfaithfulness to God had finally exhausted his patience. The rejection of Silo in the territory of Ephraim was a serious warning to the entire people (verses 59–72). When Israel had given itself up to the worship of the golden calf on Sinai, God commanded Moses to remove the tent of testimony from the midst of the people and erect it outside of the camp as a sign that the Lord was displeased with Israel and that in the future he did not wish to dwell in their midst. So also he permitted the holy tabernacle which for four hundred years stood at Silo in care of the tribe of Ephraim to be destroyed by the hand of the Philistines, and forbade the new tabernacle to be erected in Ephraim. Rather he ordered it to be erected in the territory of Juda. He no longer wished to dwell in the midst of Ephraim. As a sign of rejection, God permitted the Ark of the Covenant, the source of Israel's strength, the pride of the nation to fall into the hands of the Philistines as a booty. The army of Israel suffered a great defeat and the young men of the nation fell by the sword. So many fell in the disastrous battles that many virgins had to give up the thought of marriage and were deprived of the privilege of celebrating wedding songs. The priests Ophni and Phinees, the godless sons of Heli, fell by the sword and their widows did not mourn about them. God's judgment was just and they were more concerned about the loss of the Ark of the Covenant than about the loss of their husbands.

After Israel had been chastised and cleansed by the divine punitive judgment the Lord had mercy on them and revenged himself on his enemies. As a hero rising from a wholesome sleep takes wine and feels himself strong for action, so God now attacked the enemy and fought in favor of his people. He slew the enemy with such might that their defeat became an eternal shame for them. But when the time came to select a new sanctuary for the Ark of the Covenant which had been returned by the Philistines, God no longer chose Silo, no longer the territory of the tribe of Ephraim, but Sion in the territory of the tribe of Juda. There he built his sanctuary for all times so that in its continued existence it could be compared to the eternal heaven and the firmly-founded earth. A new era began for Israel after the Lord rejected the Benjaminite Saul and called David from his flock to be king of his people. David remained faithful to the Lord; he made himself worthy of his calling and performed the duties of his high position with wisdom and piety.

psalm 78

Deus, venerunt gentes

The Church in time of persecution prayeth for relief; it seems to belong to the time of the Machabees

1. A psalm for Asaph.
   O God, the heathens are come into thy inheritance, they have defiled thy holy temple: they have made Jerusalem as a place to keep fruit.

2. They have given the dead bodies of thy servants to be meat for the fowls of the air; the flesh of thy saints for the beasts of the earth.

3. They have poured out their blood as water, round about Jerusalem, and there was none to bury them.

4. We are become a reproach to our neighbors: a scorn and derision to them that are round about us.

5. How long, O Lord; wilt thou be angry forever: shall thy zeal be kindled like a fire?

6. Pour out thy wrath upon the nations that have not known thee: and upon the kingdoms that have not called upon thy name.

7. Because they have devoured Jacob; and have laid waste his place.

8. Remember not our former iniquities; let thy mercies speedily prevent us, for we are become exceeding poor.

9. Help us, O God, our Saviour: and for the glory of thy name, O Lord, deliver us: and forgive us our sins for thy name's sake.

10. Lest they should say among the Gentiles: Where is their God? And let him be made known among the nations before our eyes,
By the revenging blood of thy servants, which hath been shed:

11. Let the sighing of the prisoners come in before thee.
According to the greatness of thy arm, take possession of the children of them that have been put to death.

12. And render to our neighbors sevenfold in their bosom: the reproach wherewith they have reproached thee, O Lord.

13. But we thy people, and the sheep of thy pasture, will give thanks to thee forever.
We will show forth thy praise, unto generation and generation.

THE psalm was composed under the crushing impression caused by the destruction of Jerusalem and of the temple by the Babylonians in the year 587. The Gentile nation had placed its signs of victory on the pinnacles of the temple and had celebrated the defeat of Yahwe and the victory of its gods in the place of the sanctuary which had fallen into ruins. Godlessness triumphed; the people of the Lord were dispersed and its temple lay in ruins; the people were suffering in captivity. The psalm gives expressions of sorrow, but also of hope that the Lord will not let his people perish.

The sorrow is great; for God's city and temple have been desecrated (verses 1–4). The pagans have broken into the inheritance of God; for he himself had chosen Jerusalem as a dwelling place among his people. Men who were forbidden by the Law to enter the inner courts forced their way into the Holy of Holies in which only the priest or high priest was permitted to enter and housed themselves there like barbarians. Of the former glory of the temple they left nothing but a heap of ruins. Just as unscrupulously as the enemy treated the sanctuary, so also he treated the worshipers of Yahwe. The enemy killed them by the thousands; the Babylonians in their hatred even desecrated the corpses. They left them unburied and threw them to the vultures, jackals, and scavengers for devouring. The blood flowed in streams around Jerusalem. The life of an Israelite was considered as nothing. No one troubled himself about the fallen. In malicious joy the neighboring tribes, the Moabites, the Ammonites, and especially the Edomites greeted the destruction of the city. The Prophet Jeremias speaks about the heartlessness of these nations: "They said: Is this the city of perfect beauty, the joy of all the earth? All thy enemies have opened their mouth against thee and gnashed with their teeth and have said: We will swallow her up: lo, this is the day we looked for; we have found it, we have seen it" (Lamentations 2:15–16).

The divine justice cannot look long upon such conduct. Such wickedness calls for retribution (verses 5–8). Jerusalem had deserved punishment; the Lord had rightly manifested his wrath upon its inhabitants. But God's zeal for his honor cannot promise his people continued existence and redemption. The Gentiles do not only want to annihilate the people of Israel but also want to erase from the world the worship of Yahwe; for they will not acknowledge him. They will not admit him to be the only true God and will not revere and give worship to his name. The Lord has once spoken his woe upon the Assyrians through the Prophet Isaias (10:5 seq.) because they were not satisfied in punishing Israel but had in mind the complete destruction of the people. The psalmist begs God to utter a similar woe upon the Babylonians who have become guilty of the same crime. Because they hated the Lord, they greedily fell upon Israel to destroy it; like wild animals they threw themselves upon the booty to devour it; they laid waste the land, their lovely meadows. The Israelites have gravely offended God; they have acknowledged their guilt and have done penance for it. On this account may the Lord remember them with his grace and mercy. The catastrophe that had fallen on Jerusalem and Israel has exhausted the strength of the nation. Its plight must move God to be merciful.

There is no question here about the continuance of a nation or kingdom that is estranged from God. But there is concern about the people, about a kingdom established by God himself. Hence godlessness should not continue to triumph. God's honor requires speedy intervention (verses 9–13). On this account the psalmist beseeches the Lord to have mercy on Israel for his name's sake, and for his own honor's sake, and to forgive it its great guilt even if the people should not be worthy of his mercy in order that the name of the Most High may no longer be dishonored and blasphemed by the Gentiles. The victory of the godless Gentiles cannot be the purpose of the punishment upon Jerusalem. If God's arm does not intervene and if the pagan Babylon triumphs over Sion, the heathen nations will mockingly ask: Where is now the strong God who claims dominion over other gods, and over the whole world? Where is Yahwe who permits no other gods beside himself? For the sake of the honor of his justice, God must revenge the spilled blood of his believers. The prisoners in captivity are still sighing that the Lord may hear their weeping and lamenting. Many of them are still dedicated to death if the Lord does not save them from the threat by the power of his arm. May he therefore have mercy upon them and save them. It is just that the heathen neighboring nations who rejoiced in the misfortune of Sion should feel the power of the Lord because they have blasphemed the most high God. May their insult wherewith they offended God be returned to them sevenfold. How can Israel fulfill its mission in the Gentile world when it only offers to God mockery and derision. When God has once passed judgment upon the Gentiles, the people of the Lord, the sheep of his pasture will praise God forevermore and proclaim his praise through all generations.

psalm 79

Qui regis Israel

A prayer for the Church in tribulation, commemorating God's former favors

1. Unto the end, for them that shall be changed, a testimony for Asaph, a psalm.

2. Give ear, O thou, that rulest Israel: thou that leadest Joseph as a sheep. Thou that sittest upon the cherubims shine forth.

3. Before Ephraim, Benjamin and Manasses.
Stir up thy might, and come to save us.

4. Convert us, O God: and show us thy face, and we shall be saved.

5. O Lord God of hosts, how long wilt thou be angry against the prayer of thy servant?

6. How long wilt thou feed us with the bread of tears: and give us for our drink, tears in measure?

7. Thou hast made us to be a contradiction to our neighbors: and our enemies have scoffed at us.

8. O God of hosts, convert us; and show thy face and we shall be saved.

9. Thou hast brought a vineyard out of Egypt: thou hast cast out the Gentiles and planted it.

10. Thou wast the guide of its journey in its sight: thou plantedst the roots thereof, and it filled the land.

11. The shadow of it covered the hills, and the branches thereof the cedars of God.

12. It stretched forth its branches unto the sea, and its boughs unto the river.

13. Why hast thou broken down the hedge thereof, so that all they who pass by the way do pluck it?

14. The boar out of the woods hath laid it waste: and a singular wild beast hath devoured it.

15. Turn again, O God of hosts, look down from heaven, and see, and visit this vineyard.

16. And perfect the same which thy right hand hath planted: and upon the son of man whom thou hast confirmed for thyself.

17. Things set on fire and dug down shall perish at the rebuke of thy countenance.

18. Let thy hand be upon the man of thy right hand: and upon the son of man whom thou hast confirmed for thyself.

19. And we depart not from thee, thou shalt quicken us: and we will call upon thy name.

20. O Lord God of hosts, convert us: and show thy face, and we shall be saved.

THE Church has woven the thoughts of this psalm in preference to all others in her liturgy during the time of Advent. The refrain at the close of the individual strophes: "O God of hosts, convert us, and show us thy face and we shall be saved . . ." is the Advent cry of unredeemed mankind. It gives to the longing for redemption and to the restoration of grace a vivid expression. The psalm stems from the time of the Babylonian captivity. Jerusalem and its temple still lay in ruins. The land and its inhabitants were despoiled and desolate. The banished longed for their homeland and sighed for the re-establishment of the kingdom and of its sanctuary. Already the prophets saw in the exile a type of the un-redeemed condition of mankind and in their return to their native land a type and a guarantee of redemption through the Messias. The application of the psalm for the ecclesiastical advent corresponds to its deeper prophetic meaning. The contrite longing of a burdened soul for the restoration of union with God pervades the psalm.

The psalm begins with an advent call of Israel: "O Shepherd of Israel, give ear" (verses 2–4). Through the mouth of the prophets God has often pictured himself as the Shepherd of Israel and the chosen people as the sheep of his flock. We see this picture already in the blessing which Jacob gave to Joseph. He has proved himself a good shepherd. As a shepherd leads his herd, so the Lord has led his people out of Egypt, the land of captivity to Canaan, the promised land of liberty for the children of God. The imagery of a shepherd tending his flock was literally adapted to the three tribes: Benjamin, Ephraim, and Manasses, the descendants of Rachel; for in the journey through the desert these three tribes formed the division which immediately followed the Ark of the Covenant. Perhaps this fact induced the psalmist to mention only Benjamin and the two tribes, descendants of Joseph, among the tribes of Israel. He who once throned in the sanctuary at Silo and who thrones over the cherubim in heaven should show his power before these tribes, the representatives of the northern and southern kingdoms, and therefore of the entire and united kingdom. He should show his power in favor of his people and come to their rescue again. The first refrain again expresses the fervent advent petition that the Lord may again erect his dwelling place among his people and that his merciful countenance may again graciously shine from his sanctuary.

The second strophe describes the national need of Israel as the reason for the advent petition (verses 5–8). The Lord is still angry even though Israel has acknowledged its guilt for some time and humbly asked for pardon. The Prophet Baruch in his book records the penitential attitude of the captives in the fifth year after the destruction of Jerusalem. They were still sitting at the rivers of Babylon and weeping when they thought of Sion. They let their harps hang on the willows of the land and were mourning. Tears of contrition, of homesickness, and of sadness about the miseries of their captivity flowed upon their food and mixed with their drink. It is bitter for a people who above all other nations boasted about its God, who could look back to a great past, who still had an important future mission, and who looked forward to a time at which all Gentile nations would be subservient to it and to its king to be subjected to mockery and derision before the entire world. Thus again a petition is sent up to God in the second refrain: "Convert us!" It is a petition for the restoration of Israel to that greatness which it enjoyed in David's time. It is also a prayer of a sinful Christian for restoration as a child of God.

Israel's prayer has brought forth in the psalmist memories of the great past of his people. He describes the past and the present with the parable of a vine (verses 9–14). Such a parable was frequently used in the Old Testament and was easily understood by the people who had settled in Canaan, so rich in vineyards. For this reason there was placed above the entrance of the sanctuary of the Herodian temple a golden grape. We already meet with the parable in Deuteronomy and still more in detail in Isaias and in the Canticle of Canticles. God himself had transplanted the vine from Egypt to Canaan. The Gentile nations who until that time had inhabited the land, God had driven from the country and placed therein his own people. Isaias speaks about the solicitude with which God had cultivated his vineyard: "My beloved had a vineyard on a hill in a fruitful place. And he fenced it in and picked the stones out of it; and planted it with the choicest vines and built a tower in the midst thereof, and set up a wine press therein; and he looked to it that it should bring forth grapes, and it brought forth wild grapes" (Isaias 5:2). God made room for Israel and placed the people in a large land begging for expansion. With God's grace Israel struck roots and filled the entire territory. Israel with God's help conquered Canaan and gradually inhabited the entire territory. The vine covered all the mountains of Palestine and its branches to the north reached the cedars of the high mountains of the Lebanon. To the west its branches reached to the Mediterranean Sea and to the east as far as the river Euphrates. The Mediterranean Sea, Lebanon, and the Euphrates were the uttermost limits of the land in the time of David and Solomon. But what the Prophet Isaias foretold at the end of the parable of the vineyard was fulfilled. There he foretold that punishment would come upon Israel: "And now I will show you what I will do to my vineyard; I will take away the hedge thereof and it shall be wasted: and I will break down the wall thereof and it shall be trodden down" (Isaias 5:5). Fence and wall are symbols of the divine protection which lovingly and carefully encompassed the people. What happens to a vineyard without a wall happened to Israel. From all sides the Gentiles invaded it and robbed and plundered it. The wild boar of the forest, perhaps the Assyrian and Babylonian kings are meant, uprooted it. The wild beasts of the field, perhaps the other neighboring Gentile nations are meant, fed upon it. The devastated vineyard is also a picture of the sad condition of unredeemed humanity as Paul describes it in his Epistle to the Romans; it is also a picture of a soul contaminated by sin. It is deprived of the protection of divine grace and is given up to its passions and to the enticements of the world.

The psalm ends with an advent prayer: God of hosts, come again, look down from heaven and see and visit this vine (verses 15–20). It is God's creation. He loves what he has made. The vine is the child which the heavenly Father has reared. Fire has devastated the vineyard. By this the psalmist wishes to say that Israel is in its present sad condition because of the fire of the divine wrath. As once upon a time the patriarch Jacob called his darling Benjamin the son of his right hand, so may God love and glorify Israel as the nation of his right hand. If the Lord shall again favor his people and lead it back home it will never again depart from the path of God.

psalm 80

Exultate Deo

An invitation to a solemn praising of God

1. Unto the end, for the wine presses, a psalm for Asaph himself.

2. Rejoice to God our helper: sing aloud to the God of Jacob.

3. Take a psalm, and bring hither the timbrel: the pleasant psaltery with the harp.

4. Blow up the trumpet on the new moon, on the noted day of your solemnity.

5. For it is a commandment in Israel, and a judgment to the God of Jacob.

6. He ordained it for a testimony in Joseph, when he came out of the land of Egypt: he heard a tongue which he knew not.

7. He removed his back from the burdens: his hands had served in baskets.

8. Thou calledst upon me in affliction and I delivered thee; I heard thee in the secret place of tempest: I proved thee at the waters of contradiction.

9. Hear, O my people, and I will testify to thee: O Israel, if thou wilt hearken to me.

10. There shall be no new god in thee: neither shalt thou adore a strange god.

11. For I am the Lord thy God, who brought thee out of the land of Egypt: open thy mouth wide, and I will fill it.

12. But my people heard not my voice: and Israel hearkened not to me.

13. So I let them go according to the desires of their heart: they shall walk in their own inventions.

14. If my people had heard me: if Israel had walked in my ways.

15. I should soon have humbled their enemies, and laid my hand on them that troubled them.

16. The enemies of the Lord had lied to him: and their time shall be forever.

17. And he fed them with the fat of wheat, and filled them with honey out of the rock.

Accoording to the Mosaic Law (Leviticus 23:24 and Numbers 29:1 seq.) the new moon of the seventh month was to be celebrated with festive offerings and with the blowing of trombones and silver trumpets because it ushered in the month of Tishri. It was therefore called "the noisy day." It was to remind the people of the giving of the Law on Sinai which was given accompanied by the sound of trumpets, and the divine judgment on the last day will also be given accompanied by the sound of trumpets. On the tenth of the month the Feast of the Atonement was celebrated, and on the fifteenth day (full moon) the Day of the Tabernacles was celebrated with an octave. The psalm offers a meditation for this feast day. The feast was dedicated to the remembrance of the journey through the desert and of all the miracles of divine guidance through forty years; it was at the same time a thanksgiving feast for the fruit and vintage harvest.

The psalmist begins with an admonition for a correct attitude toward the feast (verses 2–6). An ecclesiastical feast of joy only brings about a religious elevation when the soul prepares for it and in joyous sentiment begins the day with thoughts of the feast. Therefore the psalmist like a herald calls upon the people to be joyous. To rejoice in God, the Lord, who has always shown himself a defender and protector of his people should be the first thought on the morning of the feast day. "This is the day which the Lord has made; let us rejoice and be glad in him." Loud music and festive song naturally add to the joyous character of the feast and incite the soul to rejoice and be glad. Therefore the request is made to the Levites to prepare their kettledrums, zithers, and harps, and to glorify the day of the Lord with song and stringed music. The spiritual joy must bodily manifest itself and must make itself known by song. That is human nature. Both body and soul want to participate in the joy. On this account a silent, songless divine service does not fit in with the character of a feast. The call goes out to the priests to blow the trumpets at the new moon in order to announce the great feast of the seventh month and to admonish the people to prepare themselves for this day of thanksgiving. The blowing of the trombones and trumpets, which was the privilege of the priests, corresponds to our ringing of the bells which on the evening before and in the morning is a prelude to the festive joy and invites the faithful to the House of God. God himself has established the feast of tabernacles on Sinai and its celebration was commanded through Moses (Leviticus 23:34 and 43): "Say to the children of Israel: From the fifth day of this same seventh month shall be kept the feast of the tabernacles seven days to the Lord, that your posterity may know that I made the children of Israel to dwell in the tabernacles when I brought them out of the land of Egypt." The celebration was intended to bring to mind that the Lord has led his people out of the Egyptian captivity and to prevent the great miracles and signs during the desert journey from being forgotten. The great feast days of the Church also obligate and have their source in the great deeds of redemption and sanctification.

In his meditation upon the feast the psalmist particularly lays stress on the thoughts of the day. God himself has inspired him with the words which he should say to the people. A direct divine instruction had not been given to him before this; therefore he calls it a language which he did not know previously. The first part of the divine instruction is a consideration of the mystery of the feast. It should be a guide to celebrate the day with a proper disposition. The Christian feastdays also remain fruitless when a reading pertaining to the mystery of the feast or a sermon does not dispose the mind and will to meditate upon the mystery commemorated.

In the first place God recalls the great benefit of redemption from the Egyptian captivity which is considered by the prophet a type of the Redemption from the slavery of sin. God took the burdensome baskets from the shoulders of the people who suffered from forced labor and freed them. Furthermore on the Feast of the Tabernacles and during the entire octave Israel should consider the time of the journey through the desert when the people had to live in huts made of tree branches. In those days as often as the people cried for help, God had mercy on them and delivered them from every need by the power of miracles. He himself led the people with a pillar of fire and smoke and from it gave to Moses his promises and Laws. When he tested their confidence, their faith in his power and goodness waned. They murmured against him at the fountain of contention when there was a lack of water. Nevertheless the Lord gave his gifts even to the ungrateful (Numbers 20:1 seq.). In a terrifying and

315

solemn manner he revealed himself on Sinai and there gave to the people his Law and commanded them to pay heed to his words. The divine admonitions were read publicly on the feast at least in the Sabbath Year. All should be reminded again of the fundamental law: "I am the Lord thy God, thou shalt not have strange gods before thee in order to love them and worship them—Hear, O Israel, the Lord is our God. He alone is the Lord. Thou shalt love the Lord thy God with thy whole heart, with thy whole soul, and with thy whole strength." (Deuteronomy 6:4) For the benefit of redemption and for the giving of rich supernatural blessings God only asks that man open his mouth, that he show a believing, hungry desire for grace and for salvation. God will satisfy those who seek after justice.

The second part of the divine instruction gives the practical application from the meditation of the feast (verses 12–17). Israel has not fulfilled its task and duty from the very beginning. The journey through the desert, Sinai itself, the graves of the obstinate who because of their obdurateness had to die in the desert give testimony that it did not pay heed to the voice of the Lord and that it did not trouble itself about God's revealed will. In the history of the chosen people from the time of the exodus God's manifestations and wonderful deeds of mercy are met by their displays of faithlessness. Because they would not hear, God finally abandoned them to their obstinacy. They should experience how bitter and wicked it is to forsake their God. Their stubborn will led them to destruction. Those whom God had redeemed from Egyptian slavery fell into the slavery of the heathen neighboring nations. There is no liberty without God. He who does not want to carry the light yoke must carry the iron one which men or nations lay upon them. From history the present generation should learn to listen to God's instructions and to walk in his way that it may have the peace and happiness which he has promised to those that fear him. Israel complains because it must submit to the authority of Gentile nations, because enemies invaded its country from all sides and destroyed it; why does it not have recourse to God? It is an easy affair for almighty God to take away the yoke of foreign rule and to make the enemy submit to Israel. The history of Israel is rich in examples of how the Lord with weak human strength has defeated and destroyed large armies of the enemies. If the nation is tired of war and oppression, it should be in earnest about its faith and religious life. Then the glorious promises will be fulfilled which the Lord has made to the faithful people. Those who hate the God of Israel should subject themselves to him and seek his mercy and the time of everlasting peace about which the prophets spoke will come. The Lord will give to his people rich harvests so that they will be nourished as the prophets had foretold. The Lord will give to his own rich harvests so that they will be nourished by the best of wheat. Flowers will cover the native soil so that the bees will obtain rich nourishment and the honeycombs in the rocky holes will overflow with honey. The rich harvest is a type of the rich spiritual blessings of Messianic times.

psalm 81

Deus stetit

An exhortation to judges and men in power

1. A psalm for Asaph.
   God has stood in the congregation of gods: and being in the midst of them he judgeth gods.

2. How long will you judge unjustly and accept the persons of the wicked?

3. Judge for the needy and fatherless: do justice to the humble and the poor.

4. Rescue the poor; and deliver the needy out of the hand of the sinner.

5. They have not known nor understood: they walk in the darkness: all the foundations of the earth shall be moved.

6. I have said: You are the gods and all of you the sons of the Most High.

7. But you, like men, shall die: and shall fall like one of the princes.

8. Arise, O God, judge thou the earth: for thou shalt inherit among all the nations.

God is the supreme Lord and Judge. All power which men have over their fellow men is from God and must be exercised according to the norms of divine justice. Judges and all persons in authority are visible representatives of the invisible Lord. Therefore in the Old Testament they are called "bene elohim," that is, "sons of God," or in one word "gods." They are called so because of their position: "persons near to God." The word *judges* is repeatedly used by the prophets. Complaints against the injustices and bribery of the Israelitic judges are found again

317

and again in the prophets. The psalmist wishes to instruct those in authority about the duty of impartiality and threatens those with divine punishment who do not want to be taught. The instruction therefore is put in the form of a court procedure which is held by God, the supreme Judge.

The judgment begins by inculcating the duties of those in authority (verses 2–4). The conduct of the judges is in direct contrast to their position; they should according to the example of God exercise their office impartially with unimpeachable justice. But on the contrary they make their decisions with partiality. They decide in favor of the guilty and refuse the innocent the protection of their rights. Because God is the refuge of the oppressed and defenseless, the defender of the widows, and the father of the orphans his representatives must also interest themselves in those who are often oppressed by the rich and mighty. Those in authority have been appointed especially to protect the poor and the orphans; it is their duty to take care of the weak and the needy. The upper classes of the population because of their social standing and their wealth are capable by themselves to secure their rights. But the great mass of the people cannot do this because to a great extent they live in a dependent condition and to secure a living they depend on those who have possessions. To see to it that the weak do not fall into the hands of unscrupulous exploiters is the most important work of the government.

Many do not want to understand that this is the duty of their calling. Therefore they must now pay heed to the divine judgment (verses 5–7). When those in authority have no understanding of their most important duty, when they do not rule according to the divine norm and standard but show partiality, when they do not walk in the light of the revealed will of the eternal Judge and do works that do not bear the light, then all the supports upon which a well-ordered state rests will crumble; for justice is the foundation of every government. Indeed God has given it the power to rule over man and to participate in the divine authority. On this account God called those in authority "bene elohim—sons of God." The name given by God is an expression of the nature of governmental authority and of its dignity. But position so near to God does not free from responsibility; it does not mean the privilege of misusing the power given. Before God all men are equal. Just as the law of death applies to all, even to kings and judges, so also the duty applies to all to give an account of stewardship to the divine Judge. He, who does not exercise his office according to the divine will, will be condemned; he will be hurled from his height as many of the worldly great have been humbled by him. The thought of the divine judgment before which those in authority will have to give an account reminds the psalmist of the other divine judgment before which all nations will be judged because the Gentile nations are also God's possession. Israel had to suffer many things from them and was oppressed by them. Therefore the psalmist beseeches God that he may also pass judgment upon them.

psalm 82

Deus, quis similis

A prayer against the enemies of God's Church

1. A canticle of a psalm for Asaph.

2. O God, who shall be like to thee? Hold not thy peace, neither be thou still, O God.

3. For lo, thy enemies have made a noise: and they that hate thee have lifted up the head.

4. They have taken a malicious counsel against thy people, and have consulted against thy saints.

5. They have said: Come and let us destroy them, so that they be not a nation: and let the name of Israel be remembered no more.

6. For they have contrived with one consent: they have made a covenant together against thee.

7. The tabernacles of the Edomites, and the Ismaelites:
Moab and the Agarens.

8. Gebal, and Ammon and Amalec: the Philistines, with the inhabitants of Tyre.

9. Yea, and the Assyrian also is joined with them: they are come to the aid of the sons of Lot.

10. Do to them as thou didst to Madian, and to Sisara: as to Jabin at the brook of Cison.

11. Who perished at Endor: and became as dung for the earth.

12. Make their princes like Oreb, and Zeb, and Zebee, and Salmana, all their princes.

319

13. Who have said: Let us possess the sanctuary of God for an inheritance.

14. O my God, make them like a wheel; and as stubble before the wind.

15. As fire which burneth the wood: and as a flame burning mountains:

16. So shalt thou pursue them with thy tempest; and shalt trouble them in thy wrath.

17. Fill their faces with shame; and they shall seek thy name, O Lord.

18. Let them be ashamed and troubled forever and ever: and let them be confounded and perish.

19. And let them know that the Lord is thy name: thou alone art the Most High over all the earth.

THE experience which the Church had again and again in its long history, namely, that men make war upon each other but in their hatred and animosity against the kingdom of God are in perfect harmony, was also the experience of the people of God in the Old Testament. This psalm stems from a time in which the Gentile neighboring nations were united with an empire to make war upon Israel in order to destroy it. Perhaps the composer had in mind the time of King Josaphat of Juda, 872–849, in which the Moabites, Ammonites, Edomites, and Agarites banded together against Juda (2 Chronicles 20). At that time the kingdom was in great danger. According to the judgment of the psalmist the Gentile nations did not go to war for mere political reasons, but because they hated Yahwe and wished to destroy his dominion upon earth. The victory of their united troops should be a triumph of their gods over the God of Israel; with the name of the people the name of their Divinity should also be erased. Thus the attack of the Gentiles was also directed against the honor of the Lord and against the fulfillment of his plan of salvation through Israel. In view of these religious backgrounds, the psalmist beseeches God for speedy divine intervention.

The psalm first of all describes the activities of the enemies (verses 3–9). It points out to God, the invisible King of Israel, how the confederate Gentile nations declared war without a just reason and that this war was mainly directed against his rule. The hatred against Yahwe, the one and only true God, is the main reason for their animosity toward Israel and the motive of their attacks. They want to strike at the people and God at the same time and destroy them. In bold arrogance they raise their head against him whom all creation should adore. As disunited as they are among themselves so as to fight each other in bloody battles, yet in their hatred against the chosen people they are united; they agree to take counsel with each other, to come to an agreement about a common plan of treachery and cunning, about the plan to defeat and destroy the kingdom and those who have placed themselves under the protection of Yahwe. They will not rest until the name of Israel is completely erased and disappears from the earth. Never again should this name be mentioned upon the earth. The kingdom of God should be forgotten forever. With a unanimity, which is rare, they formed an alliance in order that they might make common cause against the faith in the one true God and eliminate him. They acknowledge openly that the war is intended not only against the people but also against their God. The most bitter enemies of the Church are frequently such who once belonged to it and have fallen away from it or because of some other circumstances have been separated from it. Similar things happened to Israel. The fiercest enemies who with unquenchable hatred made war for centuries were Gentile nations who were related to Israel by blood. In the alliance, about which the psalmist speaks, they did not play an unimportant role. The psalmist mentions the Edomites, descendants of Esau, the son of the patriarch Isaac; and the Ismaelites who descended from Ismael, the son of Abraham and Hagar; he also mentions the Moabites and Ammonites, descendants of Lot, the nephew of Abraham; then he mentions the Agarites, an Arabian Bedouin tribe which was encamped on the border of the Syro-Arabian desert. Gebal, in the territory of the Edomites, and the Amalekites also allied themselves against them. These had even opposed the Israelites after the passage through the Red Sea on the way to Sinai. The Philistines, the most dangerous neighbors of Israel on the Mediterranean coast of Palestine, also allied themselves with the confederation. The inhabitants of the rich Tyre also became allies. The empire of Assyria assisted with well-armed troops the ruthless plans of the sons of Lot, the Moabites and the Ammonites, in order that it could itself lay hands on Palestine. The psalmist could have included the Egyptians; for all three, Sem, Cham, and Japheth, had united in making war upon Israel. The political and national interests of these nations were frequently in sharp contrast; but the hatred against the people of Yahwe bridged the chasm and united them in common purpose. Such has also been the experience of the Church through the centuries.

The present affliction makes the psalmist review the past. It was not the first time that Israel was confronted with such an alliance of its enemies. All past wars against the kingdom of Yahwe were disastrous to the opponents. The mention of those events in history is invariably connected with miraculous deeds of deliverance by the Lord. Upon these the psalmist bases his petition for divine intervention in the present tribulation (verses 10–19). From the great number the psalmist selects two victories from the time of the Judges which Israel had won only through divine intervention against such superior force: the victory of Gedeon over the Madianites and the defeat of King Jabin. May the Lord now also support the army of his people in a similar manner. The fourth and fifth chapter of the Book of Judges records the defeat of the Canaanite King Jabin of Hasor in Galilee and of his Field General Sisara at the brook Cison in the valley of Esdrelon. The poorly equipped Israelitic army, led by the Judge Debbora and the Field General Barak, stood ground near the village of Endor at Thabor. When the Canaanites advanced with their chariots and wanted to attack the weak front of the Israelites, a violent storm and a downpour of rain fell upon them so that the chariots were stuck in the soft soil of the valley. Utilizing the confusion that arose among the enemy's forces, the army of Debbora rushed down from Mount Thabor and slew the enemy and destroyed them so that the Cison was filled with corpses and the fallen were left unburied in the valley and remained lying there as dung for the soil. The seventh chapter of the Book of Kings records that Gedeon with three hundred men vanquished a Madianite army twenty times his size in the same valley. During the night he made an unexpected attack upon the Madianite's camp and the enemy troops were so confused that they began to fight each other and defeated themselves. Gedeon then occupied the fords of the Jordan in order to stop the retreat of the fleeing army. In the flight the Madianite princes, Oreb, Zeb, Zebee, and Salmana were seized and killed. God had prepared such extraordinary defeats for the enemies of his people in order to punish them; for they wanted to conquer and take possession of the lands of God which had been given to the Israelites by him as an inheritance. In so doing they laid violent hands on the kingdom of Yahwe. The victories of the kingdom of God in past times, during which its existence was seriously threatened, give confidence for the present and for all future times. Therefore the psalmist beseeches God that now also his miracles may be repeated. As it happened to the Canaanites under King Jabin and to the Madianites through Gedeon, so may it now happen through God's power to the allied enemies of Israel. In pictures which unmistakingly cover and picture the punishment already threatened to the Gentiles in the Pentateuch, the poet depicts the judgment of God which will come upon the Gentiles. They shall become as powerless as withered leaves in a whirlwind, like chaff which the wind picks up and blows away. God's wrath will come upon them like a destructive forest fire which destroys proud oaks and terebinths, like a fire which rages along the mountain side and burns all grass and shrubbery. May the wrath of God pursue them like a hurricane which carries away everything and which causes even walls to fall into ruins; may God's wrath fall upon them like a violent storm. May shame and disgrace cover them until

322

they come to realize that Yahwe is mightier than they and mightier than their gods; until the time when they bend their knees before his greatness and majesty and call upon his name, may he not have mercy on them. They should blush for shame because of their wickedness. The terror of the judgment of God shall come upon them. Their defeat shall be shameful. The composer of the second Book of Chronicles (20:29) records the defeat of the allied Moabites, Ammonites, Edomites, and Agarites, commenting that all countries were terrified when they heard that the Lord fought on the side of the Israelites. From such punishments the Gentiles will know that they have served false gods, that Yahwe alone is God and King, before whom all knees shall bend, and that they will not go unpunished if they attack and oppress his people and his kingdom. The final reason for his petition for punishment is not therefore the complete destruction of the Gentile nations, but rather their conversion.

psalm 83

Quam dilecta

The soul aspireth after heaven: rejoicing in the meantime, in being in communion of God's Church upon earth

1. Unto the end, for the wine presses, a psalm for the sons of Core.

2. How lovely are thy tabernacles, O Lord of hosts!

3. My soul longeth and fainteth for the courts of the Lord. My heart and my flesh have rejoiced in the living God.

4. For the sparrow hath found herself a house, and the turtle a nest for herself where she may lay her young ones.
Thy altars, O Lord of hosts, my king and my God.

5. Blessed are they that dwell in thy house, O Lord: they shall praise thee forever and ever.

6. Blessed is the man whose help is from thee: in his heart he hath disposed to ascend by steps,

7. In the vale of tears, in the place which he hath set.

8. For the lawgiver shall give a blessing, they shall go from virtue to virtue: the God of gods shall be seen in Sion.

9. O Lord God of hosts, hear my prayer: give ear, O God of Jacob.

10. Behold, O God our protector: and look on the face of thy Christ.

11. For better is one day in thy courts above thousands.
I have chosen to be an abject in the house of my God, rather than to dwell in the tabernacles of sinners.

12. For God loveth mercy and truth: the Lord will give grace and glory.

13. He will not deprive of good things them that walk in innocence: O Lord of hosts, blessed is the man that trusteth in thee.

THE psalmist is far away from Jerusalem, far away from his sanctuary. Perhaps one of the great feasts was approaching; for which according to the Law every male Israelite had to make a pilgrimage to the temple and to prepare himself in the land of caravans for his journey to the holy city. He was very sad because he could not join the pilgrims. Being sick at heart he composed this song of longing for the tabernacle of the Lord on Sion and praised the happiness of those who always dwelt in the holy place and as priests were permitted to serve the most high God. What a profound meaning these words of the psalm must have in their application to the Catholic house of God! What a longing must fill the heart of a Christian for the sanctuary! The temple of the Old Testament with all its beauty was after all but a shadow of the Christian place of worship. How happy the priest must be whose home is near the altar of God. Therefore the Church has him pray this psalm before any other prayer when he prepares himself to go to the altar and celebrate the most holy Sacrifice of the New Testament.

The psalm begins with an expression of longing for the sanctuary (verses 2–4): "How lovely is thy dwelling, O Lord of hosts!" It is not the palace of a ruler who separates himself from his people and has no understanding for the needs of his subjects. God indeed is the Lord of hosts. The heavenly spirits of infinite number obey him. Though he is infinitely greater than his creatures, yet he is also infinite love and goodness. Already in the Old Testament he kept his eyes and heart open to observe all the oppressions of his people and to help them. But lovelier is the dwelling of God in the New Testament because the Lord himself has really and truly set up his throne of mercy there. The heart of man finds rest only with God. He who seeks rest and peace in union with God will also desire union with him in the house of God. For this reason the psalmist longs for the courts of the sanctuary. The entire man rejoices in

324

the living and the life-giving God of the tabernacle; for there man finds his true home, his asylum. The Lord has given to every animal a home. Even the sparrow has its protection through kind Divine Providence; the swallow has its nest in which it can securely protect its brood. The home which God had given to the Israelites was the sanctuary with its two altars: the altar of holocaust and the altar of incense. In the New Testament it is the tabernacle upon our altars. When God himself, the Lord of hosts, the eternal King of Israel opens an asylum for his children, a place where they may find protection against their enemies, they are secure.

Since the sanctuary is a true home and a secure asylum, they are all happy who dwell in the house of God or make pilgrimages to it (verses 5–8). He who in the light of faith appreciates the value of the sanctuary and considers it to be a place for union with God will also consider everyone happy that is not excluded from this communion and who may be considered a member of the household of God. Blessed are the priests who as servants of God and mediators for God's community always dwell in the house of the Lord; and blessed are all whom the Lord has called to be united with him. They are therefore obligated to thank the Lord for this great grace. Blessed also is he who like the psalmist cannot appear personally in the house of God, but who has an earnest desire to be there and desires at least to make a spiritual pilgrimage insofar as in all his difficulties and needs he seeks strength, counsel, and help from God who thrones in the Holy of Holies over the cherubim. To one who in spirit patiently and with confidence goes to his God and Saviour in the tabernacle, this barren, unfruitful land changes into a fertile paradise, into a place rich in fountains and well blessed by early rains. Much richer flow the fountains of grace and God's blessings from heaven for those who with proper dispositions approach the altar of the Lord and long for the heavenly sanctuary. Christ spoke to the Samaritan woman about a water that stills all thirst and flows into eternal life (John 4:14). The grace which comes from the altar is not a mere casual drink which is drawn from the holy place, but an everlasting and ever-flowing fount of supernatural life that accompanies the pilgrim on his way to eternity in this vale of tears. Grace permeates the soul as a fruitful spring rain sinks into the soil and prepares it for the reception of further graces. Thus spiritual strength and the supernatural life grows until the recipient sees God in the sanctuary not only with the eyes of faith but will also be permitted to see him in heaven in the light of glory. The grace flowing from the altar gives a spiritual growth and maturity of manhood through Christ, so that the Christian will not permit himself to be blown about by every wind of doctrine and will in every respect grow in truth and love of him who is the head, Christ Jesus (Ephesians 4:12).

Even though he who pilgrimages to the sanctuary only in spirit is to be called blessed, the psalmist, nevertheless, desires ardently to dwell there in reality. Therefore he closes his psalm with the petition that God may permit him to go to the sanctuary (verses 9–13). The more one appreciates the value of God's house as the source of supernatural life the more he feels his separation and the more earnestly he appeals to God to put an end to the banishment from the sanctuary. Yahwe is indeed the Lord of hosts for whom there are no obstacles to any accomplishment. But in the heart of him also who dwells in the sanctuary, in the heart of the priest who daily stands in the holy place the longing for the tabernacle is daily renewed.

The more he values grace, the greater will be his desire. God is a strong fortress and a protecting shield for his people and for every member of his people. They are depending upon his assistance. It is a law of the Lord that man should seek help and protection from him and not from men. It is on this account that he erected his tabernacle among men. Therefore everyone who believes may rely on his protection, but especially his anointed may and must depend on the help of his grace.

And where should he go if the house and heart of God is closed to him? What can the world give as a substitute? It gives nothing that can equal in value living in the house of God, living in union with God and with Christ. One day in the courts of the temple brings more blessing and benefit than a thousand days in the world without blessing; for only what is done in union with God has value for eternity. It was permitted to the priests of the Old Testament to enter the inner parts of the sanctuary. But the place of the layman was in the fore-courts of the temple. However the priests and the lay people found these places more precious than dwelling in the richest tabernacles of sinners; for there is no joy of the world that can outweigh and replace supernatural joys which have their source in God alone. God alone is the light and sun of life. He gives his children more than sinners can give. He gives man his love and divine honors. To be loved by the infinite God, to be called to the communion of his Church, to the grace of divine sonship is the greatest love and the greatest honor. He who walks in innocence and does not tear asunder the bond of union with God is immeasurably rich; for God does not deny him any grace. He allows him to participate in his own eternal riches and in his own inexhaustible happiness. Enthusiastic about the great fullness of blessings received through union with God the psalmist joyfully cries out at the close of the psalm: "O Lord of hosts, blessed is he who trusts in thee."

psalm 84

Benedixisti, Domine

The coming of Christ, to bring peace and salvation to man

1. Unto the end, for the sons of Core, a psalm.

2. Lord, thou hast blessed thy land: thou hast turned away the captivity of Jacob.

3. Thou hast forgiven the iniquity of thy people: thou hast covered all their sins.

4. Thou hast mitigated all thy anger: thou hast turned away from the wrath of thy indignation.

5. Convert us, O God our saviour: and turn thy anger from us.

6. Wilt thou be angry with us forever: or wilt thou extend thy wrath from generation to generation?

7. Thou wilt turn, O God, and bring us to life: and thy people shall rejoice in thee.

8. Show us, O Lord, thy mercy; and grant us thy salvation.

9. I will hear what the Lord God will speak in me: for he will speak peace unto his people.
And unto his saints: and unto them that are converted to the heart.

10. Surely his salvation is near to them that fear him: that glory may dwell in our land.

11. Mercy and truth have met each other: justice and peace have kissed.

12. Truth has sprung out of the earth: and justice hath looked down from heaven.

13. For the Lord will give goodness: and our earth shall yield her fruit.

14. Justice shall walk before him: and shall set his steps in the way.

UPON the edict of King Cyrus who put an end to the Babylonian captivity of Israel, forty-two thousand returned to their native country and soon began to lay the cornerstone of the new temple. Yet many not having the strong faith of the Prophet Aggeus and of other

327

pious men became despondent and lost their first fervor because they felt disappointed. They had hoped that with the return home the Messianic era would begin, and now they saw that they were visited with every kind of adversity. But even upon strong souls the bad conditions made their impression. They could not doubt the truth of the divine promises, but their longing for the fulfillment of the promised salvation increased. From this religious view the psalm is to be understood. The Christian finds himself in a situation similar to that of those who returned home from the captivity. He is redeemed, but is still afflicted with adversities and spiritual needs. On this account he also desires the promised fulfillment of salvation. Thus the psalm becomes a prayer of longing.

The psalm begins with a petition for complete restoration (verses 2–8). When punitive justice fell upon the kingdom of Juda, many thousands had to go into banishment; the land too came under a curse. For sixty years or more it lay in waste; its inhabitants were plundered. The ways that led to Sion were desolate; the people mourned because no one came to the festivals. The return of the captives meant therefore the removal of the curse and the restoration to God's favor. With the fate of the descendants of Jacob the fate of their native country has also changed. The guilt of those who returned home was taken away through God's mercy; sins were forgiven and were covered forever through the infinite love and kindness of God. But penance and reconciliation were required for the ending of the exile. Now the people could again breathe more easily. The wrath of the Lord which rested upon them like a heavy burden had departed from them. They were no longer to feel the glow of the divine wrath. God's justice could have demanded a harder and longer penance than the seventy years exile; however, his mercy shortened the time of the punishment.

But the return home from exile, the forgiveness of the guilt, and the restoration to God's favor was not yet complete redemption. It did not bring the promised fulfillment, the Messianic salvation, nor the longed-for fullness of peace and blessing. The people still see themselves afflicted by hostile men, by poor harvests, and famine. The time of suffering is not yet passed; the divine wrath has not yet fully ceased. The country is still far from having the prosperous times which it had under King David. This prosperity in David's time was to the prophets a type of the Messianic times. If the Lord would always be mindful of sin, he would have to be wrathful eternally; he would have to punish constantly and no one could exist before him. Even the children and children's children would have to do penance for the sins of their fathers because no penance can make sufficient satisfaction to the divine mercy; but this cannot be, for God's mercy is so great that the Lord waits to have mercy on his people and arises to pardon them (Isaias 30:18). Thus the psalmist beseeches God for a revivification of his people and for divine mercy. May the Lord now do what he has shown to the Prophet Ezechiel in the great vision of the revival of dead men's bones which was a type of the restoration of Israel to a new life (chapter 37). Then all Israel's sorrow will cease and in the full enjoyment of the Messianic salvation Israel will rejoice in the blessings and graces of the Lord. Longing for this fulfillment the psalmist beseeches the Lord: "Let us, O Lord, behold thy grace and mercy; give us thy salvation, which thou hast promised through thy prophet." Country and people after the return from the exile are a type of the Christian soul which, though redeemed, is not yet in the condition of our first parents before original sin. Therefore the Christian too longs for this fulfillment.

Now the psalmist awaits the divine answer and is full of expectation for the final salvation (verses 9–14). "I will listen to what God the Lord promises." He speaks of peace for all who seek to be and are in union with God. No message is heard so emphatically and frequently throughout the Messianic promises as the message of peace. Original sin and the breaking of the covenant have disturbed the harmonious relations between man and God and as a consequence have brought all evil into the world and all disaster upon Israel. The restoration of harmony is the first step in effecting salvation. "He will give peace" (Isaias 26:12). "He will direct it like a stream to his people" (Isaias 66:12). "He will reveal the fullness of peace and secure existence" (Jeremias 33:6). "He will make a covenant of peace with his people" (Ezechiel 34:25). May this time of peace be ever so far in the future, it is nevertheless near for those who fear God; for they already have peace of soul and the expectation of eternal peace and its completion. For the fear of the Lord is a source of life and an escape from the snares of death (Proverbs 14:27). The sun of justice shines upon the God-fearing man (Malachias 3:20 [4:2]). When this time of peace has come, the glory of the Lord will dwell in all the land. Sacred Scripture calls the "glory of the Lord" the special presence of God over the Ark of the Covenant in the temple. In the Old Testament it was limited to this one place, but in Messianic times God's habitation will be everywhere on earth where tabernacles will be erected.

Already the time of fulfillment is near; already God's love and fidelity have descended upon earth and brought justice and peace to man. When St. Paul wrote "But when the goodness and kindness of God our Saviour appeared and brought us salvation . . ." (Titus 3:4), he saw that these divine perfections were in the person of Christ. The psalmist considered them poetically as different persons who meet each other upon earth like good friends and greet each other with a kiss. In the realization of the decree of redemption the fidelity of God works together with merciful love. Justice, the pardoning of man, and peace with God are their fruits. Fidelity sprouts from the earth; for the Messias, whom Isaias in 4:3 calls the fruit of the land, is the fulfillment of the divine plan of salvation. But justice looks down from heaven because the sanctification of men is entirely dependent on the heavenly gifts of grace and the sacraments. God's will to save, so to say, pursues the development of his work until it has come to completion at the end of time. With man the earth also is included in the Messianic blessing of salvation and to it is given again paradisaic fertility. This is a constant characteristic of the Messianic picture drawn by the prophets and a consequence of taking away the curse which has afflicted the earth since original sin. All salvation comes from God. Like a herald it goes before him by the announcement of the glad message and accompanies him at every step which he makes for the redemption and sanctification of man; for all the ways of the Lord are mercy and fidelity. What the psalmist sees in a vision of the future we see fulfilled in Christ. Yet the completion of salvation is also for us an object of promise and of longing expectation. And thus for the Christian the promise of eternal peace is the foundation of our hope in its eternal possession.

psalm 85

Inclina, Domine

A prayer for God's grace to assist us to the end

1. A prayer for David himself.
   Incline thy ear, O Lord, and hear me: for I am needy and poor.

2. Preserve my soul, for I am holy: save thy servant, O my God, that trusteth in thee.

3. Have mercy on me, O Lord, for I have cried to thee all the day.

4. Give joy to the soul of thy servant, for to thee, O Lord, I have lifted up my soul.

5. For thou, O Lord, art sweet and mild: and plenteous in mercy to all that call upon thee.

6. Give ear, O Lord to my prayer: and attend to the voice of my petition.

7. I have called upon thee in the day of my trouble: because thou hast heard me.

8. There is none among the gods like unto thee, O Lord: and there is none according to thy works.

9. All the nations thou hast made shall come and adore before thee, O Lord: and they shall glorify thy name.

10. For thou art great and dost wonderful things: thou art God alone.

11. Conduct me, O Lord, in thy way, and I will walk in thy truth: let my heart rejoice that it may fear thy name.

12. I will praise thee, O Lord my God, with my whole heart, and I will glorify thy name forever.

13. For thy mercy is great toward me: and thou hast delivered my soul out of the lower hell.

14. O God, the wicked are risen up against me, and the assembly of the mighty have sought my soul: and they have not set thee before their eyes.

15. And thou, O Lord, art a God of compassion, and merciful, patient, and of much mercy, and true.

16. O look upon me, and have mercy on me: give thy command to thy servant, and save the son of thy handmaid.

17. Show me a token for good: that they who hate me may see, and be confounded, because thou, O Lord, hast helped me and has comforted me.

M AN during this life is surrounded by many enemies and dangers which threaten the life of his soul. When the world with its enticements and temptations and godless men seeks to tempt men to faithlessness toward God, then it is Satan who goes about like a roaring lion seeking whom he may devour (1 Peter 5:8). The soul is not strong enough by its own power to withstand always and everywhere the enemies and dangers of salvation; only the power and grace of God can keep man from falling. The psalmist when he composed this prayer, thought first of all about saving his bodily life which he saw threatened. But since this prayer which all should pray, by itself enlarges thought, the psalmist passed over to the salvation of the more valuable life of the soul. The psalm gives simultaneously to the petitioner and to God the reasons upon which the confident prayer is based; hence the psalmist prays for grace to be able to walk faithfully in the way of the commandments.

The prayer of confidence draws its strength above all else from a correct knowledge of oneself (verses 1–4) especially on one's own weakness and incompetency. First of all humility gives to prayer a titanic power. Therefore the psalmist begins with the words: "Incline, O Lord, thy ear and hear me, for I am poor and needy." The Apostle Paul in the epistle to the Romans has drawn a picture of the condition in which man finds himself without the help of divine grace: "But I see another law in my members warning against the law of my mind and making me prisoner to the law of sin that is in my members" (7:23). A second reason for our confidence in prayer and for God's hearing our prayer is union with God. The Israelite was a member of the people of the covenant. Through membership in the chosen people, and on that account of a sanctified people, the psalmist could call himself sanctified and a servant of God. More intimate is a Christian's union with God through the Church united with Christ. He to whom the Lord has manifested a special love by calling him to be united to his community may confidently expect that he will continue his work and will not deny his love to the petitioner and will give him hearing and help. He may rely on this so much the more when all day long he prays with great perseverance. The just man of the Old Testament was convinced of the fact that God does not deny a hearing to persevering prayer. With this confidence Judith consoled the inhabitants of Bethulia: "Know that the Lord will hear your prayer if you continue before the Lord with fasting and prayer" (Judith 4:12). Christ has spoken the same truth in the parable of a petitioning friend (Luke 11:5 seq.). When with humility and perseverance there is also devotion, when prayer is offered with the greatest sincerity and is the fruit of a pious life requested by a true servant of God, then there will be greater certainty that the prayer will be heard.

Confidence in God is also based on a knowledge of the divine Nature (verses 5–10). To a prayerful soul it is a consolation to know that God is good and ready to help even when a sinner prays to him. He is inexhaustibly rich in love to all who call upon him. No matter how many pray to him daily, no matter how numerous their anxieties and cares, God never ceases in his love. Even he who has offended him may approach his love; for it is great in forgiving. With a confidence in this infinite love the psalmist prays that the Lord may pay heed to his petition. When the merciful God once pays heed to the needs and afflictions of a man, his sympathy is aroused and help will not be denied. On this account the psalmist is full of confidence that he will be heard as often as he calls upon the almighty and good God in the day of need. The Lord is all good and is willing to help; he is almighty and can help in every situation; he can even help when death threatens. The Gentiles boasted much about the power of their gods, but they were as nothing. God's deeds in creation and in the history of men and nations, especially in the history of the chosen people, are so awesome that the human mind cannot comprehend them, that nothing in the world may be found that will measure up to them. Before him all nations must bend their knees. Though they now refuse to do this, though they now refuse to know and acknowledge God, the time will come when all will bend their knees before the majesty of his Name, when they will appear before his throne and with Israel will join in the praises of the one and only true God. God alone is the God who can work miracles. The pages of the history of the chosen people like the pages of Church history are filled with testimonies of the powerful deeds of God.

The second part of the psalm (verses 11–17) contains a threefold petition: for instruction, for strength, and for an external sign of divine mercy and help which will be knowable to the enemy also. In order to withstand with certainty all dangers and temptations that threaten eternal salvation, it is necessary to know the way that leads to it. Only God knows the way because he has prepared it; only he can give infallible instruction. Therefore the petition is as follows: "Lord teach me the way that I may walk in thy truth." But man must make his soul receptive to divine instructions; he must direct his thoughts and desires to God. But even for this God must give his grace; he must prepare the human heart to learn to love and to fear his holy Name. When the soul is filled with the knowledge of God's greatness and love, it feels an urge to praise him. Then the praise of God will not be mere lip worship, but really an affair of the heart; then man knows something really great and worthy of praise. He knows what to proclaim about the sublime Name of the Lord. But God does not only deserve praise because of his great deeds in creation and in history, he deserves it from every individual to whom he gives the richness of his love and mercy. Is there anyone who will not admit with the psalmist that the Lord has saved his soul from the abyss of the underworld? Does not redemption mean more than being saved from the abyss of hell? Is not every grace which keeps man from sinning gravely or forgives sins committed, a deliverance from the depths of the underworld, the kingdom of the damned?

After the instruction about the way, strength must also be given in order that man may ward off all dangers. Mighty opponents rise against him, unscrupulous and brutal men, people who are not concerned about God and who do not bother about his judgments. But the Lord cannot deliver his servant into the power of his enemy even when he has sinned; for he is a merciful and kind God, long-suffering, great in love and fidelity, a God who will not always be wrathful, but who will help everyone who turns to him with a right disposition. For a proof of this divine love and fidelity the psalmist also prays: "Give me strength that I may resist my enemies and walk the way of thy commandments, give it to me because I am entirely dependent upon thee and because I belong to thee." He calls himself the servant of God and son of his handmaid; he compares himself to those who were born as children of slaves and therefore remained the life-long property of the lord. He belongs to the house of God and is God's possession. In conclusion he begs for a visible sign of grace, a miracle of the divine work of salvation in order that the enemy may see and acknowledge in shame that God is the helper and consoler of him who has been persecuted.

psalm 86

Fundamenta ejus

The glory of the Church of Christ

1. For the sons of Core, a psalm of a canticle.
   The foundations, thereof are in the holy mountains.

2. The Lord loveth the gates of Sion above all the tabernacles of Jacob.

3. Glorious things are said of thee, O city of God.

4. I will be mindful of Rahab and of Babylon knowing me.
   Behold the foreigners and Tyre, and the people of the Ethiopians, they were there.

5. Shall not Sion say: This man and that is born of her? And the highest himself hath founded her.

6. The Lord shall tell in his writings of peoples and of princes, of them that have been in her.

7. The dwelling in thee is as it were of all rejoicing.

THIS psalm was most likely composed at the time of the miraculous deliverance of Jerusalem in the year 701 when the Assyrian King Sennacherib besieged the city with 185,000 men. The angel of God destroyed the entire army in one night before it could shoot a single arrow into the city. This miraculous preservation of the city strengthened the faith of Israel in the Messianic prophecies according to which Sion was to be the center of the world-wide kingdom of God. The psalm is a prophecy of the indestructibility, unity, and catholicity of the Church of the New Testament, the mother of all nations.

Sion, the Church, is the city on the mountain established by God himself (verses 1–2). It is established in this world, but it is not of this world. Its foundation is on high places; namely, on the eternal divine power and wisdom. The Prophet Isaias (2:2) considers Mount Sion with its sanctuary a type of the Church towering over the highest mountains of the earth so that the temple becomes the center and assembly place of all nations. The Lord loves Sion because it is his creation. He loves it more than all his other works because more than all others it contributes to his glorification upon earth and to the fulfillment of his plan of salvation. The events of the year 701 were a prophetic and typical indication of its privilege. God permitted that the entire nation, all its cities and villages, should fall into the hands of the Assyrians. Jerusalem alone remained untouched in the midst of ruins. The enemy was not permitted to invade its walls; he was not permitted to shoot a single arrow into the city.

The prophets said many glorious things about Sion, the city of God, and about the Church of Jesus Christ, the mother of nations (verses 3–5). The language of Isaias becomes a spirited hymn when he describes the beauty of this new Sion and the plenitude of grace which it offers. It is endowed with divine light and with the richest blessings of heaven. It is loved and honored by all nations. It will become the spiritual mother of all nations, their true home, their father's house.

Therefore the same prophet requests Sion to enlarge its tents that all nations may find room. As the representatives of the Gentile nations that came to Sion the psalmist mentions the arrogant Rahab, a symbolic name for Egypt, and Babylon, the two world kingdoms on the Nile and Euphrates, both of which had fought for centuries for the possession of Palestine. He mentions the Philistines, the archenemy of Israel, and the rich Tyre proud of its independence, and the savage Ethiopians. All these will honor Sion as their spiritual mother who had given supernatural life to them; they will consider the holy city as their true home and birthplace because there they were reborn. Indeed, some day, when all nations shall have become members of God's kingdom and there will be but one flock and shepherd, one will be able to say of the Messianic Sion that all the world is born there. From this it is known that the Church is of divine origin, that the city of God is a heavenly establishment. Human power is not sufficient for conquering and winning such a world. Such power comes from God.

The call to the kingdom of God, the reception into the city of God is exclusively the right of God for it is an unmerited and an unmeritable grace (verses 6–7). With this meaning in mind the Apostle Paul writes to Timothy: "Who hath delivered us and called us by his holy calling, not according to our works, but according to his own purpose, and grace, which was given us in Christ Jesus before the times of the world" (2 Timothy 1:9). The psalmist gives us this truth in a picture: God alone keeps a list of the citizens of the Messianic Sion; he must keep the record that this or that man, that this or that people was born in his city; that is, born again and therefore received citizenship from him. Only to those who were called by God will the Church be a spiritual mother. No one can come to her unless God has drawn him by his grace. As a city of supernatural life and of most intimate union with God, Sion is already the city of joy and jubilation. It will be it so much the more joyful, the more graciously its members accept the divine life and with it divine peace. The joy will be perfected when the kingdom of God at the end of time will be complete and when the eternal glorification will begin.

psalm 87

Domine, Deus salutis

A prayer of one under grievous affliction: it corresponds to Christ in his passion and alludes to his death and burial

1. A canticle of a psalm for the sons of Core: unto the end, for Maheleth, to answer understanding of Eman the Ezrahite.

2. O Lord, the God of my salvation: I have cried in the day, and in the night before thee.

3. Let my prayer come in before thee; and incline thy ear to my petition.

4. For my soul is filled with evils: and my life has drawn nigh to hell.

5. I am counted among them that go down to the pit: I am become as a man without help,

6. Free among the dead. Like the slain sleeping in the sepulchres whom thou rememberest no more: and they are cast off from thy hand.

7. Thy have laid me in the lower pit: in the dark places and in the shadow of death.

8. Thy wrath is strong over me: and all thy waves thou hast brought in upon me.

9. Thou hast put my acquaintance far from me: they have set me an abomination to themselves.
I was delivered up, and came not forth.

10. My eyes languished through poverty.
All the day I cried to thee, O Lord: I stretched out my hands to thee.

11. Wilt thou show wonders to the dead? Or shall physicians raise to life, and give praise to thee?

12. Shall anyone in the sepulchre declare thy mercy: and thy truth in destruction?

13. Shall thy wonders be known in the dark: and thy justice in the land of forgetfulness?

14. But I, O Lord, have cried to thee: and in the morning my prayer shall prevent thee.

15. Lord, why castest thou off my prayer: why turnest thou away thy face from me.

16. I am poor and in labors from my youth: and being exalted have been humbled and troubled.

17. Thy wrath hath come upon me: and thy terrors have troubled me.

18. They have come round about me like water all the day: they have compassed me about together.

19. Friend and neighbor thou hast put far from me: and my acquaintance because of misery.

SADNESS because of the nearness of death pervades this psalm. One who is very sick beseeches God in prayer. He begins his supplication not with a complaint but with an act of faith and confidence. The Lord is the God of my salvation, he is the Saviour, the God that can and will help. He strikes and heals; he inflicts wounds, but cures the wounds which he has inflicted. With this faith and confidence the cry of the sick man ascends to heaven day and night. When this cry reaches the throne of God and when he pays heed to the cry, then he is sure that his prayer will be answered; for the all-good and merciful God cannot tyrannically close his heart to the needs of his creatures.

Now the sick man simply and impressively makes known his suffering to the merciful God and to the heavenly Physician. How much affliction and sorrow is contained in the few words: "My soul is filled with suffering" (verses 2–8). Life will soon come to an end; death already stands at the bedside and waits for its prize. Relatives and acquaintances have already given him up; they already count him among the dead and speak about his burial; they make the necessary arrangements and think about dividing the inheritance which he shall leave behind. They see how his strength diminishes day by day. It is only a question of time till the last remnant of strength will vanish. Thus for some time he appears as one who has already died even though he still lives. Among men he is soon forgotten like those who have fallen on the battlefield and are buried in a common grave. Soon nobody will know who lies buried therein. Over the place the plough furrows the ground so that it is not even known as a burying place. No memorial stone will be there to call him back to our remembrance. Indeed, it might seem that God considered him as one dead, as a man whose life's thread was already cut. The sick man feels as if he were encompassed by night, as if he had already entered the kingdom of the dead. God's wrath lies heavily upon him; it is hard for him to believe that love can bring such suffering to him. As surf of the sea blown by the wind rolls to the shore in unceasing waves, so likewise the Lord has permitted tribulation upon tribulation to come upon him.

Great suffering is always easier to bear when affectionate fellows are willing to help as much as they can; but it can become unbearable when the sufferer is abandoned by all men (verses 9–13). During such sufferings the sick man seems to have prayed this psalm. Even friends did not come near him; they have become strangers to him. God has permitted this sorrow. The psalmist considers this to be caused directly by God himself because he does not distinguish between willing a thing and permitting it. The friends because of their false understanding of the reason of suffering can only interpret the grave sickness of their friend as a punishment from God and therefore hold that the divine wrath has fallen upon him; they keep themselves aloof lest they themselves might be struck by the divine anger. In this lonesomeness his own home becomes a prison in which the sick man lies fettered throughout his suffering. Because of continued suffering and tears his eyes are dimmed and sight begins to leave him. Day after day from morning until night he prays God from his sickbed to help and console him. Again and again he stretches out his tired arms toward heaven in prayer that the Lord may grant him grace.

However the sickness continues; death comes nearer and nearer. Why, he asks himself and God, should I die so soon? He speaks with King Ezechias: "In the midst of my days I shall go to the gates of hell: I sought for the residue of my days . . . For hell shall not confess to thee, neither shall death praise thee: neither shall they who go down into the pit look for thy truth. The living alone shall give praise to thee" (Isaias 38:10 and 18 seq.). The dead in the underworld are no longer witnesses of the divine power of miracles which reveals itself only among the living and therefore they can no longer praise this power. For them the time of grace has ended; they no longer experience the manifestations of divine mercy and love. The promises which the Lord gave to his people are no longer for them. Therefore those in the underworld can no longer sing songs of praise about the love and fidelity of God. In the kingdom of the dead no information is given about the wonderful deeds which the Lord continues to perform for his people. There nothing is learned about events in the history of Israel, about the way God has defeated and destroyed its enemies to exalt and strengthen his people. Why then should God deliver man to death whose only joy it is to praise the Lord for his deeds and for his mercy.

Severe suffering can still be bearable, even when human consolation is wanting, as long as God gives his perceptible consolation to the sick man. But the psalmist also feels himself abandoned by God (verses 14–19). Even in the early morning he directs his prayer to God, but there is no answer. His soul hungers for consolation. Since men do not give it, he longs for a word of divine pity, but in vain. What if his former friends should be right when they consider him a man with whom God is displeased. Why has God turned his countenance away from him; why has he withdrawn his mercy and love? Why does the Lord refuse to pay attention to his need? Why does he not help him? In his sad feeling of abandonment he puts these anxious questions. If the sufferings were only from yesterday, there would be an easy explanation. But even from his youth the petitioner was weak and sick; for a long time he bore his sickness. Too long a time for human strength the fear of the wrath of God troubled him; it robbed him of spiritual peace. Like a terrible storm the glow of God's wrath came upon him. What should he still say about such visitations? Just as the dams of a swollen river break and the floods flow over the land, so God's visitations of sickness are encompassing him. No help is in sight. Those who could, perhaps, help or mitigate his suffering, his friends and acquaintances, God has kept from him in order that he may drink the chalice to the dregs.

psalm 88

Misericordias Domini

*The perpetuity of the Church of Christ in consequence of
the promise of God: which notwithstanding,
God permits her to suffer sometimes
most grievous afflictions*

1. Of understanding for Ethan the Ezrahite.

2. The mercies of the Lord I will sing forever.
   I will show forth thy truth with my mouth to generation and generation.

3. For thou hast said: Mercy shall be built up forever in the heavens: thy truth shall be prepared in them.

4. I have made a covenant with my elect: I have sworn to David my servant:

5. Thy seed will I settle forever.
   And I will build up thy throne unto generation and generation.

6. The heavens shall confess thy wonders, O Lord: and thy truth in the Church of the saints.

7. For who in the clouds can be compared to the Lord: or who among the sons of God shall be like to God?

8. God, who is glorified in the assembly of the saints: great and terrible above all them that are about him.

9. O Lord, God of hosts, who is like to thee? Thou art mighty, O Lord, and thy truth is round about thee.

10. Thou rulest the power of the sea: and appeasest the motion of the waves thereof.

11. Thou hast humbled the proud one, as one that is slain: with the arm of thy strength thou hast scattered thy enemies.

12. Thine are the heavens, and thine is the earth: the world and the fullness thereof thou hast founded:

13. The north and the sea thou hast created.
    Thabor and Hermon shall rejoice in thy name:

340

14. Thy arm is with might.
Let thy hand be strengthened and thy right hand exalted:

15. Justice and judgment are the preparation of thy throne.
Mercy and truth shall go before thy face:

16. Blessed is the people that knoweth jubilation.
They shall walk, O Lord, in the light of thy countenance.

17. And in thy name they shall rejoice all the day, and in thy justice they shall be exalted.

18. For thou art the glory of their strength: and in thy good pleasure shall our horn be exalted.

19. For our protection is of the Lord, and our king the holy one of Israel.

20. Then thou spokest in a vision to thy saints, and saidst: I have laid help upon one that is mighty, and have exalted one chosen out of my people.

21. I have found David my servant: with my holy oil I have anointed him.

22. For my hand shall help him: and my arm shall strengthen him.

23. The enemy shall have no advantage over him: nor the son of iniquity have power to hurt him.

24. And I will cut down his enemies before his face: and them that hate him I will put to flight.

25. And my truth and my mercy shall be with him: and in my name shall his horn be exalted.

26. And I will set his hand in the sea; and his right hand in the rivers.

27. He shall cry out to me: Thou art my father: my God, and the support of my salvation.

28. And I will make him my first-born forever: high above the kings of the earth.

29. I will keep my mercy for him forever: and my covenant faithful to him.

30. And I will make his seed to endure forevermore: and his throne as the days of heaven.

31. And if his children forsake my Law, and walk not in my judgments:

32. If they profane my justices: and keep not my commandments:

33. I will visit their iniquities with a rod: and their sins with stripes.

34. But my mercy I will not take away from him: nor will I suffer my truth to fail.

35. Neither will I profane my covenant: and the words that proceed from my mouth I will not make void.

36. Once have I sworn by my holiness: I will not lie unto David:

37. His seed shall endure forever.

38. And his throne as the sun before me: and as the moon perfect forever, and a faithful witness in heaven.

39. But thou hast rejected and despised: thou hast been angry with thy anointed.

40. Thou hast overthrown the covenant of thy servant: thou hast profaned his sanctuary on the earth.

41. Thou hast broken down all his hedges: thou hast made his strength fear.

42. All that pass by the way have robbed him: he is become a reproach to his neighbors.

43. Thou hast set up the right hand of them that oppress him: thou hast made all his enemies to rejoice.

44. Thou hast turned away the help of his sword: and hast not assisted him in battle.

45. Thou hast made his purification to cease: and thou hast cast his throne down to the ground.

46. Thou hast shortened the days of his time: thou hast covered him with confusion.

47. How long, O Lord, turnest thou away unto the end? Shall thy anger burn like fire?

48. Remember what my substance is: for thou hast made all the children of men in vain.

49. Who is the man that shall live and not see death: that shall deliver his soul from the hand of hell?

50. Lord, where are thy ancient mercies, according to what thou didst swear to David in thy truth?

51. Be mindful, O Lord, of the reproach of thy servants (which I have held in my bosom) of many nations.

52. Wherewith thy enemies have reproached, O Lord: wherewith they have reproached the change of thy anointed.

53. Blessed be the Lord forevermore. So be it, so be it.

IN THE history of the world there had been only one royal house which according to divine decree was destined to transcend the vicissitudes of the mundane in order to rule forever. God himself gave the guarantee of its continued existence in a solemn promise. This was the house of David. From it the Messias was to descend. David was to give to the world the Messias, the Ruler of the eternal and universal kingdom of the Messianic future, the Christ-King. The collapse of the Davidic royal house was considered, therefore, different by Israel than the collapse of Gentile dynasties. With the downfall of the Davidic kingdom an essential part of its faith and hope also seemed to be lost. Therefore the people of God could not be satisfied with the thought that this was the fate of all thrones, but it wanted a clear answer to the question that would reconcile the collapse of Israel with the divine promise. Religiously indifferent Israelites may have been inclined to entertain doubts about God's truth and fidelity. But the believer steadfastly held to the truth of the promise. This promise was a strong anchor of hope to Israel in the difficult times it had to endure even after its downfall. Israel was certain that the Lord would again re-establish the ruined house of David. The psalmist's question was: "How long, O Lord, wilt thou conceal thy countenance? When will the time of the great King come?"

Hence the psalmist begins his song with a confession of faith in the eternally true and almighty God, with a praise of the true God (verses 2–5). He does not wish to complain because the Lord has deeply humbled his people, but he will sing a song of praise about God's mercy and this song shall be sung in all generations to come. In this song he will glorify God's fidelity. In doing this the composer has given his "amen" to God's promises, the reliability of which others have doubted. He has thereby rejected at the very start everything which in his song might be considered a criticism about the conduct of the Lord. God had promised David through the Prophet Nathan that he would never withdraw his mercy even after he had been dead for a long time. He will add grace to grace; he will bring increase from increase; he will add stone upon stone to the house of David; he will add generation to generation until the structure will be completed in the Messias. Because of the divine truth and fidelity God's word stands as firm as heaven. It stands so much firmer because the Lord gave it in the form of a covenant, of a solemnly accepted duty and, so to say, sealed it with an oath. He said to David through the prophet: "And thy house shall be faithful, and thy kingdom forever before thy face, and thy throne shall be firm forever" (2 Kings 7:16).

The promise is more certain to be fulfilled if the promiser is reliable and has power to fulfill the promise. But God is not only faithful and true,

343

he is also almighty. Acknowledging this fact, the psalmist begins his song of praise about God's greatness (verses 6–19). God is exalted above the angels. Even the heavens are astounded at the deeds of the divine power, and the innumerable blessed spirits praise God's fidelity at all times. From the beginning the angels were witnesses of all the wonderful works of the Lord in his act of creation and in the history of his chosen people. They themselves are a masterwork of the power, wisdom, and love of God. But the Lord infinitely surpasses them. Even in heaven among the angels, the sons of God, there is none that can be compared to him. When God appears surrounded by his holy spirits, by the myriads of servants of his glory, his majesty and the sheen of his glory surpasses all the beauty and glory of this spiritual world even though the latter surpasses by far the glory of the visible world. In his majesty, demanding reverence, he stands before them and they bow before his immeasurable greatness.

In the kingdom of the visible creation God is also infinitely majestic. One may search the entire universe and include all the greatness, beauty, and power which exist, yet all remain infinitely less than the greatness, beauty, and power of the Creator. Mighty is God in this visible kingdom and in it too he is infinitely faithful. How immensely great and broad is the earth's ocean! How terrible is the storm of the elements! But God rules the ocean by his word. When he commands, the storm lashes the waters so that the waves tower high and form deep troughs in the sea. And again only one word of his power is needed and the storm subsides and the wild waves become quiet. Thus the Lord also stills the turmoils of war which hostile nations inflict upon Israel. With his strong arm he slew Rahab, a symbolic name for proud Egypt, as easily as if he pierced it with a sword and he destroyed it because it waged war against his people. He needed only his powerful *fiat* to still the storm. God's power is unlimited in heaven and on earth; for heaven and earth, the entire universe, are his unlimited possession. To him belongs everything that is upon earth, all animate and inanimate creatures. To him belong all plants and animals; all human beings belong to him because they are his work. He has created north and south, Thabor and Hermon, the mountains signifying the East and the West. The whole earth is God's creation and by its very existence jubilantly praises the name, the majesty of God.

God's infinite majesty has also revealed itself in the history of Israel. His arm has shown the strength of a hero; his deeds show forth the strength of his right hand. With his power is paired his incorruptible justice. Justice and righteousness are the support of his throne, the foundation of his dominion over the world. He directs the nations according to the eternal norms of his sanctity. But his infinite justice is mitigated and transfigured by his infinite love and fidelity. As servants and heralds go before the king, so also mercy and fidelity walk before the divine Majesty. Blessed, therefore, is a people who greets with jubilation this King as its Ruler, who is permitted to walk in the light of his countenance, in the glory of his mercy and grace. This blessed people is Israel which the Lord has chosen as his special possession. He has given to it what he has denied to the Gentile world. Israel may rejoice because of its God and King whose name is ineffable because of his majesty. Israel may be proud of its unique election which has as a consequence a plenitude of other graces. The great world powers may boast about the extent of their kingdom; they may be proud of their culture. Yet Israel surpasses them all in the majesty of the invisible King. Yahwe is the glory and crown of his people. His love and grace has given them a renown and moral strength to which no other nation can lay claim. In him Israel is well-secured; for he is the strong shield which covers the nation against the attacks of the enemy. Its king belongs to the Holy One of Israel; he is the representative of the Most High whose glory fills the universe.

Thus the mighty and faithful God, this majestic invisible King of Israel has given his promises to David (verses 20–38). The psalmist now describes events with poetic freedom. He speaks of visions in which the Lord revealed himself to his saints, most likely to the Prophets Samuel and Nathan. In these visions they were informed by God that he had provided a courageous youth with supernatural strength, that he had selected David, the youngest son of Jesse, from among the people and had called him to the kingship. The kingship of David stems therefore from the immediate choice and call of God. It was God also who after the rejection of Saul and his kingship gave to the Prophet Samuel the command to anoint David as the future king. The anointment was not only to give him the right to the kingdom of Israel, it was also to be a divine guarantee that the Lord would assist him and that no evil-doer was to humiliate him. Moreover God promised that he would strike his adversaries with his own hand and would destroy all who would hate him. Because of the divine fidelity and love and through the majestic name of the Lord his fame would spread, his power and renown would grow. His dominion would extend from the sea in the west to the rivers in the east, to the Euphrates and the Tigris. God's grace will always rest upon David and his house. He will be a father to him and the rock foundation of his salvation. The youngest son in the house of Jesse will be the first-born among the kings; he will have a position among them as the oldest son in a family. God assured him his mercy and grace for all times; his covenant with David will last forever and will pass on to his descendants until the Messias appears. His throne will stand firm as long as heaven stands over the earth.

Even the unfaithfulness of the generation will not change anything of this covenant and will not make ineffective the promises made to David. If the descendants will not remain faithful to the Lord, he will indeed punish them for their faithlessness, but he will neither reject the generation nor let it perish. He will never desecrate the covenant by rescinding his promises. What God's lips have once spoken will never be taken back. This applies also to the promise made to David. The promise is irrevocable and will not be changed; for God has made an everlasting oath to David which he has sworn by his sanctity, by his sublime divine nature, and by his truthfulness. This solemn form should make him realize how serious it is for the Lord to abide by his word. There was question here about the realization of the decree of the redemption that the Messias was to be a descendant of the royal house of David. As the moon remains in the heavens for all times, so true and unchangeable is the testimony which the Lord gave from heaven. As long as world order exists, so long will the dominion of David's race last. God who for many thousands of years has kept the order of nature will also keep the order of the supernatural in existence. Sun and moon are types and witnesses of the divine fidelity of God who is in heaven, who testifies, who is faithful.

The present situation of Israel and of the house of David is in sharp contrast to the glory and reliability of the divine promise (39–46). It might give the impression that God had forgotten his solemn oath, that he had rejected the descendants of David despite his promises of eternal existence, and that he had despised it and then let them feel his wrath instead of his love. The situation gives the impression that the Lord had dissolved the covenant which he had once made with his servant David and his descendants. The crown which he had placed on David's head has been desecrated and, as it were, thrown into the dust by severe defeat which could not have occurred excepting by God's will and permission. The protecting walls which, according to the description of the Prophet Isaias, the Lord had built around his vineyard, the people of Israel, are torn down so that the enemies could invade the land without difficulty and demolish the fortifications and citadels. All who came by the way plundered the unprotected vineyard. The people had to submit to the mockery and derision of their neighbors. The power of the enemies of Israel was thereby increased and they triumphed over the people of Yahwe. Israel's power of resistance, on the contrary, was diminished; God took from them the sharpness of their sword so that they could no longer continue in battle. Thus the glory of the Davidic royal house was lost and its throne completely collapsed. God shortened the days of its youthful strength and covered it with shame.

In anxious care about the fate of the people the psalmist asks the

346

question from God: "How long, O Lord; wilt thou conceal thyself forever, and how long shall thy wrath burn like fire?" The course of life which the Lord has given to man is short and fleeting and no one is excepted from the law of death. Why should the Lord be continually angry and not take into consideration the frailty of his creatures? Could the Lord really forget his promises? The people for a long time expected their fulfilment. The invectives with which the Gentile nations ridiculed the anointed ultimately are directed against God himself. Hence he cannot permit them to go unpunished.

Verse 53 forms the doxology at the end of the third Book of the Psalms.

psalm 89

Domine, refugium

*A prayer for the mercy of God: recounting the shortness
and miseries of the days of man*

1. A prayer of Moses, the man of God.
   Lord thou hast been our refuge from generation to generation.

2. Before the mountains were made, or the earth and the world was formed: from eternity to eternity thou art God.

3. Turn not man away to be brought low: and thou has said: Be converted, O ye sons of men.

4. For a thousand years in thy sight are as yesterday, which is past.
   And as a watch in the night,

5. Things that are counted nothing, shall their years be.

6. In the morning man shall grow up like grass; in the morning he shall flourish and pass away: in the evening he shall fall, grow dry and wither.

7. For in thy wrath we have fainted away and are troubled in thy indignation.

8. Thou hast set our iniquities before thine eyes, our life in the light of thy countenance.

9. For all our days are spent; and in thy wrath we have fainted away.
   Our years shall be considered as a spider:

10. The days of our years in them are threescore and ten years.
But if in the strong they be fourscore years: and what is more of them is labor and sorrow.
For mildness is come upon us: and we shall be corrected.

11. Who knoweth the power of thy anger, and for thy fear can number thy wrath?

12. So make thy right hand known: and men learned in heart, in wisdom.

13. Return, O Lord, how long? And be entreated in favor of thy servants.

14. We are filled in the morning with thy mercy: and we have rejoiced, and are delighted all our days.

15. We have rejoiced for the days in which thou hast humbled us: for the years in which we have seen evils.

16. Look upon thy servants and upon their works: and direct their children.

17. And let the brightness of the Lord our God be upon us: and direct thou the works of our hands over us: yea, the work of our hands do thou direct.

THE superscription ascribes this prayer to Moses. As to contents it would not be impossible that the psalm could be traced back as far as the period of the great leader of the people and that it would belong to the time in which the godless and rebellious generation was to die in the desert. Verses 7–8 bring this thought to mind. He compares the eternity of God with the frailty of man. God's eternity is for man a reason for confidence in his promises, and the frailty of man should be for God a motive not to be so severe with him when he must appear before his judgment, a remonstrance for mercy.

The psalm in the first place contrasts the eternity of God with the frailty of man (verses 1–6). He begins with a grateful confession that God has at all times been a refuge to his people from generation to generation. Despite all the fickleness of man he himself remained unchangeable. Throughout the centuries he has remained a protector and provider. This unchangeableness has its foundation in God's eternity. Before the mountains of Palestine which he has promised and given to his people as an inheritance came into existence, before the universe was created, God was already there; for with God there is no coming into existence and with him there is no such thing as going out of existence. With him there is no past, no present, and no future. There is no *has been*, no *being* and no *becoming*; there is only an "is" from eternity to eternity; there is no change or alteration. This eternal, unchangeable God is the Lord of life and death. He has called man into existence out of nothing;

he allows him to return to dust and lets a new generation take his place. Thus in contrast to God, in man there is a constant change, a going and a coming. What is the longest life of a man, what is the great old age of the forefathers in comparison to the eternity of God? What are a thousand years before God? A thousand of God's years are as short as a man's day, indeed, even less. They are like a night watch, like a fraction of the night. Borrowing from the thought of this psalm the Apostle Peter says that one day before God is like a thousand years and a thousand years is like one day (2 Peter 3:8). The years of man pass by as quickly as one wave in a river replaces another; they pass away as quickly as grass that sprouts in the morning under the fresh night dew and withers away in the afternoon under the hot glow of the sun.

The most profound reason for the frailty of man is sin (verses 7–12). To the first man, bodily immortality was given. The fruit of the tree of life was to preserve for him natural life and renew his strength. But original sin brought the punishment of death upon all men and their personal sins increased the wrath of God. Because the Lord was angry with man, he returned to dust. God knows man's sin and no man can say that he is just. God searches the deepest recesses of the heart; before his countenance nothing lies concealed. His omniscience pierces all darkness. Man's years pass by quickly because God is angry with him; they are as short as a thought; they are passed after they have scarcely begun. The years of the forefathers were indeed many. The patriarch Jacob tells us his years were 130 when he migrated to Egypt and he says that they are not as many as the years of his forefathers. But the greater the number of generations since the time of Adam, the fewer are the years of life. Seventy, at the most eighty years, is man's span of life. They are years of suffering and trouble and pass by as rapidly as chaff blown by the wind. But few learn much about the gravity of sin or about the greatness of the divine wrath from the swiftness and afflictions of life. Men continue in sin and by doing so heap suffering upon suffering during their life. Thus the psalmist prays that God may teach men to appreciate the number of years given them, that they may realize the shortness and transitoriness of life, that they may use them in doing God's will, that they may acquire a correct view of life in order that they may not challenge God's wrath, but rather work out their salvation as long as the days of life last.

The psalmist hopes that Israel will at least take cognizance and he concludes with a petition for mercy for his people (verses 13–17). For a long time God's wrath weighed heavily upon Israel through whom he wished to fulfill his decree of salvation. May God have sympathy with his servant who is in his special service. From the sorrowful present the psalmist looks into the Messianic future in which all transitoriness and all

349

suffering will have an end. He hopes that the night of tribulation will yield to the new day, that soon the daylight of the blessed time will come. Then all sadness will disappear; then eternally a jubilant song will be sung. May that glorious time be a compensation for the days of tribulation, for the time in which God humbled his people, and for the years of misfortune. May God make known to his servants this divine rule and let them experience it; may he give to his sons the opportunity of seeing his glory. God has promised the Messianic glory, but its fulfillment has been placed in the hands of his people. But this is not possible without his grace. On this account the psalm concludes with the petition that the Lord may give grace to his people so that they can fulfill their mission.

psalm 90

Qui habitat

The just is secure under the protection of God

1. The praise of a canticle for David.
   He that dwelleth in the aid of the Most High, shall abide under the protection of the God of Jacob.

2. He shall say to the Lord: Thou art my protector, and my refuge: my God, in him will I trust.

3. For he hath delivered me from the snare of the hunters: and from the sharp word.

4. He will overshadow thee with his shoulders, and under his wings thou shalt trust.

5. His truth shall compass thee with a shield: thou shalt not be afraid of the terror of the night.

6. Of the arrow that flieth in the day, of the business that walketh about in the dark: of invasion, or of the noonday devil.

7. A thousand shall fall at thy side, and ten thousand at thy right hand: but it shall not come nigh thee.

8. But thou shalt consider with thy eyes: and shalt see the reward of the wicked.

9. Because thou, O Lord, art my hope: thou hast made the Most High thy refuge.

10. There shall no evil come to thee: nor shall the scourge come near thy dwelling.

11. For he has given his angels charge over thee; to keep thee in all thy ways.

12. In their hands shall they bear thee up: lest thou dash thy foot against a stone.

13. Thou shalt walk upon the asp and the basilisk: and thou shalt trample under foot the lion and the dragon.

14. Because he hoped in me I will deliver him: I will protect him because he hath known my name.

15. He shall cry to me, and I will hear him: I am with him in tribulation, I will deliver him, and I will glorify him.

16. I will fill him with length of days; and I will show him my salvation.

THE Church recites this psalm at Compline on Sundays and feast days. There is an evening atmosphere pervading this psalm; it is the song of a man who at evening twilight feels himself protected against threatening visitation. The poet has given this psalm the form of a dialogue between a man and his soul.

The first three verses give us the fundamental thought of the dialogue (verses 1–3). He who lives under the protection of the Most High, who rests in the shadow of the Almighty is well protected. We find the same thought in the Epistle of St. Paul to the Romans (8:31): "When God is for us, who is against us?" On many pages of Sacred Scripture in the Old Testament the truth is written that the Lord is a shield which covers us; that he is a rock on which we stand securely; that he is a citadel which protects us against the enemy so that the sanctuary because of God's presence is a blessing like shade in the heat of noon, like a tent during storm and rain. To him who dwells and is secure in union with God the teaching of Scripture becomes a personal experience. He can speak to his Lord: "Thou, O my God art my refuge, I will depend upon thee!" With this assurance his soul may be at rest and consoled when it is threatened by physical and spiritual attacks which it cannot foresee. May treacherous men lay snares in order to bring about man's ruin; may the destroyer, Satan himself, plan harmful attacks, God protects the soul and frees it from danger.

God protects his children (verses 4–8). The thought which the psalm has already given in the introduction is now more closely meditated upon and is developed by two descriptions. The Lord protects his children like an eagle caring for its young. It hovers over its young when the fledgling makes its first attempt to fly in order to support and assist it when its weak wings grow tired; it carries it on its wings towards the sun. So God also assists his people and protects every member of his people with his love. This beautiful picture is already used by Moses as an illustration of the divine providence and care which the Lord at the very beginning of the exodus and during the journey through the desert manifested to Israel (Deuteronomy 32:11 seq.). The second illustration is taken from the military. As the little shield protects the warrior and as the shield-bearer protects and covers the whole body of the warrior with the large shield, so the Lord protects and covers the just man with his inimitable faithfulness. Under his divine protection man has nothing to fear; he need not be afraid of an open or secret attack. Whether the enemy prowls secretly as a thief in the night or whether he makes his attack by the light of day, God knows how to check the danger. In the night God's eye pierces the darkness; in the day he twists the shafts of arrows. May the danger threaten like a pestilence or come upon man suddenly like a scourge which kills in the light of day, God protects against the one as well as the other. The expression *Midday Demon* of the Greek and Latin text is a mythological expression for a contagious disease which is said to be caused by the noonday sun. May the dangers be ever so great, may the diseases rage ever so terribly, that thousands, indeed, tens of thousands in the vicinity fall victim to it, whoever stands under the protection of God will not be touched by it. Thus the Israelites in Egypt saw how the Lord afflicted their oppressors with terrible plagues, but they themselves were miraculously spared. The psalmist himself was witness of the punishments with which God afflicted evil men, but he also was spared.

God lets his children be protected by angels (verses 9–13). The meditation upon divine protection has again brought back to the mind of the psalmist the truth: He who has made the Most High his refuge, who in all dangers and visitations seeks protection and help from him, will have confidence in the Lord, and to him the Lord will be a rock foundation upon which he can confidently build. But for the Lord it was not sufficient personally to be the protector of the just. In his loving care he went still further in that no harm would befall him in body and soul, in order that no need or worry would trouble those of his house. The great world of blessed spirits, his servants, God has commissioned to look after the affairs of men; he has entrusted to them the protection of men. They should accompany the just everywhere and guard them in all their ways. Wherever they go, the angel should go with them and remain at their side; when dangers threaten, they should warn man and keep him from harm. Like a good mother who carefully takes her little child in her arms when walking on stony ground and carries it lest it stumble and fall, so maternally should the angel love and be concerned about its ward lest it may stumble and fall on life's path. Never should the angel leave man to himself but he should accompany him in all his ways; for steep and hard and stony is the path that leads to eternal life. Under his mighty protection man can walk this path until he has reached his blessed end. May lions and dragons threateningly open their jaws at him and poisonous serpents lie in the way, he who is protected by an angel and guided by him can courageously pass over all these dangers; they will do him no harm. The Lord will save and will not let him come to shame who is in union with the Almighty, who believes in him and gives him his complete confidence. The Lord will hear him who reveres his name and in confidence calls upon the majestic God. The Lord will assist him in every need; he will save him and bring him to honor. Here the psalmist may have had in mind above all else that honor which consists in the triumph of the just over the godless, but according to the epilogue of his psalm he also had in mind the Messianic transfiguration which brings about unperishable glory. In the conclusion the psalmist has in mind the Messianic salvation. It contains the divine promise that the just man will see salvation. To live at the final glory was the most ardent desire of every Israelite.

psalm 91

Bonum est confiteri

God is to be praised for his wondrous works

1. A psalm of a canticle on the sabbath day.

2. It is good to give praise to the Lord, and to sing to thy name, O Most High.

3. To show forth thy mercy in the morning, and thy truth in the night:

4. Upon an instrument of ten strings, upon the psaltery: with a canticle upon the harp.

5. For thou hast given me, O Lord, a delight in thy doings: and in the works of thy hands I shall rejoice.

6. O Lord, how great are thy works! Thy thoughts are exceeding deep.

7. The senseless man shall not know: nor will the fool understand these things.

8. When the wicked shall spring up as grass: and all the workers of iniquity shall appear:
That they may perish forever and ever:

9. But thou, O Lord, art most high forevermore.

10. For behold thy enemies, O Lord, for behold thy enemies shall perish: and all the workers of iniquity shall be scattered.

11. But my horn shall be exalted like that of the unicorn: and my old age in plentiful mercy.

12. My eye also hath looked down upon my enemies: and my ear shall hear of the downfall of the malignant that rise up against us.

13. The just shall flourish like the palm tree: he shall grow up like the Cedar of Libanus.

14. They that are planted in the house of the Lord shall flourish in the courts of the house of our God.

15. They shall still increase in a fruitful old age: and shall be well treated,

16. That they may show,
That the Lord, our God, is righteous, and there is no iniquity in him.

Gᴏᴅ is not only the cause of events that happen in the natural order, but he is also the first cause of things that happen in the course of human affairs; he is the cause of the world's history and of the history of nations. This is only a realization of the eternal plan of world dominion. Only he who has an understanding of the divine plan has a perfectly correct idea of historical events and of historical continuity. This meditation which is not possible without supernatural revelation and enlightenment lets us look into the glory of the divine power, wisdom, fidelity, equanimity, and love always giving the soul a motive to adore and praise God. The day of the Lord (Sunday) should especially be dedicated to such a meditation. This is the purpose of the psalm.

Man has the duty to praise God (verses 2–4). It is a good and precious occupation to praise God, and his holy Name, to sing to the majestic God; for no one is so worthy of praise as the infinite God. Nothing gives such rich material for praise than a meditation on God's nature and his works. Every day upon earth in the history of each individual and of all mankind we perceive acts of divine love and fidelity. With every dawn man should intone his song of praise like the lark soaring aloft sings his song dedicating the day to its Creator. The day gives testimony of so many proofs of God's mercy and fidelity that one should proclaim all night long God's deeds and benefactions. In order that the praise of God will be sung with enthusiasm it should be accompanied with the music of many harps and with the sound of the zither. Music is the transfer of the feelings of the heart into the language of the notes of music.

God's governing in the history of mankind comprises two great groups: the godless who do not trouble themselves about the deeds of the Lord and who do not want to acknowledge them; and the just who rejoice in God and in his Law. The psalmist first speaks of God's ruling of the godless (verses 5–10). It is a joy to the heart and a refreshment for the soul to be able to meditate upon and to think profoundly about God's works. In nature and in the ordered world one discovers new beauties everywhere. New worlds continually appear to our observing eyes in which the divine work reveals itself. Just as wonderful is the unfolding of the divine decrees in the history of the Old and New Covenant when God gradually unfolded his eternal plan of redemption and let it come to a reality. How great are the works of the Lord! How deep are the divine thoughts which reveal themselves in his works! How incomprehensible are the divine plans for man! Remarkably deep is the decree of the redemption even in the Old Testament preparation as the prophets reveal it. The realization of it in the Incarnation of Christ, in his atoning suffering, and in his Church is inexhaustible material for meditation. To unbelievers and to religiously indifferent all these beauties and deep thoughts remain concealed. They have no vision for the supernatural world, they have no understanding of it. They are fools and may be compared to irrational animals which have no mind for the beauty of color in a meadow covered with flowers, but only take notice of that which fills their stomachs.

To such, God's justice and fidelity will reveal themselves in his punishments; they too must be of service to the glory of the Lord in their final fate. Their end is eternal death. They now appear to be happy and prosperous and many are envious of them. But their happiness is only fiction. It may be compared to grass which sprouts forth quickly under the winter rain, but withers just as quickly when the glow of the sun has dried up the soil. Their end is eternal destruction. From the fate of godless men and nations it is evident that God alone is great and majestic. May godlessness triumph for some time and may the godless think that they have dethroned the Lord, still the hour of punishment will arrive. How quickly all pretense of glory will disappear when the wrath of the divine judgment falls upon evildoers and destroys them. How often must historians seek laboriously for traces of past glory in order to obtain examples of men who were enemies of the kingdom of God and his revealed truth?

How different is God's governing of the just (verses 11–16). While the proud and haughty godless are humbled and despised by the Lord, he exalts his children and renews and increases their strength. The description of the strength of the buffalo tends to show the measure of strength given by God. As the body is strengthened by the application of oil, so God strengthens and restores the just man to health as if he had really poured a refreshing and efficacious balm upon the body. His eyes see the punishment which the Lord inflicts upon the godless, and he rejoices at the victory of divine justice. He becomes witness of their destruction and their prosperity suddenly come to naught. He also hears that in other places and at other times divine punishment has fallen upon the enemies of the just and upon the adversaries of God. But the just man grows in supernatural life with the help of divine grace like the high palm tree and like the large cedar of Lebanon which sinks its roots deep into the earth and with its eternal green extends its branches far over the other trees and over the shrubbery of the forest. Because of his union with God the just man is planted in the house of God and grows in the courts of the sanctuary. Like a tree which draws its nourishment from the soil in which it is rooted is dependent upon the richness of the same soil for its growth, so the just man draws his strength of supernatural life from the sanctuary; that is, from union with God from whom graces constantly flow. There is no more fruitful soil than union with God for the human soul. Therefore the just man is like a tree that is planted near running waters, the foliage of which never withers and the fruit of which matures at the right time. A soul which continually draws new strength from grace will never grow old; it remains young and brings forth fruit at all times for eternal life. The eternal youth of the saints and of the Church is a constant sermon on the government of God and on the rule of his grace; it preaches that God is a protector in whom no failure can be found.

psalm 92

Dominus regnavit

The glory and the stability of the kingdom; that is, of the Church of Christ

Praise in the way of a canticle, for David himself, on the day before the Sabbath, when the earth was founded.

1. The Lord hath reigned, he is clothed with beauty: the Lord is clothed with strength, and hath girded himself.
For he hath established the world which shall not be moved.

2. Thy throne is prepared from old: thou art from everlasting.

3. The floods have lifted up, O Lord: the floods have lifted up their voice.
The floods have lifted up their waves,

4. With the noise of many waters.
Wonderful are the surges of the sea: wonderful is the Lord on high.

5. Thy testimonies are become exceedingly credible: holiness becometh thy house, O Lord, unto the length of days.

JERUSALEM was harassed by enemies, but with God's assistance the danger was miraculously averted from Sion. Indescribable joy filled the city and the courts of the temple; everybody acclaimed the victor, the invisible King and God. He has again revealed himself in power and majesty to his people and to his enemies. To the eternal King, to the unchangeable, invisible, and only God this little psalm is dedicated; it is at the same time a hymn to Christ the King.

Yahwe has again proved himself the almighty King of his realm. He is not a king like other worldly kings; he is a ruler whose robe is divinity; he is a king who clothes himself with the power of an almighty Creator. The glory of his kingdom reveals itself in the universe. We see in his works only the hem of his royal garment. Majesty and power form his being; they belong to him as a girdle to a garment. His work will last unto eternity; it will never totter; it will never collapse. Since this God and King is so mighty, it is clear that his throne also will never collapse and that it cannot be overthrown. His kingship participates in the eternity of

357

the divine nature. It existed before he created the first beings who were to serve him; it will continue to exist into eternity. No human power can put an end to his kingship which had no beginning.

Like high swollen streams which flood their shores and bring destruction upon the land the Gentile armies invaded the kingdom of Juda devastating and destroying everything. Their tumultuous cry sounded like the roaring of the sea; like a wild seething surf rolling upon the shores the great armies invaded the land threatening disaster. But they could not assail the rock of divine Protection. Wave came upon wave and flood upon flood and they were thrown back by an invisible Power and did not reach the steps of the divine throne in the heights of heaven. No kingdom can overthrow the power of God. Thus the miraculous deliverance of Jerusalem again gave proof that the testimonies and promises of the Lord are reliable and are deserving of faith and confidence. God's kingdom, his Church, cannot be destroyed; it is invincible. Sanctity belongs to the House of God. The House of God, the Church, should not be desecrated by evil hands. It must always remain inviolable in its faith and in its continuance. Therefore its structure will outlast all times and generations.

psalm 93

Deus ultionum

God shall judge and punish the oppressors of his people

A psalm for David himself on the fourth day of the week.

1. The Lord is the God to whom revenge belongeth: the God of revenge hath acted freely.

2. Lift up thyself, thou that judgest the earth: render a reward to the proud.

3. How long shall sinners, O Lord, how long shall sinners glory?

4. Shall they utter and speak iniquity: shall all speak who work injustice?

5. Thy people, O Lord, they have brought low, and they have afflicted thy inheritance.

6. They have slain the widow and the stranger: and they have murdered the fatherless.

7. And they have said: The Lord shall not see: neither shall the God of Jacob understand.

8. Understand ye senseless among the people: and ye fools, be wise at last.

9. He that planted the ear, shall he not hear? Or he that formed the eye, doth he not consider?

10. He that chastiseth nations, shall he not rebuke: he that teacheth man knowledge?

11. The Lord knoweth the thoughts of men, that they are vain.

12. Blessed is the man whom thou shalt instruct, O Lord: and shalt teach him out of thy Law.

13. That thou mayest give him rest from the evil days: till a pit be dug for the wicked.

14. For the Lord will not cast off his people: neither will he forsake his own inheritance.

15. Until justice will be turned into judgment: and they that are near it are all upright in heart.

16. Who shall rise up for me against the evildoers? Or who will stand with me against the workers of iniquity?

17. Unless the Lord had been my helper, my soul had almost dwelt in hell.

18. If I said: My foot is moved: thy mercy, O Lord, assisted me.

19. According to the multitude of my sorrows in my heart, thy comforts have given joy to my soul.

20. Doth the seat of iniquity stick to thee, who framest labor in commandment?

21. They will hunt after the soul of the just, and will condemn innocent blood.

22. But the Lord is my refuge: and my God, the help of my hope.

23. And he will render them their iniquity: and in their malice he will destroy them: the Lord our God will destroy them.

WHEN godlessness triumphs in a country and a reign of terror has been established, when laws have been enacted against the Church and its members, the injustices of which cry to heaven, then even a Christian soul resists such outrage and is tempted with the sons of Zebedee to call fire from heaven to consume the evildoers. Then it is time to consider the persecutions in the light of faith in order that the heart may find peace with God and place the fate of the enemies and persecutors in his hands. Upon Israel, the chosen nation of the Old

Covenant, many hard times had come during which godless paganism arose in order to crush it. During this time even in their own nation there were apostates who oppressed those who were faithful to the Law. The psalmist tries to console his people in such bitter hours and shows them that the Lord does not abandon his children.

The psalm begins with the petition that the divine punishment may fall upon the evildoers (verses 1–7). It is given because of the impatience of an oppressed people. The Lord once spoke to Israel through Moses: "Revenge is mine, and I will repay them in due time, that their foot may slide: the day of destruction is at hand, and the time makes haste to come" (Deuteronomy 32:35). God himself is the avenger of all wickedness that has been committed against Israel and against the just. Hence the people should give up all thoughts of personal revenge and turn to God for a just judgment. Thus the psalmist also beseeches the Lord that he may appear in judgment as he has so often held judgment upon the godless in the history of his people. The godless have deserved the intervention from heaven. Since the Lord has until now delayed his punishment, the evildoers have become more bold and arrogant. They have paid no attention to his threats. Therefore the Lord for the sake of his honor should intervene; he may no longer look quietly upon their activities. Indeed, the godless are triumphing over the just because they remain unpunished. They even boast about their wickedness. They do not fear God's judgment. They boast of their power. They commit outrages against the chosen people. They violently attack the people of God in order to destroy them. Their crime, therefore, is a rebellion against God's majesty, a defamation of his kingship. They oppress especially those whom the Lord has promised his protection: the widows, orphans, and strangers. They challenge God's wrath. They do this because they no longer believe that God troubles himself about their activities nor demands an account from them.

The godless deceive themselves (verses 8–11). They deceive themselves when they try to convince themselves that the Lord pays no attention to their conduct. Therefore the psalmist admonishes them to be discerning and understand that it is folly to believe that he who has given men eyes to see and ears to hear will not use his own powers against the evil conduct of men. History teaches the godless the truth. It shows that God has the power to punish entire nations and that he does punish them for wrong-doing against himself and against his people. Should he not also have the power to punish present evildoers? Should he, who does not let the oppression of his people by the Gentiles go unpunished, let the misdeeds of godless Israelites continue without punishment? Should he, who has given man discernment and the power of judgment, not himself perceive injustice and punish it? The Lord is all-knowing; he knows the thoughts of men. He knows their vanity, the folly of sin. Nothing lies concealed before him.

The fate of the just man is altogether different (verses 12–15). He is a boorish fool who closes his mind to the instructions of the all-wise God. But he is to be called wise whom the Lord himself has instructed through the Law, whom the Lord has instructed about his promises and threats, his blessings and his punishments. He who is instructed by God knows that he sees all things, that he rewards and punishes. He knows that evil days are permitted by the divine will and that they contribute to our salvation; such thought puts his heart at rest. He can therefore patiently wait until the evildoers have dug their own pit of destruction. God does not abandon his people and his faithful. He guides them through difficult times and does not abandon them because they are his possession and never rescinds his eternal decrees. The day of divine retribution, the day of the Lord, will come and persecuted justice will triumph. Then justice will be acknowledged by all the world and at the command of the eternal Judge all who have served him with faithful sincerity despite all persecutions will enter into the blessedness of his kingdom.

Experience confirms the victory of justice (verses 16–23). When godlessness prevails, the persecuted just man cannot depend on human help; he cannot find an advocate who will have the courage to stand up in his defense against the mighty evildoers. He is entirely dependent on God's help. If God too had withdrawn himself in such difficult times, then his soul would have long ago stood at the brink of death's kingdom; then he would have long since descended into the land of eternal silence where God's praise is no longer sung; for the malice and unscrupulousness of the evildoers knows no limits. Often the danger had been very near that the downfall of the just man was considered to be a certainty. But the Lord stood at the side of his servant and saved him from his downfall; God's love supported him. When his soul was burdened with cares, temptations, difficulties, and trials, God was always ready to console and encourage him. His consolation and encouragement made his soul confident and cheerful.

God's justice gives confidence in every persecution. He has nothing in common with judges who allow themselves to be bribed, who under the appearance of love for the law make unjust laws. But God does not permit injustice to prevail. Men may for a time continue with their injustices; they may persecute just men; they may condemn the innocent to severe punishments; they will not however obtain their purpose. They will not succeed in exterminating the just; for God does not abandon his children when they are persecuted and oppressed. He remains for them at all times an unconquerable fortress in which all oppressed may take refuge; he proves himself to be a strong and secure rock which the persecutors cannot subdue. While the Lord protects his faithful, he calls the godless to account. Every evildoer must appear before his judgment seat and will receive his deserved punishment. When God passes judgment and when the wicked see the glorious lot of those whom they have persecuted, their insolent mockery and their proud boasting will be silenced. They will be silenced when they see the malice of their works in the light of their condemnation. He who judges and brings them to silence is Yahwe, the God and King of Israel. Therefore the just man looks ahead to the day of the great judgment and to the general day of retribution with all peace and confidence.

psalm 94

Venite, exultemus

An invitation to adore and serve God and to hear his voice

Praise of a canticle for David himself.

1. Come let us praise the Lord with joy: let us joyfully sing to God our Saviour.

2. Let us come before his presence with thanksgiving: and make a joyful noise to him with psalms.

3. For the Lord is a great God, and a great King above all gods.

4. For in his hand are all the ends of the earth: and the heights of the mountains are his.

5. For the sea is his, and he made it: and his hands formed the dry land.

6. Come let us adore and fall down: and weep before the Lord that made us.

7. For he is the Lord our God: and we are the people of his pasture and the sheep of his hand.

8. Today if you shall hear his voice, harden not your hearts.

9. As in the provocation, according to the day of temptation in the wilderness: where your father tempted me, they proved me, and saw my works.

10. Forty years long was I offended with that generation, and I said: These always err in heart.

11. And these men have not known my ways: so I swore in my wrath that they shall not enter into my rest.

THIS psalm is recited by the Church as an invitatory to the daily breviary. It requests the priests to worship God in spirit and in truth. Perhaps among the Jews it was also used as an Introit to the divine service on the Sabbath. It requests worship and the service of God.

Come, let us adore (verses 1–5). Like the ringing of the bells which invites the laity to the divine service, so this psalm invites the priest and religious to adore the Lord and sing his praises. He is the Lord, the God who has solemnly made a covenant with Israel on Mount Sinai, the invisible King of his people who has promised the Messianic salvation. He is also the Lord of his Church, the foundation of our hope of salvation. This is reason enough to rejoice and praise him jubilantly. How poor are the Gentiles with their worthless gods! How poor are all who themselves make gods which they worship! How poor are such whose faith does not rest on the rock foundation of the infallible and unchangeable truth! Because God is so infinitely above human creation it is not befitting that we always approach him with complaints and petition, as if he were only Lord and King to hear our complaints and grant us favors. The first duty towards God is adoration and thanksgiving. We should approach him with praise on our lips and glorify him with songs; for the Lord is our great God and King. What are those handmade gods of the Gentiles? What are all the kings of the earth in comparison to the King of kings and to the Lord of hosts? All the world should worship him because he rules all with might and power. This power reaches into the depths of the earth, into a domain not yet entered by man much less explored by him. The highest summits of mountains which no human foot has touched are not without their Lord; for they are God's possession. The gigantic mountains are also his work. To him belongs the vast ocean and the mainland. By his word the land had risen from the primeval waters and the waters of the sea gather into the places determined by God. He has created all and called all things into being by his divine Word, the Logos. "All things were made by the Logos and without him was made nothing that was made" (John 1:3).

Come, let us listen to God (verses 6–11). For the second time the psalmist invites us to fall down on our knees and worship the almighty Creator, the great and majestic God and Lord. It is not sufficient to glorify God's majesty with songs of praise, but we must also get down on our knees before him in all humility and thankfully worship him. This sacred

363

duty rests upon every member of the chosen people and much more upon every member of the Church of Christ; for God is not only the Creator of the natural life of man, but he is also the source of supernatural life which he imparts to man through union with Christ and his Church. Just as the people of Yahwe in the Old Covenant were God's work, so also is the Church of the New Law. Only Israel among all nations of the earth could in a special sense say about Yahwe: "He is our God. We are the people of his pasture and the sheep of his land." By the making of the covenant God entered into a special relationship with Israel. He made it his special possession in order that like a shepherd he could lead and guide it. The Christian's union with God through Jesus Christ is a far more intimate and mysterious union, and therefore the Lord of the Christians is in a much deeper sense "Our Lord and God." He is the shepherd and we are the sheep of his pasture. According to St. Paul, God has left the Gentiles to themselves, but those who were his own he led to the green pastures of truth and to the refreshing waters of grace.

Since God is the shepherd of his people and Israel is his herd then it must pay heed to the voice of its shepherd. Christ says in the parable of the Good Shepherd that the sheep hear his voice and follow him because they know his voice (John 10:3). Therefore they accept the admonition: "If only today you would hear his voice." The infinite God will not allow man to go unpunished if he closes his ears to his voice. A warning example for all times was the fate of the many thousands who had been liberated from the slavery of Egypt but were not permitted to enter the promised land. When in the desert, at Massah and Meribah, on their way from the Red Sea to Sinai, they suffered for want of water and they murmured against God (Exodus 17:1 seq.). They had been witnesses of the great miracles which the Lord had wrought in Egypt; they had passed through the Red Sea; they had been fed daily by the Manna which came down from heaven; and yet they did not have the confidence that the Lord would preserve them in the desert and they doubted whether in a waterless country even he would be able to supply them with water. As in the beginning, so also the fathers sinned against God during the forty years journey in the desert and became an abomination to the Lord. They followed their own foolish evil inclinations and did not concern themselves about God who had delivered and led them from their captivity in such miraculous manner. But finally when his patience was exhausted, he swore in his holy wrath that the entire generation would die in the desert. The oath of the Lord in human language is an expression of the unchangeableness of the divine judgment. This fate of the Israelites should be an earnest warning for all to use the time given by God in order that they may not be excluded from entering into the eternal rest of heaven. The Epistle to the Hebrews has applied this admonition to the Christians: "See to it, brethren, that no one have a wicked and unbelieving heart and fall away from the living God. Admonish one another day by day, as long as it is today, that no one be hardened by the deceit of sin" (Hebrews 7:11 seq.).

psalm 95

Cantate Domino

An exhortation to praise God for the coming of
Christ and his kingdom

1. A canticle for David himself, when the house was built after the captivity. Sing ye to the Lord a new canticle: sing to the Lord all the earth.

2. Sing ye to the Lord and bless his name: show forth his salvation from day to day.

3. Declare his glory among the Gentiles: his wonders among all people.

4. For the Lord is great, and exceedingly to be praised: he is to be feared above all gods.

5. For all gods of the Gentiles are devils: but the Lord made the heavens.

6. Praise and beauty are before him: holiness and majesty in his sanctuary.

7. Bring ye to the Lord, O ye kindreds of the Gentiles, bring ye to the Lord glory and honor.

8. Bring to the Lord glory unto his name. Bring up sacrifices and come into his courts.

9. Adore ye the Lord in his holy court. Let all the earth be moved at his presence.

10. Say ye among the Gentiles, the Lord hath reigned. For he hath corrected the world, which shall not be moved: he will judge the people with justice.

11. Let the heavens rejoice and let the earth be glad, let the sea be moved, and the fullness thereof.

12. The fields and all things that are in them shall be joyful. Then shall all the trees of the woods rejoice.

13. Before the face of the Lord, because he cometh: because he cometh to judge the earth. He shall judge the world with justice, and the people with his truth.

THIS psalm is found in the first Book of Chronicles (16:23–33). According to the Chronicles it was sung by David at the solemn transfer of the Ark of the Covenant from Cariathiarim to the new sacred tabernacle at Sion. According to the superscription of the Vulgate the psalm was sung at the dedication of the post-exilic temple. It fitted the occasion because of its Messianic content. In this song Israel greets the invisible King who thrones over the cherubim of the Ark of the Covenant and enters into his sanctuary; it also greets him as King of Messianic times. The song coming from the mouth of a Christian is appropriate as a greeting to Christ the King; it is used as a greeting to the God-Man who comes on Christmas night to guide and lead the Christians. The people of God, the Gentile world, and all creation should sing with joy at the coming of the King.

The psalm begins with a mission call to Israel (verses 1–6). With the arrival of the Lord at Sion a new era began. Their God and King has set up his dwelling in the city from which the Messianic kingdom also had its beginning. With this an important step has been made in the fulfillment of the divine decree of salvation. The return home from the exile and the reconstruction of the temple also meant for Israel the beginning of a new era. Both events proved that the Lord had not completely rejected his people and that he was mindful of his promises. The return home and the reconstruction of the temple were guarantees for the coming redemption. A new era began also, in the true sense of the word, at the Incarnation of the Son of God. For the celebration of such important events which mean the beginning of a new era of salvation old songs are not appropriate; a new song must be dedicated to the Lord and sung. But it should not be sung by Israel only; all nations should join in the singing of this song. The song glorifies the great name of Yahwe, his sublime nature, his power and wisdom, his love and fidelity, all of which are so wonderfully revealed in the plan of the Redemption. The psalm is intended to glorify the plan which brings salvation and peace to all men. The gift of redemption places upon men the obligation to cooperate, to bring the good message to the Gentiles, to the nations where the light of faith has not yet penetrated, to narrate the glories of the Lord and his wonderful deeds in order that the Gentile world might also worship God and sing his praises.

The Lord is indeed worthy of the songs and praises of all nations.

What are the gods of the Gentiles in comparison to him, the one and only true God? He surpasses all as infinity surpasses measure. The gods of the Gentiles are mere idols, the work of men and the deceivers of men. May they be ever so renowned, may their power be boasted about, and may their worshipers erect the most magnificent temples, they are, nevertheless, lifeless and helpless idols. But Yahwe is almighty; all creatures are his work; they give testimony to his unlimited power and infinite wisdom. He is infinite majesty. He is surrounded by incomparable grandeur whose beauty the eyes of man cannot endure and the mind of man cannot comprehend. The heavens proclaim the power and glory of God. Innumerable spirits surround his throne and sing to the Lord of hosts: "Holy, holy, holy." Although concealed, his power and glory dwells in his earthly sanctuary of the temple, in the tabernacle of his Church.

Called to proclaim God's glory to the nations, Israel speaks through the mouth of the psalmist who calls upon the nations to acknowledge God as their king (verses 7–10). Yahwe is the Lord of the whole world. All nations should worship him and bend their knees before him. That is the purpose and end of the divine plan for man. The sanctuary on Sion, the Church, should become a house of prayer for all nations. To it all nations should come and worship because from it the Law and the Word of God have their starting point. They should make pilgrimages to the courts of the sanctuary and bring their gifts to the eternal King and worship him. But they must appear before him not in their everyday trappings of worldly thoughts, desires and anxieties, but in the precious raiment of sanctity, in the wedding garment of sanctifying grace.

Before his majesty the whole world should tremble not with a slavish fear of his power and wrath, but in reverence for his glory. Therefore to the Gentiles who wish to approach him his nature must be made known. Man must approach God with the consciousness of his own nothingness. The Lord is king; his dominion is the world; before his sceptre all nations must bow. The Lord is the creator and the preserver of the universe. He has given it a law, the natural law, which must be kept throughout all times. The Lord is the judge of the world; before his judgment seat all must appear and give an account of their allegiance to him. With an unerring justice he will pass his irrevocable judgment upon men and nations.

According to the predictions of the prophets the judgment will be a preamble to the Messianic era during which the curse resting upon the earth since original sin will be taken away. On this account the psalm closes with a call to all creatures to greet the coming King (verses 11–13). "For the expectation of the creature waiteth for the revelation of the sons of God. For the creature was made subject to vanity, not willingly, but by reason of him that made it subject, in the hope that the creature also itself shall be delivered from the servitude of corruption, unto the liberty of the children of God" (Romans 8:19–21). Thus a joy and gladness will pervade all creation when the fullness of time has come.

An indescribable joy will pervade the universe: heaven, earth, the sea and its creatures, the fields under cultivation will tremble for joy; the heavy ears of grain will bow before the coming King; the trees of the forest will rustle; the proud cedars of the Lebanon, the cypresses and fir-trees, the oaks and the elm, all of them will be ready for a joyous welcome to the Prince who will bring to them the blessing of salvation; for he will come to establish his kingdom in which eternal peace shall reign which will bring about unity among the nations. He will come to guide the universe with the sceptre of his justice.

psalm 96

Dominus regnavit

All are invited to rejoice at the glorious coming and reign of Christ

1. For the same David, when his land was restored again to him.
   The Lord hath reigned, let the earth rejoice, let many islands be glad.

2. Clouds and darkness are round about him: justice and judgment are the establishment of his throne.

3. A fire shall go before him, and shall burn his enemies, round about.

4. His lightnings have shone forth to the world: the earth saw and trembled.

5. The mountains melted like wax, at the presence of the Lord: at the presence of the Lord of all the earth.

6. The heavens declared his justice: and all people saw his glory.

7. Let them be all confounded that adore graven things, and that glory in their idols.
   Adore him, all you his angels:

8. Sion heard and was glad.
   And the daughters of Juda rejoiced, because of thy judgments, O Lord.

9. For thou art the most high Lord over all the earth: thou art exalted exceedingly above all the gods.

10. You that love the Lord, hate evil: the Lord preserveth the souls of his saints, he will deliver them out of the hands of the sinner.

11. Light is risen to the just, and joy to the right of heart.

12. Rejoice ye just, in the Lord: and give praise to the remembrance of his holiness.

THE conclusion of the preceding psalm has called upon nature to greet the King who will come to judge the world and then begin the kingdom of eternal peace. This psalm describes the appearance of the Lord for judgment which will usher in the fulfillment of salvation in the Messianic time. A parousia sentiment pervades this psalm.

The first strophe describes the coming of the Lord for judgment. The Lord is king of the whole world; his appearance should be greeted by the earth, by all islands and countries. After this request the poet envisions the Lord's appearance. With lightning and thunder God once descended upon Sinai in order to make a covenant with his people; with thunder and lightning the writers of the Old Testament books made the Lord appear for judgment. The coming of the judge for the last judgment, for the day of the Lord, will be accompanied with similar signs. The infinite majesty of God will conceal himself in the darkness of a cloud. The dark storm clouds are a symbol of his punitive and cleansing justice. Justice and righteousness will be the foundation stones of the Messianic kingdom. The Lord will judge without distinction of persons and without distinction of nations. Fire, the forerunner of his wrath, will flare up and will destroy the enemy. Lightning will constantly flash and illuminate the world. The earth will quake to its depths and will tremble; because of the uproar of the elements nothing can endure, even the massive mountains will melt like wax when the glow passes over them; they will disappear before the infinity of the great God, the Lord of all the earth. The dark and water-heavy clouds that pass over, the rolling thunder, and the flashes of lightning announce to all the world that the Lord is near and that salvation is coming, that the world will now see the glory of God.

The Lord has come, now the judgment takes place (verses 7–12). The psalm now gives a vivid description of the moment when the Judge gives his decision of separation which is to last eternally. He addresses all who did not want to acknowledge him and did not want to worship him; he addresses all who have made to themselves worthless idols, idols made by their own hands, idols that would replace the one true God. They now see the glory of the one true God exposing the worthlessness of their gods

369

and they are ashamed of their folly. How proud they had been about their gods, about the work of their own technique and art; how they had boasted about the number and the greatness of their gods; and now all their altars, the thrones of their gods, the works of men are overthrown. Now their pride is humbled and eternal shame is their portion. Sion, the kingdom of God of Messianic times, the Church, is witness to the shame of the servants of idols and of all the enemies of God. Unspeakable joy pervades the City of God at hearing the divine judgment. The righteous rejoice because now justice triumphs, because the Church has defeated all her adversaries. They rejoice because the Lord has proved himself before all the world to be the Most High, the mighty King before whom all must bend their knees. At the general judgment the infinitely majestic God stands in the glory of his divinity and his eternal majesty surrounded by myriads of angels and praised by all the saints from all races and nations; before him lie in the dust the fallen pagan idols and all the fetishes which unbelievers have adored and worshiped as their gods. That is the closing picture of world history.

The psalm now gives the practical application from this meditation (verses 10–12). He who in judgment will see the end of the sinner will find out what sin is in the mind of the just Judge, how he hates it with an infinite hatred. Therefore he who loves God must hate sin. Consequently the Lord will guide and protect him against the power of evildoers. The just man may be despised and persecuted in this life, but on the day of judgment he will radiate the light of the heavenly transfiguration; for the just man will shine like the sun in the kingdom of his father. Those who have served God with a sincere heart will shine in the light of eternal glory and will partake in eternal happiness. In view of such glory the psalmist requests the just to sing a "Te Deum." They should rejoice in the Lord and thank him always, because they have been called to be united with him. They should not tire in praising his holy Name, his wisdom, and his love.

psalm 97

Cantate Domino

All are again invited to praise the Lord for the victories of Christ

1. A psalm for David himself.

Sing ye the Lord a new canticle, because he has done wonderful things.
His right hand has wrought for him salvation and his arm is holy.

2. The Lord has made known his salvation: he hath revealed his justice in the sight of the Gentiles.

3. He hath remembered his mercy and his truth toward the house of Israel. All the ends of the earth have seen the salvation of our God.

4. Sing joyfully to God, all the earth; make melody, rejoice and sing.

5. Sing praise to the Lord on the harp, on the harp, and with the voice of a psalm.

6. With long trumpets, and sound of cornet, make a joyful noise before the Lord our king:

7. Let the sea be moved and the fullness thereof: the world and they that dwell therein.

8. The rivers shall clap their hands, the mountains shall rejoice together

9. At the presence of the Lord: because he cometh to judge the earth. He shall judge the world with justice and the people with equity.

LIKE the two preceding songs this psalm refers to the beginning of Messianic times. Israel, the pagan world, and all creation are requested to greet the coming King with jubilation. The psalm is the world's Christmas song. "A child is born to us, a son is given to us, the dominion rests upon his shoulders" (Isaias 9:5[6]).

The people of God should rejoice (verses 1–3). The deliverance from Babylonian captivity, a type of the Messianic redemption, was in itself such a miraculous deed of God that it deserved to be praised in song. As once the passage through the Red Sea was an act of deliverance which only the almighty arm of God could perform, so also in the second deliverance God revealed his infinite power and greatness. The second deliverance was more than a political success which perhaps enhanced the reputation of Daniel with King Cyrus; it was a divine deed of deliverance, an important step forward to the realization of the world's redemption. The power of the Lord and his favor and love toward the people of his choice was revealed. Thereby God's decree of deliverance was also made known to the Gentiles. The return home from the captivity was also the fulfillment of a promise made to Israel; it was a revelation of divine mercy and fidelity. Now all nations even to the end of the earth saw the salvation appear which was also to come to them. In a much deeper sense these verses may be applied to the realization of the redemption through Jesus Christ. It is a miraculous deed of divine power and justice, of mercy and fidelity which reveals itself to all the world.

371

Salvation was not to be confined to Israel, but was intended from the very beginning for the whole world. Therefore the Gentile world should also rejoice (verses 4–6). It should join in the joy of the chosen people and also take the harp in hand and accompany the jubilant orchestra of Israel. It had once rejoiced when it vanquished Israel and had celebrated its exile as a victory of its gods. But now they should be impelled by truth and grace and acclaim Yahwe, the King of the world, and greet him with trumpets and cornets, with harp and zither, and with the singing of psalms.

Irrational creatures are also included in the blessing of the Redemption; therefore they too are asked to acclaim the Lord (verses 7–9). The roaring of the sea should become a song of thanksgiving: all the millions of living creatures that live in the depths of the sea should praise their Lord and Creator in silent joy. The mainland with all that is upon it, plants in remarkable variations and animals large and small, should rejoice. May the gurgling of brooks and streams be joyful applause at the coming of the Lord. May the rustling of the forests on the mountain's side, of the cedars and cypresses of the Lebanon and of the strong oaks of Basan be a jubilant symphony which the trees dedicate to their divine Master. All should rejoice; all nature should shout for joy when the King appears to establish the kingdom of eternal peace and to guide the world with the sceptre of justice.

psalm 98

Dominus regnavit

The reign of the Lord in Sion: that is, of Christ in his Church

1. A psalm for David himself.
   The Lord hath reigned, let the people be angry: he that sitteth on the cherubim: let the earth be moved.

2. The Lord is great in Sion, and high above all people.

3. Let them give praise to thy great name: for it is terrible and holy:

4. And the king's honor loveth judgment. Thou hast prepared directions: thou hast done judgment and justice in Jacob.

5. Exalt ye the Lord our God, and adore his footstool, for it is holy.

6. Moses and Aaron among his priests: and Samuel among them that call upon his Name. They called upon the Lord, and he heard them.

7. He spoke to them in the pillar of the cloud. They kept his testimonies, and the commandment which he gave them.

8. Thou didst hear them, O Lord our God: thou wast a merciful God to them, and taking vengeance on all their inventions.

9. Exalt ye the Lord our God, and adore at his holy mountain: for the Lord our God is holy.

THIS psalm is also dedicated to the King, Yahwe; it proclaims him to be the thrice holy God, the all-powerful, the just and gracious God and King. Yahwe is a mighty king (verses 1–3). Before him all nations must tremble, even those who for a time seem to triumph in their rebellion against him and who oppress the people of his kingdom on earth. He who rules upon the cherubim of the Ark of the Covenant in the recesses of the temple is so powerful that even the earth trembles before his majesty. He has power over all nations so that they too must tremble before him sometime or other. Indeed, the Lord who rules on Sion and who has taken his abode in the tabernacle of his Church is great. From there he rules all nations of the earth. The kingdoms of the earth are no more to him than the sand on the seashore; they are no more to him than drops in the sea, than specks of dust on a scale. Therefore nations act wisely when they subject themselves to this mighty King; when they acknowledge the greatness of his name and praise him. The Lord is majestic and holy.

Yahwe is a just king (verses 4–5). He is the lord of the moral order. As a holy God he loves justice. For this reason he has revealed his holy will to Israel on Mount Sinai. He has given his holy Law to his people through Moses and has obligated them to keep the Law under threat of punishment. He himself acts and judges according to the norms of justice without respect to persons. Because of his prerogative of being the source and protector of all justice, Israel should praise the Lord and worship him before the Ark of the Covenant and bend their knees before his footstool.

In his justice Yahwe also reveals himself as the holy God. The psalmist calls the Ark of the Covenant the footstool of his throne and therefore there exists a special relation between the Ark and the glory of their King and Lord.

Yahwe is a gracious king (verses 6–9). He hears all who with a right disposition pray to him. The psalmist mentions three personalities from

373

history who as men of prayer obtained from God great things for Israel: Moses, Aaron, and Samuel. When Israel had sinned gravely by the worship of the golden calf and was to be rejected by the Lord, Moses interceded for them and was heard (Exodus 32:30). In later times after the rebellion of Core and his followers, the entire people murmured against Moses and Aaron. The Lord punished thousands with death. Then Aaron, the high priest, interceded for his faithless people and God heard his petitions and stopped the epidemic (Deuteronomy 17:11). When at the time of Samuel the Philistines invaded the Israelitic territory, the prophet offered a lamb for a sacrifice and begged God for help; the Lord sent a terrible storm upon the enemy so that their army was scattered and easily destroyed by the Israelites (1 Kings 7:2). The Lord spoke to Moses and Aaron from the pillar of a cloud; he held conversation with them (Numbers 12:8). He had conversation with him face to face (Deuteronomy 34:10). He heard them because they faithfully observed his commandments and conscientiously fulfilled his requests. This fidelity gave to their intercessory prayer a power before God. As often therefore as they prayed to God and spoke to him in behalf of the faithless people, so often was he ready to forgive them their sins and showed mercy to them. This fact should be an admonition to us and to all that by faithfulness to God's commandments we may be certain that our prayers will also be heard. God's sanctity also reveals itself in his graciousness and merciful love toward men. This love and graciousness must also be the object of our praise of God. In the sanctuary, in the tabernacle, God has erected his throne; there especially before him man should thank him for his love.

psalm 99

Jubilate Deo

All are invited to rejoice in God, the Creator of all

1. A psalm of praise.

2. Sing joyfully to God, all the earth: serve ye the Lord with gladness.
   Come in before his presence with exceeding great joy.

3. Know ye that the Lord is God: he made us, and not we ourselves. We are his people and the sheep of his pasture.

4. Go ye into his gates with praise, into his courts with hymns: and give glory to him. Praise ye his name:

5. For the Lord is sweet, his mercy endureth forever, and his truth to generation and generation.

HAVING been chosen as the people of God was the great grace of Israel. It was as unmerited as the grace by which the Christian is called by the Lord to be a member of the chosen people of the New Covenant, the Church of Christ. As often as thanksgiving offerings were made to God in the court of the sanctuary at the morning and evening sacrifices and at sacrifices on feast days commemorating the union of God with his people, Israel was to be grateful for this grace. All the elect should with a joyful heart sing jubilantly to God because he has done great things for them. He is mighty and his name is holy. He whom God has chosen for his service can with a sincere joy apply himself to it and with a holy pride bend his knees to the Lord. Only with jubilant gratitude in his heart should he appear in the house of God before the face of the most high God and before his tabernacle. Who among men, so highly favored by God, can see in the honorable service of God, a burden placed upon his liberty? In the sanctuary when the whole parish is gathered around the altar, he should with songs of jubilation confess the Lord and joyfully thank him for his great mercy and grace. The Lord alone is God; he has made us and we are his possession; we are his people, the sheep of his pasture. He has made Israel his chosen people and every member is born into this union with God by God's power and will. Every member must confess with St. Paul: "Through God's grace I am what I am" (1 Corinthians 15:10). We are also his possession because of the spiritual life that is given to us; we are his people and his flock which he leads and guides on the way to eternal happiness. These are important reasons which should impel every Israelite to come to the sanctuary with a glad heart, with songs of praise upon his lips, and with sentiments of gratitude to God in his soul. The Lord does not wish to be adored in silence alone, but also publicly; not only by the individual but also by the entire congregation. Participation in public divine service is a thanksgiving offering befitting to God. Here in the house of God hundreds and thousands should unite and praise the infinite love and eternal fidelity of the Lord. "God is good, and his mercy endureth forever, and his fidelity forevermore."

psalm 100

Misericordiam et judicium

*The prophet exhorteth all by his example, to
follow mercy and justice*

1. A psalm for David himself.
   Mercy and judgment I will sing to thee, O Lord: I will sing.

2. And I will understand in the unspotted way, when thou shalt come to me.
   I walked in the innocence of my heart, in the midst of my house.

3. I did not set before my eyes any unjust thing: I hated the workers of
   iniquities.

4. The perverse of heart did not cleave to me: and the malignant, that turned
   aside from me, I would not know.

5. The man that in private detracted his neighbor, him did I persecute.
   With him that had a proud eye; and an insatiable heart, I would not eat.

6. My eyes were upon the faithful of the earth to sit with me: the man that
   walked in the perfect way, he served me.

7. He that worketh pride shall not dwell in the midst of my house: he that
   speaketh unjust things did not prosper before my eyes.

8. In the morning I put to death all the wicked of the land: that I might cut
   off all the workers of iniquity from the city of the Lord.

THIS psalm unfolds the principles of his government. They should be
the guiding laws according to which the authorities of the country
should fulfill their duty. Mercy and justice, mildness and righteousness
must harmoniously coincide in the virtue of a ruler and especially of a
theocratic king who takes the place of Yahwe, the invisible King, whose
Nature is love and justice. Thus the psalm which sings about the mercy
and righteousness of the earthly king becomes at the same time a song of
praise of the heavenly King.

The first part of the governmental program contains the principles of
private life (verses 2–4). If a theocratic king wishes to sing the praises of
God, he may not live a life contrary to the will of God. Since every
Israelite had to be holy because God, his Lord, and invisible King is holy,

this duty applies in the first place to the king, the visible representative of the invisible King. Therefore, David will honor the Lord not only in song and by the playing of the harp but also by stainless conduct of life. But because man is not capable of doing this without the help of God's grace the psalmist prays that God may not delay with his sanctifying aid. He wants to live at home without the stain of sin. Everything that is sinful should be far from him. His eyes should not look desiringly upon things which he can enjoy only contrary to the divine Law. The Law of the Lord must be the norm of a king's life. With all his heart he will, therefore, hate and detest all falsehood; his soul shall never be stained by sins of malice. What he says should be the true expression of his thought. In what he does he will avoid every insincerity and hypocrisy. Because of his sincerity he will avoid all companionship with evil men and he will show the people that he despises all evil by whomsoever it may be committed.

A king is responsible not only to his God but also to his people. The demands of the Lord also apply to the fulfillment of the duties of his high office. King David tells us in the second part of the psalm (verses 5-8) that the norms of his private life are also the fundamental principles of government. The sword has been placed in the hands of those in authority for the protection of the weak and for the punishment of evildoers. In the Book of Proverbs the punishment of all injustice is repeatedly stressed as the first duty of a king. David, therefore, will deal strictly with calumniators and silence them. He will never treat favorably those greedy and proud men who exploit others and despise them. The king will not rely upon the godless but upon God-fearing men. Only such men who strive to live a stainless life will be accepted in his service. Cheaters and liars will never be favored by him. He who is not honest in his dealings or truthful in his speech will not have the confidence of the king because he will also cheat the king and lie to him. A means of eradicating all godlessness and wickedness from the land should be the willingness to pass correct judgment in favor of the oppressed and persecuted. Every morning he will permit all to appear before his judgment seat, even the poorest in his kingdom, in order that right and justice may prevail and crime may be banished from the city and country.

psalm 101

Domine, exaudi

A prayer of one in affliction.
The fifth penitential psalm

1. A prayer of the poor man when he was anxious and poured out his supplication before the Lord.

2. Hear, O Lord, my prayer: and let my cry come to thee.

3. Turn not away thy face from me: in the day when I am in trouble, incline thy ear to me.
   In what day soever I shall call upon thee, hear me speedily.

4. For my days are vanished like smoke: and my bones are grown dry like fuel for the fire.

5. I am smitten as grass, and my heart is withered: because I forgot to eat my bread.

6. Through the voice of my groaning, my bone hath cleaved to my flesh.

7. I am become like to a pelican of the wilderness: I am like a night raven in the house.

8. I have watched, and am become as a sparrow all alone on the housetop.

9. All the day long my enemies reproached me: and they that praised me did swear against me.

10. For I did eat ashes like bread and mingled my drink with weeping.

11. Because of thy anger and indignation: for having lifted me up thou hast thrown me down.

12. My days have declined like a shadow, and I am withered like grass.

13. But thou, O Lord, endurest forever: and thy memorial to all generations.

14. Thou shalt arise and have mercy on Sion: for it is time to have mercy on it, for the time is come.

15. For the stones thereof have pleased thy servants: and they shall have pity on the earth thereof.

16. And the Gentiles shall fear thy name, O Lord, and all the kings of the earth thy glory.

378

17. For the Lord hath built up Sion: and he shall be seen in his glory.

18. He hath had regard to the prayer of the humble: and he hath not despised their petition.

19. Let these things be written unto another generation: and the people that shall be created shall praise the Lord.

20. Because he hath looked forth from his high sanctuary: from heaven the Lord hath looked upon the earth.

21. That he might hear the groans of them that are in fetters: that he might release the children of the slain.

22. That they may declare the name of the Lord in Sion: and his praise in Jerusalem:

23. When the people assemble together, and kings, to serve the Lord.

24. He answered him in the way of his strength: declare unto me the fewness of my days.

25. Call me not away in the midst of my days: thy years are unto generation and generation.

26. In the beginning, O Lord, thou foundest the earth: and the heavens are the works of thy hands.

27. They shall perish, but thou remainest: and all of them shall grow old like a garment.
And as a vesture thou shalt change them, and they shall be changed.

28. But thou art always the selfsame, and thy years shall not fail.

29. The children of thy servants shall continue: and their seed shall be directed forever.

W HEN this psalm was composed, Israel had for some time lived in the Babylonian captivity. As long as the temple in Jerusalem still stood, the great number of the banished were not yet conscious of the full measure of the divine punishment. But when the news of the destruction of the city and of its sanctuary had reached Babylon, they were no longer indifferent but discouraged and mistrustful in their Messianic hope. Now the Prophet Ezechiel appeared as a father and spiritual guide to console and comfort them by reminding them of the divine promises. The Lord will permit Sion to be raised from dust and ashes. There will be a new and great time of divine mercy and grace. Such words from the prophet's mouth awakened in the captives an ardent desire to witness the hour of deliverance. With this sentiment the psalmist prays in the name of his fellow-citizens banished from their homes. After the return to their native country, the psalm has not lost its importance. The nearer the fullness of time approached the more vivid the longing of the Messias became among the believing Israelites. The cry for help among the banished became the advent cry of humanity for redemption. It is a prayer for everyone who is discouraged because of bodily or spiritual ailment and need.

The advent call begins with an urgent petition that the Lord may hear the suppliant's prayer (verses 2–3). "O Lord, hear my prayer and let my cry come unto thee." This is the common cry of the Church with which she sends her prayers to heaven; for when the Lord turns his countenance away from the petitioner or conceals it, when he does not want prayers, the petitioner seeks in vain. Therefore the petition that God may mercifully condescend to pay attention to our prayers and that he may not delay in sending us help is placed first.

For Israel the days of captivity were days of grave distress, the distress of a people without a home (verses 4–12). The poet adds picture upon picture to impress the people with the greatness of this need. The life of a man is of itself short and fleeting; the long banishment has consumed the strength of the nation. A cloud appearing in the sky is quickly blown away by a brief puff of wind. It is broken up by it so that every trace of it disappears in the sky. And so it happens to a people that is vanquished, made captive, and deprived of its liberty. No further act of violence is necessary to reduce and destroy it altogether. Resistance on the other hand is out of the question. When a log of wood catches fire and turns into coal, it breaks at every touch. The sufferings of a country act like fire; for they exhaust all will to resistance. The grass grows exuberantly after the winter rains, but when the hot wind comes from the southeast the grass withers and dries. So also the glowing breath of the divine wrath has dried up life's energy, has torn the people away from their native country, has deprived them of the source of grace of the sanctuary. And thus Israel languishes in exile. Sorrow and misery have caused the prophet such mental agony that he has forgotten to give his body the necessary nourishment. He can only complain and lament. All strength and vigor of life have vanished. The Book of Proverbs says: "A glad heart causes a ripe old age, and an oppressed mind dries up the bones" (17:22).

He who is sad avoids pleasant company; even the light of day troubles a gloomy soul. Like a pelican which often sits the entire day on a lonely rock shore and nests at the edge of a dismal swamp, like a night-owl who hides from the day in a crumbling wall, so the captives seek solitary places away from the activities of the Gentile world in order to mourn and weep. The solemn festivities of the Gentile gods remind them of the great feasts they had celebrated at Jerusalem; they therefore withdraw so as not to see the pageants which only increase their sorrow. They avoid meeting their conquerors that they may not be ridiculed. As a bird which has been robbed of its nest sits helpless and alone on the roof, so now they sit at the rivers of Babylon and lament the Holy City which now lies desolate; they weep for the temple which now lies in ruins; they mourn their native country which they so sincerely love. Their sorrow for being deprived of their native home is increased by the mockery of the enemy. The fate of Israel has become a curse word for many: "May it happen to thee as it happened to Israel." Thus sorrow and humiliation became their daily food: "I eat ashes like bread." In great mourning they strewed ashes upon their heads and sat in ashes that were strewed upon the ground. Thus this practice became symbolic of every great affliction and especially of spiritual sadness. On festive occasions the conquerors mixed their wine with spices in order to make it stronger and more fragrant. But the captive mixed his drink with tears. The consciousness of having caused their own sad condition by challenging God's wrath troubled the captives more than the ridicule and mockery of the enemy. When an innocent man suffers, he has at least the consolation that he himself was not the cause of his suffering and he has the assurance that the Lord will not delay with his help. But the thought of being rejected by God in his justifiable wrath deprived many of the hope of ever again returning to their native land. As evening shadows lengthen and disappear, so life reaches its rapid end and disappears in the darkness of death. Taken away from their native country, the strength of life vanished like grass that is torn up and thrown away. According to human reckoning the collapse of Israel was sealed.

Yet the thoughts and plans of God are broader than limited human knowledge. His plans are reconciliation and return, not destruction. The Lord does not wish the death of the sinner. Therefore he has not only threatened the captives through the voice of the prophets, but he has also promised the return home after the banished had acknowledged their guilt and done penance. Thus in the midst of the adversities of the exile there remained for Israel and remains for every sinner estranged from God the consolation of faith (verses 13–23). God is always the same and his plans do not change. Therefore he can never forget his people nor can he reject those whom he has chosen to be the bearers of his promises that Israel will bring salvation to the Gentile world. It is certain that he will permit Sion to rise again from its ruins as soon as the hour of mercy has arrived. The time is near. The Prophet Jeremias prophecied a period of seventy years at the end of which Babylon would fall and liberty would again be restored to the captives. The liberator Cyrus, heralded by Isaias, even now lives and rules as king of the Persian Empire and threatens the kingdom of Babylon. The captives have been converted and have done penance; the conditions for being reconciled have been fulfilled and forgiveness for their offense has been granted.

The loss of grace makes many a man appreciate its value. So also the love of Israel for Sion grew after the sanctuary had been destroyed. The homesickness of the captives increased as the vision of the renewal of the solemn divine service in the temple became more and more a possibility. Testimony to this is borne by the fact that on the fifth anniversary of the destruction of the temple a collection was taken up in order that sacrifices could be offered upon the ruins of the sanctuary requesting their return home and the reconstruction of the house of God (Baruch 1:6). When the Lord permits them to return home, a new era will begin in which the Messianic promises will be fulfilled. Then the Gentiles will experience the power of Yahwe and they will be astounded at his glory. They will hear the glad tidings of salvation and will worship the Name of the most high God in all reverence and will bend their knees to his majesty. The unexpected reconstruction of Jerusalem and its temple from the debris and ashes will be the first great revelation of the glory of Yahwe. By this the kings of the Gentile nations will know that the God of Israel has the power to fulfill his given word and that even a ruler of a pagan world kingdom will assist in fulfilling God's plans for Israel. The reconstruction of Jerusalem and its temple is for Israel a sign and a guarantee that God has forgiven his people and that he has heard their petitions in the land of captivity.

Firmly believing in God's truthfulness and fidelity the psalmist is so firmly convinced about the fulfillment of all of God's promises that he even now admonishes to mark down God's great deed of redemption for all coming generations. Later generations who have not endured the great hardships of the captivity should not forget the magnanimous deed of the Lord and should sing songs of praise for the redeemed people throughout the centuries. They should always be reminded of this great work of divine power, wisdom, and love; they should be reminded of how the Lord of mercy looked down from the heights of heaven upon the affliction of his people and of all humanity in order to redeem them; how in his infinite mercy he looked upon the distress of a people without a country. They should always be reminded of how graciously he listened to the petitions of the captives; how he cared for them who without his help would have surely perished, and how he miraculously freed them from captivity and led them back home to their native country. He did this for his honor's sake. He has chosen and made Israel his people in order that it might proclaim his name among the Gentiles and make known to them the Messianic salvation. It was God who made his dwelling on Mount Sion and erected his sanctuary in Jerusalem in order that in that place his name would receive praise and honor and that from that place truth and salvation would be propagated into the world. The restoration of the nation and its temple could only be brought about by God if both would carry out their mission in the world.

This mission the new Sion of the Messianic era, the Church, will take over from the Old Sion. It must be continued by the citizens of the New Jerusalem until all nations gather in the Holy City and all kingdoms of the earth serve the one true God, until the kingdom of God, the Church of Jesus Christ, comprises all the nations of the earth and all nations serve the Lord.

In few words the psalmist has given us a beautiful picture of the future Messianic era. It filled the hearts of the captives with an ardent desire for Sion and its temple and for the blessings of the Messianic salvation. Hence the advent call closes with an expression of longing to live this salvation (verses 24–29). It is his own supreme wish. The captivity has broken his strength and has aged him prematurely. He fears that he will not return home; he fears that he will not experience the consolation and joy of seeing his native country again. He beseeches the Lord, as later the old man Simeon did, that God may not let him see death until his eyes have seen salvation. The Lord can grant him this petition for he is the Eternal who outlives all generations; he can prolong a man's span of life and keep him. He can do this for he is the Almighty. He has formed the earth; it is his work; he has spanned the heavens and created the numberless stars; they are the creatures of his hand. Should not his power be sufficient to lengthen the life of man for a few years? Should he not have the power to bring salvation soon? All the works of the Lord are subject to change. This change is willed by the Creator. They pass away, but he alone remains unchanged in the midst of a changing world. As a cloak grows old, wears out, and is replaced by a new garment, so also times and conditions change according to the will of the divine Guide of the world. God alone is beyond all change; neither are his plans subjected to change. May all the boundaries of nations be altered, may dynasties end, the plans of the divine Ruler of the world will remain untouched. No revolutions can change or destroy the dominion of God. God always remains the same and his years will not end. Despite continuous changes his government is beyond time and events and will not be taken from him. He has all changes under his control. He accomplishes all and intends to fulfill all plans for a divine world dominion according to his law and will. In this supremacy over changes of times and nations the people of Messianic times and the Church will participate. The children of thy servants will remain, the new Sion and its temple, the Sion of Messianic times and its sanctuary, the Church of Christ, will remain; it will not be destroyed. The Church of Christ will be the home for all coming generations until the end of time.

psalm 102

Benedic, anima

Thanksgiving to God for his mercies

1. For David himself.
Bless the Lord, O my soul: and let all that is within me bless his holy name.

2. Bless the Lord, O my soul, and never forget all he hath done for thee.

3. Who forgiveth all thy iniquities: who healeth all thy diseases.

4. Who redeemeth thy life from destruction: who crowneth thee with mercy and compassion.

5. Who satisfieth thy desires with good things: thy youth shall be renewed like the eagles.

6. The Lord doth mercies, and judgment for all that suffer wrong.

7. He hath made his ways known to Moses: his will to the children of Israel.

8. The Lord is compassionate and merciful: long-suffering and plenteous in mercy.

9. He will not always be angry: nor will he threaten forever.

10. He hath not dealt with us according to our sins: nor rewarded us according to our iniquities.

11. For according to the height of the heaven above the earth: he hath strengthened his mercy towards them that fear him.

12. As far as the east is from the west, so far hath he removed our iniquities from us.

13. As a father hath compassion on his children, so hath the Lord compassion on them that fear him:

14. For he knoweth our frame: He remembereth that we are dust.

15. Man's days are as grass, as the flower of the field so shall he flourish.

16. For the spirit shall pass in him, and he shall not be: and he shall know his place no more.

17. But the mercy of the Lord is from eternity and unto eternity upon them that fear him: and his justice unto the children's children.

18. To such as keep his covenant, and are mindful of his commandments to do them.

19. The Lord hath prepared his throne in heaven: and his kingdom shall rule over all.

20. Bless the Lord, all ye his angels: you that are mighty in strength, and execute his word, hearkening to the voice of his orders.

21. Bless the Lord, all ye his hosts: you ministers of his that do his will.

22. Bless the Lord, all his works: in every place of his dominion, O my soul, bless thou the Lord.

THE Apostle Paul has called God: "The God of love" (2 Corinthians 13:11). And John summarizes his whole nature in one sentence: "God is love" (1 John 4:8). "The love of God is poured into our hearts through the Holy Spirit, whom he has given to us" (Romans 5:5). In love he has predestined us to be his children; in love he has sent us his Son in order that all who believe in him may have eternal life; in love he has redeemed us and vivified us in Christ.

About all these miracles of divine grace and mercy the Christian is reminded when he contemplates the God of love. The just man of the Old Testament could not delve so deeply into the abyss of the divine love. Yet he too has experienced in his own life and in the history of his people the love of God. He too acknowledged gladly and thankfully that God is love. So also the psalmist has experienced in his life this love and in this psalm he gives the sentiments of his soul. He meditates on God's love; he reflects upon its revelations in his own life and in the life of his people and seeks to understand the fundamental reasons of this love.

He first meditates upon the love of God as manifested in his own life (verses 1-5). It is a theme that is not only worthy to be considered and meditated upon again and again, it is also a subject that must fill the heart with joy and jubilation. One cannot meditate upon the love of God without joy and gladness. Thus the psalmist calls upon his own soul, his entire self to praise the holy Name of God, his nature, his goodness, and mercy: intellect and will, sentiment and memory should unite their powers in praising God's goodness. To praise is a duty of gratitude. Great and

385

numerous are the gifts which man has received and continually receives
from the Lord. How could the soul for one moment be unmindful of the
greatest Benefactor and of the manifestations of his love? The memory of
him should never fade; the praise of him should never be silenced. The
greatest grace is redemption from sin, the deliverance from all spiritual
ailments. If God would always be mindful of our sins, if he would not
erase them, who could continue to exist before his infinite holiness? If
sins are as scarlet, he cleanses them so that they become white as snow;
if sins are red as a crimson mantle, he cleanses them so that the soul
becomes white as wool. With the sins he also heals the effects of sin. He
gives a new heart; he puts a new spirit in the inner man. The Lord forgives all guilt may it be ever so great; he heals all moral weaknesses.
There are none which he cannot heal. The life of the body and of the soul
are protected by God. Even if man were at the brink of death, indeed,
even at the brink of eternal death God could save him with the help of his
grace. With love and kindness he protects life, as it were, with a large
shield. He stills the desires of the heart for true happiness by his blessings,
enlightenment, and consolations; for God alone can still the longings of
the human heart. With his supernatural grace he revives the strength of
man, just as an eagle renewing its feathers and being strengthened flies
towards the sun. The Christian is mindful of his renewal of life in Christ
which the Lord has granted him by imparting sanctifying grace; he is
mindful of the renewal and increase of spiritual strength through the
sacraments and all other means of grace.

Just as the Catholic placed in the life stream of divine love and grace
which flows through the kingdom of God is concerned with the preservation and spread of the Church, so also the Israelite was concerned about
the great deeds of divine Love manifested to the entire people as well as
to the individual. It was Israel's concern because of the covenant made on
Sinai between God and his people. Therefore the psalmist now begins his
meditation upon the love of God as manifested in the history of his people
(verses 6–13). The entire history gives testimony to the truth that the
Lord does justice to the oppressed. As often as the people were harassed
by the enemy God espoused their cause and sent them a deliverer.
Already at the beginning of its history the Lord proved himself to be a
merciful God. On Mount Sinai the people sinned gravely by worshiping
the golden calf. The Lord wanted to destroy them and to make Moses the
leader of a new people. Then Moses made intercession for his people and
the Lord again showed mercy and promised Moses that he himself would
lead them into the promised land. To Moses he confirmed his willingness
by manifesting his glory (Exodus 33).

At that time Israel experienced an act of God which must have convinced it that God will not always be angry and wrathful against it because of grievous guilt committed, but that he is quickly ready to forgive and bestow grace. He disciplines and punishes, but he does not destroy. Israel has by its grievous sin on Sinai well deserved to be destroyed. And its guilt grew because of its obstinacy and its faithlessness from generation to generation. But God has never punished it according to the grievousness of its guilt. He always let mercy and kindness reign. Such dealing with his people corresponds to the nature of God which is love, love without limitation. No man is capable of measuring the distance between heaven and earth and give it in numbers. So immeasurably great is God's love, so great is its effective power to all who belong to the saints, to his chosen people; for to the citizens of his chosen nation belongs his mercy in the first place. Great is the distance between the rising and the setting of the sun and for this also there is no human measurement. Just that far has the Lord removed the sins of his people from his eyes so that he will never again be mindful of them. They shall be to God as if they had never been committed. How great and strong can the love of a sacrificing father be to his child, but infinitely greater and stronger is the love of God and of his providence for his holy and chosen people. This history of divine Love for his people Israel has also been written for the consolation of Christians who know themselves to be guilty of many transgressions against God.

Why is the majestic God in heaven so merciful towards us as individuals and as a nation? What is the motive of the divine love (verses 14–22)? It is clear that man by himself did not merit this love, and the psalmist knows very well that Israel at no time has deserved it. And nevertheless this ineffable love continues. The reason for this is found in God himself, in his sympathy with human weakness and proneness to sin. He knows that men are formed from the dust of the earth; he knows the weaknesses and changeableness of the human being have their source in original sin. Man and even a whole nation may be likened to the grass of the field and the flower in the meadow. As long as the rain and dew give sufficient moisture to the soul, they sprout quickly and grow exuberantly; but as soon as the winter rains cease and the hot winds blow upon them and parch them, their beauty quickly fades and every trace of it is lost. This is a picture of the changeableness and weakness of human life. As long as God's grace and love fructify it, it sprouts forth and flourishes. But when once the hot wind of suffering falls upon it and the divine wrath passes over it, when the Lord withdraws the assistance of his grace, then everything collapses and one scarcely recognizes the place where man dwelt and worked. The unchangeableness of divine mercy and the eternal divine love outlasts the changeableness of human life. To him who fears and serves the Lord he bestows his love and remains faithful throughout all generations. God will always assist him lovingly who is determined upon keeping his divine laws. "The ways of the Lord are mercy and truth: to them that seek after his covenant and his testimonies" (Psalm 24:10).

The Lord, the eternal, faithful and kind God is the king of the universe forever. His throne is in heaven. He is surrounded by legions of blessed spirits, witnesses to his power, love, and fidelity. His power is the best guarantee for the continuation of his bounteous protection. His dominion extends over the whole world. Therefore the psalmist calls upon the whole world to praise him. The angels should praise him, the strong army of heavenly spirits, the faithful fulfillers of his commands. They are there not only in the service of his punitive justice, but also in the service of his infinite love and mercy; for he has commanded them to carry the just in their hands lest they may strike their foot against a stone. The entire host of angels should praise God; all creatures and powers in heaven and on earth which fulfill his holy will, all his works should praise him; all should give testimony everywhere of his wisdom and goodness.

psalm 103

Benedic, anima

God is to be praised for his mighty works and wonderful providence

1. For David himself.
   Bless the Lord, O my soul: O Lord, my God, thou art exceedingly great. Thou hast put on praise and beauty.

2. And art clothed with light as with a garment. Who stretchest out the heaven like a pavilion.

3. Who coverest the higher rooms thereof with water, who makest the clouds thy chariot: who walkest upon the wings of the winds.

4. Who makest thy angels spirits: and thy ministers a burning fire.

5. Who hast founded the earth upon its own bases: it shall not be moved forever and ever.

6. The deep like a garment is its clothing: above the mountains shall the waters stand.

7. At thy rebuke they shall flee; at the voice of thy thunder they shall fear.

8. The mountains ascend, and the plains descend into the place which thou hast founded for them.

9. Thou hast set a bound which they shall not pass over; neither shall they return to cover the earth.

10. Thou sendest forth springs in the vales: between the midst of the hills the waters shall pass.

11. All the beasts of the field shall drink: the wild asses shall expect in their thirst.

12. Over them the birds of the air shall dwell: from the midst of the rocks they shall give forth their voices.

13. Thou waterest the hills from thy upper rooms: the earth shall be filled with the fruit of thy works.

14. Bringing forth grass for cattle, and herb for the service of men.
That thou mayest bring bread out of the earth:

15. And that wine may cheer the heart of man.
That he may make the face cheerful with oil: and that bread may strengthen man's heart.

16. The trees of the field shall be filled, and the cedars of Libanus which he hath planted:

17. There the sparrows shall make their nests. The highest of them is the house of the heron.

18. The high hills are a refuge for the harts, the rocks for the urchins.

19. He hath made the moon for seasons: the sun knoweth his going down.

20. Thou hast appointed darkness, and it is night: in it shall all the beasts of the woods go about.

21. The young lions roaring after their prey, and seeking their meat from God.

22. The sun ariseth, and they are gathered together: and they shall lie down in their dens.

23. Man shall go forth to his work, and to his labor until evening.

24. How great are thy works, O Lord! Thou hast made all things in wisdom: the earth is filled with thy riches.

25. So is this great sea, which stretcheth wide its arms: there are creeping
    things without number:
    Creatures little and great.

26. There the ships shall go.
    This sea dragon which thou hast formed to play therein.

27. All expect of thee, that thou give them food in season.

28. What thou givest to them they shall gather up: when thou openest thy
    hand, they shall all be filled with good.

29. But if thou turnest away thy face, they shall be troubled: thou shalt take
    away their breath, and they shall fail, and shall return to their dust.

30. Thou shalt send forth thy spirit, and they shall be created: and thou shalt
    renew the face of the earth.

31. May the glory of the Lord endure forever: the Lord shall rejoice in his
    works.

32. He looketh upon the earth, and maketh it tremble: he toucheth the
    mountains and they smoke.

33. I will sing to the Lord as long as I live: I will sing praise to my God while
    I have my being.

34. Let my speech be acceptable to him: but I will take delight in the Lord.

35. Let sinners be consumed out of the earth, and the unjust, so that they be
    no more: O my soul, bless thou the Lord.

WHAT is written on the first page of Sacred Scripture in brief weighty
sentences about the work of creation by God, that the composer of
this psalm tells us in lovely picturesque language about the Creator.
There it is God's almighty power that is described as the source of all
things; here it is God's wisdom and love which we must admire and
glorify in his creatures. A veritable artist the psalmist places us in the
midst of God's creatures and displays them before our imagination. The
poet has not followed the order of the biblical narrative of creation, but
has freely made his own picture.

The psalm begins with a prelude (verses 1–4). It shows God in his
majesty and power. As the vestibule of a church is there for the purpose
of gathering one's thoughts, of directing these thoughts to the mystery
that is venerated and adored in the house of God, so also this prelude is
intended to fill the soul with holy, reverential, and awesome sentiments
with which man should meditate upon and admire the great work of the
divine Architect. As the sun rainbows itself in the dewdrops, so God's

glory mirrors itself in his creatures; but as the light of the sun is millions of times greater than the reflection in the dewdrop, so is God's glory minimally reflected in his works. Creation is only a spark of the infinite sea of light of his true nature. But despite this infinity the psalmist feels himself so near to his Creator that he calls him his Lord and his God. This is a justifiable pride that because of a covenant he stands in union with God, but this places upon him the obligation to praise the Lord in his works.

Creation is, as it were, a beautiful garment with which the Creator clothes himself and in which he shows himself to man. His garment of light is the starry heaven with its millions of sparkling stars; the sun is a reflection of the inner glory of light in God. The Lord is sublime and infinitely majestic. Who can measure the extent of the firmament? Alone God has spread this great tent over the earth without any effort, as if it were a small shepherd's tent. The vault of heaven is the garret of the world-house; it is, as it were, the huge roof over all created things. When men build a house, it must rest on a firm foundation otherwise it will not endure. God, however, built this gigantic vault upon the eternally moving sea without it being moved. The poet speaks as his limited intellect understands. When he from the mountains of his native country looked west to the sea, the firmament in the distant horizon seemed to rest on the sea. The clouds too manifest God's power. His will holds them suspended despite the heavy mass of water. At his word they speed onward in the sky; he appears upon them in order to hold judgment in the storm. The winds too must obey his holy will. They are his messengers whom he sends forth. Even the lightning flashes are in the service of the most high God. The pagans saw in them the ruling gods; but for Israel they were the servants of their God.

After the prelude the psalmist enters upon a meditation of the works of creation. He starts immediately with the second day of creation and describes the formation of the earth and mainland (verses 5–9). The formation of the earth belongs to the great natural mysteries of antiquity. The ancients thought that it rested on gigantic pillars whose foundations lay deep in the bottom of the sea so that they would not tremble. At the beginning of creation everything was covered with water. Upon the entire earth, even above the summits of the highest mountains, there was water. As the garment covers the body, so the water encompassed the mainland. Then with the thunderous voice of his power the Lord commanded the waters to recede into one place in order that the mainland might appear. The psalmist now describes picturesquely how the waters were frightened, took flight, and sought refuge in the large basin determined by God. The earth then appeared. But now a command of the Lord was given to the earth; a violent trembling and quaking went through the mass. The mountains rose from the flat land; they rose higher and higher until they reached the clouds; between the heights the earth sank and formed narrow gorges and broad valleys. It is a sketch of the earth's history as geologists have since recorded it. It is a poetic description of the great evolutions which happened in antiquity on the surface of the earth. As ancient and as violent as these movements have been, they were directed by the Creator; they were accomplished according to one eternal plan. The place of every mountain and its height, the place of every valley and its breadth was determined by God. Sacred Scripture knows nothing about the battle of the gods with the Titans in order to take from them the work of creation. God himself is the infinite power to whom everything must submit. Just as the Creator has given to mountains and valleys their places, so likewise he has determined the boundaries of the sea which it may not break through. Never again shall it cover the face of the earth with its waters. Often it is only light sand that borders the sea, but the floods must respect the apparently light barriers for they are placed there by God.

On the third day of the six days' work God had already separated the sea from the mainland and had given them each their place. The poet's description treats more minutely this work than does the first book of Moses. He does not speak about the origin of plant life, but about everything that has any bearing upon it. For watering the Creator permitted springs to come up from the mysterious depths of the mountains and brooks to run between the mountains into the valleys. They condition life in nature and give drink to the beasts in the fields. God was mindful of everything, even of the beasts of the forest and of the field that do not receive nourishment from man. For them God makes the water flow so that the wild asses, so shy of man, may not thirst. Green bands of trees and bushes surround the shores of brooks and rivers and sink their roots into the fertile soil moistened by the water. In their shady branches birds build their nests and sing their songs of thanksgiving to their Creator who so lovingly cares for them. Even the summits of the highest mountains where there are no springs and brooks are watered by the Creator. He lets rain fall upon them from heaven, from his garret, and saturates the whole earth with precious moisture which his almighty power has called into existence. From the moist soil God lets the grass sprout for the nourishment of the animal world—vegetables and grains for the use of men in order that they may obtain bread from the kernels. Besides grain the soil brings forth wine and oil, the main products of Palestine. God gives the vine to man in order that his soul may rejoice and his countenance may show gladness, as if it were anointed with oil. The bread, the mainstay of

life, should strengthen and keep him in vigor. The rain also gives drink
to the trees of God; that is, the trees that are not nurtured by men, but are
left entirely to God's care. The proud cedars of Lebanon, a plantation of
God, are kept and nourished by the Creator. At the same time he intended
the high trees to be a home for the birds. In their branches the small birds
have built their nests; in the upper branches the stork has built its house.
Even the high mountains, inaccessible to man, are not desolate. God has
given them to the chamois and the goats. In the hill caverns the badger
has taken refuge. Thus the Creator has provided for all plants, animals,
and men.

On the fourth day God created (verses 19-23) the sun, the moon, and
the stars. He intended them to be time measurements for man, and
celestial lights: the sun as the star of the day and the moon as the star of
the night. He gave them their law of movement according to which they
have run their courses for thousands of years. The sun has its time for rising and setting. It fulfills its task and runs its course according to the order
determined by God. When it sets, night begins. The east knows nothing
of a long twilight. Darkness is the time for wild animals. When the sun
has disappeared, the forests and the thickets become alive. The lion
leaves its den to seek booty; the young lion roars for its prey. The psalmist
sees in this roaring the prayers of the animals to God that he may give
them nourishment. A religious change even takes hold of wild animals.
As soon as the sun appears on the eastern horizon the savage animals
again seek their hiding places and being sated stretch their bodies upon
their lairs. Even the king of the animal world, the lion, withdraws and
clears the field for man, the king of all creation, who rules during the day;
for he is a child of the day. His work is day work; for him night is a time
for rest.

The psalmist now meditates upon God's wisdom and power in creation
(verses 24-35). Numerous are the deeds of the Lord. Everywhere there
is revealed a remarkable wisdom in the variety of creatures upon earth
in the plant and in the animal world. How wonderfully everything is
coordinated. All are dependent on one another; one must help the other
and every creature must be of service to all. The deeper the student of
nature delves into the study of the coordination of creatures the more will
he agree with the psalmist that God has done all things wisely. The
Creator has populated not only the earth but also the sea with numberless animals. As great and wide as the ocean is, it is inhabited by all kinds
of creatures, large and small, some of which even today the eyes of no
man has seen and the life of which no science has accounted for. The sea
animals alone form a wonder world of God's power and wisdom. There
are giants of creation who pass through the waters like ships. Among them

the psalmist mentions the leviathan, which despite its size and its danger to man is, as it were, a plaything in the hands of God. Probably the whale is meant by this animal which in ancient times was also in the Mediterranean Sea. All these animals large and small, depend on the providence of God. They cannot live without him. He gives nourishment to all of them; he gives them whatever they need at the right time and in proper measure. What great knowledge and wisdom this care of the animal world supposes! He, as it were, places before every animal its food and all thankfully take it from the Creator's hand. All are sated by the nourishment that is proper for them when he opens his hand and distributes his gifts. All creatures are dependent on him; they can live only so long as he provides for them. When he has decided their death, when he has taken from them the breath of life, they die and turn into dust. But they die to make room for other creatures. They continue to live in their genus and thus the appearance of the earth is continually renewed. In the plant and animal world there is a going and a coming so that in the course of a definite time a new world of living beings comes into existence.

The creation is the great work of God "*ad externum.*" It manifests his power and wisdom and the renown of the Creator as long as it exists. When God had completed his work, he looked at it and saw that it was good. It corresponded to the divine concept of creation. Therefore the Lord rejoiced at his work. And the work praises the Master. The Lord should also have his glory in the creation of man. Woe, therefore, to the man who disobeys the will of God and brings upon himself God's wrath. God is also a terrifying power. When he looks upon earth in his wrath, it quakes and shakes; when he only touches the mountains, they become firebrands. Man's duty is to strive to know the works of God and from them to know the Creator; to praise him because of his works and to glorify him in songs. It is a duty that continues during our whole life. The deeper man delves into the mysteries of God's works the more reasons he will find to praise God. Yet all the praise of God from the mouth of man is only a babbling; it is inadequate to the greatness of God and to the sublimity of his works. Hence man must humbly pray to the Lord that he may graciously accept his stammering because he finds his greatest joy in God alone and will try to obtain it in meditation upon his Word. When all creatures are praising God, the sinners who offend him cause a shrill discord in the immense choir. But this discord will cease as soon as the Messianic judgment will arrive; for in the new world only just men shall live and the godless will be excluded forever. The souls who in the time of the transfiguration want to sing the praises of the Lord for all eternity must even now praise the Lord in his creation.

psalm 104

Confitemini Domino

A thanksgiving to God for his benefits to his people Israel

ALLELUIA

1. Give glory to the Lord and call upon his name: declare his deeds among the Gentiles.

2. Sing to him, yea, sing his praises: relate all his wondrous works.

3. Glory ye in his holy name: let the heart of them rejoice that seek the Lord.

4. Seek ye the Lord and be strengthened: seek ye his face evermore.

5. Remember his marvelous works which he hath done: his wonders and the judgments of his mouth.

6. O ye seed of Abraham his servant; ye sons of Jacob his chosen.

7. He is the Lord our God: his judgments are in all the earth.

8. He has remembered his covenant forever: the word which he commanded to a thousand generations.

9. Which he made to Abraham and his oath to Isaac.

10. And he appointed the same to Jacob for a law, and to Israel for an everlasting testament.

11. Saying: to thee will I give the land of Canaan, the lot of your inheritance.

12. When they were but a small number: yea, a very few, the sojourners therein.

13. And they passed from nation to nation, and from one kingdom to another people.

14. He suffered no man to hurt them: and he reproved kings for their sakes.

15. Touch ye not my anointed: and do not evil to my prophets.

16. And he called a famine upon the land and he broke in pieces all the support of bread.

17. He sent a man before them: Joseph who was sold for a slave.

18. They humbled his feet in fetters: the iron pierced his soul,

19. Until his word came.
The word of the Lord inflamed him.

20. The king sent, and he released him: the ruler of the people, and he set him at liberty.

21. He made him master of his house and ruler of all his possessions.

22. That he might instruct his princes as himself, and teach his ancients wisdom.

23. And Israel went into Egypt: and Jacob was a sojourner in the land of Cham.

24. And he increased his people exceedingly: and strengthened them over his enemy.

25. He turned their heart to hate his people: and to deal deceitfully with his servants.

26. He sent Moses his servant: Aaron the man whom he had chosen.

27. He gave them power to show his signs, and his wonders in the land of Cham.

28. He sent darkness, and made it obscure, and grieved not his words.

29. He turned their waters into blood, and destroyed their fish.

30. Their land brought forth frogs, in the inner chambers of their kings.

31. He spoke and there came diverse sorts of flies and sciniphs in all their coasts.

32. He gave them hail for rain, a burning fire in the land.

33. And he destroyed their vineyards, and their fig trees: and he broke in pieces the trees of their coasts.

34. He spoke and the locusts came, and the bruchus of which there was no number.

35. And they devoured all the grass in their land: and consumed all the fruit of their ground.

36. And he slew all the first-born in their land: the first fruits of all their labor.

37. And he brought them out with silver and gold: and there was not among their bribes one that was feeble.

38. Egypt was glad when they departed: for the fear of them lay upon them.

39. He spread a cloud for their protection and fire to give them light in the night.

40. They asked and the quail came, and he filled them with the bread of heaven.

41. He opened the rock and waters flowed: the rivers ran down in the dry land.

42. Because he remembered his holy word which he had spoken to his servant Abraham.

43. And he brought forth his people with joy and his chosen with gladness.

44. And he gave them the lands of the Gentiles: and they possessed the labors of the people:

45. That they might observe his justifications and seek after his law.

THE history of the people of Israel has greater significance than the history of any other nation of antiquity because it had been chosen by God to be the bearer of revelation and the guardian of the Messianic promises, and salvation was to come to the world through its mediation. Israel's history is the history of redemption; it is the way determined by God which leads men to Christ. The object of the meditations to which the composers of the psalms and the prophets again and again referred was the way in which the divine decree of redemption was gradually revealed in and through Israel. The people were to remain conscious of their great mission and to walk worthily of their calling for which God had chosen them. For us also who look back to the fulfillment of the divine plan of redemption through Christ it should be of interest to follow the footsteps of God in the Old Testament. Indeed, it is a duty of thankful love for all who are redeemed to meditate upon the divine plans which were intended not only for the redemption of fallen mankind, but also for the giving of grace to those chosen by God for salvation. The composer of this psalm leads us back to the beginning of the history of the Israelitic people, to the time of the call of Abraham, and to the exodus from Egypt. The purpose of the psalm, therefore, is to give the history before the making of the covenant on Mount Sinai.

The psalm begins with a call to praise God (verses 1-6). The study of the history of redemption should not be merely to satisfy our thirst for knowledge, it should be prayerful and should fill the soul with incentives to praise God. Adoration of the sublime name of Yahwe, of his glory and majesty should be the fruit of the meditation; it should awaken the desire to spread the renown of the Lord's deeds into the Gentile world in order that it too might recognize his greatness and power and acknowledge him as God. It would be ingratitude if the people of God would conceal the works of the Lord under a bushel. The deeds of the Lord were not done for Israel alone; they had a supernatural significance. Israel must place

397

these works on a candlestick in order that all nations may see them and praise the Father who is in heaven. On this account the glad message of the power and love of God should never cease. Israel should always glorify God in its songs. The fathers should instruct their children and these should pass on the instructions to the coming generations in order that the memory of the great things which the Lord has done for his people may live on throughout all ages.

Did not Israel have sufficient reason to boast of its God before the Gentiles? Of what significance were the gods of the Gentiles? They were mere nothing and yet the Gentiles were proud of their idols. How justifiable was Israel's pride because of its God: he alone is holy; he alone is the Lord; he alone is the Most High. How it should rejoice because it is called to worship him! How the soul of man must be gratified to seek the Lord, to learn his nature and the revelations of his wisdom and power from history, to have the knowledge of his greatness, of his countenance, of the presence of his grace in the sanctuary of the tabernacle among men, and of having the privilege of visiting him there at all times. The more man learns the greatness of God from the fulfillment of his plan of salvation in history, the more he will seek union with him and the greater will be his confidence in him. Therefore it is useful to meditate frequently upon his wonders and signs, to think about his punishments and judgments. The children of Abraham especially have this duty because it was in their favor that the miracles and signs were wrought and because as descendants of the sons of the Patriarch Jacob they are the chosen people of God.

The word *chosen* leads the psalmist to the subject of his meditation; namely to the history before the selection of the chosen people through the covenant on Mount Sinai. He begins with the history of the Patriarchs (verses 7–15). He begins with the assurance which God gave that he would give to their descendants the land of Canaan as an inheritance. Yahwe, the God of Israel, is the Lord of all the earth; he rules in justice over the universe. To him belong all the countries and kingdoms of this world; he can distribute them according to his own good will. Yahwe is a God of eternal and inviolable fidelity. What he has promised he will fulfill. What he had promised he will keep for all times and for all generations, be they a thousand generations that follow one upon another. In a solemn covenant God has promised the Patriarch Abraham to give to his descendants the land of Canaan (Genesis 15:18). This promise he renewed with the Patriarch Isaac: "To thee and thy descendants I will give this whole land and thus fulfill the oath which I made to thy father Abraham" (Genesis 26:3). To Jacob God confirmed this promise as a law which he laid upon himself. In the vision of Jacob's ladder the Lord said to him: "I am the Lord, the God of thy fathers, Abraham and Isaac. The land upon which thou treadest I will give to thee and thy descendants" (Genesis 28:13). It was a covenant for all times which the Lord made with the patriarch and with all his sons.

With these promises the foundation was laid for the kingdom of God. It was still as insignificant as a mustard seed because the numbers of those that were included in the covenant were still small. It was limited to the family of the patriarchs who were strangers in the land, but it was given to the descendants as their possession. At the time of the patriarchs they had not settled places to live. They moved from place to place with their tents like homeless nomads through the territories of different peoples of Canaan and Egypt. But already at that time God had taken them under his protection and would not permit them to be oppressed. Thus he punished Pharaoh in Egypt and the king of Gerara who dared to seize Sarah and Rebecca. No one was allowed to touch his anointed and the prophets. The psalmist calls the patriarchs "anointed" because God anointed them with the Holy Spirit and distinguished them with extraordinary graces and favors. He calls them "prophets" because they were bearers of divine revelations and promises.

A second important event in the history of Israel was the immigration to Egypt (verses 16–24). It was impossible for the families of the patriarchs to live in peace and develop a strong nation in the land of Canaan so as to be able to take possession of the land. With envy and anxiety the princes of Canaan watched the growing wealth of the patriarchs; the quarrels of the shepherds about the wells and pasture lands became more numerous and violent. It was then that God so arranged it that Jacob with his whole family because of a famine migrated to Egypt. The Lord prepared a way for their reception through Joseph who had been sold as a slave to Ismaeletic merchants by his brothers and who by these was brought into Egypt. It was a hard trial for the sixteen-year-old youth. In these difficult times he may have asked himself: "Why has God permitted this?" At that time he did not yet know what blessing was to be the result of this evil deed of his brothers. Joseph came into the house of Potiphar and gained the confidence of his master. He obtained a position in this house which for a slave made life agreeable. But the Lord did not intend to have him brought to Egypt for the reason of having him serve as a steward. It happened that Joseph was accused by the wife of Potiphar for improper solicitation and without a court trial was cast into prison. Again he may have asked the question: "Why did God permit that I should be cast into prison like a criminal even though I refused to commit a sin against him?" He did not know that this hardship opened the way to freedom and renown. He suffered imprisonment for several years before the story of his dream was fulfilled; namely, the dream of the sheaves and of the stars which bowed down before him. The divine decree had to be fulfilled in Joseph. He had to be tried with suffering and humiliation before he was raised to honor and power.

His elevation began at a time when there was no wise man in Egypt who could interpret Pharaoh's dream. He therefore had Joseph brought from prison and with his own hand released him from his chains. Because of the wisdom of his advice Pharaoh raised him to the highest office in his kingdom and to the stewardship of his crown possessions. He gave him his own royal signet ring and thereby conferred on him all power in his kingdom. Joseph himself later tells his brothers that God made him counselor of Pharaoh, the master of his house, and ruler over all Egypt (Genesis 45:8). All the officials of the land had to receive their instructions from him. When appointing him the king said: "My entire people shall obey your commands: only the throne will I reserve for myself. No one in all Egypt shall move hand or foot against your will" (Genesis 41:40–44).

Through God's power and wisdom the way was now prepared to give Jacob and his family a permanent home in Egypt. Joseph himself invited his father and his brothers to migrate to Egypt and they became welcome guests in the land of Egypt, the land of Cham, who is designated the primogenitor of the Egyptians. Pharaoh gave them the fertile land of Gessen and protected them by his royal power. Here the descendants of the patriarchs could prosper in peace. God blessed them with an extraordinary fertility so that they became a powerful people. At the close of this section the psalmist indicates that in the meantime a political revolution took place in Egypt which was disastrous for the Israelites. The dynasty of the Hyksos, favorable to the Israelites, was overthrown in the year 1580 before Christ and a native dynasty under Amosis I came into power. This dynasty saw in the growing power of the Israelites a danger for the country and began to oppress them.

With this change in Egypt a new important epoch began. The history of the redemption from the Egyptian captivity was to find its climax in the making of the covenant on Sinai. This history takes in the events from the time of the exodus from Egypt until the conquest of Canaan by Josue. It is from this period that the psalmist takes the material for his meditation, namely, the miracles worked by God in Egypt which caused the liberation of Israel by Pharaoh (verses 25–36). God permitted his people to be hated and oppressed by the Egyptians that they might be glad to leave the land of Gessen which had become a home to them, to long for the promised land, and to be led by the Lord to Canaan. When according to the decree of God the time of the liberation had come, he called Moses who had been educated in all the wisdom of the Egyptians and his brother Aaron in order that they might be the leading instruments in bringing about the liberation of his people. He gave them the gift of miracles that by them they might prove to the king that they were messengers of Yahwe. They brought ten plagues upon the land when Pharaoh refused to let Israel depart. The psalmist mentions some of the plagues; it is not his intention to mention all nor does he have in mind to give them in their sequence. He first mentions the great darkness that came upon Egypt, but not upon the land of Gessen; then he mentions the change of the Nile water into blood, the plague of the frogs which entered the chambers of the king, the swarms of flies and mosquitoes that tormented men and beasts. He further mentions the terrific hailstorms that destroyed vineyards and fruit trees, and the plague of locusts that devoured the plants of the fields and destroyed grain and fruit. And finally the Lord slew all the first-born of the Egyptians from the royal house to the last of his subjects. It was the last and most terrible of all punishments that induced Pharaoh to let the Israelites depart.

Now the psalmist passes over to the last strophe (verses 37–45) to the exodus from Egypt. The Israelites should not leave their captivity poor, but should leave the land as victors laden with booty. They should receive compensation for their many years of servitude and for all they had to leave behind in Egypt. They therefore took with them silver and gold which the Egyptians voluntarily gave them or which they themselves demanded from them. All the people of the exodus, even the old men and women, were healthy and able to undertake the difficult journey. No one was obliged to remain behind because of his poor physical condition. As once Pharaoh and the Egyptian people had gladly welcomed the Patriarch Jacob, the father of their saviour Joseph, so now they rejoiced at the departure of the Israelites. Because of the plagues a great terror took hold of the Egyptians and the death of the first-born showed them the great power of the God of Israel. Thus they rejoiced when the Israelitic people prepared themselves for the exodus.

God himself undertook the leadership through the desert into the land of promise. He accompanied the people in a pillar of cloud which protected them during the day against the enemy and at night shone upon them like fire. He cared for them in a miraculous manner and fed the many thousands. At their petition he let large swarms of quail fly into the camp which could be caught easily. He also gave them manna daily. The psalmist calls it the bread of heaven. He calls it so because it was the immediate gift of the heavenly Father in contrast to the ordinary natural bread. In the midst of the barren, waterless, stony desert of the Sinai peninsula God told Moses to strike water from the rock. It flowed in such abundance that it poured over the dry land in brooks and men and beasts could drink to satiety. The Lord worked all these miracles for the sake of a people who because of their ingratitude and faithlessness did not deserve such divine miraculous intervention. God did all this because of the promises made to Abraham. He did this as a confirmation of the promise that he would give to his descendants the land of Canaan as their inheritance. Thus in leading the people out of Egypt he wrought great miracles in proof of his power. Witness the passage through the Red Sea. All this was received with great joy by Moses and the entire chosen people and commemorated with divine praises.

At the end of the forty years' journey through the desert God gave Israel the land of Canaan as a lasting inheritance. This country was inhabited by pagan tribes and had been cultivated by them. Here in Canaan the Israelites could live in peace; here they could fulfill their future mission spiritually guided by God's Law and his prophets. Only under such conditions God guaranteed the continued possession of the land.

psalm 105

Confitemini Domino

A confession of the manifold sins and ingratitude of the Israelites

ALLELUIA

1. Give glory to the Lord, for he is good: for his mercy endureth forever.

2. Who shall declare the powers of the Lord? Who shall set forth all his praises?

3. Blessed are they that keep judgment and do justice at all times.

4. Remember us, O Lord, in the favor of thy people: visit us with thy salvation.

5. That we may see the good of thy chosen, that we may rejoice in the joy of thy nation: that thou mayest be praised with thy inheritance.

6. We have sinned with our fathers: we have acted unjustly, we have wrought iniquity.

7. Our fathers understood not thy wonders in Egypt, they remembered not the multitude of thy mercies.
And they provoked to wrath going up to the sea; even unto the Red Sea.

8. And he saved them for his own name's sake: that he might make his power known.

9. And he rebuked the Red Sea and it was dried up: and he led them through the depths, as in wilderness.

10. And he saved them from the hand of them that hated them: and he redeemed them from the hand of the enemy.

11. And the waters covered them that afflicted them: there was not one of them left.

12. And they believed his words: and they sang his praises.

13. They had quickly done, they forgot his works, and they waited not for his counsel.

14. And they coveted their desire in the desert and they tempted God in the place without water.

15. And he gave them their request: and sent fullness into their souls.

16. And they provoked Moses in the camp, Aaron the holy one of the Lord.

17. The earth opened and swallowed up Dathan, and covered the congregation of Abiron.

18. And a fire was kindled in their congregation: the flame burned the wicked.

19. They made also a calf in Horeb: and they adored the graven thing.

20. And they changed their glory into the likeness of a calf that eateth grass.

21. They forgot God who saved them, who had done great things in Egypt,

22. Wondrous works in the land of Cham: terrible things in the Red Sea.

23. And he said that he would destroy them, had not Moses, his chosen, stood before him in the breach.
To turn away his wrath, lest he should destroy them,

24. And they set at nought the desirable land.
They believed not his word,

25. And they murmured in their tents: they hearkened not to the voice of the Lord.

26. And he lifted up his hand over them: to overthrow them in the desert.

27. And to cast down their seed among the nations, and to scatter them in the countries.

28. They were also initiated to Beelphegor: and ate the sacrifices of the dead.

29. And they provoked him with their inventions: and destruction was multiplied among them.

30. Then Phinees stood up, and pacified him: and the slaughter ceased.

31. And it was reputed to him unto justice, to generation and generation forevermore.

32. They provoked him also at the waters of contradiction and Moses was afflicted for their sakes:

33. Because they exasperated his spirit. And he distinguished with his lips.

34. And they did not destroy the nations of which the Lord spoke unto them.

35. And they were mingled among the heathens, and learned their works,

36. And served their idols, and it became a stumbling block to them.

37. And they sacrificed their sons and daughters to devils.

38. And they shed innocent blood, the blood of their sons and of their daughters which they sacrificed to the idols of Canaan.
And the land was polluted with blood,

39. And was defiled with their works, and they went aside after their own inventions.

40. And the Lord was exceedingly angry with his people, and he abhorred his inheritance.

41. And he delivered them into the hands of the nations: and they that hated them had dominion over them.

42. And their enemies afflicted them: and they were humbled under their hands:

43. Many times did he deliver them.
But they provoked him with their counsel: and they were brought low by their iniquities.

44. And he saw when they were in tribulation: and he heard their prayer.

45. And he was mindful of his covenant and repented according to the multitude of his mercies.

46. And he gave them unto mercies in the sight of all those that had made them captives.

47. Save us, O Lord our God: and gather us from among the nations, that we may give thanks to thy holy Name, and may glory in thy praise.

48. Blessed be the Lord, the God of Israel, from everlasting to everlasting: and let all the people say: So be it, so be it.

THE psalm sounds like an explanation of St. Paul's words: "If we do not believe, he remains faithful; he cannot deny himself." (2 Timothy 2:13) The poet reflects upon the faithlessness of his people from the time of the exodus from Egypt until the time of the Judges and upon the unwavering fidelity of God. It was because of the covenant that he did not permit the destruction of Israel. The conclusion of this psalm is found in 1 Chronicles 16:35 as a conclusion of a song of praise which was sung on the occasion of the transfer of the Ark of the Covenant to Sion under King David. The fact that the meditation ends with the time of the Judges and does not mention anything about the time of the Kings shows that it could have been written at the time of David. The petition and the gathering of the dispersed does not necessarily militate against this opinion; for already at the time of the Judges many Israelites had been taken prisoner by the enemy, sold into slavery, and lived among the Gentiles. The erection of a central sanctuary in the royal residential city must have awakened the thought of gathering the dispersed for it had the purpose of bringing about a political and religious unity of the people and of fostering its preservation. The psalm urges every petitioner to examine his own conscience to see whether in the picture which the poet has drawn about the faithlessness of the people of God there is also a portrayal of his own faithlessness. He then requests the reader to give thanks to the Lord who did not withdraw himself from him altogether, but continued in his love and fidelity toward him despite his unfaithfulness as a member of the kingdom of truth and grace and as a creature chosen by God.

The introduction (verses 1-5) gives us the purpose and reason for the psalm. It is a song of praise about the goodness and eternal love of God as revealed in the history of Israel. What was most incomprehensible was the fact that God endured the unfaithfulness of his people despite his great manifestations of love toward them. Choosing them before all other nations as the people of the covenant of the one true and infinite God, miraculously guiding them through the centuries from the first day of the exodus out of Egypt until the days of the psalmist were both unique experiences of divine mercy. God's miraculous deeds performed in behalf of Israel were undeserved manifestations of love and were so many that they could not be counted; they were so stupendous that human language could not find words sufficient to praise him worthily. Great was the goodness of God toward his entire people. Great was the love of God toward the just man. The psalmist may joyfully cry out: "Happy is he who obeys the Law of the Lord, who at all times walks steadily according to his commands." All the rich blessings which the Lord has promised to his faithful servants through Moses will come to him. But the greatest of all divine manifestations of love to the just man will be the coming of the Messianic salvation. Therefore the psalmist beseeches God to complete his work and soon to give his last and greatest proof of mercy to his people. He wishes that he himself might live during this happy era, that he might share in the joy of his people, that he might jubilate with the Israel of the new era, that he might partake of the inheritance of his God. Then he would gladly pray his *Nunc Dimittis:* "Now thou dost dismiss thy servant, O Lord, according to thy word in peace, for my eyes have seen thy salvation" (Luke 2:29).

Israel is the living witness of the goodness and everlasting love of God. It has become such by its very ingratitude and unfaithfulness. Because of its disobedience it has deserved rejection and destruction a hundredfold, but again and again God had mercy upon his people when it called upon him in the distress which it brought upon itself. The psalmist contrasts the greatness of the divine love with the greatness of the sins of their forefathers in order that the present generation may recognize their shameful actions and avoid following in their footsteps. The present generation, however, should not despise its forefathers, but should consider itself as one with the nation and pray the Confiteor with them: "I have sinned with my forefathers; I have acted unjustly and maliciously."

Israel's faithlessness began already at the exodus from Egypt (verses 7-12). It began at the moment when God performed a unique act of love upon his people. At the end of the journey through the desert, Moses already pointed to the greatness of the divine liberation: "Ask of the days of old that were before thy time from the day that God created man upon the earth, from one end of heaven to the other end thereof, if ever there was done the like thing, or if it hath been known at any time that a people should hear the voice of God speaking out of the midst of fire, as thou hast heard, and lived. If God ever did so as to go and take to himself a nation out of the midst of nations by temptations, signs, and wonders, by fight and a strong hand, and stretched-out arm and horrible visions according to all the things that the Lord your God did for you in Egypt before thy eyes" (Deuteronomy 4:32-34). Their forefathers were witnesses of the plagues that fell upon Egypt; they saw how even the Gentiles admitted the power of Yahwe. But they themselves paid little attention to these miracles; the impression they made was soon erased; for when the Lord tested them at the shores of the Red Sea, they forgot all the manifestations of his power and murmured against him who had led them out of the slavery of Egypt. But the Lord did not fulfill their foolish desires even though they deserved to be brought back into servitude. He came to their assistance even though they did not want to bear the trials and he rescued them for his name's sake in order that the Egyptians would not blaspheme him and in order that he might show his power to the enemy. By his mighty word he commanded the waters of the Red Sea to part and led Israel through the sea like a herd through pasture land. God led the people in this extraordinary manner in order to destroy the Egyptians and take from them every opportunity of hindering Israel in its journey through the desert to Canaan. God did all this in order to free his people from the power of those who hated them and of those who had for so long a time oppressed them. When Pharaoh's troops saw that a way through the sea had been opened they pursued the Israelites. But scarcely had the last in the long procession of refugees arrived on the opposite shore when the walls of water again came together and buried the army of the Egyptians in its floods and not one escaped death. Now the Israelites realized why God had led them to the Red Sea and they sang the song of praise composed by Moses: "I will sing to the Lord for he is powerful; horse and rider he cast into the sea" (Exodus 15:1).

Yet this extraordinary act of liberation by Yahwe was forgotten as soon as the waters of the sea had disappeared from sight. When the wearisome march through the desert to Sinai began, the people did not wish to place themselves submissively under God's guidance and protection. Many were the sins of which Israel became guilty during the forty years' journey. The most common sins were the numberless acts of lasciviousness. Although they had experienced the power and love of the Lord, they did not believe in the wisdom of his purposes. They did not believe that God who had led them into the desert would also feed them there. They annoyed the Lord with their impetuous demands for food and drink. Despite all this he heard their petitions and fulfilled their desires. He gave them manna daily and let quail fly into their camp in great numbers and commanded Moses to strike water from the rock.

The people committed another grave sin against God by the revolt of the faction of Core against Moses and Aaron whom God had given for leaders. Core, Dathan, and Abiron were envious of the leadership of the two brothers. About 250 joined the rebels who claimed priestly powers. At this time Moses spoke to all the people of Israel: "But if the Lord does a new thing and the earth opening her mouth swallows them down and all things that belong to them and they go down alive into hell, you shall know that they have blasphemed the Lord" (Numbers 16:30). Scarcely had Moses uttered these words when the earth split asunder and swallowed the leaders of the rebels with their families and all their possessions and closed in upon them. A fire was then sent by God which destroyed the 250 men who had the effrontery of offering incense. These with the censers in their hands had to look on how their leaders were swallowed alive. (See Numbers 16)

The most grievous of Israel's sins during the desert journey was their apostasy. They worshiped the golden calf. While Moses was tarrying on the summit of Sinai to receive directions for the making of the covenant, the people made an idol after the manner of the Egyptians, a golden calf, and celebrated a feast in honor of this idol. The celebration was accompanied with the licentious practices of the pagans. The glory of the Lord which heretofore had so wonderfully manifested itself by the miracles wrought in Egypt and on Sinai, the glory of their Creator, King and Guide, they exchanged for an idol, a senseless creature, a grass-eating beast. The punishments inflicted upon the Egyptians when Pharaoh refused departure to the Israelites were forgotten. That no Israelite was struck by the plagues had shown clearly the power of Yahwe and the helplessness of the gods of Egypt. But the Israelites forgot all the miracles in the land of Cham. (The Egyptians were Canaanites.) They even forgot the great miracle of the passage through the Red Sea. For the Israelites all these events were as if they had never happened, yet they should have been mindful of them. At that time the Lord thought of destroying Israel and creating for himself a new people worthy of his choice. Then Moses acted as a mediator between the angered God and his foolish people and offered his own life and happiness to the Lord as an atonement for sins of Israel. He said: "I beseech thee: this people hath sinned a heinous sin and they made to themselves gods of gold: either forgive them this trespass or if thou do not, strike me out of the book that thou hast written" (Exodus 32:31–32). Only because Moses interceded, God did not punish Israel.

A fourth transgression of the people was the revolt after the return of the spies. When in the second year of the desert journey Israel had reached Cades at the southern border of Canaan, Moses sent twelve men to explore the land. At the false report of the strength of the fortifications and of the gigantic size of its inhabitants the people demanded to be led back into Egypt. At the very border of the promised land they rejected that which the Lord had promised to the patriarchs and preferred the slavery of Egypt to the conquest of the promised land. They did not believe in the powerful word of God and did not put their trust in his help although they had seen the army of the Egyptians destroyed before their own eyes. In their tents they murmured against God. And all the children of Israel murmured against Moses and Aaron saying: "Would God that we had died in Egypt. And would God that we may die in this wilderness, and that the Lord may not bring us into this land lest we fall by the sword and our wives and children be led away captives. Is it not better to return to Egypt? And they said: Let us appoint a captain and let us return into Egypt" (Numbers 14:2–4). "Then the Lord swore in his wrath: As I live, the whole earth shall be filled with the glory of the Lord: but yet all the men that have seen my majesty and the signs that I have done in Egypt and in the wilderness, and have tempted me now ten times and have not obeyed my voice shall not see the land I swore to their fathers; neither shall anyone of them that hath detracted me behold it" (Numbers 14:21 seq.). But God's punishment will also fall upon their descendants if they imitate them in their faithlessness. He had threatened them through Moses: "And I will scatter you among the Gentiles, and I will draw out the sword after you and your land shall be desert and your cities destroyed" (Leviticus 26:33).

But even the new generation which had grown up in the desert after the punishment of the revolters proved themselves no better than their fathers. Having arrived at the end of their desert journey and in view of the promised land they gave themselves up to the immoral cult of Beel-phegor who was worshiped by the Moabites at the foot of Mount Phogor northeast of the Dead Sea. Although the Moabites refused them passage through their country many Israelites made friendship with them and partook of the sacrificial banquets in honor of their gods. This new sin, committed at a time when the Lord permitted them to be blessed by the Gentile seer Balaam and when he was about to give them the land of Canaan as their possession, angered the Lord so much that he afflicted Israel with a disease from which within a short time 24,000 Israelites had died. At this time Phinees, the nephew of Aaron, took things in hand in order to save his people from destruction. When he saw a prince Zambri commit a sin with a prominent Madianite woman, he pierced him with his dagger. Because of this courageous deed God put a stop to the plague. He looked upon the act of Phinees as an act of atonement and of great merit and assured to him and his tribe the priesthood for all times. In fact the descendants of Phinees held this office until the second century before the Christian era with the exception of an interim toward the end of the period of the Judges. Moses himself had to experience the severity of God's punishments. When at Meribah, at the water of contention, the people had demanded water, Moses doubted whether God would again give water in a miraculous manner to this obstinate people. Because of this doubt in the infinite long-suffering, mercy, and goodness of God, he was not permitted to enter the promised land. There were indeed ex-tenuating reasons for his conduct. The people had embittered him by their constant infidelity and obstinacy. It was an indiscreet word which he had spoken in an angry mood. Nevertheless God considered this doubt in his fidelity and inexhaustible love a grave sin in a mighty leader. Israel should realize how sincere the Lord is about his given word and with what assurance it could depend on his fidelity.

Despite the faithlessness of the people the Lord remained faithful to his promises given to the patriarchs and led Israel to the promised land of Canaan. But even here it continued in its unfaithfulness. The psalmist now gives us a brief review of the period of the Judges (verses 34–46). God had given the command to eradicate the pagan population of the country because the idolatry and immorality of the pagan tribes of Canaan was a constant danger to the faith and morals of Israel. But after the death of Josue they were unmindful of this instruction and intermarried with the Gentiles, with both male and female Canaanites, although God had expressly forbidden it without any exception because of the danger of corruption. He had forbidden it under threat of grave punishment (Deuteronomy 7:3). Being married to pagans the Israelites soon imitated them in their heathen practices. They served the gods of the Canaanites, Baal and the goddess Astarte; and like the pagans gave themselves up to the most abominable sins and crimes. They became so degraded that they sacrificed their own children, sons and daughters, God's children, to Moloch and his attendant demons and burned them in honor of the idols. They shed innocent blood and by such cruelties desecrated the land of the holy God. They who should have been a holy people, an image of the Holy One of Israel to whom they belonged, disgraced themselves by the most abominable idolatry and broke the covenant which God made with them and became like to those who committed adultery.

God's wrath fell upon this sinful people and he turned his countenance away from their abominations. They did not want to submit themselves to God's mild sceptre. Therefore he surrendered them to strange nations who oppressed them severely. They had intermingled with pagans despite the prohibition and now they were delivered to them and had to bear their heavy yoke. The God who loved them they did not want to serve; now they had to obey those whom they hated. But even now the Lord was willing to show mercy to them as often as they in their need called upon him. He sent to them liberators who broke the yoke of foreign rulers. But as soon as they felt themselves free, they again became obstinate and committed the same sins for which they had been punished. And after each relapse they fell deeper into sin. When they again cried for help and vowed conversion, God heard them in their misery, had sympathy with them, and saved them even though they did not deserve help. He did not do this on their account but because of the promises he had made to their forefathers. He remained faithful to his word despite the constant faithlessness of the people. He could not deny his nature. He showed them sympathy before the very enemy who had fettered them.

This invincible love of God toward his chosen people is a strong foundation on which the just can build their confidence and hope. If the Lord despite the unfaithfulness of the people has remained firm in the keeping of his covenant, then he will also keep all promises for the Messianic future. At the time when the Ark of the Covenant and with it God himself will enter Sion, the psalmist is certain that the Lord will gather the dispersed children of his people in order that all may praise the glory of the Lord in one sanctuary. The last verse is a doxology which closes the fourth book of the psalms. It is also found in 1 Chronicles 16:36. It expresses the approval of the people to the closing thought of the psalm.

psalm 106

Confitemini Domino

All are invited to give thanks to God for his
perpetual providence over men

ALLELUIA

1. Give glory to the Lord for he is good: for his mercy endureth forever.

2. Let them say so that have been redeemed by the Lord, whom he hath redeemed from the hand of the enemy: and gathered out of the countries.

3. From the rising and from the setting of the sun from the north and from the sea.

4. They wandered in a wilderness, in a place without water: they found not the way of a city for their habitation.

5. They were hungry and thirsty: their soul fainted in them.

6. And they cried to the Lord in their tribulation: and he delivered them out of their distresses.

7. And he led them into the right way, that they might go to a city of habitation.

8. Let the mercies of the Lord give glory to him: and his wonderful works to the children of men.

9. For he hath satisfied the empty soul, and he hath filled the hungry soul with good things.

411

10. Such as sat in darkness and in the shadow of death: bound in want and in iron.

11. Because they had exasperated the words of God: and provoked the counsel of the Most High.

12. And their heart was humbled with labors: they were weakened and there was none to help them.

13. Then they cried to the Lord in their affliction, and he delivered them out of their distresses.

14. And he brought them out of darkness, and the shadow of death; and broke their bonds asunder.

15. Let the mercies of the Lord give glory to him, and his wonderful works to the children of men.

16. Because he hath broken gates of brass: and burst iron bars.

17. He took them out of the way of their iniquity: for they were brought low for their injustices.

18. Their soul abhorred all manner of meat: and they drew nigh even to the gates of death.

19. And they cried to the Lord in their affliction: and he delivered them out of their distresses.

20. He sent his word and healed them: and delivered them from their destructions.

21. Let the mercies of the Lord give glory to him: and his wonderful works to the children of men.

22. And let them sacrifice the sacrifice of praise: and declare his works with joy.

23. They that go down to the sea in ships, doing business in the great waters.

24. These have seen the works of the Lord, and his wonders in the deep.

25. He said the word and there arose the storm of wind: and the waves thereof were lifted up.

26. They mount up to the heavens, and they go down to the depths: their soul pined away with evils.

27. They were troubled and reeled like a drunken man: and all their wisdom was swallowed up.

28. And they cried to the Lord in their affliction, and he brought them out of their distresses.

29. And he turned the storm into a breeze: and its waves were still.

30. And they rejoiced because they were still: and he brought them to the haven which they wished for.

31. Let the mercies of the Lord give glory to him, and his wonderful works to the children of men.

32. But let them exalt him in the church of the people: and praise him in the chair of the ancients.

33. He hath turned rivers into a wilderness: and the sources of waters into dry ground.

34. A fruitful land into barrenness: for the wickedness of them that dwell therein.

35. He hath turned a wilderness into pools of water, and dry land into water springs.

36. And he has placed there the hungry, and they made a city for their habitation.

37. And they sowed fields and planted vineyards: and they yielded fruit of birth.

38. And he blessed them, and they multiplied exceedingly: and their cattle he suffered not to decrease.

39. Then they were brought to be few: and they were afflicted through the trouble of evils and sorrow.

40. Contempt was poured forth upon their princes: and he caused them to wander where there was no passing, and out of the way.

41. And he helped the poor out of poverty: and made him families like a flock of sheep.

42. The just shall see and shall rejoice, and all iniquity shall stop her mouth.

43. Who is wise and will keep these things: and will understand the mercies of the Lord?

After the edict of King Cyrus many Jews under the leadership of the high priest Josue and the prince Zorobabel returned home from the Babylonian captivity and laid the foundation of the new temple in Jerusalem. At the celebration of the laying of the cornerstone the singers praised the mercy of the Lord and his eternal goodness. Perhaps this psalm has some connection with this important event. The psalmist wishes to describe the greatness of the divine work of liberation insofar as in four pictures he describes the greatness of the afflictions in exile and the impossibility of freeing themselves. He requests the people to give thanks for their deliverance. The prophets in their time already saw in the

413

deliverance from captivity a type of the Messianic future. The psalm becomes a thanksgiving song for all redeemed. The four descriptions ask for a thanksgiving for the redemption. Each description has a special thought which is expressed by a little change in the wording.

The introduction (verses 1–3) forms the antiphon to the psalm. The poet calls upon all who were redeemed by the Lord to sing along in the song of thanksgiving and to praise the Lord for his goodness and for his everlasting mercy. He who like the people of Israel and like every redeemed person has experienced in himself the goodness and mercy of God has a special reason, indeed, a sacred duty to acknowledge publicly God's love. God's breaking of the bonds and his giving to the captives their liberty was as much a work of his almighty power and infinite love as was the redemption of the people from the Egyptian captivity in former times. Israel was completely in the hands of its enemy; the kingdom of Juda had collapsed; the house of David had been dethroned; Jerusalem and its temple had been destroyed and the people banished or dispersed to different countries as refugees. All national bonds had been dissolved. Every attempt to redeem itself was folly. But what according to human reckoning was an impossibility, that the Lord has done. When Cyrus granted the return home, the word of Isaias began to be fulfilled: "And it shall come to pass in that day (of the Messias) that the Lord shall set his hand the second time to possess the remnant of his people which shall be left from the Assyrians, and from Egypt, and from Phetros, and from Ethiopia, and from Elam, and from Sennaar, and from Emath, and from the islands of the sea: and he shall set up a standard among the nations and shall assemble the fugitives of Israel and shall gather together the dispersed of Juda from the four quarters of the earth" (Isaias 11:11–12). Now the psalmist portrays in four pictures the miseries of the exile, the condition of the unredeemed, and the miracle of liberation and redemption.

The First Picture: the wandering in the desert (verses 4–9). The banishment from home into a pagan country and a life far from the sanctuary in Jerusalem was like a march through a wayless and waterless desert. The life of a man who has not the guidance of divine truth and who is cut off from the fountain of grace may also be compared to a planless roaming through a desert. It is terrible when a caravan roams about through an endless sea of sand and is deprived of water and food, when it cannot escape famishing and can escape death only miraculously. The banished were close to a spiritual famine. Who in the midst of pagan surroundings, without a sanctuary, without sacrifice, and without priest will still the hunger and thirst of the soul for truth and grace? The splendid feasts in honor of the gods made them feel more keenly the want

414

of spiritual sources. When Daniel had an upper story built on his house in Babylon and had a window built in the direction of Jerusalem, when the Jews mournfully sat at the rivers of Babylon and would not play their harps, it did not mean that they did it out of a mere love of Jerusalem; but rather because of their profound spiritual sadness and because they were deprived of the tabernacle of God.

As long as they had the house of God in their midst and could draw bounteously from the source of grace many Israelites did not appreciate fully the value of God's gift. But now since for many years they could not enjoy all this, their souls yearned for God and cried to him that he might redeem them from the misery of this spiritual desert. The Lord heard their cry and liberated them. As the Lord once led their forefathers out of Egypt and miraculously led them through the desert so now he undertook the guidance of the banished in order that they might not miss the right way to Sion. Only the God who had determined the decree of the Redemption and for its fulfillment had sent his Son into the world and gave to his Church the supernatural means of grace can lead the unredeemed who famish in the desert far away from God to the light of truth and to the source of grace. Every attempt to find one's own way out of difficulties only increases the misery. Therefore all the redeemed must thank the Lord for his great love and praise him for the miracle of grace which he worked upon them, the miracle by which he led them out of the world and placed them in the kingdom of his Son. For he who comes to him will no longer hunger and he who believes in him will no longer thirst (John 6:35).

The Second Picture: the captivity (verses 10–16). God is just in his judgments. Israel did not want to carry the light yoke of the Lord; it looked upon the Law as a shameful limitation of its liberty and independence. Now in captivity the hard yoke of a foreign rule was laid upon its shoulders. In its misery it felt as if it were fettered in iron chains. Many had ridiculed the idea of walking in the light of the Lord, of seeing in his will the light of their way of life; now they sat mourning in exile as if they were in a dark prison. In their affliction they felt themselves encompassed by the night of the kingdom of death. In their insolent pride they did not bow down before the Almighty and they opposed his holy will; they said: "I will not serve" (Jeremias 2:20). They despised his admonitions which he gave them through the prophets; they did not believe their threats and warnings. As a punishment the Lord humbled them. He punished them with the captivity. They staggered under the burden and fell on the hard way which they had to walk in pagan lands. No one was there to sympathize with them and help them; and they themselves were too weak and powerless to take courage. Since they rejected God, their only support, they had to experience the truth of the words: "Woe to him that stands alone! When he falls he has none to help him" (Ecclesiasticus 4:10).

Now they saw the folly of their arrogance; now they cried to the Lord who had so often delivered them from the misery of serfdom and from the rule of foreigners. Even though it was only affliction that taught them to pray, God nevertheless heard their cry and delivered them from their captivity. He commanded King Cyrus to break their bonds and he led them from darkness and the shadow of death into the sunny land of the promise. The Prophet Isaias often compares the deliverance from the Babylonian captivity with the deliverance from a prison. God sends the Messias, his Servant, to free the prisoners from their dungeon, to deliver those from prison who sit in darkness (42:7). Again the second refrain makes the request to the redeemed to thank God; they should praise him for his love which they did not deserve and for the wonderful deeds which he had done for their redemption. They themselves could have never torn down the iron gates of their prison; the iron bars behind which they were kept they could never have broken.

God has opened for them the prison doors and has paved the way for their deliverance. Neither can the sinner break the bonds of concupiscence or break the bars of his bad habits, the bars behind which vice keeps him a prisoner. Therefore God sends a Redeemer that he may liberate the prisoner.

The Third Picture: sickness (verse 17–22). The psalmist compares the condition of the banished and the consequences of their constant wickedness against God to a grave sickness. Sin like a fever consumes and takes away all strength and energy forever. The oppressive consciousness of guilt, the sadness in affliction which was self-acquired rob the individual of a joyous life; bring about disgust in food and drink, especially in the spiritual nourishment of the soul; and cause dissatisfaction in the heavenly manna. Both soul and body must finally succumb so that they finally stand at the gates of death. Such ailment no human physician can cure. Therefore the Israelites in their affliction cried to the heavenly Physician who inflicts wounds and heals them, who strikes and heals with his hands (Job 5:18), who through the Prophet Jeremias promises his people: "I will give thee health again and heal thee from thy stripes" (30:17). He gave them his word through the prophets of the exile, through Ezechiel and Baruch, who called them to penance and promised to the contrite of heart reconciliation, revivification, the return home, and the reconstruction of the temple of Jerusalem. To him who paid heed to his word and believed in him the Lord forgave all guilt and saved him from destruction. The third refrain again requests the giving of thanks for the undeserved miraculous healing they had received from the infinitely loving

God. The Christian too must thank God for he is rich in mercy. We must thank him in virtue of the great love wherewith he has loved us, even when we were dead because of our sins; for he brought us back to life together with Christ. By his grace we were saved (Ephesians 2:4–5). All redeemed must say with the psalmist: "I owe thee, O Lord, vows, sacrifices of thanksgiving, for thou hast saved my soul from death, thou hast kept my feet from falling that I may walk before thee in the light of the living" (Psalm 55:13). But one sacrifice of thanksgiving is not sufficient to atone for guilt; again and again we must be mindful of the Lord's deeds of love and jubilantly proclaim his works.

The Fourth Picture: the storm at sea (verses 23–32). Sacred Scripture often compares the pagan world with the ocean and the attacks of the Gentile nations upon Israel with the raging and stormy seas. Earthly interests and the seeking for wealth had already caused Solomon to establish mutual commercial relations with the pagan Phoenicians. Thus the Israelites too learned to know the vast ocean, the sea with its wonders of the divine power of creation, but they also learned its dangers. But their undertakings were only of short duration and the kingdom of Juda was later cut off from the sea; but in the spiritual sense Israel because of its political affiliations had left the peaceful shores of its native country and sailed out into the pagan world. Then the Lord permitted a violent storm to come upon the people which drove the ship of state out into the open sea where it became a toy of the towering waves. The quiet voyage, the secure development under the quiet influence of grace had ceased. By the waves of world politics it was carried high but soon sank into the deep troughs of the sea. Its soul was terrified. Like a rudderless ship in a storm it lost its hold. Like a wreck it became the plaything of wind and waves. With all its human wisdom it came to an end. Now in its great need it cried to the Lord who alone can command the storm and the waves; for the winds are his messengers which come and go according to his will. The Lord listened to their cries and his mighty word commanded the howling storm and changed it into a soft breeze; he commanded the waves and the sea became quiet. Now the Israelites rejoiced because they had escaped the dangers of the ocean into which they had ventured against God's will and because by God's grace they again reached the quiet and secure harbor of their native country and returned to union with God. The fourth refrain again requests a song and praise of thanksgiving for the miraculous deliverance. God's love had led them into the quiet harbor and his wonderful power had saved them from the stormy sea. Therefore, they should praise him before the people and glorify him in the council of the elders in order that they too may do the will of God and obey his counsel.

The close of the psalm (verses 33–43) praises the guidance of Divine

Providence and draws the conclusion from the thoughts expressed in the pictures. They tell us that all power is in the hands of God. He can bless and punish. He can change a fertile land watered by many streams into a waterless desert, a land rich in springs into a dry steppe in which all life must perish. He has the power to change orchards into salty places in order to punish the inhabitants for their sins. The psalmist evidently has in mind the Jordan valley near the Dead Sea which at the time of Abraham was still a country abounding in fruit trees, but which by the punishment inflicted upon Sodom and Gomorrha was changed into a salty steppe in which all life perished. So also sin can cause a spiritual unfruitfulness when God closes up the fountains of grace and the streams of his love no longer flow into the sinner's soul. But it is in God's power to change a waterless desert into a land well watered; to change a dried up steppe into a land rich with springs and many water courses, in a word, to change it into fertile land. For the prophet this remarkable change is a type of the spiritual change which will be effected by the blessings of the Messianic times: "I will open rivers in the high hills and fountains in the midst of the plains; I will turn the desert into pools of water and the impassable land into streams of waters. I will plant in the wilderness the cedar, and the thorn, and the myrtle, and the olive tree. I will set in the desert the fir tree, the elm, and the box tree together that they may see, and know, and consider, and understand together that the hand of the Lord hath done this, and the Holy One of Israel hath created it" (Isaias 41:18–20).

In this Messianic land of fertility, in the Church of the New Covenant, the Lord will sate the hungry. Hunger and thirst for truth and grace are presupposed for entrance into the kingdom of heaven. It is such as those who have this thirst that God makes co-citizens of the saints and inmates of the house of God. He blesses their work; for the curse of original sin no longer rests upon the land. The land gives a yield for which man need not work with the sweat of his brow. Cultivation of the fields and vineyards was the main occupation of the Israelites. These are types of the kingdom of God which was compared by Christ and the apostles to a vineyard and a field. The Messianic blessing and fruitfulness was for man and beast. A great posterity numerous as sand and stars was the promise God made to the patriarchs and is a prophetic assurance for Messianic times. Even if in the future this kingdom and its citizens will suffer adversities; even if persecutions will afflict them; even if in consequence their number will be diminished; if they suffer misfortune and sorrow, the Lord will liberate them and punish the enemy. As Babylon had to feel the wrath of God, as its princes were subjected to contempt, so will it happen to everyone that oppresses God's people. He will have to wander as one who lost his way in the desert. The poor and the oppressed he will free from their affliction and will permit them to increase and multiply. With joy the just will enjoy the providence of God, but wickedness must cease. The psalm closes with the application: He who is truly wise should take this instruction to heart and meditate well on the proofs of God's kindness.

psalm 107

Paratum cor meum

The psalmist praiseth the Lord for benefits received

1. A canticle of a psalm for David himself.

2. My heart is ready, O God, my heart is ready: I will sing, and I will give praise, with my glory.

3. Arise, my glory; arise, psaltery and harp: I will arise in the morning early.

4. I will praise thee, O Lord, among the people, and I will sing unto thee among the nations.

5. For thy mercy is great above the heavens: and thy truth even unto the clouds.

6. Be thou exalted, O God, above the heavens, and thy glory over all the earth:

7. That thy beloved may be delivered. Save with thy right hand and hear me.

8. God hath spoken in his holiness.
   I will rejoice, and I will divide Sichem, and I will mete out the vale of tabernacles.

9. Galaad is mine: and Manasses is mine: and Ephraim the protection of my head. Juda is my king.

10. Moab is the pot of my hope. Over Edom I will stretch out my shoe: the aliens are become my friends.

11. Who will bring me into the strong city? Who will lead me into Edom?

12. Wilt not thou, O God, who hast cast us off? And wilt not thou, O God, go forth with our armies?

419

13. O grant us help from trouble: for vain is the help of man.

14. Through God we shall do mightily: and he will bring our enemies to nothing.

THIS psalm is a compilation of two Davidic psalms; verses 2–6 are taken from Psalm 56:8–12; verses 7–14 are taken from Psalm 59:7–14. The king is confronted with a decisive battle against the Gentile enemies of his kingdom and as supreme general he raises his hands to God in the name of all the warriors, to the Lord of all battles that he may grant victory to his people and preserve his country from conquest by the enemy. In the victory of his people the name of the Lord will be glorified by the Gentiles. The first part (verses 2–6) forms a canticle of faith in Psalm 56, faith in God's mercy and fidelity which no affliction will cause to waver. These verses constitute a vow of thanksgiving if God in the coming battle will defeat the enemy. Then the petitioning king will take the harp in hand and sing a song of praise to God's infinite mercy and eternal fidelity. The song shall penetrate into the pagan world so that the Gentiles too may acknowledge the power of God and the reliability of his word and that his glory may be made known to all the world.

In the second part (verses 7–14) the king begs for God's help in the coming battle and for a decision in his favor. He trusts in those ancient divine promises which assured Israel the possession of Canaan and victory over the enemies. In Psalm 59 the Edomites are the enemy against whom David's march is directed. Here are the representatives of the enemy against whom war is to be waged and against the Gentile enemies of Israel and of the kingdom of God. Only God can give victory in this war; human help cannot be relied upon. But this does not give the right to slacken preparation. God gives victory and lends assistance only to those who use their own strength to accomplish and to obtain victory.

psalm 108

Deus, laudem meam

*David in the person of Christ, prayeth against his persecutors;
more especially the traitor Judas; foretelling and
approving his just punishment for his
obstinacy in sin, and final
impenitence*

1. Unto the end, a psalm for David.

2. O God, be not thou silent in my praise: for the mouth of the wicked and the mouth of the deceitful man is opened against me.

3. They have spoken against me with deceitful tongues; and they have compassed me about with words of hatred; and have fought against me without cause.

4. Instead of making me a return of love, they detracted me: but I gave myself to prayer.

5. And they repaid me evil for good: and hatred for my love.

6. Set thou the sinner over him: and may the devil stand at his right hand.

7. When he is judged, may he go out condemned; and may his prayer be turned to sin.

8. May his days be few: and his bishopric let another take.

9. May his children be fatherless, and his wife a widow.

10. Let his children be carried about vagabonds, and beg; and let them be cast out of their dwellings.

11. May the usurer search all his substance: and let strangers plunder his labors.

12. May there be none to help him: nor none to pity his fatherless offspring.

13. May his posterity be cut off: in one generation let his name be blotted out.

14. May the iniquity of his fathers be remembered in the sight of the Lord: and let not the sin of his mother be blotted out.

421

15. May they be before the Lord continually, and may the memory of them perish from the earth:

16. Because he remembered not to show mercy,

17. But persecuted the poor man and the beggar; and the broken in heart, to put him to death.

18. And he loved cursing, and it shall come unto him: and he would not have blessing, and it shall be far from him.
And he put on cursing like a garment: and it went in like water into his entrails, and like oil in his bones.

19. May it be unto him like a garment which covereth him; and like a girdle with which he is girded continually.

20. This is the work of them who detract me before the Lord: and who speak evils against my soul.

21. But thou, O Lord, do with me for thy name's sake: because thy mercy is sweet.

22. Do thou deliver me, for I am poor and needy, and my heart is troubled within me.

23. I am taken away like the shadow when it declineth; and I am shaken off as locusts.

24. My knees are weakened through fasting: and my flesh is changed for oil.

25. And I am become a reproach to them: they saw me and they shaked their heads.

26. Help me, O Lord my God; save me according to thy mercy.

27. And let them know that this is thy hand: and that thou, O Lord, hast done it.

28. They will curse and thou wilt bless: let them that rise up against me be confounded: but thy servant shall rejoice.

29. Let them that detract me be clothed with shame: and let them be covered with their confusion as with a double cloak.

30. I will give great thanks to the Lord with my mouth: and in the midst of many I will praise him.

31. Because he hath stood at the right hand of the poor to save my soul from persecutors.

WHEN through the death of the traitor Judas there was a vacancy in the apostolic college (Acts 1:16) Peter saw the necessity of an election to fill the vacancy. He did not obtain a command from the Lord to do this, but he received the inspiration from this psalm: "His office another shall receive." For him this passage was evidently more than a mere citation of words. He saw in it a prophecy which found a typical fulfillment in Judas and a divine direction to give the office of this apostle to another. Judas, by his wicked deed against the Lord, by his rejection, and by giving over his office to another disciple became a type of the Jewish nation which delivered the Messias to the Gentiles, and was, therefore, rejected by God as is seen in the destruction of Jerusalem. It too had to give up its prerogative of mediatorship of the Messianic mission to the Gentile Christians who by far outnumbered the Jews. Therefore the fathers such as Augustine and Chrysostom and theologians, among them Thomas Aquinas, have interpreted this psalm as directly Messianic. Since this psalm contains words of an ordinarily prayerful man inspired by the Holy Spirit along with various curses it offers great difficulties of interpretation to a man of Christian sentiment. Therefore the question is not out of place as to whether the psalm may be interpreted as a petition of an ordinary mortal or whether it may be looked upon not as a prayer for revenge but as a prophecy of a judgment of rejection against the Jewish people. Considered in this latter sense the prayer is a counterpart to the 21st Psalm with which we find more agreement. In Psalm 21 the blessings of the redeeming death of Christ are prophesied for the Jews who were longing for salvation for the Gentile world, while here the divine punishment passed upon the stiff-necked Jews is uttered in the form of a prophetic declaration of punishment spoken by Christ. The psalm is a prophetic answer of the Messias to the cry of the Jews: "May his blood come upon us and upon our children." The psalm was probably composed during the time of the rebellion of Absalom whose insurrection probably inspired Psalm 21 also. Just as in the passion psalm, David, the persecuted and anointed of the Lord, sees the vision of his great descendant and of his suffering. He sees in the cross the judgment proclaimed for Messianic times, the judgment of separation and destruction.

In the 21st Psalm the royal prophet has, as it were, experienced the hatred of the enemies of the Messias; a hatred which passionately demanded the blood of the Servant of God. The hatred against the Crucified and also the patience and long-suffering of the Lord had reached their climax on Golgotha. The time for the divine judgment has come (verses 2–5). God whom the Messias has glorified in his life and in his work and in whom Christ saw himself glorified has heretofore looked upon the attacks and persecutions of his Anointed with infinite patience. He bore it. The enemies fought the Saviour with the venomous weapons of lies, false suspicions, and calumnies. He was accused of blasphemy, of breaking the Sabbath day, and of inciting the people. Everywhere hateful whisperings came to the ears of the Messias; everywhere animosity was shown without any reasonable ground. They told Christ to his face that he was in league with the devil; they continually brought new accusations against him before the people although no one could really convict him of any sin. He traveled throughout the land doing good. He healed hundreds; he fed thousands and consoled numberless by his words of encouragement. But they rewarded his goodness with hatred. As the number of his miracles increased, the jealousy and hatred of his enemies also increased so that because of his love and beneficence they finally demanded his death. "What shall we do since this man works many wonders" (John 11:47). Many nights he passed in prayer for this foolish people; but all the good that he did they repaid with evil; all the love that he manifested they repaid with insatiable hatred. The Prophet Isaias has foretold this conduct of the Jews toward the Messias. He permits Christ to speak: "I have given my body to the strikers and my cheeks to them that plucked them. I have not turned away my face from them that rebuked me and spit upon me" (Isaias 50:6). And he adds: "He is near that justifieth me" (50:8).

With this last thought the second part of the psalm begins (verses 6–15). It contains the announcement of the divine judgment in the form of a prophetic demand for punishment by the Messias. In other passages of the Psalter the petitions for divine punishment upon the enemies of the anointed king or of the entire nation is only a poetic form of a threat which the Lord had announced to all his adversaries. What in this section is clothed in the form of a curse and is prayed for as a punishment by God upon the Jews has been literally fulfilled after the rejection of the Messias. At a court procedure the accuser stood at the right of the accused. When the Lord holds court upon the Jewish nation, he will entrust Satan, the wicked one, with the accusation. Satan also plays this part in the Book of Job and in the prophecy of Zacharias (Job 1:6 seq. and Zacharias 3:1 seq.). But at this judgment he will not likely appear as a calumniator with false accusations, but he will make his accusations by the command of the Lord. He, as it were, becomes the bad conscience of the people whom he mercifully accuses before the throne of the eternal Judge. The judgment will be passed upon the enemies of the Messias with the greatest severity. These enemies include the Jews. The time for mercy and forgiveness is over; the petition for consideration obtains no hearing. He who will not acknowledge his sinfulness and admit his guilt and who out of servile fear will ask only for the remission of severe punishment and for the omission of the judgment will only increase his guilt. For such is intended the threat of the Lord in the Book of Proverbs: "Then shall they call upon me and I will not hear: they shall rise in the morning and shall not find me because they have hated instruction and received not the fear of the Lord" (Proverbs 1:28–29). The days of the life of the people are numbered; rejection is the irrevocable judgment of the Judge. The office of mediatorship of salvation is taken away from the Jews and is given over to the people of the New Testament and all privileges of Israel are void.

The bond which since Sinai had united Yahwe with the chosen people of Israel was torn asunder by God himself. The mystical bond of marriage was forever dissolved. Thus Israel heretofore the bride of the Lord became a widow and the citizens of the nation became orphans. With such descriptions the prophets already portrayed the situation of the people before the time of the exile. The children of Israel will lose their native land and by the destruction of the Holy City and of the temple they will lose the center of religious worship. They will be restless, wandering from place to place; they will be strangers in all countries and dependent on others. The nations, among whom the Jews will live as strangers, will oppress them. They will give them neither rights nor protection. They will exploit them and will plunder their possessions and will leave them impoverished. Pitilessly the enemy will waste the land and will not even have sympathy with the orphans. This judgment the Lord has already threatened to the faithless people through Moses: "May the ox be slain before thee and thou not eat thereof. May thy ass be taken away in thy sight and not restored to thee. May thy sheep be given to thy enemies and may there be none to help thee. May thy sons and thy daughters be given to another people, thy eyes looking on; and languishing at the sight of them all the day, and may there be no strength in thy hand. May a people which thou knowest not eat the fruit of thy land and all thy labors: and may thou always suffer oppression and be crushed at all times" (Deuteronomy 28:31–33).

The nation will collapse and even in the following generation its name will be forgotten. These words are not to be taken literally in as much as they only express that the judgment of rejection and destruction will fall upon Israel in full measure and that the nation will not long endure. Yet we may point to the fact that already in the second generation after the death of Christ, in the year 70, a destructive punishment fell upon Jerusalem and upon the entire nation of the Jews. The people had to suffer because of the guilt of their fathers who had educated them in a spirit that would lead them to the denial of the true Messias. They had to suffer for the guilt of those who during Christ's trial called upon themselves and upon their children the curse of innocently shed blood. The guilt of the murder of the Messias rests upon the entire people as the guilt of Adam rested upon all men. The guilt is not erased but is inherited from generation to generation, and with the guilt the curse also until the hour of grace shall come for Israel.

The third part (verses 16–20) gives the reason for the divine punishment. Israel has deserved the severe divine punishments. It showed neither sympathy nor mercy toward the Messias in the agony before his death, but maltreated and derided him even in his anguish (Psalm 21). He who is heartless cannot expect sympathy from others. But is not the punishment of rejection too hard? Why does the curse of God pursue this people? The Messias himself explains: It wished the curse. It called it upon itself and upon its children when Pilate defended the innocence of the Messias and made the Jews responsible for the murder. The people disdained the blessing of the Saviour and roughly refused him. As God once proposed through Moses to Israel life and death, blessing and curse that they may choose one or the other, so Christ offered to the Jews life and death, blessing and curse. They chose death and curse and both were given them. If Israel had fulfilled its Messianic mission the Lord would have (according to Isaias 61:10) clothed it with the garment of salvation and put upon it the mantle of justice. Just as the garment belongs to the man, so also the Messianic salvation would have been the possession of Israel. It would have distinguished it and would have remained with it. But Israel had refused the wedding garment and thus the curse became its dress. The divine curse will not only clothe it, it will penetrate the inner man. It will penetrate him like the oil penetrates the skin. It will not leave him. As the garment always covers the body (the Oriental never takes off the tunic at night) and as a man always wears his girdle, so also the curse will always remain with the people because they wanted it. The judgment which the Lord will pass upon the enemies of the Messias will be a just one because they denied him and passed an unjust judgment upon him.

In the last part of the psalm (verses 21–31) the Messias utters a petition for help in the present affliction. Because the people filled with hatred still surround him, his sufferings continue. With words that remind us of the portrayal of the sufferings in Psalm 21 the psalmist pictures the greatness of his affliction. Just as in the former psalm, he calls upon the mercy of God because he trusts in his goodness. He begs the Lord to fulfill his promises because of the honor of his name. "I am poor and miserable and my heart is troubled within me." This in a few words is the thought of Psalm 21: "I am poured out like water and all my bones are scattered. My heart is become like wax melting in the midst of my bowels. My strength is dried up like a potsherd and my tongue hath cleaved to my jaws, and thou hast brought me down into the dust of death" (Psalm 21:15–16).

Life is coming to an end quickly. Like the shadows of evening, like a locust that is suddenly blown away by the wind, so will death take life and destroy it. My knees are weakened through fasting and my flesh is lacking oil. Both descriptions try to give expression to depth of sorrow and of spiritual anguish. At great mournings and grave spiritual sufferings they abstained from food and from the anointing of the body (2 Kings 12:20). Although his condition incites sympathy and must move the hearts of men, he is mocked in his misery and those who stand around him wag their heads in glee.

In his great affliction the Messias cries out again to God, his Father, at the close of his prayer. "Father the hour has come. Now glorify me in order that thy son may glorify thee" (John 17:1). In the deliverance from his deathly pain the enemies should see the divine glorification of the rejected Redeemer. From the miracles of the divine love which delivered the Anointed at the moment when his hellish enemies believed that they had triumphed, they will know that the hand of God brought about the deliverance and that his hand protected the Anointed. The enemies may now curse. The invective does not remain malignant for God changes it into a blessing for his servant. His enemies will be put to shame since their wickedness will become evident to all the world. The servant of God will be glorified by him and will enjoy the divine blessing and his transfiguration. He will be exalted and will triumph when in his glory he will appear before his enemies. The enemies will be put to eternal shame. They will be covered with reproach. Shame will be their garment for all eternity. In Psalm 21 the Messias vows: "I will proclaim thy name to my brothers; I will boast of thee in the midst of the congregation because thou didst not despise the cry of the poor, and because thou hast not concealed thy face before him." Here (verses 23–25) also he vows that he will thank the Lord publicly with his mouth and praise him before many men in the large congregation of the redeemed; for his deliverance has made known to all that the Lord stands at the right hand of the poor man to rescue him from those who curse and want to destroy him. As the accuser, so also the defender, the advocate, stood at the right side of the accused. Therefore the Lord did not leave the Messias in death; he did not let his body see corruption, but raised him from the dead and glorified him that all men may know that he does not wish the destruction of the sinner but that he may have life and have it more abundantly; that all may know that he will deliver him from the power of those who would wish to hurl him into the night of damnation, into eternal hell fire.

psalm 109

Dixit Dominus

Christ's exaltation and everlasting priesthood

1. A psalm for David.
   The Lord said to my Lord: Sit thou at my right hand:
   Until I make thy enemies thy footstool.

2. The Lord will send forth the sceptre of thy power out of Sion: rule thou in the midst of thy enemies.

3. With thee is the principality in the day of thy strength: in the brightness of the saints: from the womb before the day-star I begot thee.

4. The Lord hath sworn and he will not repent: Thou art a priest forever according to the order of Melchisedech.

5. The Lord at thy right hand hath broken kings in the day of his wrath.

6. He shall judge among nations, he shall fill ruins: he shall crush the heads in the land of many.

7. He shall drink of the torrent in the way: therefore shall he lift up the head.

No song of the Psalter has received such important confirmation as to its source and meaning as this one. Christ himself said that David in a prophetic spirit and under the inspiration of the Holy Ghost has written it and has seen in his Lord, the Messias, God's Son. Christ uses this psalm to refute his opponents in order to prove to them from the royal prophet that he must be the true Messias, a divine Being; for only then could David call his descendant expected by so many generations, his Lord. The subterfuge of the critics that the Saviour used a false Jewish interpretation for his purpose is a denial of the candid character and of the dignity of the God-Man. This opinion needs no refutation.

Every verse in the psalm reveals an important fact in the Messianic description. The vision, which is fundamental, forms the climax and conclusion of the Messianic revelations imparted to David. In the touching vision of the suffering Messias, Psalm 21, the prophet was permitted to grasp an idea of the mystery of his priesthood. He saw in it the sacrifice on the cross and in the continuation of it, the thanksgiving sacrifice of the New Testament. But how should this priesthood have any connection with the prophesied kingship of the Messias. David knew the priesthood and kingship in Israel only as two strictly distinct powers made so by the Law. How could the world dominion of the Messias, proclaimed in the Second Psalm, be fulfilled if he is a priest? These were questions for which David sought an answer. God gave the answer in the revelation of this psalm. The Messias like Melchisedech will unite both dignities and powers.

David had once received the message from Yahwe: "Ask of me and I will give thee the Gentiles for thy inheritance and the uttermost parts of the earth for thy possession" (Psalm 2:8). Now in a prophetic spirit he sees the hour of fulfillment of this divine promise. Christ takes possession of the Messianic world dominion on the day of his Ascension into heaven (verses 1-3). The psalmist becomes witness of the reception which is given for his Lord in heaven and of the solemn transfer of the world dominion to the Messias. "Sit thou at my right hand." The right hand in biblical language is the symbol of power. Sitting at the right hand of God is a description taken from the judicial custom of the East and meant not only the highest honor thinkable but also an unlimited participation in the world dominion of God. This heavenly act of solemn transfer introduces a new era in world history, the era of the kingdom of Christ over the whole world. According to the Epistle of St. Paul to the Hebrews (1:3) Christ was seated on the right of the most high Majesty after he had completed the redemption from sin. He therefore entered upon his kingship after he performed his priestly office as victim for our redemption. By the surrender of this kingdom to the Messias the power was also given to the Anointed of Yahwe to subject all the resisting nations under his rule. The second utterance of God is solemnly given at the hour of Christ's Ascension into heaven, that is, to his throne. Yahwe himself will make his enemies his footstool. It was the custom in antiquity that vanquished kings for their humiliation and as a sign of total subjection had to throw themselves on the ground so that the victor could place his foot upon their neck (Josue 10:24). Thus Yahwe will invest the Messias with the plenitude of his power and in so doing will grant him victory over all his enemies. This divine power will be put at his disposal as long as an enemy is still to be vanquished. Then wars will be at an end forever because there will no longer be any enemies. The kingdom of the Messias will never end and there will be everlasting peace. In the second verse God speaks in the third person and continues to speak to the Anointed. Yahwe and the Messias have full and equal right in exercising their power of world dominion. This power therefore is sometimes ascribed to Yahwe and sometimes to the Anointed; only the mission did the Messias receive from Yahwe. "The Lord will send forth the sceptre of thy power from Sion." Sion is the residence city of King David and of the successor to his throne. The holy city of God is a prophetic type of the Messianic kingdom, of the Church of the New Testament in which Christ the King rules and is acknowledged as King. His kingdom will grow and expand until the acknowledgment of the Messianic kingdom will become world-wide. Here Christ reigns with the sceptre of his own power. It is from Sion that Yahwe extends his kingdom into the world in order to gain the Gentile nations estranged from the kingdom of the Messias. It is God's power that extends the sceptre. It is Yahwe who put his power at the disposal of his Anointed for the spiritual conquest of the world and for the victory over the enemies of his kingdom. This conquest and victory will be successful. This is expressed in the words: "Rule thou in the midst of them." Christ will be victor and at his name all knees shall bend.

This prophecy will be fulfilled. The dominion of Christ will be an absolute one on the day of his might. It begins on the day when he takes possession in heaven of the world kingdom and continues until the day of power at the end of time when he will hold judgment upon all his enemies. The day of power is the entire time of the Messianic dominion until the day of judgment; for the gates of hell shall not prevail against his kingdom. Christ exercises his power in holy adornment, in the adorn-ment of his priesthood. In the Law the garments of the high priest are called holy. A holy adornment was the golden diadem which the high priest wore upon his head. The Latin text translates: "In the brightness of his Saints . . ." and refers the words to the redeemed. The Messias will be a king in full sacerdotal array. Melchisedech too was priest and king at the same time. The dominion is Christ's because he is the natural Son of God consubstantial with the Father. Yahwe in the Second Psalm announced the words with which he acknowledged the legitimacy of the Son on the eternal today: "This day." In this psalm it is God himself who bases the priestly kingdom of his Son on his eternal generation. "From the womb before the morning star have I begotten thee." The Son existed before the dawn of creation in eternity. The Hebrew text is generally translated: "Thy people follow thee willingly on the day of thy military campaign; in the holy adornment of the morning dawn thy youth buds forth." Without considering the linguistic difficulties that argue against this reading and without considering the fact that already the Septuagint of pre-Christian times confirms the text of the Vulgate, this kind of reading does not fit as well the great theme of the psalm as the Latin translation does. Every connection with the central thought which speaks of the royal and priestly dignity of Melchisedech is missing.

With the atoning death on the cross and with the accession to the throne the priesthood of Christ did not end. Christ remains Priest forever (verse 4). Just as God assured the Anointed eternal world power on the day of his generation, so also because of the same generation he assured him eternal continuation of his priesthood and thus a twofold dignity was assured. Therefore the Epistle to the Hebrews (5:6) also bases the priesthood of Christ on the eternal generation. The psalmist tells us that the promise was made with a solemn oath. The oath of God is an anthropomorphic expression for the absolute divine Truth and Fidelity: "Thou art priest forever according to the order of Melchisedech." The point of comparison between both personalities is not the unbloody sacrifice of bread and wine; it is rather the union of the royal and priestly dignity in one person and the uniqueness of the priesthood of Melchisedech as the Epistle to the Hebrews tells us. The priest Melchisedech appears in history not as the member of lineage. There is no predecessor nor descendant mentioned, neither father nor son. "Without father, without mother, without genealogy, having neither beginning of days nor end of life, but likened to the Son of God, continueth a priest forever" (Hebrews 7:3). So Christ also is of no human descent. Christ is not called because he is a descendant from Aaron or because he is a consecrated priest of the Aaronic tribe; he is called to this dignity immediately and solemnly by an oath at the same time that the decree of the Incarnation is made.

In the third part of the psalm (verses 5–7), David addresses God and enumerates before him the deeds of his Son, the effects of his royal power on earth. Christ holds judgment upon the nations. In the second psalm David was not only a prophetic witness of the transfer of the royal dignity to the Messias, he was also witness to the divine assurance of the power to defend his kingdom against the enemy: "Thou wilt direct them with an iron rod; thou wilt break them to pieces like pottery." The prophet sees God's word fulfilled in history and tells what he sees. The Messias is called the Lord sitting at the right hand; not because he sits at the right hand of God, but because Yahwe will assist him and because he is a divine Being and there is in him an irresistible power. Christ will crush kings on the day of his wrath. This is not only one day; it is every day on which punishment will fall upon this or that nation and upon their rulers. The history of the world is a record of God's days of wrath. How many thrones did not the Church see collapse since the world dominion of Christ began! How many nations and kingdoms which resisted his rule did she not see disappear! World history is the history of world judgment and the earth is a vast field of corpses; ancient kingdoms and their princes have turned into dust; great emperors have appeared and disappeared; only Christ's rule and his kingdom have outlasted all. "He shall crush the heads in the land of many." This verse may contain a

431

reference to the Proto-Evangelium and may remind us of the words addressed to the serpent about the offspring of the woman that will crush the head of the serpent (Genesis 3:15).

Each victory over the enemy of God's kingdom is only a part of the decisive battle of the kingdom of God against the kingdom of the world. It is in the decisive battle that the history of the world will have its end. According to the Proto-Evangelium the battle will be a difficult one and even the victor will be covered with wounds. This prophecy has been fulfilled in the sufferings of Christ and its fulfillment is continued in the sufferings of the Church. "He shall drink of the torrent in the way." Many fathers have interpreted these words as referring to the suffering which like a torrent in the way accompanied the earthly life of Christ and which does not leave the Church, which lives in Christ. Sufferings are the cause of his and her exaltation. St. Paul says: "He humbled himself and was obedient unto death, even to the death of the cross. Therefore God exalted him and gave him a name which is above all other names" (Philippians 2:8). "Therefore he raises his head." Other writers interpret the "torrent in the way" as meaning the divine help which God gives continually to the Messias in his wars and which aids him in obtaining his victories and in attaining his exaltation.

psalm 110

Confitebor tibi, Domine

God is to be praised for his graces and benefits to his Church

ALLELUIA

1. I will praise thee, O Lord, with my whole heart; in the council of the just, and in the congregation.

2. Great are the works of the Lord: sought out according to all his wills.

3. His work is praise and magnificence: and his justice continueth forever and ever.

4. He hath made a remembrance of his wonderful works, being a merciful and gracious Lord:

5. He hath given food to them that fear him. He will be mindful forever of his covenant.

6. He will show forth to his people the power of his works.

7. That he may give them the inheritance of the Gentiles: the works of his hands are truth and judgment.

8. All his commandments are faithful: confirmed forever and ever, made in truth and equity.

9. He hath sent redemption to his people: he hath commanded his covenant forever. Holy and terrible is his name:

10. The fear of the Lord is the beginning of wisdom. A good understanding to all that do it: his praise continueth forever and ever.

JESUS Sirach (17:8) says that God had endowed men with understanding that they may know his works and praise him. This means not only the works of creation but also his great deeds in history. The psalmist meditated profoundly upon the past history of his people and in it saw God's deeds of power and love. They filled his soul with admiration and holy enthusiasm. In this psalm he expresses his joy about the knowledge acquired. And in this alphabetical song he praises God before the assembled congregation. He wishes that others too would meditate upon the history of the kingdom of God and upon the great deeds of the Lord and thus fill their souls with a reverence for the majesty of God.

God's works are worthy of meditation (verses 2–3). There is no more sublime subject upon which the human mind can meditate and search out than God the Lord, the works of Creation, and the history and realization of his plan of redemption. All human science despite thousands of years of research work could not fathom the works of creation nor understand their nature. God is great in his works. Great and worthy of meditation are the deeds of the Lord which he has done for Israel in order to fulfill his plan of redemption. Indeed, in the New Testament they have not diminished; they are even today a worthy object of meditation for all who have joy in the great redemptive power of God. God's works never grow old. He who loves God cannot pass over his works without observation. The saints have found much satisfaction in meditating upon God's works. God's works are beautiful and majestic. All of them have the impress of the divine in them. This is particularly true of those works that serve the fulfillment of the decree of redemption. God's justice, that is, the divine Will to bring about the justification of man, to give him salvation, does not cease as long as the stars of heaven run their course. May the deeds of redemption that have been worked in Israel and for Israel be in the distant past, they still remain a part of the entire plan of redemption which the human mind cannot understand in its full depth unless it understands the individual deeds of redemption.

Out of the totality of the divine works of redemption the psalmist considers four great deeds of God in the history of Israel. These are especially useful for our meditation. They are monumental works of divine power and love whose importance outlasts all times. The first great deed is the miracle of the manna, a true and lasting memorial of his miraculous power. The Lord had fed the entire people in the desert with a miraculous food for forty years. He did not do this as a reward for Israel's fidelity and love. He gave them their daily bread despite their ingratitude and faithlessness. He acted out of love and mercy to his people. He did not want Israel to starve in the desert; they were the only nation who among all nations of the world revered him. That is, they acknowledged and worshiped him. He wished to remain true to his covenant which he had made with the patriarchs; namely, to give to the world salvation through their descendants. The manna is a weak type of the true Bread of Heaven which Christ gives us in the Sacrament of the Altar.

The second stupendous work of God in the fulfillment of the decree of redemption is the settling of Israel in the land of Canaan through the victories of Josue over the Canaanites and the Amorrhites, through the victory of Debbora at Thabor, through the conquest over the powerful tribes of the Madianites by three hundred followers of Gedeon. Israel could not attribute these victories to its own strength and weapons. God himself intervened in these battles and manifested his own power to his people. It was he who according to his own promise subjected the heathen nations and gave their land to the Israelites as an inheritance. In reflecting upon the fulfillment of this promise the Christian turns his mind to the conquest of the world by the Church. The divine action is fidelity and justice. "In the Lord there is no change nor a shadow of alteration" (James 1:17). All the works that he performed for Israel and against its enemies are only effects of his unchangeableness. God can never become untrue to his given word. His decrees, therefore, are absolutely reliable and a firm foundation for our confidence in him. No power in the world can make the plans of God ineffective; no one can influence God to give up his plans or to change them. His decisions were made in truth and in justice; they do not allow ambiguity or any objectionable interpretation.

A third memorial of the divine power and love is the redemption from the Babylonian captivity; for in this instance it was also God who brought about the deliverance. Long before the people were led into captivity and before the liberator Cyrus was born, the Lord had promised the redemption from exile. The fourth and most sublime work of God's love and power was preparing the way for a new and eternal covenant in order to bring to his people and all the world eternal redemption from sin. In this plan of redemption he revealed the sanctity and greatness of his being. We the redeemed members of the eternal covenant look back to its fulfillment and meditate profoundly upon the sublimity of the work of redemption brought about by Christ. We know better than Israel how to appreciate the revelation of the sanctity, greatness, power, wisdom, and love of God.

If God is so great as the meditation on his works makes known to us, if his love is as bountiful as a view into the depths of the divine plan of the redemption shows, then a reverential and thankful love is fundamental for all who acknowledge the Lord. It is the beginning of all true wisdom. With the knowledge of God's divine greatness and love true wisdom begins. However this knowledge supposes meditation on God's perfections and upon their revelations. Then too this knowledge must be practical for it alone has value before God. Only a life according to the knowledge obtained, a life of reverence for God gives us a suitable insight into God's ways of redemption, not the dry wisdom of the schools. Unto him who with meditation unites the fear of God and fidelity to the Law there is awakened an inexhaustible desire of praising God. He will never be satiated with the ever ancient and ever new beauty of the Lord and will never tire in praising him at all times.

psalm 111

Beatus vir

The good man is happy

1. Alleluia, of the returning of Aggeus and Zacharias.
   Blessed is the man that feareth the Lord: he shall delight exceedingly in his commandments.

2. His seed shall be mighty upon earth: the generation of the righteous shall be blessed.

3. Glory and wealth shall be in his house: and his justice remaineth forever and ever.

435

4. To the righteous a light is risen up in darkness: he is merciful, and compassionate, and just.

5. Acceptable is the man that showeth mercy and lendeth: he shall order his words with judgment:

6. Because he shall not be moved forever.

7. The just shall be in everlasting remembrance: he shall not fear the evil hearing. His heart is ready to hope in the Lord.

8. His heart is strengthened, he shall not be moved until he look over his enemies.

9. He hath distributed, he hath given to the poor: his justice remaineth forever and ever: his horn shall be exalted in glory.

10. The wicked shall see, and shall be angry, he shall gnash with his teeth and pine away: the desire of the wicked shall perish.

"THE fear of the Lord is the beginning of wisdom." The preceding psalm closed with this thought. In this psalm which is likewise alphabetical this thought is taken up again. It shows that the virtue of the fear of the Lord is, in truth, great wisdom because it promises great blessings. The psalmist intends to speak about these blessings. Reverence for the Lord reveals itself in the practice of love and obedience. Hence, once upon a time Moses said to Israel: "And now Israel what doth the Lord thy God require of thee, but that thou fear the Lord thy God, and walk in his ways, and love him, and serve the Lord thy God with all thy heart and with all thy soul" (Deuteronomy 10:12). The fear of God, however is unthinkable without the love of neighbor. Jesus Sirach writes that an act of love towards our fellow man is as pleasing to the Lord as sacrifice (35:4).

The fear of the Lord consists above all else in the love of God; therefore the psalmist speaks first about the blessing of the love of God (verses 1–4). "Happy is the man who fears the Lord." This promise of happiness is not given to him who like a slave is forced to obey his Lord, who obeys only out of fear of punishment. True love of God banishes fear; it rejoices to know the will of God in his Law and to serve the will of God as it is known. Only a glad obedience is pleasing in the sight of God. God loves and blesses only a cheerful service. The blessing of the love of God is threefold. He blesses the family. The most earnest desire of an Israelite was that his descendants would enjoy the happiness of Messianic times and would not be excluded from it. Parents who reared their children in the fear of the Lord could hope in the fulfillment of the divine promise. Their children possess the strength of supernatural life and grace. To the race of God-fearing men happiness is promised and thus God-fearing parents lay the foundation for the happiness of their children.

The love of God brings blessing to the honor and possession of the just man and of his whole house. The psalmist may have thought in the first place of worldly honor and perishable possessions, but in a higher sense he may also have thought of the honor and wealth of virtue and justice. The God-fearing man stores up those eternal goods and merits which neither dust nor moth consume nor thieves steal. His justice, that is, his justification in the state of grace, is for him here on earth and in heaven a safe possession.

The love of God blesses suffering. Hardships of body and soul afflict even a God-fearing man. He too can be encompassed with the darkness of suffering and sadness. But he is not sad as those who have no hope. The light of faith shines in the darkness of his suffering. He knows that all suffering which befalls the just has its source in the love of God and not in his wrath; he knows that to those who love God even adversities are blessings and that all adversities of the present time cannot be compared to the glory which is laid up for eternity by the merciful, gracious, and just God for those who hope in him.

The love of neighbor cannot be separated from the love of God and on this account it cannot be separated from the fear of God. Therefore the blessing of the fear of God shows itself also in the blessing of the love of our neighbor (verses 5–10).

Just as in the first part the psalmist explains the nature of the love of God, so now in the second part he begins with an explanation of genuine love for the neighbor. Blessedness is not meant for him who loves his neighbor in word only, but for him who loves him in deed and in truth, who assists his neighbor when he is in need. He who lends money to his neighbor without usury and aids him in his poverty so that he can continue to live, who does not cheat and take advantage of his neighbor, but in all instances acts righteously and justly, shall be blessed.

The reward of true love is a fourfold blessing of God. He who assists his neighbor in his need receives in God a strong support. Even a very just man is confronted with temptations and adversities under which he may waver and even fall if he is not sustained by the hand of God. Therefore it is a great consolation for him to know that he is upheld by the hand of God in order that he may not depart from the way of life and fall into sin and unhappiness. The name of a benefactor is held by God in eternal remembrance.

Another blessing for the love of neighbor is divine protection against calumny. He who loves his neighbor need not fear the hatred and calumny of hostile men. He may rely on the merciful goodness of the Lord and on his protection; for "God is not unjust that he should forget your work and the love which you have shown in his name, which you have ministered, and do minister to the saints" (Hebrews 6:10).

The third blessing of love towards one's neighbor is victory over the enemy. To do good gives assurance of victory especially over the enemy of our eternal salvation. God does not let those be vanquished who have comforted others. Therefore they do not have to fear any enemies; no matter how powerful they are, no matter how frequent their attacks may be. They will look down upon their enemies and will scorn them.

The fourth blessing is a growing righteousness. To do good brings wealth. He who sows bounteously will obtain a rich harvest. He who gives alms lends to God with interest. What the God-fearing man gives to his neighbor in earthly values God will return in spiritual values. His justice before God will increase and will endure forever. His honor, the respect which he enjoys, even with God, is great and his eternal reward will also be great. Here on earth the godless man may boast about his power and wealth and despise the God-fearing man. But on the day of judgment his eyes will be opened; despondency will take hold of him when he sees the lot of the just man and the reward of his love. He may gnash his teeth for anger when his own fate has been determined for all eternity. He must then see how all his hope and reckoning has come to nothing.

psalm 112

Laudate, pueri

God is to be praised for his regard to the poor and humble

ALLELUIA

1. Praise the Lord, ye children: praise ye the name of the Lord.

2. Blessed be the name of the Lord, from henceforth now and forever.

3. From the rising of the sun unto the going down of the same, the name of the Lord is worthy of praise.

4. The Lord is high above all nations; and his glory above the heavens.

5. Who is as the Lord our God, who dwelleth on high:

6. And looketh down on the low things in heaven and in earth?

7. Raising up the needy from the earth and lifting up the poor out of the dunghill:

8. That he may place him with princes, with the princes of his people.

9. Who maketh a barren woman to dwell in a house, the joyful mother of children.

THE great Hallel begins with this psalm (Psalms 112–117). This psalm was recited by the Jews at the celebration of the Paschal supper. It is, as it were, the preface to the paschal sacrifice. "It is truly worthy and just, fitting and wholesome, that we at all times, and in all places thank thee, holy Lord, almighty Father and eternal God." The psalm calls upon Israel to thank and praise God who has chosen it and despite his incomparable majesty has manifested his love to the weak and lowly. The history of the people of God is rich in testimonies of his love but still richer in the testimonies of God's love is the history of the Church of the New Covenant, the Church of those redeemed by the Lord. Thus God chooses those whom the world considers and despises as foolish and weak. No man can boast about himself. Every member of the kingdom of God has a threefold obligation to thank the Lord at all times and places.

The members of the kingdom are servants of God (verses 1–3). Without any merit of their own the Lord has called them to his covenant, while on the other hand he has excluded many millions. But as all divine activity tends to the glorification of the Lord, so also the highest purpose and last end of the call to the Church of God is to praise his Name, that is, his Being. Man must praise him for his greatness revealed in creation, for the glory of his grace, for his providence in history. He who neglects this duty is not a good and faithful servant. God must be praised at all times; for the God whom we serve is God at all times. Therefore the song of praise must never cease. Parents must teach this to their children, one generation must pass this on to the next in order that throughout the centuries honor and glory be given to the eternal God, the immortal, invisible, and only God. The Lord whom we serve is also God of the entire world and on this account he should also be praised in all places. Many millions do not know and honor him; many millions have known him but were unmindful of him. The servant of God must ardently desire that all knees shall bend before the Lord and that all men will worship him. On this account a missionary command is given to them to cooperate with all their power in propagating the worship of the name of the Lord in order

439

that all nations from the rising of the sun to its setting may praise the name of the Lord.

The Lord, whom those who are called to serve, is the only and incomparable God (verses 4–6). This service, therefore, is the highest honor. The gods of the pagans are the work of men; they are national gods which stand and fall with their people, but the Lord is the God of the universe and the King of all nations. They are before him as a drop in the ocean, like a speck of dust on a scale; they stand and fall as he wishes. The immeasurable realm of the starry heaven has its limits, but God's glory is unlimited. The heaven of heavens cannot contain him. On this account there is nothing in the entire universe that can be compared with God the Lord. He is infinitely greater than all the glories of creation. He does not stand in the world but over it. He remains untouched by the world's changeableness. His power is unattainable and untouchable; his throne is in inaccessible heights. And yet the Lord can be approached by his creatures. In his inaccessible height and in his infinite blessedness he has not isolated himself from men. More than in his power and majesty he is incomparable in his love and condescension. His providence is extended to the most insignificant of his creatures; he cares for the birds in the sky and for the grass in the field. Man especially is the object of his care and more especially his servant. The entire plan of the Redemption is a condescension of the Most High to the vessels of his election.

The third part (verses 7–9) describes the fate of two groups of persons. In this description the author uses two persons, David and Anna the mother of Samuel, as models to show that the Lord is the infinite God worthy of all praise and love and that it is a duty to serve him. It is our duty of gratitude and of a return of love to serve him. The thoughts of this section are taken from Anna's song of praise (1 Kings 2:1). God had taken King David from his flock and had chosen him to be king of his people; he had chosen him who was unknown and the youngest son in the house of his father. But the gracious elevation of weak man from the dust of the earth to the redeemed filiation of God and the enrichment of the poor and despised men with heavenly inheritance surpasses by far the elevation of David. God numbered him among the princes; but man as a child of God surpasses in dignity all the princes and mighty ones of the earth. His place is among the princes of heaven. God in his goodness has mercy upon a childless mother and makes her a happy mother of a large group of children. The fruitful Phenenna became despised, the barren Anna was praised and blessed because she gave to her people the Judge and Prophet Samuel.

psalm 113

In exitu Israel

God has shown his power in delivering his people:
idols are vain. The Hebrews divide
this into two psalms

ALLELUIA

1. When Israel went out of Egypt, the house of Jacob from a barbarous people:

2. Judea was made his sanctuary, Israel his dominion.

3. The sea saw and fled: Jordan was turned back.

4. The mountains skipped like rams, and the hills like lambs of the flock.

5. What ailed thee, O thou sea, that thou didst flee: and thou, O Jordan, that thou wast turned back?

6. Ye mountains, that ye skipped like rams, and ye hills, like lambs of the flock?

7. At the presence of the Lord the earth was moved, at the presence of the God of Jacob:

8. Who turned the rock into pools of water, and the stony hill into fountains of waters.

1. Not to us, O Lord, not to us: but to thy name give glory.

2. For thy mercy, and for thy truth's sake: lest the Gentiles should say: Where is their God?

3. But our God is in heaven: he hath done all things whatsoever he would.

4. The idols of the Gentiles are silver and gold, the works of the hands of men.

5. They have mouths and speak not: they have eyes and see not.

6. They have ears and hear not: they have noses and smell not.

7. They have hands and feel not: they have feet and walk not: neither shall they cry out through their throat.

8. Let them that make them become like unto them: and all such that trust in them.

9. The house of Israel hath hoped in the Lord: he is their helper and their protector.

10. The house of Aaron hath hoped in the Lord: he is their helper and protector.

11. They that fear the Lord have hoped in the Lord: he is their helper and their protector.

12. The Lord hath been mindful of us, and hath blessed us.
He hath blessed the house of Israel: he hath blessed the house of Aaron.

13. He hath blessed all that fear the Lord, both little and great.

14. May the Lord add blessings upon you: upon you and upon your children.

15. Blessed be you of the Lord, who made heaven and earth.

16. The heaven of heaven is the Lord's: but the earth has been given to the children of men.

17. The dead shall not praise thee, O Lord: nor any of them that go down to hell.

18. But we that live bless the Lord: from this time now and forever.

THE Vulgate comprises 114–115 of the Hebrew text into one, Psalm 113. The first part describes with dramatic vividness the miraculous passage through the Red Sea and the Jordan which opened the way from the Egyptian slavery to freedom and from the forty years' journey through the desert to the promised land. The second part shows the confidence the Israelites had that God would again return his people from the Babylonian captivity to freedom and to their native country. Both deeds of liberation are often mentioned in the Psalter as well as by the prophets. The redemption from the Egyptian slavery is a type and a guarantee of the second redemption, namely from the Babylonian exile. There is nothing, therefore, that should hinder the Septuagint from placing these two great events together in Psalm 113 and from seeing in the first part, the deliverance from Egypt, a basis for confidence in a second deliverance.

God can redeem. To show this is the purpose of Psalm 114 of the Hebrew text. For more than 200 years the house of Jacob, the descendants of the patriarchs, lived in Egypt as strangers until the time came when God had mercy upon his people and delivered them from slavery. The deliverance from a foreign country was only a preamble to the greater deeds of God; namely, the election of the chosen people and the making of the covenant on Mount Sinai. Juda, the province of the tribe of Juda by whom the people were led, became the sanctuary of God. Juda was the tribe dedicated to the Lord and Israel was its kingdom; it was to form a theocracy, a priestly kingdom. The Lord had brought about its liberation with great signs and wonders. The waters of the Red Sea had to recede at the command of God so that Israel could pass through dryfooted. The waters of the Jordan stopped flowing as soon as the priests touched its waves with the Ark of the Covenant. The mountains and hills which otherwise stood immovable, moved, or as the text says leaped like rams and young lambs; they quaked before the majesty of God revealing himself on Mount Sinai. The poet directs a question to the Sea and to the Jordan River: why do their continually moving waves recede at once or stand still forming a wall? He asks the mountains and the hills what made them move, the mountains that were otherwise so firm. The mountains answer the questioner. Their quaking and their frolicking is an act of worship to the Lord, the God of Jacob. On the peninsula of Sinai they were witnesses of the miracles during the desert journey. On the hard rocks of these mountains Moses struck his staff in the name of the Lord and water gushed forth. Streams of water issued from the rocks.

When in the Babylonian captivity Israel begs for a second deliverance, when it beseeches God to repeat the miracles of the first deliverance, the people do not expect help because they deserve it, but only for the sake of his divine Name. God should redeem them for the sake of his honor (verses 1–8) to reveal his mercy and fidelity. Among the pagans the defeat of a nation was also considered a defeat of its gods. Still more, the wars of pagan nations against the chosen people of Yahwe were wars between two opposed philosophies of life, and therefore victories over Israel were considered as victories of their gods over Yahwe. So much the more did the collapse of the Israelitic government, the destruction of Jerusalem, and their only temple mean to the pagans a triumph of polytheism over the monotheism of Israel. On this account the banished had to hear the Gentile Babylonians deride them. "Where, then, is your God whom you adore, in whom you have so much confidence?" Because Yahwe's honor is at stake the psalmist does not pray for the restoration of the national honor of his people. This has to take second place to the honor of God. But God's honor will be acknowledged by the pagans if he shows mercy to his people and fulfills his promises faithfully. Thus the Lord has spoken to the prophet Ezechiel: "It is not for your sake that I will do this, O house of Israel, but for my holy Name's sake which you have profaned among the nations whither you went. And I will sanctify my great Name which was profaned among the Gentiles, which you have

443

profaned in the midst of them, that the Gentiles may know that I am the Lord . . . when I shall be sanctified in you before their eyes" (36:22 seq.).

There is only one God in heaven and he is the Lord God of Israel. He is the creator of all; he spoke and it was made; he commanded and it came into existence; with him there are no impossibilities. But the gods of the pagans are not even living beings; they are lifeless figures. They are not creators but are made by the hands of men. The silver and gold from which they were formed is their only value. They have indeed a mouth but with it they cannot speak to men as Yahwe did so powerfully on Sinai to manifest his will to the people. They have indeed eyes but they cannot see the need of those who pray to them; they cannot even see what happens to themselves. They have received silver and golden ears, but they cannot hear. They do not hear the prayers that are offered to them; they do not hear the curses that are uttered because they do not hear. With their nose they do not smell the innumerable sacrifices that are offered. They cannot move their hands and feet. They must be carried. From their throat there comes no sound. They cannot even cry for help when they are in need. He who makes such lifeless gods and puts his confidence in them confides in nothing. He remains as helpless as his gods.

Yahwe, the Lord of Israel, is altogether different. He rewards the confidence of his adorers (verses 9–13). God is an almighty helper. He protects his people as a shield protects the warrior. The miracles during the exodus from Egypt have proved that he has the power to redeem, and the history of centuries has always confirmed this proof. On this account Israel trusts in the Lord in the time of exile as well as in all times of need. The house of Aaron, the priestly tribe, trusts in him. It has felt the destruction of the temple and the omission of the sacrificial service more than anything else. Yet all God-fearing men trust in the Lord, small and great, exalted and humble, rich and poor, young and old.

The psalmist now gives a blessing in the name of the Lord (verses 14–18). The first blessing of the Lord after creation was that of propagation which was repeated by God after the Deluge. The Lord will also give this blessing in Messianic times. Israel shall be blessed in its children and in its children's children. The source of the blessing will never be exhausted; for he who blesses is the almighty Creator of heaven and earth. He will, therefore, fulfill his promises for Israel even though the people in exile may be compared to the dead. He will not let his people be destroyed because it is their mission to glorify God. Heaven is God's palace where the angels serve him and praise his name. The Lord has given the earth to men, not as their possession, but in order that they may worship and praise him. This obligation only the living can fulfill. In the kingdom of eternal quiet all psalms and hymns are silenced. If Israel would be destroyed, death's stillness would be on earth because no one would glorify God. This mission Israel wishes to fulfill.

psalm 114

Dilexi

*The prayer of a just man in affliction with
a lively confidence in God*

ALLELUIA

1. I have loved, because the Lord will hear the voice of my prayer.

2. Because he hath inclined his ear unto me: and in my days I will call upon him.

3. The sorrows of death have compassed me: and the perils of hell have found me. I met with trouble and sorrow.

4. And I called upon the name of the Lord: O Lord, deliver my soul.

5. The Lord is merciful and just, and our God showeth mercy.

6. The Lord is the keeper of little ones: I was humbled and he delivered me.

7. Turn, O my soul, into thy rest: for the Lord hath been bountiful to thee.

8. For he hath delivered my soul from death: my eyes from tears, my feet from falling.

9. I will please the Lord in the land of the living.

WHEN God has delivered man from great affliction, when he has given consolation to the human soul by his help or has absolved it from grave sin and peace and rest have returned, then man feels the breath of divine love and his heart too is filled with love and he is inspired to return love for love. This the psalmist himself has also experienced. His soul being filled with sentiments of gratitude he can say only one thing: "I love." He, whom he means by this, need not be mentioned; for only one has claim to his love and he alone, for he is God, the Lord. The foundation of his love is faith. With the Lord there is mercy (verses 1–4). The hearing of his prayer and the return to grace has increased his confidence. Therefore in future afflictions he will not seek consolation and help among men; but with God love and confidence came from the depth of his heart and the need was great. The poet saw himself near collapse; he already felt how death laid its shackles upon all his members and powers. Fear and terror took hold of him, as if at any moment he would have to descend into the lowest depths of the underworld where night and the gruesomeness of hell would surround him. There seemed to be no escape from this distress, no help, no consoling hope in his great affliction. From this depth of misery he raised his tearful eyes to God, from his breast there came a cry for help as from one who wrestling with death utters: Save me, save my soul! It was a cry for help from the almighty and all-good God.

The need and misery was deserved, but God helped (verses 5–9). He proved himself to be a merciful and good God. He had indeed struck wounds, but he healed them again when he who was struck humbly turned to him again; for God is merciful. God sends sufferings and tribulations; he even lets man fall to cure his pride and make him humble, to bring him to the consciousness that he must depend upon the Lord. When the psalmist in his need saw that all human help was denied him and his own human strength failed him, he became humble. God then helped him; for only to the humble does he give grace. Now his soul could again be at peace because it has obtained God's mercy and has experienced his love. Sweet peace has again returned and he felt as a little child who feels itself secure when with father and mother. The Lord has saved him from death; he has dried his tears; he has kept his foot from disastrous falls and has placed it on firm ground. A sacred vow closes the psalm. The life regained should from now on belong to the Lord. The psalmist does not want to be a mere reciter of promises; he wants to love God, in deed and in truth, in his way of life before God and in his example before men that all may see God's works and praise the Father of all men.

psalm 115

Credidi

This in the Hebrew is joined to the foregoing psalm:
and continues to express the faith and
gratitude of the psalmist

ALLELUIA

10. I have believed, therefore have I spoken; but I have been humbled exceedingly.

11. I said in my excess: Every man is a liar.

12. What shall I render to the Lord, for all the things that he hath rendered to me?

13. I will take the chalice of salvation: and I will call upon the name of the Lord.

14. I will pay my vows to the Lord before all his people:

15. Precious in the sight of the Lord is the death of his saints.

16. O Lord, for I am thy servant. I am thy servant, and the son of thy handmaid. Thou hast broken my bonds.

17. I will sacrifice to thee the sacrifice of praise, and I will call upon the name of the Lord.

18. I will pay my vows to the Lord in the sight of all his people:

19. In the courts of the house of the Lord, in the midst of thee, O Jerusalem.

Days, perhaps weeks and months of great distress and of grave spiritual affliction had befallen the psalmist. He could not conceal his sorrow; he had to make known his troubles. Therefore he cried out to the Lord: "I have been humbled exceedingly." In the foregoing psalm which in the Hebrew text is incorrectly connected with this psalm the composer began with a confession of love. In this psalm he begins with a confession of faith. It is an ejaculatory prayer: "O Lord, I believe, help thou my weak faith." In his need he found out that men cannot be relied

447

upon. They promise but they do not or cannot help. God alone is reliable. Thus, the psalmist turns to the Lord and the Lord helps him. Now he wishes to thank him.

The thanksgiving is threefold (verses 3–5). The psalmist first asks himself and reflects how he can worthily thank the Lord. He has resolved for the near future on three things. He will thank God by his disposition: "I will take the chalice of the Lord." Since in the ancient Orient the father of the family gave to each one his portion of wine in a beaker, the chalice of salvation means the graces and benefits which God bestows on his children. This beaker, that is, the graces of salvation which are offered to him by God he will accept gladly and enjoy as benefits from God. They are the graces that come from the sacrifice, from the sacraments, and from men. He who refuses the gifts of God proves that he does not appreciate the value of these gifts. The second thanksgiving is in words: "I will call upon the name of the Lord." I will acknowledge him publicly as my benefactor: I will praise him before the world as the true God of my salvation; I will glorify him. I will thank him and love him. The third thanksgiving is in deed: "I will pay my vow to the Lord before all the people." The whole congregation shall be witness to my thanksgiving; they shall thank and glorify God with me.

With this the psalmist does not see his duty of giving thanks to God ended (verses 6–10). In the future too he must show signs of thankfulness. The program for the future consists of three rules of life. The first rule is: Have confidence in the divine Providence. God is not indifferent to the death of the saints, of the just and God-fearing members of his people; he will not permit them to be destroyed by the enemy; he will protect their life like the pupil of his eye. The second rule is: Be faithful in the service of God. In regard to God, man is not freeborn; he cannot even be compared to a man who has been a slave because of his debt and who is then released in the seventh year having paid his creditor six years of service. Man is never freed of his duties toward God. He may be compared to a child born during the slavery of his parents which according to law was a lifelong possession of the lord of his parents. Man must consider himself a lifelong servant of the Lord and must at all times serve him, especially because he has freed him from the bonds of fear and need. The third law is: Dedicate your life to the Lord. God has loosed the hands from the bonds of need and sin. These hands should now bring him sacrifices of praise, not only one sacrifice. During his whole life man must give God service; he must work for the honor of God. This is a vow of gratitude on the part of the psalmist. He wants to serve God, the God with whom he has made a covenant, who is his Lord and King. He wants to serve God before the entire people so that all may see it and thank and glorify God with him; he wants to serve God in the house of the Lord, in the holy city of Jerusalem, the Church of God. His thanksgiving should be a jubilant Alleluia.

psalm 116

Laudate Dominum

*All nations are called upon to praise God for
his mercy and truth*

ALLELUIA

1. O praise the Lord all ye nations: praise him, all ye people.

2. For his mercy is confirmed upon us: and the truth of the Lord remaineth forever.

THIS little psalm is, as it were, the "Te Deum" which those who had been banished to Babylonia sang on their return to their native country. But it is also the "Te Deum" for all redeemed, a jubilant thanksgiving for the grace of the Messianic salvation to which the Gentiles are called. All nations are called upon to praise the Lord, their God and Saviour, in one immense choir. The praise of the Lord is the language with which all nations from the Orient and Occident, all races and colors are familiar. First the nations should praise the Lord because of the great deed of redemption which he wrought for Israel by the deliverance from the Babylonian captivity. He did this because he loved Israel. This redemption however was of supranational significance because it was a type and a guarantee of the Messianic redemption. Since God fulfilled his promise in this instance, he will fulfill his promise of a much more valuable redemption through the Messias. He will complete that redemption by the eternal happiness of the redeemed. The Gentiles too will participate in this redemption. In the request that they too should take part and sing along in the praises of the Lord there is implied a divine request of carrying on missions, of making known to the Gentiles the glad message of salvation.

psalm 117

Confitemini Domino

The psalmist praiseth the Lord for his delivery from evils,
putteth his whole trust in him and foretelleth
the coming of Christ

ALLELUIA

1. Give praise to the Lord, for he is good: for his mercy endureth forever.

2. Let Israel now say, that he is good: for his mercy endureth forever.

3. Let the house of Aaron now say, that his mercy endureth forever.

4. Let them that fear the Lord now say, that his mercy endureth forever.

5. In my trouble I called upon the Lord: and the Lord heard me, and enlarged me.

6. The Lord is my helper: I will not fear what man can do unto me.

7. The Lord is my helper: and I will look over my enemies.

8. It is good to confide in the Lord, rather than to have confidence in man.

9. It is good to trust in the Lord, rather than to trust in princes.

10. All nations compassed me about; and in the name of the Lord I have been revenged on them.

11. Surrounding me they compassed me about: and in the name of the Lord I have been revenged on them.

12. They surrounded me like bees, and they burned like fire among thorns: and in the name of the Lord I was revenged on them.

13. Being pushed I was overturned that I might fall: but the Lord supported me.

14. The Lord is my strength and my praise: and he is become my salvation.

15. The voice of rejoicing and of salvation is in the tabernacles of the just.

16. The right hand of the Lord hath wrought strength: the right hand of the Lord hath exalted me: the right hand of the Lord hath wrought strength.

17. I shall not die but live: and shall declare the works of the Lord.

18. The Lord chastising hath chastised me: but he hath not delivered me over to death.

19. Open to me the gates of justice: I will go into them, and give praise to the Lord.

20. This is the gate of the Lord, the just shall enter into it.

21. I will give glory to thee because thou hast heard me: and art become my salvation.

22. The stone which the builders rejected; the same is become the head of the corner.

23. This is the Lord's doing: and it is wonderful in our eyes.

24. This is the day which the Lord has made: let us be glad and rejoice therein.

25. O Lord, save me: O Lord, give good success.

26. Blessed be he that cometh in the name of the Lord.
We have blessed you out of the house of the Lord.

27. The Lord is God, and he hath shone upon us. Appoint a solemn day, with shady boughs, even to the horn of the altar.

28. Thou art my God, and I will praise thee: thou art my God, and I will exalt thee.
I will praise thee because thou hast heard me, and art become my salvation.

29. O praise ye the Lord, for he is good: for his mercy endureth forever.

THIS psalm closes the big Hallel. It was composed for the dedication of the post-exilic temple, 520 before Christ, and was sung for the first time at the dedication when the people were going up to the sanctuary which according to the prophecy of the Prophet Aggeus would be still standing in Messianic times. The joy of the people pervades the entire song. It had been seventy years since the destruction of the temple by King Nabuchodonosor in 587 and twenty years since the laying of the cornerstone of the new building. Now it was completed in spite of many difficulties and could be dedicated. It was not as magnificent a temple as the one erected by Solomon, but the prophecy of the Jeremias was now fulfilled: "The voice of joy and the voice of gladness, the voice of the bridegroom and the voice of the bride, the voice of them that shall say: Give ye glory to the Lord of hosts, for the Lord is good, for his mercy endureth forever: and of them that shall bring their vows into the house of the Lord: for I will bring back the captivity of the land as at the first, saith the Lord" (Jeremias 33:11). The beginning of this psalm seems intentionally to remind the reader of this prophecy.

Later this psalm belonged to the liturgy of the Feast of Tabernacles. The people carried garlands in their hands which were waved at the beginning of the psalm. The priests walked in procession around the altar of holocausts during which they held willow branches in their hands. The song with its interpolations is sung in the procession to the new sanctuary.

At the beginning of the procession to the sanctuary (verses 1–4) the psalmist requests priests and people to praise God for his goodness and everlasting providence, for the return from exile, for the restoration of the Jewish commonwealth, for the reconstruction of the temple in the face of many difficulties. All these were proofs of the goodness, mercy, and everlasting fidelity of God. They were guarantees also that the Lord would fulfill the Messianic prophecies. All Israel, therefore, has reason to be grateful and to praise the everlasting love of God. The return home from the captivity and the reconstruction of the temple indicate that God has not rejected his people as many pessimists would have them believe. God holds firmly to his plan to give salvation to the world through Israel. God's eternal love should acknowledge the house of Aaron, the Old Testament priesthood. It was therefore their duty as servants of the Lord to glorify God in the new sanctuary. All God-fearing men, both Jew and Gentile, should praise God's mercy. The pardoning of Israel is, according to the divine promise, also a presupposition and guarantee of the call of the Gentile world. All should go up to Sion with the glad consciousness that in the temple the Lord will give the Messianic peace, that the Messias will enter, and that Christ, the glory of the Father, will take up his dwelling there to replace the Ark of the Covenant.

The procession starts (verses 5–18). On the way to the sanctuary the psalmist brings to memory the difficulties his people had to endure until the present day and the wonderful help the Lord had given them. The people had often been in great distress until finally Israel lost the character of an independent nation and was exiled to Babylon. But whenever they were in need and humbly besought the Lord, they were delivered. Even now they were led back home from their captivity. In view of such divine assistance what did Israel have to fear? What can frail men do to a weak nation whose protector and defender is God Himself? When God is with us who can successfully be against us? Since God is the helper, the victory over the enemies is certain. May they be ever so powerful and may their hatred be ever so violent, they will be humbled by the Lord. And those who were humbled by the enemies will triumph and will see the enemies' downfall. The experiences of a long history had taught the people of God that men cannot be relied upon. All covenants with the Gentile nations for the protection of their native country were not only useless but were also of great disadvantage. Only God has proved himself

452

to be a reliable helper. How often Israel seemed to be on the verge of destruction and in its need hoped to obtain assistance from Gentile nations! King Achaz turned to the Assyrian Tiglath-Pileser for help in order to defend himself against the united attack of the northern kingdom of Syria. King Ezechias sought help from the Pharaoh Shabaka to defend him against King Sennacherib. But every time they were deceived. They had to pay dearly for the Assyrian help. Juda lost its independence; the Egyptian army departed as soon as the hostile troops approached.

At the present time those who had returned home from the captivity were a small and weak minority among the pagans and were menaced by the Samaritans and by the Persian governor. These tried to hinder the construction of the temple and of the city. But the people prayed to God and thus averted all attacks by the power of his Name and made the enemy intrigues ineffective. Numerous and audacious as a swarm of bees, they encircled the little group and tried to hinder them from carrying out the plan of reconstruction. Violent and impetuous, a fire among thorns, was the hatred toward Israel. But all was of no avail against the will of God. Despite the violent and treacherous attempts to hinder the construction, the sanctuary was finished; its work was delayed for a few years but not hindered altogether. From all sides those who returned home were oppressed; everywhere hindrances were put in their way, but God showed himself to be their support and strength. He was mightier than all his enemies.

Such thoughts and memories gave joy to the souls of those who made pilgrimages to the new temple and filled them with gratitude. Just as Israel after the miraculous passage through the Red Sea sang, "The Lord is my strength and my praise; he became my salvation . . ." (Exodus 15:2). So now the people repeated the song in order to thank the Lord for the wonderful deliverance from every hostile attack. Like the passage through the Red Sea the construction of the temple meant an end to a great divine act of deliverance, the redemption from exile, and the beginning of a new epoch. The psalmist already hears the jubilation of the new, Messianic epoch, the jubilant song from the tabernacle of the just; for in the Messianic Sion only the just, the redeemed, will obtain citizenship in the new Jerusalem, on the streets through which the alleluia resounds. It is not through the merits of those who returned home that the temple was erected, but through the intervention of almighty God. The power of almighty God proved itself effective. The right hand of the Lord will again prove itself effective in bringing about the fulfillment of the plan of salvation. This plan is intimately connected with Israel for from it the Messias shall come and bring salvation to the Gentiles. Therefore it is in the divine plan of salvation that Israel shall not collapse altogether, that it shall not disappear from the kingdoms of the nations. It will continue to exist and proclaim the Lord's deeds of redemption to all the nations. The redemption from exile is in itself a sign that Israel will not perish. God has, indeed, punished Israel severely; he has deprived it of its independence, of its native country, of its home, and of its temple. But he has not permitted it to be annihilated; he has restored it and as a sign of forgiveness he has permitted it to reconstruct its temple.

The solemn procession has arrived at the sanctuary and now stands before the closed gates of the temple courts (verses 18–25). The choir asks for admission for the people to enter; it asks not only for admission into this temple of stone but also for admission into the sanctuary of Messianic times. The gates of justice shall be opened, the gates to the sanctuary in which the just and justifying God dwells, the gates from which he dispenses justice and grace. The people want to enter this gate to thank the Lord. The gate to the sanctuary is the gate to the Lord. Only the just may enter the heavenly sanctuary of Messianic times. According to Isaias the unclean may not even walk on the way to the sanctuary (35:9). Only the redeemed may make pilgrimages to Sion; only those who have been redeemed may return home to him. With jubilation they return to Sion having eternal joy in their heart. The psalmist thanks the Lord in the name of all the citizens of the nation for having heard their prayers, for having had mercy upon them, for having revealed himself to them as the God of their salvation. The Gentiles who were determined to establish great nations despised little Israel and rejected it. But God selected this despised nation for the cornerstone of his kingdom. God has given to Israel his revelations and promises for all the world. From Israel the Messias, the Saviour of all nations, was to come. In this sense Israel itself was a type and a prophecy of the Messias whom in later times it rejected. This Messias became the cornerstone of the great temple of the Holy Spirit, the Church of the New Testament. The selection of Israel was a wonderful work of divine love, grace, and power. Other nations surpassed it in the antiquity of their history, in the number of their inhabitants, in culture, in arts and science, and in the extent of their kingdoms. Despite all this the Lord chose none of the great nations, but rather the little insignificant Israel. This is a miracle of the most high God. The festive day shall be dedicated to God in thanksgiving for this gracious call to return from exile and for the erection of the new temple which is the work of God. The festive day is a day given by the Lord on which joy and jubilation are appropriate. To the jubilation and thanksgiving the psalmist adds a prayer of petition that the Lord may complete his gracious work and give salvation to the Gentiles. May God give his blessings for this mission.

At the entrance to the sanctuary (verses 26–29), the priests greet the people and give them their blessing, signifying that the divine blessing for which they prayed has come upon them. This blessing shall flow richly from the house of God. He who comes in the name of the Lord to adore and praise will receive blessings from the sanctuary; for the house of the Lord is the treasury of the divine blessings. Yahwe is the God of the covenant, the King of Israel, whose mercy rests upon the people. The people, therefore, should worship him in the courts with religious ceremonies and with palm branches in their hands. They may not enter the holy of holies. They may, however, come as far as the altar of holocausts and sing praises to the Lord in solemn procession. They may sing: "Thou art my God, I praise thee; thou art my God, I proclaim thee." The close of the psalm again takes up the introductory thought. There the request was made to celebrate worthily; here the admonition is given that it is a duty to praise God and to continue praising him; for God's goodness endureth forever.

psalm 118

Beati immaculati

Of the excellence of virtue consisting in the love and observance of the commandments of God

ALLELUIA

ALEPH

1. Blessed are the undefiled in the way, who walk in the law of the Lord.

2. Blessed are they that search his testimonies: that seek him with their whole heart.

3. For they that work iniquity, have not walked in his ways.

4. Thou hast commanded thy commandments to be kept most diligently.

5. O, that my ways may be directed to keep thy justifications.

6. Then shall I not be confounded, when I shall look into all thy commandments.

7. I will praise thee with uprightness of heart, when I shall have learned the judgments of thy justice.

8. I will keep thy justifications: O do not thou utterly forsake me.

BETH

9. By what doth a young man correct his way? By observing thy words.

10. With my whole heart have I sought after thee: let me not stray from thy commandments.

11. Thy words have I hidden in my heart, that I may not sin against thee.

12. Blessed art thou, O Lord: teach me thy justifications.

13. With my lips I have pronounced all the judgments of thy mouth.

14. I have been delighted in the way of thy testimonies, as in all riches.

15. I will meditate on thy commandments; and I will consider thy ways.

16. I will think of thy justifications: I will not forget thy words.

GIMEL

17. Give bountifully to thy servant, enliven me: and I shall keep thy words.

18. Open thou my eyes: and I will consider the wondrous things of thy law.

19. I am a sojourner on the earth: hide not thy commandments from me.

20. My soul hath coveted too long for thy justifications at all times.

21. Thou hast rebuked the proud: they are cursed who decline from thy commandments.

22. Remove from me reproach and contempt: because I have sought after thy testimonies.

23. For princes sat and spoke against me: but thy servant was employed in thy justifications.

24. For thy testimonies are my meditation: and thy justifications my counsel.

DALETH

25. My soul hath cleaved to the pavement: quicken thou me according to thy word.

26. I have declared my ways, and thou hast heard me: teach me thy justifications.

27. Make me to understand the way of thy justifications: and I shall be exercised in thy wondrous works.

28. My soul hath slumbered through heaviness: strengthen thou me in thy words.

29. Remove from me the way of iniquity: and out of thy law have mercy on me.

30. I have chosen the way of truth: thy judgments I have not forgotten.

31. I have stuck to thy testimonies, O Lord: put me not to shame.

32. I have run the way of thy commandments, when thou didst enlarge my heart.

He

33. Set before me for a law the way of thy justifications, O Lord: and I will always seek after it.

34. Give me understanding, and I will search thy law; and I will keep it with my whole heart.

35. Lead me into the path of thy commandments: for this same I have desired.

36. Incline my heart into thy testimonies and not to covetousness.

37. Turn away my eyes that they may not behold vanity: quicken me in thy way.

38. Establish thy word to thy servant, in thy fear.

39. Turn away my reproach, which I have apprehended: for thy judgments are delightful.

40. Behold, I have longed after thy precepts: quicken me in thy justice.

Vau

41. Let thy mercy also come upon me, O Lord: thy salvation according to thy word.

42. So shall I answer them that reproach me in anything: that I have trusted in thy words.

43. And take not thou the word of truth utterly out of my mouth: for in thy words, I have hoped exceedingly.

44. So shall I always keep thy law, forever and ever.

45. And I walked at large: because I have sought after thy commandments.

46. And I spoke of thy testimonies before kings: and I was not ashamed.

47. I meditated also on thy commandments, which I loved.

48. And I lifted up my hands to thy commandments, which I loved: and I was exercised in thy justifications.

ZAIN

49. Be thou mindful of thy word to thy servant, in which thou hast given me hope.

50. This hath comforted me in my humiliation: because thy word hath enlivened me.

51. The proud did iniquitously altogether: but I declined not from thy law.

52. I remembered, O Lord, thy judgments of old: and I was comforted.

53. A fainting hath taken hold of me, because of the wicked that forsake thy law.

54. Thy justifications were the subject of my song, in the place of my pilgrimage.

55. In the night I have remembered thy name, O Lord: and have kept thy law.

56. This happened to me: because I sought after thy justifications.

HETH

57. O Lord, my portion, I have said, I would keep thy law.

58. I entreated thy face with all my heart: have mercy on me according to thy word.

59. I have thought on my ways: and turned my feet unto thy testimonies.

60. I am ready, and am not troubled: that I may keep thy commandments.

61. The cords of the wicked have encompassed me: but I have not forgotten thy law.

62. I rose at midnight to give praise to thee; for the judgments of thy justification.

63. I am a partaker with all them that fear thee, and that keep thy commandments.

64. The earth, O Lord, is full of thy mercy: teach me thy justifications.

TETH

65. Thou hast done well with thy servant, O Lord, according to thy word.

66. Teach me goodness, and discipline and knowledge; for I have believed thy commandments.

67. Before I was humbled I offended: therefore have I kept thy word.

68. Thou art good; and in thy goodness teach me thy justifications.

69. The iniquity of the proud hath been multiplied over me: but I will seek thy commandments with my whole heart.

70. Their heart is curdled like milk: but I have meditated on thy law.

71. It is good for me that thou hast humbled me, that I may learn thy justifications.

72. The law of thy mouth is good to me, above thousands of gold and silver.

JOD

73. Thy hands have made me and formed me: give me understanding, and I will learn thy commandments.

74. They that fear thee shall see me, and shall be glad: because I have greatly hoped in thy words.

75. I know, O Lord, that thy judgments are equity: and in thy truth thou hast humbled me.

76. O, let thy mercy be for my comfort: according to thy word unto thy servant.

77. Let thy tender mercies come unto me, and I shall live: for thy law is my meditation.

78. Let the proud be ashamed, because they have done unjustly towards me: but I will be employed in thy commandments.

79. Let them that fear thee turn to me: and they that know thy testimonies.

80. Let my heart be undefiled in thy justifications, that I may not be confounded.

CAPH

81. My soul hath fainted after thy salvation: and in thy word I have very much hoped.

82. My eyes have failed for thy word, saying: when wilt thou comfort me?

83. For I am become like a bottle in the frost: I have not forgotten thy justifications.

84. How many are the days of thy servant; when wilt thou execute judgment on them that persecute me?

85. The wicked have told me fables: but not as thy law.

86. All thy statutes are truth: they have persecuted me unjustly, do thou help me.

87. They had almost made an end of me upon earth: but I have not forsaken thy commandments.

88. Quicken thou me according to thy mercy: and I shall keep the testimonies of thy mouth.

Lamed

89. Forever, O Lord, thy word standeth firm in heaven.

90. Thy truth unto all generations: thou hast founded the earth, and it continueth.

91. By thy ordinance the day goeth on: for all things serve thee.

92. Unless thy law had been my meditation, I had then perhaps perished in my abjection.

93. Thy justifications I will never forget: for by them thou hast given me life.

94. I am thine, save thou me: for I have sought thy justifications.

95. The wicked have waited for me to destroy me: but I have understood thy testimonies.

96. I have seen an end of all perfection: thy commandment is exceeding broad.

Mem

97. O how I have loved thy law, O Lord! it is my meditation all the day.

98. Through thy commandment, thou hast made me wiser than my enemies: for it is ever with me.

99. I have understood more than all my teachers: because thy testimonies are my meditation.

100. I have had understanding above ancients: because I have sought thy commandments.

101. I have restrained my feet from every evil way: that I may keep thy words.

102. I have not declined from thy judgments, because thou hast set me a law.

103. How sweet are thy words to my palate: more than honey to my mouth.

104. By thy commandments I have had understanding: therefore have I hated every way of iniquity.

Nun

105. Thy word is a lamp to my feet, and a light to my paths.

106. I have sworn and am determined to keep the judgments of thy justice.

460

107. I have been humbled, O Lord, exceedingly: quicken thou me according to thy word.

108. The free offerings of my mouth make acceptable, O Lord: and teach me thy judgments.

109. My soul is continually in my hands: and I have not forgotten thy law.

110. Sinners have laid a snare for me: but I have not erred from thy precepts.

111. I have purchased thy testimonies for an inheritance forever: because they are the joy of my heart.

112. I have inclined my heart to do thy justifications forever, for the reward.

SAMECH

113. I have hated the unjust: and have loved thy law.

114. Thou art my helper and my protector: and in thy word I have greatly hoped.

115. Depart from me, ye malignant: and I will search the commandments of my God.

116. Uphold me according to thy word, and I shall live: and let me not be confounded in my expectation.

117. Help me, and I shall be saved: and I will meditate always on thy justifications.

118. Thou hast despised all them that fall off from thy judgments; for their thought is unjust.

119. I have accounted all the sinners of the earth prevaricators: therefore have I loved thy testimonies.

120. Pierce thou my flesh with thy fear: for I am afraid of thy judgments.

AIN

121. I have done judgment and justice: give me not up to them that slander me.

122. Uphold thy servant unto good: let not the proud calumniate me.

123. My eyes have fainted after thy salvation: and for the word of thy justice.

124. Deal with thy servant according to thy mercy: and teach me thy justifications.

125. I am thy servant: give me understanding that I may know thy testimonies.

126. It is time, O Lord, to do: they have dissipated thy law.

127. Therefore have I loved thy commandments above gold and the topaz.

128. Therefore was I directed to all thy commandments: I have hated all wicked ways.

PHE

129. Thy testimonies are wonderful: therefore my soul hath sought them.

130. The declaration of thy words giveth light: and giveth understanding to little ones.

131. I opened my mouth, and panted: because I longed for thy commandments.

132. Look thou upon me, and have mercy on me, according to the judgment of them that love thy name.

133. Direct my steps according to thy word: and let no iniquity have dominion over me.

134. Redeem me from the calumnies of men: that I may keep thy commandments.

135. Make thy face to shine upon thy servant: and teach me thy justifications.

136. My eyes have sent forth springs of water: because they have not kept thy law.

SADE

137. Thou art just, O Lord: and thy judgment is right.

138. Thou hast commanded justice thy testimonies: and thy truth exceedingly.

139. My zeal hath made me pine away: because my enemies forgot thy words.

140. Thy word is exceedingly refined: and thy servant hath loved it.

141. I am very young and despised: but I forget not thy justifications.

142. Thy justice is justice forever: and thy law is the truth.

143. Trouble and anguish have found me: thy commandments are my meditation.

144. Thy testimonies are justice forever: give me understanding, and I shall live.

COPH

145. I cried with my whole heart, hear me, O Lord: I will seek thy justifications.

146. I cried unto thee, save me: that I may keep thy commandments.

147. I prevented the dawning of the day, and cried: because in thy words I very much hoped.

148. My eyes to thee have prevented the morning: that I might meditate on thy words.

149. Hear thou my voice, O Lord, according to thy mercy: and quicken me according to thy judgment.

150. They that persecute me have drawn nigh to iniquity; but they are gone far off from thy law.

151. Thou art near, O Lord: and all thy ways are truth.

152. I have known from the beginning concerning thy testimonies: that thou hast founded them forever.

Res

153. See my humiliation and deliver me: for I have not forgotten thy law.

154. Judge my judgment and redeem me: quicken thou me for thy word's sake.

155. Salvation is far from sinners; because they have not sought thy justifications.

156. Many, O Lord, are thy mercies: quicken me according to thy judgment.

157. Many are they that persecute me, and afflict me; but I have not declined from thy testimonies.

158. I beheld the transgressors, and I pined away: because they kept not thy word.

159. Behold I have loved thy commandments, O Lord; quicken me thou in thy mercy.

160. The beginning of thy words is truth: all the judgments of thy justice are forever.

Sin

161. Princes have persecuted me without cause: and my heart hath been in awe of thy words.

162. I will rejoice at thy words, as one that hath found great spoil.

163. I have hated and abhorred iniquity; but I have loved thy law.

164. Seven times a day I have given praise to thee, for the judgments of thy justice.

163. Much peace have they that love thy law, and to them there is no stumbling block.

166. I looked for thy salvation, O Lord: and I loved thy commandments.

167. My soul hath kept thy testimonies: and hath loved them exceedingly.

168. I have kept thy commandments and thy testimonies: because all my ways are in thy sight.

TAU

169. Let my supplication, O Lord, come near in thy sight: give me understanding according to thy word.

170. Let my request come in before thee: deliver thou me according to thy word.

171. My lips shall utter a hymn, when thou shalt teach me thy justifications.

172. My tongue shall pronounce thy word: because all thy commandments are justice.

173. Let thy hand be with me to save me; for I have chosen thy precepts.

174. I have longed for thy salvation, O Lord; and thy law is my meditation.

175. My soul shall live and shall praise thee: and thy judgments shall help me.

176. I have gone astray like a sheep that is lost: seek thy servant, because I have not forgotten thy commandments.

JUDAISM has called this psalm the great alphabet. It comprises twenty-two strophes. The strophes are arranged according to the twenty-two letters of the alphabet. Each strophe has eight verses which begin with the letter in the series of the alphabet. Each strophe is a little poem by itself which illustrates the importance of the Law under one common viewpoint. There is, however, no well-ordered sequence of thought. But in the first half of the psalm the value of the Law in general is explained and in the second half the value of the Law in times of persecution is dealt with. The concept *law* with all other expressions of the same meaning used in this psalm; for example, *word, command, instruction, statute, norm, right* cannot be taken here in the narrow sense of a precept or of the Mosaic Law, but must be interpreted in the broader sense in which the Old Testament uses the word *Torah.* It designates every divine communication which was imparted through the prophets or lawgivers of Israel for the instruction and education of men. It also includes all that has been recorded in the sacred books about God's government. It therefore comprises above all else the divine revelations, the sum total of what must be believed, and the Messianic as well as other divine promises. If we accept this meaning of *law*, then the psalm has for the Christian a very deep meaning. It is then, so to speak, a canticle of revelation fulfilled in Jesus Christ. The composer of this psalm is unknown. The psalm belongs to post-exilic times and presupposes a persecution of Jews faithful to the Law by Jews disloyal to their faith.

Aleph Strophe 1–8

When Christ in his Sermon on the Mount unfolded the Law of the New Testament, he began his sermon by giving the eight beatitudes. By these beatitudes he wished to make known to the world that his law was not a heavy yoke with which he wished to burden mankind, but a way pointed out by God to true happiness. With this viewpoint the psalmist also considers the Law of the Old Testament. Therefore at the beginning of the Canticle he also speaks in praise of happiness. For man there is only one purpose in life; namely, the possession of God. But there is also one way to God; namely, faith and obedience. Therefore, only he can be called happy who lives according to the law of the Lord. But to attain to this happiness it is not sufficient to say: "Lord, Lord." We must do the will of God. We must seek him with an undivided love. We must be united with him. We must constantly have in mind the purpose of our life and we must strive to use the God-given means to attain our end. The beatitudes are meant only for him who does not permit himself to be seduced by any enticements to evil or by temptations of disobedience to the law or to leave the way designated by revelation. Every sin takes us away from the right path and places self-will in the place of God's will. Union with God is above all a union of love and on that account a union of wills. Man must conform himself to the infinitely holy will of God. In order to make this possible God has made known his holy will in the law. It is, therefore, self-evident that this revelation had for its purpose true obedience. However, the natural power of man, even of the just, is not sufficient to meet all the demands of the Lord. There dwells in the heart of man a law of sin which wages war with the law of the spirit, the will of God. Only grace can remedy this weakness. Therefore the determination of obeying the law of God must be supported by supernatural help and this we must ask for by humble prayer. Where there is an earnest will to obey and grace is obtained by humble prayer, the just man can do all things thanks to the divine help. Such a man will not come to shame on the day of his accounting. Even today occupation in the study of the divine word gives spiritual satisfaction; for he who delves deeply into the truths of supernatural revelation and he who conscientiously strives to fulfill the instructions finds out that the yoke of the Lord is sweet and light, that his life is indeed spiritually rich and glad. Therefore his soul rejoices and thanks God for his law and his grace. For the just there can be no other program of life than: "I will keep thy commandments." For the just man there can be no greater anxiety than that the Lord because of many acts of disloyalty might withdraw his helping hand. Therefore he may never cease to pray: "Do not abandon me altogether."

Beth Strophe 9–16

The divine command, "Be ye holy; for I, Yahwe, your God, am holy . . . " (Leviticus 19:2) is meant for every period of life, even for youth. Therefore, the Book of Ecclesiastes admonishes: "Remember thy Creator in the days of thy youth, before the time of affliction comes and the years draw nigh of which thou shalt say: They please me not" (12:1). Youth also must accustom itself to walk the path that is clean, the path that keeps from sin, that aids in fulfilling the law. This path keeps the inexperienced from dangerous mistakes. The psalmist who perhaps has not attained old age speaks in the name of God-fearing youth and utters a prayer of dedication to the Lord: "I seek thee with my whole heart; let me not depart from thy admonitions." The will to lead a life of union with God may not be a passing resolution made at a religious hour of devotion, but it must be an effort anchored deeply in the soul. It must be a resolution which has in mind the coming difficulties and humbly accepts the help of God who guides and supports man in his efforts. The word of God is implanted in the heart like a seed of corn which is especially fragile in the days of youth. The spirit of the world from without and the lusts from within can smother its influence. Therefore it is necessary to cultivate it, to busy oneself with it so that at the moment of temptation man's strength is developed and the word will be for man a guide and counselor. He who in hours of decision has experienced God's power, the truth and wisdom of God's teaching and laws, will always praise and thank him for having given him his heavenly gifts. His soul will long for further divine instruction and he will delve more deeply into the riches of divine revelation. This knowledge should not be closed up within the heart. Every divine gift as well as the grace of understanding more deeply divine truths supposes the task of giving testimony to those truths. He who has learned the truth must make it known to others in order that they, too, may see God's works and praise the Father who is in heaven. For the way pointed out in the testimony of law and revelation leads to pure and holy joys. To occupy oneself with them brings more joy than all earthly riches which never satisfy the soul. The revealed word of God gives us a deeper knowledge of his infinite nature and unfathomable beauty than all visible creation. The testimonies of divine providence that are recorded in Sacred Scripture deserve to be reflected and meditated upon. It is impossible for man to stand in correct relation to God if he is in possession of all profane knowledge and yet is ignorant of the divine will and activities. Moreover, one who is called to union with God in the Church of the Old as well as of the New Testament must have joy in the law and in the entire revelation of the Lord and occupy himself with them in order that they may become for him a safe spiritual possession.

Gimel Strophe 17–24

It is the duty of every man to keep God's word. Obedience is an indispensable condition for his supernatural life. But he cannot fulfill this duty by his own strength alone. The Lord must give the power to will and to accomplish. But this grace must be prayed for; and it is given only to him who has the will to work with the talent received and thus to fulfill the law. The just man also needs supernatural enlightenment. This too he must beg from God. The ability of acquiring natural knowledge is not sufficient to search into the mysteries of the divine will and of divine providence. They are works of a higher order which can be seen only by eyes opened by God. Man must pray all the more that the heavenly light of grace may enlighten his path because he is a sojourner upon earth. We have here on earth no lasting dwelling place, but a quest for a future life (Hebrews 13:14). Life is a pilgrimage to the heavenly home, but the way to it is known to God alone. He is blessed who allows himself to be instructed by the Lord and to be led by him. On this account the desire of the just man should be to know more clearly and to comprehend more deeply the way to the eternal home designated in the Book of the Law. Truth and grace are the food which still the longing for union with God. But he who haughtily ignores God's truth and law, he who is too proud to believe and to obey will be struck by the wrath and curse of the Lord; for the most high God cannot permit those to go unpunished who want to go their own way and knowingly avoid the path designated by God. In their malicious arrogance men such as these ridicule the just to whom the observance of the law is an affair of conscience. The just man having confidence in the divine word expects the Lord to be a defender of the persecuted and a punisher of the godless. To suffer persecution for justice's sake should never make one waver in fidelity to God. Even when the princes and the great ones in the land plan and enact unjust laws against God-fearing people the laws of the Lord and a living faith in his truths should be the guiding star of life. The greater the suffering the more must the afflicted seek consolation and counsel in meditating upon eternal truth and receive therein supernatural joy. In the plan of divine Providence the purpose of persecution is that the just man seeks a more intimate union with God.

Daleth Strophe 25–32

It is indeed human when persecutions, derision, and blasphemy oppress the just man because of his virtue that his soul is deeply humbled and he is unable again to take courage by himself. But he should not forget that God has promised to support the bent reed. Trusting in God's promises he must turn to him, the Giver of all grace in prayer, that he may give him new spiritual strength. The psalmist had often been in distress. On such occasions he told the Lord his troubles; he complained about his needs and placed before him all his sufferings and cares. God always heard. If God grants the petition to be free from external adversity, he surely will not let the desire for a deeper knowledge of his teachings unnoticed. God will gladly grant the petition of a just man when he is a docile scholar and listens attentively to the words of the divine Master in order that under his safe guidance he may enrich his knowledge of the revealed truth and search more deeply into the mysteries of the eternal wisdom. In God's word there is a remedy for all of the soul's afflictions, a wonderful consolation and supernatural strength. His promises are a strong support when in suffering, spiritual strength has become exhausted. But this effect is again a gift of the divine mercy for which we must pray with faith and confidence. Another anxiety of the just man is his own weakness, his concupiscence, the law of the flesh which opposes the law of the spirit and which strives to push him from the way of the divine precepts and put him on the way of sin. Only the grace of God can keep him from going wrong; for this grace lets the soul know clearly the right way and gives it strength to follow the way of righteousness. This way the psalmist has chosen and it is his will to walk upon this way. Hence it is also his determination not to forget the norms of divine sanctity, may the enticements and temptations of the world and the concupiscences thereof be ever so great. The law shall be to him an indicator, a guide which he will follow. For him who permits himself to be guided by this spirit the petition: "Let me not be put to shame . . ." is not timid anxiety, as if God could ever deceive his children, but ardent longing for salvation which welcomes him at the end of the way. As true love takes away fear, so a strong faith removes anxiety about the dangers threatening a man on the way. He who trusts in God will courageously walk on the path of virtue. His soul is not narrow-minded; God has broadened his mental vision; he has given him determination, a magnanimous spirit willing to make sacrifices.

He Strophe 33–40

Even though the just man walks courageously on the path of virtue and perfection, he should never forget that he daily depends on the grace of God, that perseverance in good is a pure supernatural gift which he does not deserve gratuitously. Even the saint must always pray for divine instruction, enlightenment, and guidance; for only then can he with grace continue on the path of virtue to the end. If the will wishes to persevere, the saint may not be influenced by sentiment or feeling. He must be guided by a clear knowledge of the divine will. Such knowledge which, as it were, captures the will is not obtained by human studies, but is given to us by God's grace. But God gives this grace only to such who seek to obtain it. God gives it to everyone whose greatest desire is to walk the path of the divine commandments without faltering; whose greatest joy is to follow obediently the divine guidance on his way to the perfection which God in his wisdom has appointed for him. Men of the world strive for material gain; their pleasure is money and possessions. The just man has other aims than to acquire such perishable things as cannot satisfy the heart. His search is for spiritual gain, for that which is above, for the eternal and imperishable. Therefore his desire is that God may place his entire plans within the sphere of his law. This unreserved surrender to the word and will of the Lord is opposed to the lust of the eyes. Through the lust of the eyes the enticements to worldly things penetrate the inner soul. Lest the soul be enamoured by it, God must take possession of it in order that it will be turned away from the world's deceptive sham and be drawn to the glory of heavenly things. Grace must work against sensual lust in order that the just man may not succumb to it. The Lord will not deny him this assistance. He fulfills his word which the psalmist has mentioned in the Thirty-second Psalm: "Behold, the eyes of the Lord are on them that fear him: and on them that hope in his mercy, to deliver their souls from death" (32:18). For man there is no greater shame than unfaithfulness toward God, than breaking the covenant with him. The just man fears such shame, but only the grace of perseverance to the end will keep him from such degradation insofar as this grace will make him realize the beneficence of the law and the blessing that comes to him for obeying the law. He who incessantly desires to conform his will to the divine will and to be one with God in love, who desires to be strengthened and progress in his supernatural life with God's grace of redemption may confidently expect this grace.

Vau Strophe 41–48

The psalm has again and again emphasized that divine grace is the indispensable requisite for the preservation of supernatural life. But it has not exhausted the topic of the relation of grace to the law. According to the statutes of the Lord, grace cannot be dispensed without a courageous and glad confession of faith and of life. How could a man without grace refute and answer questions to those who ridicule him because of his faith and religious life? Heavenly enlightenment along with personal knowledge can put the right word on his lips after the fashion Christ promised to his disciples: "When they shall bring you before the courts be not anxious about how and what you shall speak; in that hour it will be given to you what you shall say" (Matthew 10:19). Therefore in times of persecution it is especially important that the just man by a life pleasing to God and by special fidelity to the law makes himself worthy of giving testimony to his faith. He who in such times does not strive to obtain a profound religious knowledge will be deprived altogether of the word of truth by the Lord himself. When the life of faith is subjected to grave dangers, the will must resist all influences that may weaken it; it must daily renew the pledge of making strong resistance: "I will observe the law at all times, forever and ever. I will always observe thy law. I will never be led astray by external attacks and by spiritual difficulties." The firmer a man obligates himself to do the will of God, the freer he feels himself, and the less will opposition hinder his progress and the less will it turn him from his determination. When the just man investigates the deep meaning of the divine instructions, it becomes clearer to him that they lead him along the way to true liberty. The understanding of the truth in the light of grace also gives greater courage to confess. He who has never understood the depth and sublimity of divine revelation does not know how to appreciate it; he will be ashamed of the truth when he must confess it before worldly men. But true union with God knows no fear. He who has once tasted the word of God and has found how sweet it is will love it more and more. The more he will try to draw from it its inner wealth, the more his occupation will be a source of holy and pure joy. If this was true of the imperfect Old Testament revelation, then it is much truer of the contents of the good message of Jesus Christ. The composer of this psalm is filled with such sentiments. With a yearning desire he stretches out his hand for the law of the Lord in order to receive it as a gift from God. He considers it his obligation to observe it and in his quiet hours of meditation he gains from it nourishment for his soul and receives a new urge to love God.

Zain Strophe 49–56

God by his word has promised protection and help to the just man; he has promised him to be a strong tower and a firm citadel. The God-fearing man relies on these promises when dire visitations come upon him. That the Lord has promised his strength and reward is for him a consolation when he is inclined to despondency. The Lord has promised a reward to those who suffer persecution for justice's sake. This thought enlivens his courage and gives him strength and patience to wait until God appears with his help. Proud men who in their sophisticated arrogance disobey the divine law mock at him who believes and accepts the divine revealed word and feels himself bound to obey the law. But the really just man knows no fear. Such mockery will not take him away from the right path. The Lord will not let himself be mocked. He punishes the pride of the sinner. The pages of history have recorded many punishments that were warnings for all persecutors and a consolation for the persecuted. The arm of the Lord is not shortened even now; he will punish when the time of his equanimity will come to an end. This confidence must console the afflicted and urge them on to perseverance. The just man however will not be indifferent about the activities of the godless. A just anger must lay hold of him when he sees the wicked boldly ignore the clearly revealed will of the most high God who proffers his revelations and his law. Only malice and ignorance can lead to such blindness. He who on his earthly pilgrimage has once learned the statutes of the Lord remembers them like a melodious song or psalm, like a hymn about God's wisdom, justice, and love. They are a refreshment; they quicken his steps on the path of virtue so that he advances vigorously and forgets all obstacles placed in his way. Even at night when everyone sleeps, the just man meditates upon the name of the Lord, upon the sublimity and glory of God which has revealed itself in his word. With such thoughts he goes to rest and the same thoughts occupy his mind when he awakens. The psalmist considers it a precious possession, a great gift received from God to have learned the law and to have been permitted to observe it. This grace was given him because he was a member of the chosen race.

Heth Strophe 57–64

"The Lord is my inheritance and my portion of the chalice." These words were spoken by the composer of the Fifteenth Psalm and every just man must speak in like manner. God has made himself known through revelation and through the law, and the just man must now accept God. He must accept his word and cherish it in his heart. Since the Lord has become his portion and the soul has tasted the sweetness of his word, it can have no other desire than to seek God's love and mercy in order to be able to walk perseveringly and faithfully in the way of the commandments. But in order that the divine promises might be fulfilled in him, man must daily and carefully examine his conduct, his activities, and omissions; he must conscientiously examine himself in order that he may discover his misdeeds and by the renewal of his resolutions return to the right path, to the faithful observance of the divine commandments. But he must not walk upon the way of the commandments hesitatingly; he must

471

make every effort; he must walk in rapid strides; he must have a desire to attain the end for which God has created him. Trivial considerations should not hinder him in the observance of God's holy commandments, but rather a courageous determination is demanded. The laying of snares by evil men should not deter the just man from walking along the righteous path. Many enticements and temptations lay like snares and traps obstructing the way, but he who strives for perfection is not frightened by dangers; for he who has given his word to be a light also gives strength to follow that light. The consciousness of this fills the soul with everlasting gratitude. How pitiful are men upon whom the light of truth does not shine, who lack supernatural strength, who err, stagger, and fall on the way. He whom the Lord has called to his light has every reason to thank him day and night for his love. All whom he has called, all who believe in his word are in union with God and through him in union with one another; they form a community of saints who love one another, give good example to one another, and support one another by their prayers and their fidelity to the Lord. God's infinite goodness reveals itself everywhere. God has manifested to his creatures, especially to his faithful ones, an immeasurable plenitude of love and mercy. From this plenitude the psalmist asks for himself the grace to study more earnestly and understand more fully the word of God and to acquire the science of the saints.

Teth Strophe 65–72

When the just man looks back to his former life he recalls how richly the Lord showered upon him his love. His call to the people of God, his being guided on the way of salvation are wonderful testimonies of God's goodness. The Lord has been true to his word at all times and has fulfilled his promises. In the future he will also guide him and teach him wholesome discipline because the fulfillment of the divine will demands self-conquest and mortification which combined with moderate wisdom should bring about discipline. He who believes in the disciplinary wisdom of the law and in the truth of its purpose, namely self-discipline, will come to a deeper understanding of this wisdom. The vulgar man indeed resists divine discipline because he does not appreciate its value. Therefore God humbles the proud insofar as he lets him stumble and fall. By this he should learn by himself how wholesome the discipline of the law is and surrender himself unconditionally to it. God is always good even when he punishes and humbles; for his law and his guidance have their source in his infinite love. They are intended only for what is best for his creatures. Man cannot find a better guide and teacher. Therefore he should not refuse to obey God's commandments and should always pray to God that he may not withdraw his love, grace, and instruction. He who lets himself be instructed and led by God's goodness cannot be led into error about the law by lies and calumnies which others spread about him; he cherishes in his soul the word of the Lord as a precious possession. Godless liars and detractors have a lax conscience. They have become unreceptive to the threats of God. Therefore they persecute the just with a complete lack of consideration. Yet this also does not hinder the just man from having joy in the service of God. He does not become disgusted when once he has found pleasure in it. It is even wholesome for the just man when God permits him to go through the school of suffering, when he permits him to blunder. Such experiences lead to humility, keep man from vain self-confidence, teach him that consolation and courage are to be found only with God and with his word, and impel him with God's help to study profoundly God's commandments. The more man recognizes the necessity of divine revelation and of education through the divine law, the more will he appreciate both. They surpass all the riches of the earth and cannot be outweighed or replaced. They alone show the way to God and to one's own eternal happiness which is the purpose of man's life.

Jod Strophe 73–80

Man is God's creature; his body was formed by the power of the Creator. God's love has breathed into him the breath of life; namely, the immortal soul and by doing so has made him God's image. Whatever God has called into existence should glorify him. Man should glorify God by his knowledge of what is divine and by subjecting himself to his holy will. Since God has given man this purpose, he may hope that God will give him an understanding of his word. The confidence of just men will not be disappointed. When they see in others, for example in the psalmist, how God rewards confidence in his grace and enlightenment, how he blesses those who believe in his word and trust in his promises, then they will be strengthened in faith and will persevere in their faith and confidence. They too will rejoice in the divine word. God does not humble the just arbitrarily; he does not send them visitations because he loves to trouble them. All trials that man experiences have their foundation in God's absolute justice. They are also based on God's sanctity and have for their purpose man's sanctification. Also there is God's fidelity which humbles and eradicates all pride in order that he can fulfill his divine promises of blessing. It is true that humiliation is not entirely without some bitterness even for him who has recognized God's plan of salvation. Therefore the psalmist also prays that the mercy of God may give him consolation; for he has said that every disciplinary action has for its purpose the attainment of the fruit of peace and of justice. He prays that under discipline the grace of the Lord may guide him and encourage him to lead a new life and to advance to greater progress in perfection. God grants this petition when the law has become a joy to his soul. It is from this source that new strength and energy flows. Shame befalls the haughty man who perverts justice and oppresses the just man because of this justice; for he attacks a man whose only endeavor is to obey the will of God in all things and above all else. If God would permit the godless to triumph over the just man and would let the latter succumb, then even the good would fall into error about him and have doubts about his perfections. But if God saves the persecuted, they will know that the Lord will not permit those who persecute the just to go unpunished. An irreproachable life according to the divine commandments is a condition for divine help. Therefore the psalmist again begs at the end of this strophe for the grace of fidelity and perseverance.

Caph Strophe 81–88

Surrounded by hostilities and dangers the soul of the just man longs for the salvation, for the imperishable peace with God, for the indissoluble union with him which the prophet saw as a requisite for Messianic times and which Christian revelation foretells for eternity. The just man believes firmly in the word that assures salvation to those who love God. Full of longing the just man understands that God's word and promise will be fulfilled in the time of oppression for the faith's sake. The just man sees God appearing to console and encourage. The psalmist compares his spiritual condition to a large goatskin filled with new wine. It was the custom in the ancient Orient to hang the container in the smoke of a low fire in order that the wine might more quickly mature and become mild. In the smoke the skins would become black and wrinkled. So likewise the suffering of the persecuted has taken away the external freshness. But like the wine which keeps and heightens its goodness in the smoke, so also in the just man tribulation has kept the word of God which has become more precious in value. Though suffering is of great value in the spiritual life, yet the just man longs for external peace because the life of man is so short. Therefore he begs the Lord that he will no longer delay with the punishment of his oppressors. He wishes this so much the more because the danger grows as long as the godless remain unpunished and in their arrogance lay snares for those who fear God. In their treachery they strive to bring about the downfall of the just by lies and calumny. Their conduct is in direct contrast to the laws of the Lord. This cannot please God; it must challenge the punitive justice of God. God is truth; truthful are his words and morally true are his statutes. They stand in direct contrast to the deceitful conduct of the haughty opponents of the just. The just man may rely on the help of God who will not let deceit triumph. The danger that deceitfulness might conquer was near at the time of the psalmist; he himself thought that he might be banished or killed. But in the extreme danger of his life he remained faithful to the law of his God. He felt that for a long time he would not steadfastly resist the constant attacks of his enemies if God did not give him grace and renewed strength to enliven his spirit. Only if God gave him help could he continually keep his law.

Lamed Strophe 89–96

Man can absolutely rely on the word of God; for his word is not subject to change. The word of Christ is meant for all men: "Heaven and earth shall pass away but my words shall not pass away" (Matthew 24:35). Unchangeable are the laws of the heavenly constellations. So unchangeable are the laws of God for man. His fidelity remains immutable. He says through the Prophet Isaias: "From my mouth issues only truth that is never taken back" (45:24). As the laws of the universe stand unshakable through thousands of years, so the word of the Lord remains until it has been fulfilled. All laws of nature stand firm; they can never be revoked because heaven and earth serve their almighty Creator. They have served their purpose through immeasurable periods of time until the present day. As rarely as the Lord does change the laws that have been made for the preservation of his creatures, so rarely does he change his word which he has given to man. What would creation be without the laws of nature? What would man be without the divine word and his law? In the face of the many attacks, temptations, and persecutions man would have become despondent without the supernatural source of strength and consolation; in his spiritual misery he would have perished. Because of this man should know and appreciate even more the value of God's gifts; he should at all times hold fast to the divine statutes in order to draw from them courage and consolation in all difficulties and draw new life for his wearied soul. By making himself subservient to the law, man in a sense higher than creation becomes the possession of God. Through creation man passively becomes the possession of God, but through the offering of his will in obedience he has given himself actively to the Lord. Thus being united to God in a twofold manner he has no other desire than to know God more and more, to know his holy word and will. He who is thus united with the Lord cannot waver in his fidelity to him. May evil men lie in wait for him to destroy him, he remains faithful to the law. As long as he does this with the help of divine grace, as long as God is his protector, so long the enemy cannot harm him.

475

Occupation with the divine word can never fully disclose its riches. All human work, may it be ever so perfect, is limited. Unlimited in its being and activities is God's word alone; it is unlimited in time and space. It is respected in the whole world throughout the centuries.

Mem Strophe 97–104

The divine law contains profound wisdom, that wisdom which God alone possesses and which he gave to Israel because he loved much. He who loves God must also love his word; he must respect it and meditate upon it at all times. God's word is the most excellent and sure way of coming to a clear knowledge of God. Above all, the study of the law makes us superior to the enemies in wisdom. Their wisdom is the wisdom of this world about which Jesus Sirach says: "But the learning of wickedness is not wisdom: and the device of sinners is not prudence. There is a subtle wickedness, and the same is detestable: and there is a man that is foolish, wanting in wisdom" (Ecclesiasticus 19:19–20).

God's wisdom leads to a higher knowledge than the teachers of worldly wisdom can give us. It gives us a more decisive answer to all questions of life which remain an eternal riddle to all mere human investigations. On this account Jesus Sirach remarks correctly (37:18) that the conscience of a holy man gives us better information of what is right than seven watchmen who sit on high towers to spy. May aged men have at their disposal a rich knowledge of life's experiences, this knowledge is everyday wisdom which they themselves had to acquire. Therefore it is mentioned in the Book of Job: "They that are aged are not wise men, neither do the aged understand judgment; it is the spirit in man, the breath of the Almighty that gives wisdom" (32:8). Genuine wisdom guards us against the folly of sin; for it teaches us to distinguish between good and evil; it shows us the path of righteousness and the path of evil; it promises; it threatens. Guided by divine wisdom the just man avoids the evil path so as not to transgress the law of the Lord. The way of the law gives perfect security; for God himself, the eternal Truth and Wisdom, has taught it; and he himself who can never err, nor lead men on the path of error, guides us on this way. He who is determined to be led by God experiences what the poet of the Eighteenth Psalm has said: "God's utterances are more desirable than silver and gold, sweeter than honey or the honeycomb." As precious food delights the taste, so the word of the Lord refreshes and gives pleasure to the soul of man. Man's love may not be divided between God and the world, between obedience to the law and sin. God asks for the service of the whole mind and of the entire will. He who wishes to remain united with God must hate and avoid every evil. He cannot serve God and pay heed to the spirit of the world at the same time. The study of the divine law, of God's revealed word is a necessary condition for distinguishing between truth and falsehood and for testing the tendencies of the spirit of the age.

Nun Strophe 105–112

In the chaos of men's opinions God's word is a proved guide to which man on his way through life may entrust himself. He is the light which shines into every darkness, which shows all the pitfalls and dangers, which leads the way like the pillar of fire in the desert and points out the way to the eternal land of promise. He who does not wish to be lost must allow himself to be guided by this light. He who does not wish to obey and believe has already passed judgment upon himself. Therefore the psalmist has uttered an oath that he will hold God's law sacred and will fulfill it faithfully. What he has vowed he has kept, but he also had to experience that all who wish to live piously must suffer persecution (2 Timothy 3:12); for it irks the godless when the just man will not participate in their unrestrained and licentious activities. On this account they deride him (1 Peter 4:10). Hence the psalmist beseeches God to give him grace as he has promised. For this vivifying grace he will at all times thank and praise God. He prays that the Lord may graciously accept the gifts of his mouth and that he may always permit him to know more clearly his holy will in order that he may more faithfully fulfill his holy law and even more sincerely thank him for his graces and praise him more loudly. In times of persecution and oppression God's enlightening and strengthening grace is especially necessary because man's fidelity to the law is constantly endangered. Daily his life is exposed to the danger of being lost. He needs help because even in extreme need he wishes to remain faithful to the divine will. May the godless lay snares for his soul and try to bring about his fall, he will not depart from the path of God. In the light of heavenly grace he sees the snares on the way and knows how to avoid them; for God himself keeps him from falling into them. Therefore the law is the most precious possession that the Lord can give to man. The just man may say in the words of Psalm 15: "My lot is to me a precious possession, indeed, glorious is my inheritance." The law is a possession for all times insofar as man does not lose it through his own fault. With the law the just man attains his eternal reward; for he who surrenders himself to the law with his whole heart will be blessed by God eternally for his love. The world passes away with all its pleasures, but he who does the will of God abides with him eternally (1 John 2:17).

Samech Strophe 113–120

The just man loves God with his whole heart and hates all lukewarmness and indecision in the service of God. The word of the Lord is so true and so sublime and his commandments are so decisive and binding that

477

there can be no room for indecision whether one may believe or not believe, or whether one may obey or follow his own way. Only untiring obedience to the law does justice to God's authority. A decisive "yes" to all the demands of the Lord is possible despite all external attacks and internal difficulties because the Lord not only commands, but also protects man against temptations and assists him by his grace. Therefore the God-fearing man, full of confidence, will always rely on the protection of God and on the help of his grace. With this confidence the just man should call out to those who would alienate him from fidelity to God: "Depart from me. Depart all ye tempters and seducers: I will serve God alone, and him alone will I adore." But by all determination of the will to be faithful, even a saint must say that he can do little without the grace which is absolutely necessary to lead a supernatural life. He too must pray for divine support; but he can pray with full confidence because the Lord never retracts his word; and he has said that he would hear the prayer offered with confidence. God must assist the saints in order that they overcome their common human weaknesses; he protects the saints against dangers lest they may be overwhelmed by them. When the power of the divine word proves itself to be a strong protection there arises a new impulse to search more deeply into the meaning of his promises. Those who do not believe the word of God are already judged; those who knowingly and maliciously depart from the way of the law have themselves spoken the words of their rejection; for he who judges them is the infinitely holy and true God who hates all falsehood. The way of the godless is folly; for they deceive themselves and others when they believe that on this way they can find happiness. When God's judgment which cleanses and separates comes upon them, the deception will come to light; then it will be shown that they are not pure silver, but worthless dross which is separated and thrown away. The fate of the disobedient should be an incentive for the just to a greater love of the law; for it is terrible to fall into the hands of the living God (Hebrews 10:31). When he sees so many punishments fall upon evil men or when he thinks of the eternal punishment of the godless, the just man himself shudders at the wrath of the almighty and just God. But this fear of God's judgment must confirm the just man in his fidelity to God.

Ain Strophe 121-128

In times when many fall away from their faith and those who remain faithful are subjected to persecution, the conscientious observance of the word and of the law of the Lord is especially necessary lest through carelessness the flow of divine grace may be impeded. Only he who constantly strives can rely on God's help. God himself defends the faithful servant;

he protects him to save him from the malicious acts of the oppressors. The Lord is the defender of the oppressed. Being disposed to remain faithful to the Lord, the psalmist seeks for deliverance; he begs that the Lord may free him from his distress and reveal his justice to his enemies. Since God has promised his help, may he soon fulfill his promise. The just man may not decide the time of God's fulfillment of his word. But it is a sign of God's mercy when he in a time of oppression gives a wholesome and more profound knowledge of his statutes; for the keeping of these is in itself an omen of peace with God and of eternal salvation. He whom the Lord has called to his service may hope for the grace of knowledge; for God does not do his work incompletely. To the grace of a vocation he also gives the necessary enlightenment, the insight into the law without which one cannot be a true servant of the law. At the time of the psalmist godlessness among the Jews must have become a danger for the entire people; for he considers an intervention of God absolutely necessary in order that the renegades may not corrupt the well-disposed. In order that he himself may not become a victim of the evil spirit of the time, the poet has aligned himself more firmly to the law and has learned to value and appreciate it. To him it is worth more than the best gold. Therefore he is exact in the fulfillment of all laws. Every untruthfulness and faithlessness is hateful to him.

Phe Strophe 129–136

The more men forget God and ignore his word, the more must the true servant of God desire it and be occupied with it. The divine truth and the revelations of divine Providence and of his will are wonderful testimonies of the wisdom, faithfulness, justice, and love of the Lord which captivate the human mind as much as the revelations in nature. The word of God illumines; it makes even simple men wise and intelligent; it gives them an understanding of the meaning of life, of the purpose of suffering; it makes of darkness a light which natural knowledge could not produce. He who meditates upon the glories of God strives to learn them more and more. His heart desires the law of the Lord as an open mouth longs for a refreshing drink. Such a longing for the knowledge of God and of his holy will is the result of love and the Lord cannot permit it to remain unrewarded. God cannot deny his love and grace to him who loves him and seeks salvation unless he would wish to be unjust and deny himself. One of the effects of divine love is the strengthening of faith and fidelity. In times of religious indifference and apostasy even the life of faith of a pious man can be influenced by the spirit of the world that surrounds him. Therefore he must pray for supernatural strength that he may not commit injustices. This is the more necessary when the godless put pres-

479

sure upon those who are loyal to the faith, indeed, when they are not afraid of using forceful means in order to make them waver in their fidelity. To face such storms the soul must anchor itself more firmly in truth and in the law lest it abandon the right path. But only God's mercy and grace can bring this about. God's countenance must shine upon his servant; his grace must enlighten the true path more clearly than before. He who by this supernatural light experiences the value of true faith and has been guided by the law and grace cannot remain indifferent to the godless and cannot feel secure in self-righteousness. He will rather lament with deep sorrow the disregard of truth and of the law, and the fate of the deluded.

Sade Strophe 137–144

God is just. The Book of Daniel says of him: "Thou art just in all that thou hast done to us, and all thy works are true, and thy ways right, and all thy judgments true" (3:27). All commandments of the Lord, all the decisions of his judgments, and all visitations are an expression of his unchangeable justice. Whatever he commands men to do is based upon his infinite sanctity which excludes every injustice, and upon his truthfulness which excludes every obscurity and ambiguity. All divine works have their purpose in the salvation of man; for they are done out of pure love.

On this account the God-loving soul feels the prevailing godlessness the more and is saddened at the disregard of God's word. The just man is zealous to work for God's honor even when his zeal is the cause of ridicule and persecution. God's word is above all criticism; it is pure truth and moral law; it is clean and drossless gold which resists the fire of the greatest trials. Because of this incomparable beauty everyone who strives for purity is impelled to meditate upon the law. In this pure atmosphere of truth he feels himself at home. The psalmist is still young; he cannot as yet speak of a rich experience while his opponents can appeal to their age, knowledge, and experience in order to seduce him to infidelity. But the knowledge of the law obtained through heavenly enlightenment outweighs the knowledge obtained by experience. He who acknowledges the profound wisdom which is found in the word of God will not let himself be led from the right path. He will not permit himself to be led away from the right path because justice is eternally justice and can never swerve from its course; its statutes obligate at all times. God's teaching is absolute truth which does not change as do times and men. Man must believe in the laws of God at all times; what contradicts these laws is injustice and deceit. God's truth and justice are the indestructible pillars upon which the law and revelation rest. They are firm supports in need and affliction because they never change. Especially in times of spiritual need such foundations are beneficent. One learns to appreciate them and to find joy in them. The testimonies of the Lord are eternally just; they are in full accord with the absolute divine right. They bring true life to the soul when they are appreciated. The prayer for insight with which this strophe closes is occupied with the disclosure of an inexhaustible source of life and spiritual strength.

Coph Strophe 145–152

Times of lack of faith demand a strong attachment to revealed truth and to the law; they also demand a special measure of grace. Therefore the psalmist begins this strophe with the petition for willingness and strength to remain faithful. Without the help of grace even the just man will fall and finally be lost; for perseverance cannot be acquired by man's natural power alone. Because of this fact the psalmist repeats his petition. Indeed, at his awakening in the morning he turns to God and begs for perseverance in fidelity to the law. He begs for confidence in the divine promises and for hope in God's mercy. Even during the night, from one night watch to the other, his mind occupies itself with the word of God so strong is his longing for salvation, for a new life according to the promise of the Lord. God cannot refuse to listen to the loud cries of his servant; his love and mercy will help and his justice cannot refuse the promised help. The godless oppressors seem to think that they have obtained what they sought for and pursued. But the greater their malice is, the more they depart from the law of God; and the more they challenge God's wrath and his judgment, the more they lose their chance of salvation. God is near. Therefore the wicked will not succeed in ever annulling the eternal law and his promises. The persecuted can always rely on the word of the Lord; for the Lord is near to all who invoke him. "He is near to all who honor him in truth" (Psalm 144:18). He who believes in God's word knows that time is given for all and that he does not change as do men's opinions and laws.

Res Strophe 153–160

God cannot permit his faithful who have been strong in their allegiance to his word in difficult times to be defeated. Therefore full of confidence the psalmist again prays that the Lord may look upon his misery and show mercy. God takes the affairs of his servants in hand; he delivers them from the power of the enemy and fortifies them because this he has promised to do for the just. The Lord cannot give his assistance to sinners who despise his laws. God's help cannot be expected for self-planned ways, but only through the way of faith and obedience. He who departs from this way loses God's mercy and love. But the Lord is magnanimous to all who fear him. These experience the strength of his vivifying grace. The blessings of the Lord will be bestowed upon them. Therefore they need not fear when many persecute and oppress them. The grace of the Lord is always with them that they may not depart from the law of the Lord. The activities of the godless cannot change their attitude and make them waver in their faithfulness. They will rather lament with great sorrow the faithlessness of the godless and will turn away from their conduct in disgust. Men who have no love for God's word and his law must stay away from the just. The more the godless offend the Lord, the more the love of the just grows for his statutes. The more the just see around them the terrible consequences of spiritual ruin, the more they appreciate the life that has its source in faith and in the law. The word of the Lord is a source of life that never languishes and is never exhausted. It never languishes because it is fed by infinite truth which continues forever; therefore it can never be exhausted no matter how many drink from this life-giving fountain.

Sin Strophe 161–168

Relying upon God's word and promise the just man fears no one, not even the great and mighty of the world. He fears God alone. He is mindful of the prophet's word: "Respect the Lord of hosts as holy, fear him and be terrified by him" (Isaias 8:13). He is also mindful to the Lord's word: "Do not fear those who can destroy the body but not the soul: rather fear him who can destroy both soul and body and can cast into hell" (Matthew 10:28). The fear of the Lord is conducive to joy in God's revelations. They contain glorious promises for those who suffer persecutions and persevere in them. This is the reason why the possession of truth and of the law is so conducive to happiness, as if it were rich booty taken in battle. To him who hates sin and loves the law is opened a fountain of pure joy. Again and again he will praise God and thank him for his love who has given him the great gifts of law and grace. Seven times in the day he praises the Lord because of his just judgments; his daily life is occupied with the joys of the law. The more he occupies himself with the study of the law, the more gloriously it reveals to him the greatness of this gift. This sentiment of joy is the natural expression of a rich inner peace. The Lord lets streams of peace flow to him who has regard for the law. "He who walks along the paths of God lives everlastingly in peace" (Baruch 3:13). Peace is based on the tranquil consciousness of being protected by the hand of God and of being led securely by him away from the dangerous pitfalls. And thus the psalmist longs with a lively faith and confidence and with a glad hope of salvation for deliverance from present affliction and for the promised fulfillment and transfiguration; for to him who fulfills the law is given the promise of life. As faith in God's word enlivens the hope of salvation, so hope also impels man to a greater and more faithful fulfillment of the law. And this increases love for the statutes of the Lord and for all the testimonies of divine power, love, and justice. With such sentiment the psalmist is animated. God's wisdom is his witness.

Tau Strophe 169–176

The last strophe summarizes all petitions, all utterances, and all promises. Throughout the strophes one great thought pervaded them; namely, that God's mercy and grace will grant to the petitioner the richness of the revealed word and appreciation for his law. Correct knowledge is the requisite for faith, hope, and charity. May the all-good God fulfill this wish and grant salvation and deliverance because of the promises upon which the petitioner relies. The enemies round about, the godless mockers with their derision and oppression are a great danger for the just if the Lord does not intervene. After the Lord has liberated, the psalmist shall praise him in hymns of thanksgiving. His lips shall praise God. He shall thank the Lord and praise him for the great grace of having learned his law. The tongue shall proclaim the Lord's praise for all his instructions are an outflowing of his justice, which full of wisdom meet the powers of man and which reward and punish according to man's merits. When the Lord redeems and saves, it is a work of condescension and merciful love. Man can prepare himself for the manifestations of divine love by the faithful observance of the law insofar as he fulfills the conditions upon which God has made his promise depend. He can make himself worthy by an ardent desire for salvation and by a true joy in the law of the Lord. For from him who knows how to value the gifts of the Lord, he will not withhold them. Therefore by belief in God's word the psalmist expects that his soul will acquire a renewal of life and strength and that in him supernatural life will grow and progress, that he will obtain eternal life, and that he then can praise the Lord and his judgments eternally. Relying upon himself, man is helpless and is like a sheep which is separated from the flock and is lost in the desert. By his word and grace the Good Shepherd goes after his sheep which without him go astray; he carries them by his law upon his shoulders; he rescues them from all distress and danger. God rescues his servants insofar as they in their abandonment do not forget and despise his revealed word.

psalm 119

Ad Dominum

A prayer in tribulation

A GRADUAL CANTICLE

1. In my trouble I cried to the Lord: and he heard me.

2. O Lord, deliver my soul from wicked lips, and a deceitful tongue.

3. What shall be given to thee, or what shall be added to thee, to a deceitful tongue?

4. The sharp arrows of the mighty, with coals that lay waste.

5. Woe is me, that my sojourning is prolonged! I have dwelt with the inhabitants of Cedar:

6. My soul hath been long a sojourner.

7. With them that hated peace I was peaceable: when I spoke to them they fought against me without cause.

WITH this psalm begins a series of pilgrimage songs (Psalms 119–133). They were sung on the occasions of pilgrimages to Jerusalem for the solemn feasts. The Mishna calls them the "Tractat Middot," step psalms or gradual psalms, because they are said to have been sung in late Judean worship by the Levites on fifteen steps at the place of the Nicanor gate between the women's court and the inner court. But the reliability of this assertion is questioned.

The singer of the first pilgrimage song lives in banishment far from the sanctuary. The banishment is doubly hard for him because men in his surroundings hate and calumniate him. They misinterpret first all his intentions for peace. He sees no hope for deliverance. Full of longing he turns his view to Mount Sion at Jerusalem where the Lord dwells in the temple. How often he had made pilgrimages to that place! How often he had prayed there and had found a hearing in his difficulties and help in his needs! But never had he appreciated the value of the house of God as now. The more troublesome the world around him was and the more unfeeling and inconsiderate men conducted themselves towards him, the stronger his pious heart longed for peace with God, for the peace of the sanctuary which gave him a foretaste of heavenly peace.

Toward the sanctuary the psalmist directs his petition for deliverance from his persecutors who endanger his life by their calumnies, false accusations, and slander. Against such treacherous men, especially in a strange country, a man is helpless; in such a case only God can be the defender of the persecuted. Therefore the petitioner in all confidence places his affair in the hands of the Lord. The psalmist now addresses the calumniator: "Think of it! What have you to expect from the justice of the Lord, from him who detests lies? The greatness of your punishment will correspond to the gravity of your guilt, according to the principle: Wherewith you have sinned you shall be punished." Calumnies are like sharp, poisoned arrows that are shot upon an innocent, unsuspecting victim from the rear. God's arrows will strike him as a punishment. They are sharp arrows that inflict deep and severe wounds; they are like the arrows of a hero which never miss the mark and pierce the wicked man in the center of the heart; they are burning arrows of the divine wrath. As the coal of the broomplant gives the best and constant glow, so also the judgment of God's wrath will burn.

The reason for the psalmist's petition for retaliation is his desire for peace (verses 5–7). He has no peace; he is a stranger in a pagan country, without home and without protection. There he feels himself abandoned and as helpless as if fate had banished him to the ends of the earth, to Mesech, to the wild Moschians near the Black Sea, or as if he were banished to Arabia to the enemy territory of the Kedarenes who persecuted Israel with an unquenchable hatred. Men who themselves have no peace, who are driven by the restlessness of their passions, and whose heart is like the restless sea, hate peace wherever they find it and seek to destroy it. They find satisfaction in war only, in everlasting war upon others. For anyone who loves peace and longs for it, it is difficult to live for any length of time among those who hate peace. But it is more difficult when all plans for peace are misinterpreted and ridiculed, when every attempt to keep peace is frustrated, when these attempts inspire the enemy with greater hatred and acts of persecution. Then all hope and ardent desire for peace ceases and God alone remains as the only consolation and his sanctuary as the only place of peace.

psalm 120

Levavi oculos

God is the keeper of his servants

A GRADUAL CANTICLE

1. I have lifted up my eyes to the mountains, from whence help shall come to me.

2. My help is from the Lord, who made heaven and earth.

3. May he not suffer thy foot to be moved: neither let him slumber that keepeth thee.

4. Behold he shall neither slumber nor sleep, that keepeth Israel.

5. The Lord is thy keeper, the Lord is thy protection upon thy right hand.

6. The sun shall not burn thee by day, nor the moon by night.

7. The Lord keepeth thee from all evil: may the Lord keep thy soul.

8. May the Lord keep thy coming in and thy going out; from henceforth now and forever.

P EACE and unwavering trust in God pervades this psalm. It puts to rest all disquietude in the soul and even in our days inspires us to peacefulness; for what the psalmist says of his sanctuary on Sion and of the throne of God in the Holy of Holies may be said in a greater measure about the tabernacle of the Catholic house of God. The psalm begins with a confession of confidence (verses 1–2). The Israelites when far away from the sanctuary were accustomed to pray facing Jerusalem on the Judean mountains, the Mount Sion on which the temple was built. So also the psalmist directs his view to the holy heights that greet him from the distance. There the Lord lives among his people; there his eyes are always watching the affairs and needs of those who pray to him; there his ears pay heed to their petitions. There the God-fearing man in faith and confidence may expect help in every visitation; for the God who broods there over the Ark of the Covenant is Yahwe, the invisible King and Father of Israel who has obligated himself to his people by a solemn covenant; it is the kind and eternal God, the almighty Creator of heaven and earth, for whom there are no impossibilities. If he has created the universe with one word, then he knows also how to banish the needs of men with one word.

From the house of God or from his own deeply pious soul the psalmist hears the divine *Amen* to his confession of confidence (verses 3–7). The Lord will not let him stagger and fall who in the confidence of his love takes hold of his hand. God supports everyone who in humility does not rely on his own strength alone, but in the consciousness of his weakness seeks support from God. The good Lord continually watches over such a one. God's eyes do not tire; he does not fall asleep; he does not overlook the stumbling of a petitioner. It is unthinkable that Yahwe who has taken upon himself the protection of Israel will forget and be unmindful of what he voluntarily undertook. It is therefore out of the question that the enemy will sow destruction while the Lord sleeps. Whatever happens under the watchful eyes of God happens with his will and permission. The thought that God does not bother about the sufferings of the just should never enter one's mind. Indeed, God protects his children at all times and in everything that occurs. He is not far away but stands protectingly at our right. He is mightier than the guardian angel whom he has told to carry the just in their hands that they may not stumble upon a stone. He guards them against all evil by day and by night, from the heat of the sun during the day and from lunacy at night. In the Orient those who became ill because of the chill evening temperature were said to become sick through the influence of the moon. There is no suffering from which the Lord cannot keep us; there is no danger from which he cannot save us. Under his protection is the going and coming of man; that is, man's doings and omissions are under God's powerful protection now, in the future, and throughout an entire life.

psalm 121

Laetatus sum in his

The desire and hope of the just for the coming of the kingdom of God and the peace of his Church

A GRADUAL CANTICLE

1. I rejoiced at the things that were said to me: we shall go into the house of the Lord.

487

2. Our feet were standing in thy courts, O Jerusalem.

3. Jerusalem, which is built as a city, which is compact together.

4. For thither did the tribes go up, the tribes of the Lord: the testimony of Israel, to praise the name of the Lord.

5. Because their seats have sat in judgment, seats upon the house of David.

6. Pray ye for the things that are for the peace of Jerusalem: and abundance for them that love thee.

7. Let peace be in thy strength, and abundance in thy towers.

8. For the sake of my brethren, and of my neighbors, I spoke peace of thee.

9. Because of the house of the Lord our God, I have sought good things for thee.

THREE times a year, at Easter, Pentecost, and the Feast of Tabernacles every male Israelite had to journey to the sanctuary at Jerusalem. In times when the religious life flourished a wave of religious enthusiasm pervaded the entire country. At the beginning of great feasts trumpets were sounded and reminded the people to start their journey to Sion. There was no other people that could boast of having God really dwelling among them. The psalm gives us the thoughts and sentiments which the pilgrims had at their arrival in Jerusalem and at their departure from the holy city. Sometimes the people were on the way many days before they reached the gates of the city. No matter how often in the many years they had visited the holy city on festive days, when they arrived at the spur of Mount Olivet and looked down upon the city with its walls and towers and when the extensive temple buildings lay at their feet, the impression which Sion made upon them in their first pilgrimage was never erased.

In this song the psalmist is an interpreter of the feelings of the Jerusalem pilgrims and he describes the splendor of Sion (verses 3–5). There were also other fortified cities in the kingdom of Juda but none could be compared with Jerusalem. None was protected so well by nature. It was the strongest fortified city of the country. The farmer in the open village who sought refuge in the fortifications of Jerusalem when attacked by robbers of the neighboring heathen tribes knew how to appreciate the strength of Jerusalem. Sion was for him the ideal city. The high walls that surrounded it, the narrow streets in which house was built upon house were a type of the inner and especially the religious unity of the people. A king over all the tribes of Israel, one God and one sanctuary, a common belief and a common Messianic hope, such unity, totally strange to the pagan world, came to the consciousness of the Israelites especially at the pilgrimage feasts when many thousands from all parts of the kingdom went to Sion to worship Yahwe and to praise the most high God. Not only religious unity but also political unity found public expression in Jerusalem. Here stood the throne established by David, the throne which the Messias would possess in the fullness of time. Thus the people who made the pilgrimages to the sanctuary also felt themselves one with coming generations in the great hope of the great King of the future.

Since Jerusalem was the heart of the country, the pulse of the religious life of the nation; since it was the source from which all blessings flowed, it was of great concern to all Israel whether Sion would carry on its mission peacefully or whether it would be hindered from within or from without by oppression. Therefore the pilgrim song of itself becomes a prayer for the peace of Sion (verses 6–9). When the city was besieged by the enemies, when the roads were endangered, when the city suffered hardship, the pilgrimages had to be discontinued, the religious life weakened, the stream of blessing from the sanctuary was disrupted and could not flow in a thousand channels through the land. But peace within the city and peace among the inhabitants was also necessary for the effective work of God's blessing which came from the sanctuary. What a discouraging impression it must have made upon the pilgrims when the inhabitants of the city in which the God of peace dwelt, lived in discord, where the poor were despised by the rich, where the weak were oppressed by the mighty! Therefore the pilgrims pray for peace within the walls of Jerusalem. They pray for peace for all the brethren, for all the members of the kingdom of God which has its center in Sion and is the fountain of grace. When the heart and the head are sick all the members of the body suffer. And so it was in the Old Testament kingdom of God. The spiritual welfare of each is conditioned by the free and richly unfolding religious life in Jerusalem. The pilgrims pray for the peace of Sion for the temple's sake; for when the peace of the country and of the city has waned the roads to Sion mourn because no one comes to the festivities. What Jerusalem was for Israel, that peace was for the religious mission of the holy city. Sion was a type of the Church of the New Testament. Messianically considered, we admire with the writer of this psalm the inner unity of the Church in its teaching and organization and pray for peace; for the Church, too, needs peace if it wishes to fulfill its divine mission.

psalm 122

Ad te levavi

A prayer in affliction with confidence in God

A GRADUAL CANTICLE

1. To thee have I lifted up my eyes, who dwellest in heaven.

2. Behold as the eyes of servants are on the hands of their masters.
   As the eyes of the handmaid are on the hands of her mistress: so are our eyes unto the Lord our God, until he have mercy on us.

3. Have mercy on us, O Lord, have mercy on us: for we are greatly filled with contempt.

4. For our soul is greatly filled: we are a reproach to the rich, and contempt to the proud.

As THE needle of the compass always points to the north no matter in what position it is placed, so faith points heavenward to God and directs the soul of man to divine Providence even when sorrow distracts the soul. Such firm faith is spoken about in this little psalm. In the time of need the psalmist raises his eyes to the Father who thrones in heaven as Lord and King, as the almighty King. The majesty of the Lord is the reason for his confidence. His confidence has its foundation in God. But in every man lie the motives of his belief and confidence.

One of these motives is the dependence upon God and man's own helplessness. The fate of a male or female slave lies entirely in the hands of his lord or her mistress. Their welfare and woe depends on their will. Their hand can bestow benefits and punishments; therefore the eyes of the slave are directed to that hand. Much greater is our dependence upon God. All good and all help comes from his hand. Hence our eyes should always be directed to him.

The necessity of complete dependence upon God becomes especially clear to the consciousness of a believing Christian in times of great tribulation when all attempts to free himself from adversity are of no avail. Then the greatness of the need becomes in itself a reason for confidence (verses 3–4). Where the need is greatest there God's help is nearest. In times of need the people of God make pilgrimages to the house of God: "God, our Father in heaven have mercy on us." And all of them advancing further besought God: "Have mercy on us because we are filled with reproaches." Because unbelievers in their pride despise and persecute us, have mercy on us. Thus in confidence they pray that the greatness of their affliction will impel the great mercy of God to have sympathy and give help.

psalm 123

Nisi quia Dominus

The Church giveth glory to God for her deliverance
from the hands of her enemies

A GRADUAL CANTICLE

1. If it had not been that the Lord was with us, let Israel now say.

2. If it had not been that the Lord was with us, when men rose up against us.

3. Perhaps they would have swallowed us up alive, when their fury was enkindled against us.

4. Perhaps the waters had swallowed us up.

5. Our soul hath passed through a torrent: perhaps our soul had passed through a water insupportable.

6. Blessed be the Lord, who hath not given us to be a prey to their teeth.

7. Our soul hath been delivered as a sparrow out of the snare of the fowlers. The snare is broken and we are delivered.

8. Our help is in the name of the Lord, who made heaven and earth.

THE walls of our pilgrimage churches are decorated with votive tablets which thankful love has erected. Sometimes the event of a miraculous cure is reproduced on a picture. This psalm may be compared with such a votive tablet. The Lord has helped. It is a votive tablet for an entire people in thanksgiving for a miraculous deliverance from an enemy.

First of all the psalm describes the great need (verses 1–5). If the Lord had not been with them, the need must have ended in the collapse of the entire nation. It was a need which had to be removed and for this

491

their own strength was not sufficient and every human help was wanting. Indeed, if the Lord had not been with them when the neighboring enemies had risen against Israel, when they had thirsted for blood and booty and invaded the country like merciless beasts, the entire people would have been annihilated. The great masses of the hostile army would have thrown themselves upon them and overwhelmed them like a flood. Like broken dams they would have fallen upon them devastating the entire land.

But God has helped; therefore thank the Lord (verses 6–8). He did not permit his people to become a prey for the enemy who like a savage animal would tear it to pieces and lacerate it. Israel was already like a little bird which has been caught in the net of a fowler and now seemed defenseless and given up to die. But see, as by a miracle the net broke and the bird escaped. So Israel saw that it was about to collapse; it saw no escape from being harassed by the enemy. But suddenly the Lord took things in hand; the enemy withdrew from the power of the Almighty and Israel was again freed. The psalmist may have thought here of the miraculous intervention of God in the battle of Debbora on Thabor, or of the deliverance of Israel through Gedeon and Samuel, or of the deliverance of Jerusalem from the siege of the Assyrians, or of other miraculous deeds of the Lord. The history of the Church is also rich in such miraculous deliverances. Every miraculous liberation from great need proved to Israel again and again that it was not due to its own power, that it was not due to its army and weapons, that it was not due to human alliances, but because it called on the name of the Lord and help came to it from almighty God. He who created heaven and earth, he alone had the power to deliver from enemy affliction.

psalm 124

Qui confidunt

The just are always under God's protection

A GRADUAL CANTICLE

1. They that trust in the Lord shall be as Mount Sion: he shall not be moved forever that dwelleth in Jerusalem.

2. Mountains are round about it: so the Lord is round about his people from henceforth now and forever.

3. For the Lord will not leave the rod of sinners upon the lot of the just: that the just may not stretch forth their hands to iniquity.

4. Do good, O Lord, to those that are good and to the upright of heart.

5. But such as turn aside into bonds, the Lord shall lead out with the workers of iniquity: peace upon Israel.

H E WHO has built his life upon the rock foundation of revealed truth and is in unity with the true assembly of God partakes in the firmness of its foundation. This the believing Israelite has already experienced even in the incomplete revelation and in the imperfect church of God of the Old Testament. As long as the Lord was with him, he feared nothing and did not doubt. The pilgrim who journeyed to Jerusalem saw in the temple on Mount Sion a symbol of the firmness of his faith and confidence in God. He who trusts in the Lord and believes in his fidelity stands firm in all storms of adversity and temptation like Mount Sion. May the storms rage and the winds howl, he does not waver; he is not afraid. So, likewise, he who dwells in Jerusalem, who is a child of the Church of God is not afraid. He who trusts in God is like the city of Jerusalem which God protects with a chain of mountains. He is encompassed, as it were, by protecting mountains. So also is the Sion of the New Testament, the Church, protected by God. And as the mountains encircled the holy city throughout the ages, so also God's protection continues throughout all ages until the end of time.

Despite the divine protection Jerusalem sometimes is not spared from enemy attacks (verse 3). As long as the kingdom of God has not reached its completion, it will be attacked by enemies from without and by godless men from within until the day of the last judgment. But God does not permit the sceptre of the godless to rest upon the lot of the just; he does, however, permit the godless to enter the territory of the just and afflict the Church. But in the Church they will never rule. Times of tribulation are also times of cleansing and of strengthening the faith. In times of trouble God gives to the just strength to stand firm and not to waver. God does not let wickedness enter the inner sanctuary of the soul nor of the Church.

In times of trouble God gives his grace more abundantly; he does not permit anyone to be tempted above his strength. But he wants his grace to be requested. The psalm therefore closes with a petition for grace and judgment (verses 4–5). One's own weakness and the malice of the enemy conceal many dangers. May God therefore not refuse his assistance to those who are of good will and sincerely try to walk the path of virtue. To all of these may trials bring salvation. But those who follow the crooked path and allow themselves to be led by the spirit of the world must partake of the punishment of the godless. They will be destroyed by the wrath of God; they will be cast out of the assembly of God forever. Theirs will be the lot of eternal discord; for the godless shall have no peace. When this judgment has been given, the time of eternal peace will come to Israel and also to the Church.

psalm 125

In convertendo

The people of God rejoice at their delivery from captivity

A GRADUAL CANTICLE

1. When the Lord brought back the captivity of Sion, we became like men comforted.

2. Then was our mouth filled with gladness; and our tongue with joy.
   Then shall they say among the Gentiles: the Lord hath done great things for them.

3. The Lord hath done great things for us: we are become joyful.

4. Turn again our captivity, O Lord, as a stream in the south.

5. They that sow in tears shall reap in joy.

6. Going they went and wept, casting their seeds.

7. But coming they shall come with joyfulness, carrying their sheaves.

WHEN in the year 538–537 before Christ the Persian King Cyrus published the edict which permitted the Jews to return to their native land, 42,000 joined the high priest Josue and the prince Zorobabel. Esdras returned with the second group of banished Israelites to Palestine. The psalm belongs to the period between both these events. It expresses joy over the unexpected change of events which so suddenly put an end to the exile. In the psalm the psalmist prays that God may lead back home the rest that still live in pagan lands. In this psalm we pray for the return home of many who are still outside of the Church.

The Lord has begun the work of the redemption from captivity and of the return home (verses 1–3). Cyrus's edict of deliverance came so unexpectedly despite the prophecies of Isaias and Jeremias that the permission to return home seemed like a dream to many. They could scarcely believe the fact. The long continuance of the captivity had caused many to give up hope. Indescribable was the jubilation and great was the joy when the edict became known and when the command was given by Josue and Zorobabel to the Jews to prepare for the return. During the exile Sion's joyful hymns were silenced, the harps were hanging on the willows. The glad message at once loosed their tongues; those who returned home again took their stringed instruments in hand and sang the most beautiful hymns to the Lord. The unexpected change in the fate of the Israelites also made an impression on the Gentiles. They also recognized in the work of deliverance the finger of God and acknowledged the power of Yahwe, the God of Israel. Who would have thought that the conqueror of the Babylonian Empire would bow down before Yahwe and trouble himself about the reconstruction of his temple at Jerusalem? Israel had every reason to intone a Magnificat: "The Lord is mighty and has done great things for me." What the Book of Tobias mentions has been fulfilled in Israel: "For thou art not delighted in our being lost, because after a storm thou makest calm, and after tears and weeping thou pourest in joyfulness" (Tobias 3:22).

Just as the pre-exilic prophets viewed the return home from exile and the beginning of Messianic times together in their prophecies, so the Jews returning to their native country from the captivity expected the beginning of the fullness of time in which they would be gathered together from the dispersion and be brought back to their native land. Aggeus during the construction of the new temple pointed to the Messias who would appear in that temple. But many Jews still lived in the Diaspora. Therefore the psalmist begs the Lord that he may complete his work of the return home (verses 4–6). The poet compares the ways that lead to Sion to the river beds in the winter time. In summer they are dried out; no water flows into them from the heights into the valleys. But as soon as the winter rains begin, their beds are filled with water which runs in torrents into the depths below. The ways to Sion are deserted, as it were, dried out by the glow of the divine wrath; but they will again be filled with pilgrims when the Lord fulfills his word. He will fulfill his word as surely as the harvest follows upon seeding time. When the farmer sows his seed, he is much concerned about whether he will garner in a harvest. The time of the exile was a sowing of tears. It was a time of penance. Right sentiments should have been awakened during this time; namely, a longing for the sanctuary. The time of the harvest has not yet come. But as certain as in nature the harvest follows upon seeding, so certain Israel may expect a time of joy following upon the time of tears. The picture describes the last thought more minutely. Sorrowful and anxious about the success for his trouble the farmer goes out to sow; but when the summer has come and the Lord has given him a rich harvest, he brings home the grain with great joy. So also in the life of God's people there will follow a joyful harvest upon anxious seeding.

psalm 126

Nisi Dominus

Nothing can be done without God's grace and blessing

A GRADUAL CANTICLE OF SOLOMON

1. Unless the Lord build the house, they labor in vain that build it.
   Unless the Lord keep the city, he watcheth in vain that keepeth it.

2. It is vain for you to rise before light: rise ye after you have sitten, you that eat the bread of sorrow.
   When he shall give sleep to his beloved,

3. Behold the inheritance of the Lord are children: the reward, the fruit of the womb.

4. As arrows in the hand of the mighty, so the children of them that have been shaken.

5. Blessed is the man that hath filled the desire with them; he shall not be confounded when he shall speak to his enemies in the gate.

THE psalmist speaks about the truth that all depends on God's blessing. God must bless the technique. May a building be ever so beautiful, may it have been erected with the best means of technique, it is nothing if God has not been the invisible Builder. The magnificent buildings which progress in technique built without God have not been a blessing for man. The building which science wants to erect without God may be compared to the Tower of Babel which men intended to reach the clouds, but which only led to confusion and internal struggle of soul. May a city be ever so well protected and may it be provided with the best means of defense, it is all in vain if the Lord does not protect the city. Of what use was the strong double wall to the fortified city of Jericho? It fell into

Josue's hands without much effort on his part. God did not protect this fortified city. When the Assyrian King Sennacherib and his army of 185,000 men besieged Jerusalem, he could not shoot one single arrow into the city although he thought that the taking of the town was an easy matter. As a vanquished king he had to leave the country in all haste without being able to conquer a famished people and make them surrender their strong fortification; for the Lord had given them his protection.

God must bless the work. God's blessing does not make human endeavor superfluous no matter how abundantly this blessing is given; it rather presupposes conscientious work. But it keeps man from that anxiety which accompanies a work that is done without God, in the acquisition of wealth and prosperity. For man to make himself a slave of work is of no value. The overexertion in modern business activities has not brought blessing but has taken from millions the possibility of working. Working ten hours with God has more value than twenty hours without God. It is a bread of affliction which men eat whose work is not ennobled with confidence in God. Faith and confidence take away anxiety and give peaceful sleep. In this sense the words of the psalmist that the Lord gives his loved ones peaceful sleep should be understood.

God must bless the marriage (verses 3–4). Sons are a gift of God, living vouchers of the blessing of the matrimonial bond. Barrenness is a punishment from God and God's curse. This was at all times the belief of the people of Israel. Sons begotten in the best years of manhood are for the father a support in old age and the best defenders of his honor; they form the defense of his house. As a hero who has his quiver well filled with arrows is feared by the enemy, so a father whose house is filled with living arrows, that is, with strong sons, is feared. The enemies will not besmirch the honor of the father before the gates of the city.

psalm 127

Beati omnes

The fear of God is the way to happiness

A GRADUAL CANTICLE

1. Blessed are all they that fear the Lord: that walk in his ways.

2. For thou shalt eat the labors of thy hands: blessed art thou, and it shall be well with thee.

3. Thy wife as a fruitful vine, on the sides of thy house.
   Thy children as olive plants, round about thy table.

4. Behold, thus shall the man be blessed that feareth the Lord.

5. May the Lord bless thee out of Sion: and mayst thou see the good things of Jerusalem all the days of thy life.

6. And mayst thou see thy children's children, peace upon Israel.

THE entire family going to Church together is always a renewed dedication of the family to God. The pilgrimage of the Israelitic family to the great feasts at Jerusalem was also a family dedication. Here at the place of the sanctuary a man should become conscious of the fact that his family is a unit in the great family of God, of the people who worship Yahwe as their common Father. But not every head of a family was blessed with the blessing of the Most High. He had to prepare himself for this blessing by the fear of God; for God will bless only those who fear him. God is to be found not merely on the way to Jerusalem, but on the way of piety.

It is of this blessing that the psalmist speaks, and first of all about temporal blessings (verses 2–3). The fear of God blesses man's work. It does not take away from him the obligation to work. It does not abrogate the law that was placed upon the first man and his descendants: "In the sweat of thy brow, shalt thou eat thy bread." It ennobles and sanctifies work and with the help of God secures success. Sometimes real earthly gain may not be obtained, but the eternal reward which is greater is more assured. It will go well with a man who fears God; he will prosper. The fear of God blesses man in his wife. The psalmist compares a faithful housewife and her activities within the walls of the house to a fruitful vine. The vine in appearance looks rather modest but is precious because of its fruit. It clings to the walls of the house in order to obtain support, but at the same time it adds to the beauty of the house. This is a striking description of a housewife who as a good woman must cling to the house of her husband and shed lustre to the home, who by her modesty and unpretentiousness in her work brings about the precious fruit of peace in the family. The fear of God also blesses the man in his sons. When they sit at table they may be compared to the fruit-bearing olive trees. They give hope and confidence to the father and they secure the happiness and wealth of the family. They will be the light and strength of the parents in their old age.

The earthly blessings which the God-fearing man received from the sanctuary was only the first part payment and a guarantee for the Messianic promises. Therefore in the form of an extension of the priestly blessing, the desire of obtaining the Messianic blessing is also assured to the God-fearing man (verses 4–6). He has made a pilgrimage to Jerusalem to worship the Lord and to take back with him the blessings for his home. But the Lord will not only grant him this blessing, he will also let him experience the happiness of Jerusalem all the days of his life. Jerusalem is here to be considered in the prophetic sense, the Messianic kingdom of God, the Church. The happiness of Sion means the bestowal of blessing and the source of grace in this kingdom. He shall enjoy this blessing and the Lord will permit him to draw from the source of salvation. The Lord shall give him a long life that through many generations he may enjoy the peace of Sion, the Messianic salvation.

psalm 128

Saepe expugnaverunt

The Church of God is invincible: her persecutors come to nothing

A GRADUAL CANTICLE

1. Often have they fought against me from my youth, let Israel now say.

2. Often have they fought against me from my youth: but they could not prevail over me.

3. The wicked have wrought upon my back: they have lengthened their iniquity.

4. The Lord who is just will cut the necks of sinners:

5. Let them all be confounded and turned back that hate Sion.

6. Let them be as grass upon the tops of houses: which withereth before it be plucked up.

7. Wherewith the mower filleth not his hand: nor he that gathereth sheaves his bosom.

8. And they that passed by have not said: The blessing of the Lord be upon you: we have blessed you in the name of the Lord.

THE history of the people of Israel was a long history of suffering; but to a great extent this suffering was a well-deserved way of the cross. The Gentile neighboring nations and the wicked policies of godless kings gave it no rest. The years of continued peace were few. But Jerusalem continued its existence in the midst of all storms. When the pilgrims entered the city, their conviction was strengthened and they boasted: "They can harass us but they cannot prevail against us." With greater right the Church can utter these words: "The Church may be harassed but it will never be prevailed against."

These consoling words throw light upon the past (verses 1–4). Many enemies had harassed the people of Israel from the very beginning of its history. Scarcely had the people gone out of Egypt when the Amalekites fell upon them. In Canaan it was encircled by the enemy: the Canaanites in their own land, the Moabites, the Ammonites, the Edomites in the east and south, the Philistines in the west, besides the Egyptians, the Assyrians, and the Babylonians. The country was often severely visited by wars and suffered under the severe pressure of foreign rule. But it was never eradicated. As the plower tears up the ground, so the enemy had inflicted grave wounds upon the people. They had hammered upon them, as the Vulgate put it, as the smith strikes the anvil. But Israel with God's help endured all sufferings and persecutions. In the greatest need God always sent a liberator who by his heroic deeds broke the bonds with which the people were fettered. The Lord permitted the scourges, but nothing more than what he himself had determined and what the people had deserved.

The experience of the past justified the psalmist to be confident about the future (verses 5–8). If the enemies of God's people of the Old Covenant could not vanquish them during a history of so many centuries because God protected them, then all future attacks will also be without success. They who in their hatred will wage war against God's kingdom will retreat in shame. They will be like grass on the roofs of houses. The ordinary roofs of the Palestinian homes are covered with mud and grass grows upon them during the winter rains from the seeds that are blown upon them by the wind. But as soon as the sun sends its hot rays upon the grass, it dries up before it is pulled out because it has no deep roots. What grows upon the roofs amounts to nothing; it does not pay to harvest the grass and the few stalks of grain. The cutter who takes the stalks in his hand and cuts them with a sickle cannot fill his hand with the sparse stalks and the binder of the sheaves who walks behind him does not need to gather them in the folds of his mantle. In harvest time those who passed by greeted the cutters and binders with the greeting: "The blessing of the Lord be upon you." And the latter answered: "We bless you in the name of the Lord." On the roof there is no harvest; no harvest

500

greeting is heard there. As the stalks on the roof dry up and disappear, so also the fate of the enemies of the kingdom of God shall be. They shall dry up and be cast away under the glow of the divine wrath.

psalm 129

De profundis

A prayer of a sinner, trusting in the mercies of God

The sixth penitential psalm

A GRADUAL CANTICLE

1. Out of the depths have I cried to thee, O Lord.

2. Lord, hear my voice. Let thy ears be attentive to the voice of my supplication.

3. If thou, O Lord, wilt mark my iniquities: Lord, who shall stand it.

4. For with thee there is merciful forgiveness: and by reason of thy law, I have waited for thee, O Lord. My soul hath relied on his word:

5. my soul hath hoped in the Lord.

6. From the morning watch even until night, let Israel hope in the Lord.

7. Because with the Lord there is mercy: and with him plentiful redemption.

8. And he shall redeem Israel from all his iniquities.

THIS psalm was composed during the Babylonian exile and was sung by the psalmist in the name of the people. It is a cry of profound spiritual suffering, but not the cry of a despondent person. There is a Christian sentiment pervading this psalm; it is a hopeful song for the deliverance for which the souls in purgatory sigh. It is a prayer of profound human suffering that meets the divine Love.

The first strophe (verses 1–4) is a cry for redemption. The afflicted soul cries "out of the depths." The psalmist does not think of any particular suffering such as the exile. The suffering comprises all the depths of human suffering on earth. The Church also uses this psalm for the suffering souls in purgatory. The prayer is not only a cry because of physical sufferings, but it also comes from a soul that is conscious of a grave guilt before God./The soul cries to Yahwe with whom there is a covenant and intimate union, to whom Israel can turn as a child to its father. The psalmist prays that God may graciously hear the cry of a poor afflicted heart and accept him as his child. His kind heart cannot be closed to the cry for help of him who seeks redemption and salvation. If God does not hear, then his destruction is sealed. Indeed, if God will deal according to the norms of strict justice and will not let mercy prevail upon a sinful man, then no man can continue to exist before his infinite sanctity. If God will not forgive sin but will keep a record of sin until the day of judgment, then all men will be lost eternally. God cannot be angry forever; for with him is found reconciliation and forgiveness of sin; indeed, only with him. The Lord is ready to forgive in order that we may revere and love him. He does not wish the death of the sinner, but that he may live. If there would be no forgiveness, then there also would be no love for God. How could we honor and love him from whom we were to hear only the judgment of eternal death and from whom we were to expect only eternal suffering. If God desires our love, then he must forgive.

It is upon faith in God's love that the hope of redemption rests (verses 5–8). The Lord has assured the return home to the penitent people and reconciliation to contrite sinners (Leviticus 26:40; Ezechiel 33:11). The believing soul relies upon this word and confidently expects God's mercy. As longingly as a guard of the night watch awaits morning which relieves him, so the psalmist and with him the entire people in the time of affliction await the break of the dawn of redemption. With a like longing Israel should now also hope in the Lord and for his redemption; for with the Lord there is mercy and plentiful redemption. From the depths of human misery the psalmist sinks into the depths of God's mercy. The psalmist is sure that God will redeem Israel from all its sins.

psalm 130

Domine, non est

The prophet's humility

A GRADUAL CANTICLE OF DAVID

1. Lord my heart is not exalted: nor are my eyes lofty.
   Neither have I walked in great matters, nor in wonderful things above me.

2. If I was not humbly minded, but exalted my soul:
    As a child that is weaned is toward his mother, so reward in my soul.

3. Let Israel hope in the Lord, from henceforth now and forever.

THIS little psalm gives an attractive and emotional description of peace and contentment, of a childlike humble soul which without reserve gives itself up to divine guidance and providence. It is a confession of a pious Israelite who feels himself well with God in the sanctuary at Jerusalem, who feels himself as well as a child at the mother's breast.

Humility is a requisite for peace of soul. The proud man who looks down contemptuously upon his fellow men does not acquire inner peace. Whenever his pride is not satisfied, his soul is filled with rancor. Envy, jealousy, and anger give him no peace. He occupies himself with plans that flatter his vanity. The accomplishments of these plans are above his abilities. The humble man knows nothing about envy and jealousy. Disregard does not trouble him. He knows his ability and does not occupy himself with plans which he cannot fulfill, especially when he cannot depend on God's assistance. He is mindful of the words of the pious Sirach: "Seek not the things that are too high for thee, and search not into things above thy ability, but the things that God hath commanded thee, think on them always, and in many of his works be not curious, for it is not necessary for thee to see with thy eyes those things that are hid. The suspicion of many things hath deceived many, and hath detained their minds in vanity" (Sirach 3:22 seq.).

Humility brings about peace of soul. The ambitious man is like a child not yet weaned from his mother's breast, but a humble man may be compared to a child that is weaned, that loves his mother without having the desire to be nourished by her breasts. The humble man has no passionate desires because he leaves everything to the providence of God from whom he expects everything. Whatever may cause unrest to the soul of man does not trouble the humble man. Envy, jealousy, offended ambition, dissatisfaction because the desires of the heart are not satisfied do not trouble him. Thus contented and satisfied and without worry Israel should depend in all things upon the Lord. It should not insolently make demands, but endure patiently. God in his eternal decree and in his infinite love has arranged everything for the best. One can without any anxiety depend on his love.

psalm 131

Memento, Domine

A prayer to the fulfillment of the promise made to David

A GRADUAL CANTICLE

1. O Lord, remember David, and all his meekness.

2. How he swore to the Lord, he vowed a vow to the God of Jacob.

3. If I shall enter into the tabernacle of my house: if I shall go up into the bed wherein I lie:

4. If I shall give sleep to my eyes, or slumber to my eyelids,

5. Or rest to my temples: until I find out a place for the Lord, a tabernacle for the God of Jacob.

6. Behold we have heard of it in Ephrata: we have found it in the fields of the wood.

7. We will go into his tabernacle: we will adore in the place where his feet stood.

8. Arise, O Lord, into thy resting place: thou and the ark, which thou hast sanctified.

9. Let thy priests be clothed with justice: and let thy saints rejoice.

10. For thy servant David's sake, turn not away the face of thy anointed.

11. The Lord hath sworn truth to David, and he will not make it void: of the fruit of thy womb I will set upon thy throne.

12. If thy children will keep my covenant, and these my testimonies which I shall teach them:
Their children also forevermore shall sit upon thy throne.

13. For the Lord hath chosen Sion: he hath chosen it for his dwelling.

14. This is my rest forever and ever: here will I dwell, for I have chosen it.

15. Blessing I will bless her widow: I will satisfy her poor with bread.

16. I will clothe her priests with salvation: and her saints shall rejoice with exceeding great joy.

17. There will I bring forth a horn to David: I have prepared a lamp for my anointed.

18. His enemies I will clothe with confusion: but upon him shall my sanctification flourish.

THIS psalm was composed for the dedication of the Solomonic Temple and for the carrying of the Ark of the Covenant from the holy tabernacle which David had erected on Sion to the new sanctuary. The celebration was not possible without thinking of David, the king, and his merits, and of the preparations he had made for the construction of the temple. But neither was it possible without Solomon being mindful of the promises which the Lord had made to his father, the fulfillment of which had a new guarantee in the completion of the construction of the temple. For with the commission to build the temple God also assured him the continued existence of his kingdom for all times (1 Chronicles 28:7). By this the celebration received a character which pointed to the Messianic future.

First of all the psalm reminds us of the merits of David in the construction of the temple (verses 1–5). At the completion of the great work of the construction of the temple it was befitting to remember thankfully the zeal David showed in the preparation for the structure. It was not personal ambition that prompted the king to make a resolution to build a magnificent temple that should surpass in splendor the temples of the pagan gods of Egypt. It was only reverence for the sublime majesty of God that prompted him to do so. He could not endure to live in a palace while the dwelling of the Most High was a simple tent. Out of piety he tried to give to the Lord the best he could and did not shy from personal sacrifice. He vowed not to rest until his plan was realized. The poet again made the vow at least as to its meaning and used hyperbolic expressions so that the king's determination could be clearly understood. He would not enter his house nor seek his bed until the building was completed. The psalmist wished to say that David would not be happy in his own home and would rather deny himself all comfort as long as the Lord had a more modest home than his own slave. He would deny himself sleep and would not give himself rest day or night until the great work was assured, and a worthy dwelling place was prepared for the Lord; for what he planned was the sanctuary for the Strong One of Jacob. That, as it were, was to be the title of the house of God.

It was not according to God's will that David himself should build the temple; God was satisfied with his good will and with the preparation. The work was completed by Solomon and the procession is now ready to undertake the solemn transfer of the Ark of the Covenant (verses 6–10). The psalmist makes a brief review of the last happenings to the Ark of the Covenant. After the conquest of Canaan by Josue it stood about 400 years in Shiloh in the territory of the tribe of Ephraim which is here called Ephrata. After its loss to the Philistines under the high priest Heli and after its return, it was placed in the house of Abinadab at Cariathiarim, three hours west of Jerusalem, until it was brought by David to the holy tabernacle on Sion. And now it was to receive its final place in the Holy of Holies in the temple. The choir requested all present to accompany the Ark of the Lord from the tabernacle on Sion to the temple and cast themselves down before it, the footstool of the Lord. The psalmist compares the Ark of the Covenant to the precious footstool that belonged to the throne of the king upon which the feet of the ruler rested. The throne of Yahwe is in heaven and the footstool of this throne stands on earth. The procession starts from the castle of the king. Now the people beseech the Lord to take possession of the new temple and from now on to take his throne on the Ark of the Covenant in the Holy of Holies. The poet calls the Ark of the Covenant the strong Ark because it is the footstool of the Strong One of Jacob. The Ark was permitted to be carried only by the priests. They were allowed to touch only the poles of the Ark and carry it on their shoulders. To these the request is made to clothe themselves in justice and to perform their service with holy and pious sentiments in such sublime action. Justice should be their festive garment, but not for this one service alone. Sanctity and justice should always be their garment, should be the characteristics of the priesthood; they should, as it were, clothe themselves in justice. But the people should accompany the sacred Ark of the Lord singing songs of jubilation. Their entry to the temple built by Solomon should be a guarantee that God who so richly has poured out his blessings upon David will not refuse to bless his son and for his son's sake his descendants also.

With the transfer of the Ark of the Covenant into the temple the great work which David had planned and prepared was accomplished. Now the psalm brings back to memory the promises of God to David (verses 11–13). When David, the king, had made the promise to erect the temple, God through the Prophet Nathan gave him the promise under oath that he would build him a house; that is, that he would give him great posterity, that his house would continue to exist until the Messias himself would ascend the throne. This assurance of the continuation of the Davidic dynasty depended on one condition: his descendants were to remain faithful to the law of the Lord and at all times to the covenant. This was a condition the fulfillment of which was self-evident to a theocratic king (2 Kings 7:14 seq.). That God chose Sion as the place for his dwelling upon earth was putting a seal upon his divine decree; for according to the promise David's throne at Jerusalem was to be the starting point of the Messianic world dominion. From here the grace of redemption was to fill the earth (Psalm 109:2).

By this the temple became a sign of the divine plan of salvation and at the same time a constant reminder to the king and people that they must remain faithful to the Lord.

After taking possession of the new sanctuary the first gracious act of the Lord was the confirmation of the promise of the Messianic blessing (verses 14–18). Here in the temple on Moriah God wished to dwell forever as he had dwelt in the holy tabernacle with his presence of grace. With this divine decree the temple had become the house of God, a sanctuary from which blessings would flow into the land and upon the entire people. Sion received the first blessing from the Holy of Holies; for it was the city of God. It was the Messianic blessing. The Lord will bless all provisions so that no one will famish within its walls. The nourishment of the body is a type of the spiritual nourishment of the soul, of the rich graces which flow from the temple upon its inhabitants. The citizens of the city of God, the members of God's kingdom, the Church, should have the first claim upon the graces of the Messianic salvation. The second blessing coming from the Holy of Holies God will give to the priests who serve in the sanctuary and who are the mediators of salvation. Therefore God wants to clothe them, above all else, in salvation; that is, he wants to sanctify and consecrate them, enrich them with graces and make them mediators of divine grace to all members of the kingdom of God. The greater the sanctification of the priest is the richer will be the blessing that will come to the pious who have been called to salvation. They will be jubilant because of the bounteous graces and blessings that are given them through the mediation of the priests. The third blessing pertains to the king's house. In Sion the Lord will fulfill the promise given to King David. Here he will allow a horn to sprout for him and create a light for him. The horn is a symbol of power and dominion. The light burning in the home is a symbol of continuous posterity. Both of these promises have their fulfillment in the person of the Messias. Zacharias speaks of this in his song of praise: "God has visited and redeemed his people, has erected a horn of salvation in the house of David his servant, as it has been foretold years ago by the mouth of the prophet" (Luke 1:69). For the sake of the divine Messias God will make the house of David strong and will let it triumph over its enemies. They will be covered with shame and clothed in disgrace as with a garment. Upon the head of the king a brilliant divine crown will shine: above him will be a reflection of the divine ruler which he will show visibly in his kingdom.

psalm 132

Ecce quam bonum

The happiness of brotherly love and concord

A GRADUAL CANTICLE OF DAVID

1. Behold how good and how pleasant it is for brethren to dwell together in unity.

2. Like the precious ointment on the head, that ran down upon the beard, the beard of Aaron, which ran down to the skirt of his garment.

3. As the dew of Hermon, which descendeth upon Mount Sion.
For there the Lord hath commanded blessing, and life forevermore.

G REAT feast days in famous places of pilgrimages, international Eucharistic Congresses, and similar combined celebrations are powerful manifestations of Catholic unity, of a one, holy, apostolic Church. There the participants feel themselves to be members of one great family, no matter how different their language, their education, and social standing may be. So also the great feasts in Jerusalem were days on which Israel was clearly conscious of its unity and faith. This consciousness was strengthened in post-exilic days when the Jews of the Diaspora made pilgrimages to Jerusalem in order to worship the only Lord and God in the temple. There all felt themselves brothers, members of God's people, children of the one heavenly Father. In those days it must also have been an edifying scene when tens of thousands were assembled in the large temple place, one in faith and love singing their psalms with the mountains re-echoing their songs.

In two pictures the psalmist describes the blessing of this oneness in faith and its spiritual effect on the community of saints. As at the consecration of Aaron by Moses the holy ointment dropped from the head of the first high priest upon his beard and upon the skirt of his garment and on that account the whole person was blessed and sanctified, so by the strength of unity in the true faith and love a holy stream of grace flows upon the entire community, over the entire people even to its last member. This blessing which goes out from Sion is as rich and refreshing as the dew of Hermon which in nature imparts strength and freshness of life. When the warm air passes over the snow covered summit of the

Great Hermon, it brings about a strong cooling and causes a rich fall of dew. Just as the dew from Hermon fell upon Mount Sion so the dew of grace fell from heavenly heights upon the Holy Mountain. In the religious life much spiritual fruit is obtained from great religious gatherings. When many thousands gather together in a common confession of faith and in common prayer a supernatural increase of spiritual life is noticeable. So it was also at Sion, the type of the Messianic Church. A rich and refreshing blessing came from it which fructified the life of grace. The thoughts of the psalm may be applicable in explaining the unity of the Church, the oneness of all its members in the mystical body of Christ. His divine ointment flows from him upon all members. In virtue of this union they receive from him the fullness of his grace.

psalm 133

Ecce nunc benedicite

An exhortation to praise God continually

A GRADUAL CANTICLE

1. Behold now bless ye the Lord, all ye servants of the Lord:
   Who stand in the house of the Lord, in the courts of the house of our God.

2. In the nights lift up your hands to the holy places, and bless ye the Lord.

3. May the Lord out of Sion bless thee, he that made heaven and earth.

THIS little psalm may have been said originally at the end of each nightly temple watch. As the last of the pilgrim songs it may be considered a departure song sung by the pilgrims returning home. They now return to their villages, to their daily work, and their worldly occupations which again make their demands upon them. They can no longer occupy themselves with prayer and the praises of God as they did on the festival days. The people are dismissed by the priests whom God has called to the service of the sanctuary. Thus the request is given by the departing pilgrims to the priests remaining to continue the praises of God in the temple in the name of the people. During the nights, that is, in times during which God's praises are not recited by the large masses of people, the priest should raise his hands to God; the priest who dwells in the temple should glorify God by prayer and sacrifice. This the faithful people request the priests to do and expect it from them. The priests gladly accept the obligation and give them their blessing and dismiss them. The Lord will bless them even when they are far away from the sanctuary and are occupied with worldly affairs; he will bless their work, their cares and anxieties. It is the blessing of the Almighty who with his powerful word pours forth his glory upon heaven and earth. From the house of God and his tabernacle where the priests daily offer sacrifice, his grace and blessings flow upon the people.

psalm 134

Laudate nomen

An exhortation to praise God: the vanity of idols

ALLELUIA

1. Praise ye the name of the Lord: O you his servants, praise the Lord.

2. You that stand in the house of the Lord, in the courts of the house of our God.

3. Praise ye the Lord, for the Lord is good: sing ye to his name, for it is sweet.

4. For the Lord hath chosen Jacob unto himself; Israel for his own possession.

5. For I have known that the Lord is great, and our God is above all gods.

6. Whatsoever the Lord pleased he hath done, in heaven, in earth, in the sea, and in all the deeps.

7. He bringeth up clouds from the end of the earth: he hath made lightnings for the rain. He bringeth winds out of his stores.

8. He slew the firstborn of Egypt from man even unto beast.

9. He sent forth signs and wonders in the midst of thee, O Egypt: upon Pharaoh, and upon all his servants.

10. He smote many nations, and slew mighty kings.

11. Sehon, king of the Amorrhites, and Og, king of Basan, and all the kingdoms of Canaan.

12. And gave their land for an inheritance, for an inheritance to his people Israel.

13. Thy name, O Lord, is forever: thy memorial, O Lord, unto all generations.

14. For the Lord will judge his people, and will be entreated in favor of his servants.

15. The idols of the Gentiles are silver and gold, the works of men's hands.

16. They have a mouth, but they speak not: they have eyes, but they see not.

17. They have ears, but they hear not: neither is there any breath in their mouths.

18. Let them that make them be like to them: and everyone that trusteth in them.

19. Bless the Lord, O house of Israel: bless the Lord, O house of Aaron.

20. Bless the Lord, O house of Levi; you that fear the Lord, bless the Lord.

21. Blessed be the Lord out of Sion, who dwelleth in Jerusalem.

T HE priest is the official liturgical man of prayer. Therefore in the foregoing psalm those pilgrims who were departing requested the priests remaining in the sanctuary to continue the praises of God which were sung by all the people during the solemn festivities. This vocational duty of the priest, however, did not relieve the people from the duty of praising God. Thus in this psalm there is a request to both priests and people to glorify the name of the Lord. All are servants of the Lord; they form a priestly kingdom (verses 1–5). The priests as the liturgical servants of God who stand before the Lord in the sanctuary must always be ready to do him service. But the people also who are permitted to enter the courts of the temple and participate only in a general priesthood have a duty of serving the Lord.

Three facts give the reason for this duty. Above all else it is the love of God. The name of the Lord inspires love. God by his very nature is good. The majesty of the divine Being awakens admiration and reverence; his love, however, inspires confidence and a return of love. The Israelites should then bring back to memory the wonderful ways by which the divine Providence led them. The Christian especially should be mindful of that love of the Father who gave us his only begotten Son in order that all who believe in him may not perish. This goodness alone obligates both priests and people to praise the Lord. Israel which had been chosen to be the bearer of salvation and to be distinguished above all nations of the Gentile world by being in possession of the truth and great graces could by itself make no claim upon the sanctuary. It was an act of the free love of God who shows mercy to those whom he wishes. Therefore Moses spoke to Israel: "Because thou art a holy people to the Lord thy God: The Lord thy God hath chosen thee to be his peculiar people of all peoples that are upon the earth. Not because you surpass all people in numbers, is the Lord joined unto you, and hath chosen you, for you are the fewest of any people. But because the Lord has loved you and has kept his oath, which he swore to your fathers" (Deuteronomy 7:6–8). This in a higher sense is applicable to those called to the Church of the New Testament and to those called to the priesthood because they are far superior to the Church and priesthood of the Old Covenant. The election obligates the people to praise God. On this account St. Peter admonishes: "But you are a chosen generation, a kingly priesthood, a nation, a purchased people, that you may declare his virtues, who hath called you out of the darkness into his marvelous light" (I Peter 2:9). A third reason is the greatness of God. In Egypt and Babylon Israel had seen with its own eyes with what pomp the pagans worshiped their worthless gods. Yahwe surpasses all gods; he is above all. Therefore the praise which God's people give him should not be surpassed by that which the pagans give to their idols.

The last thought leads to the main theme of the psalm; namely, to show the superiority of the God of Israel over the heathen gods (verses 6–14). The psalmist points briefly to the majesty of God who reveals himself in nature (verses 6–7). Yahwe the God and King of Israel is the almighty Creator of heaven and earth, the God for whom there are no impossibilities. Everything that he wills he also accomplishes in all realms of creation from the immeasurable heights of heaven to the deepest abysses of the sea. All creatures were created by him and are provided for by him. The clouds that appear on the distant horizon are his creation. With astonishment the Israelites looked upon them and saw in them a miracle of God's power. From the clouds God makes the lightning flash and decides when the clouds should pour down rain. At his command the wind blows and the storm rages. He holds them, as it were, in storage as long as he wills.

God's majesty is also seen in the pages of Israel's history (verses 8–14). The psalmist gives us a brief resumè of the exodus from Egypt; he mentions the plagues which God sent upon the land to show Pharaoh the weakness of his gods and the power of the God of Israel. Nine times he rebuked and warned Pharaoh with various plagues; but when he remained hardened and would not let Israel depart, God sent an avenging angel who slew all the first-born of Egypt, both men and animals. From all these signs and wonders the Egyptians should have known and acknowledged the supreme greatness of Yahwe, but they refused to acknowledge his supremacy and dared even to pursue the Israelites as far as the Red Sea in order to force them to return. He permitted them to see another great miracle. They saw how the Lord miraculously made a way for his people to pass through the sea. But when the warriors of Pharaoh attempted to pursue Israel on that same way, he engulfed them in the waters of the sea.

A second historical testimony for the majesty of Yahwe was the victories over the kings of Canaan. It was God himself who vanquished the nations and their kings, and not the strength of his people; often the victory was so remarkable that only the intervention of God could have made it possible. Among the kings vanquished by Josue the psalmist mentions only two Amorrhite princes, Sehon and Og, by name. The realm of King Sehon extended from the northern border of the land of the Moabites at the river Arnon to the Jabbok. Basan, the land of King Og, was situated next to it and east of Lake Genesareth. Its territory was settled by the tribes of Ruben, Gad, and Manasses. The kings of the Canaanites vanquished by Josue are mentioned in the Book of Josue, Chapter 12. The Lord gave the land which four hundred years earlier he had promised to the Patriarch Abraham as an inheritance to his people.

A further historical testimony of the majesty of Yahwe was the preservation of the nation of Israel. God is eternal and his name shall never vanish from the earth. The memory of his name by the nations shall remain throughout all ages; for it participates in the eternity of the Lord. Mighty nations have disappeared, mighty kingdoms have collapsed and are forgotten. But the nation of Israel to which the Lord had given his revelations and promises, Israel which was destined by God to give the Messias to the world had outlived all storms. It outlived the exile despite the destruction of the city and of the temple and the overthrow of the Davidic dynasty. This undeniable fact finds a satisfactory answer only in this that God was the defender and protector of this little nation and that faithful to his promises he was always merciful to Israel even when he had to punish it.

The majesty of Yahwe is seen even in a brighter light when it is compared to the weakness of the gods (verses 15–18). The psalmist here borrows from the 113th Psalm. God is the creator of all things; all men are created according to his image. But the gods are formed by the hands of men, valuable only because of the material from which they were formed. The Lord has given to man mouth and eyes, ears and throat which he can use. Men give to their gods a mouth and two eyes, but they remain dumb and blind. They cannot express their preferences of formation; for they cannot see what happens to them. Two ears are given to them but they cannot hear. They are given a silver throat but they cannot breathe. They are lifeless gods and cannot do anything for or against man. He, however, who trusts in God has a powerful protector; he will not be put to shame. But he who relies on these lifeless gods will be deceived and put to shame.

It is therefore the sacred duty of the entire people of Israel to praise the majestic God, the God of the covenant and their king. This duty rests particularly upon the priests. Therefore the house of Aaron from which the priests stem is first called upon to praise the Lord. The house of Levi should praise the Lord. They had taken the place of the first-born and as representatives of the entire people had dedicated their life to the Lord. On them was placed the obligation of adding to the solemnity of the divine service by music and song. The great crowds of God-fearing men shall unite with the Levites in this great choir. In later times the Gentiles who gave up their pagan gods and turned to the one true God were also added to these. Sion, the Church, should be the place where the praises of God should be proclaimed to all the world; for there God has erected his dwelling. If at any place, there the praises of the Lord should resound.

psalm 135

Confitemini Domino

God is to be praised for his wonderful works

ALLELUIA

1. Praise the Lord, for he is good: for his mercy endureth forever.

2. Praise ye the God of gods: for his mercy endureth forever.

3. Praise ye the Lord of lords, for his mercy endureth forever.

4. Who alone doth great wonders: for his mercy endureth forever.

5. Who made the heavens in understanding, for his mercy endureth forever.

6. Who established the earth above the waters; for his mercy endureth forever.

7. Who made the great lights: for his mercy endureth forever.

8. The sun to rule the day: for his mercy endureth forever.

9. The moon and the stars to rule the night: for his mercy endureth forever.

10. Who smote Egypt with their first-born: for his mercy endureth forever.

11. Who brought out Israel from among them: for his mercy endureth forever.

12. With a mighty hand and with a stretched out arm: for his mercy endureth forever.

13. Who divided the Red Sea into parts: for his mercy endureth forever.

14. And brought out Israel through the midst thereof: for his mercy endureth forever.

15. And overthrew Pharaoh and his host in the Red Sea: for his mercy endureth forever.

16. Who led his people through the desert: for his mercy endureth forever.

17. Who smote great kings: for his mercy endureth forever.

18. And slew strong kings: for his mercy endureth forever.

19. Sehon, king of the Amorrhites: for his mercy endureth forever.

20. And Og, king of Basan: for his mercy endureth forever.

21. And he gave their land for an inheritance: for his mercy endureth forever.

22. For an inheritance to his servant Israel: for his mercy endureth forever.

23. For he was mindful of us in our affliction: for his mercy endureth forever.

24. And he redeemed us from our enemies: for his mercy endureth forever.

25. Who giveth food to all flesh: for his mercy endureth forever.

26. Give glory to the God of heaven: for his mercy endureth forever.

27. Give glory to the Lord of lords: for his mercy endureth forever.

LITANIES in which God's love and mercy were praised seem to have been especially revered in Israel for the occasions of great religious festivities. They are already mentioned in the Book of Chronicles for David's time (1 Chronicles 16:41). They were sung at the dedication of the Solomonic temple (2 Chronicles 7:3) and at the cornerstone ceremony of the post-exilic temple (Esdras 3:11). This psalm is also a litany in honor of the divine mercy. At the words of the precantor the people answered: "And his mercy endureth forever." It must have been an edifying scene when many thousands expressed in unison their faith in the one God and together praised his divine goodness.

The introduction requests gratitude to Yahwe, to the good Lord, to God supreme over all gods, the King of kings, the Lord of lords.

The first part of the Litany (verses 4–9) glorifies the mercy of God revealing itself in nature. Yahwe is the only God who can perform wonderful deeds, who can perform miracles. The gods of the Gentiles are weak; they are nothing. In his infinite wisdom he has spanned the wide starry heaven; he alone has done it. He only spoke: Let the firmament be made and the wide vault be extended in immeasurable distance over the ocean. It was God who gathered the waters in order that dry land might appear; he spread the earth over the shaky foundation of water. Man must build his little house upon a firm foundation so that the heavy downpour of rain may not undermine it and make it fall together. But the Lord does not need a foundation for the huge structure of the earth. With the "Let it be done" he filled the heavenly vault with stars; he let the sun shine during the day, and the moon and innumerable stars at night. In all these wonderful works of creation God revealed his everlasting mercy; for it was for the sake of man that all these things were made. This divine love, which reveals itself in nature, man should consider and he should manifest his love in return by his gratitude and praise of God. The people answered the precantor at every call with holy admiration: "And his mercy endureth forever."

In the second part of the litany the psalmist commemorates the mercy of God as revealed in the history of Israel (verses 10–22). The first great work of divine mercy toward Israel was the deliverance from the Egyptian captivity. The psalmist recalls the killing of the Egyptian first-born which forced Pharaoh to allow the Israelites to depart. When Pharaoh repented for having allowed the Israelites passage, he with his troops pursued them having the intention of bringing them back by force. But the Lord divided the waters of the Red Sea and led the Israelites dry-footed upon the bed of the sea and when the Egyptian army followed them in hot pursuit, the Lord commanded the waves and they engulfed the pursuers. Great and many were the miracles which God worked during the desert journey in order to feed his people. When Israel recalled these miracles and read in the pages of history about the obstinacy of the people in those days and how they provoked the wrath of God because of their ingratitude and infidelity, they realized with what patience the Lord endured their unfaithfulness and praised God's mercy which was not only rich in giving but also in forgiving.

Rich in miraculous manifestations of divine power and love was also the history of the conquest of Canaan. It was God's work, and not a success which Israel attained by its own strength. It was Yahwe who slew mighty kings. The conquest of Jericho, the victory over the united Amorrhite kings by Josue in the battle at Gabaon, and many other victories were attained through the extraordinary help of God. As in the previous psalm so also this litany mentions only two conquered kings of the territory east of the Jordan, King Sehon and King Og of Basan, whose territories were settled by the tribes of Ruben, Gad, and Manasses. The land conquered in Canaan the Lord gave over to his people as a lasting inheritance.

Even after taking possession of Canaan, God's loving providence for his people did not cease. He, indeed, had to punish them often for their unfaithfulness and permit them to be harassed by their pagan neighbors, but when they called upon him for help he was mindful of their needs and delivered them from adversity. Yahwe also looked after their corporal needs and gave them rich harvests so that they would not starve. The Christian can enlarge this litany; for at all times he receives proofs of the eternal mercy of God and can add to the litany new verses until the end of time. The last verse and the last cry of "His mercy endureth forever . . ." are additions to the original psalm.

psalm 136

Super flumina

The lamentation of the people of God in their captivity in Babylon

A PSALM OF DAVID FOR JEREMIAS

1. Upon the rivers of Babylon, there we sat and wept: when we remembered Sion.

2. On the willows in the midst thereof we hung our instruments.

3. For there they that led us into captivity required of us the words of songs. And they that carried us away said: Sing ye to us a hymn of the songs of Sion.

4. How shall we sing the song of the Lord in a strange land?

5. If I forget thee, O Jerusalem, let my right hand be forgotten.

6. Let my tongue cleave to my jaws, if I do not remember thee: if I make not Jerusalem the beginning of my joy.

7. Remember, O Lord, the children of Edom, in the day of Jerusalem. Who say, rase it, rase it, even to the foundation thereof.

8. O daughter of Babylon, miserable: blessed shall he be who shall repay thee thy payment which thou hast paid us.

9. Blessed be he that shall take and dash thy little ones against the rock.

THERE may have been many Israelites who gradually felt themselves at home in their banishment because they found good income in this strange land. These forgot not only their native land but also Jerusalem, the holy city; they forgot their temple and the solemn divine services. The forty-two thousand that returned home at the end of the exile did not belong to this indifferent class. The vow of everlasting remembrance is spoken sincerely (verses 1–6). Those in banishment had constructed houses of prayer, synagogues. They had built them on the shores of the rivers or near the Babylonian canals because of the duties of the levitical purifications. There they sat on the ground like those who mourned for the dead and shed tears when they thought of Jerusalem, its temple, and its glorious feasts. They had no love for the glory of Babylon, for the beauty of its palaces, and for the pomp of its festivities in honor of the gods. The gatherings in their own places of worship could be likened to mournings for the dead. The jubilant songs of the psalms were not sung; the harps which accompanied these songs were silent. They hung on the poplars which grew on the shores of the Euphrates. Only plaintive sounds were heard from them when the wind struck their strings. Even the harp wept. The Babylonians could not understand such mourning; they could not understand why the captives did not sing the solemn hymns in honor of their God. The government did not prohibit the worship of Yahwe. Therefore they should make use of this privilege and sing the songs of Sion in the land of their captivity. The Gentiles could not understand that only in one place in the world could sacrifice be offered to Yahwe; that with the destruction of Jerusalem and the temple a deadly blow had been struck to the religious life of Israel; that the songs which had been sung at the celebration of the sacred sacrifices had lost their religious meaning without the sacrifices.

It was impossible for the Israelites who were so attached to their sanctuary to surrender to the solicitations of the Babylonians. They must have considered it a desecration of these songs if they should sing them in pagan lands. They must have considered it a sin against the holy city of Jerusalem and its temple if in their captivity they would sing these sacred songs. But they had not entirely forgotten Sion, its sanctuary, and its liturgical sacrifice. They could not and would not forget Jerusalem. The negative answer to the request of the Babylonians could be the only one which they gave. They raised their right hand for an oath of fidelity. If we ever forget Jerusalem and play the harp in heathen lands and sing

Sion's festive songs in captivity, then let my right hand be forgotten and the service of harp playing cease, then let my tongue cleave to my jaws so that my throat may not give forth a sound and that it may not be able to sing sacred songs. It is better to be dumb and lame for life than to be satisfied with a substitute. Jerusalem must remain the greatest joy for Israel, and no other joy can replace it.

The exiled raised their hands in oath never to forget Sion. They extend them now in prayer, beseeching the Lord not to forget his prophetic threats to be visited upon those who had disturbed Jerusalem and his sanctuary. Thus the prayer demanding satisfaction for the crime committed against Sion follows closely upon the oath (verses 7–9). The prophets who had foretold the Babylonian exile and the fall of Jerusalem, had also announced the judgment which was to be meted out upon the enemy. The Prophet Ezechiel (33:15) declared the punishment which was to come upon the Edomites who had mischievously welcomed the fall of Jerusalem and the exile of the Jewish brethren. May the Lord now be mindful of this threat and may he carry it out against the people so full of hatred for Israel. The judgment upon Babylon was announced by God through the Prophet Isaias (Chap. 13) and Jeremias (Chap. 50 seq.). The victor would have no sympathy for the children of Babylon; according to the then prevailing cruel custom of war, the complete destruction of an enemy involved also the dreadful destruction of its progeny. The psalmist prays that the Lord bring unto fulfillment this threatened judgment upon Babylon. The crushing of the children is an oft recurring biblical image for the uprooting of the progeny (4 Kings 8:12; Nah. 3:10) which considering the cruelty of pagan arms and warfare could very well be brought into full realization. The Prophet Nahum (3:10) threatens the city of Nineveh with the crushing of its children.

In the mouth of the Christian this psalm is an oath of loyalty for the Church and a longing for the heavenly Jerusalem in the midst of a world of allurement and seduction; it is a prayer that God may humble the enemies of the Church.

psalm 137

Confitebor tibi

Thanksgiving to God for his benefits

FOR DAVID HIMSELF

1. I will praise thee, O Lord, with my whole heart: for thou hast heard the words of my mouth. I will sing praise to thee in the sight of the angels.

2. I will worship toward thy holy temple, and I will give glory to thy name. For thy mercy, and for thy truth: for thou hast magnified thy holy name above all.

3. In what day soever I shall call upon thee, hear me: thou shalt multiply strength in my soul.

4. May all the kings of the earth give glory to thee: for they have heard all the words of thy mouth.

5. And let them sing in the ways of the Lord: for great is the glory of the Lord.

6. For the Lord is high, and looketh on the low: and the high he knoweth afar off.

7. If I shall walk in the midst of tribulation, thou wilt quicken me: and thou hast stretched forth thy hand against the wrath of my enemies: and thy right hand hath saved me.

8. The Lord will repay for me: thy mercy, O Lord, endureth forever: O despise not the works of thy hands.

Tʜᴇ history of Israel records on its pages many grave tribulations that fell upon the people, but it also records the many beneficent deeds of the Lord by which he, being mindful of his mercy and fidelity, miraculously liberated his people. The psalmist speaks in the name of all. He thanks God for his mercy and fidelity (verses 1–3). His heart is grateful; at every pulse of his heart he would give thanks and praise. When the Lord has done such great things for his nation, his soul cannot be satisfied by praying within closed doors. He is impelled to go to the house of God. In the place where the Almighty has his throne, where he is surrounded by myriads of angels in the Most Holy, there he wishes to sing his "Te Deum." The psalmist is not one of those who only go to the house of God when trouble prompts a hasty prayer. Here in the sanctuary where God

520

in his mercy blesses the people, here where a pious man is inclined to pray so well, here where the angels sing *Hosanna* unceasingly he will praise the name of the most high God. Here he will thank the Lord for the wonderful manifestations of his mercy and love. Again the Lord has made his name great above all names. Of what significance are the names of renowned kings even when they rule world empires? Of what significance are their deeds in comparison with the great deeds of the Lord? On the day when the people cried to the Lord, he heard them and freed them from all adversity and gave them new strength and courage.

Israel was not only obligated to the God of the covenant, but was also obligated to the Gentile world because of that covenant and its Gentile mission. Therefore Israel should not be satisfied if God is worshiped by its people alone; the Gentiles also should praise Yahwe (verses 4–6). Therefore the psalmist combines the praise of the Lord with the petition that all nations may praise him. All kings of the world shall praise the Lord because they have learned the words of the Lord from his mouth; that is, his revelations and promises. They should praise the acts of the Lord, his wonderful, powerful, and kind providence and the way it revealed itself in the history of the people of the covenant. They should praise his divine decree of salvation and the means he used to fulfill it. The psalmist expresses his thoughts in a song of praise. Great is the majesty of the Lord. God is supreme. His greatness reveals itself in this, that he does not consider so much what seems great in the eyes of men but that he condescends to the little and lowly. For this reason he chose the little nation of Israel and not one of the world empires of antiquity. Those who think themselves great are little before God.

Every great deed of God is not only a gift but also a responsibility for the recipient; it demands a strengthening of faith and of confidence in God's mercy and fidelity; it is an advance payment for the complete fulfillment of the divine promises. The psalmist is filled with this spirit; for he has the confidence that God will complete his work (verses 7–8). Even if the people must endure troubled times, he knows for certain that God will not permit Israel to be exterminated. When God raises his right hand, the wrath of the enemy will be of no avail. God's might right hand will save his people and his kingdom. It is not God's way of acting to let his work incomplete and to abandon it because of difficulties which his enemies put in his way. He continues with his work and his plans to the very end. He will also finish those plans that he has in mind about Israel and his Church. The love and grace of God are not limited by time, but are eternal. He does not give up his own people. Since he loves all that he has made, this is especially true about his people and his kingdom which he has established and claims as his particular possession.

psalm 138

Domine, probasti

God's special providence over his servants

1. Unto the end, a psalm of David.
   Lord thou hast proved me, and known me:

2. Thou hast known my sitting down and my rising up.

3. Thou hast understood my thoughts afar off: my path and my line thou hast searched out.

4. And thou hast foreseen all my ways: for there is no speech in my tongue.

5. Behold, O Lord, thou hast known all things, the last and those of old: thou hast formed me, and hast laid thy hand upon me.

6. Thy knowledge is become wonderful to me: it is high, and I cannot reach it.

7. Whither shall I go from thy spirit? Or whither shall I flee from thy face?

8. If I ascend into heaven, thou art there: if I descend into hell, thou art present.

9. If I take my wings early in the morning, and dwell in the uttermost parts of the sea:

10. Even there also shall thy hand lead me: and thy right hand shall hold me.

11. And I said: Perhaps darkness shall cover me: and night shall be my light in my pleasures.

12. But darkness shall not be dark to thee, and night shall be light as the day: the darkness thereof, and the light thereof are alike to thee.

13. For thou hast possessed my reins: thou hast protected me from my mother's womb.

14. I will praise thee, for thou art fearfully magnified: wonderful are thy works, and my soul knoweth right well.

15. My bone is not hidden from thee, which thou hast made in secret; and my substance in the lower parts of the earth.

16. Thy eyes did see my imperfect being, and in thy book all shall be written: days shall be formed, and no one in them.

17. But to me thy friends, O God, are made exceedingly honorable: their principality is exceedingly strengthened.

18. I will number them, and they shall be multiplied above the sand: I rose up and am still with thee.

19. If thou wilt kill the wicked, O God: ye men of blood, depart from me.

20. Because you say in thought: they shall receive thy cities in vain.

21. Have I not hated them, O Lord, that hated thee: and pined away because of thy enemies?

22. I have hated them with a perfect hatred: and they are become enemies to me.

23. Prove me, O Lord, and know my heart: examine me, and know my paths.

24. And see if there be in me the way of iniquity: and lead me in the eternal way.

THIS psalm shows a loftiness and depth of concept about God which alone gives Israel a unique place among all the people of the ancient world. It glorifies God not only in his perfections but also investigates the relations of the divine perfections one to another. The song begins with the perfection of the divine knowledge and shows its causal relation to the omnipresent God. Both perfections are explained by the causality of God. From this the psalmist argues that man has the duty of submitting himself entirely to God.

God is omniscient. Jesus Sirach says: "And he knoweth that the eyes of the Lord are far brighter than the sun, beholding round about all the ways of men, and the bottom of the deep, and looking into the hearts of men, into the most hidden parts. For all things were known to the Lord God, before they were created: so also after they were perfected he beholdeth all things" (Jesus Sirach 23:28–29). No matter how large the number of men is, no matter how manifold their peculiarities and their history are, God knows them all and knows thoroughly every individual and searches the innermost recesses of the heart. Before him there are no mysteries. He knows the sitting and standing of men; he knows man in his entire life, his activities, and omissions. The thoughts of men are known to him. He searches them from the unlimited heights of heaven; they are before his eyes in every detail. His penetrating view pierces the most secret recesses of the human heart. Just as he knows the inner life of man so also he knows his external acts, his activities, and omissions. He knows the ways of all sons of men: how they are and where they go. He knows the obstacles put in their way and their difficulties. He probes their rest, their entertainments, their joys and pleasures. He tests everything according to its value. Nothing remains hidden before God. He knows every individual's conduct of life and the way of life of the many millions; he is also acquainted with my way of life. God knows every word that I speak or have spoken even before I uttered the words. May they be a hundred million words that are daily spoken by men, not a word escapes his knowledge nor his judgment; for the Lord encompasses all. In him we live and move and have our being. He has laid his hand upon everyone. With the laying on of hands he claims man as his possession (Sirach 23:28). He is the Creator and therefore the Lord of his creatures. The omniscience of God is marvelous; it comprises not only the thoughts and words of all men, their acts and omissions; it also comprises all creatures, all the millions of living beings of the plant and animal world; all creatures that are so small that man's eye cannot see them except by manifold enlargement. Such knowledge surpasses all human comprehension.

God is present everywhere (verses 7–12). In a picturesque description the psalmist goes through the universe to see where man can conceal himself from God. Where may he go in order that he may not be observed by God? Where may he flee in order not to be seen by God's eye? There is no place in this wide world. If man ascends into heaven, he will find God; for heaven is his dwelling place. If he goes in the opposite direction into the depths of the underworld, into the kingdom of the dead in order to remain there, he does not escape God. The living God is also in the kingdom of the dead. The souls live there by his power and will. If man could take wings and fly to the east where the sun rises on the distant horizon and the morning dawn appears, or if he could fly to the opposite end of the earth, to the extreme end of the sea in the west, the Lord is both in the extreme end of the west and east. Even there at the ends of the earth God guides man by his divine providence and there he stands with his eternal decrees. Indeed, man could not even go there without being sustained and directed by his hand. There is no place in the universe in which man can escape from God. But just as little as an escape is possible in the height and depth or to the east and west, so little is it possible to escape God in extreme darkness. If black night surrounds man as the light of the sun encompasses him during the day; if the night is so dark that his eyes cannot see his hand, God sees him nevertheless. The night is a creation just as the light of the day; God himself has created the change from light to darkness, from day to night. God is the lord of the change; he has not lost his sight because of the night. The difference is only for man. For the eyes of God there is no difference between light and darkness, between day and night.

God is the cause of all (verses 13–18). To the psalmist the greatest reason for God's omniscience is that he is the cause of all things. Man, as well as every animated creature, has received his existence from the Creator and indeed even at the first moment of his existence in the womb of the mother. The poet speaks reverently about man's mysterious coming into existence in the womb of the mother. It is the work of the wisdom, miraculous power, and love of God. He is so enthusiastic about this work that he discontinues his meditation with a song of praise to the Creator: "I praise thee because thou art astonishingly great; wonderful are thy works, this my soul knows well." God is astonishingly great not only in his gigantic works, but also in the formative power by which he makes man. When the child in the womb of the mother had no consciousness, the Lord made it and formed it and the parents were only the instruments; for it is God who had created the mysterious workshop in the womb of the mother. The psalmist describes the becoming of man not according to the laws of nature, but in the simple language of a pious meditation. The depths of the earth signify the hidden darkness of the mother's womb because the event takes place unseen as if it took place in the depths of the earth. All advance in biological knowledge has not as yet unveiled the mystery of life, and we must therefore praise God because he is so astoundingly great in fabricating men in the womb of their mother. Even in his incomplete condition God's eye saw the little child. The circumstances in his life were already known to him; they already, as it were, were entered into the book of divine predestination. Every day was already known to God before the child lived its first day, before it saw the light of day. Every day was included in the plans of the divine Providence.

To thoroughly understand the perfections of the divine Being and his works is beyond man's ability. What we see is only the beginning of God's activity; we are only at the edge of God's ways. But even the little that man's intellect can comprehend is so precious to his soul that he does not tire of thinking about it and searching into it. Yet he who would keep on meditating upon thoughts of the Eternal and count them would never come to an end. God's works are more numerous than the sands on the seashore and the sands in the desert. God's nature and his works are so fascinating that a thoughtful man goes to rest thinking about them and is again occupied with thoughts of them at his awakening. He who is once truly occupied and enthusiastic about the knowledge of God's greatness will always think of it.

If God is the sole cause of man's existence, then man belongs entirely to him and the duty rests upon him to surrender himself entirely to God because he belongs to him (verses 19–24). In view of God's greatness how wicked the haters of God must appear to all others. With such, he who believes in God and loves him may not have intercourse. The close of the psalm is therefore a solemn denunciation of all the enemies of God; for he who is an enemy of God is also the enemy of the just man. He who hates and despises the most high God has lost the right to live. How can a man dare to resist the divine Truth and contradict the divine Will? What justifiable reason can man give to justify his rebellion or to excuse himself? He who loves God must hate what God hates. The hatred of God is turned against the evil, not against him who does the evil deed. The psalmist however does not differentiate between error and the erring insofar as he knows that God's punishment will come upon such men, that they will be cast out into an eternal Godless void where the love of God will cease forever. Those who are enemies of God cannot have the joy of the just; there is no relation between darkness and light, between Belial and the Lord. The psalmist therefore considers the godless as his adversaries. He has such little love for them and their wicked deeds that he can challenge the all-knowing God to search his heart to find whether he has any inclination in his soul to their deeds. If the Lord probes his conduct, he will find that he stays away from the path of iniquity. It would however be presumptuous to rely too much on his own strength to keep away from sin. God's grace must lead him on the path of justice and virtue, the path that leads him to his eternal destiny. Thus the psalmist closes with the petition that God may lead him.

psalm 139

Eripe me, Domine

A prayer to be delivered from the wicked

1. Unto the end, a psalm of David.

2. Deliver me, O Lord, from the evil man: rescue me from the unjust man.

3. Who have devised iniquities in their hearts: all the day long they designed battles.

4. They have sharpened their tongues like a serpent: the venom of asps is under their lips.

5. Keep me, O Lord, from the hand of the wicked: and from unjust men deliver me. Who have proposed to supplant my steps.

6. The proud have hidden a net for me, and they have stretched out cords for a snare: they have laid for me a stumbling block by the wayside.

7. I said to the Lord: Thou art my God: hear, O Lord, the voice of my supplication.

8. O Lord, Lord, the strength of my salvation: thou hast overshadowed my head in the day of battle.

9. Give me not up, O Lord, from my desire to the wicked: they have plotted against me: do not thou forsake me, lest they should triumph.

10. The head of them compassing me about: the labor of their lips shall overwhelm them.

11. Burning coals shall fall upon them: thou wilt cast them down into the fire: in miseries they shall not be able to stand.

12. A man full of tongue shall not be established in the earth: evil shall catch the unjust man unto destruction.

13. I know that the Lord will do justice to the needy, and will revenge the poor.

14. But as for the just, they shall give glory to thy name: and the upright shall dwell with thy countenance.

David had to suffer much from the insinuations and calumny of his enemies, Saul and his followers, before he entered upon his kingdom and later from Absalom and his associates. Against the treacherous attacks of a calumniating tongue even a king is powerless because the wrong is done in secret. But God does not let the enemy triumph over the just. The psalmist speaks of the malice of calumny and of the fate of calumniators.

First of all the psalmist gives a description of the evil of calumny (verses 2–6). Men who rob others of their good reputation by secret and treacherous whispering, by calumny and lies are very dangerous because the calumniated person cannot very easily defend himself against them. The defense is altogether impossible when the enemy remains unknown and cannot be confronted, when the lies come too late to the ears of the person attacked and he already feels the effects of the secret whisperings. Then only God who knows all can help. Therefore the psalmist begs God to keep him from the attacks of wicked men who unscrupulously undermine the honor of others. Everywhere they start quarrels and dissatisfaction by casting suspicions, and cause animosities by inciting men to have hatred one against the other. Their entire thinking and planning are directed to do evil to all whom they hate. Like the poisonous bite of the serpent calumny pierces the soul of the calumniated and like the poison of the snake it permeates the soul of the persecuted, dangerous as the glow of fever. One can defend himself against an enemy who fights with honest weapons and openly. But the detractors are often hypocrites, double-tongued persons, who in their hearts plan destruction but with their mouth speak in a friendly manner. They are genial to a hated face, but they think of nothing else than to use every means possible to bring about the downfall of those whom they despise. It makes no difference to them what means they use. In their malice they lay slings, and nets, and traps in the way in order that they may surely catch their victim and bring about his downfall. The many pictures or descriptions should give expression to their restless and passionate endeavors.

God to whom every lie is an abomination cannot let the conduct of such men go unpunished. He has also announced his judgment upon them. The psalmist begs that the punishment of the calumniators will come to pass (verses 7–12). Full of confidence the persecuted turns to God, his Lord. Being infinitely holy, God must hate and punish all falsehood. Being infinitely just, God must defend and give right to persecuted innocence; for he is the supreme Judge and the Advocate of the oppressed. Because he is the infinitely faithful God, the God of the covenant, he must fulfill his promises and give the blessings which he has promised to those who fear him; he must also punish the godless whom he has threatened to chastise. He who is calumniated also turns to the Lord because he has hitherto shown himself to be a strong helper and has proved himself to be a shield in all battles. The confidence in a helper is at the same time a thankful remembrance and an acknowledgment of frequent past helps. It also gives the greatest hope that his cry for help to God will not remain unheard.

In the faith and confidence that God's love and readiness to help has not diminished, the psalmist now prays that the Lord may also deliver him from his present enemies. God cannot and will not permit that evil men in their passionate desire to destroy others will have that desire satisfied; he cannot allow their godless plans to succeed; he cannot grant them triumph over the just. The petitioner expects with a certainty that judgment will be passed according to the principle that the godless should be punished with that wherewith they have sinned. The misery which they have planned for others will finally fall upon their own heads. Their lying and detractions will be for them their own destruction. By the divine judgment they will fall and the just will triumph. The Lord will rain glowing coals upon them; they will be hurled into fire; tremendous floods will come upon them and will drown them. These are all pictures of a strong and inescapable divine judgment. The calumniators have deserved a severe judgment; therefore it will surely come. The Lord does not let them continue on earth; he who attacks the just and the anointed of the Lord will come to an infamous end. He who commits atrocities will come to a violent end. He will be cast into the abyss; for liars and detractors cannot enter into the kingdom of heaven.

Because God hates the calumniator, the psalmist is sure that God will assist him who is calumniated and that he will hear his prayer. Therefore he closes his psalm with a confession of his confidence (verses 13–14). God himself will take in hand the affairs of the weak and persecuted and will not leave them unprotected against the power of the godless. He protects the poor. He is their advocate and mighty defender. Therefore the just do not give up hope even when they have to suffer calumny and persecution. They will rather praise God who permits only him to become a victim of calumny who has abandoned God (Ecclesiasticus 28:26). The godless he will hurl into the abyss, but the righteous he will accept into the assembly of God. They even now enjoy the graces of this assembly and hope to enjoy it in its fullness in Messianic times.

psalm 140

Domine, clamavi

A prayer against sinful words, and deceitful flatterers

A PSALM FOR DAVID

1. I have cried to thee, O Lord, hear me: hearken to my voice, when I cry to thee.

2. Let my prayer be directed as incense in thy sight: the lifting up of my hands, as evening sacrifice.

3. Set a watch, O Lord, before my mouth, and a door round about my lips.

4. Incline not my heart to evil words: to make excuses in sins.
   With men that work iniquity: and I will not communicate with the choicest of them.

5. The just man shall correct me in mercy, and shall reprove me: but let not the oil of the sinner fatten my head.

529

For my prayer also shall still be against the things with which they are well pleased.

6. Their judges falling upon the rock have been swallowed up. They shall hear my words, for they have prevailed.

7. As when the thickness of the earth is broken up upon the ground. Our bones are scattered by the side of hell.

8. But to thee, O Lord, Lord are my eyes: in thee have I put my trust, take not away my soul.

9. Keep me from the snare which they have laid for me, and from the stumbling blocks of them that work iniquity.

10. The wicked shall fall in his net: I am alone until I pass.

H E WHO walks the way of the fear of the Lord must prepare himself for trials and temptations. Therefore Jesus Sirach tells us: "Son when thou comest to the service of God, stand in justice and in fear, and prepare thy soul for temptation" (Sirach 2:1). The Lord will not permit that anyone be tempted beyond his strength; but he demands that he who is tempted pray for strength from above and that he gird himself with the weapon of prayer against the tempter. On this account Christ admonishes his disciples: "Watch and pray that you fall not into temptation" (Matthew 26:41). The psalmist also has recourse to prayer. But if God would deny his assistance, the fall would be inevitable. Prayer however receives a hearing from the Lord only when it is pleasing to him. But such a prayer too is a grace of God. Therefore the psalmist prays: "Let my prayer be pleasing to thee as the odor of the daily incense offering. Look upon my prayer which I perform with outstretched hands as pleasant in thy sight as the evening sacrifice which the priest offers daily on the altar of holocaust in the court of the temple. The psalmist asks God for two graces; namely, to be preserved from sin and for strength to suffer rather than to take part in sinful pleasures.

Man by himself is too weak to resist all temptations. He may not rely on his own strength alone. Therefore he must pray for strength to resist temptation (verses 3–4). He is surrounded by treacherous and powerful enemies who seek to bring about his downfall. Often a harsh word forces itself to his lips against his aggressor; often a curse lies on his tongue, or perhaps a murmur against God. The temptation to speak an uncharitable word is often so strong that only God's help can keep us from sin. Therefore may the Lord by his grace place a guard before the mouth that no unrighteous word may escape from it; may he place a watchman before the lips that they cannot open for sinful speech. May the Lord remove the danger to sin at its very source, may he curb in the soul every inclination to sin that it may not besmirch the soul with crime as it does those godless men who indulge in sinful pleasures.

When the psalmist sees that he is confronted with the choice of faithful service in patient suffering or sinful license in godless pleasures, he would rather suffer than sin (verses 5–6). The just God may strike him and discipline him out of love. He may let tribulation come upon him. Such chastisements that have their source in the love of God, and not in God's punitive justice, will be patiently borne. The ointment of sinners shall never come upon his head. This description wishes to say that he does not want to partake in sinful pleasures. Therefore his prayer is directed against the wickedness of sinners. He begs that enticements and temptations may not overwhelm him and bring about his downfall. The happiness of the godless is only a fleeting sham of worldly fabric which at the end of time will be rent with God's punishment. The leaders of the sinners will be hurled down from a cliff. It is said that in Jewish times those condemned to death were first hurled down from a cliff and then stoned. Perhaps here too punishment by stoning is intimated. When God's punishment falls upon them suddenly, they will find that the prayer of the persecuted was pleasing to God and indeed obtained a hearing.

Man's life is surrounded with dangers, yet confidence in God's help will not permit him to abandon hope (verses 7–10). As at plowing, the torn lumps lie at the edge of the furrows, so man lies at the edge of the underworld; at any moment he may be hurled into it and become the prey of the kingdom of the dead. During our life we are confronted by death. But the psalmist is not despondent. He believes in God, in the fidelity of Yahwe who does not abandon the just man. Full of confidence he directs his eyes toward heaven and prays: "Do not give my soul to the enemy; do not take my life." Everywhere the enemy has spread his nets; everywhere he has placed traps along the way and laid snares so that the just man is in danger at every step of being tangled in the net or of falling into a trap and of becoming a victim of the enemy. May the Lord keep him from such dangers and may he according to the norms of his justice tangle the godless in their own nets and pitfalls. When they themselves will fall into them while the just man escapes, they must acknowledge that the Lord protects his own.

psalm 141

Voce mea

A prayer of David in extremity of danger

1. Of understanding for David. A prayer when he was in the cave. (1 Kings 24).

2. I cried to the Lord with my voice: with my voice I made supplication to the Lord.

3. In his sight I pour out my prayer, and before him I declare my trouble.

4. When my spirit failed me, then thou knewest my paths.
   In this way wherein I walked, they have hidden a snare for me.

5. I looked on my right hand, and beheld, and there was no one that would know me.
   Flight hath failed me: and there is no one that hath regard to my soul.

6. I cried to thee, O Lord: I said: Thou art my hope, my portion in the land of the living.

7. Attend to my supplication: for I am brought very low.
   Deliver me from my persecutors; for they are stronger than I.

8. Bring my soul out of prison, that I may praise thy name: the just wait for me, until thou reward me.

DAVID saw himself pursued by Saul like a hunted beast. Wherever he took refuge there were men who betrayed him to Saul. Finally he concealed himself in the caves of the wilderness of Engaddi near the Dead Sea. But there too Saul pursued him with three thousand warriors. Only a miracle from God could save David from sure death. In that hour of the greatest danger of death the superscription places this psalm. It is a cry for help in the hour of need when all human assistance is of no avail and when the soul must rely on God's help alone.

Being abandoned by all men in his greatest need was David's condition at the time of this prayer. His heart was filled with the deepest sorrow; he could no longer remain silent (verses 2–5). As one who is in danger of death cries out for help that someone may hear and help, so David cries to God, his Lord; for God has promised to hear the cry of those who in all confidence turn to him for help. God indeed knows about his need, but his soul must pour out his troubles before him and weep in order to find rest. Thus the psalmist lays his complaint before God as a child before his father. In his prayer he wishes to place upon God the burden that rests upon him that he might take it away. To whom should man have recourse in such need when the spirit languishes, when from minute to minute hope for deliverance vanishes because there is no escape, no help in sight? God knows the situation; he knows also the means of escape. Men only seek his destruction. It matters not which way he goes. Wherever he flees to obtain safety snares are laid to bring about his fall. From men no help is to be expected; there is no advocate to defend him and to take care of his affairs. In Israel the defender at a court trial stood at the right of the accused. Nobody wishes to stand at his right side to defend him against the calumnies of the enemy. Indeed, no one wants to have anything to do with him. No friend shows himself; no refuge is left to him; he stands abandoned and alone in his need.

Men have forsaken him, but not the Lord. In his need he clings to God (verses 6–8). God is a sure protection; he is a secure refuge; he is ready to receive everyone. Against him who seeks protection from God all the enemies can do nothing. Anyone may seek protection from the Lord when he is his portion during life, when he is united to God by faith in him and true love for him. As long as man is united with God and seeks his joy and happiness with him, as long as this portion is not lost to him, so long does he have powerful protection from him. When the Lord stands by him, who shall prevail against him? With this faith and confidence the psalmist prays. Strength leaves him more and more and he seems to break down in the face of the persecutions and temptations. The enemies are stronger; they have powerful means at their disposal which are not at the disposal of the defenseless. They now use these powers because they believe that their success is near. But God is more powerful. He takes away the weapons from the powerful enemies and makes them helpless. Surrounded by the enemy, oppressed by anxieties and affliction, the soul feels as if it were locked in a prison. But God can open the prison and break the fetters. May he do so. Then the redeemed will be eternally thankful to him and praise his name. May he do it for the sake of the just who place their hope in the Lord. They expect God to save his anointed from the danger of death. This will be for them a great consolation when they will experience a similar situation; it will be an assurance for them when they are in the danger of death.

psalm 142

Domine, exaudi

The psalmist in tribulation calleth upon God for his delivery.
The seventh penitential psalm

1. A psalm of David, when his son Absalom pursued him (2 Kings 17).
   Hear, O Lord, my prayer: give ear to my supplication in thy truth: hear me in thy justice.

2. And enter not into judgment with thy servant: for in thy sight no man living shall be justified.

3. For the enemy hath persecuted my soul: he hath brought down my life to the earth.
   He hath made me dwell in darkness as those that have been dead of old.

4. And my spirit is in anguish within me: my heart within me is troubled.

5. I remembered the days of old, I meditated upon all thy works: I meditated upon the works of thy hands.

6. I stretched forth my hands to thee: my soul is as earth without water unto thee.

7. Hear me speedily, O Lord: my spirit hath fainted away.
   Turn not thy face away from me, lest I be like unto them that go down into the pit.

8. Cause me to hear thy mercy in the morning: for in thee have I hoped.
   Make the way known to me, wherein I should walk: for I have lifted up my soul to thee.

9. Deliver me from my enemies, O Lord, to thee have I fled.

10. Teach me to do thy will, for thou art my God. Thy good spirit shall lead me into the right land.

11. For thy name's sake, O Lord, thou wilt quicken me in thy justice. Thou wilt bring my soul out of trouble.

12. And in thy mercy thou wilt destroy my enemies. And thou wilt cut off all them that afflict my soul: for I am thy servant.

THE last of the seven ecclesiastical penitential psalms is according to the superscription likewise ascribed to David; a decisive motive, however, cannot be recognized in the psalm. The psalmist is in great distress; his enemies afflict him severely. He knows that because of his great transgression he has deserved punishment, but he relies on God's fidelity which will not deny pardon to a penitent sinner.

In the first strophe (verses 1–6) he beseeches the Lord: "Be not a judge to me." Numerous are the expressions that God does not wish the death of the sinner but that he does wish that he may be converted and live. Therefore he directs his prayer to the faithful God who has said this, to the just God who does not wish his damnation but his salvation. If the Lord would deal according to strict justice, what man could continue to exist? How could anyone obtain salvation? Because before the infinitely holy God no man is just, but is rather a sinner, weak and poor in merits; God must permit his mercy to prevail. Mercy and help are needed; for the external and internal affliction is great. The enemy harassed his soul and his temporal and supernatural life in order to harm him and to corrupt him. He threatens his life; he strives to cast him into the darkness of eternal death. The psalmist's heart is sick because of fear; his mind is confused; he knows no way of escaping the danger. He now directs his thoughts to the past. From a meditation upon the divine love which revealed itself in the history of the patriarchs, a longing for this love and hope should grow. Thus the psalmist calls back to memory the wonderful deeds which the Lord has done in times past in order to deliver the Fathers from great afflictions. This meditation creates a longing for divine mercy, strengthens faith in divine forgiveness and a confidence in God's help. In his consciousness of guilt the psalmist extends his hands in prayer to the merciful God; his soul yearns for proofs of the divine love and grace like parched land thirsting for rain.

In the second strophe (verses 7–12) the psalmist beseeches the Lord: "Be to me a Saviour." The need is great; speedy help is necessary for the mind is in great distress. All strength has vanished; all energy has been exhausted; the mind is darkened; the eyes are blurred. When God turns away his countenance, when he withdraws from the sinner his grace and mercy, then his collapse is sealed. He is like those who have been buried in the grave. The psalmist asks for three favors. The first is that the Lord may not disappoint him in his confidence and that he will again show mercy. It is impossible that God should destroy the hope of a poor man who seeks deliverance through him alone and seeks refuge with him. God would then have forgotten himself and his word. The second grace is knowledge of the way which the petitioner should walk. The end for which God created man is beyond his natural understanding. The way to

535

the end God alone knows. He alone can direct us on the way. He is the way to happiness and peace. The third grace is deliverance from the power of the enemy. Here too only the almighty power of God can deliver us. The psalmist sought refuge with God as a criminal seeks refuge in a free city of asylum. God cannot send him away; he cannot leave him without protection against his enemies. He will protect him.

To be worthy of the divine help man must walk the way of the divine commands; he must do God's will. "Not everyone who says to me, 'Lord, Lord!' shall enter into the kingdom of heaven, but everyone who does the will of my Father," says Christ (Matthew 7:21). But not only does the knowledge of God's will require divine teaching, but the walking on the way also demands divine guidance through God's grace. It is God who has given the law which cannot be observed without his revelation and grace. God therefore must give his grace. His divine spirit must lead man on the right path in order that man may not err from that path and lose himself in the labyrinth of error. "May God teach for his name's sake." Sanctity comes from God only; virtue is practiced only with the aid of God's grace. If God wishes to be glorified by man, he must give man the ability to lead a just and virtuous life. It is then an affair of God's honor to guide all who are of good will on the path of virtue and to fulfill the promises of salvation. Because of his love may he destroy the enemy of the petitioner; for he is his servant.

psalm 143

Benedictus Dominus

The prophet praises God and prays to be delivered from his enemies; no worldly happiness is to be compared with that of serving God

A PSALM OF DAVID AGAINST GOLIATH

1. Blessed be the Lord my God, who teacheth my hands to fight and my fingers to war.

2. My mercy, and my refuge: my support and my deliverer.
   My protector and I have hoped in him: who subdueth my people under me.

3. Lord, what is man, that thou art made known to him? Or the son of man, that thou makest account of him?

4. Man is like to vanity: his days pass away like a shadow.

5. Lord, bow down thy heavens and descend: touch the mountains, and they shall smoke.

6. Send forth lightning, and thou shalt scatter them: shoot out thy arrows, and thou shalt trouble them.

7. Put forth thy hand from on high, take me out, and deliver me from many waters: from the hand of strange children.

8. Whose mouth hath spoken vanity: and their right hand is the right hand of iniquity.

9. To thee, O Lord, I will sing a new canticle: on the psaltery and an instrument of ten strings, I will sing praises to thee.

10. Who givest salvation to kings: who hast redeemed thy servant David from the malicious sword.

11. Deliver me.
And rescue me out of the hand of strange children: whose mouth hath spoken vanity: and their right hand is the right hand of iniquity.

12. Whose sons are as new plants in their youth.
Their daughters decked out, adorned round about after the similitude of a temple.

13. Their storehouses full, flowing out of this into that.
Their sheep fruitful in young, abounding in their goings forth:

14. Their oxen fat.
There is no breach of wall, nor passage, nor crying out in their streets.

15. They have called the people happy, that hath these things: but happy is that people whose God is the Lord.

VERSES 1–11 of this psalm are a compilation of Davidic psalm verses. Only the closing verses are the writer's own and have a Messianic character. The lack of originality does not speak against Davidic authorship for no composer is forbidden to quote himself. But the psalm may have been ascribed to the royal singer because of its Davidic wealth of thought. The poet calls Israel blessed because Yahwe is its God and King and makes clear in his psalm the justification of calling it blessed.

The psalmist first answers the question: What until now was Yahwe to his people (verses 1–4)? Israel could say about the Lord: God is my rock. Yahwe was the foundation stone upon which the structure of the

537

commonwealth was built. He himself had laid the foundation for it on Mount Sinai. As guide of the battles he had blessed the weapons of Israel and had granted them victory whenever they went out to carry on the war of the Lord. God was for his people not only a rock, he was also manifest love. He had, so to say, marked his hand lest he might forget it; its walls were always before his eyes (Isaias 49:16). In times of adversity he proved himself a strong, invincible fortress, an impregnable citadel, a redeemer, and a protecting and covering shield. It was he and not the strength of the people who subjected the Gentile nations to Israel. In the Eighth Psalm David being astonished at the sublimity and greatness of God's works in the starry heavens asked himself the question: "When I meditate upon the heavens, the moon and the stars which thou hast made, what is man that thou art mindful of him and the son of man that thou shouldst visit him?" Here it is the greatness of God's work in the history of his people which forces astonishment and admiration from the lips of the psalmist about God's condescension. Man is but a mere breath and his days pass by like a shadow. These words may be applied to nations as well, even if the time of their existence lasts through many generations. The selection of Israel to be God's people was an undeserved grace, so also is the call to Christianity for individual men and for all nations.

The second question of the psalm is found in the following verses (5–11). What does Israel expect from Yahwe? It hopes that the Lord will hold judgment upon the enemies of Israel so that it may not collapse. The description of the appearance of the Lord for judgment is borrowed from the Seventeenth Psalm, but it is briefer. The Lord descends from heaven to earth in a heavy dark storm cloud. It is as if the entire heaven had descended in the lowering cloud and rested upon the mountains so that these seem to be enveloped, as it were, in dark smoke. Like arrows which the Lord hurls against his enemies lightning flashes here and there and terrifies and confuses men. That which David had expressed in Psalm 17 as a fact which he had experienced in his life is here clothed in the form of a petition. May the Lord save his people from the power of the enemy. May he stretch out his hand from on high and snatch it from the towering flood that it may not perish. The psalmist believes that he may expect God's personal intervention with more assurance because his opponents are not fighting with honest weapons, but with falsehood, lies, deceptions, and concealment of their true intentions. When the Lord has shown mercy upon his people and has punished the enemy, then the psalmist will sing a new psalm in his praise accompanied with the ten-stringed instrument; for it behooves to sing a new song for the glorification of the new manifestation of God's power and for the thanksgiving for it. In this song he will proclaim the greatness of God who alone has the power to

538

give victory or defeat to kings. Neither strength of armies nor of equipment brings victory, but only God's will. Therefore he also possesses the power to rescue David from the sword which serves an evil purpose, which is directed against the anointed and the kingdom of the Lord. Israel can expect from this almighty Lord and God that he will save his people and deliver it from the power of the foreign rule of the Gentiles. What their mouth speaks in falsehood they swear by stone idols and not by the one true God. Therefore their right hand which they raise to pledge an oath is a lying right hand.

The Septuagint and the Vulgate have interpreted the following verses as referring to the enemy and their prosperity; but they refer rather to the prosperity of those under the sceptre of Yahwe (verses 12–15). The description is the type which reminds us of a greeting which the Assyrians used in the hailing of a new king. Thus we read in the elevation of King Ashurbanipal, 668–626 B.C.: "Days of right and justice, rich downpourings of rain, and much water and a good purchase price. May the gods be gracious. May a joyous reverence of the king prevail everywhere and may the temples be richly supplied. May old men dance and children sing. May women and virgins marry and give birth to boys and girls. May the giving of birth to cattle succeed well. He who sins is sentenced to death; may the king give him life. Those who for many years were imprisoned thou hast liberated; those who were sick for a long time have become well; the hungry are sated, the emaciated have become fat and the naked are clothed." When after the defeat of the Gentiles the rule of Yahwe and his anointed reaches its height the Messianic blessings will pour in upon the people and upon the land. The sons will become strong and possess youthful power. They may be compared to a full-grown plant. The daughters will be beautiful and well-formed and will be like the long pillars of the palace. The Lord will give to the soil and to domestic animals an unheard-of fertility. The storehouses will be filled with the products of the field, of the vineyards, and of the trees. The steppes too will have a luxuriant growth so that the herds will have much nourishment and these too will have an extraordinary fertility. The herds will increase by the thousands. These are descriptions of the blessings of Messianic times appropriate for a people whose main occupation was agriculture and cattle raising. Even the fortified cities will receive a Messianic blessing, the blessing of invincibility. No enemy will ever make a breach in their walls; none will ever force a passage into the inner part of the city. Every attempt from the outside to conquer the city will be in vain. But in the inner part of the city there will be quiet, peace, and prosperity. In the open places there will no longer be heard the lamentations of those who are oppressed and unjustly treated. Justice will reign within the walls when Yahwe is king of Israel. In view of such expectations of the future the psalmist exclaims: "Blessed is the people that experiences this: blessed is the people whose God is Yahwe."

psalm 144

Exaltabo te, Deus

A psalm of praise to the infinite majesty of God

PRAISE FOR DAVID HIMSELF

1. I will extol thee, O God my king, and I will bless thy name forever; yea, forever and ever.

2. Every day I will bless thee, and I will praise thy name forever, yea, forever and ever.

3. Great is the Lord, and greatly to be praised: and of his greatness there is no end.

4. Generation and generation shall praise thy works: and they shall declare thy power.

5. They shall speak of the magnificence of the glory of thy holiness and shall tell thy wondrous works.

6. And they shall speak of the might of thy terrible acts: and shall declare thy greatness.

7. They shall publish the memory of the abundance of thy sweetness: and shall rejoice in thy justice.

8. The Lord is gracious and merciful: patient and plenteous in mercy.

9. The Lord is sweet to all: and his tender mercies are over all his works.

10. Let all thy works, O Lord, praise thee: and let thy saints bless thee.

11. They shall speak of the glory of thy kingdom: and shall tell of thy power.

12. To make thy might known to the sons of men: and the glory of the magnificence of thy kingdom.

13. Thy kingdom is a kingdom of all ages: and thy dominion endureth throughout all generations.

The Lord is faithful in all his words: and holy in all his works.

14. The Lord lifteth up all that fall: and setteth up all that are cast down.

15. The eyes of all hope in thee, O Lord: and thou givest them meat in due season.

16. Thou openest thy hand, and fillest with blessing every living creature.

17. The Lord is just in all his ways: and holy in all his works.

18. The Lord is nigh unto all them that call upon him: to all that call upon him in truth.

19. He will do the will of them that fear him: and he will hear their prayer and save them.

20. The Lord keepeth all them that love him; but all the wicked he will destroy.

21. My mouth shall speak the praise of the Lord: and let all flesh bless his holy name forever; yea forever and ever.

THE Talmud says of this psalm: "He who prays David's hymn of praise three times a day can be certain that he is a child of the future world" (Traktat Berakhoth 4b). This declaration is not merely based on the fact that the psalm is alphabetic, but because it praises the goodness of God who opens his hands to all. It is the only psalm which in the superscription is designated a song of praise, a title which the Jews give to the entire Psalter. Because the song praises the goodness of God it was used in the early Christian Church as a Communion hymn. The singer wished to acclaim God because he is at the same time his God and his King. Twofold are the rights of Yahwe's sovereignty over his people; there is therefore also a twofold obligation to serve the Lord, to glorify his entire Being and activity at all times. As little as God can at any time cease to be God and King, so little can there be a reason to cease singing praises to him. Therefore the psalmist will praise God every day and without end acclaim his greatness. Whether it is a day of happiness and joy or a day of suffering, the glorification of God must be independent of the vicissitudes of our life and may not be made to depend upon any condition placed by man.

God is worthy of daily praise; for God is good despite his greatness (verses 3–7). The greatness of the Lord, of his nature, and of his works is so much beyond all comprehension that no human mind can fathom or comprehend it. Of him the Book of Jesus Sirach says: "Who is able to declare his works? For who shall search out his glorious acts? And who shall show forth the glory of his majesty? Or who shall be able to declare

541

his mercy? Nothing may be taken away, nor added, neither is it possible to understand the glorious works of God. When a man hath done, then shall he begin: and when he leaveth off he shall be at a loss" (18:2 seq.). The more man delves into the mysteries of God's nature and his works, the more new beauties reveal themselves which challenge him to a renewal of God's praises. Therefore proclaiming God's greatness can never reach a height above which no further progress is possible even if hundreds of generations have studied and proclaimed it. Every new generation and every new century gives to the coming ages new proofs of God's power and new revelations of his glory. Indeed, God never ceases to make himself known to man through deeds of his power and wisdom, of his justice and love in order that all ages may speak of the glory of his majesty and meditate upon his wonderful power and greatness. The punitive judgments and the terrifying deeds of the Lord also serve the same purpose. The generation which experienced them should also narrate them to the following generation that it might fear the Lord and be on its guard against challenging his wrath through unfaithfulness. But God reveals more than his terrifying power; he also reveals the richness of his goodness and justice. From the beginning of the history of Israel the Lord erected memorials of his love. From the time of the exodus from Egypt and the journey through the desert with the great miracles of divine mercy until the centuries of the sojourn in Canaan, many memorials give testimony of the great victories which Yahwe granted to his people. His justice which wills the salvation of men causes Israel to rejoice; for the word *justice* does not only remind it of God's punitive justice but also of the decree of redemption which has for its purpose the justification and sanctification of man. It reminds it of the Messianic promise that God will send his Son to the earth so that all who believe in him may obtain eternal life.

The psalmist wishes to sing about God's goodness. He speaks first of all about God's goodness in his very nature (verses 8–13). The old covenant did not stand exclusively under the curse of the fear of God's terrifying majesty. Very frequently we meet in the Sacred Scripture of Israel this confession of faith: "Thou art a gracious and merciful God, long-suffering and rich in grace and fidelity" (Exodus 34:6). The old Tobias says: "God's ways are mercy and fidelity" (Tobias 3:2). The Lord for the believing Israelite was the Father of mercy and the God of all consolation (2 Corinthians 1:3). God in his goodness is concerned about all creatures. The Book of Jesus Sirach writes about it. "The compassion of man is toward his neighbor: but the mercy of God is upon all flesh" (18:12). It includes all the works of God for: "Thou lovest all things that are and hatest none of the things which thou hast made: for thou didst not appoint or make anything hating it" (Wisdom 11:25). There is therefore no creature and no work which the Lord abandons to itself after he has created it.

Therefore all the works of God must praise the goodness of the Creator. This duty, above all others, must be conformed to by those to whom God has manifested the greatest love; they are the saints, the members of the chosen people of God. Saints are those who are separated. The admonition which Peter wrote to the Christians applied also to Israel: "You are a chosen race, a royal priesthood, a holy nation, a purchased people; that you may proclaim the perfections of him who has called you out of darkness into his marvelous light" (1 Peter 2:9). They whom God has called to union with him, who in it experience the glory of his majesty and the richness of his love should tell others about his majesty and goodness in order that they also who walk in darkness may come to the light of truth and to the source of love. It would be ingratitude if they would remain silent about the great things which the Lord hath done for them; for from the abundance of the heart the mouth speaketh. This duty is so much the more urgent because God out of his abundant love allows some to see his glory and partake of the fullness of his grace that they who are thus favored may be heralds of his mercy to others. Through men the knowledge of God's glory and love should become the common property of all men. No time and no generation can be freed from the duty of the apostolate. The kingdom of the Lord is not a transitory kingdom, the end of which would be expected. It is not a kingdom like the kingdoms of this world which are limited in time and space. God's kingdom was established for all times and has a mission to all nations until the end of time; it is to be a mediator for all generations and nations. The kingship of the Lord is not limited like that of transitory kings; all men are subjected to it whether they realize it or not. But it is the will of the eternal King that all should acknowledge and worship him; therefore all who already know him must work for the propagation of his name.

God is good in his nature; this goodness should be magnetic, drawing all men to him. But God is also good in his work. The description of God's goodness in his providence is the theme of the second part of the psalm (verses 14–20). The Lord despite his infinite power and majesty is a good Father. He does not break the bent reed and does not extinguish the glimmering wick. With his arm he protects those who are falling, and those who are afflicted with cares and sorrows he lovingly comforts. But it is also a characteristic of God's greatness that although he thrones in the immeasurable heights of heaven where before him the earth is but a speck of dust and all men are as nothing, he should in his love take care of every creature. He is the father of the house, of the great house, the world created by him. On this account the eyes of all living creatures are directed toward him; from him they expect support, and are confident that he will give the proper nourishment at the proper time to every one of his creatures. Daily he opens his kind hand and gives to all living creatures his bounteous blessing, to the millions of animals and plants. Christ himself has described with incomparable clearness the care of his heavenly Father for his creatures: "Behold the birds of the air; they do not sow, or reap, or gather into barns, yet your heavenly Father feeds them. Consider how the lilies of the field grow; they neither toil nor spin. Yet I say to you that not even Solomon in all his glory was arrayed like one of these" (Matthew 6:26 seq.). How different are the needs of individual creatures! But to each God provides according to their needs.

God is just in all his ways and kind in all his works. He holds to the norms of his infinite goodness. He neglects none of his creatures; he slights no one, but gives to each what is necessary to attain the end which the Creator has determined for him. He is near to all his creatures; but he is especially near to human beings and above all to those who call upon him for help, who adore him in spirit and in truth. "The Lord is good to them that hope in him, to the soul that seeketh him" (Lamentations 3:25). He fulfills the justifiable wishes of those who fear him, and delivers them from all adversity. "The spirit of those that fear God is sought after and by his regard shall be blessed. For their hope is in him that saveth them, and the eyes of God are upon them that love him. He that feareth the Lord shall tremble at nothing and shall not be afraid; for he is his hope. The soul of him that feareth the Lord is blessed. To whom doth he look and who is his strength? The eyes of the Lord are upon them that fear him; he is their powerful protector" (Ecclesiasticus 34:14 seq.). Those who love the Lord will be protected by him: but the sinners will experience his strict justice. At the end of God's way when all his decrees have been fulfilled, godlessness will be exterminated. "But the just shall live forevermore: and their reward is with the Lord, and the care of them with the Most High" (Wisdom 5:16). To proclaim the praise of such a King was a glorious task for which the psalmist was very enthusiastic. He will sing and proclaim that all flesh may learn to love and praise the name of God.

psalm 145

Lauda, anima

We are not to trust in men, but in God alone

1. Alleluia of Aggeus and Zacharias.

2. Praise the Lord, O my soul, in my life I will praise the Lord: I will sing to my God as long as I shall be.
Put not your trust in princes:

3. In the children of men, in whom there is no salvation.

4. His spirit shall go forth, and he shall return into his earth: in that day all their thoughts shall perish.

5. Blessed is he who hath the God of Jacob for his helper, whose hope is in the Lord his God.

6. Who made heaven and earth, the sea, and all things that are in them.

7. Who keepeth truth forever, who executeth judgment for them that suffer wrong: who giveth food to the hungry.
The Lord looseth them that are fettered.

8. The Lord enlighteneth the blind. The Lord lifteth up them that are cast down: the Lord loveth the just.

9. The Lord keepeth the strangers, he will support the fatherless and the widow, and the ways of sinners he will destroy.

10. The Lord shall reign forever: thy God, O Sion, unto generation and generation.

THIS psalm forms with the following a chain of hymns which are connected with one another by an Alleluia. In late Judean times they were used as a daily morning prayer and were called *Hallel* like Psalms 112–117 which were sung at the celebration of the Pasch. Perhaps this psalm stems from post-exilic times and most likely from those years in which through the machinations of the Samaritans the reconstruction of the temple was forbidden. After the great advances which King Cyrus had made for the reconstruction of the temple at Jerusalem, the prohibition was for the Jews a bitter disappointment. It was for them a lesson not to rely on men and not even on the favor of princes, but to place their confidence in God who is powerful enough to set aside all difficulties. This advice forms the contents of this psalm. The poet requests his soul to praise the Lord. He will do it now and at all times as long as he lives; for one cannot praise God enough. The duty to praise God never ceases; for the Lord always remains the same in his infinite majesty and glory and always the same in his infinite mercy. He who once experienced great need and finds himself in great tribulation and seeks consolation and help from men will learn again and again the powerlessness of men and the powerfulness and goodness of God.

Man should not rely on men (verses 3–4). Even when they sit upon a throne, when they rule a great kingdom and possess great power, they are nevertheless no reliable helpers. They may make glorious promises and give positive assurances and even show a good sincere will; but they do not keep what they have promised because they do not want to or because they cannot. How many times have not those who were in power disappointed and how great is the number of those who were disappointed! Even great princes are mortal and weak men; they are not masters of their own life or of their own future. When the Lord of life takes them away, they die like all other men and they return to dust and ashes; and with their death all their plans come to nothing.

God alone is the true helper (verses 5–10). He lives eternally; his power is unlimited; he is faithful in his promises and in his agreements. Therefore he does well who does not rely upon fickle men who do not wish to help or cannot help, but who places his confidence in the God of Israel who has the power and the will and the love to help. Such a one does not build on quicksand, but on rock foundation. God can help; for Yahwe is the almighty creator of heaven and earth. With one word he has created the three kingdoms of nature and put life into them. With his almighty word he carries all and keeps all. For him there is no hindrance in giving help to those who call upon him. He must help for he is eternal fidelity. He keeps what he promises. God also wills to help because he is the infinitely good God whose very nature is love.

Witnesses to this are the innumerable oppressed whom he has helped to obtain their right. He has no respect for persons; he is not influenced by secret plottings; he is not seduced to commit injustices as human princes are; he shows mercy to all because he knows the needs of all. He feeds the hungry; he looses the fetters of those who suffer imprisonment. There is no human need gross enough to baffle him.

His love, as Saviour, is shown to all who are wearied and heavily laden. He gives sight to the blind and comforts those who are bowed down with grief. The picture which the Prophet Isaias gives us of the helping goodness of the Messias has been patterned after the divine goodness. God's love is also manifested to all who are for a great part deprived of human help. He assists the stranger who being without home has no support from his family or his relatives and who in a strange land is looked upon as one who is merely tolerated. God also takes the widows and orphans under his protection who are robbed and oppressed by unscrupulous men and who cannot find justice with the judges. The weak do not beg in vain; he gives justice to them and makes all who do them wrong feel his wrath. The eternal duration of Yahwe's kingdom is a guarantee that he will remain eternally the King of his people and that his kingdom leads to the Messianic fulfillment. No power on earth can frustrate his plans.

psalm 146

Laudate Dominum

An exhortation to praise God for his benefits

ALLELUIA

1. Praise ye the Lord, because God is good: to our God be joyful and comely praise.

2. The Lord buildeth up Jerusalem: he will gather together the dispersed of Israel.

3. Who healeth the broken heart and bindeth up their bruises.

4. Who telleth the number of the stars: and calleth them all by their names.

5. Great is our Lord and great is his power: and of his wisdom there is no number.

6. The Lord lifteth up the meek, and bringeth the wicked down even to the ground.

7. Sing ye to the Lord with praise: sing to our God upon the harp.

8. Who covereth the heaven with clouds, and prepareth rain for the earth. Who maketh grass to grow on the mountains, and herbs for the service of men.

547

9. Who giveth the beasts their food; and to the young ravens that call upon him.

10. He shall not delight in the strength of the horse; nor take pleasure in the legs of a man.

11. The Lord taketh pleasure in them that fear him: and in them that hope in his mercy.

THE psalm may be traced to the time when after the exile the temple at Jerusalem had been rebuilt and many of those who had been banished to Babylon had returned to their native country. The word spoken by the Lord that he wounds and binds the wounds, that he strikes and heals was verified in Israel (Job 5:18). God heals all wounds. This was the experience of those who saw the city, the temple, and the nation arise from ruins (verses 1–6). It is a thankful theme for a song praising God, the Lord, when his helping love and fidelity is praised; it is a lovely theme and appropriate for him who has seen and himself experienced God's healing power and kindness. He has healed the wounds of the city of Jerusalem. What a change! The weak Jerusalem arises again from its ruins. It will ever again celebrate its resurrection. The desert sand has covered the lavish temples of the gods for all times. The Lord has also begun to build up the spiritual Jerusalem and has led the captives back to their native country. He will also at some time in the future gather and lead back the dispersed members of the chosen people dispersed throughout the world. He who has again rebuilt Jerusalem will also heal the wounds of the human heart. He alone knows how to console and to cheer effectually; he has wine and oil for all wounds that afflict the human heart in so many ways. The Lord knows all things and knows the sufferings of the many who are far away from their native country and far from the sanctuary in strange lands, mourning and lamenting in pagan lands. How could the great God overlook and forget one of his children who trust in him, believe in him, and call upon him? He has numbered the innumerable galaxies; he knows every star; he knows and orders celestial courses. But man is more than the entire constellations. As God knows the many stars that are spread upon the heavens, numbers, and guides them, so he also knows all the children of Israel even if they are dispersed throughout the world. He will call them when the time has come and will lead them on their way back to their native country. The rebuilding of a nation that has lost its national independence and has been dispersed throughout the world requires great power and wisdom. With God there is mighty power and his wisdom is unlimited. All creation gives testimony of this: "It is God that maketh the earth by his power, that prepareth the world by his wisdom and stretcheth out the heavens by his knowledge" (Jeremias

10:12). This infinite power aids divine justice in order to comfort those oppressed by the malice of godless men and nations and in order to crush the blasphemers. Jerusalem and Babylon are memorials of his justice. The deeply afflicted Sion the Lord has re-established, but the proud Babylon he has forever humbled. Such is the fate of all who attack the kingdom of God and its members.

The Lord healed the wounds from which Israel bled, but his love is not exhausted. God provides also for the land (verses 7–11). For the second time the psalmist makes the request to sing a song of praise to the Lord. Again the singers should take their instruments in hand to thank the Lord for his love. The psalmist tells us about the divine providence over forests and fields, over beasts and meadows. This providence is for the psalmist a symbol of the blessings which the Lord showers upon his people. It is God who makes the clouds appear in order to provide rain for the land. If he would not provide for the watering of the soil, it would soon turn into a barren desert. By the rain he also makes the grass grow even on the peaks of the mountains and thereby provides nourishment for the beasts of the hills. He provides for the wild animals of the prairies about which no man troubles himself. Even the young raven which caws for food is not forgotten. All rely upon the good God to give them food at the right time. Thus the Lord wishes that men also will depend upon him and not anxiously provide for the morrow and trust in their own strength alone. To the almighty God what does the strength of a horse or the muscular strength of a man mean? A proof is the destruction of Babylon and the deliverance of the people of Israel. God is only pleased with those who fear, love, and worship him placing their confidence in his mercy.

psalm 147

Lauda, Jerusalem

The Church is called upon to praise God for his peculiar graces and favors to his people; in the Hebrew this psalm is joined to the foregoing

ALLELUIA

12. Praise the Lord, O Jerusalem: praise thy God, O Sion.

13. Because he has strengthened the bolts of thy gates, he hath blessed thy children within thee.

14. Who hath placed peace in thy borders: and filleth thee with the fat of corn.

15. Who sendeth forth his speech to the earth: his word runneth swiftly.

16. Who giveth snow like wool: scattereth mists like ashes.

17. He sendeth his crystal like morsels: who shall stand before the face of his cold?

18. He shall send out his word, and shall melt them: his wind shall blow, and the waters shall run.

19. Who declareth his word to Jacob: his justices and his judgments to Israel.

20. He hath not done in like manner to every nation: and his judgments he hath not made manifest to them. Alleluia.

THE second half of the 146th Psalm is considered a separate psalm (147) in the Greek, Latin, and Syriac translations. Perhaps the reason for this separation was an old tradition. According to contents both parts are related to each other and presuppose the reconstruction of the city of Jerusalem after the exile. They differ from one another in the fact that in the first part the entire nation is asked to praise God while in the second part the request is made to Jerusalem. The subject of the 147th Psalm of the Vulgate is the inner development of God's kingdom, its living in peace, and its incomparable selection to be the herald of the divine deeds of salvation for humanity. While in the first section the psalmist is occupied with the present, he here looks into the Messianic future. It is probably for this reason that the separation was made. A practical commentary justifies us to join with the Vulgate in this separation.

The request is made to the holy city of Jerusalem, the type of the Church of the New Testament to praise the Lord. It has been restored from its ruins; it is again protected by its walls; strong gates and locks give it security. Therefore Nehemias after the completion of the fortress could call for a hymn to be sung in honor of God. But Sion awaits a more glorious time, a resurrection to Messianic grace (verses 12–14). The Lord provides the new Jerusalem with mighty gates and locks so that no enemy can enter. He himself is its mighty protector who secures it against all enemy attacks. The Prophet Isaias tells us that salvation is their fortification and bulwark (26:1). Numerous are the inhabitants of the city because the Lord richly blesses the descendants. The Messianic blessing will flow from the city into the entire land. Peace will rest upon it and will no longer be disturbed by an enemy. War will no longer be inflicted upon the country to disturb its paradisaic tranquility. A paradisaic fruitfulness will accompany this peace. The curse of original sin will be taken from the world; the earth will produce such wealth that men will enjoy the best. This points to the blessings of grace which God will shower upon the Church to refresh the souls of men.

God is mighty to bring about such a change (verses 15–18); for it is brought about by his almighty word which in nature also brings about the change in seasons. When the Lord speaks the word there is no delay in carrying out the command. God commands and the winter appears. The snowflakes fall on the earth white as wool; God strews the dew upon fields and steppes as one strews ashes in the house of mourning. He freezes the water into ice by the cold sent by him. He makes spring follow upon winter. With God's word the sun rises and the ice melts and the water flows again.

The word of God is thus fulfilled for Israel. The time of the exile may be compared to winter. After it the Lord permits the spring of the return to follow and he prepares for the still more glorious spring of the Messianic times as the Canticle of Canticles so poetically describes. The word of God that comes to Israel is the word of grace and truth which he has revealed to the people. This word makes moral demands upon Israel, makes known the rights and claims of God. But the word revealed to Israel has a world-wide mission. Only Israel has become the herald of revelation and of the divine promises and not one of the great nations. The word revealed to Israel will make its strength effective. Israel shall be the herald of the divine deeds of salvation for humanity.

psalm 148

Laudate Dominum de coelis

All creatures are invited to praise their Creator

ALLELUIA

1. Praise ye the Lord from the heavens: praise ye him in the high places.

2. Praise ye him, all his angels; praise ye him, all his hosts.

3. Praise him, O sun and moon: praise ye him all ye stars and light.

4. Praise ye him, ye heaven of heavens: and let all the waters that are above the heavens

5. Praise the name of the Lord.
   For he spoke and they were made: he commanded and they were created.

6. He hath established them forever, and for ages and ages: he hath made a decree, and it shall not pass away.

7. Praise the Lord from the earth, ye dragons, and all ye deeps.

8. Fire, hail, snow, ice, stormy winds, which fulfill his word.

9. Mountains and all hills, fruitful trees and all cedars.

10. Beasts and all cattle: serpents and feathered fowls.

11. Kings of the earth and all people: princes and all judges of the earth:

12. Young men and maidens: let the old with the younger, praise the name of the Lord.

13. For his name alone is exalted.

14. The praise of him is above heaven and earth; and he hath exalted the horn of his people.
    A hymn to all his saints: to the children of Israel, a people approaching to him. Alleluia.

THE universe is a work of God; he has called all things into existence for his own honor. "The Lord has created all things for his own sake" (Proverbs 16:4). For this reason all creatures must praise and glorify him. Therefore David cries out: "Thine, O Lord, is magnificence, and power, and glory, and victory: and to thee is praise; for all that is in heaven and in earth is thine: thine is the kingdom, O Lord; and thou art above all princes" (1 Chronicles 29:11). The nation of God is only the choirmaster in the song of praise of all creation. But the invitation of the psalmist has a deeper reason. Creatures should not praise the Lord for their own sake, but because of the graces of the redemption which he has granted to his people. Creatures are invited by the psalmist to rejoice with Israel and to give thanksgiving for the glory which the Lord has prepared for his people after the humiliation of the exile. The return home in the light of prophecy is only an advance payment of the fulfillment of the Messianic promise. We participate in this song of praise and we too invite heaven and earth to give praise and thanksgiving for the grace of redemption which the Lord has given us.

The invitation is first given to heaven and to all that has any relation to it (verses 1–6). The angels in heaven should intone the song of praise; for they always look upon the face of God. In their heavenly language they should intone the praise of the Lord and give to the song of creatures the melody before God. Then the sun, moon, and the stars are invited; for the heavens especially proclaim the glory of God. They are the masterworks of his power which astound men and which they can never understand thoroughly. The vault of heaven, so high and so extensive, the clouds, the gigantic masses of water that float in the air, are all the work of God. At his word they came into existence. Without that word they would not be. And as by his word he created them, so also by his powerful word he maintains them. He has given them a law and according to it they must run their course. Readily they fulfill the divine command.

In the second strophe the earth and all that is upon it and what has relation to it are invited to praise God (verses 7–12). The psalmist first mentions the sea and all creatures that live in it. Then fire and hail, snow, ice and storm, all of them obey God's command and fulfill every command of his will. All mountains and hills, all fruit trees, all the high cedars of Lebanon shall praise the Lord. All species of the animal world, the beasts of the prairie, and the domestic animals, all that creeps upon the ground, and all that flies in the air shall praise the Lord. The invitation to praise God has come from the angels and ends with an invitation to men, to all kings and nations of the earth, to all princes and judges, to all young men and young maidens, to the aged and young.

The conclusion (verses 13–14) summarizes the entire psalm. All of those who were invited should praise the only sublime name of the Lord. His glory is infinitely greater than the universe which he has created. This great God whom all creatures glorify is the God of Israel. He is the God who has chosen it and has drawn it to himself by his eternal love. This God has again forgiven it after the exile and exalted it so that all the children of Israel praise him.

psalm 149

Cantate Domino

The Church is particularly bound to praise God

ALLELUIA

1. Sing ye to the Lord a new canticle: let his praise be in the church of the saints.

2. Let Israel rejoice in him that made him: and let the children of Sion be joyful in their king.

3. Let them praise his name in choir: let them sing to him with the timbrel and the psaltery.

4. For the Lord is well pleased with his people: and he will exalt the meek unto salvation.

5. The saints shall rejoice in glory: they shall be joyful in their beds.

6. The high praises of God shall be in their mouth: and two-edged swords in their hands.

7. To execute vengeance upon the nations, chastisements among the people:

8. To bind their kings with fetters, and their nobles with manacles of iron.

9. To execute upon them the judgment that is written: this glory is to all his saints. Alleluia.

PSALM 148 has closed with the request to praise God for the favors he has bestowed upon Israel. Now Israel itself intones a new song; for to give praise to God is the first duty of the new nation (verses 1–5). The New Covenant with its rich blessings and graces demands a new song which should be sung in the holy assembly of the redeemed. The song should praise God as the Creator of his people and as the King of the children of Sion; for the people of the New Testament are in a greater sense a creation of God than the people of the Old Testament. They make up an eternal kingdom established by God himself. Just as the victor was celebrated with timbrel and psaltery and dancing so also should the victorious God and King, the Redeemer and Saviour, be greeted. The

Lord is pleased with this redeemed people. To the humble he gives salvation. Then the righteous, the members of his kingdom, shall rejoice because of the glory which they shall behold and experience; by night they shall shout with joy upon their beds because of the peace they shall enjoy.

The people of the Messianic time, the members of the Church, have another obligation. They must fight for the Lord and his kingdom (verses 6–9). While the mouth sings praises to the Lord, the hand should carry the two-edged sword in order to carry out the judgment of God upon the pagans, to fetter the kings and princes in chains according to the written law, the law of honor for all the righteous.

psalm 150

Laudate Dominum in sanctis

An exhortation to praise God with all sorts of instruments

ALLELUIA

1. Praise ye the Lord in his holy places: praise ye him in the firmament of his power.

2. Praise ye him for his mighty acts: praise ye him according to the multitude of his greatness.

3. Praise him with sound of trumpet: praise him with the psaltery and harp.

4. Praise him with timbrel and choir: praise him with strings and organs.

5. Praise him on high sounding cymbals: praise him on cymbals of joy: let every spirit praise the Lord. Alleluia.

THE entire Psalter ends with a great doxology. It is the "Glory be to the Father, and to the Son, and to the Holy Spirit" at the end of the Book of Psalms. The praise of God should resound in his sanctuary and in Sion, his strong city. The Church of the New Covenant has the mission to glorify God in this world and its members must gather in the house of God in order to accomplish this mission. The object of this praise is the

555

wonderful deeds of God unto his people, the wonderful works of redemption and sanctification. The object of this praise is also the majesty of God which reveals itself in his works. Music should accompany song that the praise may reach to the heavens: the trumpet, the harp, the flute and cymbal should be played. By dances also shall the Lord be worshiped as the divine Victor. The whole world, heaven and earth, and all that lives and exists should sing along and join in a jubilant Alleluia.

topical index

Index

A NOTE ON THE TYPE

IN WHICH THIS BOOK WAS SET

This book is set in Caledonia, a Linotype face created in 1939 by W. A. Dwiggins, which is by far one of the best book types created in the last 50 years. It has a simple, hard-working, feet-on-the-ground quality and can be classed as a modern type face with excellent color and good readability. The designer claims Caledonia was created by putting a little of each of Scotch Roman, Bulmer, Baskerville and Bodoni together and producing a lively crisp-like book type. This book was composed by Progressive Typographers, Inc., York, Pa., printed by the Wickersham Printing Company, of Lancaster, Pa., and bound by Moore and Company of Baltimore. The typography and design of this book are by Howard N. King.